WORLD WAR I
Encyclopedia

WORLD WAR I

Encyclopedia

VOLUME III: M–R

Dr. Spencer C. Tucker

Editor

Dr. Priscilla Roberts

Editor, Documents Volume

Col. Cole C. Kingseed, USA Rtd., PhD
Dr. Malcolm Muir Jr.
Dr. Priscilla Roberts
Major General David Zabecki, USAR, PhD

Assistant Editors

FOREWORD BY

John Eisenhower

ABCCLIO

Cataloging-in-Publication data is available from the Library of Congress .

ISBN-13: 978-1-85109-420-2   ebook 978-1-85109-425-7
10   09   08   07   06   10   9   8   7   6   5   4   3   2

This book is also available on the World Wide Web as an ebook.
Visit abc-clio.com for details.

ABC-CLIO, Inc.
130 Cremona Drive, P.O. Box 1911
Santa Barbara, California 93116–1911

This book is printed on acid-free paper ∞ .
Manufactured in the United States of America

Contents

List of Entries

List of Maps

General Maps

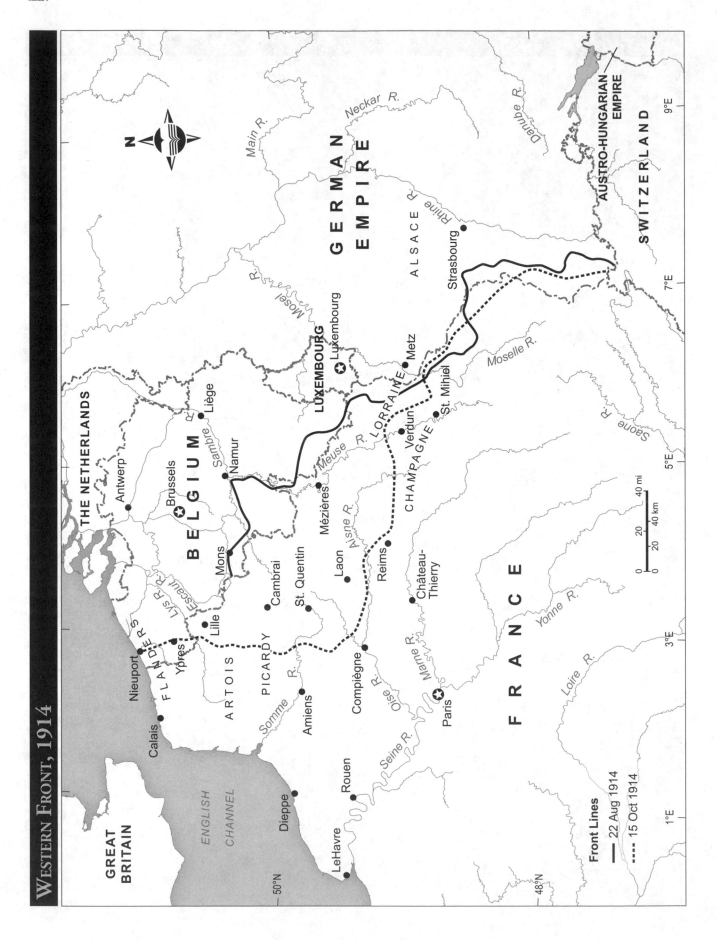

WESTERN FRONT, 1914

YPRES SALIENT, 1914 – 1918

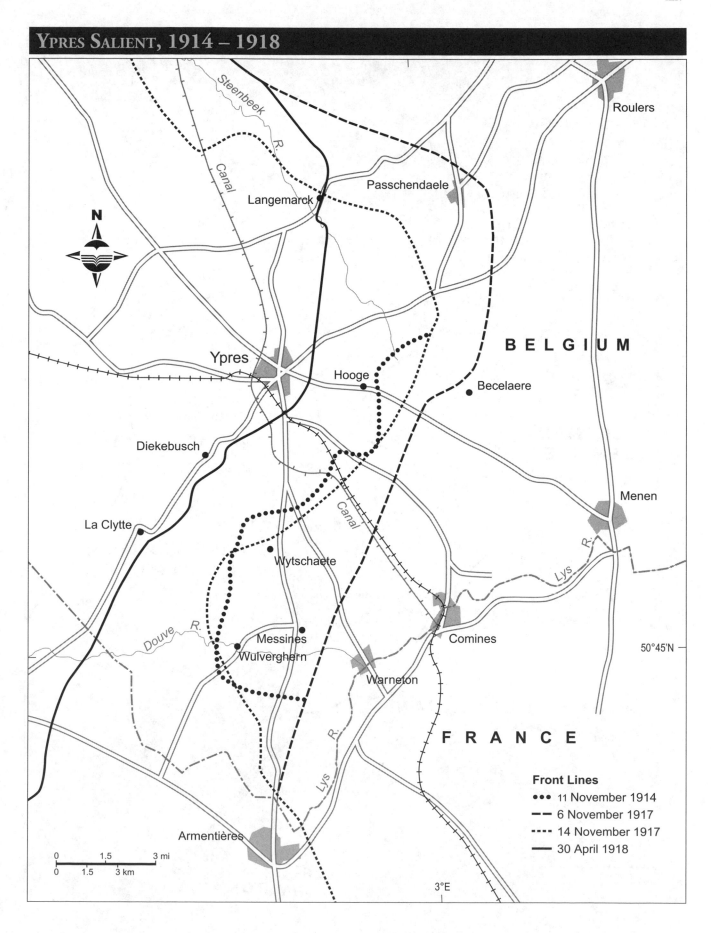

N

Steenbeek R.

Canal

Roulers

Passchendaele

Langemarck

BELGIUM

Ypres

Hooge

Becelaere

Diekebusch

Canal

Menen

La Clytte

Wytschaete

Lys R.

Douve R.

Messines

Comines

Wulverghern

50°45'N

Warneton

Lys R.

FRANCE

Armentières

3°E

Front Lines
- ••• 11 November 1914
- – – 6 November 1917
- ••••• 14 November 1917
- —— 30 April 1918

0   1.5   3 mi
0   1.5   3 km

Eastern Front, 1914 – 1918

Front Lines
— 28 September 1914
– – 1 May 1915
···· 30 September 1917
••• 1 January 1917
— Brest-Litovsk Treaty Line, March 1918

Gains
▨ German, Sept–Oct 1917
▨ Austrian, July–Aug 1917

15°E 20°E 25°E

GULF OF FINLAND

Petrograd

N

BALTIC
SEA

55°N

Konigsberg

Danzig

Tilsit

Riga

Dvina R.

Smolensk

Vilna

GERMAN
EMPIRE

Tannenberg

Minsk

Warta R.

Vistula R.

Grodno

Posen

Bialystok

Bug R.

Dnieper R.

Warsaw

Lodz

Brest-
Litovsk

RUSSIAN
EMPIRE

Komorov

San R.

Kiev

50°N

Kraków

AUSTRO-HUNGARIAN
EMPIRE

Oder R.

Dniester R.

Vienna

Danube R.

Budapest

Thesis R.

0   50   100   150 mi
0 50 100 150 km

BLACK
SEA

ROMANIA

45°N

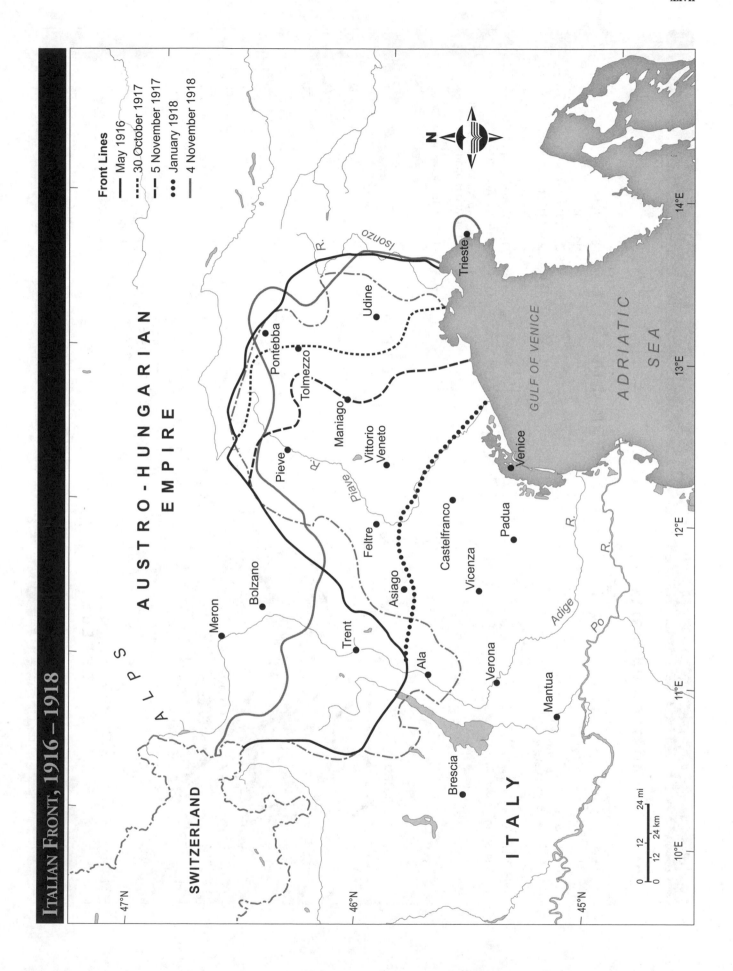

ITALIAN FRONT, 1916–1918

SWITZERLAND

ALPS

AUSTRO-HUNGARIAN EMPIRE

ITALY

ADRIATIC SEA

GULF OF VENICE

Isonzo R.

Trieste

Udine

Pontebba

Tolmezzo

Maniago

Pieve

Piave R.

Vittorio Veneto

Feltre

Castelfranco

Venice

Padua

Vicenza

Asiago

Trent

Ala

Bolzano

Meron

Verona

Adige R.

Mantua

Po R.

Brescia

Front Lines
— May 1916
-·-·- 30 October 1917
– – – 5 November 1917
· · · January 1918
— 4 November 1918

0   12   24 mi
0   12   24 km

47°N
46°N
45°N

10°E   11°E   12°E   13°E   14°E

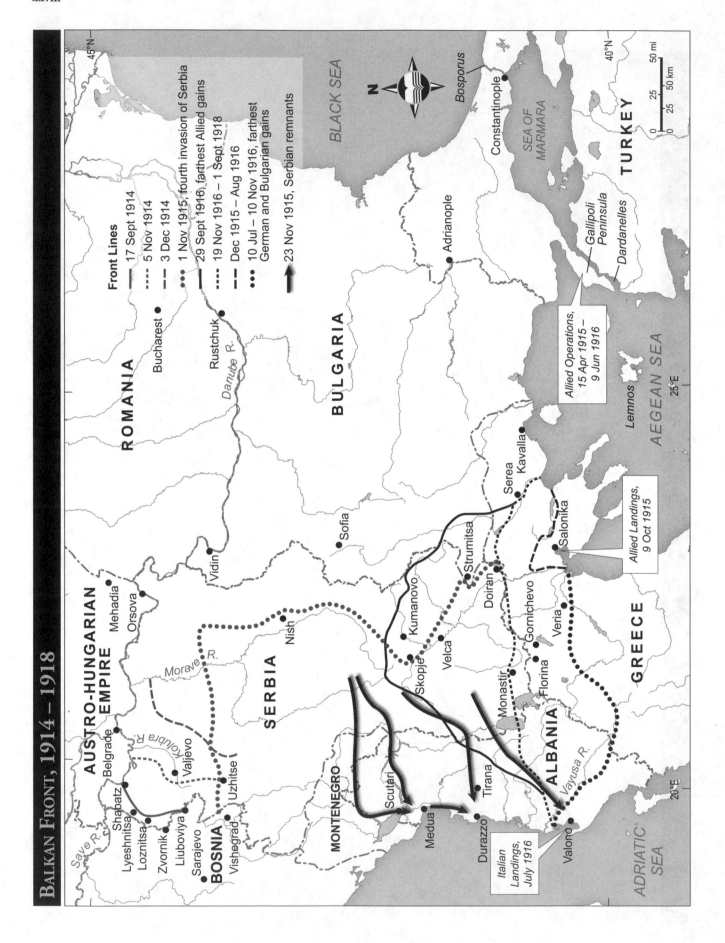

BALKAN FRONT, 1914–1918

Front Lines

—— 17 Sept 1914
······ 5 Nov 1914
— — 3 Dec 1914
•••• 1 Nov 1915, fourth invasion of Serbia
—— 29 Sept 1916, farthest Allied gains
·—·— 19 Nov 1916 – 1 Sept 1918
— — Dec 1915 – Aug 1916
•••• 10 Jul – 10 Nov 1916, farthest German and Bulgarian gains
→ 23 Nov 1915, Serbian remnants

ROMANIA
• Bucharest
• Rustchuk
Danube R.
• Vidin

AUSTRO-HUNGARIAN EMPIRE
Mehadia
Orsova
Belgrade
Shabatz
Lyeshnitsa
Loznitsa
Zvornik
Liuboviya
Valjevo
Uzhitse
Sarajevo
Vishegrad
Kolubra R.
Save R.
Morave R.

BOSNIA

SERBIA
Nish

MONTENEGRO
Scutari
Medua

ALBANIA
Durazzo
Tirana
Valona
Vayusa R.

Italian Landings, July 1916

BULGARIA
• Sofia

Skopje
Kumanovo
Velca
Strumitsa
Doiran
Monastir
Gornichevo
Veria
Florina
Serea
Kavalla
Salonika

Allied Landings, 9 Oct 1915

GREECE

BLACK SEA
• Adrianople
Constantinople
Bosporus
SEA OF MARMARA
Gallipoli Peninsula
Dardanelles
TURKEY

Allied Operations, 15 Apr 1915 – 9 Jun 1916

Lemnos
AEGEAN SEA

ADRIATIC SEA

N

50 mi
50 km
25
25
0

45°N
40°N
25°E
20°E

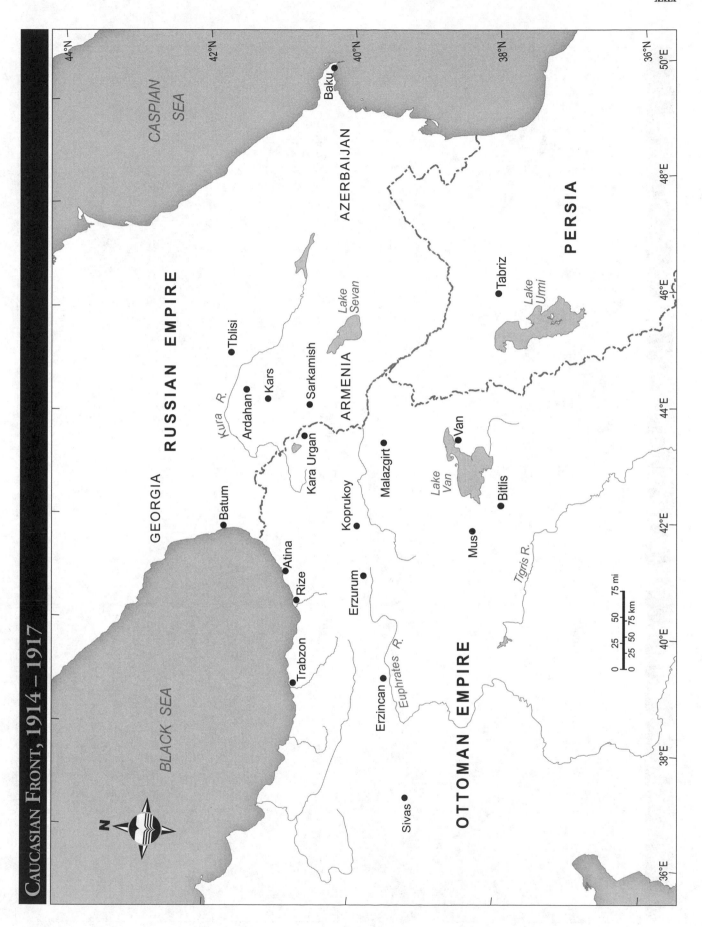

CAUCASIAN FRONT, 1914–1917

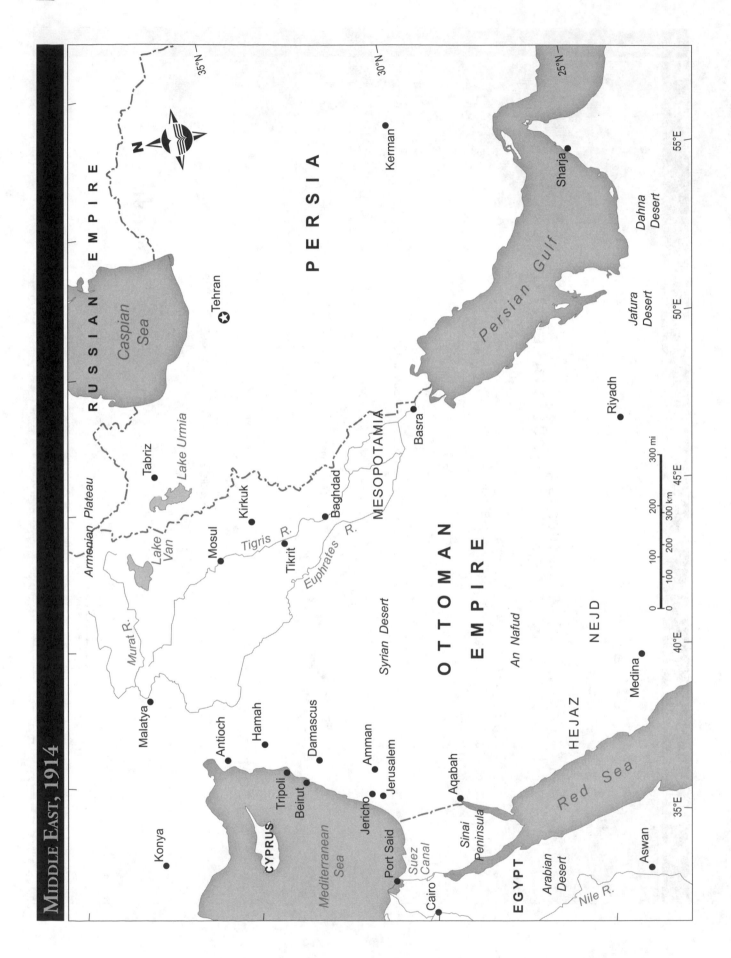

MIDDLE EAST, 1914

AFRICA, 1914

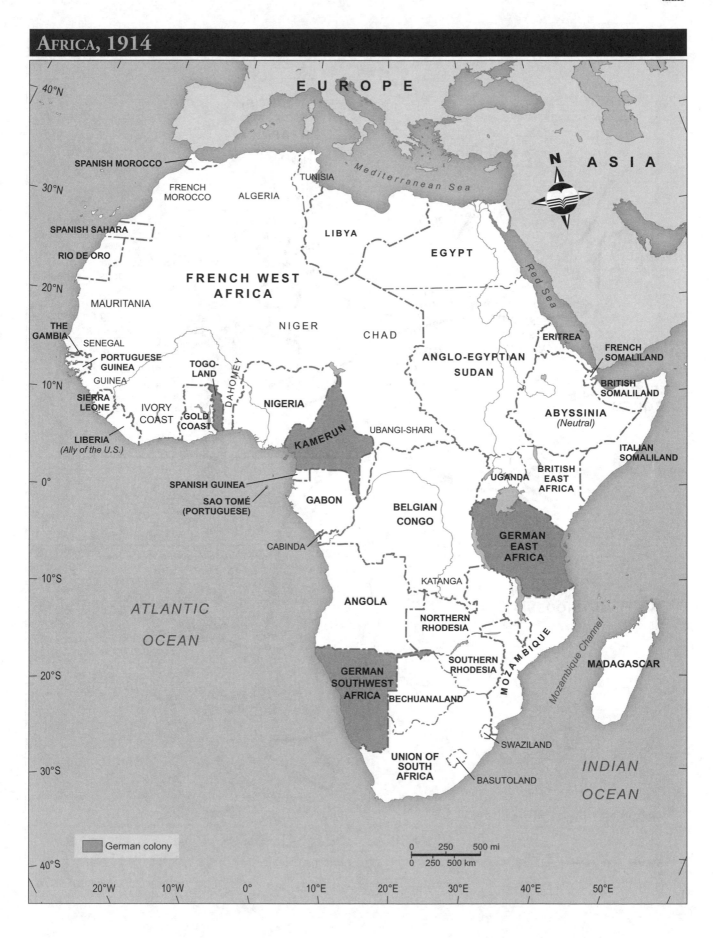

EUROPE

ASIA

N

SPANISH MOROCCO

TUNISIA

Mediterranean Sea

FRENCH
MOROCCO

ALGERIA

LIBYA

EGYPT

SPANISH SAHARA

RIO DE ORO

FRENCH WEST
AFRICA

MAURITANIA

Red Sea

NIGER

CHAD

ERITREA

ANGLO-EGYPTIAN
SUDAN

FRENCH
SOMALILAND

THE
GAMBIA

SENEGAL

PORTUGUESE
GUINEA

TOGO-
LAND

DAHOMEY

BRITISH
SOMALILAND

GUINEA

SIERRA
LEONE

IVORY
COAST

GOLD
COAST

NIGERIA

ABYSSINIA
(Neutral)

LIBERIA
(Ally of the U.S.)

KAMERUN

UBANGI-SHARI

ITALIAN
SOMALILAND

SPANISH GUINEA

SAO TOMÉ
(PORTUGUESE)

GABON

BELGIAN
CONGO

UGANDA

BRITISH
EAST
AFRICA

CABINDA

GERMAN
EAST
AFRICA

KATANGA

ATLANTIC

OCEAN

ANGOLA

NORTHERN
RHODESIA

Mozambique Channel

MOZAMBIQUE

MADAGASCAR

GERMAN
SOUTHWEST
AFRICA

SOUTHERN
RHODESIA

INDIAN

BECHUANALAND

SWAZILAND

UNION OF
SOUTH
AFRICA

BASUTOLAND

OCEAN

German colony

40°N

30°N

20°N

10°N

0°

10°S

20°S

30°S

40°S

20°W   10°W   0°   10°E   20°E   30°E   40°E   50°E

0   250   500 mi
0   250 500 km

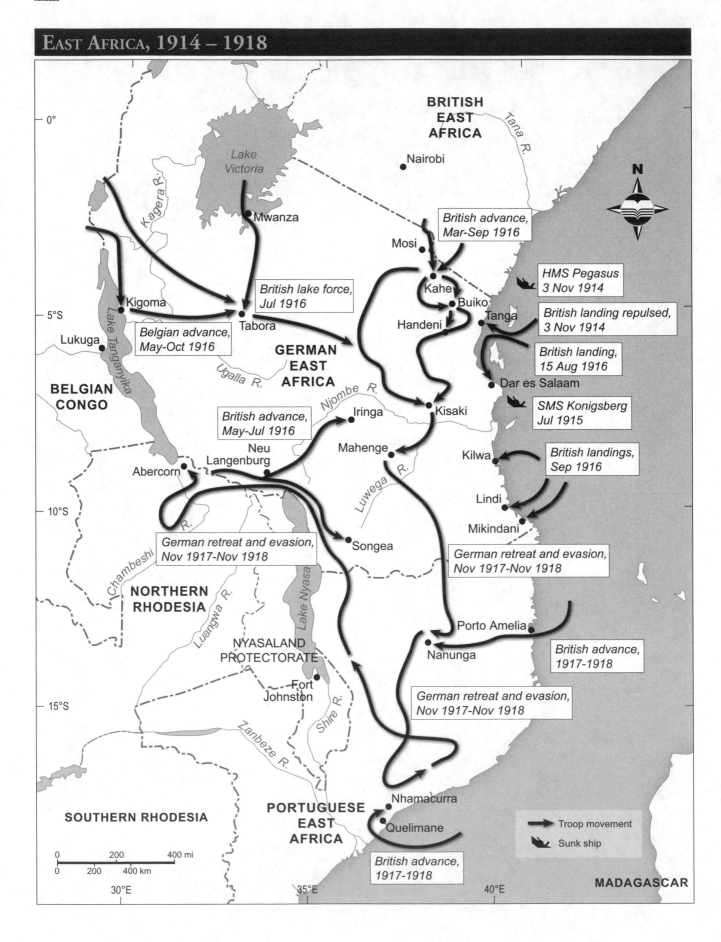

EAST AFRICA, 1914 – 1918

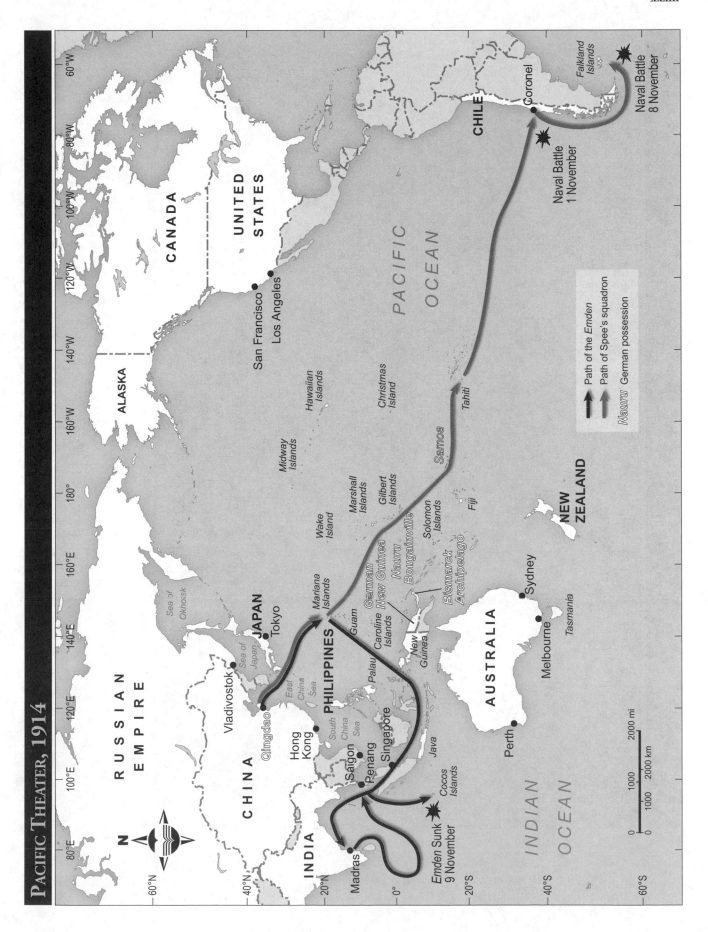

PACIFIC THEATER, 1914

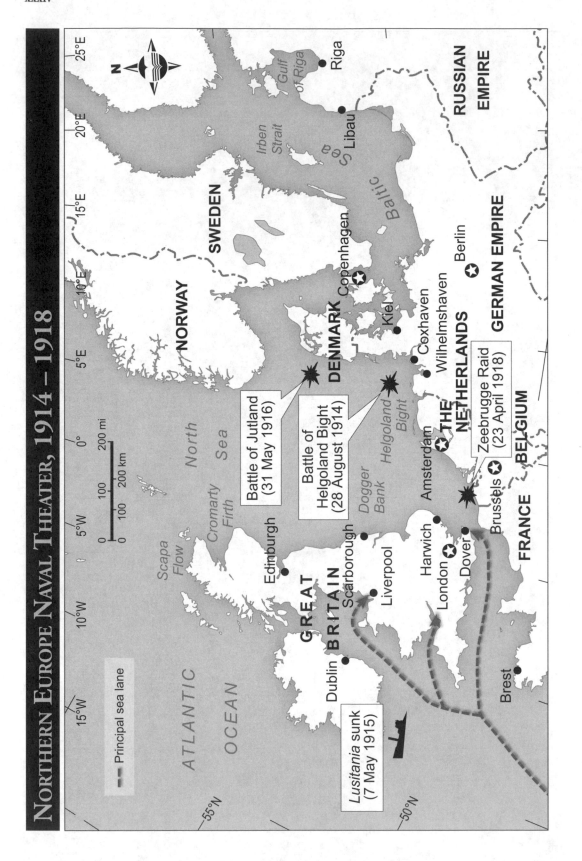

NORTHERN EUROPE NAVAL THEATER, 1914–1918

Principal sea lane

RUSSIAN EMPIRE

Riga

Gulf of Riga

Libau

Irben Strait

Baltic Sea

SWEDEN

NORWAY

Berlin

GERMAN EMPIRE

Copenhagen

DENMARK

Kiel

Coxhaven

Wilhelmshaven

THE NETHERLANDS

Amsterdam

Battle of Jutland
(31 May 1916)

Battle of
Helgoland Bight
(28 August 1914)

Helgoland Bight

Zeebrugge Raid
(23 April 1918)

Brussels

BELGIUM

FRANCE

Dogger Bank

North Sea

Scapa Flow

Cromarty Firth

Edinburgh

GREAT BRITAIN

Scarborough

Liverpool

Harwich

London

Dover

Dublin

Brest

ATLANTIC OCEAN

Lusitania sunk
(7 May 1915)

200 mi

200 km

0   100   200

0   100   200

25°E

20°E

15°E

10°E

5°E

0°

5°W

10°W

15°W

55°N

50°N

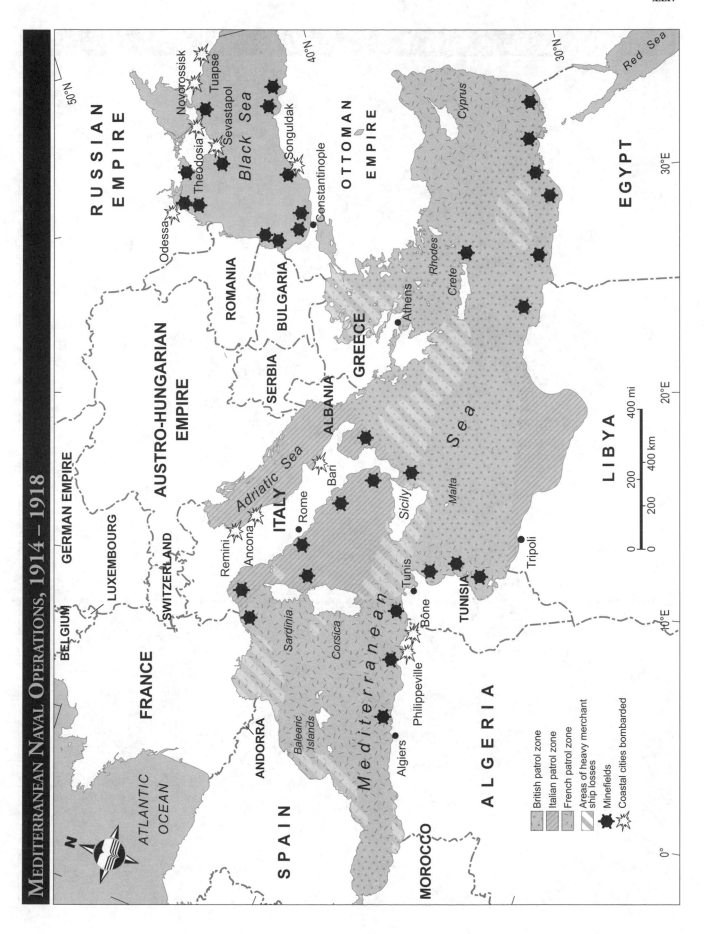

MEDITERRANEAN NAVAL OPERATIONS, 1914–1918

ATLANTIC OCEAN

SPAIN

MOROCCO

ANDORRA

FRANCE

BELGIUM

LUXEMBOURG

SWITZERLAND

GERMAN EMPIRE

AUSTRO-HUNGARIAN EMPIRE

ITALY

Rome

Remini

Ancona

Bari

Adriatic Sea

ALBANIA

GREECE

Athens

SERBIA

ROMANIA

BULGARIA

Constantinople

OTTOMAN EMPIRE

RUSSIAN EMPIRE

Odessa

Theodosia

Novorossisk

Tuapse

Sevastapol

Songuldak

Black Sea

Cyprus

EGYPT

Red Sea

Rhodes

Crete

Mediterranean Sea

Sardinia

Corsica

Balearic Islands

Algiers

Philippeville

Bône

Tunis

TUNISIA

Sicily

Malta

Tripoli

LIBYA

ALGERIA

30°N

30°E

40°N

50°N

20°E

10°E

0°

	British patrol zone
	Italian patrol zone
	French patrol zone
	Areas of heavy merchant ship losses
	Minefields
	Coastal cities bombarded

400 mi
400 km
0 200 400
0 200 400

ALLIED INTERVENTIONS IN WESTERN RUSSIA, 1918–1922

Canadians
Americans

Murmansk

British
French
Canadians
Italians
Serbs

Finns

Archangel

Shelkursk

Boundary of Russian Empire, 1914
Eastern Front, Autumn 1918
Area of Soviet Territory, Mar 1921
Main locations of Bolshevik Uprisings
Attacks by Allied Powers

NORWAY

SWEDEN

FINLAND

Finns

Helsinki

British

ESTONIA

Latts

Baltic
Sea

LATVIA
Riga

Latts

LITHUANIA

GERMANY

Baltic
Germans

Warsaw

Poles

POLAND

Petrograd

Pskov

Minsk

Kaluga

Smolensk

Moscow

Nizhni
Novgorod

RUSSIA

Kazan

Perm

Samara

Orenburg

Penza

Tambov

Saratov

Trans-Siberian Railway

Ural R.

60°N

50°N

40°N

CZECHOSLOVAKIA

HUNGARY

Dniester R.

Zhitomir

Kiev

Kharkov

Dnieper R.

Poltava

Yekaterinoslav

Don R.

Volga R.

Astrakhan

Caspian
Sea

YUGOSLAVIA

Romanians

ROMANIA

Bucharest

Odessa

Rostov

Sea
of Azov

Novorossiysk

Sevastopol

Maikop

Batumi

Baku

BULGARIA

Black   Sea

French

British

Constantinople

GREECE

OTTOMAN EMPIRE

British

Tehran

0   100   200 mi
0 100 200 km

Mediterranean
Sea

PERSIA

N

EUROPE, 1924

Reykjavik ICELAND

Norwegian Sea

SWEDEN

FINLAND

NORWAY
Christiana
Stockholm

Helsinki

Reval
ESTONIA
Riga
LATVIA

Moscow

NORTHERN IRELAND
(under British Crown)

North Sea

DENMARK

Baltic Sea

LITHUANIA
Kaunas

SOVIET UNION

IRISH FREE STATE
Belfast
Dublin
GREAT BRITAIN

THE NETHERLANDS
Amsterdam

Copenhagen

Danzig (free city)
EAST PRUSSIA (Germany)

London

Berlin
Warsaw

ATLANTIC OCEAN

Brussels
BELGIUM
Paris

GERMANY
LUXEMBOURG

Prague
CZECHOSLAVAKIA

POLAND

FRANCE

Bern
SWITZERLAND

AUSTRIA
Vienna

HUNGARY
Budapest

ROMANIA

PORTUGAL
Lisbon
Madrid
SPAIN

ANDORRA

ITALY
Rome

Belgrade
YUGOSLAVIA

Bucharest

Black Sea

Adriatic Sea

BULGARIA
Sofia

Tirana
ALBANIA

Constantinople

GREECE

TURKEY

Mediterranean
Sea
Athens

New nations (1918 – 1924)

Rhineland (German territory occupied by the Allies

Alsace-Lorraine (Ceded to France, 1918)

AFRICA

0   200   400 mi
0   200   400 km

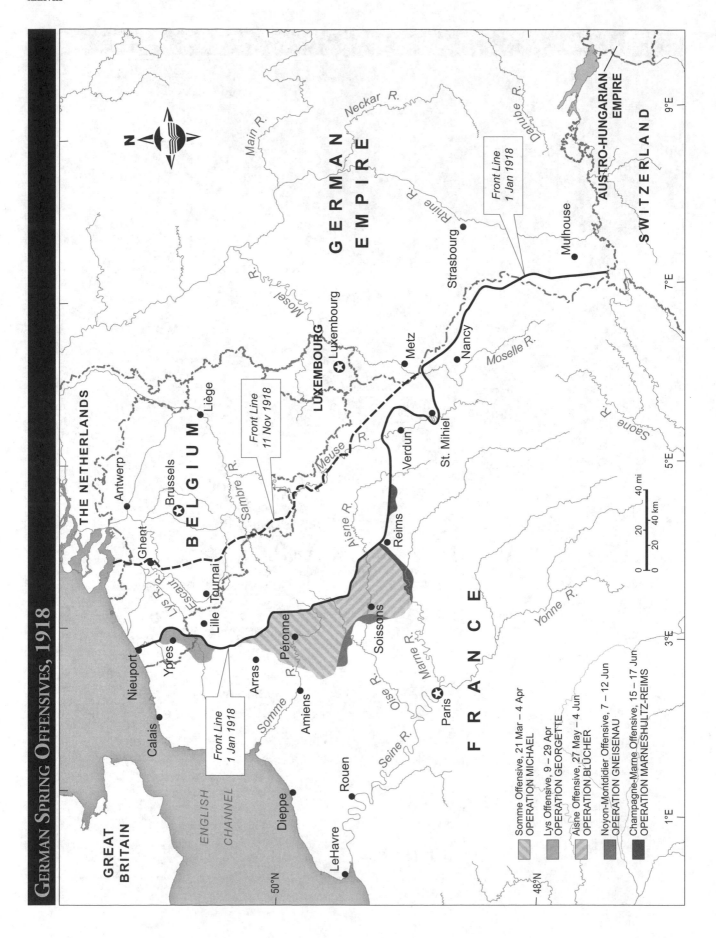

GERMAN SPRING OFFENSIVES, 1918

GREAT BRITAIN

ENGLISH CHANNEL

THE NETHERLANDS

BELGIUM

LUXEMBOURG

GERMAN EMPIRE

FRANCE

SWITZERLAND

AUSTRO-HUNGARIAN EMPIRE

Front Line 1 Jan 1918

Front Line 11 Nov 1918

Front Line 1 Jan 1918

Calais
Nieuport
Ypres
Arras
Amiens
Dieppe
Rouen
LeHavre
Paris
Lille
Tournai
Ghent
Brussels
Antwerp
Liège
Péronne
Soissons
Reims
Luxembourg
Metz
Nancy
Strasbourg
Mulhouse
Verdun
St. Mihiel

Somme R.
Oise R.
Marne R.
Seine R.
Yonne R.
Aisne R.
Meuse R.
Sambre R.
Escaut R.
Lys R.
Moselle R.
Mosel R.
Rhine R.
Neckar R.
Main R.
Danube R.
Saône R.

Somme Offensive, 21 Mar – 4 Apr
OPERATION MICHAEL

Lys Offensive, 9 – 29 Apr
OPERATION GEORGETTE

Aisne Offensive, 27 May – 4 Jun
OPERATION BLÜCHER

Noyon-Montdidier Offensive, 7 – 12 Jun
OPERATION GNEISENAU

Champagne-Marne Offensive, 15 – 17 Jun
OPERATION MARNESHULTZ-REIMS

N

40 mi
40 km
20
20
0
0

9°E
7°E
5°E
3°E
1°E
50°N
48°N

M

Ma'ān, Siege of
(17 April–28 September 1918)

Mesopotamian theater battle. The town of Ma'ān was located on the rail line between Jerusalem and Akaba and had been used as a base for Turkish operations against forces of the Arab Revolt. In early April 1918, following a halt in the British advance into the Transjordan and to the Dead Sea at Amman, Arab Northern Army commander Sharif Faisal Ibn Husayn planned an attack on Ma'ān. His goals were to secure future Allied advances in the area from attacks from the rear and to cut off Amman from reinforcement along the Hejaz railway from the south. All available Turkish troops, including most of the garrison of Ma'ān, then had been relocated to Amman in an attempt to halt the British advance there.

The attack on Ma'ān began on 17 April 1918, with Arab forces cutting the Hejaz railroad both north and south of the town. Arab Army regulars under Jafaar Pasha, supported by British armored cars and camel units, then attacked the town from the north, south, and west. Although the attacking Arab forces held a numerical advantage over the Turkish defenders, operations were suspended when Jafaar's small French artillery detachment ran short of ammunition. The majority of the Arab forces then fell back on Senna, which had been taken on 13 April. Following this stalemate, a siege began.

Turkish negotiations to surrender were broken off by the arrival of 3,000 men of the II Corps from Amman. These additional troops strengthened the Turkish defenses in Ma'ān as well as their resolve and thus prolonged the siege. Jafaar then cut off Turkish resupply into Ma'ān from Turkish-controlled Medina along the Hejaz railway to the south.

Ma'ān was now effectively isolated from the outside. The combined forces of Sharif Faisal and Major-General Sir Edward Chaytor's Australian and New Zealand Mounted Division then pursued the survivors up the Hejaz railway. On 28 September Chaytor's forces cut the Turks off and secured the surrender of 4,500 of them. Ma'ān was an important Allied victory.

Alex Correll

See also
Amman, Battle of; Faisal, Prince; Mesopotamian Theater.
References
Barker, A. J. *The Bastard War: The Mesopotamian Campaign of 1914–1918.* New York: Dial, 1967.
Buchanan, George. *Tragedy of Mesopotamia.* New York: AMS Press, 1974.
Moberly, F. J. *The Campaign in Mesopotamia, 1914–1918.* 3 vols. Nashville, TN: Battery Press, 1997–1998.

MacArthur, Douglas (1880–1964)

U.S. Army general. Born 26 January 1880 in Little Rock, Arkansas, Douglas MacArthur, the son of General Arthur MacArthur, graduated first in his class from the U.S. Military Academy, West Point, in 1903. Commissioned in the engineers, he served in the Philippines and Japan. He was aide to President Theodore Roosevelt (1906–1907) and an instructor at the General Service and Cavalry Schools (1908–1913). MacArthur participated in the U.S. occupation of Veracruz, Mexico (1914), for which he was nominated for the Medal of Honor, and was on the General Staff (1913–1917).

U.S. Army Brigadier General Douglas MacArthur in his brigade headquarters in a château at St. Benôit Chateau, France. (National Archives)

When the United States entered World War I in April 1917, MacArthur transferred to the infantry. Promoted to temporary colonel, he became chief of staff of the 42nd Infantry Division, nicknamed the "Rainbow Division" because it was an amalgam of National Guard units from across the country. The 42nd was sent to Europe as part of the American Expeditionary Forces (AEF) in October 1917. MacArthur excelled in both staff work and field command. Wounded twice, he was awarded two Distinguished Service Crosses, the Distinguished Service Medal, and six Silver Stars.

Promoted to brigadier general in July 1918, MacArthur fought with his division in the Aisne-Marne offensive and the subsequent counterattack. He then assumed command of the 84th Brigade and fought with it in the Saint-Mihiel and Meuse-Argonne Offenses. He commanded the 42nd Division in November 1918.

Following occupation duties immediately after the war, MacArthur became superintendent at West Point (1919–1922), where he introduced much-needed reforms. After service in the Philippines, he became chief of staff of the army in 1930. In 1935 he was named field marshal of the Philippine army. Designated commander of U.S. forces in the Far East in July 1941, he was later commander of the Southwest Pacific,

and, promoted to general of the army in December 1944, led the U.S. offensive in that region.

After World War II MacArthur supervised the U.S. occupation of Japan and in 1950, on the outbreak of the Korean War, assumed command of United Nations forces there. Relieved of his command by President Harry S. Truman in April 1951, MacArthur retired. He was unsuccessful in his effort to win the Republican presidential nomination in 1952. MacArthur died in New York City on 5 April 1964.

T. Jason Soderstrum

See also
Aisne-Marne Offensive; Meuse-Argonne Offensive; Saint-Mihiel Offensive; United States, Army.
References
James, D. Clayton. *The Years of MacArthur.* 3 vols. Boston: Houghton Mifflin, 1970–1985.
Manchester, William Raymond. *American Caesar: Douglas MacArthur, 1880–1964.* Boston: Little, Brown, 1978.
Perret, Geoffrey. *Old Soldiers Never Die: The Life of Douglas MacArthur.* Holbrook, MA: Adams Media Corporation, 1996.

MacDonald, James Ramsay (1866–1937)

British statesman. Born on 12 October 1866 in Lossiemouth, Scotland, James MacDonald, the illegitimate son of a maidservant, worked his way through a local school as a pupil-teacher then took a job as a clerk in Bristol in 1885. He became acquainted with the quasi-Marxist Social Democratic Federation and later joined the Fabian Society, the intellectual foundation of the British Labour Party. In 1900 MacDonald was appointed secretary of the Labour Representation Committee and was returned to Parliament in 1906 as member for Leicester. In 1911 he became leader of the Labour Party's group of parliament members in the House of Commons.

MacDonald was one of the few sitting members of parliament to take an active critical stance against the Asquith government's declaration of war in August 1914, and he resigned his post as Labour leader after the party refused to oppose the voting of war credits. MacDonald toured the country to agitate against Britain's involvement in the war, a provocative action that turned him into the "best-hated man in Great Britain" and led to numerous accusations that he was pro-German and a pacifist, both charges that he denied. In September 1914 MacDonald was one of the founders of the Union of Democratic Control, a liberal-socialist group that criticized Sir Edward Grey's handling of foreign policy.

In spring 1917 MacDonald became notorious once more when he and a group of Labour Party and independent socialist leaders attempted unsuccessfully to travel to Petrograd

Morgan, Austen. *James Ramsay MacDonald*. Manchester, UK: Manchester University Press, 1987.

Reekes, Andrew. *The Rise of Labour, 1899–1951*. Basingstoke, UK: Macmillan, 1991.

Stansky, Peter. *The Left and War: The British Labour Party and World War I*. New York: Oxford University Press, 1969.

British Prime Minister Ramsay MacDonald, Great Britain's first Labour Party prime minister. (The Illustrated London News Picture Library)

to meet with the new Russian revolutionary government. The disillusionment about the war now held by many in Labour's ranks brought a closer relationship between Mac-Donald and the more moderate party spokesmen such as Arthur Henderson.

MacDonald lost his seat in the December 1918 general election, but his career was to have a dramatic revival in the 1920s when he twice became prime minister, the first of the Labour Party to hold that office (1924 and 1929–1931). His decision to support the Conservative-dominated National Government in August 1931—he continued as premier, leading a few senior colleagues into the coalition until 1935— saw his final break with the Labour Party, which expelled him in September 1931. MacDonald died at sea en route to South America on 9 November 1937.

Alan Allport

See also

Asquith, Herbert Henry, 1st Earl; Great Britain, Home Front; Henderson, Arthur; Lloyd George, David; Peace Overtures during the War.

References

Marquand, David. *Ramsay MacDonald*. London: J. Cape, 1977.

Machine Guns

Automatic small arms, usually belt-fed, with high cyclic rates of fire. Although multiple-round firing guns, such as the Gatling, preceded the truly automatic weapons, it was the U.S.-born, naturalized British inventor Hiram Maxim who produced the first modern machine gun in the mid-1880s. It weighed 100 pounds, used recoil energy to operate its firing mechanism, and was water-cooled. The battlefield appearance of the true machine gun during the 1904–1905 Russo-Japanese War, along with the rapid-firing field artillery piece, signaled a quantum leap toward greater lethality in modern war. At 450–600 rounds per minute cyclic rate, in theory one machine gun could equal the fire of forty to eighty riflemen, although the sustained rate of fire was much less. The machine gun also had greater range than the rifle, enabling indirect fire to support an infantry attack.

Maxim and another U.S. inventor, Colonel Isaac Lewis, made a significant contribution that increased lethality. U.S. inventor Benjamin Hotchkiss moved from Connecticut to Europe to produce his excellent 8mm air-cooled guns. In fact, most of the major inventors and manufacturers of true machine guns were U.S.-born.

The technological advance of increasing the rate of fire of small-arms weapons was not accompanied by an immediate improvement in the tactical doctrine for the employment of those weapons. Well into the early years of World War I, there was confusion as to whether the machine gun should be principally a defensive or an offensive weapon. Initially they were employed as part of the defensive belts that characterized the positions in depth designed to wear down the momentum of the assault. Later in the war, light assault machine guns were a major battlefield factor and accompanied attacking forces. Unlike their heavy, manually operated predecessors, modern automatic machine guns were, with effort, man-portable. The limiting factor was the availability of ammunition.

Rapid-firing, inexpensive machine weapons tended to level the performance potential of armies. It was no longer only the wealthier states that could field highly lethal forces. The result was enormous casualty figures in dead and wounded that the machine guns and quick-firing artillery pieces could produce in the hands of skilled operators.

German troops in their front line trench around a machine gun less than 120 feet from the British lines. (Library of Congress)

The French began the war with the Saint-Étienne machine guns but soon replaced them with an improved Hotchkiss. Both took the 8mm Lebel cartridge. The Hotchkiss weighed 88 to 115 pounds, including mount; was air-cooled; and had a cyclical rate of fire of 600 rounds per minute. The British used the Vickers Mk I .303 caliber. It weighed 73 pounds including mount and was water-cooled. The Vickers, which remained the standard in the British army through World War II, fired at a cyclic rate of 500 rounds per minute and was accurate at 600 yards. Later the British also utilized the Lewis light machine gun. It used the same .303 caliber ammunition but weighed only 25 pounds and had a drum magazine. It had a rate of fire of 500–600 rounds per minute. It was also employed extensively in British aircraft. The American John Browning's .30 caliber model 1917 did not see extensive service in the Great War but became a mainstay in World War II. It weighed 41 pounds, was water-cooled, and had a cyclical rate of fire of 450–600 rounds per minute.

The standard Russian machine gun was a 1910 Maxim ("Sokolov") chambered for a 7.62mm cartridge. It weighed 90–152.5 pounds with mount, was water-cooled, and fired at a cylical rate of 500–600 rounds per minute. The American Colt 1917 design and a British Vickers type were manufactured for the Russians but did not arrive before Russia left the war. The Italian machine gun, the M1914 water-cooled Revelli, was made by Fiat. It weighed 49 pounds and fired 500 6.5mm rounds per minute from a box magazine.

American Expeditionary Forces (AEF) machine gun units were usually equipped with .30 caliber Maxim guns or the French air-cooled 8mm Hotchkiss guns. The U.S. standard, the French gun made by Benet-Mercié, was judged inferior to both those guns by the men who had to use them. The 2nd Machine Gun Battalion of the U.S. 1st Division trained in the United States with the Benet-Mercié guns. At the training center at Gondrecourt, France, they were issued the Hotchkiss. The U.S. troops preferred the Hotchkiss, which they dubbed a "He" gun, but noted that its weight of 52 pounds proved a serious handicap in battle.

Germany, the senior partner in the Central Powers coalition, made effective use of the machine gun in its units. Germany had developed both heavy and light machine guns based on the Maxim model. Austria-Hungary was the beneficiary of German technology for most of the war. The German guns were manufactured for a 7.92mm cartridge at Spandau, which is the name remembered by Allied infantrymen. By taking the Maxim MG 08 off its tripod mount, reducing the water jacket size, and adding a bi-pod near the end of the barrel and a pistol grip, the MG 08/15 [1915] was reduced from 58 to 39 pounds. A further modification in 1918 produced the 35-pound Maxim MG 08/18 [1918] that was air-cooled. It weighed just 32 pounds.

In the decade before the Great War, the Germans had begun to integrate their machine guns into infantry and cavalry regiments, with a modest reserve at the corps level. In this regard the German army was far advanced over the other powers at the onset of World War I. In fact, the Germans began the war with more machine guns than any other power. They organized them into companies, as opposed to dispersing them among infantry formations. This made it easier to concentrate the machine guns in desired sectors of the front.

Because many of the German frontline infantry formations were made up of reserve troops with minimal training in rifle marksmanship, the machine gun was a good corrective to inadequate fire volume. In 1907–1908 the Germans added a machine-gun company of six guns to each infantry regiment. In the U.S. Army a machine gun squad consisted of one gun and eight men: a corporal commanding, a gunner, a loader, and five ammunition bearers. The machine-gun company for an infantry regiment had three platoons with four squads each for a total of twelve hybrid teams.

Early in the war the machine gun was employed by all field armies as a defensive weapon. Later, notably by the Germans in their assault units, a lighter machine gun was developed so that it could be carried forward in the attack. The common deficiency for machine guns was that ammunition in sufficient quantities was difficult to move forward.

The Germans usually placed machine guns by themselves outside the frontline trenches in pairs to avoid destruction by the artillery preparations. Deep bunkers were provided for the guns and crews so that they could emerge unscathed just as the enemy infantry was crossing no-man's-land and encountering the barbed war entanglements. This was a technique that the Allies never mastered. It was this slaughter of massed infantry that led to a search for solutions, one being the tank and another being doctrinal adjustments that brought the machine gun within a system of integrated fire planning along with the artillery and rifle musketry.

German riflemen with machine gun on horse-drawn carriage, 15 October 1918. (National Archives)

During their July 1916 Somme offensive, the British sent 100,000 men against the German positions, resulting in 60 percent casualties, a third of those killed. At Vimy Ridge in September 1917, the Canadian corps used their machine guns to deliver plunging fire in the form of barrages to the German rear areas to disrupt movement of supplies and to harass the troops. The subsequent successful attack was supported by artillery creeping barrages. During the great Ludendorff offensives of March–April 1918, the Germans employed their light machine guns in special units, along with trench mortars, grenades, and flamethrowers, to infiltrate quickly and bypass Allied strong-points. Nonetheless, the British inflicted enormous casualties on the German follow-up forces, mostly because the rapid advance of the German artillery barrages from trench line to trench line did not destroy the British machine guns and infantry riflemen. In the Meuse-Argonne campaign in September–November 1918, U.S. troops faced successive defensive belts, each reinforced with multiple machine-gun positions. The importance of large numbers of machine guns was partly due to a serious shortage of artillery ammunition late in the war. After World War I, technological advances in mobility finally caught up to the earlier advances in firepower, thereby restoring the balance between fire and maneuver.

John F. Votaw

See also

Artillery; Infantry Tactics; Ludendorff Offensives; Meuse-Argonne Offensive; Somme Offensive; Tanks; Vimy Ridge, Battle of.

References

Dooly, William G., Jr. *Great Weapons of World War I*. New York: Bonanza, 1968.

Ellis, John. *The Social History of the Machine Gun*. London: Croom Helm, 1975.

Ford, Roger. *The Grim Reaper: Machine-Guns and Machine-Gunners in Action*. London: Brown Packaging, 1996.

———. *The World's Great Machine Guns*. London: Brown Packaging, 1999.

Gander, Terry J. *The Browning Automatic Rifle*. London: Parkgate, 1999.

Hogg, Ian V. *Machine Guns: 14th Century to Present*. Iola, WI: Krause Publications, 2002.

Johnson, Hubert C. *Breakthrough! Tactics, Technology, and the Search for Victory on the Western Front in World War I*. Novato, CA: Presidio, 1994.

Walter, John. *Modern Machine Guns*. London and Mechanicsburg, PA: Greenhill and Stackpole, 2000.

German Field Marshal Ludwig August von Mackensen with fur cap with death's head, 1935. (Library of Congress)

Mackensen, August von (1849–1945)

German field marshal. Born in Leipnitz near Wittenberge, Prussian Saxony, on 6 December 1849, Ludwig August Friedrich von Mackensen was completing his military obligation as a cavalry officer candidate when war with France began in September 1870. He served in that conflict, earning promotion to lieutenant and an Iron Cross for patrols behind enemy lines. Following the war he returned to the University of Halle but reentered the military in 1873. He served in the Life Hussars and Guards Cavalry Brigade, from which he had the unusual distinction of being transferred directly to the General Staff without attending the War Academy in Berlin.

Mackensen became adjutant to Chief of the General Staff General Count von Schlieffen in 1891. Accompanying him on a staff ride that year, Mackensen came to the attention of Kaiser Wilhelm II, who in 1898 appointed Mackensen one of his adjutants (Flügeladjutant), the first commoner so honored. A year later, the kaiser ennobled him.

A General der Kavallerie (lieutenant general) and commander of the XVIIth Corps in East Prussia at the beginning of World War I, Mackensen distinguished himself in the Tannenberg and Masurian Lakes battles in August and September 1914. From November 1914 until April 1915, he commanded the Ninth Army in the East, earning both promotion to colonel general (full general) and the Pour le Mérite for success in fighting at Łódź.

On 16 April 1915 Mackensen received command of the newly organized Eleventh Army, a combined German-Austrian force. Colonel Hans von Seeckt became Mackensen's chief of staff, a fortuitous arrangement for both. In May, Mackensen's combined Austro-German force began to drive the Russians from the Carpathians at Gorlice-Tarnów. Colonel Georg Bruchmüller had prepared the artillery barrage for the army, and within four hours more than 700,000 shells were fired. Within twenty-four hours the Russians fled from Gorlice, and five days later Tarnów fell. The Central Powers retook the Carpathian passes and captured 30,000 Russians. By the end of June, Przemyśl and Lemberg had fallen. The prisoner bag now exceeded a quarter million, and Mackensen received promotion to field marshal.

On 4 July 1915 Mackensen took charge of a formation that came to be known as Army Group von Mackensen. It consisted of the German Eleventh Army and the Bug Army as well as the Austro-Hungarian First Army. By the end of August it had driven the Russian army from Lublin, Cholm, and Brest Litovsk and had moved as far as the Pripet Marshes.

On 16 September Mackensen took command of a new Army Group Mackensen, consisting of the German Ninth, Austro-Hungarian Third, and Bulgarian First Armies, for operations against Serbia. Operations commenced in October, and by November Mackensen's army group had driven the Serbian army southwest from Serbia and across Albania to Greece. Mackensen spent the first half of 1916 blocking the Allied forces in northern Greece (the Salonika Front), but when Romania entered the war on the Allied side in September 1916, he moved across Bulgaria to threaten Romania from the south. His marching and countermarching along the Danube drew off Romanian forces from the Transylvanian passes, and when General Erich von Falkenhayn's German Ninth Army swept over the Transylvanian Alps, Mackensen crossed the Danube and entered Bucharest, capturing that city in December 1916. The kaiser awarded him the Grand Cross of the Iron Cross, one of only four awarded in the war. Mackensen remained in Bucharest as German commander in the Balkans and Salonika until war's end. When he attempted to return to Germany, French forces took him prisoner and held him for a year. Upon his return to Germany in December 1919, he retired from military service.

Mackensen became involved with several youth groups, most notably the "Young Storm," and veterans organizations. When Marshal Paul von Hindenburg died in 1934, Mackensen became the sole surviving German field marshal and appeared in full Death's Head Hussar's regalia at every military function. The Hitler regime gave him an estate, Brüssow, in West Prussia, and he represented the German government at the kaiser's funeral in 1941. During the war, he distanced himself from the Hitler regime. One of his sons, Eberhard, became a colonel general in the German army in World War II. Mackensen fled from the advancing Russians and died on 8 November 1945, just outside Celle at Gutshaus Burghorn.

Michael B. Barrett

See also
Bruchmüller, Georg; Falkenhayn, Erich von; Gorlice-Tarnów Offensive; Hindenburg, Paul von; Łódź, Battle of; Masurian Lakes, First Battle of the; Przemyśl; Romania, Campaign of 1916; Salonika Campaign; Seeckt, Hans von; Serbia, Conquest of; Tannenberg, Battle of; Wilhelm II, Kaiser.

References
Mackensen, August von. *Briefe und Aufzeichnungen.* Leipzig: Bibliograpisches Institut, 1938.
Showalter, Dennis E. *Tannenberg: Clash of Empires.* Hamden, CT: Archon, 1991.
Stone, Norman. *The Eastern Front, 1914–1917.* New York: Scribner, 1975.

Madden, Sir Charles (1862–1935)

British admiral. Born on 5 September 1862 at Gillingham, Kent, Charles Madden entered the Royal Navy at age 13 in 1875. Most of his early assignments were in torpedo work. Promoted to captain in 1901, he took command of an armored cruiser. Assigned to the Admiralty in 1905, Madden found himself helping to institute reforms proposed by First Sea Lord Admiral John Fisher. Madden served as naval assistant to the third sea lord and eventually became Fisher's assistant.

Madden left the Admiralty in 1907 to assume command of HMS *Dreadnought,* the world's first all-big-gun modern battleship, which he had helped to design while at the Admiralty. Until the outbreak of World War I, Madden continued to serve in administrative positions, including as naval secretary to the first lord of the Admiralty. Promoted to rear admiral, Madden served as fourth sea lord during 1910–1911. He then served with the home fleet but returned to the Admiralty at the beginning of the war.

Commander of the Grand Fleet Admiral Sir John Jellicoe secured the appointment of Madden, his brother-in-law, as his chief of staff. The two men directed the Royal Navy's most powerful force during the first two years of the conflict. Madden participated in the Battle of Jutland (31 May–1 June 1916). Although it proved an indecisive encounter militarily, the battle had important ramifications for the Royal Navy's staff. Jellicoe came under heavy criticism for his failure to achieve decisive victory and was later "promoted" to first sea lord.

As expected, Jellicoe recommended Madden as his successor as commander of the Grand Fleet. The Admiralty, however, selected Admiral Sir David Beatty. Madden became Beatty's second-in-command with responsibility for the 1st Battle Squadron, an assignment he carried out with distinction during the remainder of the war.

Advanced to full admiral in 1919, Madden assumed command of the Atlantic Fleet. That same year he received a baronetcy. He was promoted to admiral of the fleet in 1924 and became principal naval advisor to King George V. He retired in 1925 but was recalled to active service in 1927 to succeed Beatty as first sea lord, holding that post until 1930, a time of great financial constraint and disarmament. Madden opposed, unsuccessfully, many of the reductions imposed by the London Naval Conference in 1930. He retired again in 1930 and died at London on 5 June 1935.

R. Kyle Schlafer

See also

Beatty, David, 1st Earl; *Dreadnought,* HMS; Fisher, John Arbuthnot, 1st Baron; Grand Fleet; Great Britain, Navy; Jellicoe, John Rushworth, 1st Earl; Jutland, Battle of; Naval Blockade of Germany; Naval Warfare.

References

Gordon, G. A. H. *The Rules of the Game: Jutland and British Naval Command.* Annapolis: Naval Institute Press, 1997.

Halpern, Paul. *A Naval History of World War I.* Annapolis: Naval Institute Press, 1994.

Marder, Arthur J. *From the Dreadnought to Scapa Flow: The Royal Navy in the Fisher Era, 1904–1919.* 5 vols. London: Oxford University Press, 1961–1970.

Magdeburg, SMS (1912)

German light cruiser, commissioned in 1912. One of a four-ship class, *Magdeburg* displaced 4,550 tons and was armed with 12×4.1-inch (10.5cm) guns. On the outbreak of war, the *Magdeburg* was part of the Baltic Coast Defence Division and conducted several reconnaissance sweeps west of the entrance to the Gulf of Finland, shelling Russian signal stations and lighthouses.

On 25 August 1914, the *Magdeburg* and the light cruiser *Augsburg* sortied for a special mission to destroy the signal station on the island of Odensholm near Baltic Port (Estonia) inside the Gulf of Finland. While navigating in thick fog, the *Magdeburg* ran hard aground less than 200 yards from the Odensholm lighthouse. Subsequent attempts by the torpedo boat *V-26* to tow the heavily damaged cruiser free failed. Inexplicably, *Magdeburg*'s commanding officer, Lieutenant Commander Richard Habenicht, failed to order the destruction of the ship's confidential papers—including the cipher and codebooks—as his instructions demanded.

When the fog lifted in the early morning hours of the 26th, the *V-26* rescued part of the crew on board, but the torpedo

The German light cruiser *Magdeburg* seen from a Russian torpedo boat on the morning of 26 August 1914. (Courtesy of the Russian Navy)

boat abandoned the effort when the Russian cruisers *Bogatyr* and the armored cruiser *Pallada* appeared on the scene. In the confusion of Russian shells falling around the *Magdeburg*, only part of the ship was blown up, but the sensitive secret material remained intact. When the Russians boarded the wreck they captured the remainder of the crew (including the commanding officer) and retrieved the cipher and code-books—among them the secret *Signalbuch der Kaiserlichen Marine* (SKM).

The Russians were well aware of the value of their booty and made good use of it during their later campaigns in the Baltic and the Black Sea. Within days they also informed the British Admiralty through the British naval attaché in Moscow that they wished to share the information gathered from the captured documents. The cruiser HMS *Theseus* was dispatched to pick up the SKM and other material from Alexandrovsk (Polyarno) on 7 September, and on 13 October 1914 First Lord of the Admiralty Sir Winston Churchill held the *Magdeburg*'s copy no. 151 of the SKM in his hands. The captured codebook was an extraordinary windfall for Room 40, the British Admiralty's cipher-breaking organization.

The German handling of the aftermath of the *Magdeburg* incident betrayed an almost unbelievable degree of negligence, which a German postwar analysis of wireless intelligence operations singled out as the most glaring failure of German signals operations. Rear Admiral Ehler Behring, who had commanded the ill-fated sortie, stated in his report that it was not known for certain whether the *Magdeburg*'s SKM had been destroyed, and testimonies in subsequent court-martial proceedings reinforced the suspicion that the Russians had recovered the key and other sensitive material from the ship. Yet, the German naval leadership took no action. The SKM remained in force with few alterations until 1917, greatly facilitating the work of Allied signals intelligence.

Dirk Steffen

See also
Churchill, Sir Winston; Codes and Code Breaking; Room 40.
References
Beesly, Patrick. *Room 40: British Naval Intelligence, 1914–1918.* New York: Harcourt Brace Jovanovich, 1982.
Mäkelä, Matti E. *Das Geheimnis der Magdeburg* [The secret of the Magdeburg]. Koblenz: Bernard and Graefe Verlag, 1984.

Maghar Ridge, Battle of (13 November 1917)

Battle during the Palestine campaign. As part of Lieutenant General Edmund Allenby's drive through Judea, the British XXI Corps was ordered to seize Junction Station, a major Ottoman supply depot and transport hub. Junction Station was the point where the Beersheba railroad met the Jaffa-Jerusalem line, and its capture would sever the last link between the Ottoman Seventh and Eighth Armies. Standing between the British and their objective were the Ottoman 3rd, 7th, and 54th Infantry Divisions. Although seriously under-strength, these formations occupied hastily prepared positions along the Maghar Ridge and the surrounding villages of Aqir, El Maghar, Qatra, and El Mesmiye.

The British plan called for the 75th Division to push forward along the Beersheba railroad with El Mesmiye as its immediate objective, while to the north the 52nd (Lowland) Division was to attack the villages of Qatra and El Maghar at the southern end of Maghar Ridge. Once these objectives had been taken, the British infantry were to halt their advance long enough for their artillery to be repositioned before carrying on and converging on Junction Station. The flanks of the British infantry would be covered by the Yeomanry Mounted Division on the left and the Australian Mounted Division on the right.

On the morning of 13 November, following an hour-long preliminary bombardment, the British infantry launched their attack. Both divisions encountered staunch Ottoman resistance, and progress was slow. In fact, by the early afternoon it was clear that the 52nd Division's attack had become bogged down in the face of heavy Ottoman artillery and machine-gun fire. At that point the 52nd's commander, Major-General John Hill, called upon the Yeomanry Mounted Division for support against Maghar Ridge.

Unknown to Hill, the Yeomanry Division's 6th Mounted Brigade had already been dispatched to the 52nd's aid. At 3:00 P.M. two regiments of the brigade charged the Ottoman positions on Maghar Ridge in an audacious cavalry action that broke the Ottoman defense and changed the course of the battle. Before the British cavalry could close, many of the Ottoman infantry abandoned their positions and fled. The British took several hundred prisoners.

With this breakthrough the whole Ottoman line was fatally unhinged. To the south the 52nd Division captured the village of Qatra by 4:00 P.M., while the 6th Mounted Brigade and two battalions of the 52nd pressed on to take El Maghar itself. The 75th Division, with support from elements of the Australian Mounted Division, was then able to take Mesmiye before dusk.

Seeking to exploit the day's successes, the 75th Division attempted a night attack on Junction Station. But after fending off an Ottoman counterattack and a series of other encounters with Ottoman rear guards, it was decided to halt operations until daybreak. When the 75th Division resumed its advance on the morning of 14 November, the British found the Ottoman Eighth Army in full retreat, having abandoned Junction Station with most of its heavy plant and supplies left intact. British losses in the battle amounted to 1,122 casualties (most of which were suffered by the infantry), and while total Ottoman casualties remain unknown, approximately 1,700 Ottoman prisoners were taken.

Damien Fenton

See also
Allenby, Sir Edmund, 1st Viscount; Beersheba-Gaza Line, Battles of; Jerusalem, Fall of; Palestine and Syria, Land Campaign.
References
Bruce, Anthony P. C. *The Last Crusade: The Palestine Campaign in the First World War.* London: Murray, 2002.
Bullock, David L. *Allenby's War: The Palestinian-Arabian Campaigns, 1916–1918.* London: Blandford, 1988.
Falls, Cyril. *Official History of the Great War: Military Operations: Egypt and Palestine,* Vol. 1, *From June 1917 to the End of the War.* London: HMSO, 1930.
Wavell, Colonel A. P. *The Palestine Campaigns.* London: Constable, 1928.

Mahiwa, Battle of (17–18 October 1917)

Last major battle in German East Africa and the largest battle in Africa during the war. As the Great War drew to a close, German commander in East Africa Colonel Paul von Lettow-Vorbeck claimed a victory in the isolated southeast corner of German East Africa. Mahiwa is located just southwest of Nyangao, a scene of fighting several weeks before. On 24 September British General Gordon Beves attempted to use the Anglo-Nigerian brigade of his Linforce (named for its base of Lindi, a port in present-day Nigeria) to block Lettow's retreat from Nyangao. Beves then ordered an attack employing columns under Brigadier General Henry de Courcy O'Grady and Colonel Harry Christopher Tytler. Meanwhile, Lettow-Vorbeck was withdrawing to the southwest from Nyangao to Mahiwa, attempting to salvage the majority of his forces.

Beves pursued, and the Battle of Mahiwa began at daybreak on 17 October 1917 as Tytler's infantry column attacked southward, supported by both the artillery and General O'Grady's infantry column on its right. The battle pitted fewer than 5,000 British troops against about 3,000 Germans. The engagement continued throughout the day and into the night, escalating the next day. The battle, fought at close quarters, produced heavy casualties on both sides.

The British attacks appeared to be succeeding but were repeatedly rebuffed by German counterattacks. Lettow-Vorbeck had fortified a ridge line, where he employed 1,500 men and two field guns. Following two failed frontal assaults by the Anglo-Nigerian brigade, Beves ordered O'Grady and Tytler to end the attacks. The British side sustained 2,348 casualties (528 Nigerians), and they also lost more than 350 bearers. German casualties came to 519; the British claimed in addition they had taken 918 prisoners. Lettow-Vorbeck also abandoned the *Königsberg* gun.

Lettow-Vorbeck, although victorious, was convinced that his troops could not sustain further fighting. He continued his retreat southward with 3,000 men, escaping and outmaneuvering the British pursuers. The British resumed the advance on 6 November. After the conclusion of hostilities in Europe, Lettow-Vorbeck finally surrendered on 25 November 1918.

Jon Anderson

See also
Africa, Campaigns in; Askaris; Lettow-Vorbeck, Paul Emil von.
References
Farwell, Byron. *The Great War in Africa, 1914–1918.* New York: Norton, 1986.
Hoyt, Edwin P. *Guerilla: Colonel von Lettow-Vorbeck and Germany's East Africa Empire.* New York: Macmillan, 1981.
Lettow-Vorbeck, Paul von. *My Reminiscences of East Africa.* London: Hurst and Blackett, 1920.
Miller, Charles. *Battle for the Bundu: The First World War in East Africa.* New York: Macmillan, 1974.

Maistre, Paul (1858–1922)

French army general. Born on 20 June 1858 at Joinville, Paul-André-Marie Maistre graduated from L'École Spéciale Militaire de Saint-Cyr in 1877 at the head of his class. He later served there as an instructor. Promoted to captain in 1887 and major in 1898, he made general of brigade in 1912.

At the onset of World War I Maistre was chief of staff of the Fourth Army. In 1914 he was promoted to general of division. After the First Battle of the Marne in September 1914, Maistre took command of XXI Corps. While with XXI Corps Maistre saw action at Vimy, Verdun, the Somme, and Armentières.

In May 1917 Maistre assumed command of the Sixth Army following the failure of the Second Aisne (Nivelle) offensive and the crisis of mutinies in the French army. Maistre intended to resume the offensive against the Germans on the Western Front, but word of this led to a resurgence of mutinies in the Sixth Army and caused Maistre to renounce offensive plans. By early June 1917, eleven of seventeen divisions in the Sixth Army were experiencing disciplinary problems. In October 1917, with discipline at last restored, Maistre's army went on the offensive and was victorious at Malmaison. The Germans withdrew at a cost of 12,000 prisoners and 200 guns.

In late October 1917 Maistre briefly commanded French forces in Italy. In the spring of 1918, he was assigned to command the Tenth Army on the Western Front during the Ludendorff offensive. In the Allied counteroffensive of July 1918, Maistre commanded Army Group Center, which won the Second Battle of the Marne. In 1920 he became general inspector of infantry, retaining that position until months before his death. Paul Maistre died in Paris on 25 July 1922.

Bache M. Whitlock

See also
France, Army Mutiny; Marne, First Battle of the; Marne, Second
    Battle of the; Ludendorff Offensives; Nivelle Offensive.
References
Clayton, Anthony. *Paths of Glory: The French Army, 1914–18.*
    London: Cassell, 2003.
Williams, John. *Mutiny, 1917.* London: Heinemann, 1962.

Makino Nobuaki, Count (1861–1949)

Japanese diplomat, Lord Privy Seal. Born in Kagoshima on
22 October 1861, Makino Nobuaki, the second son of
Toshimichi Ōkubo, a leader of the Meiji Restoration, became
heir to the family title at one year of age. At age 11 he joined
Iwakura Mission to visit Western nations, and he studied in
the United States for three years.

Makino then became a diplomat, and during 1880–1882
he was third secretary in the Japanese Embassy in London.
He was minister to Italy during 1897–1899 and minister to
Austria and Switzerland in 1899–1902. During February
1913–April 1914, Makino was minister for foreign affairs. He
tried to promote economic relations with China, but his plan
was not successful.

In 1919, following the Allied victory in World War I,
Makino was appointed as one of the Japanese plenipoten-
tiaries to the Paris Peace Conference. Makino was effectively
head of the Japanese delegation, as the nominal head Saionji
Kimmochi was in poor health and lacked Makino's experience and connections in European diplomacy. Makino proposed that a racial nondiscrimination clause should be
included in the Covenant of the League of Nations. The Japanese delegation held that this was extremely important as a
sign of Japan's international status. The proposal failed to win
approval, a major rebuff to the Japanese. Makino believed
that Japanese diplomacy should be based on international
cooperation, but the Tokyo government insisted that he not
concede any interests in the Shandong (Shantung) Peninsula.
Makino also helped obtain a Japanese mandate over the German Pacific islands north of the equator. Makino generally
followed the Japanese practice during the conference of
remaining silent on those issues that did not directly affect
Japanese interests.

Makino was appointed minister of the imperial household
in 1921 because Saionji trusted him. He became Lord Privy
Seal and was named a count in 1925. One of the most important advisors to Emperor Hirohito when he was at court,
Makino was a voice of moderation in an increasingly strident
nationalist government. Makino resigned in 1935. In the 25
February 1936 coup attempt, he narrowly avoided assassination because he was a leader of the internationalists. Makino
died in Chiba prefecture on 25 January 1949. Yoshida

Baron Nobuaki Makino, Japanese delegate to the Paris Peace
Conference, 1919. (Library of Congress)

Shigeru, the most powerful political figure in postwar Japan
until the mid-1950s, was his son-in-law.

Sakai Kazuomi

See also
League of Nations Covenant; Paris Peace Conference; Saionji
    Kimmochi, Prince; Shandong Settlement.
References
Dickinson, Frederick R. *War and National Reinvention: Japan in the
    Great War, 1914–1919.* Cambridge: Harvard University Press,
    1999.
MacMillan, Margaret. *Paris, 1919: Six Months That Changed the
    World.* New York: Random House, 2002.
Naoko Shimazu. *Japan, Race and Equality: The Racial Equality
    Proposal of 1919.* London and New York: Routledge, 1998.

Maklakov, Nikolai Alekseevich (1871–1918)

Russian political figure. Born in 1871, Nikolai Maklakov
graduated from Moscow University in 1892 and joined the
state treasury bureaucracy. From 1984 until 1900 he was clerk

in the Moscow branch of the Treasury and a tax inspector of Suzdal. He also headed a section of the Tambov branch of the Treasury, and by 1906 he was head of the Poltava branch. An influential friend helped him secure appointment in 1909 as governor of Chernigov.

In December 1912 Maklakov was appointed minister of the interior, in part because Tsar Nicholas II liked Maklakov's autocratic views. Maklakov formally took control of the ministry in early 1913. Considered a staunch monarchist, Maklakov pandered to the tsar and rightist groups and did not initiate any major reforms to address Russia's staggering internal problems. Indeed, he opposed concessions to the Duma.

Hostile to universal suffrage, Maklakov sought to exploit Russian nationalism and anti-Semitism to roll back democratic reforms. In the July Crisis of 1914, Maklakov believed that Russia must support Serbia and remained confident of victory against both Germany and Austria-Hungary.

As the war progressed badly for Russia, Tsar Nicholas II came under mounting pressure from the Duma to remove his most reactionary ministers, and Maklakov resigned under pressure from his post on 6 June 1915. He continued to exercise influence as a member of the state council. In January 1917 Maklakov had charge of gerrymandering districts to manipulate the elections to the Fifth Duma.

Maklakov lost his posts after the Bolshevik Revolution of November 1917. He was executed in Petrograd, along with more than 500 other political prisoners, during 31 August–1 September 1918.

Vadim K. Simakhov

See also
Nicholas II, Tsar; Russia, Civil War; Russia, Home Front; Russia, Revolution of March 1917; Russia, Revolution of November 1917.

References
Figes, Orlando. *A People's Tragedy: The Russian Revolution, 1891–1924.* New York: Viking Adult, 1997.

Gurko, Vladimir Iosifovich, and J. E. Wallace Sterling, eds. *Features and Figures of the Past: Government and Opinion in the Reign of Nicholas II.* Trans. Laura Matveev. Stanford, CA: Stanford University Press, 1939.

Kochan, Lionel. *Russia in Revolution, 1890–1918.* New York: The New American Library, 1966.

Warth, Robert D. *Nicholas II: The Life and Reign of Russia's Last Monarch.* Westport, CT: Praeger, 1997.

Malazgirt, Battle of (5 August 1915)

Caucasian Front battle involving Turkish and Russian forces. The battle ended offensive actions initiated in the summer of 1915 by Turkish Minister of War Enver Pasha to drive Russian forces from Armenia. In mid-July Enver's Turkish Second Army had forced the Russians to retreat west of Lake Van.

Despite actions by rebel Armenians that prevented the Turks from concentrating fully on the Russians, a tenuous supply line, and troop shortages, Enver continued the attacks on Russian Caucasus Army Commander Nikolay Yudenich's forces. By 10 July the Turks had forced Russian forces to withdraw from west of Lake Van. By the 27th the Turks had taken Mus. Meanwhile, Yudenich prepared his forces for a counterattack on the thinly stretched Turkish northern flank.

On 5 August 1915 on the Plain of Malazgirt, Yudenich's forces fell on the extended Turkish forces and defeated them. Yudenich followed up this victory with attacks all along the line, forcing the Turks into a general and costly retreat. By August the front had been stabilized on a line east of Rize on the Black Sea, Erzurum, and Bitlis. With Russian forces then struggling on the Eastern Front and having just undertaken the "Great Retreat" from Poland, Yudenich's accomplishment at Malazgirt proved to be the sole victory of the year for Russian troops.

Yudenich was not able to capitalize on the situation. Many of his own forces were soon siphoned to other fronts, and he knew that further pursuit of Enver's armies could reverse his own earlier success. The Battle of Malazgirt, however, marked the end of Turkish offensive action on Caucasian Front until the next year.

Jon Anderson

See also
Caucasian Front; Enver Pasha; Yudenich, Nikolay.

References
Allen, George H. *The Great War,* Vol. 4, *The Wavering Balance of Forces.* Philadelphia and London: George Barrie's Sons, 1919.

Erickson, Edward J. *Ordered to Die: A History of the Ottoman Army in the First World War.* Westport, CT: Greenwood, 2000.

Halsey, Francis Whiting. *The Literary Digest: History of the World War,* Vol. 7, *Russian Front, August 1914–July 1919,* and Vol. 8, *Turkey and the Balkans, August 1914–October 1918.* New York and London: Funk and Wagnalls, 1919–1920.

Stone, Norman. *The Eastern Front, 1914–1917.* New York: Scribner, 1975.

Malinov, Alexandur (1867–1938)

Bulgarian political leader. Born into a Bulgarian family in Russian Bessarabia on 21 April 1867, Aleksandur Malinov spent his early life in Russia. He earned his doctorate of law at the University of Kiev in 1891. Malinov then returned to Bulgaria, immersed himself in politics, and in 1901 became head of the Democratic Party in the Bulgarian National Assembly. Tsar Ferdinand appointed him minister-president (premier) in January 1908.

Known for his pro-Russian views and regarded as a moderate liberal, Malinov supported a formal alliance with Russia and the other Entente powers of France and Great Britain. He introduced minor reforms that included reinstatement of dismissed academic heads, easing press censorship, and institution of proportional representation in local provincial elections. Malinov oversaw Bulgaria's declaration of independence from the Ottoman Empire in 1908. Tsar Ferdinand forced him from office in March 1911. Malinov recommended that Bulgaria remain neutral in World War I, but Tsar Ferdinand eventually concluded that the Central Powers would win, and in September 1915 Bulgaria entered the war on their side. Ferdinand urged Malinov to join the cabinet of Premier Vasil Radoslavov in a show of national unity, but Malinov refused.

By spring 1918 civilian unrest, including bread riots and an opposition bloc that formed in the Sobranie, led Tsar Ferdinand in June to call on Malinov to form a new government. Malinov was unable to form the coalition government he had desired because Tsar Ferdinand refused to release Agrarian Party members from prison. Their representatives in the Sobranie (Bulgarian Parliament) would not support Malinov's government. Hostile relations with Romania complicated Bulgaria's position. With military defeat looming by the summer of 1918, Malinov was in open defiance of the tsar, who was determined to fight to the end. Malinov and his cabinet finally secured an armistice with the Allies on 30 September, ending Bulgaria's participation in the war.

Malinov resigned as minister-president on 28 November 1918 to protest Romanian occupation of the southern Dobrudja. He continued to play an important role in Bulgarian politics, although he refused to participate in Aleksandŭr Stamboliyski's government in 1922 and continued to oppose the Agrarian Party-led government. Malinov supported the coup that ousted Stamboliyski and formed a new government in October 1931. Malinov died on 20 March 1938 in Sofia.

Joshua J. Robinson

See also
Balkan Wars; Ferdinand I, Tsar of Bulgaria; Radoslavov, Vasil Hristov; Stamboliyski, Aleksandŭr.

References
Crampton, R. J. *A Short History of Modern Bulgaria.* Cambridge: Cambridge University Press, 1987.
Hubatsch, Walther. *Germany and the Central Powers in the World War, 1914–1918.* Lawrence: University Press of Kansas, 1963.

Malvy, Louis-Jean (1875–1949)

French politician. Born in Figeac (Lot) on 1 December 1875, Louis-Jean Malvy earned a doctorate in law. He rose to prominence as a Radical-Socialist deputy in the decade before 1914, developing close ties with Joseph Caillaux. He served the government of Gaston Doumergue (1913–1914), first as minister of commerce, industry, posts, and telecommunications, and then as minister of the interior.

Malvy remained minister of the interior from 13 June 1914 until 31 August 1917, serving the governments of René Viviani, Aristide Briand, and Alexandre Ribot. As such, he was responsible for Carnet B, the government list of 3,000 suspected agitators and aliens recommended for arrest in the event of war. In order to preserve France's wartime political truce, the Union Sacrée, Malvy did not implement the list.

In February 1917 Malvy declined a warning from French army commander-in-chief General Robert Nivelle, who advised him to take action against antiwar activity. When Nivelle's disastrous spring offensive provoked a mutiny in the army, many officers and right-wing commentators blamed internal "defeatists." Armed with leaked information from French intelligence sources, Senator Georges Clemenceau attacked Malvy on 22 July 1917 for his apparent lassitude toward the pro-German newspaper, *Le Bonnet Rouge.* When that paper's editor, Miguel Vigo (aka Almereyda), committed suicide in jail on 14 August, the political right claimed that he had been assassinated. Malvy resigned on 31 August, and Ribot's government fell a week later. On 4 October the right-wing journalist Léon Daudet wrote to French President Raymond Poincaré charging Malvy with treason. The Union Sacrée was in tatters.

When Clemenceau formed his government in November 1917, one of his prime objectives was to crack down on "defeatism." This campaign led to a wave of arrests, including that of Caillaux and the staff of *Le Bonnet Rouge.* Clemenceau took a lenient attitude toward Malvy. However, Malvy had little faith in Clemenceau's good will, so he took the initiative by asking the National Assembly to investigate Daudet's charges. This maneuver backfired. A nine-month trial by the Senate dismissed the flimsy treason charge but found Malvy guilty of negligence and banished him from France for five years.

Malvy returned from Spain in 1924 and was reelected to the Chamber of Deputies. He served briefly as minister of the interior under Briand in 1926, but the resulting outcry prompted him to resign, and he subsequently reduced his political activity. Malvy died in Paris on 9 June 1949.

Robert K. Hanks

See also
Briand, Aristide; Caillaux, Joseph; Carnet B; Clemenceau, Georges; France, Army Mutiny; France, Home Front; Nivelle, Robert; Nivelle Offensive; Poincaré, Raymond; Ribot, Alexandre; Viviani, René.

References
King, Jere Clemens. *Generals and Politicians: Conflict between France's High Command, Parliament, and Government, 1914–1918.* Berkeley: University of California Press, 1951.
Daudet, Léon. *Clemenceau: A Stormy Life.* London: William Hodge, 1940.
Malvy, Louis. *Mon Crime.* Paris: Flammarion, 1921.

Parry, D. L. L. "Clemenceau, Caillaux and the Political Use of Intelligence." *Intelligence and National Security* 9(3) (July 1994): 472–494.

Mandates

The system of administration of the former German overseas colonies and non-Turkish territories of the Ottoman Empire in the Middle East after the Great War under the aegis of the League of Nations. During the course of war the aforementioned territories fell into the hands of the Allied Powers. British Empire and Commonwealth forces drove the Turks from Mesopotamia, Palestine, and Syria. In Africa, the Union of South Africa had seized German South-West Africa (present Namibia), while British and South African forces had captured most of German East Africa and the Belgians had occupied the remainder; British and French forces had also taken Kameroun and Togoland. In the Pacific, New Zealanders had seized German Samoa, the Australians had captured German New Guinea and adjacent islands, and the Japanese had occupied the German islands north of the equator.

Following the war the question of the disposition of these occupied territories arose. U.S. President Woodrow Wilson, who dominated the Paris Peace Conference, refused to allow the distribution and outright annexation of colonial territory by the victorious powers. But an immediate grant of independence to the colonial peoples was considered hardly feasible either. To solve this matter the conferees at Paris created the mandate system in Article 22 of the Covenant of the League of Nations.

Colonial areas acquired from Germany and the Ottoman Empire would be in a transitional status until the people of these territories "could stand by themselves." These territories were entrusted to certain victor states until such time as they were ready for independence. Mandates were divided into three categories: Class-A mandates were the former Ottoman territories in the Middle East; Class-B mandates were mostly in Tropical Africa; and Class-C mandates were those territories of South-West Africa and the Pacific. The local populations in Class-A mandates were to have a higher degree of autonomy, whereas those in Class-C would have the lowest. A Permanent Mandates Commission (PMC) was established within the League of Nations machinery to examine the annual administration reports submitted by the mandatory states and advise the League Council concerning them.

Views of the mandate system vary widely. Some accuse the system of representing veiled annexation of the conquered territories by the victorious imperial powers. Others saw it as a denial of the right of conquest and the forerunner of decolonization. The truth lies somewhere in between.

The British mandate of Iraq was terminated in 1932, when Iraq became an independent state (it joined the League of Nations the same year). Other mandates were expected to follow the same model, and the Middle Eastern mandates gained independence during or immediately after World War II. After Adolf Hitler came to power in Germany in 1933, the future status of the mandated territories that had belonged to the German Empire became the focus of fierce argument. Hitler demanded the return of Germany's overseas colonies, and there was some debate in Britain and France concerning possibly appeasing Germany by rearranging the mandates in Africa. Most of the former German colonies under the mandate system remained in Allied hands throughout the war, however.

In the years leading to World War II, Japan constructed military bases in its mandated Pacific islands and sharply restricted foreign access to the area. These islands later became the scene of fierce fighting between Japanese and U.S. forces. Those mandates that remained at the end of World War II passed under the control of the United Nations Trusteeship system in 1947.

Tohmatsu Haruo

See also
Arab Revolt; Balfour Declaration; Fourteen Points; League of Nations Covenant; Lugard, Frederick, Lord; Mesopotamian Theater; Pacific Islands Campaign; Palestine and Syria, Land Campaign; Paris Peace Conference; Smuts, Jan Christian; Sykes-Picot Agreement; Wilson, Thomas Woodrow; Zionism.

References
Crozier, Andrew J. *Appeasement and Germany's Last Bid for Colonies.* London: Macmillan, 1988.
Hall, H. Duncan. *Mandates, Dependencies, and Trusteeship.* New York: Carnegie Endowment for Peace, 1948.
Khoury, Philips S. *Syria and the French Mandate: The Politics of Arab Nationalism.* Princeton, NJ: Princeton University Press, 1989.
Louis, William Roger. *Great Britain and Germany's Lost Colonies, 1914–1919.* Oxford, UK: Clarendon, 1967.
Maanen-Helmer, Elizabeth van. *Mandates System in Relation to Africa and the Pacific.* London: P. S. King, 1929.
Smuts, Jan Christian. *The League of Nations: A Practical Suggestion.* London: Hodder and Stoughton, 1918.
Wright, Quincy. *Mandate under the League of Nations.* Chicago: Chicago University Press, 1930.

Mangin, Charles (1866–1925)

French army general. Born on 6 July 1866 in Sarrebourg (Lorraine), which was lost to Germany as a consequence of the Franco-Prussian War of 1871, Charles-Marie-Emmanuel Mangin graduated from L'École Spéciale Militaire de Saint-Cyr in 1888. Most of his early military career was spent in the French colonies. Known as an aggressive commander, Mangin was three times wounded in colonial service. His first assignment was in Senegal, and in 1898 he led the advance

French General Charles Mangin. (Library of Congress)

guard of Colonel Jean Baptiste Marchand's expedition across Africa to the Nile River at Fashoda. Admitted to the École de Guerre in 1899, Mangin was assigned to Tonkin before returning to western Africa.

In Africa Mangin found time to write a book, *La Force noire,* which he published in 1912. In it he suggested that France could offset her population imbalance with Germany by utilizing troops from its African possessions. Such troops could be employed effectively in north Africa, freeing up French forces there. Mangin also believed that native soldiers, once they had completed their service, would form the nucleus of a new colonial elite, loyal to France. That same year the French Chamber of Deputies authorized the raising of several battalions of Senegalese troops. Under Mangin's command, they carried out military operations in southern Morocco.

Returning to metropolitan France at the end of 1913, Mangin was promoted to general of brigade. Mangin fought in the earliest battles of World War I near Charleroi and at the Marne and Artois. He was promoted to general of division in early 1915. Mangin greatly admired African troops and used them whenever possible in his attacks. Once of France's most skillful commanders, his hallmarks were careful coordination with attacks launched on time and in an aggressive fash-

ion. Utterly fearless, Mangin often inspected his troops at the front and was wounded several times. He was also reckless with the lives of his men, winning him the sobriquet of "The Butcher."

In the spring of 1916, Mangin was sent to Verdun in command of the 5th Infantry Division of General Robert Nivelle's III Corps. Mangin's division succeeded in recapturing from the Germans Forts Douaumont and Vaux, and he soon became Nivelle's favorite commander. Raised to command the Sixth Army, Mangin led it in the ill-fated Nivelle offensive in Champagne in the spring of 1917 but failed to capture his objective of the Chemin des Dames. Attempting to shift the blame for his own failure, Nivelle relieved Mangin in May.

Absolved of any fault by a board chaired by General Ferdinand Foch, Mangin received command of the Tenth Army, which he led with distinction in helping to halt the last attacks of the German Ludendorff offensives in mid-June 1918. Foch selected Mangin to launch the first counterattack. Mangin's forces then drove toward Laon, which he seized in October. At the end of that month he was assigned command of an army group then in the process of formation.

Following the war, Mangin commanded French occupation troops in Lorraine in the Metz area. In this capacity, he supported Rhineland autonomy movements. His last assignment, which he retained until his death, was the inspectorate of French colonial troops. He also wrote his recollections, *Comment finit la guerre,* published in 1920. Mangin died in Paris on 12 May 1925.

Philippe Haudrère and Spencer C. Tucker

See also

Aisne, First Battle of the; Artois, First Battle of; Chemin des Dames Offensive; Foch, Ferdinand; Frontiers, Battle of the; Marne, First Battle of the; Nivelle, Robert; Verdun, Battle of.

References

Horne, Alistair. *The Price of Glory: Verdun, 1916.* New York: St. Martin's, 1963.

King, Jere Clemens. *Generals and Politicians: Conflict between France's High Command, Parliament, and Government, 1914–1918.* Berkeley: University of California Press, 1951.

Mangin, Charles M. *Comment finit la guerre.* Paris: Plon, 1920.

———. *Mangin: Lettres de guerre, 1914–1918.* Ed. Louis Eugène Mangin. Paris: Fayard, 1950.

Mangin, Louis Eugène. *Le Général Mangin.* Paris: F. Landre, 1986.

Mannerheim, Carl von, Baron (1867–1951)

Finnish field marshal and president of Finland. Born on 4 June 1867 near Turku in southwest Finland (then part of the Russian Empire), Carl Gustav Emil von Mannerheim graduated from the prestigious Nikolaevskoe Cavalry School in St. Petersburg in 1889. Initially commissioned into a Russian

Finnish President Carl Mannerheim. (Library of Congress)

dragoon regiment based in Poland, in 1890 Mannerheim transferred to the elite Chevalier Guards Regiment in St. Petersburg. In 1903 he served under future Russian army commander Aleksey Brusilov.

During the 1904–1905 Russo-Japanese War, Mannerheim volunteered for combat. Lieutenant Colonel Mannerheim participated in several cavalry raids and won promotion to colonel. During 1906–1908 Mannerheim led a special mission gathering political and military intelligence along Russia's Far Eastern borders. His excellent reports made a favorable impression on Tsar Nicholas II, who met Mannerheim in 1908. Mannerheim then commanded cavalry units in Poland and was promoted to major general.

During World War I Mannerheim saw a great deal of combat, mostly commanding cavalry divisions under General Aleksey Brusilov. He witnessed and opposed the Russian Revolution of March 1917, urging Tsar Nicholas II to suppress it. In June Mannerheim once again commanded a cavalry division under Brusilov in Galicia and was there when the Bolshevik Revolution occurred that November.

Mannerheim then retired from the Russian army and returned to Finland, which soon erupted into civil war paralleling that of Russia. Mannerheim commanded the anticommunist White Guards that crushed the Communist Red Guards in Finland in 1918.

Finland secured its independence from Russia as a consequence of the war. Mannerheim served as regent of Finland during November 1918–July 1919 and ran for the presidency, but he was defeated. He then retired.

In 1931 Mannerheim returned to public service as supreme commander of the Finnish armed forces. As part of a strong defensive strategy, he oversaw construction of a defensive line, which became known as the Mannerheim Line. It held Soviet troops for several months during the Russo-Finnish War when Mannerheim commanded Finnish forces. Mannerheim then negotiated an armistice with the Soviets in 1940 and, following Finnish reentry into the war (the Continuation War) against the Soviet Union in 1941, negotiated another in 1944. Mannerheim was elected president of Finland in 1944, but poor health forced him to retire in 1946. He spent his remaining years in Switzerland and died in Lausanne on 28 January 1951.

Michael Share

See also

Brusilov, Aleksey Alekseyevich; Finland, Role in War; Nicholas II, Tsar.

References

Jagerskiold, Stig. *Mannerheim: Marshal of Finland.* Minneapolis: University of Minnesota Press, 1986.

Mannerheim, Carl. *Memoirs of Marshal Mannerheim.* New York: Dutton, 1954.

Screen, Joseph E. O. *Mannerheim: The Years of Preparation.* London: C. Hurst, 1970.

Warner, Oliver. *Marshal Mannerheim and the Finns.* London: Weidenfeld and Nicolson, 1967.

March, Peyton Conway (1864–1955)

U.S. Army general and chief of staff during World War I. Born at Easton, Pennsylvania, on 27 December 1864, Peyton March attended Lafayette College, where he graduated with honors in classics in 1884. He graduated from the U.S. Military Academy in 1888. March commanded an artillery battery in the Spanish-American War in 1898, participating in the campaign leading to the capture of Manila. After serving briefly as aide-de-camp to U.S. commander General Arthur MacArthur, March participated in several campaigns during the Philippine-American War and served as a provincial governor. At the conclusion of hostilities, he returned to Washington in 1903 to serve on the new War Department General Staff and as a military observer of the Russo-Japanese War in 1904.

In 1916–1917 Colonel March commanded the 8th Field Artillery Regiment along the tense Mexican border, after which he was promoted to brigadier general and placed in command of the 1st Field Artillery Brigade, 1st Division, American Expeditionary Forces (AEF), and deployed to Europe. Following promotion to major general in August 1917, March became chief of AEF artillery, a duty he held until his return to Washington in March 1918 to serve as acting chief of staff of the U.S. Army as part of an overhaul of the War Department by Secretary of War Newton D. Baker.

Baker handpicked March, whom he knew as "an energetic and effective administrator," to supervise the mobilization, training, equipping, and deployment of U.S. forces sent to Europe; to establish the organization, control, and effectiveness of its supply; and to ensure the base of support and cooperation upon which the success of General John Pershing and the AEF depended. In this role as the first modern military manager, March performed brilliantly, and he established the primacy of the chief of staff in the army hierarchy. During his tenure significant numbers of U.S. forces were trained and transported to France. March also created new branches in the U.S. Air Service, Tank Corps, Chemical Warfare Service, and Motor Transport Service. Under his leadership the War Department became an efficient and powerful agency, and its General Staff functioned as the brain of the army. At war's end, March supervised the AEF's return to the United States, the demobilization and discharge of the bulk of the army, and the integration of the AEF regulars into the peacetime army. The army released more than 3 million men in the ten months following the armistice, an accomplishment March viewed with justifiable pride. However, his plan for demobilization created friction between him and Pershing and with a U.S. Congress eager to reassert itself after the war. This friction worsened when March's plans for a strong General Staff, a 500,000-man postwar army, and a three-month universal training program clashed with congressional preferences for a stronger role for the National Guard and more robust universal military training. Pershing's opposition to the March proposal in testimony to Congress in 1920 proved its death knell.

March retired as a major general in November 1921; however, in 1930 he was advanced to general on the retired list. He published a memoir of his wartime service in 1932. Brutally frank, *The Nation at War* harshly criticized Pershing and engendered a strong counterattack from the latter's followers. Ironically, March was respected by two later chiefs of staff who were Pershing men, Douglas MacArthur and George Marshall. March followed closely the course of the Second World War and the Korean War and in 1953 was recognized by a concurrent congressional resolution for his "selfless and patriotic interest in the U.S. Army since his retirement." March died in Washington, D.C., on 13 April 1955.

Charles F. Brower IV

See also
Baker, Newton Diehl; Pershing, John Joseph; United States, Army.
References
Coffman, Edward M. *The Hilt of the Sword: The Career of Peyton C. March.* Madison: University of Wisconsin Press, 1966.
March, Peyton C. *The Nation at War.* Garden City, NY: Doubleday, 1932.
Palmer, Frederick. *Newton D. Baker: America at War.* 2 vols. New York: Dodd, Mead, 1931.
Pershing, John J. *My Experiences in the World War.* 2 vols. New York: Frederick A. Stokes, 1931.
Vandiver, Frank E. *Black Jack: The Life and Times of John J. Pershing.* 2 vols. College Station: Texas A&M University Press, 1977.

March First Movement, Korea

Caught in the crossfire during decades of political intrigue and war among China, Russia, and Japan, Korea was annexed by Japan in 1910. Resistance groups based in Manchuria fought the occupation, but without international support their cause was doomed.

World War I temporarily changed the situation. Encouraged by U.S. President Woodrow Wilson's Fourteen Points, on 1 March 1919 a group of thirty-three Korean students, many of them Christian idealists, issued a declaration of Korean independence. It was timed to coincide with the funeral of Yi dynasty Emperor Ko-Jong (1852–1919), in many respects the last symbol of Korean autonomy. It was also secretly coordinated with protests by nearly 2 million Koreans in nationwide demonstrations against Japanese occupation. This event was dubbed the Sam-Il, or March First Movement.

The protestors did not expect international support, but they did have the sympathies of Western diplomats, missionaries, and journalists in Korea. The West had initially backed Japan's takeover of Korea in 1905 and its subsequent annexation in 1910 as a means of stabilizing the region, but by 1919 many Westerners were outraged by the brutality of Japanese rule there. Thus, many Koreans hoped that Japan, rather than risk aggravating the Western powers, would end its occupation.

Instead, the Japanese responded with overwhelming force. In Seoul, where the declaration was read, Japanese soldiers and police acted ruthlessly, shooting down the unarmed protestors. An estimated 7,500 Koreans died in the Japanese repression. In the weeks that followed, thousands more Koreans were arrested. Many were assaulted, raped, and tortured. Protestant missionaries, thought by the Japanese to be behind the movement, were among those jailed or deported. The Japanese also looted and burned many Christian churches. Tokyo denounced the March First Movement as a puppet of Western radicals and linked it to resistance groups in

Japanese soldiers executing Koreans who took part in the March First Movement. (Library of Congress)

Manchuria. Anxious to maintain friendly relations with Japan, the Western powers did nothing. Although the March First Movement had been crushed, it remained very much the symbol of Korean nationalism and resistance to Japan.

Arne Kislenko

See also
Fourteen Points; Japan, Home Front; Wilson, Thomas Woodrow.
References
Kim, Chung S. *The Korean Paekjong under Japanese Rule: The Quest for Equality and Human Rights.* London: Routledge, 2003.
Lone, Stewart, and Gavan McCormick. *Korea since 1850.* New York: St. Martin's, 1993.
Schmid, Andre. *Korea between Empires, 1895–1919.* New York: Columbia University Press, 2002.

Marghiloman, Alexandru (1854–1925)

Romanian politician and premier. Born in Buzau, Wallachia, on 4 July 1854, five years before Wallachia and Moldavia formed an autonomous Romanian state, Alexandru Marghiloman studied law and political science in Paris. In 1884 he began his political career in Romania's Conservative Party and was its leader when World War I began in 1914. Romanians, including Conservatives, were divided over whether to support the Entente or the Central Powers. From 3 August

1914 Marghiloman, who had favored close prewar links with Germany, consistently supported Romanian neutrality, although he also tried to use the exigencies of war to extract from Austria-Hungary better treatment for Romanian minorities within the Dual Monarchy.

Marghiloman deplored the October 1915 Treaty of Bucharest, whereby Prime Minister Ionel Brătianu pledged that Romania would eventually join the Allies. He correctly believed that this would bring military disaster, which indeed resulted from Romanian intervention in August 1916. German troops then occupied much of the country, including Bucharest, and Marghiloman, also president of the Romanian Red Cross, remained in Bucharest to mediate between Germans and Romanians. He was credited with persuading German officials to leave King Ferdinand in place. Thanks to Brătianu's backing and machinations, on 18 March 1918 Marghiloman became premier, in the hope that Germany would therefore grant Romania more favorable peace terms. In spring 1918 Germany did indeed allow Romania to annex Bessarabia from Russia, but otherwise the projected peace terms were harsh.

Marghiloman tried to maintain himself in power through rigged elections and by persecuting prominent Liberal politicians, but in autumn 1918 Allied military successes undercut the fundamental rationale of his premiership, and he left office on 6 November. Romania abrogated its peace agreements with Germany, declaring war one day before the armistice, while King Ferdinand reinstalled Brătianu as premier to represent Romania at the Paris Peace Conference.

Marghiloman remained politically active, justifying his wartime behavior as impelled by a patriotic desire to moderate German hostility toward defeated Romania, but his collaboration with Germany permanently compromised his political standing. Marghiloman died in Buzau on 10 May 1925.

Priscilla Roberts

See also

Brătianu, Ionel; Bucharest, Treaty of; Ferdinand I, King of Romania; Romania, Role in War.

References

Marghiloman, Alexandru. *Note politice.* Ed. Stelian Neagoe. 2 vols. Bucharest: Editura Scripta, 1993–1994.

Seton-Watson, R. W. *A History of the Roumanians: From Roman Times to the Completion of Unity.* Cambridge: Cambridge University Press, 1934.

Torrey, Glenn E. *The Revolutionary Russian Army and Romania, 1917.* Pittsburgh, PA: Center for Russian and East European Studies, University of Pittsburgh, 1995.

———. *Romania and World War I: A Collection of Studies.* Iasi, Romania, and Portland, OR: Center for Romanian Studies, 1998.

Marne, First Battle of the (5–12 September 1914)

Decisive series of engagements fought between Paris and Verdun along the Marne River during the German invasion of France in September 1914. By late August the German advance still reflected the outline of the Schlieffen Plan, which assumed correctly that the French would react to war with an offensive aimed to recover Alsace and Lorraine. While the Germans held their left flank with two weak armies, the five larger armies of the right wing swept through Belgium and northern France. In front of them the shattered French armies and the British Expeditionary Force (BEF) retreated in good order. By 1 September the Germans were within 30 miles of Paris, prompting government evacuation. French army commander General Joseph Joffre had maintained good communications with his subordinate commanders, and he sought an opportunity for a counterattack. Around Paris he constituted a new Sixth Army to guard the capital while he regrouped his remaining armies along the Somme-Verdun line.

Fortunately for the Allies, the friction of war in the form of extended logistics, inadequate command and control, and human exhaustion began to exert a significant effect on German operations. Although the original German plan had called for about fifty-nine divisions in a right wing north of Metz and nine for a southern left wing, chief of staff General Helmuth von Moltke had modified the ratio of forces by placing approximately fifty-five divisions on the right flank and twenty-three south of Metz. As the offensive progressed, forces from the right wing were detached to deal with fortresses at Antwerp and Maubeuge. Believing that Allied defeat was imminent, Moltke also ordered two corps (five divisions) to the Eastern Front where Russian mobilization occurred faster than expected. Thus the remaining forces on the right wing were weaker than Schlieffen had planned. The Germans were also exhausted after continuous marching and fighting over 300 miles, whereas the French could rely on their excellent railroad system and interior lines to shift forces and bring up reserves.

Perhaps more critical to German operations were inadequate communications systems that failed to provide Moltke with timely or accurate information from the front. Moltke remained at his headquarters in Luxembourg over 200 miles from the front and lost touch with his commanders, leading to German failure to exploit operational opportunities at decisive points in the offensive.

This disintegration began when aggressive German First Army commander General Alexander von Kluck ordered his army to swing east of Paris to roll up the flank of the retreating French Fifth Army. Kluck's speed of advance moved him far ahead of the other German armies and exposed his right flank to the French Sixth Army and the Paris garrison. Unaware of the true situation, Moltke ordered Kluck to guard the flank of General Karl von Bülow's Second Army, an action that caused the First Army to move south of the Marne River on 4 September.

The Allies quickly identified the exposed German flank in aerial reconnaissance and radio intercepts. Joffre was concerned about attacking prematurely until the Fifth Army was out of danger and the BEF could be induced to rejoin the battle. He planned the attack for 6 September, but General Joseph Gallieni, military governor of Paris, ordered the Sixth Army of more than 150,000 men to attack Kluck's exposed corps on 5 September. As Kluck turned to deal with this threat, he moved the First Army northwest and away from Bülow, an action that opened a gap of almost 30 miles between the two German armies.

Meanwhile, the remaining French armies held the line to the east, attacking or defending where needed to contain any German breakthrough. The battle along the Marne raged for three days and was fought between seven German and eight Allied armies in an area little more than 100 miles wide. At one point the French called upon the Paris garrison to rush 6,000 reserves to the front in requisitioned taxicabs and buses.

Because he closely coordinated the actions of his forces, Joffre quickly identified an opportunity to exploit the gap between the German armies using the battered Fifth Army and the BEF. On 9 September the BEF crossed the Marne

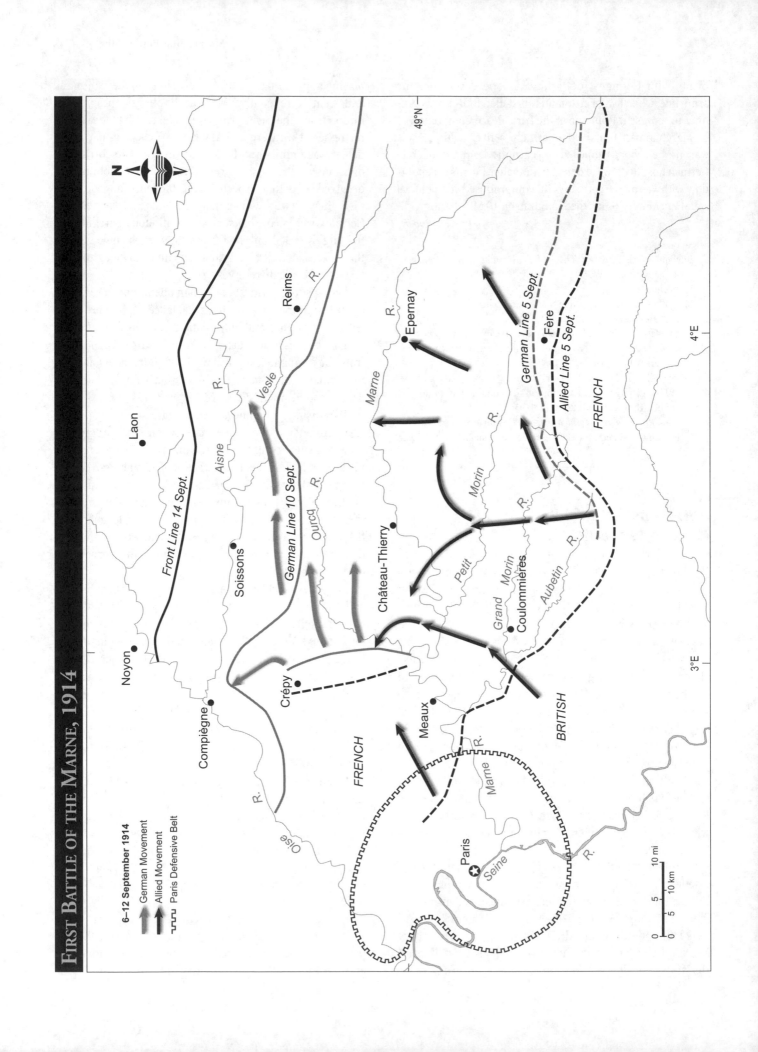

FIRST BATTLE OF THE MARNE, 1914

6–12 September 1914

German Movement
Allied Movement
Paris Defensive Belt

N

Noyon

Compiègne

Laon

Soissons

Crépy

Reims

Front Line 14 Sept.

German Line 10 Sept.

Aisne R.

Vesle R.

Ourcq R.

Château-Thierry

Marne R.

Epernay

Petit Morin

Grand Morin

Coulommières

Aubetin R.

FRENCH

Meaux

Marne R.

Paris

Seine R.

BRITISH

Oise R.

German Line 5 Sept.

Allied Line 5 Sept.

Fère

FRENCH

49°N

4°E

3°E

10 mi

10 km

5

5

0

0

Retreat of the Germans at the Marne. (John Clark Ridpath, *Ridpath's History of the World,* Vol. 10, Jones Bros., Cincinnati, 1921)

and moved unopposed into the gap, but cautious British commanders failed to exploit the opportunity to strike deep into the German rear.

Frustrated by inadequate communications, on 8 September Moltke sent a General Staff officer, Lieutenant Colonel Richard Hentsch, forward to coordinate the actions of his army commanders. Hentsch arrived at Bülow's headquarters just as the German Second Army flank was being turned by the French Fifth Army and the BEF threatened Kluck's rear. Hentsch approved Bülow's request to retreat and in Moltke's name ordered the First Army to withdraw to the Aisne River to avoid envelopment. The battle had been lost for the Germans. During 10–12 September the Germans conducted a 40-mile fighting withdrawal to the Aisne River, where they halted and made defensive preparations. Moltke was at the end of his tether. Relieved on 14 September, he was replaced by General Erich von Falkenhayn. Soon both sides began extending their front over 200 miles from Switzerland to the sea. The First Battle of the Marne was one of the most important battles of military history. Sometimes called the "Miracle of the Marne," the battle was a strategic victory for the Allies and was the closest the Germans ever came to victory.

Without this Allied victory, there would have been no second chance. Casualties amounted to more than a quarter million men on each side during the battle. The First Battle of the Marne ended hopes on both sides for a short war and opened the way to the longer struggle of stalemate.

Steven J. Rauch

See also

Bülow, Karl von; France, War Plan XVII; French, John, 1st Earl of Ypres; Hentsch, Richard; Joffre, Joseph; Kluck, Alexander von; Moltke, Helmuth von, Count; Schlieffen Plan.

References

Barnett, Correlli. "The Tragic Delusion: Colonel-General Helmuth von Moltke." In *The Swordbearers: Supreme Command in the First World War*. New York: William Morrow, 1964.

Blond, Georges. *The Marne.* Trans. H. Eaton Hart, Harrisburg, PA: Stackpole, 1966; reprint, London: Prion, 2002.

David, Daniel. *The 1914 Campaign: August–October 1914.* New York: Combined Books, 1987.

Palmer, Alan. "The Marne." In *Decisive Battles of the Twentieth Century: Land-Sea-Air,* ed. Noble Frankland and Christopher Dowling. New York: McKay, 1976.

Strachan, Hew. *The First World War,* Vol. 1, *To Arms.* Oxford: Oxford University Press, 2001.

Marne, Second Battle of the
(15–18 July 1918)

With the failure of its Operation GNEISENAU (the Noyon offensive) in June 1918, the German army no longer had the slightest chance of winning a military victory in World War I. Each of General der Infanterie (equiv. to U.S. lieutenant general) Erich Ludendorff's four great offensives since March had only left the German army more weakened and more extended, with larger sections of front line to man and defend. Germany's strategic situation was in fact desperate. By the middle of June the Americans had twenty divisions in France, and each of these was twice as large as a European division and could field three times the actual trench strength of the understrength German divisions. Ludendorff, however, still could not bring himself to abandon his grand scheme of driving the British Expeditionary Force (BEF) off the Continent, which he was convinced would cause a general Allied collapse. The plans for that attack, Operation HAGEN, remained on the books, and Ludendorff still believed that he could somehow muster the necessary forces to win the war.

Before the Germans could launch Operation HAGEN, however, they had to address two very immediate problems. Although Operations BLÜCHER (the Chemin des Dames offensive) and GNEISENAU had managed to draw some of their strong reserves south of the Somme River, the Allies were still too powerful in the north for HAGEN to succeed. More immediately, the German forces in the huge salient caused by the BLÜCHER attack were daily becoming weaker. With no major rail line under German control into the salient, and with major road networks and waterways running in the wrong direction, the Germans could not supply those forces. Ludendorff had no alternative but to attack again in the same sector.

Almost as soon as Operation GNEISENAU ended, the German high command (OHL) sent Crown Prince Wilhelm's Army Group the warning order to begin preparing another massive offensive. The overly ambitious plan called for a double envelopment of the French city of Reims, which was on the eastern base corner of the salient created by the BLÜCHER offensive. By threatening to cut off Reims, Ludendorff was convinced that the Allied Supreme Commander,

French soldiers in the ruins of a church during the Battle of the Marne. (National Archives)

General Ferdinand Foch, would be forced to pull all of his remaining reserves from Flanders. Capturing Reims also would give the Germans control of the Reims-Soissons rail line that ran through the center of the BLÜCHER salient, thereby easing the severe logistics problem in that sector. Ludendorff planned, within days of cutting off Reims, to shift rapidly to the north and launch Operation HAGEN.

The attack around Reims would be the farthest south and east of all the great German 1918 drives. It was in a location where the overall frontline trace ran east and west, which meant that the Germans would be attacking from north to south. West of Reims a large section of the front line ran along the Marne River. The German Seventh Army would have to start its attack with a deliberate river crossing. East of Reims, in Champagne, the Marne was anywhere from 12 to 20 miles south of the line of departure. The German First and Third Armies would have to attack over relatively open ground and then conduct a hasty crossing of the Marne. The western wing of the First Army also had the mission of conducting a holding attack against the front of Reims itself.

The official name of Ludendorff's fifth great drive was Operation MARNESCHUTZ-REIMS. The operation's cover name, the one the German troops heard, was FRIEDENSTRUM (peace offensive). It was an unfortunate code name because it gave German troops in the trenches the impression that it would be the last attack and would end the war. On the French side, the Fourth Army held the ground east of Reims. The Fifth Army was on the west side, extending almost to Château-Thierry on the Marne River, at the tip of the BLÜCHER salient. The overall correlation of forces gave the attackers an advantage, with forty-eight German divisions facing thirty-six French.

As with Noyon, the Germans failed to achieve the same level of surprise they had for the attacks in March, April, and May. The Germans had sufficient time to prepare, but the conditions did not favor secrecy. Short, bright nights aided Allied observation, and the prevailing northeasterly winds carried the sounds from the German lines. Once again, OHL put Colonel Georg Bruchmüller in charge of the artillery planning and preparations. Although he managed to mass 6,353 German guns to only 3,080 Allied guns, this did not match the tube superiority ratios of the earlier attacks.

The French anticipated the German attack as early as 1 July. On the night of 14 July a trench raid captured a number of German prisoners who divulged that the attack was scheduled to commence the following morning, with the artillery preparation starting at 1:10 A.M. At midnight, the French artillery began an enhanced program of harassing and interdicting fire. At 1:20 A.M., ten minutes after the beginning of German artillery preparation, the French artillery began a full-scale counterpreparation, the intensity of which caught the Germans by surprise. At 4:50 A.M. the German infantry started moving forward behind a double creeping barrage. Although

the direction of the wind favored the attackers, it was too strong and quickly dissipated the effects of the German gas.

West of Reims the French counterpreparation almost immediately separated the Seventh Army's infantry from their creeping barrage. The infantry attack stalled, but the barrage kept moving forward on schedule. French fire also disrupted the German bridging operation. As the engineers struggled to build the bridges under heavy fire, small groups of infantry crossed the Marne in boats. For the most part, they landed in the wrong locations and had little support because they could not get their artillery across. After the third try the Germans got some bridges across the river. By nightfall on 15 July they had some six divisions on the south bank but hardly any artillery. The bridgehead was then about 12 miles wide and 3 miles deep. At that point the French artillery, working in conjunction with their air force, began concentrating on the bridges to cut off the German force on the south bank.

East of Reims the German First and Third Armies encountered far heavier French artillery fire than anticipated but almost no resistance on the ground. Despite taking stiff casualties from the French fire, the German infantry advanced rapidly at first. At about 7:30 A.M. their creeping barrage reached its maximum range and lifted. The attackers then found themselves facing a fully manned zone defense that hardly had been touched by the preparation or the barrage. The Germans had walked into a trap. Knowing the exact timing of the attack, troops of the Fourth Army had abandoned their frontline positions except for a very light security force. They reestablished the main line of defense along their intermediate position, between their first and second sets of trench lines. The massive German artillery preparation had mostly struck empty ground.

Operation MARNESCHUTZ-REIMS was already a failure by nightfall of 15 July. The fighting, however, dragged on through the next day. Ludendorff knew he was not going to accomplish another spectacular land-grab, but he still believed he could scare the Allies into shifting their theater reserves if the Germans took Reims. He ordered the Third Army on the east flank to halt its attack and the Seventh Army on the west flank to consolidate its gains. Early on 17 July, OHL began shifting much of the reinforcing artillery away from the Seventh Army to support the First Army's attack on Reims.

Early on 18 July, however, the French launched a surprise counterattack. Two French armies, heavily augmented with U.S. divisions, hit the BLÜCHER salient on both sides of Château-Thierry. That was exactly the same area OHL had stripped of most of the reinforcing artillery the day before. This time the French had a 2.3 to 1 tube superiority. They also committed almost 750 tanks. The French counterattack spelled the end of Operation MARNESCHUTZ-REIMS, and it also aborted Operation HAGEN. After 18 July 1918 the Germans never again regained the initiative in the Great War. By 3 August the Germans had been pushed back to their original 27 May starting line for Operation BLÜCHER. The slightly more than two weeks of fighting cost the Allies 160,000 casualties and the Germans 110,000 casualties and 600 irreplaceable guns.

David T. Zabecki

See also
Bruchmüller, Georg; Chemin des Dames Offensive; Foch, Ferdinand; HAGEN, Operation; Ludendorff, Erich; Ludendorff Offensives; Noyon Offensive; Wilhelm, Crown Prince.

References
Essame, Hubert. *The Battle for Europe, 1918.* London: Batsford, 1972.

Holmes, Richard. *The Western Front.* New York: TV Books, 2000.

Paschall, Rod. *The Defeat of Imperial Germany, 1917–1918.* Chapel Hill, NC: Algonquin, 1989.

Pitt, Barrie. *1918: The Last Act.* New York: Ballantine, 1963.

Wynne, Graeme. *If Germany Attacks: The Battle in Depth in the West.* London: Faber and Faber, 1940.

Zabecki, David T. *Steel Wind: Colonel Georg Bruchmüller and the Birth of Modern Artillery.* Westport, CT: Praeger, 1994.

Marshall, George Catlett (1880–1959)

U.S. Army officer. Born in Uniontown, Pennsylvania, on 31 December 1880, George Marshall graduated from the Virginia Military Institute in 1901 and was commissioned in the infantry in 1902. After service in the Philippines during 1902–1903, he served with the 30th Infantry Regiment at Fort Reno, Oklahoma Territory, until he was posted to the Infantry and Cavalry School at Fort Leavenworth in 1906. He graduated first in his class in 1907. Promoted to first lieutenant in 1907, Marshall was an instructor at Fort Leavenworth during 1908–1910 and then held several other brief assignments before returning to the Philippines (1913–1916), where he was aide to General Hunter Liggett. Marshall won promotion to captain in 1916.

When the United States entered World War I in April 1917, Marshall was serving on the staff of Major General J. Franklin Bell, first in the Western Department and then in the Eastern Department. As the 1st Expeditionary Division was made ready for service in France, its commander Major General William Sibert requested Marshall as his operations officer. Promoted to temporary lieutenant colonel, Marshall prepared the plans and wrote the orders for the 1st Division's attack at Cantigny on 28 May 1918. Marshall's skill was validated when the village was taken in less than thirty minutes. In July, American Expeditionary Forces (AEF) commander General John Pershing ordered Marshall to AEF headquarters to serve in the operations section of the staff as a temporary colonel. Marshall made his most important contributions to the U.S. war effort in the Saint-Mihiel and Meuse-Argonne campaigns of September through November 1918. Marshall learned important lessons about organization, logistics, personnel, and training from the war.

U.S. Army Colonel George C. Marshall. (Marshall Library)

Perhaps the most important lesson, however, was an appreciation of the conduct of warfare within a coalition of allied nations. Marshall was one of a number of U.S. officers whose contributions during the war had both immediate and lasting effects on the organization and efficiency of the U.S. Army.

Between the wars, Colonel George Marshall learned from his mentor General Pershing and performed those tasks of education and training that an army dwells upon in peacetime. Recommended for promotion to brigadier general in 1918, Marshall finally attained that rank in October 1936. On 1 September 1939, he was made army chief of staff and promoted to general. He attained five-star rank as general of the army on 16 December 1944. After World War II he served the United States as ambassador, secretary of state, and secretary of defense. He died on 16 October 1959 in Washington, D.C. Among his many decorations and honors was the Nobel Peace Prize awarded in December 1953 for his role in the European Recovery Program (Marshall Plan). George Marshall was an extraordinary soldier and a gifted statesman.

John F. Votaw

See also

Cantigny, Battle of; Meuse-Argonne Offensive; Pershing, John
Joseph; Saint-Mihiel Offensive; United States, Army.

References

Cooke, James J. *Pershing and His Generals: Command and Staff in the
AEF.* Westport, CT: Praeger, 1997.

Marshall, George C. *Memoirs of My Services in the World War
1917–1918.* Boston: Houghton Mifflin, 1976.

Nelsen, John T., II. "George C. Marshall as Chief of Staff, U.S. Army
1939–1941: The Influences of His World War I Experiences."
In *Cantigny at Seventy-Five: A Professional Discussion,*
110–113. Wheaton, IL: Robert R. McCormick Tribune
Foundation, 1994.

Pogue, Forrest C. *George C. Marshall: Education of a General,
1880–1939.* New York: Viking, 1963.

Marshall, Sir William Raine (1865–1939)

British army general. Born on 29 October 1865 at Stranton in
Durham, William Marshall was educated at Repton and the
Royal Military College, Sandhurst. He joined the Sherwood
Foresters in 1885 and was stationed in Ireland, India, and
Malta. Marshall served in the 1897 Malakand campaign, the
1897 Tirah Expedition, and the 1899–1902 Boer War. In 1912
he was appointed to command his regiment's 1st Battalion,
then stationed in India.

Having served most of his career with his regiment and
having never attended the Staff College or held influential
War Office appointments, Marshall was relatively unknown
outside of his regiment. However, he made a rapid rise during World War I, from a battalion commander at its outset to
the commander of an army of 500,000 men by its conclusion.

In 1914–1915 Marshall commanded his battalion in
France, including at Neuve-Chapelle where he was slightly
wounded. In January 1915 he received a brigade command
and served in the Gallipoli landings. Commanding at "X"
Beach, Marshall defeated Turkish counterattacks and
secured the landing. Surviving another minor wound, Marshall was promoted to major general and appointed to command a division. He participated in the failed attack at
Scimitar Hill and in the final evacuation of the peninsula.

From January to September 1916, Marshall commanded
a division at Salonika, and late in the year he was sent to
Mesopotamia to command a corps. He participated in the
victory at Kut-al-Amara, the capture of Baghdad, and in operations north of the city. After the death of Lieutenant-General
Frederick Maude, Marshall was chosen to command the
Mesopotamia Expeditionary Force.

Other theaters of war were by then of more strategic
importance to the British, and Marshall had to release several
divisions from his command. Nonetheless, Marshall occupied Kirkuk in May 1918 and broke the Turkish defensive
line at Fathah Gorge in October 1918. After the armistice
with Turkey, Marshall pushed forward and entered Mosul
and thereafter enforced the Turkish surrender on the upper
Tigris.

Marshall was promoted to lieutenant-general in 1919 and
returned to India later in the year to head the Southern Command. He retired in 1924 and died at Bagnoles de l'Orne,
France, on 29 May 1939.

Bradley P. Tolppanen

See also

Baghdad, Fall of; Gallipoli Campaign; Kut, Second Battle of;
Mesopotamian Theater; Neuve-Chapelle, Battle of; Salonika
Campaign.

References

Barker, A. J. *The Bastard War: The Mesopotamian Campaign of
1914–1918.* New York: Dial, 1967.

Marshall, William. *Memories of Four Fronts.* London: Ernest Benn,
1929.

Moberly, F. J. *The Campaign in Mesopotamia, 1914–1918.* 3 vols.
Nashville, TN: Battery Press, 1997–1998.

Marterer, Ferdinand von, Baron (1862–1919)

Austro-Hungarian army general. Born on 30 October 1862 in
Prague, Ferdinand von Marterer enrolled in the Infantry
Cadet School in Prague in 1879 and later served with the
infantry in Bohemia and Moravia. He attended the War
Academy from 1887 to 1889. Promoted to captain in 1892,
Marterer then served with the General Staff. In 1904 Emperor
Franz Joseph appointed him to his military chancellery.
Marterer was promoted to colonel in 1905, ennobled in 1908,
and made deputy to the chancellery head and promoted to
major general in 1910.

During the Great War Marterer ran the military chancel-
lory and carried out various missions between the government and the fighting fronts. In late 1916 Emperor Karl
appointed Marterer adjutant general and chief of the military
chancellery. In 1917 the emperor promoted him to general of
infantry after General Conrad von Hötzendorf was relieved
as chief of the General Staff. The emperor also made Marterer
a baron that same year. Marterer retired from the army in 1917
because of poor health. He died in Vienna on 29 January 1919.

Brandon H. Turner

See also

Conrad von Hötzendorf, Franz, Count; Franz Joseph I, Emperor;
Karl I, Emperor.

References

Herwig, Holger H. *The First World War: Germany and Austria-
Hungary, 1914–1918.* New York: St. Martin's, 1997.

Rothenberg, Gunther. *The Army of Francis Joseph.* West Lafayette,
IN: Purdue University Press, 1976.

Martin-Leake, Arthur (1874–1953)

British military surgeon and the first man ever twice awarded the Victoria Cross. Born at Standen, Hertfordshire, England, on 4 April 1874, Arthur Martin-Leake was educated at Westminster School and University College Hospital, London, and became a surgeon. Martin-Leake then joined the Indian Railway Service, spending thirty-four years as chief medical officer of the Bengal-Nagpur Railway. As a surgeon-captain with the South African Constabulary during the 1899–1902 Boer War, he received his first Victoria Cross, the highest British gallantry award, given for self-sacrifice and devotion to duty. On 8 February 1902, at Vlakfontein in the Transvaal, Martin-Leake ignored intense fire from forty Boer riflemen to go forward within 100 yards of the enemy in order to dress an injured soldier's wounds. While attending another badly wounded officer Martin-Leake himself was shot and wounded, but he continued working until he was entirely exhausted.

After the Boer War Martin-Leake returned to India. When World War I began in 1914 he feared that his age would bar him from military service. He therefore traveled independently to Paris, where he enlisted at the British Embassy and forthwith attached himself to the 5th Field Ambulance, the first medical unit he encountered. In late October 1914 Martin-Leake took part in the First Battle of Ypres. Throughout the battle, he showed conspicuous courage and determination to assist the wounded, repeatedly risking fierce enemy fire to rescue many British wounded who were lying near German positions. His heroism was recognized with a bar to his Victoria Cross, making him the first individual so honored and one of only three men—the others being Captain Noel G. Chavasse, also of the Royal Army Medical Corps, during World War I, and Captain Charles H. Upham of the Canterbury Regiment of New Zealand, during World War II—ever to win the award twice.

Martin-Leake served throughout the war and after demobilization returned to the Indian Railways until he retired in 1932. During World War II he commanded a mobile Air Raid Patrol unit. Martin-Leake died at Ware, Hertfordshire, on 22 June 1953.

Priscilla Roberts

See also
Medals and Decorations; Medicine in the War; Ypres, First Battle of.

References
Buzzell, Nora. *The Register of the Victoria Cross.* 3rd ed. Cheltenham: This England, 1997.

Clayton, Ann. *Martin-Leake: Double VC.* London: L. Cooper, 1994.

Gliddon, Gerald. *VCs of the First World War: 1914.* Stroud, UK: Sutton, 1994.

Marwitz, Georg von der (1856–1929)

German army general. Born on 3 July 1856 near Stolp (Slupsk) in Pommerania to an aristocratic family, Georg von der Marwitz attended school in Stolp; he transferred to a cadet training academy in Potsdam and later to the main cadet academy in Berlin. In 1875 he began his military career as a second lieutenant in the 2nd Uhlan Guards Regiment. Marwitz served in cavalry regiments and on the General Staff. Promoted to Generalmajor (equiv. to U.S. brigadier general) in 1908 and Generalleutnant (equiv. to U.S. major general) in 1911, in 1912 he became inspector general of all the cavalry.

On 4 August 1914 Marwitz commanded the II Cavalry Corps, which he led into Belgium in an effort to decoy the advance of the First and Second Armies. Promoted to General der Cavalerie (general of cavalry, lieutenant general) on 19 August, he fought with General Alexander von Kluck's First Army against the British in the Battle of Le Cateau. His force was then ordered to the Ourcq River to cover the exposed left flank of the First Army during the First Battle of the Marne. His cavalry next helped cover the German withdrawal behind the Aisne. In October his cavalry fought in the Battle of Arras as a part of Bavarian Crown Prince Rupprecht's Sixth Army. In command of eight cavalry divisions, Marwitz then took part in the so-called Race to the Sea, fighting at both Lille and Ypres.

Following occupation duties in Belgium during the winter of 1914–1915, Marwitz was transferred to the Eastern Front where he assumed command of the new XXXVIII Reserve Corps. He took part in the Second Battle of the Masurian Lakes in February and March 1915, trapping the Russian XXII Corps. His success there won him the coveted Pour le Mérite and a new command at the head of the Beskiden Corps in late March, fighting the Russians from the Carpathian Mountains on the southern flank of the Russian advance into Galicia. By the end of June 1915, he had helped push the Russians out of Lemberg (Lviw) and back to the Bug River. Illness in July took him out of action until November.

After a brief stint in France as commander of VI Army Corps at Péronne in France, Marwitz returned to the Eastern Front in June 1916 to help blunt the Brusilov offensive in command of VI Corps in the Carpathians. At Kovel, Marwitz took command of an army group of German and Austro-Hungarian units, halting Brusilov's advance.

From December 1916 to September 1918, Marwitz commanded the Second Army near Saint-Quentin in France. In November 1917 his forces at Cambrai were pushed back by the surprise British tank attack, but Marwitz rapidly counterattacked on the northern and southern flanks of the advance and drove the attackers back. In the final German

German General der Cavalerie Georg von der Marwitz, commander of the Second Army on the Western Front. April 1917. (National Archives)

offensives on the Western Front in March 1918 (the Ludendorff or spring offensives), Marwitz's troops at first advanced rapidly but failed to take Amiens and thereby split the British and French forces. After the German offensives were turned back by Allied troops, Marwitz's exhausted and understrength Second Army bore the brunt of the British attack in the Battle of Amiens on 8 August, what General der Infanterie (lieutenant general) Erich Ludendorff termed the "black day of the German Army" in the war. In September 1918 the Second Army was dissolved, and Marwitz took command of the Fifth Army in the Champagne area.

Marwitz retired in December 1918 and returned to his estate of Wundichow in Pommerania. He served as local party chairman of the German National People's Party and died at Wundichow on 27 October 1929.

Gregory Zieren

See also
Amiens Offensive; Arras, First Battle of; Belgium, Overrun; Brusilov Offensive; Cambrai Offensive; Kluck, Alexander von; Le Cateau, Battle of; Ludendorff, Erich; Ludendorff Offensives; Marne, First Battle of the; Masurian Lakes, Second Battle of the; Saint-Quentin Offensive.

References
Cooper, Bryan. *The Ironclads of Cambrai: The First Great Tank Battle*. London: Souvenir Press, 1967.
Gies, Joseph. *Crisis 1918: The Leading Actors, Strategies and Events in the German Gamble for Total Victory on the Western Front*. New York: Norton, 1974.
Marwitz, Georg von der. *General von der Marwitz Weltkriegsbriefe*. Ed. Erich von Tschischwitz. Berlin: Steiniger Verlage, 1940.
Stone, Norman. *The Eastern Front, 1914–1917*. New York: Scribner, 1975.

MAS Boats

Italian navy attack boats during and after World War I. "MAS" originally stood for a pre–World War I project designated "*motoscafo armato di siluri*" (torpedo-armed motorboat). As early as 1906 FIAT, following developments in Great Britain, Germany, and the United States, produced a prototype attack boat capable of a speed of about 15 knots, and a 1914 project by Maccia Marchini of Milan claimed 30 knots, but the contract for MAS 1 and 2 was awarded by the Italian navy to designer Attilio Bisio of the firm Societá Veneziana

Automobili Navali (SVAN). "MAS" thus soon came to represent "Motobarca Armata SVAN" (SVAN Armed Motorboat), and as design variations and improvements followed the first constructions in 1915, this more generic acronym was applied to a range of developments including torpedo boats, gunboats, antisubmarine boats, and minecraft.

Essentially prototypes, MAS 1 and 2 were slender craft, 52'6" in length with a beam of 8'6", displacing 12 tons with a nominal speed of 30 knots. Two forward-facing 18-inch torpedoes were launched over the stern—an awkward arrangement that by 1916 led to conversion of these boats into minelayers and to a more successful forward-launching torpedo boat. Achieving better results with the next group of 20 SVAN boats, the Italian navy ordered 400 more MAS 12- and 19-ton SVAN and Orlando derivatives, as well as 40-ton ELCO boats from U.S. and Italian yards. Of these, 244 entered service by November 1918; the torpedo variants were specifically designed for Adriatic service, where the MAS forces achieved their most conspicuous successes.

The developing fast-attack forces of the Italian navy had a champion in naval chief of staff Admiral Paolo Thaon di Revel, whose faith in these small craft was rewarded on 7 June 1916 with the sinking of Austro-Hungarian transport steamer *Lokrum* by torpedo boats MAS 5 and 7 in the port of Durazzo (Durres, Albania). Further successes ensued, including another torpedoed steamer at Durazzo, and the sinking of the battleship *Wien* on 10 December 1917 by Lieutenant Commander Luigi Rizzo, who had piloted MAS 9 into the harbor of Trieste with silent electric motors. The crowning achievement of Italian torpedo boat warfare was Rizzo's open-sea attack on the Austro-Hungarian navy in the early hours of 10 June 1918. Patrolling off Zara (Zadar) near the island of Premuda, Rizzo's MAS 15 and MAS 21 intercepted Admiral Miklos Horthy's battle group, including the dreadnoughts *Szent Istvan* and *Tegetthof.* Rizzo's craft mortally wounded the *Szent Istvan,* which capsized and sank within three hours.

While the torpedo MAS squadrons were in the Adriatic spotlight, the inherent flexibility of the boats' designs allowed a range of wartime activities for the Italian navy's burgeoning MAS administration, the squadrons of which were based along Italy's coasts, in the Aegean, and in Libya. They undertook such operations as minesweeping, mine laying, escort duties, seaplane and dirigible support, harbor policing, support for coastal and riverine army operations, and the insertion and recovery of intelligence agents or saboteurs. In the last MAS raid of the war and an underwater attack that presaged MAS operations in World War II, a silent, slow torpedo with detachable warheads (called "Mignatta," or leach) was positioned off Pola (Pula) the night of 31 October 1918, by MAS 95. The torpedo was then piloted into the harbor by Lieutenants Raffaele Rossetti and Raffaele Paolucci, who used their two warheads in the early hours of 1 November to sink the former Austro-Hungarian dreadnought *Viribus Unitis,* ceded earlier that same day to the neutral South Slav federation (which planned to rename her *Frankopan* or *Jugoslavija*), as well as the steamer *Wien.*

Italy, along with other navies the MAS forces had influenced, continued to pioneer small assault craft development in the interwar period.

Gordon E. Hogg

See also
Adriatic Theater; Austria-Hungary, Navy; Italy, Navy; Rizzo, Luigi; Thaon di Revel, Paolo; Torpedo Boats.
References
Bagnasco, Erminio. *I MAS e le Motosiluranti Italiane, 1906–1968.* Roma: Ufficio Storico della Marina Militare, 1969.
Bagnasco, Erminio, and Achille Rastelli. *Navi e Marinai Italiani nella Grande Guerra.* Parma: Albertelli, 1997.
Halpern, Paul G. *The Naval War in the Mediterranean, 1914–1918.* Annapolis: Naval Institute Press, 1987.
Kemp, Paul. *Underwater Warriors.* Annapolis: Naval Institute Press, 1996.

Masaryk, Tomáš Garrigue (1850–1937)

Politician, statesman, professor, and first president of Czechoslovakia. Born in Hodonin, Moravia, on 7 March 1850, Tomáš Masaryk excelled in languages and studied at the universities of Vienna and Leipzig, earning a doctorate in philosophy. Masaryk was a professor of philosophy at the Czech University in Prague from 1882 to 1914. In 1881 he published a book, *Suicide and Modern Civilization.* Masaryk became leader of the Young Czechs, a Czech nationalist organization agitating for autonomy and reform. Elected to the Austrian Reichsrat in 1891, he supported Czech interests but resigned his post in 1893 to devote himself full-time to the Young Czech organization.

In 1893 Masaryk founded a monthly magazine, *Atheneum,* and a monthly review, *Our Epoch,* as forums for his ideas. He was also editor of a political weekly, *Time.* In 1898 he published another book, *Philosophical and Sociological Foundations of Marxism.*

Masaryk also helped organize what became the Realist Party and later the Progressive Party, which supported a democratic yet federally–organized Austria-Hungary. Masaryk again served in the Austrian Reichsrat from 1907 until 1914. Early on he championed the rights of Slav minority leaders brought to trial by the government. He also strongly opposed war with Serbia in 1914.

Masaryk escaped arrest by fleeing abroad. In late 1914 he established the Czech National Council in London. As head of this organization, he worked tirelessly with his younger colleague, Edvard Beneš, to promote an independent Czech

Tomáš Garrigue Masaryk, the first president of an independent Czechoslovakia. (Library of Congress)

state. Masaryk traveled extensively to meet with world leaders and promote his program. Among these were visits to Geneva, Paris, Moscow, Petrograd, Tokyo, Chicago, Washington, and New York.

Masaryk helped establish the Czech Legion in Russia to fight against Austria-Hungary, and he took the lead in Paris in the creation of a Czech government-in-exile, his goal being establishment of an independent Czech and Slovak state. A large number of Czechs lived in the United States, and President Woodrow Wilson received Masaryk and supported his aims.

The Czechoslovak Republic was proclaimed in Prague on 14 October 1918, and a month later Masaryk was elected the new state's first president. To ensure legitimacy he ordered a national election in 1920, which he also won. Masaryk was reelected in 1927 and 1934. He and other Czech leaders implemented land reform within the democratic process, assuaged nationalist tendencies among the country's minorities, and created conditions that gave the nation the highest standard of living in central Europe. In foreign affairs, Masaryk championed an alliance with France, signed in 1924, and the activities of the League of Nations.

Failing health forced his retirement from office in 1935, leaving the government in the hands of his trusted colleague

Beneš. The recognized "Father of Czechoslovakia," Tomáš Masaryk died in Prague on 17 September 1937.

Annette Richardson

See also
Beneš, Edvard; Czech Legion; Czechoslovakia, Role in War and Formation of State; Wilson, Thomas Woodrow.
References
Bolton, Glorney. *Czech Tragedy.* London: Watts, 1955.
Martin, William. *Statesmen of the War in Retrospect, 1918–1928.* New York: Associated Faulty Press, 1970.
Selver, Paul. *Masaryk: A Biography.* London: Michael Joseph, 1940.
Skilling, H. Gordon. *T. G. Masaryk: Against the Current, 1882–1914.* London: Macmillan, 1994.
Szporluk, Roman. *The Political Thought of Thomas G. Masaryk.* Boulder, CO: East European Monographs, 1981.
Zeman, Z. A. B. *The Masaryks: The Making of Czechoslovakia.* London: Weidenfeld and Nicolson, 1976.

Masurian Lakes, First Battle of the (8–15 September 1914)

One of the initial series of battles in East Prussia between the Russian and German armies that initiated action on the Eastern Front in World War I. Conducted between 8 and 15 September 1914, this battle occurred shortly after the Russian defeat at Tannenberg.

Outnumbering the defending German Eighth Army waiting behind the north-south line of the Masurian Lakes by nearly two to one, Russian General Yakov Zhilinski's Northwestern Front, consisting of General Pavel Rennenkampf's First Army in the north and General Aleksandr Samsonov's Second Army in the south, entered East Prussia on 15 August 1914. Between the two Russian armies lay a countryside strewn with natural obstacles: forests, rolling hills, marshes, and the Masurian Lakes that canalized the Russian advance and forced their deployment on relatively narrow fronts, slowing their march and diffusing their mass. Zhilinski failed to establish effective communications between the two armies in order to synchronize their actions, and, making coordination even worse, the two army commanders refused to communicate with each other, allegedly because of a grudge between the two dating from the Russo-Japanese War of 1904–1905.

These Russian command failings allowed German General Paul Hindenburg, who had replaced General Max von Prittwitz as Eighth Army commander following the latter's panic after his defeat at Gumbinnen, to throw his Eighth Army against Samsonov, routing the Second Army at Tannenberg, while Rennenkampf essentially dawdled after his victory at Gumbinnen. Hindenburg was now free to turn his whole strength against the Russian First Army.

Having failed to support the Second Army at Tannenberg, Rennenkampf had spent the end of August deploying his army in defensive positions stretching from the Baltic coast to the northern end of the Masurian Lakes. His troops were well-rested and entrenched but spread too thin, with twelve divisions covering a front of more than 80 miles and four reserve divisions concentrated to meet an expected German attack from the fortress of Königsberg. Reinforced from the west with two corps, Hindenburg and his chief of staff, Generalmajor Erich Ludendorff, planned a double attack against the Russians. Four corps were to pin their main positions in the north, and two corps were to strike and break through the thin Russian lines near the lakes.

The Eighth Army opened its attack on 8 September 1914 with the Russian line holding against the attack in the south. By 9 September the holding attack in the north had also ground to a stop. However, on that day the German corps under General Hermann von François, after marching 80 miles in four days, crashed through the southern end of the Russian line. Rennenkampf, fearing his force would be cut off, ordered a general retreat. Leading the retreat in a near panic himself, Rennenkampf had sufficient presence of mind to order a sacrificial spoiling attack with two divisions directly at the German center. Driving the German XX Corps back in disarray and leaving the flanking units exposed, the Russians' suicidal attack caused Ludendorff to hesitate and halt the Eighth Army's pursuit. The remainder of the First Army was allowed to escape—clearing East Prussia of all Russian forces—but not before losing 125,000 men, large amounts of guns and supplies, and nearly half of its transports. A Russian counterattack between 25 and 28 September—the Battle of Nieman—retook much of the ground lost in the battle.

In his headlong retreat, Rennenkampf severed all communication with General Zhilinski, leaving the army group commander completely unaware as to First Army's whereabouts. Eventually reports reached him that Rennenkampf had abandoned his army and fled to the Russian fortress of Kovno, farther to the rear than anyone expected. Within days of the retreat, Grand Duke Nikolai Nikolaevich, supreme commander of Russia's armed forces, relieved Zhilinski from command. However, Rennenkampf's friends at court were able to protect him from the grand duke's wrath.

On the other hand, as a consequence of Tannenberg and the Masurian Lakes victory, Hindenburg and Ludendorff were hailed as heroes in Germany. Eventually, in 1916, Hindenburg succeeded General Erich von Falkenhayn as chief of the German General Staff, and Ludendorff became his first quartermaster general.

Arthur T. Frame

See also
East Prussia, Campaigns in; Eastern Front Overview; François, Hermann von; Gumbinnen, Battle of; Hindenburg, Paul von; Ludendorff, Erich; Mackensen, August von; Masurian Lakes, Second Battle of the; Nikolai Nikolaevich, Grand Duke; Prittwitz und Gaffron, Maximilian von; Rennenkampf, Pavel Karlovich; Russia, War Plan; Samsonov, Aleksandr Vasiliyevich; Tannenberg, Battle of; Zhilinski, Yakov Grigorevich.

References
Knox, Sir Alfred. *With the Russian Army, 1914–1917: Being Chiefly Extracts from the Diary of a Military Attaché.* 2 vols. New York: Dutton, 1921.

Lincoln, W. Bruce. *Passage through Armageddon: The Russians in War and Revolution, 1914–1918.* New York: Simon and Schuster, 1986.

Stone, Norman. *The Eastern Front, 1914–1917.* New York: Scribner, 1975.

Masurian Lakes, Second Battle of the (7–22 February 1915)

The Second Battle of the Masurian Lakes was part of Central Powers commander on the Eastern Front Field Marshal Paul von Hindenburg's plan for a simultaneous Austrian-German decisive thrust along the Eastern Front to defeat Russia and

German soldiers during the Second Battle of the Masurian Lakes maintaining continuous fire from their shield-protected machine guns. They are directed by an officer who watches the results through binoculars. (Francis J. Reynolds and C. W. Taylor, *Collier's Photographic History of the European War,* P. F. Collier & Son, New York, 1916)

force it from the war. Also known as the Winter Battle of Masuria, the battle opened in the midst of a *metel,* the Russian word for severe blizzards in which gale force winds from the east whip blinding sheets of snow for days on end. This metel blew from Russia across Poland and into East Prussia just as the German Ninth Army attacked in early February 1915 toward Bolimów to fix the Russian Tenth Army in place. The metel quickly ground that attack to a standstill.

The German plan called for the commitment of two armies—the Eighth and Tenth—in East Prussia. The Tenth, formed from four corps recently transferred from the West, was to attack south from staging areas near Tilsit, Insterburg, and Gumbinnen into the right flank of the Russian Tenth Army deployed north of the Masurian Lakes. Meanwhile, the German Eighth Army would drive east toward Lyck and Augustów from bases at Lötzen, Ortelsburg, and Thorn. General Rudolph Sievers, commanding the Russian Tenth Army, believed that the Germans could not attack in such severe conditions and was caught by surprise when German forces struck on 7 February 1915. With most of his staff nearly 70 miles in the rear at Grodno, Sievers threw up a hasty and stubborn defense focused around infantrymen of the III Siberian Corps. Fighting with limited means because most of their ammunition and supplies were snowbound at railroad depots, the Russians were forced on 10 February to fall back when the German XXI Corps cut the rail line to the Russian fortress at Kovno and the XXIX Reserve Corps captured 10,000 Russian soldiers near Wirballen. On 14 February the Germans entered Lyck and seized that vital rail junction.

On 21 February advanced elements of the German Eighth and Tenth Armies met at Lipsk, south of the Augustów Forest, closing the ring on remnants of the Russian Tenth Army. Fighting primarily with fixed bayonets on empty rifles, the men of Sievers's III Siberian Corps, accompanied by the badly mauled XXVI Corps, forced their way out of the ring the next day. While German casualties were relatively low, the Russians lost 100,000 killed and another 110,000 captured, along with 300 guns. Further German progress eastward ended when Russian General Pavel Pleve's Twelfth Army attacked the German right flank on 22 February.

Although a tactical success, the German victory proved to be of little strategic importance. The Austro-Hungarian army effort in the south had been less than effective, and the Russians, having great recuperative ability, were not driven from the war. However, the Second Battle of the Masurian Lakes caused the Russian public to doubt a positive outcome to the conflict.

Arthur T. Frame

See also
East Prussia, Campaigns in; Eastern Front Overview; Hindenburg, Paul von; Ludendorff, Erich; Masurian Lakes, First Battle of the; Pleve, Pavel Adamovich.

References
Falls, Cyril. *The Great War, 1914–1918.* New York: Capricorn, 1961.
Knox, Sir Alfred. *With the Russian Army, 1914–1917: Being Chiefly Extracts from the Diary of a Military Attaché.* 2 vols. New York: Dutton, 1921.
Lincoln, W. Bruce. *Passage through Armageddon: The Russians in War and Revolution, 1914–1918.* New York: Simon and Schuster, 1986.
Stone, Norman. *The Eastern Front, 1914–1917.* New York: Scribner, 1975.

Mata Hari (1876–1917)

Alleged German spy. Born in Leeuwarden, Holland, on 7 August 1876, Margaretha Geertruida Zelle married Rudolph MacLeod, an officer in the Netherlands Colonial Army, in 1895. After a posting to Java, the marriage crumbled and Margaretha decided to use the knowledge she had acquired of the East Indies to become an exotic dancer in France. Adopting the Malay stage name of Mata Hari (the sun at dawn), she became a 1905 Paris sensation. Surrounded by an aura of exoticism and mystery, she used her allure to become one of the Belle Époque's most famous courtesans.

When war began, Mata Hari was in Berlin enjoying the attentions of a police commissioner while attempting to

The infamous exotic dancer Mata Hari who was convicted and executed for espionage in 1917. (Underwood & Underwood/Corbis)

revive her dance career. She quickly departed for the Netherlands. There she received 20,000 francs from Karl Kroemer, a member of German Intelligence, who hoped to benefit from her French connections. Mata Hari agreed to undertake small assignments for Kroemer and received the code name "H21," but beyond accepting his money did nothing.

Arriving in Paris, perhaps with the aim of dancing again, she drew the attention of informers suspicious of the numerous lovers she had indiscriminately chosen from all ranks, ages, and nationalities. In August 1916, she met with Georges Ladoux, head of French Counterintelligence, agreeing to provide the French with information in exchange for 1 million francs. Mata Hari had, in the meantime, fallen in love with a Russian army officer in France. Evidently she believed that wealth would give her a better chance of securing his family's approval of the match. Ladoux had no intention of paying this sum and assigned Mata Hari no specific mission but simply sought proof that she worked for the Germans. The British then confused the ex-dancer with a notorious German spy, took her off a Channel ship, and detained her for several days. Ladoux took the British mix-up as evidence of guilt and believed that he received further proof of her complicity when Mata Hari sought a pass to visit Vittel in the military zone. Her lover had been injured and sent to the military hospital at Vittel, unbeknownst to Ladoux.

In order to earn the money from Ladoux, Mata Hari approached a German military attaché in Spain who had charge of an intelligence network in Barcelona. Identifying her clumsy attempts to gather secrets as an attempted betrayal of German intelligence, this officer deliberately sent a message to be intercepted by the French that implicated Mata Hari. When the would-be spy returned to France to report her findings to Ladoux, she was arrested on 13 February 1917 for espionage and passing secrets to the enemy.

Tried before a military tribunal, Mata Hari, despite protestations of innocence, was found guilty on 25 July 1917. She was executed in Paris by a firing squad on 15 October 1917.

Caryn E. Neumann

See also
France, Home Front; Intelligence and Counterintelligence; Women in the War.

References
Howe, Russell Warren. *Mata Hari: The True Story.* New York: Dodd, Mead, 1986.

Keay, Julia. *The Spy Who Never Was: The Life and Loves of Mata Hari.* London: Michael Joseph, 1987.

Maude, Sir Frederick Stanley (1864–1917)

British army general. The son of a general and holder of the Victoria Cross, Frederick Maude was born at Gibraltar on 24 June 1864. He attended Eton and the Royal Military College, Sandhurst, before joining the Coldstream Guards in 1884. Known throughout the army as "Joe" Maude, he served in the Sudan in 1885 and in the 1899–1902 Boer War. During the latter conflict he permanently damaged his right shoulder in a fall from his horse. In 1901 Maude was appointed military secretary to the governor-general of Canada, and in 1905 he became private secretary to the British secretary of war.

Upon British mobilization for World War I, Maude was appointed to the staff of III Corps and served in the early battles in France. In October 1914 he was appointed commander of the 14th Brigade, and in April 1915 he was wounded while inspecting trenches at St. Eloi. Promoted to major-general in June 1915, Maude was sent to Gallipoli to take command of the 13th Division.

Following the evacuation of the Gallipoli Peninsula, Maude brought the 13th Division to Egypt and then to Mesopotamia. In July 1916 he was selected to command the Tigris Corps and the following month replaced Lieutenant-General Sir Percival Lake as commander of the Mesopotamia Expeditionary Force.

British attempts early in 1916 to capture Baghdad had met disaster with the humiliating fall of Kut. Determined to redeem their position in the region, the British dispatched reinforcements and additional weapons, including armored cars and modern fighter aircraft, to this theater. A stickler for dress and discipline, Maude applied his thoroughness and energy to the systematic reorganization of the army. He improved the lines of communication and built a solid logistical base before he moved. Maude recaptured Kut in February 1917 and entered Baghdad in March. He was promoted to lieutenant-general in 1917.

After a pause to guarantee his logistics, Maude undertook further operations intended to destroy the Turkish ability to counterattack and threaten Baghdad. He captured Samarrah in April 1917, defeated the Turks at Ramadi that September, and occupied Tikrit in November. Maude died of cholera in Baghdad on 18 November 1917. His death deprived the British of one of their best generals of the war.

Bradley P. Tolppanen

See also
Baghdad, Fall of; Gallipoli Campaign; Kut, First Battle of; Kut, Second Battle of; Lake, Sir Percival; Mesopotamian Theater; Ramadi, Battles of; Tikrit, Battle of.

References
Barker, A. J. *The Bastard War: The Mesopotamian Campaign of 1914–1918.* New York: Dial, 1967.

Callwell, C. E. *The Life of Stanley Maude.* New York: Houghton Mifflin, 1920.

Moberly, F. J. *The Campaign in Mesopotamia, 1914–1918.* 3 vols. Nashville, TN: Battery Press, 1997–1998.

Maud'huy, Louis Ernest de (1857–1921)

French army general. Born on 17 February 1857 at Metz in Lorraine, the province later ceded to the new German Reich after the Franco–German War of 1870–1871, Louis Maud'huy joined the army and had risen to general by 1912. When French army commander General Joseph Joffre created the Tenth Army as part of an attempt to envelop the German right flank during the so-called Race to the Sea, he gave Maud'huy command of it. Maud'huy's army fought hard in Flanders in October 1914 and during the First Battle of Artois in December 1914, suffering enormous casualties.

In 1915 Maud'huy was relieved of command of the Tenth Army as it was preparing for the next Artois offensives, and Joffre sent him to a quieter sector. In command of the Seventh Army in the Vosges, Maud'huy undertook a series of small but costly attacks. In April 1916 he took command of XV Corps and saw action at Verdun on the west bank of the Meuse. He moved to command of XI Corps in January 1917 after it was pulled from the Verdun sector. Some elements of his corps were involved in General Robert Nivelle's disastrous Chemin des Dames offensive, but later the corps took part in the successful recapture of the fort of La Malmaison in the same area in October 1917. This latter operation was one of French army commander General Henri Philippe Pétain's so-called *batailles de redressement*, small offensive actions that restored the French army's faith in its ability to secure a victory through limited but well-prepared operations.

Maud'huy was still on the Chemin des Dames when the German Ludendorff offensives broke through the French lines there in May 1918. Despite Pétain's orders for an elastic defense in-depth, General Denis A. Duchêne, commander of the Sixth Army (of which Maud'huy's corps formed a unit) had not wished to concede the front line because it ran along the River Aisne. Duchêne's decision resulted in a rout of French forces and near disaster. Maud'huy fell victim to Premier Georges Clemenceau's purge of generals after parliamentary criticism because of the German breakthrough. Allied supreme commander General Ferdinand Foch had been forced to agree to the purge, but he rewarded Maud'huy for his great efforts in 1914 when, on 26 November 1918, he appointed Maud'huy military governor of Metz, Maud'huy's home town and newly restored to the French Republic. Maud'huy died in Metz on 16 July 1921.

Elizabeth Greenhalgh

See also
Artois, First Battle of; Chemin des Dames Offensive; Clemenceau, Georges; Duchêne, Denis Auguste; Joffre, Joseph; Ludendorff Offensives; Nivelle, Robert; Nivelle Offensive; Pétain, Henri Philippe; Race to the Sea.

References
Clayton, Anthony. *Paths of Glory: The French Army, 1914–18.* London: Cassell, 2003.
Gies, Joseph. *Crisis 1918: The Leading Actors, Strategies and Events in the German Gamble for Total Victory on the Western Front.* New York: Norton, 1974.
Spears, Sir Edward. *Liaison, 1914: A Narrative of the Great Retreat.* London: Eyre and Spottiswoode, 1968.

Maunoury, Michel Joseph (1847–1923)

French army general and marshal. Born on 11 December 1847 in Maintenon (Eure et Loire), Michel Maunoury was commissioned into the artillery from the École Polytechnique in 1869 and saw service during the Franco-Prussian War of 1870–1871. In 1901 he was promoted to general of brigade. After periods spent as instructor at the military academy at Saint-Cyr-L'École, as military governor of Paris (1910–1912), and as a member of the French Supreme War Council (Conseil Supérieur de la Guerre), Maunoury retired from the army at the statutory age of 65 in 1912.

Recalled to active service in August 1914, Maunoury received command of the Army of Lorraine and was entrusted with the investment of Metz. On 26 August Maunoury's army was ordered west and, reinforced with reservists and detachments from other armies, became the Sixth Army. The expeditious move of Maunoury's Sixth Army westward toward Paris provides a good example of the command of logistics possessed by French army commander General Joseph Joffre. Between 27 August and 2 September, thirty-two trains were used to transport the Sixth Army and its equipment to the Paris area.

The Sixth Army played an important role in the First Battle of the Marne. Maunoury's attack on the west flank of German General Alexander von Kluck's First Army marked the opening of the battle. Maunoury then joined, but cautiously, the pursuit of the Germans to the Aisne River where the battle lines became trench lines.

Wounded during an inspection of the front in March 1915, Maunoury was partially blinded and forced to retire. After a short period as military governor of Paris from November 1915 to March 1916, he played no further role in the war. Maunoury died on 28 March 1923. For his role in the First Battle of the Marne, he became posthumously one of the group of marshals of France created after the war.

Elizabeth Greenhalgh

See also
Kluck, Alexander von; Marne, First Battle of the; Race to the Sea.

References
Asprey, Robert B. *The First Battle of the Marne.* Philadelphia: Lippincott, 1962.

Clayton, Anthony. *Paths of Glory: The French Army, 1914–18.* London: Cassell, 2003.

Spears, Sir Edward. *Liaison, 1914: A Narrative of the Great Retreat.* London: Eyre and Spottiswoode, 1968.

Max von Baden, Prince (1867–1929)

German chancellor. Born on 10 July 1867 at Baden-Baden, Germany, Max joined the Prussian army and achieved the rank of a cavalry Generalmajor before leaving the service in 1911. He then pursued a doctorate of jurisprudence. In 1907 Max was designated heir apparent to his childless cousin, Grand Duke Friedrich II of Baden, and as such he was automatically president of the Upper House of Baden's Diet. Max had a lively interest in the intellectual and artistic currents of his time.

At the beginning of World War I in August 1914, Max joined the headquarters staff of the XIV Corps as the representative of the grand duke. He was promoted to general of cavalry à la suite (an honorary attachment without duties). Due to his dissatisfaction with his post and poor health, Max returned home in October 1914 to busy himself with alleviating the plight of the thousands of prisoners of war (POWs)

now held in Germany. He became honorary chairman of the board of Baden's Red Cross and, in large part due to his efforts, a vast system to aid POWs was built up. He cooperated with the YMCA World Union and was nominated honorary president of its American-German POW assistance organization in 1916.

On 3 October 1918 following the resignation of Count Georg von Hertling, Max succeeded as imperial chancellor. He took over the most difficult of circumstances, with Germany having been defeated on the battlefield. Urged to do so by the Supreme Command of the Army (OHL), Max asked U.S. President Woodrow Wilson for an armistice and peace agreement based on the Fourteen Points. During the thirty-two days of his chancellorship, Max carried on an exchange of notes with the U.S. government concerning an end to the war.

Ironically, Max, a prince of the blood, presided over the first parliamentary government in German history when Kaiser Wilhelm II agreed to institute genuine ministerial responsibility. When the OHL demanded an end to negotiations with Wilson because the generals found the U.S. peace conditions unacceptable, Max helped secure Ludendorff's dismissal. He also urged Wilhelm to abdicate to save the monarchy as an institution. With the kaiser wavering and to stave off possible revolution, Max publicly announced without authorization the abdication of both Wilhelm II and Crown Prince Wilhelm on 9 November 1918. Later that day, Social Democrat Philipp Scheidemann proclaimed the establishment of a German republic, frustrating Max's hopes for a continuation of the monarchy.

Max then handed over the chancellorship to the leader of the largest party in the Reichstag, Social Democrat Friedrich Ebert. This unusual step made the transfer of power from monarchical to parliamentary government more acceptable to the elite classes, especially the civil servants who formed the core of the conservative establishment. Max's resignation was also widely respected by the Entente governments.

After the war, Max wrote his memoirs and he and Kurt Hahn founded the Salem boarding school at Lake Constance, which aimed to educate a new German elite. The ideals of the school, especially its call for a sense of community, were imitated both inside and outside Germany. Max died at Konstanz, Germany, on 6 November 1929.

Bert Becker

German Chancellor Prince Max of Baden, who presided over the first parliamentary government in German history. (Francis A. March, *History of the World War*, United Publishers, Chicago, 1918)

See also

Ebert, Friedrich; Fourteen Points; Germany, Revolution in; Hertling, Georg Friedrich von, Count; Ludendorff, Erich; Scheidemann, Philipp; Wilhelm, Crown Prince; Wilhelm II, Kaiser; Wilson, Thomas Woodrow.

References

Deuerlein, Ernst. *Deutsche Kanzler von Bismarck bis Hitler.* Munich: Paul List Verlag, 1968.

Herwig, Holger H. *The First World War: Germany and Austria-Hungary, 1914–1918.* New York: Arnold, 1997.

Matthias, Erich, and Rudolf Morsey. *Die Regierung des Prinzen Max von Baden.* Duesseldorf: Droste, 1962.

Max von Baden. *Erinnerungen und Dokumente.* Newly edited by Golo Mann and Andreas Burckhardt. Stuttgart: E. Klett, 1968.

Maxse, Sir Ivor (1862–1958)

British general known for his excellence in training troops. Born in London on 22 December 1862, Frederick Ivor Maxse was the son of British admiral Frederick Augustus Maxse. Educated at Rugby and Sandhurst, Ivor Maxse served in India, Egypt, and South Africa until 1900. In 1910 he took command of the 1st Guards Brigade and soon demonstrated his talent for training, stressing clear instruction, relentless drill, and the responsibility of junior officers for the well-being and performance of their men.

In 1914, Maxse's brigade participated in the British retreat from Mons, and his outspoken exasperation with inadequate staff work and an argument with General Douglas Haig, his corps commander, may have contributed to Maxse's assignment to Colchester to train the 18th Division, a volunteer unit recruited for Kitchener's New Army. When the Somme offensive began on 1 July 1916, the 18th's advantageous position on the front and the high caliber of its training preserved it from the carnage that befell other units of the New Army, and in September it distinguished itself in fighting around Thiepval.

In January 1917 Maxse received command of the newly formed XVIII Corps. After six months it joined the Fifth Army under General Hubert Gough, serving in the Third Ypres (Passchendaele) campaign from July to November 1917. In the major German offensive of March 1918, XVIII Corps retreated in good order, and while some criticized Maxse for withdrawing too precipitately, Gough later credited him for preventing a catastrophic gap in the Allied lines. Maxse afterward served under General Henry Horne of the First Army, whom he soon confronted about tactics, supplies, and training. This friction played a part in Haig's decision in April 1918 to appoint Maxse inspector general of training for the entire British Expeditionary Force, a post he kept for the remainder of the war.

From 1919 to 1923 Maxse held the northern command at York, continuing to sustain his training standards and providing one of his staff officers, Basil Liddell Hart, support to begin his career as a military theorist and historian. In 1926 Maxse retired and spent the remainder of his life operating a fruit-growing business. Maxse died at Midhurst, Sussex, on 28 January 1958.

John A. Hutcheson Jr.

See also

Aisne, First Battle of the; Great Britain, Army; Gough, Sir Hubert de la Poer; Haig, Douglas, 1st Earl; Kitchener, Horatio Herbert, 1st Earl; Liddell Hart, Sir Basil Henry; Somme Offensive; Western Front Overview; Ypres, Third Battle of.

References

Baynes, John. *Far from a Donkey: The Life of General Sir Ivor Maxse.* London: Brassey's, 1995.

Griffith, Paddy. *Battle Tactics of the Western Front: The British Army's Art of Attack, 1916–18.* New Haven, CT: Yale University Press, 1994.

Maxwell, Sir John Grenfell (1859–1929)

British army general. Born on 11 July 1859 at Liverpool, John Maxwell was educated at Cheltenham and the Royal Military College, Sandhurst. He joined the 42nd Highlanders in 1879 and served in the 1882 Egyptian campaign. Maxwell later transferred to the Egyptian army and saw extensive service in the Sudan. During the 1899–1902 Boer War, he commanded a brigade and served as military governor of Pretoria. Promoted to major-general in 1906, Maxwell was selected to command the British forces in Egypt in 1908. Following his promotion to lieutenant-general in 1912, Maxwell relinquished his appointment and went on half pay.

Maxwell was recalled to active service in World War I. In the first month of the war Maxwell served as head of the British mission at French army headquarters, but he was soon sent back to Egypt to resume command of British forces there. Maxwell faced a series of daunting challenges in Egypt. His first task was to enforce martial law that had been declared throughout the country on 2 November 1914.

When Turkey entered the war that same month, Maxwell had to secure the Suez Canal against possible Turkish attack. He oversaw improvements in the canal's fortifications and allocation of troops to its defence. In February 1915 the defenders easily defeated a Turkish attack on the canal. Maxwell then provided administrative support for the Allied expeditions to Gallipoli and Salonika. He also had to deal with an uprising by the Senussi in western Egypt, which was largely suppressed by early 1916.

By 1916 an inefficient command system had developed in Egypt. There were three independent structures under Maxwell, Lieutenant-General Archibald Murray, and Major-General Edward Altham operating there. This situation was resolved in March 1916 when Maxwell was recalled at his own request.

Upon his return to Britain, Maxwell was presented with another difficult task as he was sent to Ireland as commander-in-chief to deal with the Easter Rising. In quick order he forced the surrender of the rebellion's leaders, restored order in Dublin, and governed Ireland under martial law.

In 1916 Maxwell was appointed to head the Northern Command in Britain. In 1919 he was promoted to full general, and he served on Lord Alfred Milner's mission to Egypt. Maxwell retired in 1922 and died in Cape Town, South Africa, on 20 February 1929.

Bradley P. Tolppanen

See also
Egypt; Gallipoli Campaign; Ireland, Role in War; Murray, Sir Archibald James; Salonika Campaign; Senussi and Sultan of Darfur Rebellions; Suez Canal.
References
Arthur, George. *General Sir John Maxwell.* London: Murray, 1932.
Bruce, A. P. C. *The Last Crusade: The Palestine Campaign in the First World War.* London: Murray, 2002.
Wavell, Colonel A. P. *The Palestine Campaigns.* London: Constable, 1928.

Mayo, Henry Thomas (1856–1937)

U.S. Navy admiral. Born on 8 December 1856 at Burlington, Vermont, Henry Mayo was commissioned in the navy on graduation from the U.S. Naval Academy, Annapolis, in 1876. He was assigned to the Asiatic Squadron of the Pacific Fleet. In 1883 he participated in the Greely relief expedition in the Arctic. Promoted to commander in 1905, two years later Mayo assumed his first sea command, the cruiser *Albany,*

U.S. Navy Admiral Henry Mayo, commander of the Atlantic Fleet. (Corbis)

off South America. Promoted to captain in 1908, Mayo took command of the cruiser *California.* He made rear admiral in 1913 and was assigned as aide to Secretary of the Navy Josephus Daniels.

In 1913 Mayo took command of the 4th Division of the Atlantic Fleet in the Caribbean. In April 1914 Mexican authorities at Tampico arrested some of Mayo's sailors. Mayo demanded their immediate release as well as a public apology, causing a brief international crisis that almost led to war between the United States and Mexico. The incident made Mayo a public hero and led to his promotion to vice admiral in June 1914 and to full admiral and commander of the Atlantic Fleet in June 1916.

After the United States entered World War I in April 1917, Mayo commanded all U.S. warships in the Atlantic and European waters. Mayo represented the United States at a naval conference in London where he pushed for more aggressive action. He endorsed construction of a large antisubmarine force and recommended such measures as a mine barrage from Scotland to Norway.

Mayo commanded the redesignated U.S. Fleet after the war and kept that position until June 1919, when he reverted to his permanent rank of rear admiral. Following service on the General Board, Mayo retired in December 1920. During 1924–1928 he was governor of the Philadelphia Naval Home. In 1930 he was advanced to the rank of admiral on the retired list. Mayo died at Portsmouth, New Hampshire, on 23 February 1937.

Christopher J. Richman

See also
Daniels, Josephus; United States, Navy.
References
Jones, Jerry W. *U.S. Battleship Operations in World War I.* Annapolis: Naval Institute Press, 1998.
Lewis, Charles Lee. *Famous American Naval Officers.* Boston: L. C. Page, 1948.

McAdoo, William Gibbs (1863–1941)

U.S. secretary of the Treasury. Born on 31 October 1863 into poverty in Marietta, Georgia, William McAdoo had an irregular education before entering the University of Tennessee. He abandoned his studies in 1882 to accept a position as deputy clerk of the U.S. Circuit Court. Admitted to the Tennessee Bar in 1885, he served as a railroad attorney and became president of an electrified railway, steering the company into bankruptcy in 1892. Starting afresh in New York City in 1897, McAdoo sold railroad bonds and spearheaded an effort to improve rail service by building additional lines. In 1891 the construction of twin rail tunnels under the Hudson River made McAdoo into one of New York City's leading figures. As president of the Hudson and Manhattan Railway Company, he gained a reputation as a progressive manager.

In 1910, McAdoo supported Woodrow Wilson's New Jersey gubernatorial campaign and briefly led Wilson's presidential bid in 1912. Rewarded with a cabinet position in 1913, McAdoo presided over a dramatic increase in the economic power of the federal government as treasury secretary. Following his wife's death in 1912, McAdoo married Wilson's daughter Eleanor in 1914. Three of McAdoo's sons from his first marriage would serve in the navy during World War I.

When World War I began, McAdoo opposed sending U.S. troops, preferring to employ economic rather than military power to advance U.S. interests. McAdoo believed that to prevent the collapse of the U.S. economy and the failure of the Allied war effort, the United States had to lend the European powers the money they needed to continue buying supplies in U.S. markets. To this end, he coordinated massive loans and mandated that the Europeans could only spend federal money in the United States. He also helped establish the War Risk Insurance Bureau in 1914 to issue insurance on ships and cargoes that had been refused reasonable rates by private companies and also helped establish the U.S. Shipping Board to maintain transatlantic traffic. McAdoo created and promoted the enormously successful Liberty Loan campaigns, which raised almost $17 billion from the American public in less than two years. When the rail system almost collapsed because of the press of war shipments, Wilson ordered a government takeover and appointed McAdoo as the railroad director in 1918. McAdoo coordinated lines, eliminated the backlog of shipments, and, true to his progressive roots, intervened on behalf of railway employees to increase wages and improve working conditions.

Financial obligations forced McAdoo to tender his resignation three days after the signing of the armistice in 1918, having filled his promise to stay throughout the war. Returning to his law practice, he moved to California and made a run for the 1924 Democratic presidential nomination. Unfortunately, McAdoo became embroiled in the Teapot Dome oil scandal and saw his hopes dashed. In 1932 he won a U.S. Senate seat from California. Defeated for reelection in 1938, he died in Washington, D.C., on 1 February 1941.

Caryn E. Neumann

See also
United States, Home Front; Wilson, Thomas Woodrow.
References
Broesamle, John J. *William Gibbs McAdoo: A Passion for Change, 1863–1917.* Port Washington, NY: Kennikat, 1973.
McAdoo, William Gibbs. *Crowded Years: The Reminiscences of William G. McAdoo.* Boston: Houghton Mifflin, 1931.
Shook, Dale N. *William G. McAdoo and the Development of National Economic Policy, 1913–1918.* New York: Garland, 1987.

Medals and Decorations

Military awards fall into three basic categories. Medals are widely awarded to recognize service in a war, a campaign, or a battle or for periods of long peacetime service. Decorations are selective individual awards presented for significant or distinguished service or for valor in combat. Qualification or skill badges are awarded to recognize proficiency with a particular weapon or piece of equipment. As today, most armies during World War I had some system of proficiency badges. With the exception of pilots' wings and marksmanship badges, almost none of the proficiency badges of today's armies bears much resemblance to their World War I counterparts.

Medals and decorations consist of a metal badge suspended from a ribbon with a color scheme unique to that specific award. Many countries had and still have special ways of draping the ribbon that are readily identifiable and unique to that country. The full award, the ribbon and the badge, is worn generally only on special occasions and on the dress uniform. During normal occasions the award is represented by a ribbon bar worn on the service uniform. In most World War I armies, soldiers wore their decorations and medals, at least in the form of the ribbon bar, on their uniforms in combat. Virtually no army today follows that practice.

The badge of the medal generally, but not always, consists of a round, bronze medallion. Decorations generally tend to have badges in some shape, with stars and crosses being the most common. The badges of the higher decorations are often made from silver or gold and sometimes have enameled or even jeweled portions.

Following the end of World War I, all the Allied armies issued their participating soldiers a medal of almost identical design. The Allied Victory Medal recognized service in any theater of operation between 1914 and 1920, including post–November 1918 operations in the eastern Baltic and Russia. The design of the medallion featured a winged female figure with a shield and the sword of victory. The ribbon featured a rainbow pattern. A series of bars attached to the suspension ribbon specified participation in a given battle or campaign. The Allied Victory Medal was unique to World War I. No similar medal has ever been awarded, before or since. Supreme Allied Commander Marshal Ferdinand Foch suggested the idea to the members of Paris Peace Conference, and the proposal was adopted on 24 January 1919.

The world's first true campaign medal awarded to soldiers of all ranks was probably the British Waterloo Medal for the 1815 battle that resulted in Napoleon's final defeat. In 1847 the British also established a Military General Service Medal, with bars to designate service in specific battles between 1793 and 1814. In the early years of World War I, the British deviated

British Sergeant Alexander Edwards of the Seaforth Highlanders being decorated by King George V for gallantry north of Ypres. (Sir J. A. Hammerton, *A Popular History of the Great War: A Year of Attrition, 1917,* Vol. 4, The Fleetway House, London, 191–)

briefly from the design norm and established two campaign medals with badges in the shape of stars. (Britain would again follow that practice for all of its World War II campaign medals.) The 1914 Star was awarded for service in battles between 5 August and 22 November 1914. The 1914–1915 Star recognized service through the end of 1915. From 1916 through 1920 British soldiers received the British War Medal. Those who received the earlier Stars also received the War Medal, and all British soldiers also received the Allied Victory Medal.

French soldiers participating in the war received the Commemorative Medal of the 1914–1918 War. Belgium also issued a Commemorative Medal 1914–1918 as well as a medal for Volunteers 1914–1918 and a special Croix de Feu for those who served on the front lines. In addition, Belgium awarded a separate Yser Medal for participation in that 1914 battle. Italy awarded its soldiers a Medal of War 1915–1918. All French, Belgian, and Italian soldiers also received the Allied Victory Medal.

Russia issued only one service medal for World War I, the Medal for Distinguished Efforts in the General Mobilization of 1914. After late 1917, the attentions of the interim provisional government and then finally the Soviet government were so consumed with the Russian Civil War and its

aftermath that there apparently was little interest in recognizing service in what came to be known as the Great Imperialistic War.

U.S. soldiers received only the Allied Victory Medal for service between 1917 and 1920, including service in Russia. Those who performed occupation duty between 12 November 1918 and 11 July 1923 also received the Army of Occupation of Germany Medal. That award, however, was not established until 1941. Many returning U.S. soldiers were awarded special war service medals by their home states or home towns, and in some cases by both. Although these were not official U.S. military awards, many discharged soldiers wore them on their uniforms.

Despite its name and shape, the German Cross of Honor of the 1914–1918 World War was essentially the German Empire's (and Prussia's) World War I service medal. Two versions of the medal existed, one for frontline soldiers and one for the widows and parents of those killed in action. In both cases, the badge was the same, but the color schemes of the ribbons were different. The various German kingdoms (Bavaria, Saxony, Württemberg), dukedoms (Baden), lesser states, and even the Hanseatic city-states (Bremen, Lübeck, Hamburg) all issued war service medals for their citizens.

Modern military decorations evolved from the system of chivalric and noble orders that had been in existence in Europe for hundreds of years. In most of the World War I European armies (and Japan), the system of military decorations at the higher end merged with the system of orders. Orders were always awarded only to officers. Some countries, such as Great Britain, even had a dual system of decorations, one for officers and one for enlisted men.

The United States had no system of chivalric or noble orders. It was also the first modern nation to confer military awards on common soldiers. In 1780 the Continental Congress authorized decorations for three New York militiamen for their roles in capturing British intelligence officer Major John André. The so-called André Medals were one-time creations. The first standing U.S. military decoration was the Badge of Military Merit, established by General George Washington in 1782. The badge consisted of a purple cloth heart and was awarded only three times. After the War for American Independence, the award fell into disuse until it was reestablished in its modern form in 1932 as the Purple Heart, awarded for wounds (including mortal wounds) received in combat. The Purple Heart was made retroactive to service in World War I. Prior to that, World War I wounds were indicated by a small inverted chevron (point down) for each wound received, worn on the soldier's lower right sleeve. The same type of chevron worn on the lower left sleeve indicated six months overseas service in World War I.

The U.S. Army established the Certificate of Merit in 1847, awarded to army privates and noncommissioned officers for acts of heroism. Originally it consisted only of a certificate and an entry in the soldier's record. In 1905 a medal was authorized for all holders of the certificate. The Certificate of Merit became obsolete in 1918. Initially, all holders of the Certificate of Merit were authorized to convert their award to the newly established Distinguished Service Medal. Later, that was changed to the Distinguished Service Cross.

The Medal of Honor (often erroneously called the Congressional Medal of Honor) was established for the U.S. Navy on 12 December 1861 and for the U.S. Army on 12 July 1862. The highest U.S. military decoration for battlefield heroism, it is awarded by the president in the name of Congress to those members of the U.S. Armed Forces who distinguish themselves by gallantry and intrepidity at the risk of their lives above and beyond the call of duty while engaged in combat against an armed enemy of the United States.

Though they were originally authorized only for enlisted men, officers became eligible for the Army Medal of Honor in 1863 and for the Navy Medal of Honor in 1915. The Army and Navy Medals of Honor also differed in that from the start the Army Medal of Honor could be awarded only for acts of combat valor. The Navy Medal of Honor could be awarded for peacetime acts of heroism until 1942. Between 1917 and 1942,

the navy actually had two different designs for the Medal of Honor, one for combat and one for noncombat. The suspension ribbon was the same for both medals.

The Medal of Honor was awarded 125 times in World War I. In one of the quirks of history, U.S. Marines who fought as part of the U.S. Army's 2nd Infantry Division received army rather than navy decorations, including the army version of the Medal of Honor. In the early 1920s, 4 of those marines were also awarded the navy version of the Medal of Honor for the exact same act, using the exact same citation. To this day they are counted as two-time Medal of Honor recipients.

The modern system of U.S. military decorations came into being during World War I. Until that time the only U.S. decorations were the Medal of Honor and the Certificate of Merit. With the establishment in 1918 of the Distinguished Service Cross, the Navy Cross, and the Distinguished Service Medal, Congress created the concept of the Pyramid of Honor. For the first time in U.S. history, degrees of military service to the nation were established, each worthy of its own level of recognition. In the years following World War I, some dozen lower-level decorations for valor, distinguished service, or both have been added to the Pyramid of Honor.

The Medal of Honor is at the apex of the Pyramid of Honor. Some levels of the Pyramid of Honor had more than one decoration because the army and the navy each had their own unique award. During World War I there was no separate air force, the air service being part of the army. The U.S. Marine Corps was and still is part of the Navy Department. Both the army and the navy had their own unique design for the Medal of Honor, but both medals have the same ribbon. At the second level, the decorations even had slightly different names and completely different designs and ribbons; however, the Army Distinguished Service Cross and the Navy Cross rank equivalent as the second highest combat decorations in the United States. At the third level, the army and navy Distinguished Service Medals have the same names but completely different designs and ribbons. The Distinguished Service Medal is the highest U.S. military award for noncombat service.

On the fourth and primary level of the World War I Pyramid of Honor, the Silver Star was awarded by both the army and the navy. The third highest U.S. decoration for combat valor was authorized in 1918 as the Citation Star, affixed to the ribbon of the Allied Victory Medal to recognize soldiers who had distinguished themselves in combat. It was a mirror of the British Mentioned in Dispatches award. In 1932 the United States converted the Citation Star to a decoration in its own right and renamed it the Silver Star.

Unlike many European systems of decorations, both officers and enlisted soldiers were eligible for all U.S. military awards during World War I. In some countries soldiers wore multiple medals or ribbons for subsequent awards of the same decoration. Each subsequent award of a U.S. Army decoration is indicated by a Bronze Oak Leaf Cluster device attached to the suspension ribbon or to the ribbon bar. A Silver Oak Leaf Cluster represents five subsequent awards. The U.S. Navy and U.S. Marine Corps use a Gold Star device to represent subsequent awards, and a Silver Star Device (not to be confused with the silver Citation Star) for five subsequent awards. The most decorated American of World War I, and arguably of all time, was aviation ace Edward Rickenbacker, who in addition to the Medal of Honor received the Distinguished Service Cross with seven Oak Leaf Clusters.

Imperial Russia's decorations were an outgrowth of its system of orders. Russia had a number of orders that recognized various levels of both civilian and military service, but its principal military decoration was the Order of St. George. Instituted in 1769, the order came in four classes and was awarded only for battlefield heroism or for distinguished service by the most senior commanders. As with the orders of all other countries, it was reserved only for officers. In 1807 Russia established its first permanent award for noncommissioned officers and privates. The St. George Cross was an extension of the Order of St. George, and like it the St. George Cross was awarded in four classes and only for extreme bravery in the face of the enemy. In 1878 the Russians again extended the system by establishing the even lower level St. George Medal, which also came in four classes. Between 1914 and 1917, Russia awarded an estimated 200,000 St. George Crosses and more than 1 million St. George Medals.

Britain too entered World War I with a wide system of orders to recognize distinguished military and civilian service. Originally established in 1399, the Order of the Bath (Military Division) was the most significant recognition for distinguished military service at the highest levels. In 1856, Queen Victoria established the Victoria Cross as the premier British decoration for combat heroism. From its inception until the end of the cold war period, the Victoria Cross was the only British combat decoration for which officers and enlisted men were both eligible. Significantly, the Victoria Cross ranked in order of precedence ahead of all British orders, even the Order of the Garter, seldom awarded outside the Royal Family. Until 1920, the Victoria Cross ribbon was crimson for the army and blue for the Royal Navy, when it was changed to crimson for all services. The Victoria Cross was awarded 636 times during World War I, accounting for 47 percent of the medals ever awarded. Among the World War I winners was Captain Noel G. Chavasse, who won the Victoria Cross in 1916 and again, posthumously, in 1917. Only two other British or Commonwealth soldiers have won the Victoria Cross twice.

Below the level of the Victoria Cross, the British awards system split into distinct groups for officers and enlisted men. Although technically decorations, the enlisted awards were called gallantry medals. In order of precedence, the decoration for the lowest-level officers ranked above the highest enlisted gallantry medal. The British finally abandoned this dual system in the 1990s.

Despite its name, the Distinguished Service Order was a decoration for officers of all three services and recognized gallantry or distinguished service in the face of the enemy. The second highest British combat award, it was established in 1886. Just below the level of the Victoria Cross, the highest enlisted gallantry medals were the Distinguished Conduct Medal for the army and the Royal Air Force and the Conspicuous Gallantry Medal for the Royal Navy.

Below the level of the Distinguished Service Order, each of the services had distinct decorations for combat gallantry: Military Cross, Army; Distinguished Service Cross, Royal Navy; and Distinguished Flying Cross, Royal Air Force. The enlisted equivalents were the Military Medal, the Distinguished Service Medal, and the Distinguished Flying Medal, respectively.

British decorations were awarded to soldiers of all the countries of the British Empire that fought in World War I—Canada, Australia, New Zealand, and India. The receipt of any of the above-noted decorations entitled the recipient to add the appropriate postnominal to his official name. Subsequent awards of the same decoration were indicated with a metal bar on the decoration's suspension ribbon. The correct postnominal for a three-time recipient of the Military Cross, for example, would be "MC and 2 Bars." On the service ribbon bar, the bar was represented by a small metal device in the shape of a Tudor heraldic rose.

The primary level of recognition for acts of gallantry or distinguished conduct by British officers in combat operations was the Mention in Dispatches. Officers so-mentioned were authorized to wear a bronze oak leaf device on the ribbon of the Allied Victory Medal. As noted above, the U.S. version of this practice in World War I later evolved into the Silver Star.

Although France was a republic by the time of World War I, its highest decoration was established by Emperor Napoleon I in 1802. The Légion d'Honneur was awarded to French military soldiers and civilians (and even foreigners) for distinguished civilian or military service or for combat valor. It came in five classes. Although open to everyone in theory, French NCOs and privates almost never received the Légion d'Honneur, especially during World War I. As a result, the French established one of the most peculiar systems of military decorations, which exists to the present day.

In 1852 President Louis-Napoléon Bonaparte (later Emperor Napoléon III) established the Médaille Militaire as France's highest strictly military decoration. That decoration, however, could only be awarded to NCOs and privates and to senior generals and admirals. Officers from lieutenant to colonel were not eligible. The underlying notion behind this odd system was based on the dual nature (distinguished service or combat valor) of the Légion d'Honneur and the assumption that an enlisted soldier would almost never receive France's highest decoration. Generals and admirals, on the other hand, would almost certainly receive the Légion d'Honneur for their service virtually as a matter of course. The Médaille Militaire, therefore, would identify those French flag officers who actually distinguished themselves in combat.

The basic French decoration of World War I was the Croix de Guerre. Established in 1915, it was awarded to soldiers of all ranks who had been mentioned in the dispatches of a regimental or higher-level commander. The level of the command was indicated by the type of device attached to the suspension ribbon: Bronze Star for regiment and brigade; Silver Star for division; Gold Star for corps; and Bronze Palm for army.

Belgium and Italy, as with Britain, had a number of orders to recognize distinguished civilian and military service. The most important Belgian military order was the Order of Leopold, which came in five classes. Prior to World War I, the Belgian military also had a Military Decoration for Acts of Heroism for NCOs and privates. In 1915 Belgium instituted its own Croix de Guerre, patterned very closely after the French version. The principal Italian decoration for officers was the Military Order of Savoy, which came in five classes. The first Italian decoration for junior officers and enlisted men was established in 1793. Italy established the Medal for Military Valor and the Medal for Naval Valor in 1833 and 1836, respectively. By World War I there were Gold, Silver, and Bronze Classes for each of these decorations, which were open to all ranks. In 1918 Italy also introduced the War Cross of Valor and the War Cross of Merit.

The German Empire, being an empire composed of four distinct kingdoms and a collection of lesser states, had a bewildering array of orders. But since the German emperor was also the king of Prussia, and since the Great General Staff of the Prussian army controlled all wartime field operations of the combined German army, the principal German decorations of World War I were those of the Prussian army. They were awarded to all German soldiers regardless of their state army of origin (Bavarian, Saxon, Baden, etc.). Quite often, however, the individual states also continued to confer their own decorations and awards on their own soldiers.

The Iron Cross is undoubtedly one of the world's best-known military decorations. It was established in 1813 by King William Frederick III of Prussia. Although during the period of World War II Adolf Hitler more than doubled the number of classes of the Iron Cross, there were only four during World War I. The Iron Cross could be awarded for either individual acts of combat heroism or for distinguished wartime service. In other words, it could be awarded to a successful commander for winning a battle, even though he may never have come under fire. Another peculiar feature of the Iron Cross is that it had to be earned one class at a time. Regardless of the nature of the act of heroism, the soldier always received only the lowest class. A second act of valor would bring the next higher class.

The Iron Cross 2nd Class was the basic level of the award. It consisted of an iron cross badge suspended from a black and white ribbon. Unlike other medals worn over the left breast, the Iron Cross 2nd Class was worn looped through the second and third buttons of the uniform tunic. Two versions of the ribbon existed, one for frontline combatants and one for noncombatants. The Iron Cross 1st Class consisted of the badge only, without the ribbon, worn on the left breast pocket of the uniform. The Iron Cross 1st Class and 2nd Class were available to all German soldiers in World War I. As a general rule, however, the award of the Iron Cross 1st Class to enlisted men was far less common than to officers. Hitler was one of those enlisted men who received the Iron Cross 1st Class for his World War I service. He served four years in the German army as a company runner, an extremely hazardous job.

The two highest levels of the Iron Cross were awarded only a few times during World War II, and only to very senior commanders. The Iron Cross Grand Cross was worn from a neck ribbon, similar to the Iron Cross Knight's Cross of World War II. The badge of the Grand Cross, however, was much larger. It was awarded to only five senior commanders, including Generals Paul von Hindenburg, Erich Ludendorff, Prince Leopold of Bavaria, and August von Mackensen. The kaiser also awarded the Grand Cross to himself. The Star to the Iron Cross Grand Cross (also known as the Blücher Star), was awarded only once, to Hindenburg. An iron cross badge surmounted on an eight-pointed star, it was worn on the left breast pocket, along with the Iron Cross 1st Class.

One other Prussian decoration available only to officers ranked between the Iron Cross 1st Class and the Iron Cross Grand Cross. First established in 1667 as the Order of Generosity, the Ordern Pour le Mérite was renamed in 1740 by Prussian King Frederick II. Its popular, if somewhat irreverent, name was the "Blue Max," after aviation ace Max Immelmann. The Pour le Mérite was also worn from a neck ribbon, and it came in two classes. The higher class added a small cluster of oak leaves (mit Eichenlaub) to the top arm of the eight-pointed cross of the badge. During World War I the Pour le Mérite was awarded 687 times, and the Oak Leaves was awarded only 122 times. As with the award system for the Iron Cross, recipients of the Oak Leaves first had to earn the basic Pour le Mérite. Although considered World War I Germany's premier decoration for combat heroism, the Pour le Mèrite also was awarded for distinguished war service at the higher levels. For example, Germany's artillery genius, Colonel Georg Bruchmüller, received the Pour le Mérite in 1917 as a lieutenant colonel for his work as an artillery commander on the Eastern Front. In 1918 he received the Oak Leaves for planning the artillery fires for Operation MICHAEL, the great Ludendorff offensive.

David T. Zabecki

r, Georg; Chavasse, Noel Godfrey; Foch, Ferdinand;
urg, Paul von; Hitler, Adolf; Immelmann, Max Franz;
, Prince of Bavaria; Ludendorff, Erich; Mackensen,
August von; Martin-Leake, Arthur; Wilhelm II, Kaiser.

References

Brinkmann, Jürgen. *Die Ritter des Ordens Pour le Mérite, 1914–1918*. GmbH, Hannover: Schäfer Druckerei, 1982.

Decorations United States Army: 1862–1926. Washington, DC: U.S. Government Printing Office, 1927.

Hall, Donald. *British Orders, Decorations, and Medals*. St. Ives, UK: Balfour Publications, 1973.

Kerrigan, Evans. *American Medals and Decorations*. London: Balfour Publications, 1990.

Register of the Victoria Cross, The. Cheltenham, UK: This England, 1988.

Rosignoli, Guido. *Ribbons of Orders, Decorations, and Medals*. New York: Acro, 1977.

Werlich, Robert. *Orders and Decorations of All Nations*. Washington, DC: Quaker Press, 1965.

———. *Russian Orders, Decorations, and Medals*. Washington, DC: Quaker Press, 1981.

Williamson, Gordon. *The Iron Cross: A History, 1813–1957*. Poole, UK: Blandford, 1984.

Medicine in the War

World War I was the first major conflict in which scientific principles of surgery, anesthesia, asepsis, and infection control were widely adopted. As recently as the Boer War, the British army's only medical units comprised litter bearers and one fixed field hospital for each brigade. Litter companies and field hospitals were combined under a single command as field ambulances in 1905. (In World War I terminology, "ambulance" refers to the whole transport and hospital system rather than just the means of transportation.) The mobile casualty clearing station, usually sited next to a rail line and used to stabilize patients and dispatch them to the next appropriate level of care (triage), was not devised until 1907. In their war with Russia, the Japanese added evacuation hospitals between field hospitals at the front and base hospitals on the home islands. They deployed sophisticated hospital ships to augment land-based facilities and, recognizing the importance of early wound treatment, Japanese physicians (many of whom trained in German hospitals) employed stabilizing surgery in the forward areas.

From the first days of World War I, the vast military mobilization stressed civilian medical capabilities. The French and Germans incorporated virtually their entire physician populations into the military from the beginning. They sent younger doctors to the front and used older men in rear-area hospitals where their experience better equipped them to manage difficult cases. As the war progressed, all belligerents suffered from lack of physicians. There were too few doctors to satisfy either military or civilian requirements. The first Americans officially to enter the war were medical personnel assigned to the British army the month after the United States entered the war, in May 1917. Before any U.S. soldiers had been sent to Europe, 1,400 physicians, 1,000 nurses and 2,600 enlisted members had been deployed in addition to six base hospitals.

Although the usefulness of trained female nurses had been recognized since the Crimean War, none of the European armies had an adequate number when the war started. In 1914 there were fewer than 300 nurses in Queen Alexandra's (QA) Imperial Military Nursing Service (the nursing arm of the Royal Army Medical Corps). As a result of aggressive recruitment and training programs, there were 10,404 QAs with 9,000 VADs (partially trained nursing personnel in Voluntary Aid Detachments) working under their supervision by 1918.

From 1914, Americans had provided hospital and transportation services on the Western Front with several motor ambulance services voluntarily manned and funded and a series of university-based teams of physicians and nurses operating primarily under the auspices of the American Hospital in Paris. The American Red Cross initially provided volunteers to both the Entente and the Central Powers but stopped service to Germany and Austria after the sinking by a German submarine of the passenger liner *Lusitania*.

The American Army Medical Corps rapidly expanded after the United States entered the war. In June 1916 there were only 443 American medical officers; by 1918 there were 30,591 (more men than were in the entire 1916 U.S. Army). There was a shortage not only of doctors and nurses but also of hospitals. When the war started, there were only 18,000 hospital beds in the whole empire; by the end of the war there were 637,000.

World War I saw significant advances in military medicine with consequent better outcomes. The earliest improvements were in transportation and triage. Litter bearers retrieved men from the field and took them to aid stations (*postes de secours*) just behind the front lines. After bandaging and stabilization, the men were transported—increasingly by motor ambulance—to casualty clearing stations (CCSs) just beyond the reach of artillery fire where wounds were débrided (dead tissue removed) and redressed, fractures braced, and minor injuries definitively treated. From the CCS, men were taken to field hospitals where surgical teams could perform emergency operations. Field hospitals were usually adjacent to a rail line allowing further transport to base hospitals where more complex surgery, convalescence, and rehabilitation could take place. For the most severely wounded there were specialized hospitals in the zone of the interior where long-term rehabilitation and complex reconstructive procedures could be done.

Relatively stable front lines and an abundance of roads behind the immediate combat zone encouraged the development of motorized ambulance transport. Prior to U.S. entry

A shattered church in Neuilly provides temporary shelter for American wounded, 20 September 1918. (National Archives)

into the war, most ambulance services were operated by military transport rather than medical services and served strictly as modes of conveyance. The services were partially manned and supplied by troop transport divisions, but a significant number were under the auspices of various volunteer organizations such as the St. Johns' Ambulance, the Society of Friends, and the American Ambulance Field Service. John Dos Passos, Ernest Hemingway, and E. E. Cummings served as volunteer drivers and described their experiences in later published works.

Initiating treatment at CCSs made it possible to manage wounds within minutes to hours rather than the one to two days that had been usual early in the war. Early treatment decreased blood loss and the risk of infection, and survival rates improved. The heavily fertilized fields of northern France were rife with Clostridium perfringens and the related Clostridium tetani, responsible for gas gangrene and tetanus, respectively. Early wound débridement decreased the inci-

dence of gas gangrene, and an effective antiserum (11 million doses of which had been administered by war's end) virtually eliminated tetanus.

Chemical sterilization of wounds also contributed to the decrease in secondary infection. Direct application of chlorine was replaced by continuous irrigation with a combination of hypochlorites and boric acid developed by French physician Alexis Carrel and British chemist H. D. Dakins. In the absence of antibiotics, which were not developed until the interwar years, the Carrel-Dakins method provided a remarkably effective way to limit wound infections. The death rate in hospital from wounds was 4.5 per 1,000 as compared to 10.48 per 1,000 in the American Civil War.

Trench warfare with machine guns, shrapnel, high explosives, land mines, grenades, and mortars caused a unique assortment of injuries. Wounds to the head came from exposure over trench rims, and extremity injuries came from mines protecting the space between opposing lines. The prevalence of extremity injuries necessitated improvements in orthopedic reconstruction and prostheses and in diagnosis and repair of nerve injuries. The high number of head injuries led to better intracranial surgery (particularly under the auspices of American Harvey Cushing), and the complex facial injuries engendered innovative techniques in plastic and reconstructive surgery. Improvements in anesthesia and the general application of aseptic surgical techniques benefited all areas of surgery. Although the case mortality rates of head, chest, and extremity wounds improved during World War I, the lack of antibiotics meant that improved survival from penetrating abdominal wounds would have to wait until the next war.

Unlike prior wars, the rate of death from injury was more than twice that from disease in World War I, even when the high mortality of the 1918 influenza epidemic is included. Although not as lethal as in prior conflicts, disease was still a serious problem in World War I. Recruits, many of whom came from sparsely populated rural areas, were thrown together in close quarters with urbanites whose immune systems were accustomed to high population density and carried protection against many contagious diseases. The nonimmune recruits were subject to and suffered in great numbers from measles, mumps, scarlet fever, and meningitis. Diseases such as smallpox, typhoid, tetanus, diphtheria, and some forms of dysentery that had previously devastated armies were effectively controlled with vaccines. Some diseases carried by arthropods, such as louse-borne typhus and trench fever, were at least partially controlled by chemical pest control, especially with DDT.

Disease was an especially serious problem in Africa and the Middle East. The East African campaign had the highest incidence of disease of any in the war, mostly malaria. The British in Mesopotamia suffered from malaria and dysentery with as many as 10 percent of all personnel reporting sick every day during the siege of Kut. At Gallipoli, 85,000 men

Members of the Medical Corps removing wounded from Vaux, France, 22 July 1918. (National Archives)

were hospitalized (most often evacuated to Egypt) for disease, with dysentery being the most common problem.

All combatants recognized the risk of infection in the squalid conditions of trench warfare, and separate sanitary sections were organized to minimize the risk. The German trenches were more often concrete-lined, easier to clean, and less prone to infection than those of the British and French.

The Germans first used chlorine gas as a weapon at Ypres nine months after the war started. Later in the war chlorine was replaced by mustard and phosgene gases. By July 1915 effective gas masks had been developed, and 27 million were produced by the war's end. As a weapon, gas was relatively humane with a much lower mortality rate than other types of war injury; of 185,000 British gas casualties, only 9,000 were fatal.

Among the major improvements in military medicine during World War I, one might list generalized use of hypodermic syringes, retractors, forceps, rubber gloves, thermometers, sterile gauze, motor ambulances, mobile laboratories, diagnostic x-rays, vaccinations, trained nurses, and iodine solutions.

Jack McCallum

See also

Casualties, Combatant and Noncombatant; Chemical Weapons; Gallipoli Campaign; Influenza Pandemic; Kut, Siege of; Literature and the War; Red Cross; Shell Shock; Trench Fever; Trench Foot; Trench Warfare; Women in the War.

References

Fauntleroy, A. M. *Report on the Medico-Military Aspects of the European War from Observations Taken behind the Allied Armies in France.* Washington, DC: Government Printing Office, 1915.

Garrison, Fielding. *Notes on the History of Military Medicine.* Washington, DC: Association of Military Surgeons, 1922.

Ireland, M. W., ed. *The Medical Department of the United States Army in the World War, 1917–1918.* 15 vols. Washington, DC: Government Printing Office, 1921–1929.

Lovegrove, Peter. *Not the Least Crusade: A Short History of the Royal Army Medical Corps.* Aldershot, UK: Gale and Polden, 1952.

Macdonald, Lyn. *The Roses of No Man's Land.* New York: Atheneum, 1989.

Medina, Siege of (1916–1919)

Significant event during the Arab Revolt. One of the three holy cities of Islam and terminus of the Hejaz railroad, Medina was a natural target for the Arab insurgents in the Hejaz from the outset of the revolt. In fact, the standard of revolt was first raised on 5 June 1916 near the city, and a first attempt at capturing it failed the next day. While the forces of the Grand Sharif of Mecca Husayn ibn 'Alī, aided by Egyptian field artillery and British warships, were able to capture most important cities and ports in the Hejaz, among them Jidda, Mecca, Taif, and Yanbo, the Turks reinforced Medina and held it for almost three years.

In spite of a warning by their German allies that trying to defend both the Hejaz and Palestine in the face of the British buildup could result in losing both, the Ottoman leadership, fearing for its legitimacy when giving up the holy places, decided to hold the Hejaz. To this end, they turned Medina into an impregnable stronghold and reinforced its garrison. The Turkish VIII Corps was tasked with defending the Hejaz railroad on its entire length of some 430 miles from Syria to the Hejaz. The principal component of this force, the Medina garrison itself that was called the Hejaz Expeditionary Force, numbered 14,000 men by the fall of 1916. The Turkish commander at Medina, Khairy Bey, felt strong enough to stage repeated successful sorties against the weakly organized Arab forces that were more blockading than actually besieging the town, and he even planned a counteroffensive aimed at recapturing Mecca, though it never materialized.

In the summer of 1917, Prince Faisal's Arab Army, backed by British warships, moved north from al-Wejh, taking Aqaba and conducting raids on the Hejaz railroad, the sole artery of supply for the Medina garrison. When the British Egypt Expeditionary Force (EEF) and its Arab allies continued their advance into Palestine and Syria in late 1917 and 1918, the task of protecting the railroad increasingly imposed a heavy strain on the Turkish forces. Including the Medina garrison, the Ottoman Empire needed 22,000 troops in 1918 to keep the Hejaz railroad open. The men were distributed among some major garrisons and numerous small blockhouses along the track from which they usually dared not venture.

In April 1918 Arab forces finally cut the Hejaz railroad around Ma'ān. Evacuation of the 12,000-man Turkish garrison still in Medina, for a long time advocated by Ottoman officers but always refused by the government, was now out of the question. Fakhri Pasha refused to surrender well into January 1919, when his officers finally revolted and turned the influenza-plagued garrison over to the Arabs. Some 8,000 Turkish troops were evacuated to Egypt, while many Arabs joined the victors' cause. Holding on to Medina may have been a political necessity for the Ottoman government, but the fall of the empire made it a vain sacrifice.

Dierk Walter

See also

Allenby, Sir Edmund, 1st Viscount; Beersheba-Gaza Line, Battles of; Faisal, Prince; Falkenhayn, Erich von; Husayn ibn 'Alī, King; Palestine and Syria, Land Campaign.

References

Bruce, Anthony P. C. *The Last Crusade: The Palestine Campaign in the First World War.* London: Murray, 2002.

Bullock, David L. *Allenby's War: The Palestinian-Arabian Campaigns, 1916–1918.* London: Blandford, 1988.

Erickson, Edward J. *Ordered to Die: A History of the Ottoman Army in the First World War.* Westport, CT: Greenwood, 2000.

Falls, Cyril. *Military Operations: Egypt and Palestine, from June 1917 to the End of the War.* London: HMSO, 1930.

MacMunn, George, and Cyril Falls. *Official History of the Great War: Military Operations, Egypt and Palestine, from the Outbreak of the War with Germany to June 1917.* London: HMSO, 1928.

McKale, Donald M. *War by Revolution: Germany and Great Britain in the Middle East in the Era of World War I.* Kent, OH: Kent State University Press, 1998.

Mediterranean Theater, Naval Operations (1914–1918)

Virtually all the warring naval powers, including the Pacific nation of Japan, contributed naval units to the war in the Mediterranean. While there was no Jutland-like naval clash between great battle fleets in the Mediterranean, events there played a significant role in the war's outcome.

In August 1914 France was the dominant naval power in the Mediterranean. An agreement of 1912 between France and Britain conferred on France the primary responsibility for the Mediterranean. Britain withdrew many ships from the Mediterranean to the North Sea, promising to protect the French coasts against a German naval attack. Control of the Mediterranean was important to France, which relied on both troops and resources from its North African possessions.

Before the war Austria-Hungary and Italy had engaged in a major naval-building contest in the Mediterranean, including the construction of modern dreadnought battleships. Italy already had an oceangoing navy, but Austria-Hungary did not. Vienna's decision to turn its limited coast-defense force into a blue water fleet had a substantial effect on the Mediterranean balance of power (and also the outcome on land, as the naval-building absorbed significant resources that would otherwise have gone to the Austro-Hungarian army). Additionally, Germany had established a permanent naval presence in the Mediterranean in the form of a squadron. If the naval resources of Germany, Austria-Hungary, and Italy in that sea were combined, they would pose a considerable danger to France and even to Britain. The latter's imperial lifeline to India and the Pacific ran through the Suez Canal. As events transpired, in August 1914 Triple Alliance member Italy proclaimed its neutrality and in 1915 joined the Allied Powers.

Germany's Mediterranean naval force, the Mittelmeerdivision, consisted of the new powerful battle cruiser *Goeben* and light cruiser *Breslau.* On the outbreak of the war the *Goeben* was the most powerful ship in that sea. To bolster the French position and maintain Allied regional superiority, Britain sent several battle cruisers to the Mediterranean.

On 28 July, with the Dual Monarchy's declaration of war on Serbia, river monitors of the Austro-Hungarian Danube flotilla fired the opening shots of the war. Italy's decision to remain neutral, announced on 2 August, assured the British and French of naval superiority, at least in surface warships, in the Mediterranean for the remainder of the conflict.

The Italian declaration of neutrality placed Mittelmeerdivision commander Rear Admiral Wilhelm Souchon in a vulnerable position. Souchon's primary missions were to disrupt Allied lines of communication and to prevent the transfer of French troops to southern France from North Africa. Steaming for the Algerian coast on news of the formal declaration of war by Germany against France, his ships fired the first shots in the Mediterranean on the morning of 4 August against the Algerian ports of Bône and Philippeville but caused little damage. Later that afternoon Souchon received orders to steam for Constantinople.

Vice Admiral Augustin Boué Lapeyrère, commander of the French fleet in the Mediterranean, the *1ère armée navale,* concentrated his naval assets on protecting convoys of troops from North Africa to France and was subsequently accused of letting the *Goeben* escape. Too late, he took up the chase, believing that the Germans were aiming for the Austrian naval base at Pola or attempting to reach the Atlantic. His fleet was therefore out of position on 6 August, and owing to a combination of unfortunate decisions and faulty intelligence, the French forces missed the German ships when they set out for the Dardanelles after recoaling at Messina.

The task of intercepting the Mittelmeerdivision now fell to the British. British commander in the Mediterranean Vice Admiral Sir Archibald Milne was directed to destroy the German ships, but Milne was hamstrung by Italian neutrality (limiting how and where he could pursue the Germans), poorly drawn orders, and faulty intelligence. Rear Admiral Sir Ernest Troubridge, commander of the 1st Cruiser Squadron of four armored cruisers, might have engaged the *Goeben,* but he believed this would violate his orders that called on him to avoid action with superior forces. Indeed, the *Goeben*'s heavier guns would have enabled her to sink the British cruisers before they had come within range.

Thus the two German ships escaped and steamed into the Dardanelles, anchoring off Constantinople on 10 August. Souchon transferred the two ships to nominal Turkish control but then used them to attack Russian naval bases on the Black Sea and bring about Turkey's entrance into the war on the German side. This latter was most unfortunate for the Allies, since it cut Russia off from access to its western allies via the straits and helped precipitate the economic dislocations that would lead to the Russian revolutions and drive Russia from the war at the end of 1917. The Allies now had almost uncontested control of the Mediterranean, that is, until Austro-Hungarian and German submarines became a serious threat. The Ottoman Empire's entry into the war also prompted the British "peripheral strategy" that led to the failed Dardanelles campaign to force those straits and the Gallipoli land campaign in April. This combined effort, led by

From the opening of the war France kept the greater part of its navy in the Mediterranean to guard its southern coast and protect routes of communication to North Africa. Pictured here are French and English ships near the Dardanelles. (Francis J. Reynolds and C. W. Taylor, *Collier's Photographic History of the European War*, P. F. Collier & Son, New York, 1916)

the British and supported by the French, had the goal of driving Turkey from the war and opening up a supply route to Russia though the straits into the Black Sea.

As Souchon initiated his dash to Constantinople on 6 August, British and French representatives met in London to hammer out their respective duties in the Mediterranean. The Anglo-French Convention of that date placed British naval units in the Mediterranean under French command. The agreement proved short-lived, for as the war dragged on the British were unwilling to entrust their interests in the Mediterranean completely to France. The Royal Navy assumed the task of defending Allied interests in the eastern Mediterranean, including the Aegean Sea, while the French Navy protected the western Mediterranean and blockaded the narrow Strait of Otranto in order to prevent the Austro-Hungarian navy from making sorties from the Adriatic.

Despite the absence of a major fleet action, both sides undertook many minor naval operations. For example, both the Austrians and French conducted small actions along the Montenegrin coast. On 1 September 1914 the French conducted a naval bombardment of Cattareto, and on 20 December the Austrians captured a French submarine entering Pola harbor. During the first six months of the war Austrian submarines sank two French cruisers.

On 10 May the French and British negotiated a naval convention with the Italians, who demanded a major Allied naval commitment if they joined the war. This agreement established a First Allied Fleet of four British battleships, four British light cruisers, twelve French destroyers, and many French torpedo boats, submarines, and minesweepers. The First Allied Fleet operated from the Italian ports of Taranto and Brindisi under Italian Fleet Vice Admiral Luigi Amedeo di Savoia. If this First Allied Fleet were deployed to the northern Adriatic, a second Allied Fleet would come into existence under the French naval commander to include French battleships, cruisers and destroyers, and Italian and British warships not already assigned to the Italian fleet commander. Although the Italian fleet was larger than the Austro-Hungarian fleet, Italian appeals for Allied naval support were

chiefly based on the geographical configuration of the Adriatic, which favored the concentrated Austro-Hungarian fleet.

The Italians entered the war on the Allied side against the Austro-Hungarian Empire on 24 May 1915. Chief of the Italian Naval Staff Vice Admiral Paolo Thaon di Revel opposed a major fleet action in the narrow Adriatic and insisted on the employment there of smaller naval units and submarines. This meant that the Italian battle fleet remained essentially inactive at Taranto throughout the war, and this led to some bitterness on the part of the British and French, who questioned Italian naval competence. Indeed, Austro-Hungarian naval units bombarded Italian ports on the first day Italy entered the war and sank an Italian destroyer. In June 1915 Austro-Hungarian navy units again raided the Italian Adriatic coast, and during the next month the Italians lost two cruisers. In December there was an inconclusive larger naval action off the southern port of Durazzo in which an Austrian cruiser and five destroyers attacked that port and sank some cargo ships and a submarine but lost two destroyers in a minefield. The remainder of the attackers succeeded in escaping.

The major threat to the Allies at sea, in the Mediterranean as elsewhere, turned out to be the submarine. The initial effort was mounted by the Austro-Hungarian navy, but Germany sent its first submarines into the Mediterranean in April 1915 in response to the Anglo-French Dardanelles campaign. They arrived by sea and were also sent overland in sections to Pola and then assembled. The Mediterranean was an attractive target for the war against commerce because a substantial amount of British and French shipping passed through that sea. Unlike in the Atlantic, submarines could operate more effectively year-round. Also, there were several choke points, such as the Suez Canal, the central Mediterranean near Malta, and the Strait of Gibraltar, that Allied shipping had to traverse. Another advantage for the Central Powers in the Mediterranean was that their submarines would encounter far fewer risks of sinking neutral shipping there.

The Germans organized a separate U-boat task force in the fall of 1915 at Cattaro, under Kapitänleutnant Lothar von Arnauld de la Perière, the most successful U-boat commander in history (he ultimately sank 446,708 tons of shipping). The Central Powers employed both Pola and Cattaro as U-boat bases. In October 1915 the Germans intensified their U-boat operations in the Mediterranean. In the last three months of the year, they sank seventy-nine merchant ships totaling 290,471 tons.

The French navy, theoretically in charge of Allied naval operations in the Mediterranean, suffered from a critical shortage of antisubmarine equipment, and its role in the Mediterranean steadily declined as the Royal Navy took up the slack, in part by dispatching additional destroyers there. Leaders in both countries also realized that they needed to intensify their efforts, and on 3 December 1915 Britain, France, and Italy signed the Paris Agreement dividing the Mediterranean into eighteen patrol zones. The British and Italians would each patrol four zones and the French ten. The patrol zones were located close to each country's territory, and the powers involved agreed to assign all the destroyers they could spare to their zones.

An Allied conference at Malta during 2–9 March 1916 reduced the number of Mediterranean patrol zones from eighteen to eleven. The British took responsibility for most of the Aegean and instituted a system of patrolled sailing routes. However, the Allies continued to resist a convoy system. Allied countermeasures reduced the effectiveness of the German submarine effort in the first six months of 1916, with only twenty-four Allied ships sunk in the Mediterranean in that period. As 1916 wore on, Allied shipping losses increased again. Austrian submarines also registered some successes.

At Taranto on 30 October 1916, the Allies agreed that they would improve defenses in the Strait of Otranto, through which Central Powers submarines had to pass to reach the Mediterranean. The Allies established a barrage in the straits, formed of trawlers with drift nets. These unarmed trawlers were protected by Allied warships. This did not prevent the Austro-Hungarian navy from carrying out raids against the barrage, however.

The most important of these, the second largest naval engagement in the Adriatic during the war, took place on 15 May 1917. In the resulting Battle of the Otranto Straits, Captain Admiral Miklós Horthy de Nagybánya led three cruisers and two destroyers, supported by three submarines and thirteen aircraft, against the barrage. En route Horthy's ships sank an Italian destroyer and ammunition ship. They also broke through the barrage, sinking fourteen trawlers and damaging four others. The far more powerful Allied reaction force was slow to close, and all the Austrian ships reached home safely.

Meanwhile, the Italians suffered further losses. Two battleships were lost, one much earlier in the war and one in 1917 to sabotage, and another succumbed to a minefield. The Italian navy had its principal success late in the war, achieved by small craft, principally MAS boats. These sank the predreadnought battleship *Wien* in December 1918 and the dreadnought *Szent Istvan* in June 1918.

Another Allied meeting in January 1917 led to a new system that combined several previous methods to combat submarines. It too was unsuccessful, especially after the Germans introduced unrestricted submarine warfare. Finally, the British assumed control of the Mediterranean antisubmarine effort.

After Berlin adopted unrestricted submarine warfare in February 1917, Vienna pledged its submarines to the effort outside the Adriatic. This contributed to the worsening situation facing the Allies. The Royal Navy soon ordered its shipping in the western Mediterranean to use Spanish territorial waters owing to Spain's neutrality, even though this added considerable time and distance to the voyages. In the eastern Mediterranean, the British employed a dispersal system whereby ships would follow different and erratic courses. Finally, at the Corfu Conference of 28 April–1 May 1916, the Allies adopted a limited convoy system, but their most important step was to introduce a separate command staffed by Allied naval officers designed to defeat the U-boats. The Direction Général was the result; it was tasked with protecting transports and the major shipping lanes. The Allies also pledged to increase the number of destroyers deployed in the Mediterranean. In April, Japan also sent a cruiser and eight destroyers to the Mediterranean as part of the antisubmarine effort.

On 4–5 September 1917, yet another Allied naval conference, this time in London, discussed the situation in the Mediterranean. The creation of a Mediterranean convoy system proved extremely difficult because of the complex route configuration necessary and because, unlike the Atlantic, virtually the entire Mediterranean was considered a danger area. Finally the Allies, now including the United States, inaugurated an extensive convoy system that would protect Italian coal shipments, the Egypt via Bizerte lane, and the southern France to French North Africa route. U.S. forces concentrated their ships along the approaches to Gibraltar and, as their numbers grew, took increasing responsibility for areas eastward. Thanks to the success generated by these efforts, the British expanded their convoys in October to cover the entire British Isles-Port Said route. Although Allied cooperation was not always flawless, the convoy system plainly worked, and the tonnages sunk began to fall while U-boat losses mounted.

The Germans, disturbed by their increasing losses, split the U-boat command on 1 January 1918. The First Mediterranean U-boat Flotilla used Pola, and the Second Mediterranean U-boat Flotilla operated from Cattaro. The German navy also reinforced its flotillas. The U-boats were increasingly plagued by maintenance and supply problems, and sheer exhaustion took a toll on the crews and sailors. The Central Powers' submarine effort also faced the growing antisubmarine "net" of the Otranto Barrage and increasing Allied air strikes against the submarine bases.

Allied shipping losses in the Mediterranean continued to decline in the last year of the war. Nonetheless, the Central Powers' submarines sank more than 3.35 million gross tons of shipping in the Mediterranean.

The Turks surrendered on 30 October, and a combined Allied fleet entered the Dardanelles and anchored off Constantinople on 12 November. The Germans began withdrawing U-boats from Pola and Cattaro on 28 October. On 1 November the Italians employed a manned torpedo to sink the dreadnought *Viribus Unitis* at Pola. She had been transferred by Austria-Hungary to Yugoslavia the day before. On 9 November, two days before the armistice with the Germans, one of the returning German U-boats off Cape Trafalgar sank the British battleship *Britannia*, the last British warship sunk in World War I.

William P. McEvoy and Spencer C. Tucker

See also

Adriatic Theater; Antisubmarine Campaign, Allied Powers; Arnauld de la Perière, Lothar von; Austria-Hungary, Navy; Balkan Wars; Battleships; Black Sea, Naval Operations; Cruisers; Dardanelles Campaign; Destroyers; France, Navy; Gallipoli Campaign; Germany, Navy; *Goeben* and *Breslau*, Escape of; Great Britain, Navy; Horthy de Nagybánya, Miklós; Italy, Navy; Japan, Navy; MAS Boats; Monitors; Naval Armament and Gunnery; Naval Balance; Naval Warfare; Otranto Barrage; Otranto Straits, Battle of; Ottoman Empire, Navy; Savoia, Luigi Amedeo di, Duke of Abruzzi; Souchon, Wilhelm; Submarine Warfare, Allied Powers; Submarine Warfare, Central Powers; Submarines; Thaon di Revel, Paolo; Troubridge, Sir Ernest; United States, Navy.

References

Halpern, Paul G. *A Naval History of World War I.* Annapolis: Naval Institute Press, 1994.

———. *The Naval War in the Mediterranean, 1914–1918.* Annapolis: Naval Institute Press, 1987.

Laurens, Adolphe. *Le Commandement naval en Méditerranée, 1914–1918.* Paris: Payot, 1931.

Marder, Arthur J. *From the Dreadnought to Scapa Flow: The Royal Navy in the Fisher Era, 1904–1919.* 5 vols. London: Oxford University Press, 1961–1970.

Sokol, Hans H. *La Guerra marittima dell'Austria-Ungheria, 1914–1918.* 4 vols. Rome: Ufficio Storico della Marina Militare, 1932.

Ufficio Storico della Marina Militare. *La Marina italiana nella grande guerra.* 8 vols. Florence: Vallecchi, 1935–1942.

Megiddo, Battle of (19–21 September 1918)

Opening stage of the final British offensive on the Palestinian Front. It is also known as the Battle of Armagedden. After his Egyptian Expeditionary Force (EEF) had taken Jerusalem in December 1917, Lieutenant General Edmund Allenby planned to launch a final offensive to drive the remaining Turkish-German forces from Palestine. The Allied Supreme War Council at Versailles assumed that victory on the Western Front would not be possible until 1919 and so urged Allenby to proceed. Operations on this front also had the enthusiastic backing of British Prime Minister David Lloyd George.

Accordingly, in late February Allenby took Jericho in preparation for a Transjordan offensive. Prince Faisal's Arab Northern Army (ANA) raided along the eastern and southern shores of the Dead Sea, and in March the EEF launched an unsuccessful attack across the Jordan River toward Amman. A second EEF attack in April was also unsuccessful. Meanwhile, fighting on the Western Front interceded. The massive German Ludendorff offensives there began in March 1918. Desperate for manpower, London ordered Allenby to transfer two complete divisions to France plus separate battalions sufficient to constitute three more, a total of some 60,000 men. Two Indian divisions from Mesopotamia and fresh troops from India replaced them, but all of these men had to be trained, dashing hopes of an early offensive in Palestine. Allenby was limited to small operations east of the Jordan River in cooperation with Arab forces led by Faisal and Major T. E. Lawrence. By the time he was ready to resume the offensive, Allenby had at his disposal some 67,000 men: 56,000 infantry and 11,000 cavalry, along with 552 guns.

Turkish commander German General Otto Liman von Sanders was also experiencing difficulties. Tensions ran high between the Germans and Turks as Turkish Minister of War Enver Pasha siphoned off troops to send to the Caucasian Front. Supplies were also difficult to obtain, and many Turkish soldiers were deserting.

It was no secret that Allenby would soon resume offensive operations, so the British resorted to an elaborate deception. Allenby used his virtual total air superiority to screen his enemy's reconnaissance from the point of actual attack. This time he would feint inland and deliver the main blow along the left, or Mediterranean Sea, flank. In the meantime he used cavalry to patrol aggressively in the Jordan Valley and even staged two large cavalry raids toward the city of Amman, which was supporting Turkish forces at Medina. This new threat forced Liman von Sanders to deploy a third of his troops east of the Jordan River.

Allenby then transferred substantial resources northward until he had three-quarters of his resources along only one-quarter of the front. His deception measures for the Jordan Valley included 15,000 canvas-stuffed horses, a dummy headquarters, false radio traffic, sledges to kick up large clouds of dust, and even men marching about to give the false impression of large numbers.

Allenby brilliantly combined the principles of mass and surprise. Forward observers adjusted artillery fire, and armored cars operated with horse cavalry. All arms—infantry, cavalry, artillery, engineers, and the Royal Flying Corps—worked smoothly together, and irregular Arab forces, advised by Lawrence, provided useful support. Allenby planned to use fire and maneuver to secure key mountain passes and envelop the principal Turkish units.

The ensuing battle began early on the morning of 19 September with an intense fifteen-minute artillery barrage. The infantry then attacked and created a lane for the cavalry, which drove north. By day's end one division controlled the pass near the small village of Megiddo, which gave its name to the campaign. The next morning another division hit Turkish headquarters at Nazareth, nearly capturing Liman von Sanders. By 21 September the British had 25,000 prisoners. For all intents and purposes, the Turkish Seventh and Eighth Armies ceased to exist. Only part of the Turkish Fourth Army managed to escape through Dar'a. A large portion of Turks surrendered at Amman on 25 September, while the remainder surrendered with the fall of Damascus, occupied by the Desert Mounted Corps and ANA on 1 October.

Brett Mills and Spencer C. Tucker

See also
Allenby, Sir Edmund, 1st Viscount; Enver Pasha; Liman von Sanders, Otto; Lloyd George, David; Ludendorff Offensives.

References
Bruce, Anthony P. C. *The Last Crusade: The Palestine Campaign in the First World War.* London: Murray, 2002.
Bullock, David. *Allenby's War: The Palestine-Arabian Campaigns, 1916–1918.* London: Blandford, 1988.
Falls, Cyril. *Armageddon, 1918: The Final Palestinian Campaign of World War I.* Philadelphia: University of Pennsylvania Press, 2003.
———. *Military Operations: Egypt and Palestine, fFrom June 1917 to the End of the War.* London: HMSO, 1930.
Liman von Sanders, Otto. *Five Years in Turkey.* Trans. Carl Reichmann. Annapolis: Naval Institute Press, 1927.
Perrett, Bryan. *Megiddo, 1918: The Last Great Cavalry Victory.* Oxford, UK: Osprey, 1999.
Wavell, Colonel A. P. *The Palestine Campaigns.* London: Constable, 1928.

Mehmed V, Sultan (1844–1918)

Ottoman sultan during 1909–1918. Born on 2 November 1844 in Constantinople (Istanbul), Mehmed Reshad led a reclusive life until he succeeded his elder half brother Abdul Hamid after the latter's forced abdication by the Committee of Union and Progress (CUP) in 1909. Described as a gentle and educated person, Mehmed V was a weak politician and as such effectively little more than a figurehead whose actions were directed by Enver Pasha of the CUP and commanding general of the Third Army at Salonika, Mahmud Shevket Pasha.

Mehmed V presided over the disastrous Balkan Wars in 1912–1913 and war with Italy in 1912, in which the Ottoman Empire lost almost all of its European possessions and

Sultan Mehmed V of Turkey ascended the throne in 1909. (Francis J. Reynolds and C. W. Taylor, *Collier's Photographic History of the European War,* P. F. Collier & Son, New York, 1916)

Tripoli, its last remaining North African province. His lack of control over his country's fortunes worked to his advantage, and the CUP was largely blamed for the military failures.

In 1914 Mehmed V initially resisted the alliance with Germany. After Enver had engineered the Ottoman Empire's entry into the war on the side of the Central Powers, however, Mehmed as sultan-caliph issued a call for jihad (Holy War) against the Allied Powers in order to rally his Arab subjects as well as those living under British and French control. Although the Ottoman Arab subjects remained loyal for the most part, the caliph's proclamation failed to generate any significant response in the Arab regions under the control of the Entente powers. Otherwise, Mehmed V exerted no significant influence on Ottoman wartime policy. Mehmed V died on 3 July 1918 as the Ottoman Empire was quickly approaching the point of collapse. He was succeeded by his younger brother, Mehmed VI.

Dirk Steffen

See also
Arab Revolt; Balkan Wars; Enver Pasha; Italo-Turkish War; Ottoman Empire, Home Front.

References
Kent, Marian, ed. *The Great Powers and the End of the Ottoman Empire.* London: Allen and Unwin, 1984.
Macfie, A. L. *The End of the Ottoman Empire, 1918–1923.* London: Longman, 1998.

Palmer, Alan. *The Decline and Fall of the Ottoman Empire.* London: Murray, 1992.

Palmer, Alan. *The Decline and Fall of the Ottoman Empire.* London: Murray, 1992.

Mehmed VI, Sultan (1861–1926)

Ottoman sultan, 1918–1922. Born on 14 January 1861 in Constantinople (Istanbul), Mehmed Vahideddin was a capable leader, though short-tempered and narrow in outlook. He succeeded his weaker brother, Mehmed V, as sultan after the latter's death on 3 July 1918.

Mehmed VI presided over the terminal decline of the Ottoman Empire, but he was determined to exercise as much control as possible over the course of events in order to ensure the survival of the dynasty. He vigorously suppressed and persecuted nationalist groups and cooperated with the Allies following the Ottoman Empire's unconditional surrender on 30 October 1918 and the flight of the Young Turks administration on board a German ship on 1 November 1918.

On 8 December 1918 Mehmed VI accepted an Allied military administration in Istanbul. In his efforts to maintain domestic control, he dissolved parliament on 21 December 1918 and reaffirmed his commitment to suppress nationalist ideologies of all colors. Nevertheless, the nationalist movement, led by Mustafa Kemal, forced the sultan to agree to new elections in 1919. When the nationalists gained a sweeping victory in the parliamentary elections, Mehmed VI dissolved parliament once more on 11 April 1920, prompting the nationalists either to exile themselves or flee to Ankara, their provisional capital in Anatolia.

The sultan's subsequent signing of the Treaty of Sèvres and the Allied dismemberment of the Ottoman Empire were the death blows to the sultanate. The nationalists deeply resented the far-reaching concessions to the Greeks and, in addition to civil war, precipitated a war in which they defeated Greece and ejected the Greek minority from Turkey. Mustafa Kemal abolished the sultanate with the help of the Grand Assembly on 1 November 1922, and shortly thereafter Mehmed VI fled the country to Malta on a British warship.

Mehmed's attempts to reestablish himself as caliph in the Hejaz (western Saudi Arabia), following the official abolition of the caliphate in Turkey in 1924, resulted in failure. Mehmed VI died in San Remo, Italy, on 16 May 1926.

Dirk Steffen

See also

Enver Pasha; Izzet Pasha, Ahmed; Kemal, Mustafa; Ottoman Empire, Postwar Revolution; Sèvres, Treaty of.

References

Kent, Marian, ed. *The Great Powers and the End of the Ottoman Empire.* London: Allen and Unwin, 1984.
Macfie, A. L. *The End of the Ottoman Empire, 1918–1923.* London: Longman, 1998.

Mercier, Désiré-Joseph (1851–1926)

Roman Catholic cardinal. Born on 22 November 1851 at Braine-l'Alleud, Belgium, Désiré-Joseph Mercier was ordained a priest in 1874 and soon distinguished himself as both a theologian and philosopher. In 1882 Mercier was awarded the new chair of Thomistic theology at the University of Louvain. In his writings he attempted to reconcile Thomistic philosophy and modern science. In 1906 Pope Pius X named Mercier archbishop of Malines, and in 1910 he became a cardinal and the Roman Catholic primate of Belgium.

At the beginning of World War I the Germans conquered most of Belgium. With King Albert and his government continuing the struggle from France, Mercier became the spokesman for his nation and a Belgian patriot. On the death of Pope Pius X in late August 1914, Mercier traveled to Rome. When he returned to Belgium he found Louvain in ruins,

Roman Catholic Cardinal and Primate of Belgium Désiré-Joseph Mercier. (John Clark Ridpath, *Ridpath's History of the World,* Vol. 10, Jones Bros., Cincinnati, 1921)

destroyed by the Germans in an act of reprisal, and most of the country under German military control. Through publication of ecclesiastical letters, such as "Patriotism and Endurance," issued at Christmas in 1914, Mercier criticized the German occupation and reminded Belgian churchgoers of their loyalty to King Albert.

German authorities would have deported Mercier but believed this step would only heighten anti-German sentiment in Belgium and would also stir up anti-Catholic sentiment in Germany. Mercier continued to campaign against German excesses in Belgium, including the forced deportation of workers to Germany and German incitement of Flemish separatism.

After the war Mercier toured the United States and Canada, where he was received as a war hero. During the last years of his life he took up ecumenism in an effort to bridge the divisions in European Christianity. Mercier died in Brussels on 23 May 1926.

Shelley K. Cox

See also
Albert I, King of Belgium; Belgium, German Occupation of; Louvain, Destruction of.

References
Gade, John. *The Life of Cardinal Mercier.* New York: Scribner, 1935.
Long, Edward LeRoy, and Robert T. Hardy. *Theology and Church in Times of Change.* Philadelphia: Westminster Press, 1970.
Mercier, Désiré. *An Appeal to Truth: A Letter Addressed by Cardinal Mercier, Archbishop of Malines, and the Bishops of Belgium, to the Cardinals, Archbishops and Bishops of Germany, Bavaria, and Austria-Hungary.* London: Hodder and Stoughton, 1916.
———. *Cardinal Mercier's Story.* New York: Doran, 1920.
———. *The Voice of Belgium, being the War Utterances of Cardinal Mercier.* London: Burns and Oates, 1917.
Toynbee, Arnold J. *The German Terror in Belgium: An Historical Record.* New York: Doran, 1917.

Mesopotamian Theater

The 29 October 1914 entry of the Ottoman Empire into World War I on the side of the Central Powers threatened British interests in the Near East, especially the Suez Canal and the newly discovered oil fields in the area around Basra in Mesopotamia. At the end of September the British had discussed sending reinforcements to the area, and they now did so, seeking to protect these important assets and to encourage the Arabs to revolt against Ottoman rule. On 7 November a brigade of the Indian army and 600 British troops landed at Fao at the head of the Persian Gulf. The initial British goal was to capture Basra.

The campaign began well. British and Indian forces captured Basra on 22 November and Qurna, at the confluence of the Tigris and Euphrates, on 9 December. On 12 April 1915 the Turkish army attacked both Basra and Qurna in an effort to dislodge the British and Indians. At Shaiba, southwest of Basra, 6,000 British and Indian defenders routed 10,000 Turks. The British sustained some 1,357 casualties, the Turks 2,435. The British were unable to follow up the victory, however, as they had no transport. The ease of the victory gave the British forces a false sense of Turkish military inferiority.

Through 1915 Whitehall left much of the decision making for Mesopotamia to the government in India, which did not necessarily have the same interests as those in London. On 9 April General Sir John Nixon, commander of the Indian Northern Army, assumed command in Mesopotamia. Nixon's orders were to secure Basra and Lower Mesopotamia; protect the oil fields, the refinery at Abadan, and the pipeline; and prepare for an offensive against Baghdad.

To carry out these missions and expand the British defensive perimeter, Nixon called for drives up the Tigris and Euphrates rivers. In May 1915 Major General Charles Townshend's 6th Indian Division proceeded up the Tigris, routing the Turkish defenders and pursuing them in a series of quick, successful amphibious operations. The conclusion of the pursuit came at Amara where an amphibious reconnaissance force of about 100 soldiers and sailors captured the town, its stores, and its garrison. The Turkish troops there surrendered on the assumption that the main Anglo-Indian force was close on the heels of the reconnaissance force, when in reality it was nearly 100 miles away. Subsequently, Major-General George Gorringe led the 12th Indian Division up the Euphrates and captured Nasiriyah, in another amphibious operation, on 25 July. The Basra region and Lower Mesopotamia were now secure, and the oil fields were held safe from Turkish attack.

These easy campaigns on the Tigris bred a sense of overconfidence among the British and convinced Nixon that he could capture Baghdad and bring a speedy close to the campaign. Despite Townshend's objections that his men were not prepared for such an effort in the heat of the summer and that he lacked sufficient logistical support, Nixon ordered the 6th Division to continue its advance up the Tigris. River towns fell in quick succession to Townshend's force as it drew closer to Baghdad. On 28 September 1915, following two days of fighting, the British occupied Kut-al-Amara, 90 miles from Baghdad. British supply lines now stretched 380 miles from Kut to the sea, and their transportation capacity was far from adequate.

Despite mixed opinion on the advisability of an advance on Baghdad, Townshend continued his push upriver on 11 November. Eleven days later he was within 25 miles of Baghdad. At Ctesiphon during 22–26 November 1915, Townshend attacked an entrenched Turkish force of 18,000 men and fifty-two guns commanded by German General Colmar von der Goltz. The British lost 4,600 men, almost one-third of the force of three infantry brigades, without displacing the Turks.

British infantry passing over the Jebel Hamrin during the fighting in Mesopotamia. (National Archives)

The Turks at Ctesiphon suffered 9,500 casualties, twice as many as Townshend's force, but rather than breaking, they counterattacked.

Lacking sufficient reserves and supplies, Townshend had little option but to retreat to Kut, sending his sick and wounded on a torturous 400-mile trek (thirteen days by boat) to the Persian Gulf. Townshend's exhausted troops needed a rest, and he halted at Kut to wait for reinforcements. From 7 December the Turks placed Kut under siege. Townshend had 10,000 effectives; there were also 2,000 casualties and 3,500 Indian noncombatants.

In January 1916 Lieutenant-General Sir Fenton Aylmer led a British effort to raise the siege. The main constraint in Aylmer's attempt, as in all such British efforts in the campaign, was the supply situation. In January 1916 the rivers were the only viable means of transport open to the British. Although materials to build a narrow-gauge railway from Basra to the front lines at Ali Gharbi were available in India, no thought had been given to sending these to Mesopotamia, and by the time the Turks surrounded Townshend in Kut it was too late. The British forces in Mesopotamia also faced a chronic shortage of boats for river transit. Aylmer faced the task of lifting a siege in an area that was a three-week round-trip boat journey from Basra. That port also left much to be desired. Its port facilities were so inadequate that it could take up to six weeks for oceangoing transports to unload their cargoes. Aylmer's relief force was therefore sent forward as troops arrived, and the maximum size of his force was set by the army's supply limitations, rather than the number of troops estimated to be necessary to lift the siege.

On 3 January 1916 Aylmer's force of 19,000 soldiers and forty-six guns advanced up both banks of the Tigris toward Kut. On 7 and 8 January they fought and failed to dislodge a Turkish force at Sheikh Sa'ad about 19 miles from Kut. The Turks, who had their own supply problems, soon withdrew, however. On 9 January Aylmer's force occupied Sheikh Sa'ad, but the fighting had claimed 4,000 of his men. Responding to pressure from Nixon, Aylmer continued to press the attack. On 13 January he engaged the Turks in the Battle of the Wadi 12.5 miles from Kut, suffering another 1,600 casualties in the process.

Under pressure from Nixon and spurred on by reports from Townshend of dwindling supplies within Kut, Aylmer ordered his remaining forces to take the Hanna Defile in preparation for a final assault on Kut. Aylmer now had about 12,000 men, while the Turks had about 30,000 men between Aylmer and Kut. The attack on the Hanna Defile began with a

British artillery barrage at midday on 20 January that continued until the next morning. It did little more than warn Turkish Commander Khalil Pasha where the attack was coming.

On 21 January, 4,000 British soldiers set out across 600 yards of flooded terrain separating the two forces, only to be cut down by Turkish machine-gun fire. Having sustained 2,700 casualties, Aylmer believed his force was now inadequate to lift the siege. Nevertheless, Nixon ordered him to continue. With additional British reinforcements, Aylmer tried again, and on 8 March he reached the Dujaila Redoubt, 2 miles from Kut. The Turkish Sixth Army, reinforced by 36,000 men transferred from Gallipoli after the British evacuation there at the end of December, repulsed the British, leading Nixon to replace Aylmer with General Gorringe.

Gorringe made one last attempt to relieve Kut. His command was bolstered to 30,000 men by the arrival of Major-General Sir Stanley Maude's 13th Division. Von der Goltz drew on Turkish reserves in Baghdad to match that number. Maude's division attacked the Hanna Defile at dawn on 5 April only to find the Turkish frontline trenches unoccupied. Maude regrouped, attacked, and captured Fallahiyeh while a diversionary attack on the other bank of the Tigris enjoyed similar success. Although these successes had cost 2,000 British casualties, Gorringe prepared to attack Sannaiyat the following day. The Turks fought off attacks on Sannaiyat on 6, 7, and 9 April, inflicting further casualties on the British. On 17 April, Gorringe switched targets to the other side of the river and took Bait Asia with light casualties. Turkish counterattacks failed to dislodge the British and cost the Turks about 4,000 casualties. The loss of 1,600 men of the British-Indian force, however, made it impossible for Gorringe to continue in that sector on the bank of the river. On 22 April, Gorringe chose to resume his attack on Sannaiyat and failed, at a cost of 1,300 more casualties. This was the last effort to relieve Kut. In all, the British had suffered 23,000 casualties trying to rescue the 10,000 survivors at Kut.

Townshend surrendered unconditionally to Khalil Pasha on 29 April 1916. Goltz, who had masterminded the Turkish siege, did not live to see the British surrender. He died of typhus on 19 April, although rumors persisted that the Turks had poisoned him. The Turkish victors forced some 8,000 British and Indian prisoners to march to camps in Anatolia without sufficient water or provisions. Through mistreatment and neglect, nearly 5,000 died before the end of the war.

In August 1916, General Sir Stanley Maude replaced Nixon as commander of British forces in Mesopotamia, having replaced Gorringe as commander of British forces on the Tigris the previous month. Maude reorganized the forces at his disposal, revamped the system of medical care, and improved the supply train. He then resumed the offensive up the Tigris on 13 December with a force of 59,000 British and 107,000 Indian soldiers. The force recaptured Kut on 25 February 1917.

After a brief rest and consolidation, Maude resumed his march on Baghdad on 5 March. Khalil did not take effective advantage of the pause. He abandoned construction of defenses around Ctesiphon, giving up on the idea of a forward defense, and ordered his 33,000 soldiers to dig in on both sides of the Tigris and along the Diyala River about 20 miles south of Baghdad. By 10 March Maude had forced a crossing of the Diyala. Khalil, ignoring German arguments for a counterattack, withdrew to the northwest to protect the Berlin to Baghdad railroad and then decided to evacuate Baghdad entirely. On 11 March Maude's forces entered Baghdad without a fight. This was a major propaganda coup at a time when the Allies needed any victory, although the capture of the city carried little strategic significance.

To consolidate his newly won position, Maude dispatched columns up the Tigris, Euphrates, and Diyala rivers in an effort to destroy the Turkish army in the field. This renewed effort, which sought ultimately to capture the terminus of the Baghdad-Samarrah railway, began just two days after Maude's forces took Baghdad, pitting 45,000 British troops against 25,000 Turks. Although the Turks carried out a skillful fighting withdrawal, notable British successes, including capture of the flood control works at Falluja on 19 March, prevented the Turks from flooding the plains between the Tigris and Euphrates. The British then took Samarrah on 23 April. In the campaign, Maude's forces had sustained 58,000 casualties (40,000 from disease), and this forced a cessation of offensive action until the autumn.

On 28 September 1917 the British offensive resumed. Its most notable success was the capture of Tikrit on 6 November. Maude died of cholera on 18 November. His replacement, Lieutenant-General Sir William Marshall, followed Maude's policy of advancing up the rivers to keep the pressure on the Turks. Maude's death, however, gave General Sir William Robertson, chief of the Imperial General Staff, the opportunity to limit the resources earmarked for the Mesopotamian theater.

British efforts resumed in the spring of 1918 against dwindling Turkish resistance. The capture of 5,000 Turks at Khan Baghdad on the Euphrates on 26 March 1918 showed that the Turkish army had lost its will to fight. In October a British force drove up the Tigris and captured the oil fields around Mosul shortly before the leaders of the Ottoman Empire asked for an armistice. The last battle in the Mesopotamian theater took place near the ancient Assyrian capital at Asshur. The Turks signed an armistice at Mudros on 30 October 1918. It went into effect the next day, ending Turkish participation in the war.

Following the war, Mesopotamia received its modern name of Iraq and became a British mandate. Fighting there during the war had cost the British and Indians 92,000 casualties, including 27,000 dead (13,000 of disease). In the same period the Ottoman army had sustained an estimated 325,000 casualties in what historian Michael Lyons has called "perhaps the most unnecessary campaign of the entire war."

John Lavalle

See also

Amara, Battle of; Arab Revolt; Baghdad, Fall of; Ctesiphon, Battle of; Gallipoli Campaign; Goltz, Colmar von der, Baron; Hanna, Battle of; Kut, First Battle of; Kut, Second Battle of; Kut, Siege of; Maude, Sir Frederick Stanley; Nasiriyah, Battle of; Nixon, Sir John Eccles; Qurna, Battle of; Robertson, Sir William Robert; Samarrah Offensive; Sheikh Sa'ad, Battle of; Sykes-Picot Agreement; Tikrit, Battle of.

References

Barker, A. J. *The Bastard War: The Mesopotamian Campaign of 1914–1918.* New York: Dial, 1967.

Erickson, Edward J. *Ordered to Die: A History of the Ottoman Army in the First World War.* Westport, CT: Greenwood, 2000.

Moberly, F. J. *The Campaign in Mesopotamia, 1914–1918.* 3 vols. Nashville, TN: Battery Press, 1997–1998.

Messines Ridge, Battle of (7–14 June 1917)

Preliminary attack to the Third Battle of Ypres. In 1917 Britain had built up its military resources in France to the point that Field Marshal Sir Douglas Haig was finally free to launch the offensive in Flanders that he had long postponed in deference to French wishes.

Before the general offensive could occur, several preliminary attacks were necessary. One of these was to take Messines Ridge, from which the Germans could observe preparations for the larger offensive. Taking the ridge fell to General Sir Herbert Plumer's Second Army. Plumer was an apostle of the "bite and hold" technique that combined extensive artillery preparation and support with seizing limited objectives and crushing counterattacks.

At Messines, Plumer had a unique advantage. The British had begun mining in the area two years earlier, and he could initiate his assault with extensive explosions. The soil in the area had made mining feasible, and the bulk of this was accomplished before countermining techniques became effective. Although there was a war underground, no other comparable operation occurred during the war. In all, the British would explode twenty-one mines with 1 million pounds of high explosive.

Plumer initially planned to shell the defenders for four days and, with the help of the mines, take the German first line of defense on the first day of the attack. On the second he would seize the rest of the high ground, including the village of Wytschaete; then, having advanced about 1,500 yards, he would conclude the operation. Haig, always an optimist, urged that the attack push forward 20–30 miles and offered several hundred extra artillery pieces to support his version. Plumer agreed to take both the villages of Messines and Wytschaete on the first day, but he did not wish to consider going farther until he knew what additional forces would be available to him.

After a pause because of the Canadian attack at Arras, Plumer's plan was finalized. It called for taking the two fortified villages and then pushing forward to the Oostaverne Line, an intermediate defensive position on the reverse slope of the ridge. This meant an advance of 3,000 yards through well-wired German defensive positions supported by pillboxes. Although it doubled his original plan, Plumer seems to have been satisfied.

British employment of artillery had become much more sophisticated during the war, and meticulous calculations about destruction of defensive positions, wire cutting, and counterbattery fire (previously often an afterthought) were made. More than 2,000 guns were required, and 144,000 tons of ammunition were brought forward. Observation from Kemmel Hill and Hill 63 was good, and because the German position was a salient their first defensive lines were enfiladed. The final element was good weather so that observation—from ground and air—would be unimpeded. For once, nature cooperated.

British wire-cutting fire began on 21 May, and the barrage grew from there. By the end of the month German artillery counterfire was clearly slackening. At 3:10 A.M. on 7 June, the mines were exploded with a blast that was felt across the English Channel, even startling Prime Minister David Lloyd George in his London office. The assault then went forward in four stages. First the German front line was taken. The remaining German defenders were stunned and, except for Australian forces on the southern flank who unluckily advanced into a gas barrage, the attackers faced little resistance.

The second step was taking the crest of the ridge, where there was some patchy resistance. New Zealanders attacking the village of Messines had some trouble, but Wytschaete fell to the 16th Division with hardly a shot fired. By 9:00 A.M. the British held the crest of the ridge.

The third step was consolidation to meet German counterattacks. These were minimal. Finally, the plan called for moving forward to the Oostaverne Line, which proved much more difficult. German artillery, supposedly captured, had actually fallen back and shelled the attackers on the ridge. British artillery observers thought such shelling represented a counterattack and shortened their range, resulting in many casualties from friendly fire. The Oosterverne Line was taken only when the Germans discovered that it was not a good defensive position and fell back a week later.

Plumer was too slow to follow up the victory, and despite his success Haig replaced him, causing additional delays that the Germans put to good use. The good weather was also lost. In some ways, then, the victory at Messines was squandered, and the subsequent attacks of Third Ypres bogged down in the mud and suffered enormous casualties. How much more might have been accomplished by Plumer and his methods cannot be known.

Fred R. van Hartesveldt

See also
Arras, Second Battle of; Haig, Douglas, 1st Earl; Plumer, Sir Herbert; Tunneling and Mining Operations; Ypres, Third Battle of.

References
Oldham, Peter. *Messines Ridge.* Barnsley, UK: Leo Cooper, 1998.
Passingham, Ian. *Pillars of Fire: The Battle of Messines Ridge, June 1917.* Stroud, Gloucestershire, UK: Sutton, 1998.
Powell, Geoffrey. *Plumer, the Soldier's General: A Biography of Field-Marshal Viscount Plumer of Messines.* London: Leo Cooper, 1990.
Prior, Robin, and Trevor Wilson. *Passchendaele: The Untold Story.* New Haven, CT: Yale University Press, 1996.

Metaxas, Ioannis (1871–1941)

Greek army general. Born on 12 April 1871 at Ithaca, Greece, Ioannis Metaxas was educated at the Athens Military Academy. He received a commission in the engineers and fought in the Greco-Turkish War of 1897. He then studied at the War Academy in Berlin from 1899 to 1903. He was a General Staff officer during the 1912–1913 Balkan Wars and carried out planning for the capture of the Dardanelles by the Greek army.

At the beginning of World War I, Metaxas was deputy chief of staff of the Greek army. At that time Premier Eleuthérios Venizélos and King Constantine were in sharp disagreement over Greek foreign policy. Metaxas favored a Greek alignment with the Central Powers, believing that they would win the war and dominate Europe.

In late 1914 Metaxas opposed the British appeal that Greece join the war against Turkey and land troops on the Gallipoli Peninsula in return for the island of Cyprus. Despite Allied pressure, Metaxas worked to maintain Greek neutrality. Venizélos favored accepting the Allied proposal, but King Constantine was against it in large measure because of Metaxas. This stance helped drive Venizélos from office.

After the Central Powers defeated and occupied Serbia, Metaxas urged Constantine to form a closer relationship with Berlin, and he himself was the king's liaison with Berlin. He and other Greek officers saw a German advance in Salonika as a means of freeing Greece from an Anglo-French invasion. In January 1916 Metaxas urged Constantine to move to northern Greece to rally support and troops, but the king rejected this advice. Metaxas, however, cooperated with the Central Powers, providing intelligence, purging pro-Allied officers from the army, and in May 1916 allowing the Bulgarians to seize the strategic border post of Fort Rupel.

Under heavy Allied pressure, Constantine began to tilt toward the Entente in 1916. Greek troops engaged French and British marines in the December 1916 "Battle of Athens," which marked Constantine's final days. Again Metaxas urged Constantine to flee to the north and lead the Greek army alongside the Germans, while he would organize guerrilla forces in Macedonia. The king refused, and in June 1917 Constantine was deposed and exiled. Metaxas and other members of the General Staff were exiled to Corsica.

After the war Metaxas remained active as a monarchist, antirepublican politician. Following a military coup in 1936, he became dictator of Greece. Although he was a fascist, he did not ally Greece with Italy and instead led the Greek army to repel an Italian invasion in 1940. Metaxas died in Athens on 29 January 1941, before his nation was overrun by the Germans.

Christopher J. Richman

See also
Constantine I, King of Greece; Greece, Role in War; Venizélos, Eleuthérios Kyriakos.

References
Adams, John Clinton. *Flight in Winter.* Princeton, NJ: Princeton University Press, 1942.
Leon, George. *Greece and the Great Powers, 1914–1917.* Thessaloniki: Institute for Balkan Studies, 1974.
Theodoulou, Christos A. *Greece and the Entente, August 1, 1914–September 25, 1916.* Thessaloniki: Institute for Balkan Studies, 1971.
Woodhouse, C. M. *A Short History of Modern Greece.* New York: Praeger, 1968.

Methuen, Paul, 3rd Baron (1845–1932)

British field marshal. Born on 1 September 1845 at Corsham, England, Paul Sanford Methuen was educated at Eton College. He purchased a commission in the Scots Guards in 1864 and fought in the 1873–1874 Second Ashanti War, the 1882 Egyptian campaign, and the 1884–1885 Expedition to Bechuanaland.

Following a stint as commander of the Home District during 1892–1897, Methuen was promoted to lieutenant-general and given a divisional command in the 1899–1902 Boer War. In 1904 he was promoted to full general and given command of IV Corps and, later, the Eastern Command. After serving as Britain's last commanding general in South Africa (1908–1910), Methuen retired as a field marshal in 1911.

In February 1915 Methuen came out of retirement and was appointed governor-general and commander-in-chief of Malta. The previous governor-general, Sir Leslie Rundle, had proposed handing Malta over to the Royal Navy when World War I began. Methuen, however, saw the benefits of maintaining and utilizing its garrison and advocated army control. Throughout the war, he sent detachments of the garrison to Cyprus and Egypt. In addition, he recruited several hundred Maltese for active service in British and local regiments.

Malta's significance in the war, however, lay in its strategic position. In March 1915, with the launching of the Dardanelles campaign, Malta became a crucial way-station, and British and French ships were repaired and refitted in its dockyards. Methuen was quick to recognize the possibility of transforming the island into the "nurse of the Mediterranean." In May 1915, when the first patient arrived, there were only a few hundred hospital beds. By war's end, Malta's general hospital could care for up to 25,000 patients at a time. For his service during the war, Methuen was honored by both the British and French governments. In 1919 he returned to England and retirement. Methuen died at Corsham on 20 October 1932.

Stephen M. Miller

See also

Gallipoli Campaign; Medicine in the War; Mediterranean Theater, Naval Operations.

References

Dobie, E. *Malta's Road to Independence.* Norman: University of Oklahoma Press, 1967.

Miller, Stephen. *Lord Methuen and the British Army.* London: Cass, 1999.

British soldiers resting after capturing German second-line trenches in a hotly contested section of the Argonne. (Edgar Allen Forbes, ed., *Leslie's Photographic Review of the Great War,* Leslie-Judge Co., New York, 1919)

Meuse-Argonne Offensive (September–November 1918)

The Allied campaign designed by Marshal Ferdinand Foch to cut the German lines of communication and support between their armies on the Western Front and bases to Metz and the East. Foch had agreed to allow American Expeditionary Forces (AEF) commander General John Pershing and his U.S. First Army, newly formed in August 1918 after the campaign to reduce the Marne salient, to conduct the attack on the Saint-Mihiel salient as a prelude to this operation. Foch gave Pershing a time limit and told him that his army would have to be available for the attack in the Meuse Valley toward Sedan. Pershing wished to reduce the Saint-Mihiel salient, then continue to attack northeast directly toward Metz, but Foch would not permit that divergence of forces from the main effort. The attack at Saint-Mihiel went very quickly and was concluded in only four days, partly due to the withdrawal of German forces in the salient just as the attack began on 12 September.

In masterful staff work, Colonel George Marshall, a General Headquarters AEF operations officer, planned the movement of both the combat forces and the extensive logistical support forces from the Saint-Mihiel Front to the Meuse Argonne Front. The reorientation of 820,000 U.S. and French troops, with all their supporting artillery, engineers, and trains, was accomplished by the night of 25–26 September.

On 3 September Foch had directed the British to continue operations to the east in the direction of Saint-Quentin and Cambrai, the Belgians to clear the Channel coast, and the French to force the Germans back from the Aisne River line and to cooperate in the Champagne area with the U.S. troops on their right. The U.S. and some French units were to drive north between the Meuse River and the Argonne Forest. If successful, the Germans would be deprived of their vital rail communications to the east through Metz.

In order to protect those communications, which were within 35 miles of the front in the Meuse River valley, the Germans had built defensive belts in depth. It was those tough, reinforced positions that the U.S. First Army attacked on 26 September. Moreover, the Germans had excellent observation of the battle area from the heights at Montfaucon and other hills. The terrain in front of the U.S. troops was quite rugged with many east-west ridges and the Argonne Forest on the left flank of the zone. All along the Western Front, from the English Channel to Verdun, the converging Allied armies shortened their front as the Germans fell back. Foch was most concerned to set boundaries between the national armies and insisted on adequate lateral liaison to prevent any German exploitation of gaps in the line.

In the U.S. First Army, Major-General Hunter Liggett's I Corps and Major General George H. Cameron's V Corps spearheaded the advance. Liggett had his 77th, 28th, and 35th Divisions in line (west to east) and the 92nd and the French 5th Cavalry Divisions in corps reserve for an advance northward through the German defenses. The New Yorkers of the 77th National Army Division had fought with the French Sixth Army in the Champagne region and needed more than

4,000 replacements as they joined Liggett's I Corps and readied to plunge into the Argonne.

The attack began in thick fog on the morning of 26 September. Major General Robert Alexander deployed the 77th Division in standard attack formation with all four infantry regiments on line. By 2 October, nearly 5 miles deep in the forest, six companies from two battalions of the 308th Infantry Regiment found themselves isolated and surrounded by the Germans. This was the so-called Lost Battalion, consisting of 670 men commanded by Major Charles Whittlesey. By the time the isolated force was rescued on 7 October, it was down to fewer than 200 men.

Liggett received most of the 82nd Division from First Army reserve during the night of 6–7 October and committed them against the eastern flank of the Germans in the Argonne. During this attack, Corporal Alvin C. York of the 328th Infantry Regiment performed the acts for which he later received the Medal of Honor. Hunter Liggett remembered Foch's directive to use his "initiative and energy" in unhinging the German defenses.

The U.S. V Corps drew the tough assignment of taking the high ground in the center of the First Army zone. The high ground of Montfaucon at the eastern edge of the V Corps boundary dominated the zone. Cameron placed three divisions—the 91st, 37th and 79th—in line west to east with the 32nd Division in corps reserve. The 79th was to reduce the Montfaucon position. Cameron planned to penetrate the German defenses and drive on the heights at Romagne, with Liggett's I Corps on his left and Major General Robert Bullard's III Corps on his right providing artillery support.

The U.S. troops enjoyed success all along the line except at Montfaucon, which held out until the 27th and gave the Germans time to reinforce their subsequent defensive positions. Phase One of the attack concluded at the German line known as the Hindenburg (Siegfried) Line on 3 October.

On 4 October replacements of men and equipment were ordered up. On 12 October Pershing made changes to the command, elevating General Liggett to command the First Army and moving General Bullard to command the new Second Army. Major General Edwin P. Summerall replaced Cameron at V Corps, while Major General Joseph Dickman took over I Corps and Major General John Hines replaced Bullard at III Corps. Pershing relinquished field command but retained overall command of the new group of U.S. armies, which continued to grow even in the midst of combat operations.

During the second phase of the attack that began on 4 October through the German defensive belts toward Mézières and Sedan on the Meuse River, V Corps mishandled the 1st Division's advance across the front of the divisions of I Corps, now commanded by General Dickman, but it was Pershing himself who launched that convergence on Sedan, hoping to

Ditched British tank by the Fampoux Road during the 1917 Battle of Arras. (Edgar Allen Forbes, ed., *Leslie's Photographic Review of the Great War*, Leslie-Judge Co., New York, 1919)

liberate it from German occupation before the French could do so. George Marshall called it a "typical American 'grandstand finish,'" words he considered a compliment, not a criticism. The offensive halted with the final push and the armistice on 11 November 1918.

A total of twenty-three American divisions participated in the forty-seven-day campaign, the largest ever to that date involving U.S. troops. The 1.2 million troops engaged suffered perhaps 120,000 casualties (about 10 percent of force). German casualties totaled some 100,000 men and 847 guns captured. Although many Americans did not fully comprehend the details of the recently concluded campaign, all recognized that their country's forces had won a famous victory.

John F. Votaw

See also

Foch, Ferdinand; Liggett, Hunter; Lost Battalion; Pershing, John Joseph; Saint-Mihiel Offensive; Siegfried Line; York, Alvin Cullum.

References

Braim, Paul F. *The Test Of Battle: The American Expeditionary Forces in the Meuse-Argonne Campaign.* Shippensburg, PA: White Mane, 1998.

Coffman, Edward M. *The War to End All Wars: The American Military Experience in World War I.* Lexington: University Press of Kentucky, 1998.

Foch, Ferdinand. *The Memoirs of Marshal Foch.* Trans. T. Bentley Mott. New York: Doubleday, Doran, 1931.

Marshall, George C. *Memoirs of My Services in the World War, 1917–1918.* Boston: Houghton Mifflin, 1976.

McHenry, Herbert L. *As a Private Saw It: My Memories of the First Division, World War I.* Indiana, PA: A. G. Halldin, 1988.

U.S. 66th Congress, 2nd Sess., House of Representatives, Document No. 626. Final Report of Gen. John J. Pershing, Commander-in-Chief American Expeditionary Forces. Washington, DC: Government Printing Office, 1920.

Mexico

When World War I began, Mexico was in the midst of domestic political and military upheaval. The overthrow of the regime of General Victoriano Huerta in July 1914 led to a civil war from 1914 to 1916 in which different revolutionary factions vied for control. Mexico was one of the world's leading oil producers and exporters, so Mexican affairs were of great interest to the warring powers in Europe.

The United States was greatly concerned over what it viewed as a German threat in Mexico and particularly along the U.S.-Mexican border. U.S. concern was justified, since Germany sought to keep Mexico in turmoil, hopefully provoking a large-scale U.S. intervention that would limit possible U.S. involvement in the European war. Germany made a financial commitment of almost $12 million in a failed 1915 effort to restore ousted dictator General Huerta. The Germans then turned their attention to Francisco "Pancho" Villa, a leading revolutionary general who had lost out in the struggle for power in 1914–1915. The Germans supplied Villa with arms and equipment in late 1915 and early 1916. On 9 March 1916, Villa's forces attacked Columbus, New Mexico, killing seventeen Americans. There was no evidence linking the Germans to the decision to attack Columbus, but the attack certainly produced the major U.S. military intervention hoped for by the Germans. By June 1916 most of the U.S. Army's combat forces were tied down with the Pershing Punitive Expedition into Mexico. In addition, President Woodrow Wilson had federalized the National Guards of all the United States (more than 100,000 troops) and sent them to the border. While war between the United States and Mexico was avoided, the last U.S. troops did not leave Mexico until February 1917.

Having failed to use Huerta and Villa to overthrow the regime of Venustiano Carranza, the Germans decided to work with Carranza to achieve their international designs. The highly nationalistic Carranza was feuding regularly with the U.S. government over border security issues and oil policy. In this context of closer relations, the incident of the Zimmermann Telegram took place. In that telegram, German Foreign Secretary Arthur Zimmermann instructed the German ambassador to Mexico to offer a military alliance to Mexico in the event that the United States entered the war against Germany. After the telegram became public knowledge on 1 March 1917, Carranza publicly denied that Germany had ever offered Mexico an alliance, but he privately indicated to the German ambassador that an alliance might be feasible should war break out between the United States and Mexico.

U.S.-Mexican relations continued problematic after U.S. entry into the war. Several Latin American nations showed their solidarity with the United States by breaking relations with Germany or even declaring war. The Carranza government, however, maintained strict neutrality throughout the war, despite U.S. pressure. The German secret service moved its North American headquarters to Mexico City after U.S. entry and even prepared a submarine base on Mexico's Gulf coast, although it was never used. The Wilson administration remained convinced throughout the war that Carranza's supposed neutrality was only a disguise for a pro-German policy. Despite wartime personnel demands, the Wilson administration still kept approximately 30,000 troops on the U.S.-Mexican border.

Don M. Coerver

See also
Latin America and the War; Pershing, John Joseph; Wilson, Thomas Woodrow; Zimmermann, Arthur; Zimmermann Telegram.
References
Coerver, Don M., and Linda B. Hall. *Texas and the Mexican Revolution: A Study in State and National Border Policy, 1910–1920.* San Antonio: Trinity University Press, 1984.
Hall, Linda B., and Don M. Coerver. *Revolution on the Border: The United States and Mexico, 1910–1920.* Albuquerque: University of New Mexico Press, 1988.
Katz, Friedrich. *The Secret War in Mexico: Europe, the United States and the Mexican Revolution.* Chicago: University of Chicago Press, 1981.

Michaelis, Georg (1857–1936)

German civil servant and imperial chancellor. Born on 8 September 1857 at Haynau (Silesia), Georg Michaelis studied law at the universities of Breslau and Leipzig and qualified to practice law in 1879. He was appointed a junior barrister in 1884 and received a doctoral degree in law at the University of Goettingen in 1885. In the fall of 1885, he became lecturer in law and national economy at the German Law School in Tokyo, Japan.

Returning home in 1889, Michaelis began a career as a law-court official but soon joined the Prussian government service. From 1892 he held different positions in the administration of the provinces of the Rhine, Westphalia, and Silesia. In 1905 he was appointed commissioner for the regulation of the Oder River. Known for his energetic character and managerial skills, in 1909 Michaelis was promoted to undersecretary of state in the Prussian Ministry of Finance.

After the war began, Michaelis became head of the supervisory committee of the War Grain Corporation

(Kriegsgetreideges ellschaft) in November 1914. He was additionally appointed imperial commissioner for grain and flour under the federal Ministry of the Interior in March 1915. When the Imperial Grain Corporation (Reichsgetreidestelle) was established in July 1915, Michaelis became chairman of its board. In 1916 he proposed establishment of an independent War Food Office (Kriegsernährungsamt) to organize the entire German food supply on the home front. Due to bureaucratic rivalries, he did not head the new office. In February 1917, he became Prussian state commissioner for food distribution and soon demonstrated his energetic style of leadership.

Following the resignation of Theobald von Bethmann Hollweg on 13 July 1917, Michaelis was appointed imperial chancellor and Prussian minister-president. Opposed to democratic reforms and the Reichstag Peace Resolution of 1917, which he considered meddling by the Reichstag in the chancellor's area of foreign affairs, Michaelis soon encountered difficulties with the major party leaders in the Reichstag, who also criticized his autocratic behavior. The German response to the Papal peace note of August 1917, drafted by Foreign Minister Richard von Kuhlmann, was extremely vague because Michaelis and Kuhlmann sought to retain Belgium as a pawn for future negotiations with the Entente. When these secret maneuvers were revealed, it led to an accusation by Matthias Erzberger that the government had let slip a real chance for peace. Michaelis's final downfall came with naval unrest in August 1917, which he and Admiral Eduard von Capelle handled poorly. During the 100 days of his chancellorship, Michaelis did carry out an important bureaucratic reform that brought the establishment of a federal Ministry of Economic Affairs on 21 October 1917. His plan for social welfare reform to win the support of the Social Democrats could not be published before he left office. Michaelis resigned on 1 November 1917.

Appointed lord lieutenant of the Province of Pomerania in March 1918, Michaelis left the civil service in April 1919. He then devoted his time to welfare work on behalf of students. Michaelis died at Bad Saarow/Mark near Berlin on 24 July 1936.

Bert Becker

See also
Bethmann Hollweg, Theobald von; Capelle, Eduard von; Erzberger, Matthias; Germany, Home Front; Hertling, Georg Friedrich von, Count; Kuhlmann, Richard von; Reichstag Peace Resolution.

References
Becker, Bert. *Georg Michaelis: Ein preussischer Jurist im Japan der Meiji-Zeit: Briefe, Tagebuchnotizen, Dokumente 1885–1889.* Munich: Iudicium, 2001.
Deuerlein, Ernst. *Deutsche Kanzler von Bismarck bis Hitler.* Munich: Paul List, 1968.
Michaelis, Georg. *Für Staat und Volk: Eine Lebensgeschichte.* Berlin: Furche-Verlag, 1922.
Morsey, Rudolf. "Michaelis, Georg." In *Neue Deutsche Biographie,* 17:432–434. Berlin: Duncker and Humblot, 1994.
Yaney, George. *The World of the Manager: Food Administration in Berlin during World War I.* New York: Lang, 1994.

Michel, Victor (1850–1937)

French army general. Born on 30 January 1850 in Auteuil (outside Paris), Victor Michel became a member of the French Supreme War Council (Conseil Supérieur de la Guerre) in 1907. Michel's appointment as vice-president of that body in January 1911 meant that he would become ex officio the commander-in-chief of the French army in case of war. The appointment came at a time when French strategic thinking was in a state of transition. The German threat seemed more patent after the Moroccan crises of 1905 and 1911, and Michel was concerned that the French projected response was inadequate.

Accordingly, in February 1911 Michel submitted to the minister of war his proposed revisions to the French strategic plan (number XVI). Michel's thinking on how to counter the German threat foreshadowed the Schlieffen Plan. He believed that the Germans would make a deep incursion into Belgium in order to strike at France through the Franco-Belgian border, rather than invading from Lorraine. Such an invasion plan would allow room for the mass armies that Michel believed the German high command intended to deploy, utilizing reservists on the front line to boost the active army.

In order to counter this, Michel proposed first that the French also make use of their reservists to increase numbers, although he recognized that reserve formations would require stiffening with a strong cadre. He also proposed to reduce the troops defending the eastern border in favor of concentrating eleven army corps along the Belgian border. These troops would be in position both to counter any German incursion from Belgium and to counterattack if the opportunity arose, this operation being justified by the German violation of Belgian neutrality.

These proposals received much praise after the war for their prescience. But in one other area, Michel was proved wrong. He opposed the high command's calls for more heavy artillery. As it turned out, the French army suffered greatly from lack of heavy artillery at the start of World War I.

Although Michel's assumptions about German intentions proved correct, his proposals were rejected. Neither the political right nor the left accepted the use of reservists, and the army high command rejected the idea of a defensive counterattack. It was the thinking of Michel's successor General Joseph Joffre, who advocated concentration in Lorraine and an immediate offensive should war come, that became War Plan XVII.

The fierce opposition to Michel's ideas, both within the high command and in the press, led him to resign on 21 July

1911. Michel became military governor of Paris, but he was relieved of his post at the end of August 1914, ostensibly because the defenses of Paris had not been completed when war broke out, but probably also because he had been proven correct and his successor proven wrong. Michel died in Meulan (Yvelines) on 7 November 1937.

Elizabeth Greenhalgh

See also
France, War Plan XVII; Joffre, Joseph; Schlieffen Plan.
References
Herrmann, David G. *The Arming of Europe and the Making of the First World War.* Princeton, NJ: Princeton University Press, 1996.
Porch, Douglas. *The March to the Marne: The French Army, 1871–1914.* Cambridge and New York: Cambridge University Press, 1981.
Tanenbaum, Jan Karl. "French Estimates of Germany's Operational War Plans." In *Knowing Your Enemies,* ed. Ernest R. May, 150–171. Princeton, NJ: Princeton University Press, 1984.
Williamson, Samuel R., Jr. *The Politics of Grand Strategy: Britain and France Prepare for War, 1904–1914.* Cambridge: Harvard University Press, 1969.

Micheler, Joseph Alfred (1861–1931)

French army general. Born in Phalsbourg (Moselle) in 1861, Joseph Micheler became an officer in the army and enjoyed routine advancement and promotion. At the beginning of World War I Micheler commanded the 53rd Infantry Division; during the mobilization he also commanded the 3rd GDR (Groupe de Divisions du Réserve) but only until 15 September 1914. He continued to command the 53rd Infantry Division until March 1916 and participated in the second Champagne offensive.

In 1916, following a very brief period in charge of XXXVIII Army Corps, Micheler assumed command of the Tenth Army during the Battle of the Somme. The Tenth Army held the front south of the River Somme and joined in operations on 4 September, continuing to fight until the end of the battle on 15 November 1916. Micheler's performance was sufficient for him to be promoted to command the Reserve Army Group for the 1917 campaign. Plans called for the Reserve Army Group to exploit the breakthrough that French army commander Robert Nivelle anticipated on the Chemin des Dames.

Micheler had little faith in Nivelle's plans, and he also had the ear of Antonin Dubost, president of the Senate. War Minister Paul Painlevé was another skeptic, and he encouraged Micheler and the other army group commanders to voice their doubts. Painlevé, Premier Alexandre Ribot, and President Raymond Poincaré confronted Nivelle in front of his army group commanders at a conference in Compiègne on 6 April 1917. Unfortunately for the French army, the politicians' courage failed them, and Nivelle's offensive was allowed to proceed.

The Nivelle offensive began on 16 April, and Micheler's Reserve Army Group took part in attacks along the whole of its front, advancing to the Chemin des Dames ridge where it organized defensive positions. In the renewed fighting in May, the Tenth Army took part in the operations to relieve Reims and to capture Craonne. The Tenth Army was dissolved on 8 May.

Micheler took over command of the Fifth Army on 22 May 1917, a post he still occupied when the German assault on the Chemin des Dames took place in May 1918. As an offensive-minded general, Micheler had been among those who disapproved of French army commander General Henri Philippe Pétain's new defense methods and, as with Generals Denis Duchêne and Louis de Maud'huy in the Sixth Army alongside, he had deployed too many troops in forward trenches. Clemenceau subsequently sacked Micheler with the rest to satisfy parliamentary opinion. Micheler died in Nice (Alpes Maritimes) on 18 March 1931.

Elizabeth Greenhalgh

See also
Champagne Offensive, Second; Chemin des Dames Offensive; Clemenceau, Georges; Duchêne, Denis Auguste; Ludendorff Offensives; Maud'huy, Louis Ernest de; Nivelle, Robert; Nivelle Offensive; Painlevé, Paul; Pétain, Henri Philippe; Poincaré, Raymond; Ribot, Alexandre; Somme Offensive.
References
Clayton, Anthony. *Paths of Glory: The French Army, 1914–18.* London: Cassell, 2003.
Duroselle, Jean-Baptiste. *La Grande Guerre des Français: 1914–1918.* Paris: Perrin, 1994.
Herbillon, Emile. *Le Général Alfred Micheler (1914–1918) d'après ses notes, sa correspondance et les souvenirs personnels de l'auteur.* Paris: Plon, 1933.
King, Jere Clemens. *Generals and Politicians: Conflict between France's High Command, Parliament, and Government, 1914–1918.* Berkeley: University of California Press, 1951.
Spears, E. L. *Prelude to Victory.* London: Jonathan Cape, 1939.

Mikhail Alexandrovich, Grand Duke (1878–1918)

Russian grand duke. Born at the Anichkov Palace, St. Petersburg, on 8 December 1878, Mikhail (Michael) Romanov was the third son of Tsar Alexander III of Russia and Princess Dagmar (Marie Fyodorovna) of Denmark. After the death of his elder brother Georgi in 1899, Mikhail was heir to the throne and, following the birth of Nicholas II's son Alexis in 1904, a potential regent. Mikhail served in the Horse Guards and, after 1902, as squadron commander of his mother's elite Chernigov Hussars (Blue Cuirassiers). After several unsuitable romantic entanglements, Mikhail eloped with twice-divorced Nathalia Wulfert, by whom he had a son, George, in 1910. Their October 1912 marriage by a Viennese Serbian

Russian Grand Duke Mikhail Alexandrovich, commander of II Corps of the Seventh Army. (Underwood & Underwood/Corbis)

Orthodox priest enraged the imperial family, and he was banished and all his property put into trusteeship.

Mikhail lived in exile in rural England and Paris from 1912 until the outbreak of war in August 1914, when he was recalled and given command as a major general of a new division, the Caucasian Native Cavalry, composed of volunteer Muslim Caucasian horsemen, that quickly won the sobriquet the "Savage Division" for its fighting on the Galician Front in November 1914 and in the Carpathian Mountains in January 1915. In February 1916 Mikhail was promoted to command II Corps of the Seventh Army, which took part in the 1916 Brusilov offensive.

Despite Mikhail's popularity and his military experience, Tsar Nicholas II and Alexandra refused to consider naming him as regent during the February 1917 crisis, a move that might have stabilized the throne. On Nicholas II's abdication on 2 March 1917, Mikhail, then technically the tsar, issued a manifesto refusing the crown unless it was offered by a future Constituent Assembly and pledging his support to the provisional government. Mikhail was discharged from the army on 5 April 1917 and then lived as a private citizen, although he fell under intense suspicion because of the Savage Division's

participation in the Kornilov Plot. In November 1917, he helped smuggle Aleksandr Kerensky out of the country under a Danish passport obtained from his royal relatives. The Cheka Bolshevik secret police arrested Mikhail on 7 March 1918 and exiled him to Perm, from which he was kidnaped on orders of the Ural Soviet and murdered in the woods outside the city on 12 June. His wife and family had him declared legally dead by a London court in 1924. There was no official Russian confirmation of his death until 1989.

Margaret Sankey

See also
Alexandra Fyodorovna, Tsarina; Brusilov, Aleksey Alekseyevich; Kerensky, Aleksandr Fyodorovich; Kornilov, Lavr Georgyevich; Nicholas II, Tsar.

References
Crawford, Rosemary, and Donald Crawford. *Michael and Natasha.* New York: Scribner, 1997.
Gray, Pauline. *The Grand Duke's Woman: The Story of the Morganatic Marriage of Michael Romanoff, the Tsar Nicholas II's Brother and Nathalia Cheremerevskaya.* London: Macdonald and Jane's, 1976.
Majolier, Nathalie. *Stepdaughter of Imperial Russia.* London: S. Paul, 1940.

Military Board of Allied Supply (MBAS)

Allied agency for coordinating logistical support of the Allied forces in France and Belgium. The growth of the American Expeditionary Forces (AEF) in early 1918 highlighted the need for better coordination of the logistical support of the Allied armies in the field in France and Belgium. In March 1918 Colonel (later Brigadier General) Charles G. Dawes, AEF general purchasing agent, recommended to AEF commander General John Pershing the creation of an agency to coordinate transportation and storage in the rear of the Allied armies. Pershing approved Dawes's recommendation and discussed with French Premier Georges Clemenceau the idea of pooling of supplies, storage facilities, and transport for the Allied armies. Clemenceau agreed to the creation of an interallied agency to coordinate Allied supply efforts. Accordingly, the Military Board of Allied Supply (MBAS) was established on 14 May 1918. The agreement of the British, Italians, and Belgians was then obtained, and the MBAS's first meeting was held in Paris on 28 June.

The French representative, General Jean Marie Charles Payot, was elected president of the MBAS. Colonel R. H. Beadon, and later Major General Sir Reginald Ford, represented Great Britain. Italy was represented by General Errico Merrone and Belgium by Colonel Eugene Cumont. Brigadier General Dawes represented the United States. The MBAS principals were assisted by an interallied staff that worked closely with the staff of the Allied commander-in-chief Marshal Ferdinand Foch. MBAS decisions required unanimous consent but once made were binding on all the Allied armies, each of which otherwise remained responsible for its own support and maintained its own logistical organization and procedures.

The MBAS quickly set to work devising and implementing measures to pool resources, establishing common policies and procedures, and coordinating support in the rear of the armies. The MBAS developed a comprehensive picture of the storage facilities in France and standard regulations for motor traffic, the use of railroads and narrow-gauge (60 centimeter) railways, the supply of gasoline, and the construction and operation of telephone and telegraph systems. Schools were also set up to instruct Allied officers in motor transport and railway regulating procedures and in the maintenance of narrow-gauge railways. French and U.S. representatives reached an agreement on the use of French timber resources and also agreed to pool their artillery ammunition. The MBAS also established a standard Allied forage ration and studied the possibility of a common ration for all Allied troops.

By 11 November 1918, the MBAS had already accomplished much by reducing competition for scarce resources and making more efficient use of the available storage, transport, and materials. The last meeting of the MBAS was held on 3 December 1918, but until 1921 its staff continued to compile statistical data and prepare comparative studies of the logistical services of all the Allied armies. A model of inter-Allied cooperation and coordination, the MBAS was largely forgotten in the postwar years, and the principles and procedures it developed had to be rediscovered in World War II and after.

Charles R. Shrader

See also
Clemenceau, Georges; Foch, Ferdinand; Pershing, John Joseph.
References
Dawes, Charles G. *A Journal of the Great War.* 2 vols. Boston: Houghton Mifflin, 1921.
Goedeken, E. A. "Charles Dawes and the Military Board of Allied Supply." *Military Affairs* 50(1) (1988): 1–6.
Jadwin, John S. "The Military Board of Allied Supply." United States Army War College Historical Study No. 22. Washington: Historical Section, U.S. Army War College, August 1942. Reprinted in Charles R. Shrader, ed., *United States Army Logistics, 1775–1992: An Anthology,* 2:445–447. Washington, DC: Center of Military History, U.S. Army, 1997.
Supreme War Council, the Allied Armies under Marshal Foch in the Franco-Belgian Theater of Operations. *Report of the Military Board of Allied Supply.* 2 vols. Washington, DC: United States Government Printing Office, 1924–1925.

Military Organization

Armies are hierarchical organizations, and long ago military commanders learned through trial and error that a given number of soldiers operating on the battlefield as part of a coordinated and synchronized team were far more effective than an equal or even a larger number of individual combatants. In the classical period the ancient Greeks developed the phalanx, and the Romans developed the century, the cohort, and the legion. By World War I there was a great deal of similarity in the names and the structures of the various echelons of most of the world's armies. There was somewhat less similarity among the navies and especially the newly emerging air services of the various nations.

Armies

The primary unit in almost all armies was the section, or squad (German Gruppe), consisting of 8 to 12 soldiers and led by a junior ranking noncommissioned officer (NCO), usually a corporal or lance corporal. By the middle years of the war the Germans had reorganized their infantry squads completely around the light machine gun. In artillery units the section made up the crew of a single gun. In the tank units that emerged in the last year of the war, the crew of a single tank was the primary unit.

The platoon (German Zug) consisted of three or four squads and up to 30 soldiers, commanded by a junior lieutenant who was assisted by a sergeant. In the British army the lieutenant was called a platoon commander. In the U.S. Army, however, he was known as a platoon leader. In the U.S. Army the company was the lowest level at which an officer exercised full command authority. As World War I progressed, attrition of combat units forced many armies to put NCOs in charge of platoons and even companies. Some NCOs eventually won battlefield commissions in this manner. The term "platoon" derived from the French word *peloton,* which simply means a group of men. The term was first used to describe any group of soldiers who fired their weapons in unison.

The company (German Companie), consisting of three or four platoons, is one of the oldest of all military organizations, tracing its lineage directly to the Roman century, commanded by a centurion. By World War I companies in most armies numbered between 100 and 200 soldiers, depending on the type of company. In artillery units the company-sized unit was called a battery (between two and six gun sections, depending on the size of the gun), and in a cavalry unit the company-sized unit was known as a troop. The company commander was assisted by a senior first lieutenant, as the executive officer, and a senior NCO. In almost all armies except those of the British Commonwealth, the company, battery, or troop commander was a captain. The British assigned majors as company commanders and still do to this day. The senior NCO in a British company was called the company sergeant-major, while in the U.S. Army he was called the first sergeant.

In the early seventeenth century, Maurice of Nassau introduced the battalion, patterned on the ancient Roman cohort.

Commanded by a lieutenant colonel, the World War I battalion (German Battallion) consisted of three to five companies totaling anywhere between 400 and 1,000 soldiers, depending on the type of unit. In cavalry organizations the battalion-sized unit was called a squadron, which was in no way equivalent to a naval squadron or an air force squadron. In most armies the equivalent artillery unit was also called a battalion, but in the German army it was known as an Abteilung and in the British army it was called a brigade. The battalion is the lowest echelon at which a commander had a dedicated staff to assist him in planning and conducting operations.

The regiment (German Regiment), commanded by a colonel, is another of the oldest of military formations. Evolving from the ancient Roman legion, the World War I regiment consisted of three or four battalions and numbered between 1,000 and 3,000 soldiers. The next echelon above the regiment was the brigade (German Brigade), commanded by a brigadier general, but there was a great deal of variation at this particular level from army to army.

The division (German Division) first appeared at the end of the eighteenth century. In 1914 French, German, and Russian infantry divisions all had two brigades of infantry, each with two regiments. Each regiment had three infantry battalions except the Russian, which had four. The British division had three infantry brigades, each consisting of four infantry battalions, and no intermediate regimental headquarters. By 1918 the typical German division had a single brigade headquarters that controlled three regiments of three battalions each. The U.S. division of 1918, which had almost twice the trench strength of the European divisions, had two brigades of two regiments of three battalions each. All World War I divisions also had organic artillery units as well as other supporting arms and services. The World War I division was the lowest echelon capable of semi-independent combined arms operations. Depending on its type (infantry or cavalry), the division had anywhere from 8,000 to 14,000 soldiers, but because of high attrition rates the actual field strengths were often significantly lower. In most armies the division was commanded by a major general, but in the German and Russian armies by a lieutenant general. Despite the difference in rank titles, a divisional commander in all cases was the equivalent of a two-star general. Because of high attrition rates among senior officers in the German army, it was not uncommon for a German division to be commanded by a colonel. Two or more divisions comprised a World War I corps (German Korps). A product of the mass armies of the French Revolution, a corps of Napoleon's day was commanded by a marshal. During World War I the standard rank of a corps commander was a lieutenant general (or three-star equivalent). In practice, however, many corps commanders were senior major generals who had successfully commanded at the divisional level. In addition to its subordinate divisions, a corps also had a number of separate battalions and brigades of supporting arms and services. Depending on the number of subordinate divisions, a corps could have anywhere from 20,000 to 50,000 soldiers. Corps were always designated in Roman numerals, for example, V Corps. All echelons below the corps were always designated in Arabic numerals, for example, 3rd Infantry Division.

The echelon above the corps was the army (German Armee), sometimes called the field army or the numbered army to distinguish it from the army as a whole (German Heer). Most numbered armies in World War I were actually commanded by lieutenant generals. Armies are designated by spelling out their numerical designation, for example, Third Army.

The army group (German Heeresgruppe), which first appeared in World War I, is the largest battlefield command in military history. An army group was commanded by either a full general (four-star equivalent) or by a field marshal (or a five-star equivalent general). In the Russian army the army group was known as a front. Army group designations used Arabic numerals, for example, 12th Army Group.

The French army of World War I had only two general officer ranks, general of brigade (one star, or brigadier general equivalent) and general of division (two star, or major general equivalent). The rank of marshal of France existed on paper, but no French commander held that rank during the war. Joseph Joffre received the rank after he was relieved of his command of the French forces following the Battle of Verdun, and Henri Philippe Pétain and Ferdinand Foch were advanced to marshals of France after the war. Although the corps, army, and army group commanders, and even Foch as Supreme Allied Commander, wore the rank of general of division, there were certain distinctions that indicated their higher levels of command and responsibility and authority. In the early 1920s the French added the ranks of general of corps and general of army.

Above the army group level most armies had high command headquarters that exercised command and control of all field operations. Both the British Expeditionary Force (BEF) and the American Expeditionary Forces (AEF) were headed by a General Headquarters (GHQ). The French army was headed by the Grand Quartier Général (GQG). The German army in the field was commanded by the Oberste Heeresleitung (OHL), which essentially was the forward command post on the Western Front of the Great General Staff. The German headquarters on the Eastern Front, Oberost, answered to OHL.

Marines

Almost all marine organizations of World War I were small and specialized. Although components of their respective navies, they were all organized along army lines. In World

War I the U.S. Marine Corps operated in the field under U.S. Army command. One of the two brigades of the U.S. 2nd Infantry Division was a Marine formation, and the division's commander, Major General John Lejeune, was a Marine.

Air Forces

Air power was a new and not completely understood concept in World War I, and all the major powers placed their aerial units under one of the dominant military arms, either the army or navy, or gave both services an aerial component. Britain and France established their first aerial units, balloon observation companies, in the late 1870s and 1860s, respectively. France established its first fixed-wing units in 1906, while Britain added fixed-wing aircraft to the Royal Engineers' balloon battalion in 1907. Britain's Royal Engineers trained and equipped the pilots of the army and Royal Navy as well as the observation balloon and kite units. However, it took Winston Churchill as First Lord of the Admiralty and King George V's concern over German aviation developments to force Britain into pursuing development of an aerial arm. Britain formed the Royal Flying Corps (RFC) as part of the army in 1912, although it had a naval component and was to provide naval aviation detachments. France established the Aeronautique Militaire (Military Air Service) that same year. By 1914 the Royal Naval Air Service had broken away from the RFC to serve as the Royal Navy's air arm. Germany's aviation development was fostered by the chief of the General Staff General Helmuth von Moltke, who directed the formation of the German Fliegertruppen (Flying Troop) in October 1912. Austria-Hungary followed suit a few months later.

All the major powers treated aircraft as reconnaissance units at war's start, except that German leaders saw the dirigible (e.g., Count von Zeppelin's rigid lighter-than-air aviation craft) as a potential offensive strike unit and organized their aerial units accordingly. Squadrons constituted the lowest echelon of aerial unit in British service and were considered company-level commands led by a captain. British squadrons had a nominal complement of twelve aircraft or four balloons. As with Britain, French Escadrille (squadrons) were considered a company-level command. Initially they contained six aircraft, but by 1916 squadrons consisted of two flights of four to six aircraft for a total of eight to twelve aircraft each. At war's start, French bomber units were called Groupe de Bombardment and contained three sections of six aircraft each. Germany and Austria-Hungary used six-plane truppen commanded by a Leutnant (army lieutenant) as the lowest echelon of aerial unit with one Lufttruppe assigned to each Regular Army corps and fortress garrison (German), or Armee (Austria-Hungary). The German and Austria-Hungarian navies also had aerial units. The former had Zeppelin Geschwader and Seeflieger Geschwader, while the latter

opened the war with a single Seefliegertruppe of three seaplanes. Russian aviation was structured along lines very similar to German aviation, using squadrons (otryad) of six to ten planes of varying types commanded by captains.

By 1915, all services began to group their aviation units to better concentrate their capabilities. The RFC grouped two to three squadrons of a similar type into "wings" that were commanded by a major. Plans called for two aircraft wings and one kite-balloon battalion to form an aviation brigade and for a brigade to be assigned to every army. The French, who provided most of the aviation units on the Western Front, grouped their Escadrille as required to achieve air superiority over a given section of front. As with the RFC's wings, French fighter groups were commanded by majors. By 1916, French bombers and fighters had standardized squadron organizations of ten aircraft each. Unlike fighters, however, the bombers were often grouped into three squadron units for bomber missions in support of an army. Generally, however, the French assigned three squadrons to every army corps, one of each aircraft type (fighter, reconnaissance, and bomber) as well as an observation balloon battalion.

By 1916, the Germans had begun to collect their jaegerfliegeren (hunting flyers) into Jadgstafflen (hunting or fighter squadrons) of twelve aircraft, commanded by a Hauptmann (captain). Later, several of these squadrons were concentrated in Jagdgeschwader (hunting or fighting wings) under an Oberstleutnant (lieutenant colonel) or Oberst (colonel). Operational experience led the Germans to establish a formal intermediate organization, the Jagdgruppen (hunting or fighter groups) of three to six squadrons that were commanded by a major or Oberstleutnant (lieutenant colonel).

The German navy treated its dirigible or zeppelin units as a scouting force and organized it into flotillas (Geschwader) of the Naval Airship Division under Fregattekapitaen (CDR) Peter Strasser. Individual dirigibles were commanded by a Kapitaenleutnant (lieutenant commander). Organizationally they had the same status as destroyer flotillas, although they gained far more importance and a higher operational priority, as the Zeppelin-led bombing campaign against Great Britain acquired a greater strategic priority in the eyes of Kaiser Wilhelm II. German seaplane squadrons consisted of ten to twelve seaplanes, led by an Oberleutnant (navy lieutenant, equivalent to an army captain).

Austria-Hungary's Seeflieger never numbered more than a dozen aircraft, but the army's Luftfahrtruppen (aviation troops) eventually expanded into a force commensurate with other elements of Austria-Hungary's vastly underequipped armies. Der Fliegerkompanie (flying company) became the basic flying unit at the front. Initially it consisted of two Fliegertruppen (flying troup) of six planes each, but in practice its strength varied between five and ten aircraft. A Fliegertruppenpark was established in each sector of front to support the flying companies assigned. Gruppen were established to control flying companies concentrated for a specific mission or operation. Operational control rested with the aviation staff officer of the supported army unit's staff, while administrative and logistics support remained the responsibility of Oberst Emil Uzerlac, who had commanded the Kaiserliche und Königliche Luftfahrtruppen (Royal and Imperial Flying Troops [LFT]) from its 1912 inception to war's end.

Despite being the country where the first manned powered flight had occurred, the United States was a latecomer in the world of aviation, having established its first formal aerial units in 1913. The AEF followed the French pattern of organization but practiced tactics that more closely followed the aggressiveness of the Royal Flying Corps. AEF squadrons had eighteen to twenty-four aircraft, depending on aircraft type. As with the French, they treated aviation units like specialist troops to be allocated and concentrated as required to support a corps for a specific mission or operation. By 1918, then-Lieutenant Colonel Billy Mitchell was the staff officer controlling the planning and allocation of U.S. aviation units under the AEF, but in practice the units enjoyed great independence as long as they operated within the designated sector of the unit they were assigned to support.

Italy was the last major European power to establish a formal aviation unit, although Italian forces had pioneered aerial bombing and reconnaissance in modern-day Libya during fighting there with the Ottoman Empire during 1911–1912. Italy established its Corpo Aeronautico Militarre (Military Aeronautics Corps) in January 1915, just four months before it entered World War I. Its squadrons (Squadriglia) were equipped with varying numbers and types of aircraft. As with other countries in the war, its squadrons were considered company-level commands, and by 1917 it was beginning to mass its aviation units into larger formations for bombing and aerial superiority purposes. These Gruppo consisted of several squadrons and fell under the direction of the aviation staff officer (typically a major) assigned to the supported Italian army (next echelon above corps). The Italian navy never organized its aerial units into squadrons, treating each seaplane or airship as an independent unit under the overall direction of the navy's aviation staff.

The Royal Flying Corps (RFC) and Royal Naval Air Service (RNAS) were consolidated in April 1918 to form the Royal Air Force, making it the world's first independent air arm. Squadrons consisting of two sections of eight to twelve aircraft became the basic building block of RAF units. Airfield commanders, typically a major or lieutenant colonel, became responsible for the aircraft assigned to their airfield, and all the airfields within a sector came under a group commander. By war's end, the RAF had established the basic rank structure and command organization that would take it, with some minor modifications, into the early days of World War II.

All the major powers in World War I walked away from that war with a vision of air power's future potential, but only those countries that had conducted strategic bombing campaigns (Britain, Germany, and Italy) saw a need for an independent air force and established such a force during the interwar years that preceded the Second World War. Although prohibited from possessing aircraft by the Versailles Treaty, Germany studied the lessons of the Great War and applied them to the Luftwaffe (German Air Force) when Adolf Hitler chose to violate that treaty after coming to power in 1933. France, Russia, and the United States retained control of their air forces within the army until after World War II.

Navies

All the major navies of World War I entered that conflict with organizational structures little changed from those of the late nineteenth century. Ships of the line (battleships) were the queens of the sea, and most naval commanders expected naval engagements to follow along traditional lines, with modern technology changing only the ranges and speeds, not the tactics, of naval combat. The submarine and aircraft were not yet seen as major threats.

Battleships were organized in divisions of the same class led by a rear admiral, with two to four battleships each. Lesser major combatants that supported the battle line but were not considered suitable to "fight in the line" were organized into squadrons. As with the second-rates and third-rates of the nineteenth century and before, these ships were considered extensions of the battle fleet, suitable for scouting ahead or patrolling and showing the flag in areas where the main fleet's presence wasn't required or practical. In port, they were assigned to squadrons of two to four units (cruisers, battle cruisers, and, in the Royal Navy, seaplane carriers) commanded by a rear admiral (battle cruisers) or a senior captain (other units). All the major navies concentrated these units into scouting forces in areas where the main battle fleet was stationed or assigned them to forces (Royal Navy) or squadrons (all other navies) operating under a regional commander-in-chief whose rank varied with the size and importance of his command (in the Royal Navy, usually a rear admiral but occasionally a vice admiral). Forces and deployed squadrons were generally commanded by the senior officer present unless the squadron commander was also the naval commander for the region or body of water in which the squadron patrolled. In that case, the commander usually was a rear admiral. Commanders-in-chief were subordinate to the Admiralty (the first sea lord acting as the overall fleet commander under the direction of the first lord of the Admiralty). The most senior of the commanders-in-chief was Admiral Sir John Jellicoe, commander-in-chief of the Grand Fleet, who commanded the main battle fleet and all of its supporting units.

Flotilla units, that is, lesser combatant ships (destroyers and submarines) and auxiliary vessels, were organized in flotillas, generally commanded by commander (equiv. to a lieutenant colonel) or captain (equiv. to a colonel). With electronic communications in its infancy, most navies employed a light cruiser to serve as flotilla flagship since most destroyers and submarines could carry at best only a single morse code operator and carried only a short-ranged wireless set, if any. The Royal Navy assigned a destroyer to British submarine flotillas before 1915 to serve as the submarine flotilla leader and relay communications because of the limited range and reliability of submarine wireless equipment. Communications with the fleet was relayed by the destroyer via the cruiser serving as the flotilla flagship. Flotilla units were assigned to ports, forces, fleets, and commanders-in-chief as required by the Admiralty.

Other navies followed these same general organization guidelines, but there were some minor differences. In the U.S. Navy, squadrons were a higher-level formation. For example, two to three battleship divisions of two to three battleships each constituted a battleship squadron. The U.S. Navy had a single such squadron at war's start. However, it was more than just a battleship formation. Before World War I, the navy deployed in squadrons commanded by a commodore (one-star flag rank) or rear admiral. A typical U.S. Navy squadron overseas consisted of one to two cruisers supported by a mixture of lesser surface craft. All squadron commanders reported to the commander-in-chief of the U.S. Fleet, who was the organizational equivalent to the Royal Navy's first sea lord, unless they were detached from a fleet commander.

In 1913, the U.S. Congress authorized the establishment of the U.S. Atlantic Fleet, which contained the entire U.S. battle fleet, all but two of the navy's cruisers, most of its destroyers, and all but two if its submarines. Commanded by an admiral, the Atlantic Fleet would grow to a force nearly equaling Britain's Grand Fleet by 1918. The Atlantic Fleet commander had the authority to detach "squadrons" as circumstances dictated, and he did indeed deploy a Mediterranean Squadron of several destroyer and antisubmarine flotillas into the Mediterranean in late 1917. There was no Pacific Fleet in 1914. Instead, the U.S. Navy had an Asiatic Squadron and a Flying Squadron, consisting of a single cruiser (later two) and a handful of supporting ships. The former operated in the western Pacific, while the latter was stationed along the U.S. west coast.

The German navy employed a similar structure to the Royal Navy, with its Asiatic and Mediterranean "squadrons" under the fleet commanders (equiv. to Royal Navy commanders-in-chief) for the oceans areas to which they were deployed. These deployed "fleets" were commanded by rear admirals. The High Seas Fleet was the Imperial German Navy's primary battle element and, like its British counterpart the Grand Fleet, was commanded by an admiral and included several battleship divisions, a scouting force of several battle cruiser squadrons led by a vice admiral, and several flotillas of lesser units. The much smaller Baltic Fleet, commanded by the kaiser's younger brother Heinrich, was initially a fleet in name only, consisting mostly of older units organized in subordinate squadrons. Its opponent, the Russian navy, was organized along similar lines, except that its flotilla units were organized into brigades of two to three flotillas.

Prior to World War I, shore-based regional commanders-in-chief primarily served as intelligence and logistics providers to the naval units operating in their area of authority. They relayed strategic-level orders from the Admiralty, modifying those orders only if they had more recent information that changed the circumstances shaping the Admiralty's instructions. The same rule applied to U.S. squadron commanders deployed overseas. The introduction of wireless communications and the installation of wireless equipment to a growing number of naval units was to prove more disruptive to traditional command arrangements than the advent of steam and long-range gunnery.

It is important to understand that wireless communications was less than fifteen years old in 1914, and its implications were not fully understood. It had increased the range of maritime communications, but naval commanders were reluctant to surrender their independence to increasingly distant commanders. Most fleet commanders wanted only flagships to have wireless equipment, fearing the impact of having shore-based commanders and higher authority gaining access to a fleet or squadron commander's subordinates. This induced a certain level of friction and misunderstandings during the war's early months. For example, the German battle cruiser *Goeben*'s escape to Turkey was facilitated by the contradictory and confusing orders sent out by the Admiralty to British Mediterranean naval units.

There were other instances where the traditional command structure based on the days of flag and semaphore communications proved impractical or irrelevant to modern naval operations. For example, port captains commanded all ships in their port until they were underway or out of territorial waters. Once underway, the senior officer present afloat (SOPA) commanded all ships either assigned to him or within his area of control (line of sight or within communications range, depending on his interpretation of the situation). This was not a major problem in the Royal and U.S. Navies, where SOPA's authority was preeminent and personal initiative took precedence over orders if local circumstances dictated. However, it was a source of problems and confusion in the Austria-Hungarian, German, and Russian navies, where traditions derived from army subordination had led to a system of the shore-based commander's authority being dominant. In those navies, forces operating offshore under the port commander's authority reported to him and not to SOPA. Shore commanders preferred to monitor the situation before dispatching the ships and remain in command until the ships were out of sight or communications range (again dependent on the commander's interpretation of which applied). This often delayed fleet reaction to surprise attacks and, worse, complicated the fleet's response in situations where the shore-based commander refused either to authorize deployment until the situation was clearer to him or relinquish command once SOPA sighted the enemy. Germany changed its command structure to give command to SOPA after Britain's Harwich Force successfully raided the High Seas Fleet's main operating base near Wilhemshaven on 25 December 1914. Austria-Hungary and Russia did not change their command structures in this regard until their respective empires were near collapse in 1918.

Submarines and mines forced all the navies of World War I to change their basic operating procedures. Flotilla units, particularly destroyers and antisubmarine vessels, gained importance. The Royal Navy felt that the war had validated its concept of establishing ad hoc "forces" of mixed naval units for specific missions and the employment of flotilla units as convoy escorts to combat submarines. However, disappointment over the zeppelin as an antiship weapon and the inability of the war's aircraft to damage anything larger than a light cruiser led fleet commanders to underestimate air power's potential impact on future naval operations. As a result, all major naval commanders came out of the war believing that "lines of battle" would still dominate the later naval engagements of the twentieth century. It would take either extensive study and debate during the interwar years or devastating combat experience in the next war to change their minds.

David T. Zabecki and Carl O. Schuster

See also

Churchill, Sir Winston; Foch, Ferdinand; George V, King; *Goeben* and *Breslau,* Escape of; Heinrich, Prince of Prussia; Hitler, Adolf; Jellicoe, John Rushworth, 1st Earl; Joffre, Joseph; Lejeune, John Archer; Mitchell, William; Moltke, Helmuth von, Count; Pétain, Henri Philippe; Verdun, Battle of; Versailles, Treaty of; Wilhelm II, Kaiser; Zeppelins.

References

Bodansky, Stephen. *Air Power.* London: Viking, 2004.

Chant, Christopher. *Austro-Hungarian Aces of World War I.* Oxford, UK: Osprey, 2003.

Griess, Thomas E., ed. *Definitions and Doctrine of the Military Art: The West Point Military History Series.* Wayne, NJ: Avery, 1985.

Halpern, Paul. *Naval History of the War at Sea.* Annapolis: Naval Institute Press, 1998.

Hough, Richard A. *The Great War at Sea, 1914–1918.* Oxford: Oxford University Press, 1983.

House, Jonathan M. *Toward Combined Arms Warfare: A Survey of 20th Century Tactics, Doctrine, and Organization.* Fort Leavenworth, KS: U.S. Army Command and General Staff College, 1984.

Ireland, Bernard. *War at Sea: 1914–1945.* London: Cassell, 2002.

Morrow, John H., Jr. *The Great War in the Air: Military Aviation from 1909 to 1921.* Smithsonian History of Aviation Series. Washington, DC: Smithsonian Institution Press, 1993.

Millerand, Alexandre (1859–1943)

French politician. Born in Paris on 10 February 1859, Alexandre Millerand studied law at the University of Paris. As a young lawyer he gained a reputation for defending strikers and socialists. A socialist himself, Millerand also wrote for a number of newspapers and was editor of *La Lanterne* in 1898. Primarily interested in politics, Millerand won election to the Paris Municipal Council in 1884 and the Chamber of Deputies in 1885, beginning a fifty-five-year parliamentary career.

In 1899 Millerand became minister of commerce, prompting a crisis that disrupted the Second International because of Millerand's opposition to revolution and his belief that socialists could work within the political system. Many on the political left accused him of undermining working-class solidarity by his reforms. As minister of public works during 1909–1910, Millerand instituted old age, accident, and unemployment benefits.

French President Alexandre Millerand. (Library of Congress)

In January 1912 Premier Raymond Poincaré appointed Millerand minister of war. He served in that post until January 1913. A leading figure in the nationalist revival in France just before the Great War, Millerand worked to increase the size of the French army and navy. Returning to the post of minister of war in the René Viviani government during August 1914 to October 1915, Millerand played a significant role in mobilizing the French economy for war by enlarging existing factories, adding new ones, and vastly increasing production. Some 500,000 skilled workers were also recalled from the front and returned to work in the armament factories.

Millerand believed that in wartime the civilian leadership should defer to the military, and he shielded French army commander General Joseph Joffre from civilian political interference and control. This did not sit well with the politicians, and when in mid-1915 Joffre dismissed politically connected Third Army commander General Maurice Sarrail, left-wing politicians in the Chamber forced the Viviani government to overrule Joffre's decision for the first time during the war and secured Sarrail's appointment as commander of the newly created French army in the Balkans. Millerand, who had defended Joffre's prerogatives, was forced to resign in October 1915. His departure from office demonstrated a shift in power away from the army high command toward the civilian politicians.

Millerand had an illustrious postwar career. He first took charge of the administration of the recovered provinces of Alsace and Lorraine. Then, as leader of the Bloc national, he was premier and foreign minister (January–September 1920) followed by president of the Republic (September 1920–June 1924). Millerand's parliamentary career ended in the Senate (1925–1927 and 1927–1940), where he pointed out the growing danger posed by Germany. Millerand died at Versailles on 6 April 1943.

Spencer C. Tucker

See also
Joffre, Joseph; Poincaré, Raymond; Sarrail, Maurice; Viviani, René.

References
Derfler, L. *Alexandre Millerand: The Socialist Years.* The Hague: Mouton, 1977.
Farrar, Majorie Milbank. *Principled Pragmatist: The Political Career of Alexandre Millerand.* New York: Berg, 1991.
King, Jere Clemens. *Generals and Politicians: Conflict between France's High Command, Parliament, and Government, 1914–1918.* Berkeley: University of California Press, 1951.
Weber, Eugen. *The Nationalist Revival in France, 1905–1914.* Berkeley: University of California Press, 1959.

Milne, Sir Archibald Berkeley (1855–1938)

British admiral. Born in London on 2 June 1855, Archibald Milne was the son of Admiral of the Fleet Sir Alexander Milne.

Milne followed his father into the navy in 1869. He fought ashore and was wounded during the Zulu War of 1879, but much of his naval service was in royal yachts as a close friend of the Prince of Wales, the future King Edward VII. Milne rose rapidly through the higher echelons of the navy, being promoted to rear admiral in 1904 and to full admiral in 1911. Milne has been the subject of much criticism. Many within the navy, including the venerable Admiral John "Jacky" Fisher, regarded Milne with contempt, believing that he had attained his advanced rank through royal favoritism rather than ability. Nonetheless, in November 1912 Milne reached the pinnacle of his career when he was appointed commander-in-chief of British naval units in the Mediterranean.

Milne's naval career ended for all practical purposes in the first month of World War I. At the beginning of the war it was uncertain whether Italy would remain neutral; also, Milne had conflicting orders from the Admiralty, having been asked to give priority to protecting French troops ships from North Africa to metropolitan France but also to destroy the new German battle cruiser *Goeben,* flagship of the German Mittelmeerdivision, and her consort the light cruiser *Breslau.* Simultaneously, however, Milne's orders called for him to avoid engagement with a superior force, by which the Admiralty meant the Austro-Hungarian navy, unless acting in concert with the French fleet. With Italy's declaration of neutrality, the Admiralty also ordered Milne to respect Italian territorial waters, which Milne believed prevented him from entering the narrow Strait of Messina between Italy and Sicily. Coordination with the French was also poor. Thus, the two German ships were allowed to escape to the Dardanelles and thence to Constantinople, where their presence helped bring the Ottoman Empire into the war on the side of the Central Powers. Milne's subordinate Rear Admiral Ernest Troubridge did pursue the German ships but interpreted the Admiralty "superior force" order to mean that he should not engage, as each of his own armored cruisers was inferior to the *Goeben.* Troubridge was later court-martialed but acquitted.

Milne came under heavy criticism in Britain for the escape of the *Goeben,* even though an Admiralty investigation exonerated him. He was nonetheless removed from his command and never again employed at sea. He formally retired in November 1919 and wrote a book justifying his conduct. Milne died at Musselburgh, Midlothian, Scotland, on 5 July 1938.

Raymond Westphal Jr. and Spencer C. Tucker

See also
Fisher, John Arbuthnot, 1st Baron; *Goeben* and *Breslau,* Escape of; Mediterranean Theater, Naval Operations; Troubridge, Sir Ernest.

References
Lumby, E. W. R., ed. *Policy and Operations in the Mediterranean, 1912–1914.* London: Navy Records Society, 1970.
Marder, Arthur J. *From the Dreadnought to Scapa Flow: The Royal Navy in the Fisher Era, 1904–1919.* 5 vols. London: Oxford University Press, 1961–1970.

Miller, Geoffrey. *Superior Force: The Conspiracy behind the Escape of Goeben and Breslau.* Hull, UK: University of Hull Press, 1996.

Milne, Sir Archibald B. *The Flight of the Goeben and the Breslau: An Episode in Naval History.* London: Eveleigh Nash, 1921.

Wegener, Oliver. *The Naval Strategy of the World War.* Annapolis: Naval Institute Press, 1989.

Milne, Sir George Francis (1866–1948)

British army general. Born on 5 November 1866 at Aberdeen, Scotland, George Milne was educated at Aberbeen University and the Royal Military Academy, Woolwich. He joined the Royal Artillery in 1885 and served in the 1898 Sudan campaign and the 1899–1902 Boer War. In 1913 he was appointed artillery commander of the 4th Division as a brigadier-general.

Deployed with his division to France in 1914, Milne served at the battles at Le Cateau, the Marne, Aisne, and Ypres. After a period as chief staff officer of III Corps during early 1915, Milne was promoted to major-general and appointed chief staff officer to the Second Army. In mid-1915 he was selected to command the 27th Division. Late in the year the division was ordered to Salonika. Shortly after its arrival, Milne was

British Lieutenant-General Sir George Francis Milne, commander of the British Salonika Army. (Corbis)

appointed to command the XVI Corps. In May 1916, with the British strength on the Macedonian Front expanded, Milne took command of the British Salonika Army. In 1917 he was promoted to lieutenant-general.

The British forces at Salonika were part of a French-led Allied command structure. Until December 1917 the overall commander was General Maurice Sarrail, in whom Milne had little confidence. He regularly complained back to London of Sarrail. In addition to his French allies, Milne also had to contend with a harsh and inhospitable environment. These conditions, which included malaria, took a terrible toll on his forces.

Despite London's attempts to limit its commitment to the Macedonian Front, by 1918 Milne's army consisted of four infantry divisions and one cavalry brigade with a total strength of 140,000 troops. While his attacks in the Lake Doiran sector in 1917 made little progress, Milne participated in the Vardar offensive of September 1918 that successfully concluded the war on the Macedonian Front. After the armistice he directed his forces to Constantinople, and British forces entered that city in mid-November 1918.

After the war Milne served from 1926 to 1933 as chief of the Imperial General Staff. He presided during a period in which budget restrictions and general stagnation inflicted great damage on the British army. Promoted to general in 1920 and field marshal in 1928, Milne died in London on 23 March 1948.

Bradley P. Tolppanen

See also
Aisne, First Battle of the; Lake Prespa, Battle of; Le Cateau, Battle of; Marne, First Battle of the; Salonika Campaign; Sarrail, Maurice; Vardar Offensive; Ypres, First Battle of.

References
Nicol, Graham. *Uncle George: Field Marshal Lord Milne of Salonika and Rubislaw.* London: Reedminster, 1976.

Palmer, Alan. *The Gardeners of Salonika.* New York: Simon and Schuster, 1965.

Milner, Alfred, Viscount (1854–1925)

British administrator and statesman. Born on 23 March 1854 in Giessen, Hesse-Darmstadt, where his father studied medicine, Alfred Milner was a brilliant student at Oxford University. He became a passionate Liberal whose zeal to spread reform and social improvement beyond Britain made him a fervent imperialist. Following administrative service in Egypt and as chairman of the Board of Inland Revenue, from 1897 to 1905 Milner was high commissioner for South Africa, where his relentless efforts to establish British dominance over the Dutch-descended Boers aroused bitter controversy. He was created a peer in 1901.

Milner's imperialist principles aligned him with the most uncompromising opponents of the Liberal government

British Secretary for War Alfred Milner. (Hulton-Deutsch Collection/Corbis)

elected in 1906. After the Great War began in 1914, he became a focus for critics of Prime Minister Herbert H. Asquith's leadership and led the movement demanding conscription. When David Lloyd George replaced Asquith in December 1916, he included Milner in his five-man War Cabinet. Without a departmental portfolio, Milner involved himself in food supply, shipping allocations, and institution of convoys, and he arranged for the Dominion prime ministers to join an Imperial War Cabinet. He supported Lloyd George's efforts to reform the General Staff, and at the Doullens Conference in March 1918 Milner was instrumental in negotiating a unified Allied command structure under French General Ferdinand Foch.

Appointed secretary for war in April 1918, Milner was unjustly blamed for British defeats during the German offensive of March and April 1918. In mid-1918 rumors spread that he favored a negotiated peace with Germany at Russia's expense. Shortly before the armistice of November 1918, Milner did call for moderate terms that would not degrade Germany's position as a possible bulwark against the spread of Russian Bolshevism.

Following the election of December 1918, Milner became colonial secretary. He attended the Paris Peace Conference of 1919, and from November 1919 to March 1920 he visited Egypt to deal with nationalist challenges to the British protectorate. His conclusion that Britain should treat Egypt as fully sovereign, insisting only on a few safeguards for British interests, met heavy criticism, and in February 1921 he resigned. Milner died at Sturry Court, his home near Canterbury, on 13 May 1925.

John A. Hutcheson Jr.

See also
Armistice; Asquith, Herbert Henry, 1st Earl; Doullens Conference; Foch, Ferdinand; Lloyd George, David; Paris Peace Conference.
References
Gollin, Alfred M. *Proconsul in Politics.* New York: Macmillan, 1964.
Marlowe, John. *Milner: Apostle of Empire.* London: Hamish Hamilton, 1976.
O'Brien, Terence. *Milner.* London: Constable, 1979.
Wrench, John Evelyn. *Alfred Lord Milner.* London: Eyre and Spottiswoode, 1958.

Milyukov, Pavel Nikolayevich (1859–1943)

Russian statesman. Born on 27 January 1859 in Moscow, Pavel Milyukov was a historian by training. He taught at the University of Moscow and wrote a number of important works on Russian history, including *Studies in the History of Russian Culture.* Milyukov's political views, which were liberal-democratic, led to his dismissal from the university and exile. He spent most of the next decade abroad.

Milyukov was lecturing at the University of Chicago when the Russian Revolution of 1905 occurred. Believing that the autocratic tsarist regime was about to give way to democracy, he returned to Russia. Milyukov was promptly jailed for one month, but upon his release he played a major role in founding the Constitutional Democratic (Kadet) Party. He was elected to the Third and Fourth Dumas, in which he was instrumental in forging a coalition of center-left political parties known as the Progressive Bloc.

Milyukov supported Russia's entry into the war despite his opposition to the government. His support, however, turned to increasingly vehement criticism of the government's incompetence and corruption as the war dragged on. Milyukov and other members of the Progressive Bloc called for the establishment of a government of public confidence to take control of the war effort from inept and corrupt tsarist bureaucrats such as Ivan Goremykin and Boris Stürmer. Those calls, however, were rejected by reactionary elements at court centered around the fanatically autocratic Tsarina Alexandra.

On 1 November 1916, Milyukov voiced his mounting frustration in a pivotal speech before the Duma. Milyukov's speech, in which he listed the regime's many failings and

Pavel Milyukov, leader of the Russian Constitutional Democratic Party. (Library of Congress)

inquired rhetorically whether those shortcomings were the result of treason or stupidity, electrified the opposition and signaled the beginning of the end of the tsarist regime.

Following the March 1917 revolution, Milyukov became the foreign minister of the provisional government. Finding himself politically to the right in the new government, Milyukov publicly reiterated Russia's continuing commitment to the war and pursuit of tsarist war aims, including the annexation of the Dardanelles. Such pronouncements not only put him at odds with the new government, which had proclaimed a policy of "peace without indemnities," but they also aroused the wrath of the increasingly powerful Petrograd Soviet, which was suspicious of Milyukov's moderate politics. Nor were they popular with the war-weary public, and in the wake of demonstrations in Petrograd, Milyukov resigned on 2 May 1917.

Following the November 1917 revolution, Milyukov made his way to southern Russia and assisted in the formation of the anti-Bolshevik Volunteer Army. After the collapse of the White effort, Milyukov returned to exile. He then became a journalist and writer in France until his death in Paris on 31 March 1943.

John M. Jennings

See also
Alexandra Fyodorovna, Tsarina; Goremykin, Ivan Logginovich; Nicholas II, Tsar; Russia, Home Front; Russia, Revolution of March 1917; Stürmer, Boris Vladimirovich.
References
Hasegawa Tsuyoshi. *The February Revolution: Petrograd, 1917.* Seattle: University of Washington Press, 1981.
Lincoln, W. Bruce. *Passage through Armageddon: The Russians in War and Revolution, 1914–1918.* New York: Simon and Schuster, 1986.
Riha, Thomas. *A Russian European: Paul Miliukov in Russian Politics.* Notre Dame, IN: Note Dame University Press, 1989.
Stockdale, Melissa Kirschke. *Paul Miliukov and the Quest for a Liberal Russia, 1880–1918.* New York: Cornell University Press, 1996.

Mine Warfare, Sea

Mine warfare had been employed by the Russians in the Crimean War of 1854–1856 and more extensively by both sides in the American Civil War of 1861–1865. The mass use of sea mines during World War I set new standards in the aims and scope of mine warfare. The general aim of mining in the war was either tactical, to destroy enemy ships, or strategic, to dislocate enemy war efforts and to contribute to the security of friendly sea lines of communications through the destruction or threat of destruction of enemy naval forces. Conversely, the challenge for mine countermeasures lay in allowing friendly warships and merchant vessels to use the seas and enter and leave ports, which was essential to their own war effort and maintenance of the civilian population, without unacceptable damage or losses from mines.

In 1914 only Germany and Russia had thoroughly studied the employment of mines and intended to use them to the fullest extent possible. Both countries had substantial stocks of well-designed material and numerous suitable or purpose-built surface vessels and submarines for mine laying. Japan, Italy, and France were also aware of the potential of the mine, but they lacked adequate numbers of them for large-scale operations. Great Britain was by and large unprepared for modern mine warfare on any scale.

Germany's first naval activities at the start of the war consisted of mine laying. In the last five months of 1914, German minelayers placed with good effect a total of 1,220 mines in the Thames, Tyne, and Humber estuaries; the Firth of Forth; the northwest coast of Ireland; and the approaches to Yarmouth and Scarborough. The most spectacular British mine casualty of these efforts was the new 25,000-ton battleship *Audacious,* which foundered on a minefield laid by the armed merchant cruiser (AMC) *Berlin* on 27 October 1914.

By mid-1915, however, the British Navy had compelled the German navy to abandon the use of auxiliary minelayers

Explosion of an underwater mine, March 1917. (National Archives)

in British waters and instead turn to submarine minelayers. The use of AMCs by the Germans for mine-laying operations continued, however. On 6 January 1916 the British battleship *King Edward VII* sank from mines laid by the outbound German raider *Möwe* north of Scotland, and in 1917 the raider *Wolf*, on a legendary fifteen-month cruise, laid minefields in South African, New Zealand, Indian, and Singaporean waters that claimed over 70,000 tons of allied shipping and damaged another 50,000 tons.

In the Baltic Sea the German mine-laying campaign aimed to bottle up the Russian fleet in the Gulf of Finland to provide flanking cover for the advancing German army there, but this activity was largely preempted by Russian defensive mine-laying activity in the same area. Unable to penetrate the Russian mine defenses, the German campaign in 1915 turned instead against the Russian trade routes in the Gulf of Botnia, where it temporarily interrupted seaborne traffic between Sweden and Russia. German mine-laying operations in the White Sea inflicted serious losses on shipping involved in munitions supply from Britain to Russia. Of even greater strategic value in isolating Russia from its Western Allies was the Turkish barrage in the Dardanelles. Minefields there,

reinforced and improved with German assistance, also claimed the largest single tactical success of the war: on 18 March 1915, following ten days of futile Allied sweeping attempts, the French predreadnought *Bouvet* and the British predreadnoughts *Ocean* and *Irresistible* foundered on a tactical minefield while attempting to force the Dardanelles.

The Russians also lived up to their reputation in the mastery of mine warfare, which they had acquired during the Russo-Japanese War. In July and August 1914, they laid 3,485 mines in defensive fields in the Gulf of Finland (Central Position) and flanking positions for the protection of the Russian coast. The able Russian commander-in-chief of the Baltic Fleet, Admiral Nikolai von Essen, extended the mining campaign along the German coast as far west as Stolpmünde in Pomerania until heavy ice halted general naval activities in February 1915. The Russian campaign severely circumscribed German naval activities in the region and claimed one German armored cruiser, four minesweepers, and fifteen merchantmen between August 1914 and February 1915. The German navy remained unable to penetrate the Russian mine defenses to provide meaningful flanking assistance to the German army until the collapse of Russia and the capture of the Baltic islands Dagö and Ösel in Operation ALBION in October 1917. Even then, difficulties encountered by the superior German naval forces against Russian ships fighting from inaccessible positions behind minefields made ALBION an instructive lesson in the tactical use of minefields as a force multiplier.

The Russian mining campaigns in the Black Sea met with equal success. By persistently mining the northern entrance of the Bosporus throughout 1915 and 1916, the Russian navy effectively reduced the supply of coal to the Ottoman navy and the Mittelmeerdivision (the German Mediterranean Squadron), depriving the latter of much of its strategic leverage during that period of relative Russian naval weakness.

By 1915 it had become clear to the Royal Navy that it too was committed to an extensive mine-laying campaign. As the British increased their stocks of mines, they carried the mine war into the German Bight in the summer of 1915 in an effort to restrict the High Seas Fleet's freedom of movement. The decision was by no means uncontroversial. Many British naval leaders, including commander of the Grand Fleet Admiral Sir John Jellicoe, argued that a mining campaign would also restrict the Grand Fleet's freedom of movement.

At the same time, however, British minesweeping capabilities increased dramatically. Great Britain's minesweeping forces in 1914 had consisted of 82 trawlers of the Trawler Reserve and a handful of fleet sweepers (which were, in fact, old torpedo boats). Faced with the German mine threat, those forces expanded rapidly. The construction of the Flower- and Acadia-class fleet sweepers provided the Grand Fleet with the necessary organic mine countermeasure capability, while smaller paddle-wheel minesweepers and auxiliary vessels swept the home waters. By 1918, the British Minesweeping Service comprised 726 ships of every description.

The focus of British mine-laying operations soon shifted to interdicting the movement of German U-boats. A major effort was thus made to mine the exit routes of the German Flanders U-boat flotilla in April and May 1916. The use of mines in extensive barrage systems, first in the Folkstone-Cape Gris Nez Barrage (Dover Barrage) and later between the Orkney Islands and the southwestern coast of Norway (Northern Barrage), established the mine in a new and quite unforeseen role as the primary antisubmarine weapon of the war. Of a total of 240 submarines lost in the war by Germany, Austria-Hungary, Italy, France, and Great Britain, 68 (38 German) fell victim to mines or mine-nets. The introduction of the more reliable British H.II mine, based on a captured German EM-type, greatly improved the quality of the British mine-laying effort in 1917 and 1918.

A total of 16 German U-boats were lost to mines during the last year of the war alone, but the real effect of the campaign was strategic: the enhancement of the Dover barrage in 1918 compelled U-boats of the High Seas Fleet to take the lengthy northern route around Scotland into the Atlantic, thus decreasing their numbers and the effective patrol times in the areas of operations. The improved Dover Barrage almost completely deprived the small UB-type boats of the Flanders flotilla of their only egress route. The number of monthly U-boat transits through the English Channel declined from 29 in February 1918 to only 5 in June and 9 in July. The last passage by a U-boat of the Flanders flotilla into the Bay of Biscay was made on 14 August 1918 by UB-103, which upon its attempt to return by the same route was sunk by a mine on 16 September.

By the end of the war, the Allies had laid a total of 9,500 mines in the Dover Barrage and 24,739 mines off the Flanders coast. The massive, primarily U.S., effort to close the northern exit of the North Sea was less successful. A total of 71,126 mines were laid in the Northern Barrage between March and October 1918, but only 4 U-boats were definitively lost there, while the number of transits remained relatively constant at 35 outbound passages per month until the last month of the war.

Over the course of the war, the roles in mine warfare at sea had thus been reversed. Of 309,800 mines laid during the war, Great Britain accounted for 129,000, the United States for about 57,600, and Russia for 52,000. Against that figure the German tally of 45,000 mines and Austria-Hungary's 6,000 appear paltry. Nevertheless, German mines accounted for over 1 million tons of Allied merchant shipping sunk during the war. On balance, however, the western Allies had reached a better understanding of the strategic potential of the mine than had the Germans, who were too focused on the tactical aspects of mine warfare.

Dirk Steffen

See also
ALBION, Operation; Antisubmarine Campaign, Allied Powers; Armed Merchant Cruisers; Auxiliary Vessels; Dardanelles Campaign; Dover Barrage; Essen, Nikolai Ottovich von; Jellicoe, John Rushworth, 1st Earl; Mine Warfare and Escort Vessels; Mines, Sea; *Möwe,* SMS; Northern Barrage; U-Boat Operations, U.S. Coastal Waters; *Wolf,* SMS.

References
Cowie, J. S. *Mines, Minelayers and Minelaying.* London: Oxford University Press, 1949.
Ledebur, Gerhard Freiherr von. *Die Seemine* [The Sea Mine]. Munich: J. F. Lehmanns Verlag, 1977.
Tarrant, V. E. *The U-Boat Offensive, 1914–1945.* London: Cassell, 1989.

Mine Warfare and Escort Vessels

The widespread use of mines and submarines in World War I spurred the development of a new type of craft, the escort vessel. Strictly speaking, this was a misnomer because these ships at first did not escort at all; they were employed primarily as minesweepers. Mine warfare and escort vessels of World War I fell into four categories: the submarine chaser, the minesweeper, a larger vessel capable of performing both

German mine-laying U-boat captured by the British. (John Clark Ridpath, *Ridpath's History of the World,* Vol. 10, Jones Bros., Cincinnati, 1921)

tasks and often referred to as sloop or fleet sweeper, and the minelayer.

Submarine chasers were fast, low-freeboard vessels, somewhere between a small destroyer and a very large motor launch operating near the shore, usually in a group, and relying on speed to close with any submarine sighted. The most representative type of this class was the U.S.-built 110-foot subchaser (SC 1-444), of which 331 were completed between 1917 and 1919. Several subchasers were fitted with hull-mounted or towed passive listening gear. Armament usually consisted of a single 3-inch gun and a Y-gun depth charge projector. The Germans built a total of 47 subchasers (Unterseebootszerstörer) between 1916 and 1918. These boats measured 86–90 feet in length and were armed with a single 2-inch gun, two depth charges, and minesweeping gear. Considered inadequate by the Germans, most of them were subsequently converted into motor minesweepers or patrol craft.

Dedicated minesweepers evolved from the relatively small, tuglike Russian Albatross-class (100 tons) of 1910 into the very substantial 950-ton U.S. Bird-class of 1918. The German M-1 type of 1915 represented an effective, inexpensive, and reliable middle-of-the-road solution. These rugged 425-ton boats were powered by commercially available coal-fired triple-expansion engines, which gave them a top speed of 16 knots. Their draft of only 7 feet was characteristically shallow for minesweepers in order to avoid contact mines. The initial armament of 1×8.8cm (3.5-inch) and 1×3.7cm (1.5-inch) guns was later increased to 2×8.8cm guns. Later M-type boats carried up to 3 guns of that calibre or 2×10.5cm (4.1-inch) guns, which, in conjunction with their good speed, increased their survivability and gave them some escort capabilities as well. An unusual approach was the 32 British paddlewheel minesweepers of the Racecourse-class and Improved Racecourse-class, built under the Emergency War Programme. Their paddlewheel arrangement gave them the distinct advantage of a shallow draft of less than 7 feet at a relatively large displacement of over 800 tons.

The Allies additionally employed larger vessels, more seaworthy and capable of escort duties, that often doubled up as fast minesweepers (fleet sweepers). The British 1,200-ton Flower-class sloops were the first British reaction to counter both the U-boat and the mine. The British built 72 of these ships between 1915 and 1916. The Acadia-class and Hunt-class represented similar designs. The British P-boat, on the

German M-Type minesweepers in transit, c. 1918. (Courtesy of Dirk Steffen)

other hand, was a unique type of small utility destroyer, displacing a mere 613 tons. Its principal armament consisted of 2 × 4-inch guns, 2 × 14-inch torpedo tubes, and a depth-charge rack. The success of the early Q-ships led to some Flower-class and P-boats being modified to give them a mercantile silhouette. The 36 French antisubmarine gunboats (Cannonières Contre-Sousmarins) of the Friponne-class and Ardent-class were similar in layout, although considerably smaller at a displacement of only 350 tons. The boats carried depth charges in addition to their 2 × 3.9-inch guns and minesweeping gear.

The purpose-designed minelayer was a rare breed, and very few of them were built before the war, most of them by the Russian navy. The basic design was that of a very large destroyer or of a small, fast (17–20 knots) scout cruiser with a typical displacement of 1,500–4,500 tons. Since speed and a low silhouette were emphasized in the designs, mine capacity was limited compared to the roomier, but slower and more conspicuous, auxiliary minelayers that were converted from short-sea liners. At nearly 3,000 tons displacement, the Russian Amur-type and the slightly smaller German Albatross-class minelayers carried only 240 and 288 mines, respectively.

Dirk Steffen

See also

Antisubmarine Campaign, Allied Powers; Auxiliary Vessels; Mine Warfare, Sea; Mines, Sea; Q-Ships.

References

Gardiner, Robert, ed. *Conway's History of the Ship: The Eclipse of the Big Gun.* London: Conway Maritime, 1992.

Moore, John. *Jane's Fighting Ships of World War I.* London: Random House, 1990.

Mines, Sea

Explosive devices laid in the sea with the intention of damaging or sinking enemy ships or deterring ships from entering that particular area. Mines had been utilized at sea since the mid-nineteenth century. The most widely used type of mine in World War I was the moored contact mine consisting of a spherical or cylindrical mine case, a sinker (an anchor to hold the mine in place), and a mooring rope (or wire) to connect the two and hold the buoyant mine case at a predetermined depth. The Germans and Russians—and later the British—relied mostly on the Herz horn-type firing mechanism (invented in 1866) for their mines. Herz horns were glass tubes encased in metal that snapped if the horn was bent by contact. The released battery electrolyte then activated the firing mechanism.

In 1914 only the German and Russian navies possessed state-of-the-art mine technology. Germany had stocked essentially two types of moored contact mines, which remained in use throughout the war: the EMA with a 331-pound gun-cotton charge and the EMB with a 497-pound TNT charge. Germany also developed and issued antisubmarine mines. The UMC, with a charge weight of 88 pounds, could be deployed in depths of up to 1,300 feet. For laying by UC-type submarines, EM-type mines (frequently referred to as UC-mines) were adapted to that role. Corrosion due to exposure of these mines to sea water during transit, however, impaired the function of the depth-setting and arming mechanisms. The introduction of the UE-type submarine minelayer in 1917 resolved the problem by allowing dry transportation of mines (UE-mines).

In 1917 the T1 and T2 mines were developed for laying from a submarine's torpedo tube or by large torpedo seaplanes.

Russia possessed the largest stock of mines in 1914, ranging from the Herz horn designs M-04 and M-08 to the more innovative M-12, with a charge of 199 pounds of TNT, which used a sensitive inertia weight-firing mechanism suitable only for the tideless conditions of the Baltic. All Russian mines were designed for surface and submarine minelaying. A Herz horn modification of M-12 mine was additionally configured for parachute air-drop. Other innovative features of Russian mine design included the sprocket wheel sweep evader (proposed in 1911 by Royal Navy Assistant Paymaster C. Bucknell) or the 22-pound inshore "Fish Mine" for use against motor boats. Russian mines were generally utterly reliable and easy to operate. North Korea still used stocks of the original M-08 during the Korean War, and Iraq laid licensed copies of the same mine during the First Gulf War in 1980–1988.

The 1905 design of the British Naval Spherical Mine, also known as the Service Mine, was the only domestically developed independent mine available to Great Britain in 1914. Only 1,000 pieces had been produced, and the rest of Britain's small stock of 4,000 mines were chiefly commercially acquired Italian Elia mines, German Herz horn type Carbonit mines, and Swedish oscillating Leon mines. As a stop-gap measure, production of the Spherical Mine and a similar mine derived from the Italian 1901 Elia design was instituted in 1914. Both mines used a combination of a firing lever and a cocked spring-driven striker for the firing mechanism. In 1915 small numbers of S.IV Herz horn type submarine mines were issued for laying from the torpedo tubes of E-Class submarines.

British mines were unreliable and prone to premature detonations until 1917, when the H.II, a spherical Herz horn moored mine based on a captured German EM-type mine, came into service. The H.II carried a 320-pound amatol (a 50/50 mix of TNT and ammonium nitrate) charge. The H.II* antisubmarine modification had a 170-pound charge and a practical depth limit of 250 feet. In August 1918 Great Britain deployed the first ground magnetic mine in the form of the Sinker Mk I (M), a crude concrete device with a 1,000-pound TNT charge. Moored acoustic mines were issued in November 1918 but did not become operational.

The United States was the only other major wartime producer of mines. For deployment in the Northern Barrage, the United States mass-produced the Mk-6 moored antenna mine with a 300-pound TNT or TNX charge. A lower antenna (parallel to the mooring rope and insulated against it) and a 35-foot-long copper antenna suspended above the mine by a tiny float increased the vertical danger space. The potential in the sea water between copper and a steel hull of a submarine in contact with the antenna operated a relay, which fired the mine. France and Italy used a variety of largely prewar contact mines, some employing rather unique hydrostatic firing mechanisms and inertia firing gears.

Japan, with no immediate demand for mines, relied on an obsolete 1904 type electro-mechanical moored mine with an inertia firing gear and a 70-pound charge.

Dirk Steffen

See also
Dover Barrage; Mine Warfare, Sea; Northern Barrage.
References
Cowie, J. S. *Mines, Minelayers and Minelaying.* London: Oxford University Press, 1949.
Ledebur, Gerhard Freiherr von. *Die Seemine* [The Sea Mine]. Munich: J. F. Lehmanns Verlag, 1977.

Minorities Treaties

The territorial settlements at the Paris Peace Conference of 1919 created thirteen states in central and eastern Europe. From Finland in the north to Greece in the south, they included 100 million people. In 1914, 80 percent of this population lived within the former Russian, Austro-Hungarian, and German Empires. Well aware of this situation, the delegates at Paris included within the treaties the defeated powers' provisions to protect the rights of their ethnic, religious, and linguistic minorities. The victorious powers also insisted that the governments of the newly established European states of Czechoslovakia, Greece, Poland, Romania, and the Kingdom of Serbs, Croats and Slovenes (the later Yugoslavia) sign such treaties. Enforcement of the treaties came under the new League of Nations. Member states had the right to bring to the attention of the League Council alleged treaty violations.

The first minority treaty was signed with Poland. It provided that Poland "protect the interests of the inhabitants of Poland who differ from the majority of the population in race, language, or religion." Polish Prime Minister Ignacy Paderewski issued a statement on 16 May 1919 in which he strongly opposed the concept of a minorities treaty that, he pointed out, would impinge on Polish sovereignty. The leaders at Paris ignored his pleas and informed the Polish government that it would be allowed to sign the peace treaty with Germany only when it had accepted its provisions regarding minority rights. Poland had no other choice but to submit,

and on 28 June 1919 it signed a minorities treaty, referring to it as "the Little Versailles Treaty." The treaty consisted of twenty-one articles. Its preamble unequivocally stated that Poland had gained its independence thanks to the military effort of the Allied Powers. The essence of the treaty was expressed in Article 7: "All Polish nationals shall be equal before the law and shall enjoy the same civil and political rights without distinction as to race, language or religion."

The Polish minorities treaty served as a model for the treaties with other states. Provisions regarding the protection of minority rights were also included in peace treaties with Austria, Bulgaria, Hungary, and Turkey. In addition, Albania, Estonia, Latvia, and Lithuania were obliged, on entering the League of Nations, to legislate similar arrangements. As the Allied governments were well aware, the new states born of the war had no choice but to sign such treaties or enact similar legislation. They desperately sought international recognition and ties with the West.

The minorities treaties, while noble in their inception and sparked by liberal impulses, nonetheless helped prolong racial passions and encourage separatism in the states involved. Adolf Hitler capitalized on this in 1938 in the case of Czechoslovakia, and Hitler's insistence that Poland was violating the rights of Germans there became one of the justification for the German invasion that led to World War II.

Łukasz Kamieński

See also
Fourteen Points; Paris Peace Conference; Versailles, Treaty of.
References
Mair, Lucy Philip. *The Protection of Minorities: The Working and Scope of the Minorities Treaties under the League of Nations.* London: Christophers, 1928.
Musgrave, Thomas Duncan. *Self-Determination and National Minorities.* Oxford: Oxford University Press, 2000.

Mišić, Živojin (1855–1921)

Serbian army field marshal. Born on 19 January 1855 at Struganik, Serbia, the thirteenth child of a peasant family, Živojin Mišić was educated at the Serbian Military Academy at Belgrade and served with distinction in the Serbo-Turkish War of 1877–1878 and the Serbo-Bulgarian War of 1885.

From 1898 to 1904 Mišić taught strategy at the Serbian Military Academy. Forced to retire in 1904, he returned to serve on the staff of General Radomir Putnik during the Bosnian annexation crisis of 1908. After commanding the Drina Division in the Balkan Wars of 1912–1913, Mišić was again forced to retire, but he was recalled in July 1914 as Serbian army deputy chief of staff. In the temporary absence of Field Marshal Putnik, Mišić directed the mobilization of the Serbian army and its initial deployment. In November 1914 he was named to command the First Army and was advanced to field marshal for rallying his troops and leading them to victory over the Austrians in the Battle of the Kolubara River in December 1914.

Severely debilitated during the Serbian winter retreat through Albania in November–December 1915, Mišić recuperated in France until September 1916, when he reassumed command of the First Army on the Salonika Front. He led the First Army in the successful fall 1916 Monastir offensive. When aged Field Marshal Putnik could no longer perform his duties, Mišić became the de facto commander of the Serbian army.

Formally appointed army chief of staff in July 1918, Mišić led the Serbs in the Vardar offensive of 1918, soundly defeating the Bulgarians and liberating Serbia. His forces then penetrated deep into Austro-Hungarian territory, thereby facilitating the formation of a South Slav State.

Bold, persistent, and a skilled tactician, Mišić repeatedly rallied his Serbian troops in moments of crisis and led them to victory against great odds. Second only to the great Field Marshal Putnik in modern Serbian military history, Mišić died in Vracar on 20 January 1921.

Charles R. Shrader

See also
Alexander Karageorgević, Prince; Balkan Front; Balkan Wars; Drina River, Battle of the; Jadar River, Battle of the; Kolubara River, Battle of the; Monastir Offensive; Peter I Karageorgević, King; Putnik, Radomir; Salonika Campaign; Serbia, Conquest of; Serbia, Role in War; Vardar Offensive.
References
Falls, Cyril. *History of the Great War: Military Operations: Macedonia*, Vol. 1, *From the Outbreak of War to the Spring of 1917.* London: His Majesty's Stationery office, 1933.
Thomas, Nigel, and Dusan Babac. *Armies in the Balkans, 1914–18.* Oxford, UK: Osprey, 2001.

Mitchell, William (1879–1936)

U.S. Army Air Corps general. Born to American parents in Nice, France, on 29 December 1879, William "Billy" Mitchell attended Columbian College (today a division of George Washington University) until 1898 when he enlisted in the 1st Wisconsin Volunteer Infantry during the Spanish-American War.

U.S. Army Air Service Brigadier General Billy Mitchell. (Library of Congress)

Receiving a commission in the Signal Corps, Mitchell subsequently served in Cuba, the Philippines, and Alaska. In 1903 Mitchell joined an observation balloon unit and, later, the Signal Corps Aeronautics and Flying Section. In 1909 Mitchell graduated from the army's School of the Line and Staff College (Army Staff College), and during 1912–1916 he served on the General Staff.

Major Mitchell learned to fly and briefly directed army aviation. He participated with the 1st Aero Squadron in the 1916–1917 Punitive Expedition into Mexico under Brigadier General John Pershing and then went to France as an observer, arriving there a few days after the United States entered World War I. In France, Mitchell was deeply influenced by air power visionaries such as Major General Hugh Trenchard, commander of the Royal Flying Corps (RFC), a staunch proponent of a separate air arm and the employment of airplanes as offensive weapons.

In early 1918 commander of the American Expeditionary Forces (AEF) General Pershing placed Brigadier General Mason Patrick in overall command of the American Air Service in France, but he gave Colonel Mitchell operational air command. In September 1918 Mitchell planned the air support for the Saint-Mihiel offensive, leading 1,481 aircraft against German air and ground targets with great success. He pioneered mass, large-scale bombing raids. By the end of the war Mitchell was a brigadier general.

After the war Mitchell was assistant chief of the Air Service and campaigned in the press and with Congress for an independent air force modeled after the Royal Air Force. He also published *Our Air Force* (1921) and *Winged Defense* (1925), both designed to sway public opinion. Mitchell demonstrated the potential of air power in a mock attack on New York City and the sinking of the German prize battleship *Ostfriesland*. Mitchell's abrasive approach won him many enemies in the navy and army. Reduced in rank to colonel, Mitchell was transferred to a minor assignment at San Antonio, Texas.

Mitchell refused to curb his public campaign. Following the 1925 crash of the navy airship Shenandoah, Mitchell accused the national defense establishment of "incompetency, criminal negligence, and almost treasonable administration of the national defense." Court-martialed for his comments, Mitchell was convicted of conduct "prejudicial to good order and military discipline" and suspended from duty without pay for five years. He resigned his commission in January 1926. In retirement Mitchell continued to write and publicize his views. He died in New York City on 19 February 1936.

World War II revealed the accuracy of Mitchell's predictions. The noted medium bomber, the North American B-25, was named the Mitchell in his honor. His cherished independent air force became reality in 1947. That July the U.S. Congress voted Mitchell posthumous promotion to major general and awarded him a special Medal of Honor.

William Head

See also
Pershing, John Joseph; Saint-Mihiel Offensive; Trenchard, Hugh Montague, 1st Viscount.

References
Cooke, James J. *Billy Mitchell*. Boulder, CO: Rienner, 2002.

Davis, Burke. *The Billy Mitchell Affair*. New York: Random House, 1967.

Flogel, Raymond R. *United States Air Power Doctrine and the Influence of William Mitchell and Giulio Douhet at the Air Corps Tactical School, 1921–1935*. Norman: University of Oklahoma Press, 1966.

Head, William P. *Every Inch a Soldier: Augustine Warner Robins and the Building of U.S. Air Power*. College Station: Texas A&M University Press, 1995.

Hurley, Alfred F. *Billy Mitchell: Crusader of Air Power*. Bloomington: Indiana University Press, 1982.

Lane, Spencer. *First World Flight: The Odyssey of Billy Mitchell*. Daytona Beach, FL: U.S. Press, 2002.

Mitteleuropa

German for "Middle Europe." Definitions of the term vary greatly, but here it is taken to mean a vague plan by German leaders to enhance national power by securing at least economic hegemony over the nations of central and eastern Europe located between the North and Baltic Seas in the north and the Aegean and Black Seas in the south.

As a result of the punitive peace imposed on France following the Franco-Prussian War of 1870–1871, Germany faced a hostile neighbor to the west. Germany was also not a major naval power, so the path of least resistance for expansion of influence was in Europe and to the east and south. In 1879 Germany had chosen as its chief ally Austria-Hungary, even though this meant that Germany would have to involve itself increasingly in Balkan affairs. In the years before World War I, Kaiser Wilhelm II had sought to expand ties with the Ottoman Empire in order to secure the resources of southern and central Europe as well as Asia Minor.

A few weeks after the beginning of the Great War, Chancellor Theobald von Bethmann Hollweg set forth in the "September Program" the German war objectives. The main theme of this was German economic dominance over central Europe by the creation of a customs union with France, Belgium, the Austro-Hungarian monarchy, Denmark, the Netherlands, and Poland. The program was put aside as German hopes of quick victory faded.

The plan reemerged in the autumn of 1915, following the Central Powers victory over Serbia. Chief of the German General Staff General Erich von Falkenhayn sought to establish a Central-European federation based on a strong German-Austro-Hungarian alliance. Besides economic and political integration, it also called for military cooperation by placing the allied military forces under German command. The Austro-Hungarian monarchy raised objections to the plan, and it was abandoned in 1916. Germany's plans for a Mittleleuropa were certainly realized, at least as far as central Europe was concerned, in the Treaties of Brest Litovsk with Russia in March 1918 and Bucharest with Romania that May. Had Germany been able to defeat the Western Allies in the spring of 1918, it would have dominated all Europe and had under its direct rule or economic control a vast stretch of Middle Europe.

Anna Boros

See also

Bethmann Hollweg, Theobald von; Brest Litovsk, Treaty of; Bucharest, Treaty of; Falkenhayn, Erich von; War Aims; Wilhelm II, Kaiser.

References

Fenyõ, D. Marió. "Része-e Magyarország Mitteleurópának? Magyarország a Harmadik Birodalom életterében" [Is Hungary part of Mitteleurope? Hungary in the lebensraum of the Third Reich]. *Rubicon* (August 1994): 8–11.

Graydon, A. Tunstall. "A Pángermánizmus víziója: Német Mitteleurópa elképzelések az elsõ világháború alatt" [The vision of pan-Germanism: German Mitteleuropa plans during World War II]. *Rubicon* (August 1994): 11–13.

Hardach, Gerd W. *The First World War, 1914–1918.* Trans. Peter and Betty Ross. London: Allen Lane, 1977.

Strachan, Hew. *The First World War,* Vol. 1, *To Arms.* Oxford: Oxford University Press, 2001.

Welch, David. *Germany, Propaganda, and Total War, 1914–1918: The Sins of Omission.* New Brunswick, NJ: Rutgers University Press, 2000.

Moltke, Helmuth von, Count (1848–1916)

German army general and chief of the German General Staff at the outbreak of World War I. Helmuth Johannes Ludwig von Moltke was born to a noble family on 23 May 1848 in Gersdorff, Mecklenburg. Often referred to as "Moltke the Younger," he lived in the shadow of his uncle, Helmuth Karl Bernhard von Moltke (known as "Moltke the Elder"), architect of military victories that led to the creation of modern Germany. Moltke the Younger entered the Prussian army in 1869 as an infantry lieutenant and served during the Franco-Prussian War. In 1882 he was promoted to captain with duty as adjutant to his uncle and later to Kaiser Wilhelm II, where his knowledge of military science was deemed less important than his interest in the arts and occult religions. An "organization man" with the right name, Moltke was promoted to colonel in 1895 and to Generalmajor (brigadier general) in 1899. By 1900 he was a Generalleutnant (major general) commanding the 1st Guards Division, and in 1904 he became quartermaster general to German army chief of staff Alfred von Schlieffen. Upon Schlieffen's retirement in 1906, the kaiser appointed Moltke as his successor. The appointment shocked Moltke, who fully admitted that his personal shortcomings and lack of self-confidence did not suit him for the demands of the position.

Moltke inherited the problem of how to defend Germany simultaneously against two major powers on different fronts. Schlieffen's planning had been designed to meet this challenge by concentrating German resources against France, with only a weak force to hold a slow-moving Russia until France could be defeated. The invasion of France would be carried out through Belgium. Emphasis would be on the right wing, which would sweep up the Channel ports and Paris, then smash the French armies against German Lorraine. Moltke's challenge was to turn what many believe was an academic concept into a viable operational plan that included logistical and political considerations largely ignored by his predecessor.

Moltke's efforts from 1906 to 1914 reflected the changing strategic situation and caused him to modify (or dilute, according to his critics) the original concept. As new units came on line, he changed the ratio of forces between the left and right wings by strengthening the left wing in order to rebuff an anticipated French thrust into Aslace and Lorraine. Whereas Schlieffen planned for fifty-nine divisions north of Metz, Moltke deployed fifty-five; to the south, where Schlieffen had called for nine divisions, he placed twenty-three.

Moltke also decided to respect Dutch neutrality, thereby forcing the two largest flank armies into a constricted area of maneuver that necessitated the capture of Liège to clear their path. Austria-Hungary, moreover, demanded additional troops to face Russia, which had achieved a quicker-than-expected recovery from the Russo-Japanese War. Considering these new conditions, one might argue that Moltke should have scrapped the whole concept rather than implement a compromised version.

As early as 1912 Moltke had argued for a preventive war. He saw a general war as inevitable and believed that it was better to fight before Russia had completed its military expansion and new strategic railway network that would render the Schlieffen Plan meaningless. Recent historians, including Annika Mombauer and David Fromkin, have argued that during the July Crisis of 1914 preceding the outbreak of World War I, Moltke took the lead in pushing for war.

Certainly, just before the outbreak of the Great War, when Kaiser Wilhelm II contemplated fighting only Russia, Moltke did act decisively. He confronted the kaiser and insisted that failure to implement the complex war plan would mean that Germany would be defeated before a shot was fired; it simply could not be done. The kaiser replied, "Your uncle would have given me a different answer."

Moltke's performance during the war clearly validated his own reservations over his abilities in high command. In the early fighting Moltke failed to exercise from his headquarters in Luxembourg effective control over the seven German field armies in the West and one in the East. On 25 August Moltke detached five divisions from the critical right wing and sent them to East Prussia, where the Russians had moved faster than anticipated. These divisions were in transit when the key Battle of Tannenberg occurred.

Moltke then abandoned his usual noninterventionist leadership style and instructed his commanders to push the Allies away from Paris to the southwest, resulting in the pivotal First Battle of the Marne, although Moltke issued no orders whatsoever to his commanders during 5–9 September.

His nerves shattered, Moltke, profoundly depressed, sent a staff officer, Lieutenant Colonel Richard Hentsch, on a liaison mission, probably entrusting him with full authority to make strategic decisions. By 9 September Hentsch had ordered a German withdrawal from the Marne. This maneuver ended all hopes of a rapid German victory in the war.

On 14 September the kaiser removed Moltke from command, replacing him with General Erich von Falkenhayn. Moltke then served as deputy chief of staff. He died of a heart attack in Berlin on 18 June 1916.

Steven J. Rauch

See also
Falkenhayn, Erich von; Hentsch, Richard; Marne, First Battle of the; Schlieffen, Alfred von, Count; Tannenberg, Battle of.

References
Bucholz, Arden. *Motlke, Schlieffen and Prussian War Planning*. Oxford, UK: Berg, 1991.

Craig, Gordon A. *The Politics of the Prussian Army, 1640–1945*. London: Oxford University Press, 1955, 1964.

Framkin, David. *Europe's Last Summer: Who Started the Great War in 1914?* New York: Knopf, 2004.

Görlitz, Walter. *History of the German General Staff, 1657–1945*. New York: Praeger, 1953.

Mombauer, Annika. *Helmuth von Moltke and the Origins of the First World War*. Cambridge and New York: Cambridge University Press, 2001.

Monash, Sir John (1865–1931)

Australian army general. Born in Melbourne on 27 June 1865, John Monash earned a degree in engineering from Melbourne University in 1891. He then pioneered the construction of reinforced concrete bridges in Tasmania and Melbourne. Monash also joined the Australian militia, eventually reaching the rank of colonel. When the Great War began in 1914, Monash joined the Australian Imperial Force (AIF) as a brigadier-general and organized the 4th Infantry Brigade, which he led in the Gallipoli campaign. Monash then commanded the 3rd Australian Division, which he trained and took to France as a major-general. Monash earned a reputation for careful and efficient planning and organization as part of General Sir Herbert Plumer's British Second Army in fighting at Messines and Broodseinde. Monash demanded perfection from his subordinates and replaced several during his tenure.

Monash was present at the Battle of Vimy Ridge to watch the new Canadian tactics and subsequently established contact with the Canadian Corps and its commander after July 1917, Sir Arthur Currie. While the bloody Battle of Passchendaele (Third Ypres) did not enhance Monash's reputation, it did not prevent him from succeeding General Sir William Birdwood as commander of the Australian Corps in June 1918, when he was advanced to lieutenant-general.

Monash's style of command led him to plan regular conferences and meetings with divisional staffs as well as with brigade and battalion commanders. Monash believed that there was nothing worse than indecision. An Australian nationalist, he nonetheless got on well with the British, especially British Expeditionary Force commander Field Marshal Sir Douglas Haig.

Monash's corps was successful at Le Hamel, in the Amiens offensive, and against the Hindenburg Line as part of General Sir Henry Rawlinson's Fourth Army. Monash pioneered the "Peaceful Penetration" tactics in which small groups of soldiers raided German lines and outposts, dominating no-man's-land. Monash also relied heavily on combined arms, incorporating artillery, tanks, machine guns, and aircraft into the infantry assault. Indeed, the Australians may have been the preeminent practitioners of infantry-tank cooperation. The Le Hamel attack has been called the first modern battle because of its integration of infantry, tanks, and aircraft.

Monash argued during the war that scientifically and technically trained civilians were better equipped than regular officers to grasp the potentialities and uses of innovations in warfare. He viewed war as essentially a problem in engineering, and he believed that the conduct of warfare was a "plain business proposition," much like directing a large industrial undertaking. After the war Monash returned to civilian life. He became a strong supporter of the Jewish Lads' Brigade, a youth organization established before the war to integrate Russian and Polish immigrant Jewish boys into British society. In 1921 Monash headed the State Electricity Commission of Victoria, and in 1928 he became president of the Zionist Federation in Australia. Regarded as the finest senior Australian commander of the war, Monash recorded his war experiences in *The Australian Victories in France in 1918* (1920) and *War Letters* (1933). Monash died in Melbourne on 8 October 1931. Monash University in Melbourne is named after him.

Britton W. MacDonald

See also
Amiens Offensive; Australia, Army; Birdwood, Sir William Riddell; Currie, Sir Arthur William; Gallipoli Campaign; Haig, Douglas, 1st Earl; Le Hamel, Battle of; Plumer, Sir Herbert; Rawlinson, Sir Henry Seymour; Ypres, Third Battle of.

References
Andrews, Eric M. *The ANZAC Illusion: Anglo-Australian Relations during World War I*. Cambridge: Cambridge University Press, 1993.

Edwards, C. *John Monash*. Melbourne, Australia: State Electricity Commission of Victoria, 1970.

Monash, John. *The Australian Victories in France in 1918*. New York: Dutton, 1920.

Pederson, Peter A. *Monash as Military Commander*. Carlton, Victoria: Melbourne University Press, 1992.

Serle, Geoffrey. *John Monash: A Biography*. Melbourne, Australia: Melbourne University Press, 1982.

Monastir Offensive
(12 September–11 December 1916)

Autumn 1916 Allied offensive on the Salonika Front. In mid-1916, Allied forces on the Salonika Front under the command of French General Maurice Sarrail numbered some 320,000 men (201 battalions and 1,025 guns) deployed in five sectors on a 160-mile front. The six French and one Italian divisions, plus two Russian brigades, were organized into three corps-sized "Groups of Divisions" commanded by the French General Victor Louis Emilien Cordonnier. The Allied left flank from the Albanian border to Lake Prespa was held by the French 3rd Division Group. The Franco-Russian 2nd Division Group held from Lake Prespa to Gradesnica, while the reconstituted Serbian army (three field armies and a cavalry division) held the central sector from Gradesnica to the Crna River. The Franco-Italian 1st Division Group manned the line from the Crna to the Vardar, and the British Salonika Army (two corps with six divisions) held the right flank from the Vardar to the Strumna.

Facing the Allies were some 172 German, Bulgarian, and Turkish battalions and 900 guns. The Bulgarian First Army (under General Kliment Boyadieff) held the front from Lake Prespa to Mount Duditsa. In the center, the German Eleventh Army (under General Max von Gallwitz) held from the Duditsa mountain to Lake Doiran east of the Vardar River. The Bulgarian Second Army (under General Georgi Stoyanov Todorov) held the Central Powers left facing the British Salonika Army along the Belashitza Mountains and the Strumna River.

General Sarrail planned an offensive for August 1916 in the Monastir-Crna sectors to retake Monastir and turn the Bulgarian fortifications along the Serbo-Greek frontier in the Vardar Valley. However, the Allied offensive was preempted by an attack by the Bulgarian First Army under General Boyadieff. The main Bulgarian attack was launched on 17 August against the Serbs in the western Kenali Valley leading from Monastir to Florina.

Outnumbering the Serbs two to one, the Bulgarians quickly took Florina, the brunt of the attack being borne by the Serbian Third Army. Meanwhile in the East, the Bulgarian Second Army advanced south from Fort Rupel to drive a wedge across Eastern Macedonia, and the Allied forces were pushed back across the Strumna from Seres. On 22 August the Bulgarians attacked west of Lake Ostrovo but were held by the Serbs, and the Bulgarian offensive ended by 1 September. On 26 September General Arnold von Winckler, recently named to command the German Eleventh Army, assumed responsibility for the defense of Monastir from General Boyadieff, who was replaced as commander of the Bulgarian First Army by General Dimitri Ivanov Geshov.

The planned Allied offensive was rescheduled for 5 September. Given the demonstrated German and Bulgarian strength, an attack in the Vardar Valley or from the line of the Strumna River into Eastern Macedonia was out of the question, and General Sarrail thus staked everything on an attack in the West, where the Serbs were eager to retake Monastir and liberate Serbian territory. The offensive was finally launched on 12 September, with the main effort directed against the German and Bulgarian forces between Lake Prespa and the great loop of the Crna River. The Serbian "Drina" Division attacked on 12 September and took Mount Kajmakchalan in the Moglena Mountains by 30 September. The 2nd Division Group (two French divisions and a Russian brigade) attacked on the Bulgarian right flank and, after hard fighting, retook Florina on 2 October. Meanwhile, on the Allied right flank the British XII and XVI Corps conducted secondary operations designed to hold the Bulgarian Second Army in place.

After a brief pause, the Allied offensive resumed on 11 November 1916 with an attack by two Serbian divisions and a regiment of French Zouaves along the Crna River, and on 13 November the Serbs broke through the German positions. The Franco-Russian 2nd Division Group attacked again on 14 November and took Kenalia in blizzard conditions. On 17 November the Allies again moved forward, and on the morning of 19 November French and Serbian cavalry, followed by French and Russian infantry, entered Monastir. Operations were suspended on 11 December.

During three months (12 September–11 December 1916) of hard fighting in difficult mountainous terrain, the Allies had retaken the ground lost to the Bulgarians in August and liberated some 400 square miles of Serbian territory. However, the cost was heavy. Allied casualties, including those in the British sector, were about 50,000 men, the bulk of whom (27,000) were Serbs. German and Bulgarian casualties were even higher: some 61,000 men, including at least 8,000 Germans and 53,000 Bulgarians killed, wounded, or missing.

Charles R. Shrader

See also

Balkan Front; Gallwitz, Max von; Milne, Sir George Francis; Mišić, Živojin; Salonika Campaign; Sarrail, Maurice.

References

Falls, Cyril. *History of the Great War: Military Operations: Macedonia*, Vol. 1, *From the Outbreak of War to the Spring of 1917*. London: HMSO, 1933.

Larcher, Maurice. *La Grande Guerre dans les Balkans: Direction de la Guerre.* Paris: Payot, 1929.

Palmer, Alan. *The Gardeners of Salonika.* New York: Simon and Schuster, 1965.

Thomas, Nigel, and Dusan Babac. *Armies in the Balkans, 1914–18.* Oxford, UK: Osprey, 2001.

Monitors

Specialized shore bombardment warships. These heavily armed and protected ships evolved from John Ericsson's iron-turreted *Monitor* of the American Civil War. During that war, the U.S. Navy laid down some fifty-five monitor-type warships. The British employed monitors for coastal defense but chose to concentrate on the battle fleet rather than rely on coastal defense.

Monitors returned to vogue in World War I with the need for a shallow-draft vessel that could deliver heavy firepower in support of troops ashore. The British produced thirty-five monitors by 1916. These warships had a 10-foot draft, one twin big-gun turret, protection especially against mines and torpedoes, and seagoing capability. They measured about 350 feet long and displaced 5,683–6,900 tons. An antitorpedo bulge developed by British Director of Naval Construction Eustace Tennyson d'Eyncourt was a new protective measure. The monitors were quite slow, with a top speed of between 6 and 7 knots, and fuel consumption was considerable.

Their broad beam and shallow draft made the monitors stable gun platforms, although they maneuvered awkwardly. The large monitors mounted 12-, 14-, or 15-inch guns. They also carried a secondary battery of 12-pounders and 3-inch guns. Because of its tremendous weight the monitor's turret was fitted amidship. In 1918 three monitors—the *General Wolf, Lord Clive,* and *Prince Eugene*—mounted single 18-inch guns taken from HMS *Furious.*

Monitors saw action in the North Sea and the Mediterranean. The *Abercrombie, Havelock, Roberts,* and *Raglan* went to the Dardanelles for the Gallipoli campaign. There they were instrumental in destroying Turkish shore batteries and other targets near the coast. They were also useful as artillery support for troops ashore. After their tour in the Mediterranean, *Havelock* went to Lowestoft and *Roberts* to Yarmouth, where they acted as guardships. In January 1918 *Raglan* and *M.28* were sunk in Kusu Bay, Imbros, by the German battle cruiser *Goeben* (*Sultan Yavuz Selim*) and light cruiser *Breslau* (*Midilli*).

Monitors also played an important role off Belgium. They protected the Allied left flank ashore and shelled German U-boat bases. In addition, monitors helped protect Allied convoys passing through the Dover Straits.

The Royal Navy also built smaller monitors, fourteen of which were half the length of the regular monitors and mounted 9.2-inch guns taken from other ships. These warships had a 6-foot draft and a speed of 12 knots. Another class of small monitors was armed with 6-inch guns taken from the Queen Elizabeth-class battleships. These five ships had a 4-foot draft and could make 10 knots. Smaller monitors were employed in a variety of tasks such as bombardment, patrol, and blockade duties in the Mediterranean, North Sea, and Aegean Sea.

Monitors were also employed in World War II. HMS *Terror*'s 15-inch guns helped defend Malta against possible attack by the Italian navy and also provided shore bombardment to support operations in North Africa. HMS *Erebus* acted as a guard ship at Madagascar and participated in the invasions of Sicily and Normandy. The last of the British monitors were the 15-inch-gun *Roberts* (1941) and *Abercrombie* (1942), which took part in the Normandy invasion.

William L. Padgett

See also
Gallipoli Campaign; *Goeben* and *Breslau,* Escape of.
References
Buxton, Ian L. *Big Gun Monitors: The History of the Design, Construction and Operation of the Royal Navy's Monitors.* Annapolis: Naval Institute Press, 1980.

Paloczi-Horvath, George. *From Monitor to Missile Boat: Coast Defense Ships and Coastal Defense since 1860.* Annapolis: Naval Institute Press, 1996.

Monro, Sir Charles Carmichael (1860–1929)

British army general. Born at sea aboard a passenger vessel bound for England on 15 June 1860, Monro was educated at Sherborne and the Royal Military College, Sandhurst. He joined the 2nd Foot in 1879 and served in the 1897 Mohmand Expedition, the 1897 Tirah Expedition, and the 1899–1902 Boer War. In 1907 he was appointed to command a brigade in Dublin. Monro was promoted to major-general in 1910, and in 1912 he was selected to command a division.

With the outbreak of the war, Monro was transferred to command the 2nd Division in France. He served in the retreat from Mons and the first battles of the Marne, Aisne, and Ypres. On 31 October 1914, Monro narrowly escaped being killed at Hooge Château when a German shell hit the building he was in and killed a number of officers. In December 1914 Monro succeeded Lieutenant-General Sir Douglas Haig in command of I Corps and led the formation at the battles of Aubers Ridge, Festubert, and Givenchy. In July 1915 Monro took command of the newly created Third Army. He was promoted to lieutenant-general in 1915.

In October 1915 Monro replaced General Sir Ian Hamilton in command of the Mediterranean Expeditionary Force. Shortly after he arrived and reviewed the situation, Monro formed the opinion that Gallipoli should be evacuated. Only after Secretary of War Field Marshal Lord Kitchener conducted a personal visit to the front and reported to the British cabinet did Monro receive permission for this move. The evacuation of the peninsula, conducted from December 1915 to January 1916, was accomplished without the loss of a single soldier and minimum loss of equipment and matériel. It stands as one of the most outstanding British operations of the war.

In early 1916 Monro returned to France and took command of the First Army. That October he was promoted to full general and appointed commander-in-chief of India. Although the position was one of immense responsibility, India was not an active military theater. Instead, Monro provided support to the Mesopotamian campaign, directed border operations on the Northwest Frontier, and provided internal security in India.

Created a baron in 1921, Monro was appointed governor and commander-in-chief of Gibraltar in 1923. He retired in 1928 and died in London on 7 December 1929.

Bradley P. Tolppanen

See also

Aisne, First Battle of the; Gallipoli Campaign; Haig, Douglas, 1st Earl; Hamilton, Sir Ian; India, Army; Kitchener, Horatio Herbert, 1st Earl; Marne, First Battle of the; Mons, Battle of; Neuve-Chapelle, Battle of; Ypres, First Battle of.

References

Barrow, George de S. *The Life of General Sir Charles Carmichael Monro, Bart, G.C.B., G.C.S.I, G.C.M.G.* London: Hutchinson, 1931.

Carlyon, Les A. *Gallipoli.* London: Bantam, 2003.

Hickey, Michael. *Gallipoli.* London: Murray, 1995.

James, Robert Rhodes. *Gallipoli: The History of a Noble Blunder.* New York: Macmillan, 1965.

Moorehead, Alan. *Gallipoli.* New York: Harper, 1956.

Mons, Battle of (23–24 August 1914)

First major battle of World War I between British and German forces. Shortly after Britain entered World War I, the British Expeditionary Force (BEF) was dispatched to the Continent. Its size of four infantry divisions and one under-strength cavalry division was laughable by the standards of other major belligerents. Indeed, Kaiser Wilhelm II of Germany referred to it as a "contemptible little army." Later its few survivors would glory in the name of "Old Contemptibles." The BEF was, however, well trained and had seen considerable action in colonial fighting before the war. Mons was its first battle of World War I.

The BEF was formed of two corps. Lieutenant-General Sir Douglas Haig commanded I Corps, and Lieutenant-General Sir Horace Smith-Dorrien commanded II Corps. Major-General Sir Edmund Allenby led the cavalry. BEF commander

Wounded British and Belgium soldiers following the Battle of Mons, August 1914. (Three Lions/Getty Images)

Field Marshal Sir John French had gained his military reputation leading cavalry in the 1899–1902 Boer War. Neither his personality nor his experience stood him in good stead on the Western Front, and problems emerged at Mons.

Secretary of State for War Field Marshal Horatio H. Kitchener had instructed Field Marshal French to cooperate with the French military, although without taking undue risk of losing his force. Accordingly, when it landed on the Continent, the BEF moved northward through Belgium and took up a position on the French left. By 23 August the British II Corps was along the Mons-Condé Canal, and, with a dogleg around the village of Mons, I Corps was angled southwest. The French V Corps, commanded by General Charles Lanrezac, held the BEF's right. French and Lanrezac were soon in contact and as quickly at odds. Although exacerbated by the fact that neither general was fluent in the other's language, the central problem was ego, with each perceiving the other as arrogant and untrustworthy.

Meanwhile, the French high command, Grand Quartier Général (GQG), headed by General Joseph Joffre, believed that the Germans might probe the BEF's position but only with limited forces. Indications that this assessment might be mistaken were ignored. In fact, French intelligence estimates were largely concocted to support the official doctrine of the all-out offensive and drive into Alsace-Lorraine.

The German Schlieffen Plan, however, called for enveloping of the French left, capturing Paris, and smashing the French armies that would turn back from attacking Germany to defend the capital. To achieve this the German right wing had to pass through Belgium. Rather than the light force consisting largely of cavalry that French intelligence predicted, some 200,000 men of General Alexander von Kluck's First Army were about to attack the BEF of perhaps 75,000 men.

Fortunately for the British, the Royal Flying Corps and Allenby's cavalry reported more German troops on the left of the Anglo-French line than the GQG assessment. Field Marshal French declined appeals from the French that he advance, but he did agree to hold his position. The British were also fortunate in that von Kluck did not realize they had moved so far forward. The result was that the initial German blow of 23 August arrived piecemeal, mostly against II Corps.

The fact that the British soldiers were professionals rather than short-term conscripts and reservists was soon clear. Typically for the beginning of the war, the BEF had only two machine guns per battalion, but rapid, aimed British rifle fire was greatly superior to that of other armies. The men could fire fifteen aimed rounds a minute and did so with such effect at Mons that the Germans reported that the BEF was heavily equipped with machine guns. The BEF was also more effectively dug-in than was typical for Continental forces. Helped by valiant artillerymen, the British infantry held through the day. Fighting died down at dark, and the British then fell back to a prepared position south of the canal.

Then word arrived that Lanrezac was falling back, opening the British flank. The BEF had little choice but to retreat as well. It had, if briefly, blocked the Schlieffen Plan. BEF performance at Mons spawned one of the well-known myths of the war. Almost immediately after the battle, it was reported that the British retreat had been covered either by bowmen from Agincourt raised by St. George or a mysterious cloud from which angels rebuked the Germans when they tried to advance. The story of the angels of Mons remains a popular tribute to the efforts of the BEF in its first battle.

Fred R. van Hartesveldt

See also
Allenby, Sir Edmund, 1st Viscount; Great Britain, Air Service; Haig, Douglas, 1st Earl; Joffre, Joseph; Kitchener, Horatio Herbert, 1st Earl; Kluck, Alexander von; French, John, 1st Earl of Ypres; Lanrezac, Charles; Le Cateau, Battle of; Schlieffen Plan; Smith-Dorrien, Sir Horace.

References
Ascoli, David. *The Mons Star: The British Expeditionary Force, 5th Aug.–22nd Nov. 1914.* London: Harrap, 1981.
Cave, Nigel. *Mons.* London: Leo Cooper, 1999.
Clowes, Peter. "Fire Over Mons." *Military History* 18(3) (August 2001): 59–65.

Macdonald, Lyn. *1914: The First Months of Fighting.* London and New York: Atheneum, 1988.

Montecuccoli degli Erri, Rudolf Count (1843–1922)

Austro-Hungarian admiral and commander of the navy during 1904–1912. Born on 22 February 1843 to a prominent noble family in Modena, Rudolf Montecuccoli entered the navy in 1859 on graduation from the Naval Academy at Trieste-Barcala. He saw his first naval action that year and took part in the Austrian naval victory over Italy at Lissa in 1866. He subsequently spent much of his time at sea, including commanding a cruiser squadron dispatched to China in 1900 to assist in quelling the Boxer Rebellion. In 1903 he was appointed to serve as the second-in-command of the navy, succeeding to the top post in 1904.

Concerned about the expansion of the Italian navy, Montecuccoli was determined to build up the Austro-Hungarian fleet so that it could match its Italian rival in the Adriatic and Mediterranean. Montecuccoli proved to be an astute politician, and he was able to muster a number of influential supporters for his cause, including members of the newly formed Austrian Naval League (a pronaval lobbying organization modeled on the highly successful German Naval League) and heir to the throne Archduke Franz Ferdinand. As a result, the naval budget as a percentage of the overall military budget nearly doubled during Montecuccoli's tenure.

Despite the budget increases, Montecuccoli was continually in search of ever more funding for naval expansion. News that Italy had laid down its first dreadnought battleship in the summer of 1909 caused Montecuccoli to accelerate his own plans for building an Austrian dreadnought fleet. Faced with a lengthy delay in receiving funding from the parliament, Montecuccoli resorted to securing loans from private banking concerns to begin dreadnought construction immediately. Although these efforts ultimately led to the launch of four dreadnoughts of the Viribus Unitis-class, Montecuccoli's financial maneuverings caused a scandal, forcing him into retirement in 1912. His successor, Grand Admiral Anton von Haus, led the fleet into war in 1914. Regarded by many as the father of the modern Austro-Hungarian navy, Montecuccoli died at Baden, near Vienna, on 16 May 1922.

John M. Jennings

See also
Austria-Hungary, Navy; Haus, Anton von, Baron.
References
Sondhaus, Lawrence. *The Naval Policy of Austria-Hungary, 1867–1918: Navalism, Industrial Development, and the Politics of Dualism.* West Lafayette IN: Purdue University Press, 1994.

Vego, Milan N. *Austro-Hungarian Naval Policy, 1904–1914*. Portland, OR: Cass, 1996.

Montenegro

The only Allied state to lose its independence in World War I. The small Balkan principality of Montenegro (latinized form of the Serbo-Crotian words *Crna Gora,* which means "Black Mountain") gained its independence from the Ottoman Empire and doubled its territory as a result of the Treaty of Berlin (13 July 1878) following the successful 1876–1877 war against the Turks. Led by Nikola I Petrovic-Njegos (prince during 1860–1910 and king during 1910–1918), Montenegro was modernized in the late nineteenth century and became a small but viable European state. In 1905 Nikola I granted constitutional government with an elected National Assembly. He subsequently led Montenegro in the Balkan Wars of 1912–1913 in which Montenegro again doubled its territory but failed to realize all of its territorial ambitions.

With the outbreak of World War I, King Nikola I of Montenegro supported his son-in-law, King Peter I Karageorgević of Serbia, and tiny Montenegro declared war on Austria-Hungary on 5 August 1914. With a population of just over 436,000 people, Montenegro mobilized some 60,000 troops, who were placed under the command of the Serbian Major General Bozidar Jankovic. General Jankovic deployed the bulk of the Montenegrin army toward Bosnia-Herzegovina and the remainder toward Albania.

The Austro-Hungarian XVI Corps of the Sixth Army invaded Montenegro on 9 October 1914, but the small Montenegrin army, modernized by Nikola I in 1906, fought bravely and repelled the initial Austrian attack. The Montenegrins later covered the retreat of the Serbian army through Albania in November–December 1915 by engaging the Austrians in Eastern Herzegovina and the Sanjak, winning an important victory at Mojkovac on 6–7 January 1916.

Following the Serbian withdrawal, the Montenegrin army fought on against the Central Powers. On 8 January 1916, 50,000 Austrian and Bosnian troops began an offensive against Montenegro, took Mount Lovcen, and forced the Montenegrins back on their capital of Cetinje, which fell on 11 January 1916. On 17 January the Montenegrin army was forced to surrender to Austro-Hungarian forces after having suffered heavy casualties. King Nikola I went into exile in Italy, and some Montenegrin troops escaped to Corfu where they joined the survivors of the Serbian retreat and subsequently served with the Yugoslav Division of the Serbian army on the Salonika Front during 1917–1918.

King Nikola had long clashed with the "Greater Serbia" ambitions of his son-in-law, King Peter I Karageorgević, and Serbian Prime Minister Nicola Pašić. Following the surrender of the Montenegrin army in January 1916, King Nikola compromised his own position by seeking a separate peace with the Central Powers. On 23 October 1918 the Serbian Second Army occupied Montenegro, and on 26 November 1918 King Nikola I was deposed by the Montenegrin National Assembly meeting in Podgorica. Serbia then annexed Montenegro. It became the province of Zeta in the new South Slav Kingdom of the Slovenes, Croats, and Serbs. An unsuccessful uprising of Montenegrin patriots led by Colonel Krsto Popovic began in January 1919 and lasted until 1926.

Charles R. Shrader

See also
Balkan Front; Balkan Wars; Nikola I Petrovic-Njegos, King; Pašić, Nicola; Peter I Karageorgević, King; Serbia, Conquest of; Yugoslavia, Creation of.

References
Thomas, Nigel, and Dusan Babac. *Armies in the Balkans, 1914–18.* Oxford, UK: Osprey, 2001.
Treadway, John D. *The Falcon and the Eagle: Montenegro and Austria-Hungary, 1908–1914.* West Lafayette, IN: Purdue University Press, 1983, 1998.

Morel, Edmund Dene (1873–1924)

British anti-imperialist, peace activist, and member of Parliament. Born in Paris on 15 July 1873, Edmund Morel settled in England after the death of his father in 1877. His mother was a member of the Society of Friends, which influenced the development of Morel's political ideas.

Forced to leave school at age 15 because of family financial difficulties, Morel went to work im Liverpool for the Elder Dempster steamship company. His diligence and bilingualism led to his being appointed to liaise with officials of the Congo Free State, with which Elder Dempster held a trading monopoly. Morel noted the shipment of quantities of arms and munitions but relatively few trade goods to the Congo, certainly in insufficient amount to account for the rubber and ivory secured in return. Morel soon learned that European merchants were forcing Africans to perform unpaid labor. In 1900, he published a series of articles revealing these trade practices, and this cost him his position.

In 1904, Morel founded the Congo Reform Association and took a leading part in the movement against misrule in that Belgian colony. He published pamphlets and went on speaking tours throughout Britain and the United States. In 1909, he took part in the formation of the International League for the Defence of the Natives of the Conventional Basin of the Congo. Morel was also a member of the West African Lands Committee in the Colonial Office during 1912–1914 and vice-president of the Anti-Slavery Society.

An active member of the Liberal Party, Morel became an outspoken critic of British policy in the months leading up to World War I. Morel alleged that the British government had entered into secret agreements with other governments that would tie its hands in the event of hostilities. Soon after Britain entered the conflict, Morel joined Charles Trevelyan, Norman Angell, and Ramsay MacDonald in forming the Union of Democratic Control (UDC) to oppose the war. Morel became UDC secretary and its initial driving force. The UDC's stated objectives were parliamentary control over foreign policy, an end to secret diplomacy, international understanding after the war, self-determination of peoples, and a just peace settlement. Over the next four years the UDC became the most important of antiwar organizations in Britain.

Morel was the dominant figure in the UDC. He also wrote most of its pamphlets published during the war. The *Daily Express* led the campaign against the UDC, and in April 1915 it printed wanted posters of Morel, MacDonald, and Angell, suggesting that the UDC was working for the German government. The police refused to protect UDC speakers, and there were several assaults and physical attacks on Morel. In August 1917, Morel's house was searched and evidence was discovered that he had sent a UDC pamphlet to a friend in Switzerland, technically a violation of the Defence of the Realm Act. This led to Morel's arrest, trial, and sentence of six months at hard labor.

Upon release from prison in 1918, Morel, in poor health, resumed his speaking and writing. He finally left the Liberal Party and, like other UDC colleagues, joined the Labour Party. After the war Morel criticized the Treaty of Versailles and warned that it would lead to another war. In 1922, Morel became the Labour Party candidate at Dundee and, in a vigorous campaign dominated by foreign policy issues, managed to defeat Liberal Party candidate Winston Churchill.

When Morel's UDC colleague Ramsay MacDonald became prime minister in 1924, Morel expected to be named foreign secretary, but MacDonald kept that portfolio himself. Morel did advise MacDonald on foreign policy matters and helped persuade him to recognize the communist government in the Soviet Union. Edmund Morel died in London on 12 November 1924.

Katja Wuestenbecker

See also
Angell (Lane), Sir Ralph Norman; Churchill, Sir Winston; MacDonald, James Ramsay; Union of Democratic Control; Versailles, Treaty of.

References
Bedford, Hastings William Sackville Russell. *Diplomacy and War Guilt: A Tribute to the Vision and Peace Aims of the Late E. D. Morel, MP.* Glasgow, Scotland: Strickland Press, 1945.
Cline, Catherine Ann. *E. D. Morel, 1873–1924: The Strategies of Protest.* Belfast: Blackstaff Press, 1980.

Morhange-Sarrebourg, Battle of
See Lorraine, Invasion of

Morogoro Offensive (5 March–8 September 1916)

Major British offensive in German East Africa named for the town of Morogoro, 115 miles west of Dar-es-Salaam. In November 1915 the British Imperial Committee of Defence recommended that East Africa be conquered "with as little delay as possible." The British government in fact needed a military victory somewhere in the world. Command of the offensive went to General Sir Horace Smith-Dorrien, but he fell ill and was replaced by South African Jan Christian Smuts, commissioned a lieutenant-general (at age 46 the youngest in the British army). Smuts arrived to take up his command at Mombasa on 19 February. The problems confronting him were vast. German East Africa was larger than France and Germany combined, and there were formidable difficulties of terrain, weather, disease, and logistics to be overcome.

Smuts commanded some 27,350 men, along with 71 artillery pieces and 123 machine guns. These included British troops from East Africa and a South African expeditionary force under Major-General Jacob ("Japie") van Deventer of two brigades as well as a battalion of "colored" (mixed-blood) troops. Smuts also had a squadron of the Royal Flying Corps (RFC). After sorting out problems and assessing the situation, Smuts took the offensive almost immediately, on 5 March 1916. By mid-March Smuts had secured the towns in the north in the Kilimanjaro area as well as the railway terminus at Moshi, taken on 13 March. On the 18th Smuts began to advance down the Usambara railway to Kahle. Smuts repeatedly attempted to envelop the German defenders, but each time they eluded him, inflicting small defeats at times and places of their own choosing and then quickly withdrawing. Lettow-Vorbeck intended to inflict the maximum number of casualties on the attackers while minimizing his own casualties. The British were also inhibited by a lack of knowledge of the area in which they were campaigning, and casualties mounted from disease.

All of Smuts's efforts to surround German Colonel Paul von Lettow-Vorbeck's main force failed. The British believed that he would fight for the major cities and railways, enabling them to defeat him, but he refused. As they withdrew, the Germans took everything of possible use and destroyed what was left, including all bridges. Lettow-Vorbeck's aim was to draw the British deeper into the vast German territory and tie down as many of their troops as possible so that they might not be sent to more strategically important theaters of war. At least

Smuts was measuring his progress in miles rather than the yards of the Western Front. Heavy rains and disease then forced Smuts to regroup.

The offensive resumed in April. Smuts led a column east along the Usambara line while another column under Deventer drove south to the Central Railway. At the same time, smaller Allied attacks occurred from Northern Rhodesia (Zambia), the Belgian Congo (Zaïre), and Mozambique (Portugal had declared war on Germany on 9 March).

After losing half his 4,000-man force to sickness, Deventer came under German attack on 9–10 May, forcing him to halt at Kandoa Irangi until late June. Meanwhile, Smuts marched east in late May and took Amani before heading south toward Morogoro on the Central Railway. Meanwhile, 500 Indian troops under Smuts's command captured the railway terminus of Tanga on 7 July and Bagamoyo on 15 August 1916.

The Allied columns reached the Central Railway in late August. As German troops retreated, Smuts's men occupied Morogoro on 26 August, although the Germans had carried off or destroyed anything of military value. The next day the British 1st and 2nd Divisions linked up on the rail line 12 miles east of Kilosa. Dar-es-Salaam fell on 4 September, taken by the Royal Navy, which discovered there 450 unarmed Germans and four wrecked steamers. British supplies were soon moving through the port.

Smuts's advance came to a halt in fighting at Kisaki on the Mgeta River some 125 miles south on 7–8 September, when 2,600 Germans defeated 1,700 South Africans. Smuts then returned to Dar-es-Salaam. By 6 October the Allies controlled the entire Central Railway. German forces under Colonel Paul von Lettow-Vorbeck had been driven back into the southeastern corner of the colony. Although Allied public opinion considered the long struggle for East Africa at an end with control of the Central Railway and the Allied capture of Tabora on 19 September, Lettow-Vorbeck's troops remained very much at large, able to strike the occupying Allied troops at will. He still had 1,100 European troops along with 7,300 askaris, sixteen field guns, four 105mm guns from the German cruiser *Königsberg,* and seventy-three machine guns. The force was small but well trained and fit, and Lettow-Vorbeck had no intention of surrendering. Indeed, fighting continued in East Africa until November 1918. It has been estimated that overall in the fighting in German East Africa, Lettow-Vorbeck tied down more than 130,000 Allied troops, preventing their use on the Western Front.

Spencer C. Tucker

See also
Africa, Campaigns in; Lettow-Vorbeck, Paul Emil von; Smuts, Jan Christian; Tabora Offensive.

References
Farwell, Byron. *The Great War in Africa, 1914–1918.* New York: Norton, 1986.
Hordern, Charles. *History of the Great War: Military Operations, East Africa,* Vol. 1, *August 1914–September 1916.* London: HMSO, 1941.
Miller, Charles. *Battle for the Bundu: The First World War in East Africa.* New York: Macmillan, 1974.
Morrow, John H., Jr. *The Great War in the Air: Military Aviation from 1909 to 1921.* Smithsonian History of Aviation Series. Washington, DC: Smithsonian Institution Press, 1993.

Mortars

Mortars constitute one of the three primary technological categories of artillery weapons. Guns fire projectiles at high muzzle velocities, flat trajectories, and at low angles of fire, that is, the angle of the gun's tube is 45 degrees or less in relation to the ground. Mortars only fire at high angles—45 degrees and greater—and at much lower muzzle velocities and shorter ranges than guns. The howitzer combines the best characteristics of both the gun and the mortar. It can fire at both high and low angles, and it fires at lower muzzle velocities than the gun but much higher than the mortar. The howitzer's range is somewhat less than the gun but far greater than the mortar. Because of the flexibility of the howitzer, the mortar was all but obsolete by the start of the twentieth century.

With the advent of trench warfare in World War I, the mortar came back into its own. Since it fired only at high angles and all its recoil was directed into the ground, the mortar did not need the elaborate recoil mechanisms of guns and howitzers. Being more compact, it could fire from small and restricted positions. Since it fired at high angles, it could fire from directly behind defensive emplacements, and the projectile's angle of fall meant that it would drop on the target from almost straight above. The mortar was the ideal weapon for heavy firepower in the forward trenches.

Throughout the course of the war both sides built up large trench mortar organizations. In some armies these so-called trench artillery units were part of the artillery; in some they were part of the infantry; and in the German army they were part of the pioneers (combat engineers). Since World War I, mortars have been considered infantry weapons almost universally.

The categories of German mortars often cause confusion. The German term *Mörser* is translated literally as "mortar," but a German Mörser of World War I was actually a heavy howitzer, usually larger than 210mm. The German World War I term for a trench mortar was *Minenwerfer* (mine launcher). By World War II, however, the Germans changed the term for an infantry mortar to *Granatenwerfer* (grenade launcher).

Throughout most of World War I mortars bore little resemblance to the modern mortars of today, until the British later in the war introduced the Stokes Mortar. It was the forerunner of all modern muzzle-loading, gravity-fed, light-

Australian soldiers preparing to fire a trench mortar against the German lines, near Villers-Bretonneux, France, on 10 July 1918. (Australian War Memorial E02677)

weight, "stovepipe-type" infantry mortars. Most World War I mortars were breach-loading weapons and were much larger and heavier than modern infantry mortars.

German light trench mortars weighed up to 300 pounds and fired a 76mm round to a range of 1,400 yards. The crew of six could fire up to forty-four rounds per minute. German medium trench mortars weighed up to 1,100 pounds but fired a 170mm round to only 1,240 yards. The crew of twenty-one could fire only thirty-five rounds per hour. The German heavy trench mortars weighed up to 1,500 pounds and fired a huge 250mm round to only 1,070 yards—in some cases, not even far enough to get across no-man's-land. Its twenty-eight-man crew could fire only twenty rounds per hour.

Mortars were effective defensive weapons. Because of their short range and relative immobility, the medium and heavy mortars were of little value in supporting an attack once the infantry started moving forward. Light mortars, however, could be fitted with wheels and manhandled forward by their crews to support the advancing infantry. The main drawback was that the ammunition also had to be carried forward on the backs of men.

David T. Zabecki

See also

Artillery; Infantry Tactics; Trench Warfare.

References

Bailey, J. B. A. *Field Artillery and Firepower.* 2nd ed. Annapolis: Naval Institute Press, 2003.

Hogg, Ian V. *The Guns, 1914–1918.* New York: Ballantine, 1971.

———. *The Illustrated Encyclopedia of Artillery.* London: Quarto, 1987.

Zabecki, David T. *Steel Wind: Colonel Georg Bruchmüller and the Birth of Modern Artillery.* Westport, CT: Praeger, 1994.

Motono Ichiro (1862–1918)

Japanese ambassador. Born in Saga province, Japan, on 23 February 1862, Motono Ichiro studied at the universities of Paris and Lyon and joined the Japanese Foreign Ministry in May 1890. Beginning in December 1901, he was minister to France. He served in that post until January 1906, when he became minister to Russia.

In this position Motono played an important role in restoring relations with Russia following the Russo-Japanese War of 1904–1905. For his accomplishments in this regard,

Motono was made a baron in September 1907. When the Japanese diplomatic mission in Russia was upgraded to an embassy in May 1908, Motono became the ambassador. Motono believed in Russo-Japanese cooperation and helped negotiate four understandings with Russia in the period 1907–1916 concerning the Far East. His accomplishments resulted in his being made a viscount in 1916.

Motono ascended to the apex of Japan's foreign policy apparatus when he was appointed foreign minister in the cabinet of Terauchi Masatake in November 1916. Since Terauchi lacked a strong political base in the Parliament, he established the Emergency Foreign Affairs Research Council in June 1917 to garner support from party politicians including Seiyukai President Hara Takashi. Motono became the inaugural member of the council, which was virtually the top government organ for coordinating foreign and military policies during World War I. Although Motono was a capable diplomat, his standing in domestic politics was tenuous, and this tended to undermine his effectiveness as foreign minister.

Following the Bolshevik seizure of power in Russia in November 1917, Motono, no doubt motivated by his emotional attachment to imperial Russia, supported a proposal to dispatch Japanese troops to Siberia. Encountering skepticism on the part of Hara and others, Motono resigned as foreign minister in April 1918. He died in Tokyo on 17 September of that year, only a month and a half after Japan announced its participation in the Siberian Expedition.

Kurosawa Fumitaka

See also
Hara Takashi; Siberian Intervention, Japan; Tanaka Giichi.
References
Nish, Ian. *Alliance in Decline*. London: Athlone, 1972.
Van der Oye, David Schmmelpenninck. *Toward the Rising Sun: Russian Ideologies of Empire and the Path toward War with Japan*. DeKalb: Northern Illinois University Press, 2001.

Mountbatten, Louis Alexander (1854–1921)

British admiral of the fleet. Born in Graz, Austria, on 24 May 1854, Prince Louis von Battenberg was the son of Prince Alexander of Hesse and Countess Julie Hauke. Tutors prepared him for entry into the British navy in 1868, allowing him to be naturalized as a British citizen, and he enjoyed a lifelong friendship with future King Edward VII. Battenberg pursued a career in the Royal Navy and held a variety of commands. He also invented the Battenberg Compass, which was later used in naval gunnery.

Battenberg married Victoria of Hesse, a granddaughter of Queen Victoria and sister of the future Empress Alexandra of Russia. They had four children: Alice, who married Prince

British Admiral Lord Louis Mountbatten, First Sea Lord at the beginning of World War I. (Getty Images)

Andrew of Greece and was mother of Prince Philip, Duke of Edinburgh (husband of Queen Elizabeth II); Louise, who married King Gustav of Sweden; George, the 2nd Marquess of Milford Haven; and Louis, who became Earl Mountbatten of Burma.

In 1899 Battenberg was appointed assistant director of Naval Intelligence and then was director from 1902 until 1905, making significant improvements in Naval Intelligence activities. Promoted to rear admiral in 1904, he commanded the 2nd Cruiser Squadron during 1905–1907. Promoted to vice-admiral, during February–August 1907 he was second-in-command, Mediterranean Station, then commander-in-chief, Atlantic Fleet, during 1907–1910. In 1911 Battenberg commanded the 3rd and 4th Divisions, Home Fleet. Known as a naval reformer, Battenberg advocated improvements in living conditions for seamen as well as the institution of a modern staff system.

Battenberg became first sea lord in December 1912, where he worked to improve fleet readiness and also acted as a buffer against First Lord of the Admiralty Winston Churchill, who had no naval experience. Both men advocated the use of aircraft at sea.

Churchill and Battenberg had the fleet ready for hostilities at the outbreak of war, and under Battenberg the British Expeditionary Force (BEF) was transported to France without loss, a blockade of Germany was implemented, and three German cruisers were sunk. There were also setbacks for Britain at sea. The German battle cruiser *Goeben* and light cruiser *Breslau* reached Turkish waters; German submarines sank three British cruisers in one day; and Germany scored a clear victory in the Battle of Coronel. Invasion hysteria swept Britain, and the Admiralty came under criticism in the press. The final blow to Battenberg's prestige occurred on 27 October 1914, when the dreadnought *Audacious* was sunk by a German mine.

On 28 October 1914, Prime Minister Herbert Asquith asked for Battenberg's resignation, which he tendered. He spent the remainder of the war as a member of the King's Privy Council. In 1917 he anglicized the name of Battenberg to Mountbatten and became marquess of Milford Haven to protect his family from anti-German bias. Mountbatten retired from the navy in 1919 and died in London on 11 September 1921.

Annette Richardson

See also
Aboukir, Cressy, and *Hogue,* Sinking of; Asquith, Herbert Henry, 1st Earl; Churchill, Sir Winston; Coronel, Battle of; *Goeben* and *Breslau,* Escape of; Great Britain, Navy.

References
Hatch, Alden. *The Mountbattens: The Last Royal Success Story.* New York: Random House, 1965.
Kerr, Mark. *Prince Louis of Battenberg.* London: Longmans, Green, 1934.
Ziegler, Philip. *Mountbatten: The Official Biography.* London: Collins, 1985.

Möwe, SMS

German commerce raider, the most successful of the war. The Germans were concerned about the ease with which Allied shipping steamed across the Atlantic and the possibility that the United States would enter the war if numbers of noncombatants were lost when their ships were sent to the bottom by German submarines. The answer was to send a number of commerce raiders to sea to attack enemy shipping as did the U-boats, but to do so in accordance with the Declaration of London of 1909 by rescuing survivors.

The *Möwe* (Seagull) began its life as the *Pungo,* launched in 1914. Built to haul bananas for a private firm, it had a sturdier construction and faster speed than most cargo ships. Commissioned in November 1915, it displaced 4,788 tons and was 405'10" in length. Slower, at 13.3 knots, than most auxiliary cruisers, the *Möwe* would rely on stealth. False plating that

would swing away masked its 4 × 150mm (5.9-inch) deck guns. Aft, camouflaged to resemble an emergency steering apparatus, it mounted a 105mm (4.1-inch) gun that could fire through a 180-degree field. The refitting at Wilhelmshaven also added two torpedo tubes. The *Möwe* had a range of 8,700 nautical miles at 12 knots. The ship's appearance would be varied as much as possible by new paint every few weeks.

The *Möwe,* masquerading as a tramp steamer, set sail from Kiel for the British base on Scapa Flow on 29 December 1915. Korvettecapitän Nikolaus Graf und Burggraf zu Dohna-Schlodien had command with orders to lay all 500 mines aboard before pursuing enemy ships. One of these mines sank the British battleship *King Edward VII* off Cape Wrath on 6 January 1916. Another batch of the mines claimed two more ships off the mouth of the Gironde River in France.

The *Möwe* then began to prey on shipping, using the ruse of flying the British merchant flag. Before returning home on 4 March, the *Möwe* took fifteen ships totaling 57,520 tons, claiming one as a prize and sinking the others. No passengers or enemy crewmen were harmed. It then served briefly in the Baltic as a commerce raider, taking one ship of 3,326 tons.

On its second Atlantic voyage, from 22 November 1916 to 22 March 1917, the *Möwe* took twenty-five ships, totaling 125,265 tons. But on 10 March the *Möwe* encountered the British cruiser *Otaki.* In the ensuing engagement, several of the crew on the German commerce raider were killed, but the *Möwe* escaped.

The *Möwe* then served as the auxiliary mining vessel *Ostee.* Following the war it was given to Britain as war reparations but was sold back to Germany in 1933 and renamed the *Oldenbourg.* On 7 April 1945 it was attacked by Allied aircraft and grounded in Norway. The ship was broken up in 1953 as a hazard to navigation.

Caryn E. Neumann

See also
Auxiliary Vessels; Germany, Navy; Mine Warfare, Sea; Mines, Sea; Naval Warfare.

References
Chatterton, E. Keble. *The Sea-Raiders.* London: Hurst and Blackett, 1931.
Hoyt, Edwin P. *The Phantom Raider.* New York: Crowell, 1969.
Walter, John. *The Kaiser's Pirates: German Surface Raiders in World War One.* Annapolis: Naval Institute Press, 1994.

Mulhouse, Battles of (August 1914)

Battles between French and German forces during the French offensive into Alsace at the beginning of World War I. Recapture of the provinces of Alsace and Lorraine had been the dream of every French officer since their loss to Germany in 1871. France's War Plan XVII reflected this goal. The French planned their major effort for Lorraine. The rugged Vosges Mountains separated their south thrust, which was to be by the Belfort gap into the Sundgau area and thence to Colmar. Mulhouse (Mülhausen), capital of Sundgau, was only 3 miles west of the Rhine.

French army commander General Joseph Joffre sought a quick victory in Alsace but planned to accomplish this with only one provisional corps of 20,000 men under General of Division Bonneau, consisting of the 14th and 41st Infantry Divisions and the 8th Cavalry Division. Bonneau was given no clear military objectives and simply ordered to press home the attack relentlessly.

The Germans had only second-line Landwehr troops defending Alsace. The Seventh Army, commanded by Generaloberst (equiv. to U.S. full general) Josias von Heeringen, was to prevent any serious French advance toward the Rhine but was authorized to withdraw and even to regroup on the right bank of the Rhine if necessary. The Germans had erected numerous defensive positions and were completely familiar with the area. Von Heeringen intended to let the French attack deep into Sundgau before counterattacking with reinforcements.

On 2 August a German cavalry patrol crossed the French border to reconnoiter the Belfort Road. Near the small village of Delle, the patrol charged French sentries from the 44th Infantry Regiment. During the resulting fight the French suffered their first dead soldier of the war, André Peugeot, while the Germans lost their first officer, Camille Mayer.

Following several days of skirmishing Bonneau's corps crossed the frontier into Alsace on the morning of 7 August. The French quickly took the town of Altkirch. German resistance was light, but Bonneau suspected a trap and ordered a halt. Joffre was so angry that Bonneau, under protest, ordered the advance resumed the next day. On 8 August Mulhouse fell to the French 14th Infantry Division, the citizens cheering the French as liberators.

That same day German reserves, the XIV and XV Corps from Strasbourg, moved into position supported by the XIV Reserve Corps on the right bank of the Rhine. Bonneau's force was soon in danger of envelopment. The German attack on 9 August failed because of the strength of French defensive positions and because the Germans did not have their heavy artillery, which could outrange the French 75mm guns. Bonneau decided to retire to the French border that night, abandoning Mulhouse and its Francophile inhabitants. Bonneau's withdrawal was skillfully executed and saved the French from being crushed by overwhelming German strength. Joffre, however, was furious and dismissed Bonneau.

The French then formed a new force of two army corps and an independent mountain troops brigade—115,000 men under General Paul Pau—to retake Mulhouse. Von Heeringen had dispatched his two corps to the north along the Vos-ges Mountains to strengthen the Bavarian Sixth Army's left in Lorraine and had only his XIV Reserve Corps to defend Sundgau. Pau, a retired general at the beginning of the war, moved cautiously. On 14 August the French took the passes above Colmar and Mulhouse. Then, after having secured his positions, Pau resumed his offensive in Sundgau. On 18 August the French again fought in the Mulhouse area, taking twenty-four guns in a bayonet charge.

On 19 August Mulhouse was again in French hands. Unfortunately for the French, with the defeat at Mohrange and Sarrebourg, they were forced to shorten their front and Pau had to retire southward. The Germans retook Mulhouse on 24 August. The city would not welcome the French again until 17 November 1918.

Gilles Boué

See also

Alsace and Lorraine; France, War Plan XVII; Joffre, Joseph; Pau, Paul; Schlieffen Plan.

References

Barres, Maurice. *Chroniques de la Grande Guerre.* Vol. 1. Paris: Lavauzelle, 1915.

Clayton, Anthony. *Paths of Glory: The French Army, 1914–18.* London: Cassell, 2003.

Guichard, Louis. *Guide illustré Michelin: Colmar, Mulhouse et Schleschstadt.* Clermont Ferrand: Michelin édition, 1919.

Keegan, John. *Opening Moves: August 1914.* New York: Ballantine, 1971.

Ministère de la Guerre, État-Major de l'Armeé Service Historique. *Les Armées françaises dans la Grande Guerre.* Vol. 1. Paris: Imprimerie nationale, 1922.

Tuchman, Barbara W. *The Guns of August.* New York: Macmillan, 1962.

Müller, Georg Alexander von (1854–1940)

German navy admiral. Born on 24 March 1854 in Chemnitz, Georg von Müller entered the navy in 1871. In 1895 he was appointed adjutant to Prince Heinrich of Prussia, brother of Kaiser Wilhelm II, and in 1897 he was appointed to the post of commander of the 2nd Division of the 1st Squadron. When Prince Heinrich was appointed chief of the East Asian Cruiser Squadron in 1899, Müller became his chief of staff. In 1900 he was appointed to the Naval Cabinet with direction of officer personnel. In 1904 he was appointed adjutant to Wilhelm II and in 1905 to the honorary position of admiral à la suite in the imperial retinue. In July 1906 Müller became chief of the Naval Cabinet.

In this position Müller laid great emphasis on maintaining good relations with Britain. Working against this was his close association with Naval Secretary Alfred von Tirpitz from the time he first served with him in a torpedo unit in

Along with Jagow, Müller saw no strategic imperative for a battleship clash, always aware of diplomatic and political requirements in which the navy might be lost as a political lever. He was also opposed to Tirpitz's policy of unrestricted naval warfare, well aware of the effect such a policy would have upon neutrals. This view in particular fostered enmity in his former mentor Tirpitz, although he retained the support of the kaiser himself.

The increasing power of the Third Supreme Command dominated by Field Marshal Paul von Hindenburg and General Erich Ludendorff led to Müller's marginalization. He tendered his resignation in January 1918, but this was rejected by Wilhelm II. Müller was formally retired upon Admiral Reinhard Scheer's appointment as chief of the Naval Staff in August 1918. Müller's important war diaries were subsequently translated and published in English. He died in Hagelsberg on 18 April 1940.

Peter Overlack

See also

Heinrich, Prince of Prussia; Hindenburg, Paul von; Jagow, Golltieb von; Ludendorff, Erich; Scheer, Reinhard; Tirpitz, Alfred von; Wilhelm II, Kaiser.

References

Herwig, Holger H. *"Luxury" Fleet: The Imperial German Navy, 1888–1918*. London: Allen and Unwin, 1980.
Hildebrand, Hans, and Ernest Henriot. *Deutschlands Admirale, 1849–1945*. 3 vols. Osnabrück: Biblio Verlag, 1988–1990.
Müller, Georg von. *The Kaiser and His Court: The Diaries, Note Books and Letters of Admiral Georg Alexander von Müller, Chief of the Naval Cabinet, 1914–1918*. Ed. Walter Görlitz. New York: Harcourt, Brace and World, 1964.
Röhl, John G. C. "Admiral von Müller and the Approach of War, 1911–1914." *Historical Journal* 12(4) (1969): 651–673.

Australian newspaperman Keith Murdoch, Gallipoli Peninsula, September 1915 (*Australian War Memorial* G01212)

1879. Müller then became an avid supporter of Tirpitz's battleship expansion program. His position as chief of the Naval Cabinet gave Müller an unusual degree of influence over naval policy, since all naval documents had to pass through his hands before reaching Wilhelm II. His opponents saw him as a negative influence associated with the cautious Foreign Secretary Gottlieb von Jagow.

With the commencement of war in 1914, Müller shared the Kaiser's disinclination to risk the High Seas Fleet in action against the Royal Navy. Müller's task was to advise Wilhelm II of the wartime realities and the capabilities of the navy, but the longer this inactivity lasted, the more his competency was questioned within the navy. Müller wanted to hold naval warfare within manageable bounds and declined an aggressive policy merely to justify the navy's existence and maintain its honor as a large section of the officer corps demanded.

Murdoch, Sir Keith Arthur (1885–1952)

Australian war correspondent who became a powerful newspaper magnate. Born on 12 August 1805 in Melbourne, Keith Murdoch studied at the London School of Economics and then began a career in journalism with the Melbourne Age. In 1907 Murdoch left Australia for London, returning three years later. In 1915 he was once more dispatched to London as managing editor of the United Cable Service of the *Sun* and the *Melbourne Herald*.

In late August 1915 Murdoch received permission from Lieutenant General Sir William Birdwood to visit Gallipoli for four days. This was ostensibly only to investigate alleged mismanagement of mail sent to Australian soldiers serving in the campaign. Once there Murdoch expressed concern not only at what he perceived to be the bungling mismanagement of the campaign—a charge levied against the commander General Sir Ian Hamilton—but also at the manner in which Allied press reports were rigorously censored so that little criticism reached Britain.

Murdoch composed an 8,000-word letter to Australian Prime Minister Andrew Fisher, which he sent on 23 September. Fisher was already dissatisfied with the British organization of the Australian forces, particularly operations in Gallipoli that were resulting in heavy losses. Murdoch praised Australians lavishly, but he strongly criticized the British army at all levels. Although containing some errors and exaggerations, this account provided ammunition for the anti-Dardanelles faction in London. Murdoch was supported by press baron Lord Northcliffe, backing that helped not only to bring about Hamilton's recall from Gallipoli on 17 October but also to bring the campaign to its ignominious close. Murdoch's exposure of British mismanagement also contributed to the Light Horse (the Australian cavalry units) being reformed, these troops having been detoured to Gallipoli.

Following the war, Murdoch concentrated on consolidating and expanding his newspaper interests to include radio stations. He consistently supported conservative politicians and was a confidant of British press magnate Lord Northcliffe, who assisted his endeavors. Known as a supporter of the arts, Murdoch became a noted art collector in his own right. Knighted in 1933 (in 1919 he had refused the honor from Prime Minister David Lloyd George), Murdoch subsequently served as Australian director-general of information during June–December 1940 and formed a U.S. section of this department to try to promote U.S. entry into the war. Murdoch died at Cruden Farm outside Melbourne on 5 October 1952. His son Rupert became an even more prominent international media magnate.

Peter Overlack

See also
Anzac; Australia, Army; Australia, Role in War; Birdwood, Sir William Riddell; Fisher, Andrew; Gallipoli Campaign; Hamilton, Sir Ian; Lloyd George, David; Monash, Sir John.

References
Liddle, Peter H. *Gallipoli 1915: Pens, Pencils, and Cameras at War.* Washington, DC: Brassey's, 1985.

Serle, G. "Sir Keith Murdoch." In *Australian Dictionary of Biography,* ed. B. Nairn and G. Serle, 10:622–627. Melbourne, Australia: Melbourne University Press, 1986.

Williams, John F. *ANZACs, the Media, and the Great War.* Sydney, Australia: University of New South Wales Press, 1999.

Zwar, Desmond. *In Search of Keith Murdoch.* South Melbourne, Australia: Macmillan, 1980.

Murray, Sir Archibald James (1860–1945)

British army general. Born on 21 April 1860 at Woodhouse, Hampshire, Archibald Murray was educated at Cheltenham and the Royal Military College, Sandhurst. He joined the 27th Foot in 1879 and served in the 1888 Zululand campaign and the 1899–1902 Boer War. Murray was promoted to major-general in 1910 and appointed inspector of infantry in 1912. In early 1914 he was selected to command the 2nd Division.

Upon the mobilization of the British Expeditionary Force (BEF) at the beginning of World War I, Murray was appointed chief of the General Staff to BEF commander General Sir John French. He served in the Battle of Mons and the retreat as well as at the Marne and the Aisne and in First Ypres. However, Murray's health could not withstand the tremendous stress involved in this post. On two occasions during the retreat from Mons, he fainted and collapsed. By January 1915 Murray had lost the confidence of French, who replaced him with Major-General Sir William Robertson. Murray, however, retained the confidence of Secretary of State for War Field Marshal Lord Kitchener, who appointed him deputy chief of the General Staff in February 1915 and chief of the Imperial General Staff in September 1915. Murray was promoted to lieutenant-general in October 1915. His brief tenure as chief of the Imperial General Staff ended in December 1915 when he was dismissed by Prime Minister Sir Herbert Asquith, who considered Murray too weak to stand up to Kitchener, and he was once again replaced by General Robertson.

In January 1916 Murray was appointed commander of the Egyptian Expeditionary Force. Soon after his arrival in Egypt, his command was weakened by the transfer of several divisions to other theaters. Murray, however, defeated a Turkish attack on the Suez Canal at Romani in August 1916. Late in the year Murray received permission to take the offensive on the Palestinian Front. The British soon cleared the Turkish forces from Rafah and Magheba and closed up the Palestine border. However, Murray's attempts to invade Palestine were defeated at the First Battle of Gaza in March 1917 and at the Second Battle of Gaza a month later. These failures cost Murray his command, and he was replaced by Lieutenant-General Sir Edmund Allenby in June 1917.

Murray was appointed to lead Aldershot Command in Britain in 1917 and was promoted to full general in 1919. He retired in 1922 and died at Makepeace, Reigate, on 23 January 1945.

Bradley P. Tolppanen

See also
Aisne, First Battle of the; Allenby, Sir Edmund, 1st Viscount; Asquith, Herbert Henry, 1st Earl; French, John, 1st Earl of Ypres; Gaza, First Battle of; Gaza, Second Battle of; Kitchener, Horatio Herbert, 1st Earl; Marne, First Battle of the; Mons, Battle of; Palestine and Syria, Land Campaign; Robertson, Sir William Robert; Romani, Battle of; Sinai Campaign; Ypres, First Battle of.

References
Bruce, A. P. C. *The Last Crusade: The Palestine Campaign in the First World War.* London: Murray, 2002.

Bullock, David L. *Allenby's War: The Palestinian-Arabian Campaigns, 1916–1918*. London: Blandford, 1988.

Wavell, Colonel A. P. *The Palestine Campaigns*. London: Constable, 1928.

Music of World War I

The world of music became increasingly fragmented in the years before World War I. Among many different trends, nationalism emphasized the use of folk music and folklore in conjunction with a patriotic desire to establish a national identity. This can be seen in works such as *Finlandia* (1900) by Jan Sibelius (1865–1957) and the folk opera *Jenufa* (1903) by Czecho-Slovak composer Leoš Janáček (1854–1928). Impressionism (roughly defined as music that sought to evoke fleeting sensations and moods in the manner of the French painters of the 1870s) was also an important trend. *La Mer* (The Sea) (1905) by Claude Debussy (1862–1918) and *Daphnis et Chloé* (1911) by Maurice Ravel (1875–1937) as well as works by American composer Charles Griffes (1884–1920) are examples of this style.

Of great significance during these years was the formation of a new radical aesthetic that sought to break away from the seductive illusions of nineteenth-century romanticism. Austrians Arnold Schoenberg (1874–1951) and Alban Berg (1885–1935) developed a style called expressionism, which emphasized distorted representations of reality to express the inner tensions of modern society. During this period the Russian composer Igor Stravinsky (1882–1971) developed a musical language mixing nationalism with a raw primitivism that would become highly influential.

Ultimately, it was the more radical composers who seemed best equipped to deal with the issues and images that would come define the war. This is perhaps best seen in two works that seemed to anticipate the war: Schoenberg's *Pierrot Lunaire* (Moonstruck Pierrot) and Stravinsky's *Le Sacre du Printemps* (The Rite of Spring).

Pierrot Lunaire, written for speaker—using an innovative form of declamation called *Sprechstimme* (speech-song)—and chamber ensemble was premiered in Berlin on 16 October 1912. The text (by Albert Giraud, German translation by Otto von Hartleben) depicts Pierrot (a character from the

Willliam Simmons, Marie Tiffany, and A. W. Kramer performing for the troops at Camp Upton, Long Island, New York, 1918. (National Archives)

Group of World War I soldiers gathered around a piano, framed by war song sheet music covers. (Library of Congress)

commedia dell'arte usually shown as a love-struck simpleton) as a deeply alienated Everyman who is driven mad by an increasingly hostile and violent world. Schoenberg's score brilliantly reflected the disintegration of prewar European culture through a dissonant musical language, dubbed atonality, that completely broke with musical convention. In spite of the score's musical demands, Pierrot experienced considerable success before the outbreak of the war.

Stravinsky began planning a new ballet in 1911 based on "legends from pagan Russia" that would ultimately become *Le Sacre.* The now notorious premiere in Paris on 29 May 1913 generated enormous controversy and a near-riot. Scored for large orchestra, the ballet depicted scenes from a decidedly precivilized and pre-Christian Russia that culminated in the brutal image of a young girl forced to dance herself to death under the watchful eyes of nameless tribal elders. Stravinsky's music, like Schoenberg's, made a radical break from European musical tradition, writing the piece in a language of primitive

energy and extraordinary power. While the violence of the work is unmistakable, it is the death of a "chosen innocent" before watching "elders" that seems most chillingly prophetic (the work was originally titled *The Victim*).

The war brought U.S. popular music to Europe, including the earliest forms of jazz. This was at the height of popularity for published sheet music; songs in this form were plentiful, inexpensively produced, and widely disseminated. When the war broke out it was inevitable that this form of entertainment be used to serve the war effort. As a result, many of the songs are upbeat in both music and lyrics. While this positive tone was considered necessary in order to respect the sensibilities of the people at home, mostly it was a product of the popular musical language of the time.

Since both sides on the Western Front shared a common musical heritage, many songs were adapted and shared either through translation or the addition of new texts. This shared repertoire was evident in such events as the Christmas Truce of 1914. For the most part there were no "official" songs of protest, although the soldiers themselves would often come up with new words for songs that expressed their experiences in a more realistic fashion. Some popular songs of World War I have been appropriated as World War II songs; for example, "Colonel Bogey's March" was written in 1916 but is now associated with David Lean's film *The Bridge Over the River Kwai*. Some famous songs predate the war; "It's a Long Long Way to Tipperary" was written in 1912.

The songs show a wide range of attitudes about the war, from the pacifist "I Didn't Raise My Boy To Be a Soldier" to George M. Cohan's stirringly patriotic "Over There!" There were comic songs ("K-K-K-Katy: The Sensational Stammering Song Success Sung by the Soldiers and Sailors" and "How 'Ya Gonna Keep Them Down on the Farm [After They've Seen Paree?]") as well as sentimental songs ("Roses of Picardy," "The Rose of 'No Man's Land,'" and "Madelon, I'll be True to the Whole Regiment," based on a French soldier's song "Quand Madelon"). There were nostalgic songs of the home front (such as the English songs "Take Me Back to Dear Old Blighty" and "Keep the Home Fires Burning") as well as unabashedly patriotic songs ("America, I Love You," and Irving Berlin's "Let's All Be Americans Now"). Traditional songs also became associated with the war, such as the German song "Die Wacht am Rhein" (The Watch on the Rhine), which was sung for Kaiser Wilhelm II upon the announcement of general mobilization in 1914.

Soldiers would often take well-known tunes and write new words that had satirical bite. Some of these have taken on the status of "unofficial classics," such as one sung to the tune of "Auld Lang Syne," the text of which consisted entirely of "We're here because we're here." Another, sung to the tune of "What a Friend We Have in Jesus," stated "When this lousy war is over, no more soldiering for me, / When I get my civvy clothes on, oh how happy I shall be. / No more sergeants bawling, 'Pick it up' and 'Put it down' / If I meet the ugly bastard I'll kick his arse all over town." There were also original songs of this kind. "Hanging On the Old Barbed Wire" had numerous verses running through the full range of soldier's complaints; while the battalion was "hanging on the old barbed wire," other verses suggested that you would find "the company sergeant lying on the latrine floor" and "the brasshats drinking claret at Brigade HQ." "The Mademoiselle from Armentières" existed in versions that ranged from the harmless to the obscene. Another song had a refrain that ran "Oh, oh, oh, it's a lovely war," which became the title of Richard Attenborough's 1969 film, *Oh! What a Lovely War*. This film intentionally contrasted the upbeat lyricism of the war songs with the brutality of the war itself.

On the whole, the songs were designed to help improve morale among soldiers and those at home. The low cost of producing sheet music made it an invaluable source for fund-raising, recruitment, and propaganda. The words were positive and optimistic, if somewhat at odds with the actual savagery of the fighting. Many of the sentiments expressed in these songs, written as they were by people who had no concept of the war's realities, undoubtedly seemed as absurd during the war years as they do now. Nevertheless, through the titles and texts of these songs, one can get a glimpse of the prevailing attitudes of the time.

In the years following the armistice, composers searched for an appropriate way to respond to the postwar world. Schoenberg and his followers continued to devote their energies toward the development of a new musical language, as it was strongly felt that the earlier romantic language was no longer valid, particularly in light of the war experience. Stravinsky developed a style called neoclassicism, which retained elements of the past while incorporating new materials. One of his first works in this style was his *The Soldier's Tale* (1918), for speaker and chamber ensemble (text by C. F. Ramuz). This work adapted popular musical forms to tell the story of a soldier who is sidetracked by the Devil and as a result finds himself unable to return to his homeland (a theme that resonated with many after the war). Stravinsky's *Symphony of Psalms* (1930) is a different kind of memorial: it is a powerfully reconciliatory work of deep spirituality. There were also works such as the enormously popular *Threepenny Opera* (1928) by Kurt Weill (1900–1950) that combined art and politics in a biting satire of postwar life.

Finally, in Alban Berg's opera *Wozzeck* (1922), based on a play by Georg Büchner, the title character is depicted as an alienated soldier relentlessly tormented by his superiors. Tragically, Wozzeck ultimately murders those he loves, thus blurring the divide between victim and perpetrator, leaving behind an innocent child whose fate is unknown. The final scene of the opera shows the innocent child alone on stage, a fitting image for war-torn Europe.

Jeffrey Wood

See also

Art and the War; Propaganda.

References

Butler, Christopher. *Early Modernism: Literature, Music and Painting in Europe, 1900–1916*. Oxford: Oxford University Press, 1994.

Eksteins, Modris. *Rites of Spring: The Great War and the Birth of the Modern Age*. Boston: Houghton Mifflin, 1989.

Kinkle, Roger D. *The Complete Encyclopedia of Popular Music and Jazz, 1900–1950*. 4 vols. New Rochelle, NY: Arlington House, 1974.

Palmer, Roy. *What a Lovely War! British Soldiers Songs from the Boer War to the Present Day*. London: M. Joseph, 1990.

Scheele, Carl H. *Praise the Lord and Pass the Ammunition: Songs of World Wars I and II*. New York: New World Records, The Recorded Anthology of American Music, 1977.

Whittall, Arnold. *Music since the First World War*. Oxford: Oxford University Press, 1988.

Mussolini, Benito (1883–1945)

Socialist leader and advocate of Italian intervention in World War I; later dictator of Italy. Born on 29 July 1883 near the village of Predappio in the Romagna, Benito Mussolini grew up a radical. His father Alessandro was a blacksmith, and his mother Rosa was a schoolteacher. They named him for Mexican revolutionary and president Benito Juárez. His mother wanted him to be a schoolteacher, and Mussolini became a substitute elementary school teacher at age 18 but found it to be boring.

Already as an adolescent Mussolini had joined the revolutionary or syndicalist section of the Italian Social Democratic Party, helping to establish unions and foment strikes. From his youth Mussolini seemed to have been a violent person. At age 18 he took as his mistress the young wife of a soldier away on station. He mistreated her and at one point stabbed her with his pocket knife.

At age 19 Mussolini fled Italy in order to escape compulsory military service. He lived in Switzerland for three years doing odd jobs and relying in part on money sent by his mother. He occasionally attended university lectures, but his radical socialist views led to his expulsion from one Swiss canton after another, and he eventually served time in prison.

An amnesty caused Mussolini to return to Italy. He submitted to compulsory military service and then resumed the agitator's role, supplementing it with radical journalism. In 1912 he was named editor of *Avanti!,* the national daily newspaper of the Socialist Party. Arrested for antimilitarist activities, Musasolini served five months in prison.

When World War I began, Mussolini revealed his opportunism by supporting Italian participation on the Allied side in order that the country might secure its "unredeemed" lands in the Tyrol and along the Adriatic. He founded his own newspaper, *Il Popolo d'Italia* (The People of Italy), to promote this end. The former pacifist wrote, "Neutrals have never dominated events. . . . It is blood that moves the wheels of history." This stance led to Mussolini's expulsion from the Socialist Party.

In October 1914 Mussolini founded the prowar group Fasci Rivoluzionario d'Azione Internazionalista (Revolutionary Fasci for International Action) to bring about intervention in the war. In December of that year it became the Fasci di Azione Rivoluzionaria (Fasci for International Action). The word *fascio* recalled the bundle of sticks carried by the lictors of ancient Rome, representing state power; one stick might be broken, but fastened together they were unbreakable. Mussolini liked to call up ancient glories, and this later became the emblem of Fascist Italy.

Following Italy's entrance into the war on the Allied side in 1915, Mussolini volunteered for war service. He fought on the Isonzo Front, rose to the rank of caporalmaggiore (equiv. in the U.S. Army to sergeant), and was seriously wounded when an artillery piece exploded. Following a period of hospitalization, he was discharged in June 1917 and returned to Il Popolo d'Italia.

On the return of peace in November 1918 and with hard economic times, the Socialists resumed their agitation. Mussolini's reaction came in March 1919 when he organized demobilized ex-soldiers into the first Fascio di Combattimento (combat bands). They did battle with Socialists and Communists the length of Italy.

Government paralysis in the crisis gave Mussolini his chance, and in October 1922 he ordered the "March on Rome." King Victor Emmanuel III refused to order martial law, and Mussolini was appointed premier. Gradually the fascists took control of Italy, and Mussolini assumed dictatorial powers as Il Duce (leader). Although he restored order, Mussolini failed to achieve the economic advances for which Italians had yielded their liberties. Instead, he gave his people an opportunistic, expansionary foreign policy. In 1940 he led Italy into World War II, a conflict for which his nation was unprepared. Overthrown by his own Fascist Grand Council in 1943, he was rescued by German commandoes on the orders of Adolf Hitler. Mussolini then headed a fascist rump state in north Italy until the end of the war when, trying to flee, he was captured by partisans at Dongo near Lake Como on the Swiss border and shot on 28 April 1945.

Arne Kislenko and Spencer C. Tucker

See also
Italy, Home Front; London, Treaty of; Paris Peace Conference.

References
Farrell, Nicholas. *Mussolini: A New Life.* London: Weidenfeld and Nicolson, 2003.
Lamb, Richard. *Mussolini as Diplomat: Il Duce's Italy on the World Stage.* New York: Fromm International, 1999.
Mack Smith, Denis. *Mussolini.* New York: Knopf, 1982.
Neville, Peter. *Mussolini.* London: Routledge, 2004.
Ridley, Jasper. *Mussolini.* New York: St. Martin's, 1997.

N

Nahr-al-Kalek, Battle of (26 February 1917)

Mesopotamian Front naval battle. Following the British recapture of Kut-al-Amara on 25 February 1917, three Royal Navy gunboats, the *Mantis, Moth,* and *Tarantula,* proceeded up the Tigris River. These 645-ton gunboats were each armed with 2 × 6-inch and 2 × 12-pounder guns and 6 machine guns. Ever since the envelopment of Major-General Sir Charles Townshend's forces at Kut-al-Amara in December 1915, British naval units in Mesopotamia had served largely as artillery support for troops on land, and the crews were anxious for independent action.

Under the command of Captain W. Nunn, the three gunboats moved quickly up the Tigris, mistakenly believing that men on the riverbanks moving north toward Baghdad were advancing British troops. The gunboats soon encountered the Turkish rear guard and came under howitzer fire. The three gunboats sustained damage and were hit many times, but they continued upriver.

At Nahr-al-Kalek, approximately 20 miles north of Kut-al-Amara, the *Mantis, Moth,* and *Tarantula* encountered a hairpin turn in the Tigris. When they made that turn, four Turkish vessels lying in wait opened fire on them. In the ensuing battle the British gunboats sank three of the Turkish boats and captured the fourth, the former British naval gunboat *Firefly,* lost at Umm-al-Tabul in the British retreat from Ctesiphon. Despite this decisive victory, the gunboats suffered grave losses in personnel. On the *Moth,* for example, four of the five officers died and half of the enlisted crew perished. The *Mantis* also lost its pilot and quartermaster.

Hundreds of Turkish soldiers, fearing reprisals if they surrendered to Arabs, swarmed the riverbanks after the battle to surrender to the astonished British sailors. This river battle marked the effective end of the Turkish river force on the Mesopotamian Front; what remained—two small Thorneycroft patrol boats—stayed above Tikrit, well out of harm's way for the rest of the war.

John Thomas McGuire

See also
Ctesiphon, Battle of; Mesopotamian Theater; Tikrit, Battle of.
References
Barker, A. J. *The Bastard War: The Mesopotamian Campaign of 1914–1918.* New York: Dial, 1967.
Corbett, Julian S., and Henry Newbolt. *Naval Operations: History of the Great War Based on Official Documents.* 5 vols. London: Longman, 1920–1931, 1938, 1940.
Gray, Randal, ed. *Conway's All the World's Fighting Ships, 1906–1921.* Annapolis: Naval Institute Press, 1985.
Moberly, F. J. *The Campaign in Mesopotamia, 1914–1918.* 3 vols. Nashville, TN: Battery Press, 1997–1998.

Namur, Siege of (20–24 August 1914)

Namur was one of the two great Belgian fortress cities protecting the Meuse River valley from invasion in either direction. Namur lies at the confluence of the Sambre and Meuse rivers. A renovation program between 1888 and 1892 made these two Belgian fortresses among the most modern in the world. The nine fortresses at Namur were built in a rough circle on the high ground around the city, about 5 miles from the city center. In the years between their construction and the beginning of World War I, the Belgian government had not maintained the fortresses. The forts were also short on ammunition, and the garrisons were undermanned. The defenders were complemented by the Belgian 4th Infantry Division, which was to hold the areas in front of and between the forts, yet the work of digging trenches to connect the forts and clearing new fields of fire did not begin until 2 August 1914.

The fortresses at Liège and Namur stood in the path of the right wing of the German army. Liège, which was closer to Germany, came under attack first. When the fortresses fell on 16 August, the German First Army began its march to the northwest, while the Second and Third Armies advanced along the Meuse toward Namur. The 37,000 soldiers in Namur stood in the path of 107,000 German soldiers. The defenders' morale was low. Liège, which most military experts had expected to hold for months, had fallen in a matter of days, and King Albert of Belgium had made the fateful decision to withdraw the bulk of his army toward Antwerp and away from Namur. Namur was to hold out until General Charles Lanrezac's French Fifth Army, on the opposite bank of the Sambre, could link up with the Belgian 4th Division.

On 20 August, units of General Karl von Bülow's German Second Army, which had the assignment of taking Namur, approached Fort Marchovelette, the easternmost fort in the ring around Namur, and began to probe its defenses. Simultaneously Bülow detached part of his army to cross the Sambre and attack Lanrezac near Charleroi in order to keep the French from reinforcing Namur. On 21 August the Germans crossed the Sambre. As these troops fought their way across the river, the Germans began their main attack on Namur with more than 400 pieces of artillery. By now the German artillery besieging Namur included the superheavy-caliber Skoda 305mm and Krupp 420mm "Big Bertha" guns that had been used with such devastating effect at Liège.

German gunners now began to pound the Namur fortresses into submission, and on 23 August, as the forts guarding the eastern approaches to Namur surrendered under the weight of the German onslaught, it became impossible to hold the city, and the defenders in Namur withdrew. Only one of Lanrezac's infantry regiments had succeeded in making contact with the defenders. With the gates to the city open, it was only a matter of time before Bülow's troops occupied Namur and reduced the remaining forts. That task was completed on 24 August. Lanrezac's army withdrew from the Sambre, and the German Second Army and the entire German right wing were now free to continue their sweep toward Paris. The defenders of Namur had purchased for the Allies a few days of valuable time.

John Lavalle

See also
Albert I, King of Belgium; Big Bertha; Bülow, Karl von; Charleroi, Battle of; Frontiers, Battle of the; Lanrezac, Charles; Liège, Siege of; Schlieffen Plan.
References
Macdonald, Lyn. *1914: The First Months of Fighting.* London and New York: Atheneum, 1988.
Strachan, Hew. *The First World War*, Vol. 1, *To Arms.* Oxford: Oxford University Press, 2001.
Tuchman, Barbara W. *The Guns of August.* New York: Macmillan, 1962.

Narev Offensive (13–22 July 1915)

Battle in the northern part of the Polish salient on the Eastern Front that helped prompt the Russian "Great Retreat" in late July 1915. The city of Narev is located about 25 miles north of Warsaw in the northeastern portion of the Polish salient. The German attack there was part of a three-pronged offensive against the Russians in 1915 that included Galicia, Narev, and Courland (Kurland).

The Germans had tried to break through west of the Narev River in February and March 1915 and had failed. This time they were determined to leave nothing to chance. For the attack, German General Max von Gallwitz, commanding Army Group Gallwitz, assembled in East Prussia twenty divisions and 200,000 men, supported by 1,000 guns in the charge of master artillerist Lieutenant Colonel Georg Bruchmüller. Facing the Germans at their point of attack, the inner wings between the First and Twelfth Russian Armies, were seven weak Russian divisions of some 100,000 men, supported by only 377 guns with fewer than 40 rounds of ammunition available per gun. The German attack opened with a four-hour artillery barrage on 13 July. German infantry then moved forward. Striking to the southeast toward the Narev River, they split the Russian First Army from the Twelfth Army and opened a gap in the Russian lines 25 miles wide. Too late, chief of staff of the Russian army General Mikhail Alekseyev ordered reserves to this area, and they were still many miles from the front when the German blow fell. Coordination between the First and Twelfth Armies was inadequate, and the Russian positions were poorly prepared, not being designed for defensive operations.

By the 17th the Germans had advanced some 5 miles and had inflicted 70 percent losses on the Russian defenders, including 24,000 prisoners. Alekseyev had no choice but to pull back his troops to the Narev, with corresponding withdrawals to the flanks. Alekseyev fought the battle well, and as the Germans advanced they encountered increasing numbers of Russian troops.

Gallwitz would have had great difficulty in forcing the Narev line, but at this point the Russian high command

(Stavka) lost its nerve. With the Russians suffering reversals elsewhere, on 22 July Stavka ordered Alekseyev to withdraw the Narev forces to the east and, if necessary, evacuate Warsaw. The "Great Retreat" now began, involving seven Russian armies in a withdrawal several hundred miles to the east. This wiped out the Polish salient and saw the Germans push into Byelorussia along a line north of the Pripet Marshes. Alekseyev, however, conducted the retreat with great skill, denying the Germans any opportunity to break through and trap major units in the process.

Jon Anderson

See also
Alekseyev, Mikhail Vasilyevich; Bruchmüller, Georg; Eastern Front Overview; Gallwitz, Max von.

References
Clark, Alan. *Suicide of the Empires: The Battles on the Eastern Front, 1914–18.* New York: American Heritage Press, 1971.
Stone, Norman. *The Eastern Front, 1914–1917.* New York: Scribner, 1975.

Nasiriyah, Battle of (24 July 1915)

Significant British military victory over the Turks in Mesopotamia. As a result of this success, the British continued to drive toward Baghdad, ultimately resulting in the catastrophe of the siege and their surrender at Kut-al-Amara.

The British first sent an expeditionary force to southern Mesopotamia in October 1914 to protect the oil fields and refineries there. The troops for this effort came from the Indian army. These forces easily captured Basra and other towns in southern Mesopotamia. By early 1915 British strength had grown to more than two divisions. General Sir John E. Nixon favored the capture of Baghdad. Any British advance to that place would have to be made up the Tigris and Euphrates rivers, since they were the only practical routes for communications and logistics in Mesopotamia. By 3 June the main British force under Major-General Charles V. F. Townshend had scored easy victories over weak Turkish opposition and had advanced upriver on the Tigris to Amara.

At the same time, in order to protect Basra and Townshend's western flank, Nixon sent Major-General George F. Gorringe and a reinforced brigade of about 5,000 men up the Euphrates River to attack a Turkish force at Nasiriyah, the central supply depot for Turkish troops in southern Mesopotamia. Nixon signaled his intentions to the Indian government on 11 June. Gorringe's command started the advance on 27 June. At the time seasonal flooding covered most of the district, but the troops moved by small boat through canals, creeks, and marshes, supported by shallow-draft steamers and gunboats. Daytime temperatures soared to over 100 degrees Fahrenheit, and the water levels quickly dropped.

The first obstacle for the British to overcome was an improvised dam constructed by the Turks to deny the British access to the Euphrates. British sappers working under fire blew a gap in the dam, and the boats were dragged through the rushing water. Gorringe soon encountered more forward defenses, with two Turkish field guns covering the river. On 5 July two Indian battalions outflanked the Turkish defenders, while others drew their attention in a frontal assault. The poorly trained Turks were driven out. A Turkish officer captured by Arabs revealed the location of mines in the Euphrates, clearing the way for the British flotilla to advance.

The main Turkish defenses of Nasiriyah were located 6 miles below the town. Turkish infantry were dug in on both sides of the river with their flanks covered by marshes. As the banks were significantly higher than the river, this prevented British gunboats from providing effective support. The Turks had also cleared fields of fire. Gorringe called for reinforcements. Another brigade was brought up, but falling water levels in the river delayed its arrival until 13 July.

On the 13th Gorringe tried to outflank the Turkish right flank. A British assault force crossed the marsh, but an attack by Arab irregulars caused heavy British losses and failure of the scheme. Over the next several weeks sickness decimated both armies. By 24 July, each side had about 5,000 men. A single British aircraft helped Gorringe reconnoiter Turkish defenses and develop a new plan to attack the Turkish left flank, which was behind a creek too deep to wade.

As dawn broke on 24 July, a barge was towed to the mouth of the creek. British sappers then attempted to construct a bridge over the barge. Although the attempt failed with heavy losses to the sappers, the barge dammed the creek sufficiently to allow British and Indian soldiers to wade across below the barge. They soon mopped up the Turkish defenders in the first position. As the Turks fell back to their second line of trenches, the British flotilla was able to fire directly on them. The Turkish withdrawal then became a rout. On 25 July Nasiriyah surrendered to Gorringe.

British losses for the month-long campaign came to 533 men. The Turks lost at least that many dead and more wounded. They also had 1,000 men and seventeen guns captured.

Tim J. Watts

See also
Mesopotamian Theater; Nixon, Sir John Eccles; Townshend, Sir Charles.

References
Barker, A. J. *The Bastard War: The Mesopotamian Campaign of 1914–1918.* New York: Dial, 1967.
Davis, Paul K. *Ends and Means: The British Mesopotamian Campaign and Commission.* Toronto: Associated University Presses, 1994.
Erickson, Edward J. *Ordered to Die: A History of the Ottoman Army in the First World War.* Westport, CT: Greenwood, 2000.
Moberly, F. J. *The Campaign in Mesopotamia, 1914–1918.* 3 vols. Nashville, TN: Battery Press, 1997–1998.

Naval Armament and Gunnery

Naval armament underwent tremendous change in the decades preceding World War I. The battleship remained the largest and most formidable naval vessel. The standard gun caliber for battleships in most major navies in 1906 was the 12-inch (304.8mm or in France 305mm). German battleships, however, mounted 11-inch (actually 183mm, or 11.14-inch). Until HMS *Dreadnought* (1906), battleships carried a mixed armament of guns for short-, medium-, and long-range fire. The Japanese *Mikasa*, completed in Britain in 1902 and rated at the time as the largest and most powerful vessel in the world, had 4 × 12-inch guns in two turrets but also 14 × 6-inch and 20 × 3-inch guns to deal with torpedo boats. Such armament enabled it to fight at close, intermediate, and long range. The *Dreadnought* was the first all-big-gun battleship. It mounted 10 × 12-inch guns, all of which could be centrally controlled and aimed at a single target. It also had 27 × 12-pounders and some smaller guns to deal with the threat of torpedo boats and mounted 5 × 18-inch torpedo tubes. The *Dreadnought*'s 10 large guns gave it a firepower 2.5 times that of the *Mikasa*. With central gunnery control and presenting less of a target, the *Dreadnought* might even be the equivalent of four or five *Mikasa*s. The *Dreadnought* immediately made all other capital ships obsolete.

Britain went to 13.5-inch (342.9mm) guns in its new superdreadnoughts. Completed in 1910–1911, the four Orion-class ships mounted 10 × 13.5-inch and 16 × 4-inch guns. The largest superdreadnoughts before the First World War, although they did not actually join the fleet until 1915, were the five Royal Navy superdreadnoughts of the Queen Elizabeth-class. They were to mount 13.5-inch guns, but because the Japan and the United States were moving to larger guns, they mounted 8 × 15-inch (381mm) guns in two superfiring turrets fore and aft. They also carried 12 × 6-inch guns as well as 2 × 3-inch antiaircraft guns, 4 × 3-pounders, 5 machine guns, and 4 × 21-inch broadside torpedo tubes. Fourteen-inch (355.6mm) guns were not a standard British caliber but were on the *Canada* (the ex-*Almirante Latorre,* a dreadnought being built by Armstrong for Chile and purchased by the British government in September 1914).

The first German dreadnoughts, the four-ship Nassau-class, mounted 12 × 11-inch guns along with 12 × 150mm (5.9-inch) guns. In 1908 Germany laid down four Helgoland-class ships mounting 12 × 12-inch as well as 14 × 5.9-inch guns. In 1909–1910 the Germans laid down a new class of dreadnought. Completed in 1911, the *Kaiser* was the first of a new type of dreadnought that would eventually develop into the *Bismarck* and *Tirpitz* of World War II. The Germans built five of this class, completed during 1911–1912. Their main armament was 10 × 12-inch (305mm) guns. Secondary armament consisted of 14 × 5.9-inch guns. Other ships mounting 12-inch guns followed. The German answer to the Queen Elizabeth-class came late in the First World War in two ships: the *Baden* and *Bayern*. Each mounted a main battery of 8 × 15-inch (actually 14.96-inch) 380mm guns. Their secondary batteries included 16 × 5.9-inch guns as well as antiaircraft protection and torpedo tubes. The Germans projected 520mm (20.47-inch) guns for battleships they planned to build in 1918.

The first U.S. dreadnoughts, the South Carolina-class ships, mounted 8 × 12-inch guns plus a secondary armament that included 14 × 3-inch guns. The first U.S. superdreadnoughts, the two Texas-class ships laid down in 1911, were the first U.S. ships to carry 14-inch guns. They mounted 10 × 14-inch and 16 × 5-inch guns. Other superdreadnoughts with 14-inch guns followed. Their number one and number four turrets had 3 guns each; numbers two and three—the two superimposed turrets—had 2 guns each. The last prewar U.S. superdreadnoughts were two Pennsylvania-class ships mounting 12 × 14-inch guns, 3 to a turret, as well as 14 × 5-inch guns. In 1918 the United States had battleships under construction with 16-inch guns. Japanese main gun batteries went from 14-inch to 16.14-inch (410mm) for ships under construction in 1918. Japan's Nagato-class of 1919 were the world's first battleships to mount 16-inch guns.

French battleship armament also increased in caliber. The first French dreadnoughts completed in 1910–1912, the four-ship Courbet-class, mounted 12 × 12-inch and 22 × 5.5-inch guns. The three Bretagne-class ships laid down in 1912 had 10 × 13.39-inch (340mm) guns along with 22 × 5.5-inch. Russia's four Gangut-class battleships carried 12 × 12-inch guns, but during the war Russia had some battleships mounting 14-inch (355.6mm) guns. The largest Italian naval guns were 15-inch (381mm), but these were for floating batteries. The largest guns in the Austro-Hungarian navy during the war were 12-inchers (305mm).

The first six British battle cruisers had a main battery of 8 × 12-inch guns. The secondary battery included 12 × 4-inch guns. The equivalents of the superdreadnoughts among the battle cruisers mounted 8 × 13.5-inch guns and had a secondary armament including 16 × 4-inch guns. The first German battle cruiser, the *Von der Tann,* mounted a main armament of 8 × 11.1-inch (280mm) guns, while the two Moltke-class battle cruisers (the *Moltke* and *Goeben*) and the *Seydlitz* were armed with a main battery of 10 × 11.1-inch guns. The excellent Derflinger-class (*Derflinger* and *Lützow*) battle cruisers mounted 8 × 12-inch (305mm) guns. Japan's Kong-class battle cruisers mounted a main battery of 8 × 14-inch guns.

Of smaller warships, heavy cruisers usually mounted 8-inch (8.2-inch for Germany) guns while light cruisers

Night firing by the British Navy battleship *Hercules*. (National Archives)

mounted 6-inch or even 4-inch guns. Destroyers were generally armed with a maximum of 4-inch (Germany 3.4-inch) guns as well as torpedo tubes.

Length of naval guns is most usually expressed in calibers or number of diameters of the bore. Most naval guns were about 45 calibers. Thus, a 12-inch/45-caliber gun would be 540O in length. Some guns were as long as 50 calibers, while others were as short as 40. The advantage of the longer gun was that the propellant charge could act on the projectile over a longer period, thus producing greater range. The German and Austro-Hungarian navies used brass cartridge cases for all or a part of the propellant charge, while other navies used bags of powder. Projectile weights varied greatly depending on type. The weight of a 12-inch armor-piercing shell during the war varied from 850 pounds in the British navy to 1,038 pounds in the Russian navy, with the average for the eight major navies being 934 pounds. Muzzle velocities varied sharply, depending on projectile weight and powder charge. They might range from 2,472fps to 2,920fps.

In the United States, Bradley Fiske produced an electric rangefinder as early as 1889; two years later he patented a naval telescopic sight. Mounted on a sleeve around the gun barrel, the sight did not recoil when the gun was fired. Fiske may also have been the first person to attempt to control a ship's gunfire from aloft, when he was stationed in the foremast of the USS *Petrel* at the Battle of Manila Bay in 1898. Later he wrote, "Ninety percent of the art of naval gunnery seems to me to be the art of merely shooting to the correct distance." Another innovator, Captain William Sims, succeeded in reducing firing time and improving accuracy in gunnery aboard U.S. Navy ships.

The most important figure in the dramatic change in naval gunnery practice was Royal Navy Captain Percy Scott, "the pocket Hercules," who had charge of the HMS *Excellent* gunnery school. In 1898, while commanding the *Scylla* in the Mediterranean, Scott invented a technique of continuous aiming. In the Mediterranean Fleet annual firing competition, the average for the ships participating was only 30 percent hits, but the *Scylla* scored a staggering 80 percent. Scott also introduced salvo firing.

The 1905 Battle of Tsushima seemed to confirm sentiment that the big gun was the key at sea and that only the largest shells could inflict crippling damage on a ship's hull. Increasing attention thus came to be paid to gunnery practice and methods, and in the decade after Tsushima naval gunnery was transformed. Until the early 1890s the chief method of pointing a naval gun was a simple tangent sight. In 1892 the Royal Navy had adopted the new Barr & Stroud range-finder device, which had two mirrors set 4.5 feet apart. The Japanese navy adopted it the next year and the U.S. Navy soon thereafter. Later longer-base instruments were much more precise. For the first time, gunners could obtain a reasonably accurate range to their targets. In the mid-1890s Zeiss in Germany also developed an improved stereoscopic rangefinder for naval use. Longer base-length rangefinders were adopted, capable of accurate range measurement out to 10,000 yards. Early analogue computer systems appeared to help solve the considerable problem of calculating the precise location of the target ship when the shells arrived.

The Royal Navy turned down a privately developed fire-control computer system, in effect an early analogue computer, designed by a civilian, Arthur Pollen, in favor of an inferior, less-sophisticated system developed by Admiral Sir Frederic Dreyer. There is disagreement over whether the Pollen system would have improved Royal Navy gunnery sufficiently to have made a difference during the First World War.

In 1905 Scott perfected a system of "director firing." Taking advantage of new electrical circuitry, he developed a system that, in normal circumstances, concentrated control of all the big guns in the hands of one man, the "director" or first gunnery officer. Along with his enlisted assistants, the director was located in a "director tower" high in the foremast. From this observation platform with its master sight, cables ran to a central transmitting station, which produced firing data for the director, and to the individual turrets. This gave the director control over laying and firing all the main guns, eliminating individual gunlayers having to make their own calculations of range and bearing. In emergency circumstances or if the director tower was out of action, individual turrets could still fire on their own.

The Admiralty long resisted this change, but in November 1912 the superdreadnought *Thunderer,* fitted for director firing, achieved a hit ratio six times that of its sister ship, *Orion,* which employed the older independent method. This result could not be ignored, but the Admiralty moved so slowly in response that on the outbreak of the First World War, only a third of Royal Navy dreadnoughts were fitted with director towers. Nonetheless, during the war capital ships could engage their opponents at ranges out to 5 miles or more, double that of the Battle of Tsushima less than a decade before.

Elevation in ship guns reflected this change. Those ships constructed before the fire control revolution had gun mounts capable of only modest elevation. In the Royal Navy, gun elevation was 13.5 degrees until 1909, when in new ships it became 15 degrees. In 1911 it became 20 degrees, and in 1915 it was increased to 30 degrees.

By 1912, with assistance from instruments to plot range changes (the dumaresqs or trigometric slide rule developed in 1902 by Royal Navy Lieutenant John S. Dumaresq), Vickers range clocks to determine changes of range rate, and new Barr and Stroud rangefinders, British capital ships could conduct firing practice out to 14,000 yards. The next year British battle cruisers experimented with 12,000-yard fire under tactical conditions of high speed and sharp turns. If ships during World War I scored about the same number of hits as the U.S. Navy had registered at Manila Bay and Santiago, it should be noted that it was in considerably more difficult circumstances and at up to ten times the range.

Spencer C. Tucker and Raymond Westphal Jr.

See also
Battle Cruisers; Battleships; Cruisers; Destroyers; Sims, William Sowden; Submarines; Torpedoes.

References
Baer, George W. *One Hundred Years of Sea Power: The U.S. Navy, 1890–1990.* Stanford: Stanford University Press, 1994.
Gardiner, Robert, ed. *The Eclipse of the Big Gun: The Warship, 1906–45.* Annapolis: Naval Institute Press, 1992.
George, James L. *History of Warships: From Ancient Times to the Twenty-first Century.* Annapolis: Naval Institute Press, 1998.
Kennedy, Paul M. *The Rise and Fall of British Naval Mastery.* London: The Ashfield Press, 1997.
Moore, John. *Jane's Fighting Ships of World War I.* London: Random House, 1990.
Tucker, Spencer C. *Handbook of 19th Century Naval Warfare.* Stroud, UK: Sutton, 2000.

Naval Arms Race, Anglo-German

One of the most celebrated arms race in modern history, and one that had profound implications for World War I. Much of the responsibility for this arms race rests with Kaiser Wilhelm II. Even before he became ruler of Germany, Wilhelm had been deeply interested in naval affairs. As kaiser he became convinced that a powerful German navy was necessary to support his new foreign policy of world involvement (Weltpolitik).

Initially there was little sentiment in Germany for a powerful navy. Most Germans believed that such a force was unfeasible, given the large size of the army. In 1895 the German navy ranked fifth behind Italy, although Germany was then second in world trade. Support for a stronger navy came from German imperialists, represented in the German Colonial League and the Pan-German League, and the Rhineland industrialists. Highly influential was the publication in German in 1897 of American Alfred Thayer Mahan's book, *The Influence of Sea Power upon History* (1890). Mahan asserted that world power demanded a strong seagoing navy.

In 1896 Wilhelm took advantage of rising sentiment for the navy to appoint as its head Rear Admiral Alfred von Tirpitz, commander of the German Far East Squadron. Tirpitz insisted that the emphasis on building a navy be in capital ships rather than the cruisers and destroyers favored by Wilhelm, and he immediately launched a great propaganda effort in favor of naval construction. In March 1898 the Reichstag, which had rejected the naval-building program of his predecessor only the year before, overwhelmingly approved a bill that called for the construction by 1905 of eleven battleships, five heavy cruisers, and seventeen light cruisers. Although such a fleet would be too small to challenge Britain, Tirpitz argued that it would force the British to take a more conciliatory attitude toward Germany. Indeed, British official volumes of documents treating the origin of the First World War begin with the year 1898. German Chancellor Otto von Bismarck had steadfastly warned that building a powerful fleet would drive Britain into the arms of France, but the German Foreign Office and the kaiser believed in the permanence of the Franco-British and British-Russian rivalries.

Tirpitz had announced, probably for British consumption, that this bill would fill Germany's requirements, but already by the summer of 1899, before the first program was barely underway, he concluded that a new one was necessary. Tirpitz sought to take advantage of sentiment aroused by the Boer War, when a British warship seized a German merchant ship. The government also had the enthusiastic backing of the newly organized Navy League. Heavily financed by German steel interests, it soon had a membership of more than 100,000, its own publications, and an active group of lecturers. The Reichstag passed the second naval bill in June 1900. It called for a fleet of thirty-eight battleships to be completed in twenty years and built regardless of cost. Apparently the kaiser and Tirpitz desired a fleet large enough to challenge the British Home Fleet of thirty-two battleships.

Meanwhile, Britain was not idle. As early as 1889 the British government had adopted a two-power naval standard; that is, maintaining a navy as powerful as that of the next two naval powers combined. It seemed to the British that the German program was shaped largely to satisfy the ego of the kaiser, who indeed derived great satisfaction from possessing and reviewing his fleet. The British believed that for their island nation, heavily dependent on imports of food and raw materials, a powerful fleet was a "necessity," while for Germany it was a "luxury."

Tirpitz's counterpart in Britain, First Sea Lord Admiral Sir John Fisher, was a radical innovator no less driven than Tirpitz. Fisher pushed the construction of a superbattleship. HMS *Dreadnought*, launched in 1905, revolutionized capital ship design and made every other battleship in the world, including those of Britain itself, obsolete. The *Dreadnought* was the first modern all-big-gun battleship. Its 10×12-inch guns could all be centrally controlled. Driven by a steam-turbine engine, it was also the fastest battleship afloat. The advantage of the *Dreadnought* was, of course, short-lived. The Germans soon replied with their own superbattleships, but Britain relied on its greater ship-building resources to keep ahead.

Fisher was also responsible for the introduction of a new ship type, the battle cruiser. Really a supercruiser, it introduced battleship guns on a heavy cruiser hull, sacrificing armor for speed. Again, the Germans followed suit, building ships with heavier armor protection, better range-finding equipment, and superior fire-control. The Germans also had better shells.

In 1906 the Reichstag passed a new navy law providing for construction of six dreadnoughts. Although these were less heavily gunned than their British counterparts, they proved to be almost unsinkable. Tirpitz ordered the Kiel Canal widened to allow the new bigger ships to pass easily between the Baltic and North Sea. He then increased the number of shipyards and gun factories and laid down battle cruisers. Fisher introduced the 13.5-inch gun while Tirpitz increased the German heavy gun caliber from 11 to 12 inches. Tirpitz also ordered long-range submarines and pushed the development of naval airships, the zeppelins.

Tirpitz saw the navy as crucial to Germany's future. He claimed from the beginning of his tenure that this was for Germany a "question of survival" (*Existenzfrage*). Failure to build a great battle fleet would bring Germany's decline and second-rank status. It was very much in this spirit that the Reichstag passed the supplementary naval bill of 1906, following a foreign policy crisis with France over Morocco.

Tirpitz justified his initiatives on the basis of the "risk theory." He argued that the German navy's ultimate strength would deter any potential opponent from risking an all-out naval encounter with Germany because even if that country should emerge victorious from a fleet encounter, the enemy force would have been crippled to the point that it would find itself at the mercy of a third naval power, or even a coalition. The fleet would also enhance Germany's value as an ally. Tirpitz saw as the greatest danger a preemptive British strike before the German navy was sufficiently powerful. He believed that by 1914 or 1915 this danger would have passed and that by 1920 the German navy would stand a good chance of defeating any attacking British force.

German historian Gerhard Ritter has described this "risk theory" as a "gruesome error" and the entire German naval policy as a "monstrous error of judgement." In reality, the risk theory was a smokescreen designed to mask other considerations. Tirpitz and the kaiser believed that Germany was losing the imperial race and that only a strong battle fleet would enable the nation to become the preeminent world power. Tirpitz calculated that the very existence of his battle fleet in the North Sea would pressure the British to grant Germany overseas concessions. Thus the German High Seas Fleet was stationed permanently in the North Sea. If in the future Great Britain should refuse to yield to this pressure, Tirpitz was willing to stake Germany's fate on a single decisive naval battle, which he called *Der Tag* (The Day).

By 1908, however, the British had effectively countered many of Tirpitz's initial calculations. In the first place, Tirpitz underestimated Britain's, and overestimated Germany's, financial power. The Royal Navy not only kept pace with new German construction but pulled ahead of it. Britain, after all, had only a small army to maintain. Great Britain also broke free of "splendid isolation," and it was Germany rather than Britain that was isolated in Europe. In 1904 Britain concluded the entente cordiale with France and in 1907 reached an understanding with Russia. Then in 1912, Great Britain and France agreed that the French would patrol the Mediterranean Sea while the British guarded the English Channel and the North Sea. This arrangement enabled the Royal Navy to recall units from the Mediterranean and station them in the North Sea, and thus achieve overwhelming naval superiority vis-à-vis the German High Seas Fleet. Then, by 1907–1908, the German army again received priority in armaments production and military strategy.

There were efforts to relieve the friction between Germany and Britain. In 1909 new Chancellor Theobald von Bethmann Hollweg discussed with London the possibility of an agreement, proposing that each country retard naval construction. But he also demanded that this be accompanied by a political agreement whereby Great Britain would have to promise not to attack Germany and to remain neutral if Germany were attacked by a third power. The British Foreign Office doubted the sincerity of the German proposals and in any case viewed them as an attempt to break up the Triple Entente.

Following the Second Moroccan Crisis of 1911, German imperialists demanded that the navy be further increased, and early in 1912 Wilhelm announced to the Reichstag that a supplementary naval bill would be introduced. Britain sent War Minister Lord Haldane to Germany, and he met with the kaiser who agreed to slow construction of recently proposed ships. But again Bethmann Hollweg sought to link the naval understanding with a diplomatic agreement. In Germany Tirpitz and his followers opposed any change in Germany's naval program, while in the British Foreign Office there was great reluctance to accept the political formula suggested by Bethmann Hollweg lest it antagonize Russia and France. In the end the Haldane Mission failed.

Germany's Third Supplementary Naval Law (Novelle) of May 1912 created a new squadron that would eventually include three dreadnoughts and brought the total projected strength of the German fleet to forty-one battleships, twenty large cruisers, and forty small cruisers. Thereafter Germany slowed its naval construction somewhat, although by 1914 it had the second largest navy in the world. Unfortunately, Germany, without actually having built a navy sufficiently strong to challenge Britain on the seas, had succeeded in thoroughly alarming the British and pushing them firmly to the side of France and Russia.

Germany's naval-building program was a colossal blunder. It not only alienated Britain, but it also turned out to be but little used as an instrument of war. With the exception of submarines, the German High Seas Fleet remained in port during most of the war. The great exception was the Battle of Jutland in 1916, and that ended in a strategic British victory. Although this must remain speculation, it seems reasonably clear that if the resources expended on the navy had been applied to the army instead, Germany would have won the First World War.

Spencer C. Tucker

See also

Bethmann Hollweg, Theobald von; *Dreadnought*, HMS; Fisher, John Arbuthnot, 1st Baron; Germany, Navy; Great Britain, Navy; Haldane, Richard Burdon, Viscount; Tirpitz, Alfred von; Wilhelm II, Kaiser; Zeppelins.

References

Art, Robert J. *The Influence of Foreign Policy on Seapower.* London: Sage, 1973, 1978.

Herwig, Holger H. *"Luxury" Fleet: The Imperial German Navy, 1888–1918.* London: Allen and Unwin, 1980, 1987.

Kennedy, Paul M. *The Rise of the Anglo-German Antagonism, 1860–1914.* Boston: Allen and Unwin, 1980, 1987.

Massie, Robert K. *Dreadnought: Britain, Germany, and the Coming of the Great War.* New York: Random House, 1991.

Padfield, Peter. *The Great Naval Race: Anglo-German Naval Rivalry, 1900–1914.* New York: McKay, 1974.

Naval Balance (1914)

In terms of numbers of capital ships (battleships and battle cruisers) the Allied Powers of Britain, France, Russia, and Japan had a clear advantage over Germany, Austria-Hungary, and the Ottoman Empire. This does not take into account qualitative differences. Nor does it calculate the reluctance of some powers to hazard capital ships in combat for fear of possible loss of national prestige or upsetting the balance of power in a given theater of war.

The Allies, thanks particularly to the Royal Navy, had a global reach, enhanced by numerous naval bases around the world. The German navy was concentrated in the North Sea. But the well-trained German navy was superior to other navies in such technologically advanced areas as fire control, internal subdivision, quality of gun propellant, and gunnery. Moreover, all navies, with the exception of the Russian and Japanese, had little experience in modern naval combat, and for the most part the admirals were conservative, especially regarding the commitment of resources to combat.

On some seas the Allies did not have the advantage. Thus the German navy dominated the Baltic, and the Central Powers contested control of the Black Sea. In the Adriatic the Austro-Hungarian navy, though inferior in strength to the uncoordinated Allied naval resources there, was still able to protect most of its coastal trade in the Adriatic littoral, and Central Powers submarines were able to operate in the Mediterranean Sea throughout the entire war.

The most critical point of contact in 1914 was the North Sea. In number of capital ships, the British dominated with twenty-five battleships and battle cruisers to oppose sixteen in German service. The British were also able to add to that total by requisitioning ships under construction for other navies (two for the Ottoman Empire and one for Chile) and completing several others of their own. In capital ships, however, the Germans had only the battle cruiser *Goeben* stationed overseas at the start of the war, while Britain had capital ships in the Mediterranean and the Far East. And, as the war progressed, Britain found it necessary to send dreadnought battleships and battle cruisers elsewhere in the world, while Germany only detached them for duty in the nearby Baltic Sea.

Britain had an additional advantage in the number of its predreadnoughts and armored cruisers. While slower and inferior to a dreadnought in power and number of guns, many of its predreadnoughts were quite modern, some not even a decade old. Britain also had two modern semidreadnoughts which, although predating HMS *Dreadnought,* had powerful mixed armaments. Germany had nothing comparable to these ships. In predreadnought battleships, Britain had forty to Germany's twenty, while in armored cruisers Britain enjoyed a massive thirty-eight to nine advantage.

Although the German navy was inferior in overall numbers of capital ships and its guns tended to be smaller, it had the advantage in low visibility and night fighting due to superior optics and training. Combat also revealed that German gunnery was superior to British gunnery. The Germans enjoyed better shells and better-built warships ton for ton. The latter reflected in part the fact that German ships could be designed for short-range operations, that is, in the North Sea and Baltic, while British ships required worldwide reach and thus greater attention to crew accommodations and long-range cruising requirements.

Table N1 lists the actual numbers of ships available in August 1914. Totals include both ships in service and others nearing completion.

Although Germany had the world's second most powerful navy, it was inadequate to challenge the British for naval mastery, especially given the support of the French and other Allied navies. Germany also began the war with too few submarines. In 1914 the submarine was not viewed as a weapon against commerce. Indeed, Germany had been late to build them. In turn the destroyer and other smaller ships would take on new roles of convoy protection and antisubmarine warfare.

In 1914 Germany and Austria-Hungary would not seriously challenge the Allies with their surface fleets. The Allies dominated the sea lanes and placed the Central Powers under a strangling naval blockade, a key factor in the eventual Allied victory in the war. Only with the submarine would Germany seriously threaten that naval dominance. The Allied naval advantage only increased by 1917 with the addition of the Italian and U.S. navies.

Jack Greene

See also

Australia, Navy; Austria-Hungary, Navy; Battle Cruisers; Battleships; France, Navy; Germany, Navy; Great Britain, Navy; Italy, Navy; Japan, Navy; Mediterranean Theater, Naval Operations; Russia, Navy; Submarine Warfare, Allied Powers; Submarine Warfare, Central Powers; United States, Navy.

Table N1.
Ships Available in August 1914

	Dreadnoughts	Battle Cruiser	Semidreadnoughts	Armored Predreadnoughts	Light Cruisers	Cruisers	Torpedo Destroyers	Boats	Submarines
Great Britain	32	10	2	38	38	98	238	70	96
Germany	17	6	—	20	9	45	152	47	39
Russian Baltic	4	—	2	2	6	4	80	16	13
Russian Black Sea	3	—	—	5	—	3	26	10	11
France	7	—	6	13	18	12	87	153	93
Italy	6	—	—	8	9	11	43	75	20
Austria-Hungary	4	—	3	9	3	7	19	85	14
Ottoman Empire	—	—	—	2	—	2	8	13	—

Note: The battle cruiser *Goeben* and light cruiser *Breslau* are assumed to be German warships.

References

Halpern, Paul G. *A Naval History of World War I*. Annapolis: Naval Institute Press, 1994.

Hythe, Viscount, and John Leyland, eds. *The Naval Annual, 1914*. London: William Clowes and Sons, 1914.

Marder, Arthur J. *From the Dreadnought to Scapa Flow: The Royal Navy in the Fisher Era, 1904–1919*. 5 vols. London: Oxford University Press, 1961–1970.

Moore, John. *Jane's Fighting Ships of World War I*. London: Random House, 1990.

Naval Blockade of Germany

British naval blockade that was a primary factor in the defeat of Germany in World War I. The implementation of blockades, whereby naval vessels prevented an enemy nation from receiving overseas supplies in an attempt to damage its war effort, had been a common practice for Great Britain in time of war since the eighteenth century. The potential of such a blockade, however, was not apparent to British planners in the prewar years when they drafted strategic plans for a possible conflict with Germany. This planning resulted from diplomatic and military factors that surfaced in the years between the mid-nineteenth century and the war.

The great expansion of international law that protected neutral rights at sea proved a hindrance to the use of blockades. The 1856 Declaration of Paris, which was the product of the Congress of Paris that ended the 1854–1856 Crimean War, placed restrictions on belligerents that instituted blockades. Great Britain supported this arrangement largely from the desire to placate the war's most powerful neutral, the United States, that championed the rights of neutrals through its call for freedom of the seas. Critics at the time rightly maintained that in case of a future war with a continental European power, the agreement allowed neutral merchantmen to transport supplies having a military purpose, known as contraband, to a neutral European port. Once there, the goods could be transported to the belligerent power and thus subvert any blockade.

The ability of Great Britain to institute a blockade in wartime was further eroded by the 1909 Declaration of London. This agreement specified lists of items that were either absolute contraband, meaning munitions of war that were always open to seizure; conditional contraband, including all goods that might be used for a military purpose; or commodities that could never be seized in time of war. The agreement greatly limited the use of naval blockades in the age of total war, where all goods contributed to a country's war effort. The agreement further hindered Britain's future ability to implement a blockade through the abolition of the doctrine of continuous voyage when applied to conditional contraband. The doctrine of continuous voyage held that

goods destined for an enemy but consigned to a neutral port were open to seizure.

Despite the fact that the British Parliament did not ratify this agreement, the British government felt compelled to uphold it, since it had initiated the conference in an effort to enhance the security for British trade in times of war when Britain was a neutral power. The Declaration of London therefore magnified the problem posed by the Declaration of Paris through the abolition of the doctrine of continuous voyage.

These laws undermined any future British blockade of Germany. Although Britain could seize all merchant ships sailing through the North Sea for Germany, naval strategists noted that neutral commerce, even in contraband items, would continue unabated to those countries contiguous to Germany, and the onus of proof of destination rested with Britain rather than the neutral. Germany would simply import contraband supplies from these countries.

The second factor stemming from the growth of neutral rights in time of war that hindered the use of blockades was that of its definition. The Declaration of Paris set forth the principle that a blockade, in order to be a legitimately recognized instrument in terms of international law, had to consist of a force strong enough to prevent access to the ports or coast of an enemy. In essence, a blockading power had to position a large number of ships within proximity of the coast in order to accomplish this condition. Naval officials viewed this stipulation as problematic, since they had little faith in the traditional, close blockade of an enemy's shores, due to technological innovations such as the torpedo. A blockaded nation could break up a close blockade consisting of larger, more powerful vessels through the use of small ships armed with these weapons. Mines, submarines, and more accurate coastal artillery could also permit a country to fend off blockaders.

The British had not resolved these problems at the outbreak of World War I, but they implemented a blockade since their war plans still attached some importance to it. The blockade was conducted in two theaters: the Mediterranean Sea and the North Sea. In the Mediterranean, a British squadron stationed at Gibraltar policed traffic with the aid of the French navy. These activities, however, paled in comparison to those in the North Sea, which was the principal theater for the blockade. Upon the outbreak of war in August 1914, the British immediately instituted a blockade of the North Sea. By early November the British had declared it to be a war zone; all ships entering the North Sea would do so at their risk.

The blockade of the North Sea consisted of two separate forces. One was the Dover Patrol that sealed off the Dover Straits through the use of minefields, cruisers, and destroyers. The other, more significant force was the 10th Cruiser Squadron under the command of Rear Admiral Dudley De Chair.

The 10th Cruiser Squadron's mission was to intercept all ships trying to pass through the northern entrance to the

North Sea and to send any vessels suspected of carrying contraband for Germany into a port for examination. De Chair's force initially comprised eight of the oldest cruisers of the Grand Fleet that were poorly suited to the task of chasing down more modern ships attempting to run the blockade. Indeed, in many cases neutral vessels managed to outdistance their pursuers. This problem was exacerbated by the confusion of the prewar years in terms of how to implement a blockade under the Declaration of Paris in an age when naval weapons made such an effort either extremely costly or impossible.

Indecision in the British Admiralty meant there was no clear definition at the outbreak of the war of where this force should conduct its patrols. In order to prevent the heavy losses that would ensue from a close blockade of Germany's shores, the British chose to violate the Declaration of Paris and operate the patrol between an area north of Aberdeen, Scotland, to the coast of Norway in the vicinity of Jutland. This position exposed the squadron to German submarine attack and resulted in the sinking of a cruiser on 15 October 1914. The force was consequently withdrawn farther north to a patrol line that extended from the Shetland Islands to the coast of Norway, where it remained for the rest of the war.

Hard upon the resolution of where to conduct the blockade came the replacement of the old cruisers by twenty-three armed merchant cruisers in December 1914. These warships were civilian-owned vessels that were taken over by the government and equipped with light guns. Armed merchant cruisers were much faster than the obsolete cruisers that they replaced, enabling the force to run down any vessel that tried to flee from the blockaders. Despite this improvement, the efforts of the squadron in 1914 did not produce the desired results. Although German commerce in its own merchant ships virtually ceased, it was clear that the European neutral powers were shipping contraband goods to Germany by utilizing their own ships calling at their own ports. Substantial quantities of these goods flowed from the United States, which at that time was a neutral power.

This lackluster British performance continued in 1915. Germany's war effort, although experiencing some hardship on the home front from increasing British restrictions, was largely unaffected, as goods continued to pass through via neutral countries. The reason for the ineffectiveness of the blockade was Whitehall's reluctance to openly contravene the Declaration of London. Prime Minister Herbert Asquith's government, and particularly Foreign Secretary Sir Edward Grey, had championed this agreement and the power of international law in general and therefore hesitated to compromise its principles or anger the United States, which not only supplied Germany but also Great Britain. Meanwhile, the blockading force was endangered by mines, rough weather in the patrol area, and submarine attack. Each of these threats claimed one merchant cruiser of the squadron during 1915.

These losses and the continuing poor results from the squadron created great diplomatic pressure on the Asquith government to reform the administration of the blockade. Calls for change came not only from political opponents of the Asquith administration in Parliament but also from the Royal Navy. Commander-in-chief of the Royal Navy Admiral John Jellicoe called for stricter measures, viewing the loss of armed merchant cruisers as senseless waste caused by the blockade's ineffectiveness. The first significant step toward a tighter blockade came in early 1916 when the Asquith government yielded and created the Ministry of Blockade, which immediately produced new, stricter blockade procedures that were tightened further after 7 December when David Lloyd George succeeded Asquith as prime minister.

Unlike Asquith, Lloyd George favored any measure that could better prosecute the war. The powers of the Ministry of Blockade were strengthened enormously in April 1917 when the United States entered the war on the side of the Entente. These developments produced a far more effective blockade, even though many of the policies of the Ministry of Blockade, such as imposing restrictions on the tonnage of goods shipped to the European neutral states, contravened international law. Even so, by 1917 wartime necessity overrode considerations of international law, since Germany still remained relatively unaffected and the war was exacting an increasingly grievous toll in manpower and equipment. These measures bore fruit by the end of 1917, as the German civilian sector reached the point of collapse and the army was undersupplied because far fewer supplies were penetrating the blockade.

This feat came at great cost to the 10th Cruiser Squadron. In 1916 the force, now under the command of Rear Admiral Reginald Tupper, lost another ship in a battle with the German raider *Greif,* while three more ships were lost in 1917 to submarine attack. On 8 December 1917, the 10th Cruiser Squadron was disbanded and its remaining ships assigned to convoy duty. The squadron had intercepted and boarded 12,979 vessels at sea and failed to prevent 642 ships from running the blockade, at a cost of 9 ships sunk and the loss of 1,165 officers and men. In March 1918 a giant minefield, the Northern Barrage, replaced the squadron. By this point, however, the blockade was a diplomatic rather than military endeavor. The United States was the greatest supplier of all the European neutrals. Its entry into the war meant that neutral powers could be forced not to trade with Germany on pain of having their own supplies decreased or cut off altogether. New administrative machinery to institute punitive measures made this threat much more viable. In December 1917, the Allied Blockade Council was created in an attempt to organize a unified policy among the Entente powers and the United States toward blockade matters. This body proved quite effective in closing some of the few remaining loopholes that allowed some goods into Germany.

The blockade contributed to economic ruin and widespread unrest within Germany that led to the final collapse. The blockade was not lifted entirely until 12 July 1919, when the German government ratified the Treaty of Versailles.

Eric W. Osborne

See also

Armed Merchant Cruisers; Asquith, Herbert Henry, 1st Earl; Cecil, Robert, 1st Viscount; Germany, Home Front; Great Britain, War Plan; Grey, Edward, 1st Viscount of Fallodon; Hoover, Herbert Clark; Jellicoe, John Rushworth, 1st Earl; Northern Barrage.

References

Chatterton, E. Keble. *The Big Blockade.* London: Hurst and Blackett, 1932.

Hardach, Gerd. *The First World War, 1914–1918.* Trans. Peter and Betty Ross. London: Allen Lane, 1977.

Osborne, Eric W. *Britain's Economic Blockade of Germany, 1914–1919.* London: Cass, 2004.

Poolman, Kenneth. *Armed Merchant Cruisers.* Wiltshire, Trowbridge, UK: Redwood Burn, 1985.

Siney, Marion. *The Allied Blockade of Germany, 1914–1916.* Ann Arbor: University of Michigan Press, 1957.

Naval Warfare

The last great European war, the culmination of the age of fighting sail, had ended in 1815 and was followed by a century of comparative peace. During World War I, 1914–1918, naval warfare appeared in three dimensions—surface, subsurface, and aerial—and was manifested on even greater scale. During the nineteenth century, extraordinary advances in metallurgy, ordnance, structures, ship types, design, construction, and technology had progressed unabated. In the days of sailing ship warfare, a critical factor was the supply of wood; during the nineteenth century, it was coal. Beginning with the twentieth century, it became access to oil. This sparked the quest for oil, as First Lord of the Admiralty Winston Churchill decided to take "the fateful plunge" in 1912 to convert the Royal Navy from coal to oil. The strategic implications of this decision were momentous.

Ship structures changed from wood to iron and steel, sails gave way to more reliable and predictable steam propulsion, and gun power and range massively increased. In the run-up to the war, innovative and original ship types were introduced, including the torpedo boat; the torpedo-boat destroyer; the submarine; and the battle cruiser, a cheaper, faster, but more vulnerable capital ship. Existing types were enhanced, beginning with the *Dreadnought,* the first all-big-gun capital ship. The *Dreadnought* was so revolutionary that all predecessors were dubbed "predreadnoughts."

Mines, torpedoes, and aircraft (both lighter- and heavier-than-air) were introduced, along with the earliest aircraft carrier, in an already unprecedented pace of technological change in surface naval warfare. The lighter-than-air craft, utilized for reconnaissance and bombing raids, was not to survive into the next war. In any case, such innovations precipitated changes in the concepts of sea power, strategy, tactics, and blockade. The use of blockade, seen as decisive in the eventual Allied victory, was transformed from the traditional "close" to "far," adapting to the innovations in weapons and platforms. Arms races, invasion scares, naval panics, the usual concerns over the trading rights of neutral powers, and accusations of encirclement resulted as inevitable consequences.

Despite warning signs discernable from the American Civil War and the Sino-Japanese and Russo-Japanese Wars of the late nineteenth and early twentieth centuries, many predicted that a future war would be short. When war finally came, the principal participants at sea were Great Britain, Germany, France, Russia, Austria-Hungary, Japan, Turkey, Italy, and the United States. Germany was the senior partner of the Central Powers, which also included Austria-Hungary and Turkey. The Allies, eventually two dozen states, were initially led by Britain, France, and Russia. Other sea states included the British self-governing Dominions and China.

The most volatile and enduring of the naval antagonisms of 1914 were those between Britain and Germany. During the two decades of the prewar period, personal leadership in the naval realm became so prominent that historians have named those periods after British Admiral of the Fleet Sir John "Jackie" Fisher and German Admiral Alfred von Tirpitz, respectively, the Fisher era and the Tirpitz era. Tirpitz viewed the German navy as the means to make the nation a world power; the British dreamed of another Battle of Trafalgar (1805) that would give them complete maritime dominance.

When developing naval strategy before the war, the British stressed naval blockade, a type of economic warfare. Technological advances in the nineteenth century forced alterations. An early and continuous strategy of the Allies was the implementation of the naval blockade of the Central Powers, something that did not end with the armistice of November 1918 but was extended through the first half of 1919, ending only with the signing of the Versailles Treaty in June 1919. Although controversial then, the British blockade obviously proved effective. Germany initiated its own version of blockade with unrestricted submarine warfare against the British Isles.

Blockade has several features. It is a technical legal term used in international law, initiated by a declaration published by a belligerent power forbidding trade with a designated enemy power. In military terms it means obstructing movement of enemy naval forces and commercial vessels from their ports. Close blockade, common in the days of sailing ship warfare, entailed continuous operations outside enemy ports. Long-range guns, mines, torpedoes, the submarine, and the airplane forced changes from the "close" blockade to the "far" blockade, which included trade interception out at sea. After a

British battleships *Agincourt* and *Benbow*. (National Archives)

review of the maneuvers of the Royal Navy in the late 1880s and subsequent debate, Britain concluded that close blockade was tactically too costly. Nevertheless, the Central Powers could be isolated by patrolling the narrow entrances to the English Channel and North Sea. The British, French, and Italian navies, and later the U.S. Navy, all participated in the blockade of the Central Powers, intercepting, diverting, or seizing hundreds of merchant vessels. Citizens of the Central Powers suffered significantly, and that suffering intensified over time.

During the war, the navies of the belligerents operated worldwide, in the Pacific and Atlantic oceans east and west of South America, in the Far East, in the Indian Ocean, in the Black Sea, and even along the Danube River. However, most operations were concentrated in the English Channel and the North Sea and in the Mediterranean and Baltic Seas. British sea power dominated worldwide, which was confirmed within a short time of the war's beginning. In the first few months there were dozens of individual actions, instances of German surface raiders sinking British merchant ships, and two important naval battles.

The most significant example of amphibious warfare during the war at sea was the 1915 Anglo-French naval expedi-tion against the Dardanelles in the eastern Mediterranean, which led to the Gallipoli campaign on land. Here the Allied strategic objective was to bypass the stalemate on the Western Front, drive Turkey from the war, and open up a southern supply route to Russia. British Admiralty planners, backed by the French, proposed to breach the defenses of the Dardanelles Straits by bombardment from capital ships, proceed into the Sea of Marmara, steam to Constantinople, and then threaten the city with naval bombardment to drive Turkey from the war and then proceed into the Black Sea to aid the Russians. Although Allied naval forces began attacking the forts, the Turks mined the waters. Minesweepers were brought in, but they could not sweep due to fire from the land forts and to the current, so the bombarding ships could not silence the forts. Following an attempt to force the straits in which three capital ships were sunk, ground forces were called in and the British and French mounted an invasion of the Gallipoli Peninsula. Anzacs, troops from Australia and New Zealand, participated along with the British and French. The Turks, with German assistance, contained the landings. The Turks admitted later that the naval effort almost succeeded and the invasion almost broke through, but success

Ships of the German High Seas Fleet steaming to the surrender rendezvous in the North Sea. (National Archives)

eluded the Allies. Their withdrawal in December 1915 was the only successful aspect of the campaign, as it took place with no casualties.

On 7 May 1915, a sensational naval incident occurred with both immediate and long-term consequences. The then largest and fastest passenger ship in the world, the Cunard liner *Lusitania,* en route from New York to Britain, was torpedoed off the coast of Ireland, near Kinsale, by the German *U-20.* Twelve hundred people, including 128 Americans, were lost, 61 percent of all aboard. Complications, controversies, and conspiracy theories arose then and later. American public opinion fast turned against the Germans.

On 31 May–1 June 1916, what the British hoped would be another battle of Trafalgar and the Germans hoped would be *Der Tag* (The Day) failed to materialize in both cases. In the North Sea, opposite Denmark, 151 ships of the British Grand Fleet and 101 ships of the German High Seas Fleet met in the late afternoon of 31 May. The Germans had hoped to cut off and destroy a portion of the British Grand Fleet. The British, who had fairly accurate knowledge of the German plans, hoped to destroy the German High Seas Fleet.

There were several confrontations in the Battle of Jutland, first of battle cruiser squadrons, then two episodes involving the main battle fleets, the Germans turning away both times, and, during the night of 31 May–1 June, a melee of confused night fighting, mostly by destroyers. The Germans had deployed both submarines and aircraft and the British an aircraft carrier, but they played no roles in the battle. The Germans escaped and returned to port. The Germans sank fourteen British ships and only lost eleven of their own. Casualties were 6,094 British and 3,058 German. The Germans claimed victory, but in fact the Battle of Jutland (known by the Germans as the Battle of the Skagerrak) represented a strategic victory for the British. Effectively, the Grand Fleet was ready for action the next day, while the ships of the High Seas Fleet required months of repairs. The German fleet never again ventured such a gamble, and many of its best junior officers and ratings were drawn off for the submarine campaign against Britain. Conditions in the German ships continued to deteriorate, and eventually, at the end of the war, mutinies occurred when the High Seas Fleet commanders attempted to take it out on a last "death ride."

Two German Navy sailors push a torpedo into the torpedo tube of a U-boat docked during World War I. (Corbis)

The Germans first implemented unrestricted submarine warfare at the beginning of the conflict, then had second thoughts and canceled it after the sinking of the *Lusitania*. They resumed it dramatically in February 1917. The results were almost fatal to the British, with the Germans sinking more tonnage than could be replaced and Britain's stocks of food fast dwindling. Far from driving Britain from the war, as the German Admiralty Staff had anticipated, the campaign had fatal consequences for Germany in that it brought the United States into the war that April.

German submarine successes beginning in February 1917 precipitated a desperate Allied search for countermeasures. A major focus of the scientific and invention initiatives of Britain and the United States was antisubmarine warfare. That massive effort, ultimately achieving increasing success, incorporated a variety of approaches, through trial and error, on hydrophones, depth charges, mines, minesweeping, nets, and, most important, the development of convoy tactics. Intelligence organizations also came into their own during the war. Among the most important was the famous Room 40 within British Admiralty headquarters in London.

Other episodes of the war at sea included the escape of the German warships *Goeben* and *Breslau* in the Mediterranean Sea to Turkey, helping to bring about its entry in the war on the side of the Central Powers; Anglo-German confrontations such as Coronel, the Falklands, and a series of Channel encounters such as Helgoland Bight and the Dogger Bank; the institution of massive underwater barriers to block U-boat exit routes; and U.S. and Japanese participation in the war, with deployment of their naval forces to European waters.

Final activities at sea in the war included the ineffective Zeebrugge landings, the surrender of much of the German battle fleet as a consequence of the armistice of 11 November 1918, and the sensational scuttling of that fleet, which had been interned at the British anchorage at Scapa Flow. The Allies purposely prolonged the blockade to force German acceptance of the peace settlement of 28 June 1919, which imposed sharp limits on German naval strength, including a ban on submarines. The Allies agreed to restrictions on their own at a conference held in Washington during 1921–1922, the first in a series of interwar naval disarmament conferences.

Eugene L. Rasor

See also

Antisubmarine Campaign, Allied Powers; Churchill, Sir Winston; Coronel, Battle of; Dardanelles Campaign; Dogger Bank, Battle of the; Falklands, Battle of the; Fisher, John Arbuthnot, 1st Baron; Germany, Navy; *Goeben* and *Breslau,* Escape of; Great Britain, Navy; Helgoland Bight, Battle of; Jutland, Battle of; Naval Blockade of Germany; Ostend and Zeebrugge Raids; Room 40; Scapa Flow, Scuttling of German Fleet at; Submarine Warfare, Central Powers; Tirpitz, Alfred von.

References

Corbett, Julian S., and Henry Newbolt. *Naval Operations: History of the Great War Based on Official Documents.* 5 vols. London: Longman, 1920–1931, 1938, 1940.

Frothingham, Thomas G. *The Naval History of the World War: The United States in the War, 1917–1918.* Cambridge: Harvard University Press, 1926.

Halpern, Paul G. *A Naval History of World War I.* Annapolis: Naval Institute Press, 1994.

Hough, Richard A. *The Great War at Sea, 1914–1918.* Oxford: Oxford University Press, 1983.

Marder, Arthur J. *From the Dreadnought to Scapa Flow: The Royal Navy in the Fisher Era, 1904–1919.* 5 vols. London: Oxford University Press, 1961–1970.

Millett, Allan R., and Williamson Murray, eds. *Military Effectiveness,* Vol. 1, *The First World War.* Boston: Unwin Hyman, 1988.

Newbolt, Henry. *A Naval History of the War, 1914–1918.* London: Hodder and Stoughton, 1920.

Netherlands

The Netherlands is strategically located along the North Sea. An important trading entrepôt, with much international trade passing through its great port cities of Rotterdam and Amsterdam, the Netherlands on the outbreak of the First World War immediately declared its neutrality. Still, there were concerns that the Germans might try to seize the strategically important Limburg territory as an easier route west or else invade to establish submarine bases along the North Sea. Dutch leaders also feared that the British might invade to secure the Scheldt River. Although many Dutch came to favor the Allies, particularly after heavy losses to the nation's merchant marine from German submarines, Queen Wilhelmina's government maintained strict neutrality throughout the conflict.

The 200,000-man Dutch military mobilized at the beginning of the war and remained under arms throughout the conflict, a considerable national expense. The army was not tested, which was fortunate because it was poorly trained and equipped and had insufficient stocks of ammunition.

The Netherlands became the reluctant host to numerous refugees. Following the siege of Antwerp, some 35,000 Belgian troops escaped across the border, where they were interned and remained the rest of the war. By war's end, nearly a million Belgians had fled to the Netherlands.

Cartoon showing Holland holding finger in "German contempt" leak of "neutrality dike," with "war" looming in the background, c. 1914–1918. (Library of Congress)

Although the Netherlands traded with both sides in the war, it was hard hit economically. The economy early on suffered severe disruption thanks to the refugees, the British naval blockade, and London's decision to declare goods bound for the Netherlands as contraband because the Dutch government could not guarantee that they would not be exported to Germany. The only positive aspect to this was that during the war the Dutch built up their industrial capability. Food stocks sharply decreased during the war, and in 1917 the government was forced to introduce rationing. Economic suffering during the war resulted in demands for constitutional change, which in turn provoked widespread support for the House of Orange. In November 1917, however, the Dutch introduced proportional representation and universal suffrage at age 25.

On 10 November 1918, in a controversial decision that brought considerable criticism from the Allied governments, Queen Wilhelmina's government decided to grant asylum to Kaiser Wilhelm II of Germany. He remained in the kingdom until his death in 1941.

Spencer C. Tucker

See also
Naval Blockade of Germany; Wilhelm II, Kaiser.
References
Frey, Marc. *Der Este Weltkrieg und die Nederlande: Ein Neutrales Land in politischen und wirtshaftlichen Kalkül der Kriegsgegner.* Berlin: Akademie Verlag, 1998.
Newton, Gerald. *The Netherlands: An Historical and Cultural Survey, 1795–1977.* Boulder, CO: Westview, 1978.
Schmitt, Hans A., ed. *Neutral Europe between War and Revolution, 1917–23.* Charlottesville: University of Virginia Press, 1988.
Tuyll van Serooskerken, Hubert P. van. *The Netherlands and World War I: Espionage, Diplomacy and Survival.* Leiden, Netherlands: Brill, 2001.
Voorhoeve, Joris J. C. *Peace, Profits and Principles: A Study of Dutch Foreign Policy.* The Hague: Martinus Nijhoff, 1979.

Neuilly, Treaty of (27 November 1919)

The treaty of peace between the victorious Allied and Associated Powers and Bulgaria. Signed in the Paris suburb of Neuilly-sur-Seine on 27 November 1919, the Treaty of Neuilly was a product of the Paris Peace Conference. Ostensibly founded on the principle of national self-determination, the treaty was actually the outcome of intense diplomatic pressure on the part of Bulgaria's victorious neighbors, dictated by the extremely complex history of national sovereignty in that part of Europe.

Rival territorial claims in the area dated back at least to the Treaty of Berlin of 1878, which had created the Principality of Bulgaria. However, many Bulgarians remained in territory such as Macedonia, controlled by the Ottoman Empire, or in Serbia and Romania. Bulgaria was the chief victor in the First Balkan War in 1912, securing a significant portion of Macedonia. In the Second Balkan War of 1913, Bulgaria recovered more of Macedonia and secured access to the Aegean Sea in Thrace, but it also yielded more land to Greece and Serbia elsewhere.

In World War I Bulgaria saw an opportunity to further its claims in Macedonia and to make good its losses in the Second Balkan War. Although most Bulgarians favored joining the Triple Entente because of ties to Russia, Tsar Ferdinand and Premier Vasil Radoslavov joined the Triple Alliance in October 1915. At the end of the war, the army overthrew Ferdinand, who abdicated in October 1918 and was succeeded by his son Boris III and a new premier, Aleksandŭr Stamboliyski; however, this did not change the fact that Bulgaria was on the losing side. Its Balkan rivals Greece and Serbia had chosen the winning side, and they pressed the conferees in Paris to favor their interests.

As with the other peace treaties, Part I of the Treaty of Neuilly reproduced the twenty-six articles of the League of Nations Covenant. Part II defined the new Bulgarian frontiers. Article 27-1 required Bulgaria to recognize the "Serb-Croat-Slovene State," which became Yugoslavia, and its new frontiers. The future Yugoslavia gained part of western Bulgaria and also regained some of the Strumitsa Valley area, which had been ceded to Bulgaria in 1913. Article 27-2 defined the new frontier with Greece, with grievous consequences for Bulgaria since it lost western Thrace to Greece and thus port facilities on the Aegean Sea at Dedeagats (Alexandroupolis in Greek). Articles 27-4 and 27-5 confirmed the Bulgarian frontier with Romania, with the definitive loss of Southern Dobruja (Dobrudza in Bulgarian), which had been part of Bulgaria since 1878 but ceded in 1913. Article 27–3 delineated the only gains made by Bulgaria; not surprisingly, these minor acquisitions were at the expense of another vanquished power, the Ottoman Empire.

Part III contained the "political clauses." Article 59 compelled Bulgaria to recognize the changes in central and southwestern Europe, including the new frontiers of Austria, Hungary, Greece, Poland, Romania, the Serb-Croat-Slovene state, and the Czecho-Slovak state. As a result of these territorial changes, Bulgaria, which had suffered 100,000 men killed in the war, now lost another 300,000 people.

The "Military Clauses" of Part IV demilitarized Bulgaria, abolished obligatory military service (Article 65) and stipulated that the Bulgarian army "shall be exclusively employed for the maintenance of order within Bulgarian territory and for the control of the frontiers" (Article 66). Article 69 limited the army to 20,000 men, supported by 10,000 policemen and 3,000 frontier guards. Article 78 banned construction of new fortifications in Bulgaria, while Article 81 prohibited manufacture or importation of arms, munitions, and war matériel.

Part VII dealt with reparations. Article 121 stipulated reparation payments in the amount that Bulgaria would be able to pay, $445 million—a realistic sum, especially as it was subsequently reduced considerably by the Reparation Commission.

The Treaty of Neuilly went into effect on 9 August 1920, and Bulgaria joined the League of Nations on 16 December 1920. The country remained bitterly divided politically. The Macedonian question was particularly vexing and led to a succession of governments in addition to costing Stamboliyski his life in 1923.

Antoine Capet

See also
Bulgaria, Role in War; Ferdinand I, Tsar of Bulgaria; League of Nations Covenant; Paris Peace Conference; Radoslavov, Vasil Hristov; Stamboliyski, Aleksandŭr.
References
Carnegie Endowment for International Peace. *The Treaties of Peace, 1919–1923,* Vol. 2, *Containing the Treaties of Neuilly and Sèvres, The Treaties between the United States and Germany, Austria and Hungary respectively.* New York: Carnegie Endowment for International Peace, 1924.
Crompton, R. J. *A Concise History of Bulgaria.* New York: Cambridge University Press, 1997.

Genov, Georgi P. *Bulgaria and the Treaty of Neuilly.* Sofia: H. G. Danov, 1935.

MacMillan, Margaret. *Paris 1919: Six Months That Changed the World.* New York: Random House, 2002.

Treaty of Peace between the Allied and Associated Powers and Bulgaria, and Protocol: Signed at Neuilly-sur-Seine, November 27, 1919. London: HMSO, 1920.

Neuve-Chapelle, Battle of (10–12 March 1915)

First major offensive effort by the British on the Western Front in the war. In October 1914 the Germans had forced a bulge in the Allied line. British First Army commander Lieutenant-General Sir Douglas Haig proposed retaking Neuve-Chapelle and also Aubers Ridge. If this were accomplished, the British would be in position to threaten the German rail center of Lille. Operational planning for the attack fell to Major-General Sir Henry Rawlinson, commander of IV Corps, who was unenthusiastic over pushing beyond Neuve-Chapelle. Haig insisted, and Rawlinson planned an assault, coordinating attacks by his IV Corps and the Indian Corps, that started with a short but intense bombardment lasting only thirty-five minutes—the British Expeditionary Force (BEF) lacked ammunition for an extended barrage. Rawlinson's plan called for a concentration of artillery fire from 342 guns that remained unequaled for two years. The most serious flaw in the plan, however, was the failure to delineate the attack on Aubers Ridge.

The attack on 10 March went very well, achieving complete surprise. Before 9:00 A.M. the British held the main street of Neuve-Chapelle, while the Indian Corps advanced to secure the right flank. On the left, however, there was trouble. Two howitzer batteries had arrived from Britain only the day before, and the guns were not properly registered. Their fire missed the German defenses, and wire-cutting fire also failed. On the left the attacking troops stopped and summoned artillery support. Despite communication problems, artillery fire was renewed and the British troops pushed forward, although at a high cost in casualties. By midday, the attackers had taken the initial objectives and were in position for the largely unplanned attack on Aubers Ridge.

The fog of war now took hold as battlefield communications deteriorated. Rawlinson had ordered telephones to be triple-wired with crossing connections, hoping to keep some lines open. These efforts failed. The lead battalions on the right had asked for permission to advance from Neuve-Chapelle in mid-

British soldiers fighting at close quarters at Neuve-Chapelle, France. (Francis J. Reynolds and C. W. Taylor, *Collier's Photographic History of the European War*, P. F. Collier & Son, New York, 1916)

morning but were told to wait for a coordinated attack. Some reserves were ready, but others had been used to fill holes in the line. Still other reserves were performing logistical support tasks and had to be reassembled. Coordination never occurred, and attacks, often unsupported because other units had differing or no orders, occurred piecemeal. A little ground was gained on the left and by the Indian Corps on the far right, but overall that afternoon saw only minimal progress.

Overnight the British prepared a coordinated attack by six battalions. The Germans, however, had deployed reserves and had prepared new defensive lines. The British artillery was firing without having registered on its new targets, making that fire inaccurate, and units attacking on 11 March were cut down by German machine-gun fire. Increased German shelling cut the British telephone wire, and confusion deepened. While Rawlinson insisted on pressing attacks, local commanders resisted and called for additional artillery support. Messages in each direction reached their intended recipients only sporadically.

Conditions were so desperate that battalion commanders refused to make supporting attacks when requested to do so by neighboring units, as they had received no official orders to do so. Units with orders ended up attacking alone, while other battalions received orders canceling attacks for which instructions had not arrived. The second day of the battle ended in failure for the BEF.

The third day of the battle, 12 March, began with a German counterattack. At dawn some 10,000 German troops assaulted the British line, but the German artillery barrage that was supposed to prepare the way failed for lack of target registration. The Germans penetrated the British lines at a few points, but after several hours the attack was defeated. Meanwhile, new British attacks had been planned in the illusory hope that artillery registration could be accomplished. Once again communications failed. British attacks were sporadic, with some commanders refusing outright to order their exhausted, battered units forward. Information reaching Rawlinson was consistently late and sometimes wrong. There were no significant British gains on the third day, and the battle then ended.

In the battle the British had straightened their line and retaken the village of Neuve-Chapelle. But this small gain had come at a cost of 11,652 casualties. The Germans suffered almost as many casualties due to their counterattack on the 12th. In the long run Neuve-Chapelle provided some lessons on the role of artillery fire in offensive actions, including the need for more accurate preparatory fire from heavier guns. The British, however, chose to concentrate on the destruction of obstacles in the path of the infantry, and this led to longer and heavier preliminary bombardmenets. The British also concluded that future attacks needed to take place across a broader front to allow exploitation by reserves. The Germans concluded that relatively small numbers of troops, properly dug in and supported, could repulse a numerically superior enemy force.

Fred R. van Hartesveldt

See also
Artillery; French, John, 1st Earl of Ypres; Haig, Douglas, 1st Earl; Rawlinson, Sir Henry Seymour; Shell Scandal.

References
Cassar, George H. *The Tragedy of Sir John French*. Newark: University of Delaware Press, 1985.

Johnson, J. H. *Stalemate! The Great Trench Warfare Battles of 1915–1917*. London: Arms and Armour, 1995.

Prior, Robin, and Trevor Wilson. *Command on the Western Front: The Military Career of Sir Henry Rawlinson 1914–1918*. Oxford, UK: Blackwell, 1992.

New Zealand, Army

On 4 August 1914, the New Zealand government cabled London with the offer of an expeditionary force to aid the "Mother Country" in the conflict ahead. Within forty-eight hours this offer had been accepted, and recruitment for the "New Zealand Expeditionary Force" (NZEF), consisting of an infantry brigade, a mounted rifles brigade, a field artillery brigade, and supporting arms, began in earnest. A pioneer battalion drawn specifically from the indigenous Maori population was also formed.

While the main body was under organization, a small 1,400-strong force was dispatched to seize German Samoa. This task was carried out on 29 August without bloodshed, although 215 of these men would later die on the battlefields of Europe and the Middle East.

Escorted by British and Japanese warships, the convoy carrying the first 8,500 officers and men of the NZEF left New Zealand on 16 October 1914, bound for Egypt. Once there, the New Zealanders were joined by two Australian brigades to form the "New Zealand & Australian Division," which, together with the 1st Australian Division, made up the newly christened Australian and New Zealand Army Corps (Anzac). It was in these formations that the soldiers of the NZEF fought throughout the 1915 Gallipoli campaign at the cost of 7,473 casualties. NZEF battalions also saw action that year along the Suez Canal and against the Senussi on the Egyptian-Libyan frontier.

In the aftermath of Gallipoli the NZEF was rebuilt and expanded. Two additional infantry brigades and two field artillery brigades were raised, allowing the formation of a "pure" New Zealand Division in March 1916. That division was sent to France a month later, while the Mounted Rifles Brigade remain in Egypt where they were incorporated into the "Australia & New Zealand Mounted Division," alongside three Australian light horse brigades.

New Zealand infantry corporal in full pack. (National Archives)

The New Zealand Division spent two months in the relatively quiet Armentières sector of the line before participating in the later stages of the 1916 Battle of the Somme. In three separate attacks in September and October 1916, the New Zealanders seized all of their objectives, despite suffering 7,408 casualties in the process. This set the pattern for the division's operations on the Western Front over the next two years. Only once, on 12 October 1917, during the Battle of Passchendaele, did the division fail to take an objective, and on that occasion it suffered its highest losses in a single day: 1,190 dead and 2,106 wounded.

The New Zealanders also proved themselves resolute in defense, most notably in March–April 1918 when they helped stop the German drive on Amiens. After taking part in the battle to break through the Hindenburg Line, the division finished the war by storming the ancient fortress town of Le Quesnoy on 4 November 1918, capturing 2,000 German prisoners and sixty guns in the process.

Accordingly, all of its British corps and army commanders rated the New Zealand Division highly as an aggressive and reliable formation. Another factor commending the division to some British observers was a better disciplinary record out of the line than its Australian and Canadian coun-terparts. The division was also numerically larger than its British and Dominion counterparts during most of its service on the Western Front. From May 1917 to February 1918, it had a fourth infantry brigade attached, which was only broken up in the aftermath of the losses incurred at Passchendaele. Even then, thanks to the introduction of conscription at home, the division was able to maintain four battalions per brigade through to the end of the war, whereas British and Australian brigades were reduced to three battalions.

The New Zealand Mounted Rifles Brigade enjoyed a similar record of operational success, with far lighter casualties, in Sinai and Palestine. From the Battle of Romani in August 1916 to the capture of Amman in September 1918, the New Zealand horsemen were a constant mainstay of the British effort to expel Ottoman forces from the Holy Land.

In addition to these major NZEF formations, a large number of smaller NZEF units or detachments also served with the British armies in Europe and the Middle East. These included a cyclist battalion, a tunneling company, and a light railway company in France; a stationary hospital in the Salonika campaign; a pack wireless troop in Mesopotamia; and two companies of the Imperial Camel Corps in Sinai and Palestine.

To sustain these units in the field, NZEF base organizations were established in Egypt and the United Kingdom. A large and elaborate network quickly developed in the latter, and by November 1917, 17,700 NZEF personnel (which includes those recovering from wounds or sickness) were in the United Kingdom as opposed to 23,870 in France. The New Zealand network in the United Kingdom ranged in size and function from three general hospitals to a gift section in London.

A total of 124,211 men, or approximately 45 percent of the New Zealand male population between the ages of 18 and 45, mobilized for the NZEF, and 550 women served in the New Zealand Army Nursing Service. Of those mobilized, 100,444 men were sent overseas. The NZEF suffered a total of 59,483 casualties, including 18,166 dead. Given these figures, it is interesting to note that only 501 soldiers of the NZEF were made prisoners of war.

Damien Fenton

See also

Anzac; Anzac Convoy; New Zealand, Role in War; Pacific Islands Campaign.

References

Boyack, Nicholas. *Behind the Lines: The Lives of New Zealand Soldiers in the First World War.* Winchester, MA: Allen and Unwin, 1989.

Carbery, Andrew D. *The New Zealand Medical Service in the Great War, 1914–18.* Sydney, Australia: Angus and Robertson, 1935.

Drew, H. T. B., ed. *Official History of New Zealand's Effort in the Great War,* Vol. 4, *The War Effort of New Zealand.* Wellington, New Zealand: Whitcombe and Tombs, 1923.

McGibbon, Ian. *The Path to Gallipoli: Defending New Zealand, 1840–1915.* Wellington, New Zealand: GP Books, 1991.

Powles, Charles G. *Official History of New Zealand's Effort in the Great War*, Vol. 3, *The New Zealanders in Sinai and Palestine*. Wellington, New Zealand: Whitcombe and Tombs, 1922.

Pugsley, Christopher. *The ANZAC Experience: New Zealand, Australia and Empire in the First World War*. Auckland, New Zealand: Reed, 2004.

———. *On the Fringe of Hell: New Zealanders and Military Discipline in the First World War*. Auckland, New Zealand: Hodder and Stroughton, 1991.

Stewart, Hugh. *Official History of New Zealand's Effort in the Great War*, Vol. 2, *The New Zealand Division, 1916–1919*. Wellington, New Zealand: Whitcombe and Tombs, 1921.

Studholme, John. *Some Records of the New Zealand Expeditionary Force, Unofficial, but Compiled from Official Records*. Wellington, New Zealand: Government Printer, 1928.

Waite, Frederick. *Official History of New Zealand's Effort in the Great War*, Vol. 1, *The New Zealander's at Gallipoli*. Wellington, New Zealand: Whitcombe and Tombs, 1921.

New Zealand, Role in War

The British Dominion of New Zealand loyally followed Britain into World War I. A large proportion of the population served in the war: 128,449 New Zealanders volunteered for the New Zealand Expeditionary Forces (NZEF) from a population of only 1.09 million people. On 29 August 1914, some 1,400 NZEF troops landed unopposed in German Samoa and remained there throughout the war.

The chief military employment of the NZEF came in the Middle East. In February 1915 New Zealand troops helped repulse a Turkish attack on the Suez Canal. New Zealanders were combined with Australians into the Australian and New Zealand Corps (Anzac) and were primarily identified with the Allied campaign on the Gallipoli Peninsula in 1915.

The NZEF reorganized, and most of it then sailed for France. New Zealand troops saw extensive service on the Western Front and then served in the occupation of Germany until June 1919. In the entirety of the war, New Zealand troops suffered 59,483 casualties, including 18,166 dead, a casualty rate of nearly 60 percent.

In addition to the NZEF, New Zealand also contributed some 700 ground and aircrew troops to the Royal Flying Corps, the Royal Naval Air Service, and the Australian Flying Corps and at least 500 men to the Royal Navy.

Before the war New Zealand paid for the battle cruiser *New Zealand*, commissioned in 1912 and donated to the Royal Navy as New Zealand's contribution to imperial defense. The Royal New Zealand Navy's only warship during the war was the *Philomel*, an old Pearl-class cruiser completed in 1890 and armed with 8 × 4.7-inch and 8 × 3-pounder guns and 2 torpedo tubes. The *Philoeml* helped escort the force that occupied German Samoa and then served in the Mediterranean and the Persian Gulf. Several hundred New Zealanders also served in the Royal Navy Motor Boat Reserve, and a number of them took part in the raids on Zeebrugge and Ostend in April 1918. New Zealand also made other important contributions to the war effort, chiefly in the export of food to Britain.

M. Taylor Emery

See also

Anzac; Anzac Convoy; Gallipoli Campaign; Jutland, Battle of; New Zealand, Army; Ostend and Zeebrugge Raids; Suez Canal; Suvla Bay Offensive; Vimy Ridge, Battle of; Ypres, Third Battle of.

References

Livingston, William S., and Wm. Roger Louis, eds. *Australia, New Zealand, and the Pacific Islands since the First World War*. Austin: University of Texas Press, 1979.

Pugsley, Christopher. *The ANZAC Experience: New Zealand, Australia and Empire in the First World War*. Auckland, New Zealand: Reed, 2004.

———. *Gallipoli: The New Zealand Story*. Auckland, New Zealand: Hodder and Stoughton, 1984.

Robertson, John. *The Tragedy and Glory of Gallipoli: ANZAC and Empire*. Darlinghurst, Australia: Mead and Beckett, 1990.

Newfoundland

Now a province of Canada, during World War I Newfoundland was a separate Dominion of the British Empire. The Dominion of Newfoundland consisted of Newfoundland Island and Labrador on the mainland. The small, sparsely settled Dominion depended on its fishing fleets, mining, and timber. As a loyal and staunchly pro-British part of the empire, Newfoundland raised more than 8,500 men for service, representing a sizable proportion of all able-bodied young men in the Dominion. Of those, 7,000 thousand served in the army and Forestry Corps, with the remainder serving in the Royal Navy. Of the 5,482 in the army and Forestry Corps who served outside of Newfoundland, 1,300 were killed and another 2,314 wounded. Of those in the Royal Navy, 180 died and 125 were invalided home.

Most Newfoundlanders in the army formed the 1st Newfoundland Regiment and shipped first to Britain for training and then to France for service. The Newfoundlanders went into combat at Beaumont-Hamel in the Battle of the Somme on 1 July 1916. British commanders, disbelieving reports that the first wave had failed, sent the Newfoundlanders forward in the second wave. The regiment attacked straight from its reserve trench, without artillery support and in full daylight, and struggled to cross a half mile of no-man's-land. Within an hour, the attack was over. All 26 officers and 658 of the 752 soldiers who left the trench were killed or wounded. The effect on Newfoundland was catastrophic, and the emotional bond with Britain that had kept Newfoundland out of the Canadian Confederation was broken. In 1949, following the Great Depression and another world war, Newfoundland abandoned Dominion status and joined Canada.

Barry M. Stentiford

See also
Canada, Role in War; Great Britain, Colonies; Somme Offensive.
References
Harris, Leslie. *Newfoundland and Labrador: A Brief History*. London: J. M. Dent and Sons, 1968.
MacKay, R. A., ed. *Newfoundland: Economic, Diplomatic, and Strategic Studies*. Toronto: Oxford University Press, 1946.
Middlebrook, Martin. *The First Day on the Somme, 1 July 1916*. New York: Norton, 1972.
Perlin, A. B. *The Story of Newfoundland Comprising of a New Outline of the Island's History from 1497 to 1959*. St. Johns, Newfoundland: Guardian, 1959.

Nicholas II, Tsar (1868–1918)

Emperor of imperial Russia and last of the Romanov dynasty that ruled Russia for two and a half centuries. Born on the feast day of Job the Sufferer, 16 May 1868, Nicholas Alexandraevich Romanov was the eldest son of Tsar Alexander III and Tsarina Marie Fyodorovna, daughter of the king of Denmark. Nicholas became tsar of all the Russians on 20 October 1894 when his father died unexpectedly of nephritis, a disease of the kidneys, at age 49. Temperamentally unfit to carry the burden of ruling Russia in a period of upheaval and great change as it struggled to industrialize and modernize, the new tsar was shy and reserved in relations outside his family and intimate circle. He had enjoyed only limited exposure to Russian political affairs and social conditions. Nicholas was unsure in his decision making and lacked the singleness of purpose that had marked his father's rule. Less than a month after his ascension, Nicholas married Princess Alix (Alice), from the small German duchy of Hesse-Darmstadt, who had been brought up in Kensington Palace by her grandmother, Queen Victoria. Taking the Russian name of Alexandra Fyodorovna, Alix wholeheartedly embraced Russian Orthodoxy and, like her husband, exercised unshakeable faith in the mystical union of the Russian autocracy and the people, blessed by the Orthodox Church. Nicholas adored his wife and was dominated by her. He preferred sports, recording weather data, gathering mushrooms in the forests around St. Petersburg and Tsarskoe Selo, and being with family to the official functions required of the tsar. However, he could be unshakable in holding to a position once he had taken it, and he was resolute in his belief in the traditional as well as the tsar's divine right to autocratic rule. Nicholas also harbored a disdain for Jews, intellectuals, and liberal democratic ideologies and institutions.

Early in Nicholas's reign revolutionary activity gained momentum, spurred on by Russia's defeat in the 1904–1905

Tsar Nicholas II of Russia. (Library of Congress)

Russo-Japanese War and the resulting revolution of 1905 that caused the tsar to agree to the establishment of an elected parliament, the State Duma. The era became one of increased personal freedom and economic progress but also one of heightened revolutionary activity, agents provocateurs, and government reaction.

Nicholas II and Alexandra were extremely devout, profoundly believing in miracles, faith healing, and guidance and comfort provided by men of God. Into this atmosphere of mysticism came the reputed faith healer Grigory Rasputin. Tsarevich Aleksey Nikolaevich, heir to the throne, was a hemophiliac. Called to the boy's bedside on occasions of distress, Rasputin was apparently able to stop the tsarevich's hemorrhaging. Rasputin's success in controlling Aleksey's bleeding endeared him to the tsarina and gave him an intimacy with and access to the royal family enjoyed by few. His unfettered advice soon interfered in state business and influenced the tsar's decisions in relation to ministerial and military matters, particularly after the outbreak of World War I.

Initially, Nicholas sought to avoid war and suggested that the crisis between Austria-Hungary and Serbia be submitted to the Hague International Court, despite pressure from militarists. Nicholas vacillated on the issue, but in late July he finally authorized mobilization of the Russian army, which brought a German declaration of war against Russia. Nicholas then appointed his popular uncle, Grand Duke Nikolai Niko-laevich, as commander-in-chief of the armed forces. Envious of the grand duke's popularity and fearing it threatened the throne, Alexandra pressed her husband to assume his right-ful position as commander-in-chief in an effort to reverse Russia's early military defeats.

When the tsar took personal command of the war effort on 21 August 1915, the tsarina gained increased sway in han-dling domestic affairs and fell completely under the sway of Rasputin. With the war effort going badly and conditions at home deteriorating, resentment of Alexandra's relationship with Rasputin fed building revolutionary fervor. Yet the fall of the monarchy, in March 1917, came not from a revolu-tionary coup d'état but from civil disturbances brought on by food shortages in the capital that incited general strikes and work stoppages.

Forced to abdicate when his council of ministers collapsed on 12 March 1917 and his generals urged political conces-sions to restore order, Nicholas renounced his throne to his brother Grand Duke Mikhail on 15 March. When Mikhail declined the throne, he brought an end to the Romanov dynasty. Nicholas and his family went into virtual house arrest in Tsarskoe Selo when a promise of asylum in England was withdrawn by Nicholas's cousin King George V.

As conditions in the nearby capital worsened, the provi-sional government moved the former tsar and his family to a governor's mansion in Tobolsk, western Siberia. When the Bolsheviks seized control in November 1917, the family was moved yet again, to Yekaterinburg in the Urals. It was here during the civil war that Bolshevik leader Vladimir Lenin ordered local officials to "liquidate" Nicholas and his family to prevent them from becoming a rallying point for White opposition. At midnight on 16–17 July 1918, Nicholas, Alexandra, and their son and four daughters along with their doctor and three servants were executed by their guards and their bodies thrown into a nearby abandoned mine shaft.

Arthur T. Frame

See also
Lenin, Vladimir Ilyich; Nikolai Nikolaevich, Grand Duke; October
    Manifesto; Rasputin, Grigory Yefimovich; Russia, Army; Russia,
    Home Front; Russia, Revolution of March 1917; Russia,
    Revolution of November 1917.

References
Carrère d'Encausse, Hélène. *Nicholas II: The Interrupted
    Transition.* Trans. George Holoch. New York: Holmes and
    Meier, 2000.
Ferro, Marc. *Nicholas II: Last of the Tsars.* Trans. Brian Pearce. New
    York: Oxford University Press, 1993.
Florinsky, Michael T. *The End of the Russian Empire.* New York:
    Collier, 1931.
Massie, Robert K. *Nicholas and Alexandra.* New York: Atheneum,
    1967.
———. *The Romanovs: The Final Chapter.* New York: Random
    House, 1995.
Mazour, Anatole G. *Rise and Fall of the Romanovs.* Princeton, NJ: D.
    Van Nostrand, 1960.
Radzinsky, Edvard. *The Last Tsar: The Life and Death of
    Nicholas II.* Trans. Marian Schwartz. New York: Doubleday,
    1992.
Sulzberger, C. L. *The Fall of Eagles.* New York: Crown, 1977.
Warth, Robert D. *Nicholas II: The Life and Reign of Russia's Last
    Monarch.* Westport, CT: Praeger, 1997.

Nicolai, Walter (1873–1947)

German (Prussian) army colonel and head of the intelligence section of the German Supreme Command. Born in Braun-schweig on 1 August 1873, Walter Nicolai grew up in an impoverished officer's family and joined the 82th Infantry Regiment in 1893. Promoted to major in 1912, he became act-ing head of the General Staff's subsection for intelligence (Sektion IIIb).

Given the federal law enforcement structure of Germany, a notorious lack of funding, a general lack of interest in intelli-gence matters in the army, and a navy that was eager to prove the independence of its own agency, Nicolai faced a compli-cated task. During the war this task grew to include military intelligence, counterintelligence, censorship, attaché service, and war propaganda. In June 1915 IIIb was upgraded to a full section (Abteilung), but within the headquarters' hierarchy Nicolai lost influence to the more political soldiers on the staff, such as Max Bauer and Hans von Haeften. Nicolai began to delegate intelligence matters to subordinates in order to con-centrate fully on propaganda, and in 1917 he introduced the "Patriotic Instructions," a propaganda document aimed at bolstering support for the German war effort from soldiers and the home front. His promotion to lieutenant colonel fol-lowed in January 1918, but the armistice ended Nicolai's career. Regarded as a representative of the Supreme Com-mand's dictatorial regime in domestic policy, Nicolai was given leave until his formal retirement at the rank of colonel on 27 February 1920.

The Reichswehr showed no interest in reintegrating Nico-lai into the writing of the official history of the service or the reorganization of the Abwehr (military intelligence). He spent his retirement in political activities in a nationalist youth organization and writing his memoirs. In September 1945, the 72-year-old Nicolai was arrested by the Soviet NKVD, which wrongly took him for a figure in the Nazi intel-ligence web. He was deported to Moscow for interrogation and died there on 4 May 1947.

Markus Pöhlmann

See also
Intelligence and Counterintelligence; Oberste Heeresleitung;
    Propaganda; Sabotage.

References

Nicolai, Walter. *The German Secret Service.* Trans. George Renwick. London: S. Paul, 1924.

Welch, David. *Germany, Propaganda, and Total War, 1914–1918: The Sins of Omission.* New Brunswick, NJ: Rutgers University Press, 2000.

Nikola I Petrovic-Njegos, King (1841–1921)

Prince (1860–1910) and then king (1910–1918) of Montenegro. Born at Njegos on 7 October 1841, Nikola Mirkov Petrovic-Njegos, the son of Duke Mirko Petrovic-Njegos and Anastasia Martinovich, was educated in Trieste and Paris. When his uncle, Prince Danilo, was assassinated in 1860, Nikola became the ruling prince of Montenegro and embarked on a long process of modernizing his tiny, backward principality. He introduced many administrative, legal, and educational reforms and oversaw the construction of transportation and communications systems. He granted constitutional government in 1905 and subsequently declared himself king on 28 August 1910. Nikola married Milena Vukotic in 1860. Of their twelve children, five daughters and one son married into European royal families, earning Nikola the sobriquet of "the father-in-law of Europe."

With the support of his friend Tsar Alexander II of Russia, Nikola proved an able military leader. Under his leadership the Montenegrins repelled a Turkish attack in 1862 and conducted a brilliant campaign against the Turks during 1876–1877, thereby winning their independence from the Ottoman Empire while doubling the size of their country. King Nikola also led Montenegro effectively in the Balkan Wars of 1912–1913 and supported Serbia against the Central Powers in World War I. The small but courageous Montenegrin army covered the retreat of the Serbian army through Albania in November–December 1915 but was forced to surrender to the Austro-Hungarians on 17 January 1916. King Nikola then went into exile in Italy. On 26 November 1918 he was deposed by the Montenegrin National Assembly, and Montenegro was annexed by Serbia, thus becoming the only Allied state to lose its independence in World War I.

King Nikola I transformed Montenegro from a remote Balkan principality into a modern European state and led her effectively in peace and war only to lose his kingdom to the "Greater Serbia" ambitions of his son-in-law, King Peter I of Serbia, and the rising tide of South Slav nationalism. He died in exile at Cap d'Antibes, France, on 2 March 1921 and was buried at San Remo, Italy. In 1989 his remains were reinterred at Cetinje.

Charles R. Shrader

King Nikola I Petrovic-Njegos of Montenegro. (Library of Congress)

See also

Balkan Front; Balkan Wars; Montenegro; Yugoslavia, Creation of.

References

Glenny, Misha. *The Balkans: Nationalism War and the Great Powers, 1804–1999.* New York: Viking, 2000.

Nikola I Petrov'c Njegos. *Autobiografija; Memoari; Putopisi.* Eds. Dimitrije Joveti'c and Branko Bankev'c. Cetinje, Montenegro: ISRO Obod, 1988.

Treadway, John D. *The Falcon and the Eagle: Montenegro and Austria-Hungary, 1908–1914.* West Lafayette, IN: Purdue University Press, 1983, 1998.

Nikolaevsk Massacre (25 May 1920)

Massacre of Japanese soldiers and civilians by Bolshevik partisans during the Russian Civil War. Nikolaevsk was a small city in eastern Siberia at the mouth of the Amur River. A thriving fishing industry sustained the population of 15,000 people, including approximately 350 Japanese merchants.

Japanese forces intervening in Siberia in 1918 imposed harsh policies on the inhabitants of that territory. This helped build support for the Bolsheviks there during the Russian Civil War and set the stage for Bolshevik retaliation.

In November 1919 Yakov Ivanovich Triapitsyn led a Bolshevik group of partisans down the Amur River. His initial force of only 10 men eventually grew to some 2,000. This force arrived at the fortress of Chnyrrakh near Nikolaevsk in early February 1920. The counterrevolutionary White (Russian) and Japanese military detachment there then retired to Nikolaevsk, and the partisans followed, shelling the city. On the 24th the two sides signed a cease fire, and the partisans moved into the city. Several weeks later White and Japanese forces mounted a counterattack, which culminated in the partisans storming the Japanese consulate in Nikolaevsk on 15 March, ending all resistance.

The Bolsheviks soon learned of a planned Japanese counterattack. Preparations for the defense of the city began with the evacuation and voluntary departure of approximately 6,000 Russian inhabitants. On 25 May Triapitsyn ordered the execution of the Japanese at Nikolaevsk. Conservative accounts estimate the number killed at 350 civilians and 306 soldiers.

The Japanese government used the incident to incite popular support against the Bolsheviks and revitalize its Siberian operations. By July, Japanese forces had extended their occupation to include the important areas of the Siberian coast. Bolshevik partisans captured Triapitsyn and executed him for his crimes on 25 July 1920. The last Japanese troops in Siberia departed Vladivostok in October 1922, and the Japanese evacuated north Sakhalin Island following a treaty with Russia in January 1925.

Jason W. Crockett

See also

Japan, Army; Siberian Intervention, Japan.

References

Connaughton, Richard M. *The Republic of Ushakovka: Admiral Kolchak and the Allied Intervention in Siberia, 1918–1920.* London: Routledge, 1990.

Kawamura, Noriko. *Turbulence in the Pacific: Japanese-U. S. Relations during World War I.* Westport, CT: Praeger, 2000.

Unterberger, Betty Miller. *America's Siberian Expedition, 1918–1920: A Study of National Policy.* New York: Greenwood, 1969.

White, John Albert. *The Siberian Intervention.* Princeton, NJ: Princeton University Press, 1950.

Nikolai Nikolaevich, Grand Duke (1856–1929)

Russian army general and commander of the Russian army early in World War I. Born in St. Petersburg on 18 November

Russian Grand Duke Nikolai Nikolaevich of Russia. (Francis J. Reynolds and C. W. Taylor, *Collier's Photographic History of the European War,* P. F. Collier & Son, New York, 1916)

1856, Nikolai Nikolaevich ("the Younger") was a member of the Russian imperial family and received the customary military education. He completed the Nikolaevsky Engineering School in 1873 and graduated from the General Staff Academy in 1886.

During the 1877–1878 Russo-Turkish War, Nikolai Nikolaevich served first as an aide to the Russian field commander, his father Grand Duke Nikolai Nikolaevich ("the Elder"), and then in the Guards Cavalry. A major general by 1885, he next served from 1895 to 1905 as the army's inspector general of cavalry.

In 1901 during the reign of his nephew, Tsar Nicholas II, Grand Duke Nikolai was promoted to general of cavalry. Four years later during the October Revolution of 1905, he enhanced his reputation as a political liberal by refusing to suppress unrest and pushing the tsar toward constitutional reform.

The grand duke gained the reputation of a military reformer during the period after the 1904–1905 Russo-Japanese War. He headed the Council of State Defense during 1905–1908, coordinating the operational tasks of the army and navy. In response to unjust criticism from the Duma, he resigned from the Council on State Defense in 1908 and became inspector general of cavalry and commander of the St. Petersburg Military District.

On 2 August 1914 during the Russian mobilization for war, Tsar Nicholas II appointed his uncle commander-in-chief of the army. This came as a surprise in military circles because of the grand duke's lack of combat experience and the tactical and administrative skills required in this post. Grand Duke Nikolai ordered a series of offensives that proved to be his primary contribution to the 1914 campaign, but he did not control daily operations. Continued military reversals, though hardly the fault of the grand duke, led Tsar Nicholas II to sack his uncle on 21 August 1915 and take command of the army himself. The grand duke then became the head of the Caucasus Military Region.

In the wake of the 1917 March revolution, Grand Duke Nikolai urged his nephew to abdicate. He himself retired and moved to the Crimea. In March 1919 he went abroad, living out his final years in Italy and France. He died in Antibes on 5 January 1929.

Joseph D. Montagna

See also
Eastern Front Overview; Nicholas II, Tsar; Russia, Army; Russia, Revolution of March 1917.
References
Ferro, Marc. *Nicholas II: Last of the Tsars.* Trans. Brian Pearce. New York: Oxford University Press, 1993.
Lincoln, W. Bruce. *The Romanovs: Autocrats of All the Russias.* Garden City, NY: Doubleday, 1981.
Stone, Norman. *The Eastern Front, 1914–1917.* New York: Scribner, 1975.
Wildman, Allan K. *The End of the Russian Imperial Army.* 2 vols. Princeton, NJ: Princeton University Press, 1980–1987.

Nitti, Francesco Saverio (1868–1953)

Italian statesman. Born on 19 July 1868 in Melfi, Francesco Nitti graduated with a degree in law from Naples University in 1890 and worked on the staff of the newspaper *Xorriere di Napoli.* In 1892 he began to teach political economy at the University of Napes, and from 1898 he also taught economics. In 1903 Nitti published *Principi di scienza delle finanze* (Principles of Financial Science). He also wrote additional books on politics and economics.

In 1904 Nitti won election as a Radical to the Chamber of Deputies of the Italian parliament. During 1911–1914 he served in the cabinet of Giovanni Giolitti as minister of agriculture, industry, and trade. During the First World War Nitti, unlike Giolitti, urged Italian intervention on the Allied side, although he saw this not as a vehicle for Italian territorial aggrandizement as much as a means to preserve European democracy.

In mid-1917 Nitti traveled to the United States to secure U.S. economic and financial aid for Italy. Nitti served as minister of the Treasury in the Vittorio Orlando cabinet during October 1917–January 1919. Second in stature in the cabinet only to Orlando, Nitti had a major impact on the war effort, demanding that Italian resources be fully mobilized in

Italian premier Francesco Saverio Nitti (with cane). (Edgar Allen Forbes, ed., *Leslie's Photographic Review of the Great War,* Leslie-Judge Co., New York, 1920)

order to achieve victory. He also managed to secure both financial and food aid from Italy's allies. Nitti also influenced military policy in supporting new army commander General Armando Diaz's pleas to defer offensive military action until the army had been rebuilt following the Caporetto debacle.

Disgruntled by postwar developments, especially the failure of the government to adopt his economic plans for a peacetime economy, Nitti resigned his post in January 1919. After the fall of the Orlando government, Nitti was himself premier, from June 1919 until June 1920. During this period Nitti tried to convert industry to peacetime production, but he also had to deal with internal unrest brought on by the Socialists and an international crisis unleashed by Gabriele D'Annunzio's occupation of Fiume. The use of force to compel D'Annunzio to abandon Fiume, while necessary to maintain solidarity with Italy's Entente allies, was nonetheless highly unpopular in Italy. This weakened Nitti's position in the November 1919 election and led to the collapse of his government the next June.

Nitti at first worked with Benito Mussolini, hoping to moderate his Fascist movement. In 1924, however, he broke with the Italian dictator and went into exile in Switzerland. He settled in Paris the next year, where he organized anti-Fascist Italians in exile.

Arrested by the Germans in August 1943, Nitti was freed at the end of the Second World War and returned to Italy. He resumed his political activity and continued to write books, becoming known as a staunch anticommunist and neutralist. Nitti died in Rome on 20 February 1953.

Alessandro Massignani

See also
Caporetto, Battle of; Diaz, Armando; D'Annunzio, Gabriele; Giolitti, Giovanni; Italy, Home Front; Mussolini, Benito.

References
Barbagallo, Francesco. *Francesco S. Nitti.* Turin, Italy: Unione tipografico-editrice torinese, 1984.
Bosworth, R. J. B. *Italy and the Approach of the First World War.* New York: Macmillan, 1983.
Burgwyn, H. James. *The Legend of the Mutilated Victory: Italy, the Great War, and the Paris Peace Conference, 1915–1919.* Westport, CT: Greenwood, 1993.
Lowe, Cedric J., and Frank Marzari. *Italian Foreign Policy, 1870–1940.* London and Boston: Routledge and Kegan Paul, 1975.
Monticone, Alberto. *Nitti e la Grande Guerra (1914–1918).* Milan: Giuffré, 1961.
Thayer, John A. *Italy and the Great War: Politics and Culture, 1870–1915.* Madison: Wisconsin University Press, 1964.

Nivelle, Robert (1856–1924)

French army general and commander-in-chief. Born in Tulle on 15 October 1915, Robert Nivelle, the son of a Protestant officer and an English mother, graduated from the École Polytechnique in 1878. Commissioned in the artillery, he saw duty in China, Korea, and Algeria. By August 1914, he was a colonel commanding the 4th Artillery Regiment.

Nivelle embodied the school of the offensive. During the Battle of Frontiers in 1914, he earned acclaim by charging a battery of 75mm field guns through a retreating group of French infantry toward the advancing Germans and halting them with rapid short-range artillery fire. Enjoying quick promotion thereafter, Neville won further renown during the Battle of Verdun as commander of the Second Army, where his use of counterbattery fire, the creeping barrage, and aggressive small-unit tactics recaptured Forts Vaux and Douaumont. With these successes to his credit, he appeared to be the brightest star in the French army. Nivelle's Protestantism further enhanced his popularity with anticlerical center-left politicians.

In December 1916, Premier Aristide Briand selected Nivelle to replace General Joseph Joffre as French commander-in-chief over such established generals as the older Ferdinand Foch and the more cautious Henri Philippe Pétain. Hoping to convert his local tactical methods into a grand operational success, Nivelle promised that he could win the war with a single great breakthrough if he were given sufficiently large reserves, a *masse de maneuvre.* Briand's cabinet, which was deeply concerned by the ever-worsening strain of the war on France's manpower and international finances, found this argument compelling. Many French officers were afraid that France would be eclipsed by Britain and accordingly wished it to play the starring role in 1917. The English-speaking Nivelle also appealed to British Prime Minister David Lloyd George, who deeply distrusted his own commander on the Western Front, Field Marshal Sir Douglas Haig. Nivelle was thus able to persuade the British government to make him the overall commander on the front and to extend the lines of the British Expeditionary Force (BEF) in order to release sufficient French troops for his offensive.

Both Haig and his ally, Chief of the Imperial General Staff General Sir William Robertson, opposed placing the BEF under Neville. Only after a bitter civil-military crisis did they agree to subordinate the BEF to Nivelle for the duration of his attack. Shortly after this compromise, the Briand government lost a vote of confidence and was replaced by the Ribot government. The new minister of war, Paul Painlevé, had little confidence in Nivelle, especially after the Germans withdrew the bulk of their forces in the threatened Aisne region to the heavily fortified Siegfried (Hindenburg) Line. Yet in spite of the changed strategic landscape, Nivelle silenced his doubters by threatening to resign if he were not allowed his way.

On 9 April 1917 Nivelle set the Allied armies in motion. After a preliminary attack by the BEF in the Arras sector captured Vimy Ridge but failed to draw off substantial German reserves, Nivelle launched his main assault with the French Sixth and Tenth Armies on the night of 15–16 April. Although the French captured 20,000 German prisoners by 9 May, they only advanced 4 miles and suffered almost 130,000 dead and wounded. Coming in the wake of three years of terrible casualties, this offensive proved to be the last straw for many French soldiers. More than half of all French divisions mutinied in the spring and summer of 1917. For France, this setback represented the nadir of the war. Nivelle was relieved of command on 15 May 1917, leaving it to his successor, General Henri Philippe Pétain, to rebuild morale and to implement more cautious and thorough offensive tactics.

In spite of the disaster brought on by Nivelle, a determined attempt was made to rehabilitate his reputation. He and his supporters attributed his failure to the effects of defeatist propaganda in the rear and to interference from civilians, which he claimed halted his attack just as he was on the verge of success. An official military inquiry, consisting of Generals Foch, Henri Gouraud, and Henri Joseph Brugère, actually commended Nivelle for his boldness and thorough preparation. In 1918 Premier Georges Clemenceau appointed him to command French troops in Algeria, but Nivelle never again enjoyed senior command in the field. After serving on the Conseil Supérieur de la Guerre, Nivelle died in Paris on 23 March 1924.

Robert K. Hanks

See also
Briand, Aristide; Clemenceau, Georges; Foch, Ferdinand; France, Army Mutiny; Gouraud, Henri; Haig, Douglas, 1st Earl; Joffre, Joseph; Lloyd George, David; Nivelle Offensive; Painlevé, Paul; Pétain, Henri Philippe; Robertson, Sir William Robert; Verdun, Battle of; Vimy Ridge, Battle of.

References
Clayton, Anthony. *Paths of Glory: The French Army, 1914–18.* London: Cassell, 2003.
———. "Robert Nivelle and the French Spring Offensive, 1917." In *Fallen Stars. Eleven Studies of Twentieth Century Military Disasters*, ed. Brian Bond, 52–64. London: Brassey's, 1991.
Pedroncini, Guy. *Les Mutineries de 1917.* Paris: Presses universitaires de France, 1967.
Spears, E. L. *Prelude to Victory.* London: Jonathan Cape, 1939.
Watt, Richard M. *Dare Call It Treason.* New York: Simon and Schuster, 1963.

Nivelle Offensive (16 April–9 May 1917)

Major World War I French offensive. No Allied operation of the entire war inspired such confidence for so little gain. Touted by its commander, General Robert Nivelle, as a way to win the war quickly, the offensive ended without significant Allied gains and led directly to mutinies that involved half the French divisions on the Western Front.

In December 1916 General Joseph Joffre stepped down as commander of the French army. Parliament had grown frustrated with his obstinacy and failure to recognize civilian oversight. The bloody battles at Verdun and the Somme had also discredited his leadership. General Robert Nivelle succeeded him. A glib and charismatic officer who had begun the war as a colonel, Nivelle had risen in just two and a half years to army commander. He had become well known for his innovative tactics in the Battle of Verdun. Nivelle had employed artillery in a "creeping barrage" in advance of infantry and had retaken the operationally and symbolically important forts of Douaumont and Vaux. He nonetheless lacked experience in the conduct of strategic operations.

By early 1917, although the French and British armies had been badly weakened, Nivelle sought to resume the offensive. The Italian government warned the British and French governments that if Germany were permitted to focus its 1917 efforts on the Isonzo Front, it was likely that Italy would be driven from the war. Despite formidable gains achieved by General Aleksey Brusilov in 1916, the Russian Front also seemed in danger of collapse. Moreover, at the end of January Germany decided to resume unrestricted submarine warfare, placing tremendous pressure on Great Britain and its fragile supply lines. All these factors worked to promote a French Western Front offensive.

Nivelle promised that the same tactics he had used at Verdun would bring victory. He argued that the Germans had been just as affected by the bloodletting of 1916 as had the Allies. Nivelle exuded confidence and promised new tactics that, he assured, would gain more land for fewer lives. He contended that the time was propitious for an attack. To politicians accustomed to the dour pronouncements of Joffre and British Expeditionary Force (BEF) commander General Douglas Haig, Nivelle's confidence and assurance were intoxicating. British politicians were especially susceptible to his charms because Nivelle, who had an English mother, spoke fluent and idiomatic English and understood British society and politics. He was thus immune to the suspicions of Anglophobia that had plagued Joffre. Nivelle seemed to be the exact opposite of his predecessor. He even disbanded Joffre's political and insular headquarters at Chantilly, reestablishing it at Beauvais with new personnel and a more open atmosphere.

British Prime Minister David Lloyd George had such confidence in the French commander that he agreed to place Haig and the BEF under Nivelle's orders for the duration of the offensive. Almost everyone seemed carried away by Nivelle's charisma. Only the British generals demurred, but Lloyd George saw their opposition as resentment over having being subordinated to the French.

The focus of the offensive was the German salient that bulged into Allied lines between Bapaume and Laon. Nivelle's plan called for the British to make diversionary attacks in the northern part of the salient between Arras and Compiègne to draw German reserves to that sector. The main weight of the attack would be mounted by a new army group, consisting of the French Fifth, Sixth, and Tenth Armies, under the command of General Joseph Micheler. It would strike the southern half of the salient between Soissons and Reims. Nivelle proposed to minimize French casualties by employing massive artillery barrages before the attack and precisely timed creeping barrages during it. He promised to open a 70-mile gap in German lines through which Allied reserves would then pour and win the war.

Nivelle's preparations inspired further confidence. Eventually he assembled 1.2 million men and more than 700 heavy guns for the offensive. He trained the troops to attack in relays, with one unit advancing as another rested. He replaced cautious commanders such as General Émile Fayolle with more aggressive ones such as General Charles Mangin; he organized massive artillery support; and, in order to ensure coordination and boost morale, he arranged wide dissemination of orders down to the battalion level. Nivelle's optimism inspired confidence. Told that they would win the war and be home for Christmas, the morale of French troops soared.

But from February on, events conspired against Nivelle. His wide dissemination of orders proved fatal when a German trench raid that month seized a complete copy of orders for the offensive. Partly in response, the Germans in Operation ALBERICH retired a large element of their forces back to a prepared set of defenses on commanding terrain known as the Siegfried Line (the Allies called it the Hindenburg Line). By evacuating the salient voluntarily, the Germans had eliminated the operational justification for the offensive. Nivelle nevertheless announced that his offensive would go ahead as scheduled, even if Allied forces would now have to attack much stronger positions.

New French War Minister Paul Painlevé met with Nivelle and expressed considerably less faith in the offensive than had his predecessor, General Louis Lyautey. Even Lyautey had begun to have his doubts. Painlevé informed Nivelle that important details of the plan, including its starting date, were well-known in the military circles of Paris. Wide dissemination of his plan had led to an important breach of security. Nivelle assured Painlevé that his plan could, and would, succeed.

Continuing to harbor doubts, Painlevé met with Nivelle's three top subordinates, Generals Louis Franchet d'Esperey, Alfred Micheler, and Henri Philippe Pétain. All three expressed considerable pessimism about the chances of success. Former Army Group Commander Ferdinand Foch and former War Minister Adolphe Messimy also opposed the plan. Painlevé thus scheduled a conference on 4 April 1917 to discuss the offensive. The timing was critical, as the preparatory artillery bombardment had already begun and the British diversionary attacks were scheduled for 9 April, with the main French attack to begin one week later.

Nivelle remained supremely confident, despite the discouraging news that on 4 April another German raid had captured up-to-date copies of the Allied plan. Painlevé expressed his reservations, whereupon Nivelle threatened to resign if the offensive was canceled. Painlevé, fearful of the political fallout if Nivelle resigned before even conducting an offensive, yielded. He did force a promise from Nivelle to stop the offensive if the projected breakthrough did not occur within forty-eight hours.

The Germans were well prepared for the French attack. They built concrete emplacements for machine guns with interlocking fields of fire. They also built underground bunkers to protect themselves from French artillery. Whereas in February the Germans had just nine divisions in the sector to meet forty-four French divisions, by April they had forty-three divisions in place. Many of these were specially trained to conduct counteroffensive operations.

The Nivelle offensive was over before it even began on 16 April. Rain and sleet the night before turned the battlefield into a morass. The wet, sloppy terrain forced advancing French troops to move more slowly than anticipated, meaning that their rolling barrage moved too far ahead to offer the men any protection. By midafternoon, clouds and snow grounded all Allied aircraft, depriving the French of aerial observation.

The first day went so badly for the French that rather than achieving a breakthrough, by late afternoon they were fending off German counterattacks. The French medical corps, told to prepare for 15,000 wounded, instead had to deal with 90,000. Nivelle soon turned on his subordinates, especially Mangin, for failure to push hard enough. Nivelle's headquarters was soon the scene of intense infighting.

Nivelle reneged on his promise to stop the offensive after forty-eight hours, continuing the attack for five days and sustaining 120,000 casualties for scant territorial gain. By the time he finally halted the offensive on 20 April, French army morale was in ruins. By 29 April mutinies had begun, and on 15 May Nivelle was relieved of command. General Henri Philippe Pétain replaced him as commander of the French army. Pétain quelled the mutinies and restored order, promising his men that he would wait for U.S. troops before resuming the offensive.

Michael S. Neiberg

See also

ALBERICH, Operation; Brusilov, Aleksey Alekseyevich; France, Army; France, Army Mutiny; Haig, Douglas, 1st Earl; Joffre, Joseph; Lloyd George, David; Lyautey, Louis; Micheler, Joseph Alfred; Nivelle, Robert; Painlevé, Paul; Pétain, Henri Philippe; Siegfried Line; Verdun, Battle of.

References

Smith, Leonard. *Between Mutiny and Obedience: The Case of the French Fifth Infantry Division during World War I*. Princeton, NJ: Princeton University Press, 1994.

Watt, Richard. *Dare Call it Treason: The True Story of the French Army Mutinies of 1917*. New York: Simon and Schuster, 1969.

Nixon, Sir John Eccles (1857–1921)

British general. Born on 16 August 1857 at Brentford, England, John Nixon was educated at Wellington College and Sandhurst. He joined the 75th Foot in 1875 and fought in the 1879–1880 Afghan War and the 1899–1902 Boer War. He then served in India. In 1904 he was promoted to major-general and in 1909 to lieutenant-general. In 1912 Nixon received command of the Indian Southern Army, and in 1914 he won promotion to full general. In 1915 he received command of the Indian Northern Army.

In April 1915 Nixon assumed command of British forces in Mesopotamia. Policy makers in London favored a defensive strategy to protect the oil fields, but before Nixon left India, India's commander-in-chief Sir Beauchamp-Duff instructed him to advance on Baghdad. This was not known in London until later.

Having received reinforcements, although not a requested cavalry brigade, Nixon ordered his field commander, Major General Charles Townshend, to take the offensive. In June 1915 Townshend captured Amara, followed by Kut-al-Amara in September. London then authorized Nixon to march on Baghdad, promising two Indian divisions from France. Nixon was prepared to gamble to achieve success, and he depreciated the ability of Turkish troops. Townshend was more realistic, opposing an advance on Baghdad without reinforcements. After registering his objections, in late November Townshend moved toward Baghdad. Blocked by the Turks at Ctesiphon, Townshend was forced back on Kut where he was besieged by the Turks in December and forced to surrender in April 1916, the promised reinforcements not having arrived.

In January 1916 Nixon gave up his command, ostensibly for reasons of health. The Mesopotamia Commission, which between August 1916 and April 1917 investigated the military failure, found Nixon had to make do with "wholly insufficient means," but it also concluded that "the weightiest share of responsibility lies with Sir John Nixon, whose confident optimism was the main cause of the decision to advance." Plans to bring Nixon before a special court of inquiry were overtaken by the end of the war, but his career was in tatters. Nixon died at St. Raphael, France, on 15 December 1921.

Spencer C. Tucker

See also
Ctesiphon, Battle of; Kut, First Battle of; Kut, Seiege of; Mesopotamian Theater; Townshend, Sir Charles.
References
Barker, A. J. *The Bastard War: The Mesopotamian Campaign of 1914–1918*. New York: Dial, 1967.
Moberly, F. J. *The Campaign in Mesopotamia, 1914–1918*. 3 vols. Nashville, TN: Battery Press, 1997–1998.

Njegovan, Maximilian (1858–1930)

Austro-Hungarian admiral. Born at Agram (Zagreb), Croatia, on 13 October 1858, Maximilian Njegovan graduated from the Naval Academy in Fiume in 1877 and entered the navy. During his career he served many posts and participated in expeditions to the coast of West Africa and to Brazil. He commanded various naval units after 1893, including the armored vessel *Budapest* during 1906–1907. Promoted to captain in 1907, Njegovan then commanded a squadron. In 1909 he was appointed chief of the Operations Chancellery in the Naval Section of the War Ministry. Advanced to rear admiral in 1913, he then commanded units of the navy during the international blockade of Montenegro. He next served as the royal representative in the admiralty council in Skutari.

On the outbreak of the World War I, Njegovan had command of 1st Squadron of the fleet at Pola. He commanded the naval bombardment of Ancona in May 1915. In February 1917, on the death of Admiral Baron Anton von Haus, Njegovan took command of the Austro-Hungarian fleet. He was also appointed chief of the Naval Section of the War Ministry.

Criticized for not being sufficiently aggressive, Njegovan was not entirely to blame. The navy was chronically short of supplies, and the sailors were weary of war and ready prey for propaganda urging a breakup of the Dual Monarchy and an end to hostilities. Njegovan was successful in expanding port facilities at Cattaro (today Boka Kotorska) for submarine use, but he retired following mutinies in October 1917 and February 1918. The position of head of the navy was then divided among three individuals. Rear Admiral Miklós Horthy de Nagybánya became fleet commander, Vice Admiral Franz von Holub was appointed as the head of the Naval Section of the War Ministry, and Vice Admiral Franz von Keil became naval advisor to Emperor Karl. Njegovan died at Agram on 1 July 1930.

Joseph D. Montagna

See also
Austria-Hungary, Navy; Haus, Anton von, Baron; Horthy de Nagybánya, Miklós; Karl I, Emperor.
References
Halpern, Paul G. *The Naval War in the Mediterranean, 1914–1918.* Annapolis: Naval Institute Press, 1987.
Sokol, Anthony Eugene. *The Imperial and Royal Austro-Hungarian Navy.* Annapolis: Naval Institute Press, 1968.
Sondhaus, Lawrence. *The Naval Policy of Austria-Hungary, 1867–1918: Navalism, Industrial Development, and the Politics of Dualism.* West Lafayette, IN: Purdue University Press, 1994.

No-Conscription Fellowship

British antiwar organization. On 27 November 1914, two pacifists, Fenner Brockway and Clifford Allen, formed the No-

Conscription Fellowship (NCF) in London to encourage men to refuse war service. The group soon received support from public figures such as Bertrand Russell, Philip Snowden, Bruce Glasier, Robert Smillie, and the Reverend John Clifford.

Few at this point believed that the government would introduce conscription, which had never happened in any previous war. By July 1915, however, it was becoming clear that the government intended to do just that. Despite the millions of men who had joined up in the first months of the war, the unprecedented military losses were rapidly thinning the ranks of the army. It had also become clear that the war would last a long time.

The NCF established a network of branches across the country to fight the Military Service Bill. An enormous campaign was launched against the legislation; the NCF printed more than 1 million leaflets and sent many deputations to the House of Commons. NCF members did succeed in securing "the conscience clause" in the 1916 Conscription Act: the right to claim exemption from military service. About 16,000 men made that claim. The grounds of objection varied. Some, such as Quakers, objected on religious grounds, while others were opposed on political grounds. These men became known as conscientious objectors (COs). They were required to attend a tribunal, an interviewing panel with legal authority, to have the sincerity of their claims assessed. The government meant well: these tribunals were intended to be humane and fair, but it was left to local councils to select their actual members.

Conscription began on 2 March 1916 for single men between the ages of 18 and 41, and in June it was extended to married men as well. The government also gained the right to reexamine men previously declared medically unfit for service. According to NCF figures, 6,312 men were arrested for resisting conscription, and more than 800 of them served more than two years in prison. About 7,000 pacifists agreed to perform noncombatant service. This usually involved working as stretcher bearers in the front lines, an occupation that had a very high casualty rate.

The NCF mounted a vigorous campaign against the punishment and imprisonment of conscientious objectors. Ranged against them was the full might of the government, the police, the army, most churches, and the press, which mobilized public opinion against COs and their supporters. Allen was eventually sent to prison and served sixteen months there until his release in December 1917. Brockway was also sent to prison in 1916.

The NCF was meticulously organized, keeping records of every CO: the grounds of his objection; his appearances before tribunals, civil courts, and courts-martial; and even which prison or Home Office settlement he was in. It also maintained contact with COs, arranging visits to camps, barracks, and prisons across the country. Pickets of prisons were held. The NCF also had a press department, which constantly sought to draw public attention to what happening to COs and the ill-treatment and brutality to which many were subjected. It also published leaflets and pamphlets, briefed members of Parliament, and drafted questions to ministers.

Women were extensively involved in the NCF. As the mothers, wives, girlfriends, or friends of COs, they encountered hostility from family and neighbors. They also figured prominently in NCF work, especially as male members were imprisoned. Some held important positions in the organization, and several were imprisoned.

Despite all attempts at suppression, the NCF continued its opposition to war and assisted those victimized until its final convention, which was held in London at the end of November 1919.

Katja Wuestenbecker

See also
Conscientious Objectors; Pacifism; Russell, Bertrand.
References
Central Board for Conscientious Objectors. *Troublesome People: A Reprint of the No-Conscription Fellowship Souvenir, Describing Its Work during the Years 1914–1919.* London: Central Board for Conscientious Objectors, 1958.
Chamberlain, W. J. *Fighting for Peace: The Story of the War Resistance Movement.* New York: Garland, 1971.
Kennedy, Thomas C. *The Hound of Conscience: A History of the No-Conscription Fellowship, 1914–1919.* Fayetteville: University of Arkansas Press, 1981.

Northern Barrage

Minefield laid by U.S. and British forces that blocked the northern passage to and from the North Sea. The genesis of the Northern Barrage was Germany's renewal of unrestricted submarine warfare in February 1917. The subsequently high losses in Allied merchant shipping forced the Entente to change its naval strategy against Germany. Throughout the war the Entente had relied on a naval blockade to prevent the passage of merchant vessels into the North Sea to supply Germany. The submarine crisis of 1917 made prevention of German submarines and raiders leaving the North Sea the primary strategic goal.

The British considered numerous methods to bar vessels from exiting the North Sea, but the idea of a huge minefield was a U.S. innovation. In May 1917, a little over one month after the entry of the United States into the war, Washington proposed a minefield that would extend eastward from the Orkney Islands to the territorial waters of Norway. This scheme was actually opposed by some U.S. naval officials, but the chief impediment was posed by the British, who believed that existing supplies of mines were insufficient for the project and questioned its effectiveness. The Admiralty also believed that such a huge minefield would hinder operations of British naval forces.

The scheme resurfaced in September 1917 at an inter-Allied conference held in London. There the representatives agreed to execute the project. The British dropped much of their opposition in the belief that the desperate straits produced by Germany's renewal of unrestricted submarine warfare justified any measure that might produce success. Politicians in Whitehall also decided to agree in the hope of not alienating their new and powerful ally.

The construction of the barrage did not begin until 3 March 1918, owing to the huge number of mines required. The minefield was in a constant state of development from this point until 24 October. It was divided into three different sectors that stretched approximately 250 miles over the northern entrance to the North Sea. The largest, laid by the U.S. Navy, was the 130-mile-long Area A that formed the central portion of the minefield. The 50-mile-long western portion, Area B, and the 70-mile-long eastern portion, known as Area C, were deployed by the Royal Navy. The entire minefield comprised 70,263 mines at a cost of some $40 million.

Historians still question the effectiveness of the Northern Barrage. By the time of its construction, the convoy system had greatly diminished Allied losses to German raiders and submarines. When the armistice was declared in November 1918, the barrage had only destroyed six submarines and damaged an additional three. By 1920 all the mines had been swept, a major naval operation.

Eric W. Osborne

See also

Antisubmarine Campaign, Allied Powers; Dover Barrage; Mine Warfare, Sea; Mines, Sea; Naval Blockade of Germany; Submarine Warfare, Central Powers; *Wolf*, SMS.

References

Halpern, Paul. *A Naval History of World War I.* Annapolis: Naval Institute Press, 1994.

Osborne, Eric W. *Britain's Economic Blockade of Germany, 1914–1919.* London: Cass, 2004.

Trask, David F. *Captains and Cabinets: Anglo-American Naval Relations, 1917–1918.* Columbia: University of Missouri Press, 1972.

U.S. Navy Department, Office of Naval Records and Library. *The Northern Barrage and Other Mining Activities.* Washington, DC: Government Printing Office, 1920.

———. *"The Northern Barrage" (Taking Up the Mines).* Washington, DC: Government Printing Office, 1920.

Norway

At the outbreak of war in 1914, all three Scandinavian countries—Sweden, Denmark, and Norway—sought to remain neutral. Norway had no national aspirations that might be satisfied through war, and the nation's leaders concluded that its interests could indeed be seriously hurt by participation in the conflict. Norway had secured its full independence from Sweden only in 1905. King Haakon VII presided over a number of democratic reforms, including the introduction of full parliamentary government and near universal suffrage, including the right of women to vote (1907), the first country in Europe to do so.

In December 1914, on Swedish government invitation, the kings of Denmark, Norway, and Sweden (Christian X, Haakon VII, and Gustavus V) met at Malmö to discuss ways to maintain their neutrality. The meeting led to improved relations especially between Sweden and Norway, which had been acrimonious since their 1905 break and because of claims over the sovereigny of a group of submarine skerries, Griesbaaerne. Other meetings of the premiers and foreign ministers of the three states were held in Copenhagen (March 1916), Oslo (September 1916), Stockholm (May 1917), and Copenhagen (June 1918).

In 1907 Norway had secured a treaty signed by Germany, Britain, and France guaranteeing its neutrality, but Norway also took steps to improve its defenses by building up its armed forces, including beginning a navy. On the outbreak of the war, Norway proclaimed its neutrality but also announced that it was prepared to fight to maintain that neutrality. It also mobilized its coast defense forces and navy.

At the beginning of the war, purchases of Norwegian products by both sides led to an economic boomlet. Norwegian national sentiment was overwhelmingly pro-Entente. This increased with shipping losses to the sizable Norwegian merchant marine that resulted from German submarine warfare. This is not to say that relations with Britain were all harmonious. The British naval blockade of Germany adversely affected Norwegian trade. The British were particularly concerned about exports from the substantial Norwegian fisheries industry to Germany. At first the British merely outbid the Germans; later, the British threatened to halt exports of coal and oil to Norway unless the trade with Germany was halted. Finally, a secret agreement was negotiated whereby the British would buy Norwegian fish at maximum prices, provided Norway cut exports to Germany to a minimum. British pressure also led Norway to halt exports of copper ore, which brought German protests.

During the first two years of the war, Norway benefited economically from the conflict. This changed with German unrestricted submarine warfare and British determination to hold down expenses. In 1916 the government introduced rationing of grain, sugar, coffee, and tea, and it passed legislation prohibiting strikes and lock-outs. In the first half of 1917 Norway suffered heavy losses of merchant ships and lives to German U-boats. There was some popular support for the arming of merchant ships, but in the end, an arrangement was reached with London providing for British vessels to carry cargoes between the two nations while a similar number of Norwegian vessels would be chartered by the British and sail under their flag. By 1918 Norwegian economic conditions had sharply deteriorated. The national debt swelled, and the government imposed rationing. In April 1918 Norway signed a trade arrangement with the United States whereby Norway agreed to a substantial reduction in its trade with Germany in return for imports from the United States.

In September 1919 the Allied Supreme Council awarded Norway sovereignty over the island of Spitsbergen, which Norway annexed in February 1920. Norway joined the League of Nations the next month.

Spencer C. Tucker

See also
Denmark; Sweden.
References
Larsen, Karen. *A History of Norway.* Princeton, NJ: Princeton University Press, 1950.
Popperwell, Ronald G. *Norway.* New York: Praeger, 1972.
Riste, Olav. *The Neutral Ally: Norway's Relations with Belligerent Powers in the First World War.* Oslo: Universitetsforlaget, 1965.
Salmon, Patrick. *Scandinavia and the Great Powers, 1890–1940.* Cambridge and New York: Cambridge University Press, 1997.

Noske, Gustav (1868–1946)

German political figure. Born on 9 July 1868 in Brandenburg, Gustav Noske was apprenticed as a boy to a basket maker. He joined the Social Democratic Party (SPD) in 1884, rising in the ranks of the party and its unions and serving as editor of SPD newspapers in various Prussian cities such as Chemnitz and Königsberg.

Elected to the Reichstag in 1906, Noske became the SPD expert in military and colonial matters. He was closely associated with Friedrich Ebert and Philipp Scheidemann and the conservative wing of the Social Democratic Party. When in August 1914 Kaiser Wilhelm II proclaimed the *Burgfrieden* or pledge of political truce (a medieval custom whereby when a castle was besieged the inhabitants pledged to forego their individual differences as long as the siege lasted), Noske became an ardent supporter of the war. By 1917 his support had cooled, and he endorsed the Reichstag Peace Resolution that year.

In November 1918 Chancellor Prince Max von Baden sent Noske to quell the Kiel Mutiny. He understood that the mutinous mood among sailors stemmed from war-weariness and dissatisfaction with harsh discipline, and he defused the situation with extraordinary political skill. The mutineers even selected him to lead their soviet (council). Chancellor Friedrich

German politician Gustav Noske who directed the suppression of the Spartacis Uprising. (Getty Images)

Ebert accordingly ordered Noske to return to Berlin in December as Defense Minister to de-escalate a menacing situation caused by rebellious troops and sailors converging on the capital. When Berlin exploded into the Spartacist Uprising of January 1919, the energetic Noske raised volunteer units (Freikorps) to suppress the rebels when the army could not provide sufficient forces. His bloody crushing of that uprising and others with his newly raised Freikorps gained him the support of the officer corps and permanent enmity from his fellow Socialists, who called him the "bloodhound." Noske's denunciation of rebels as "hyenas of revolution" created a riot in the Reichstag, and from then on the working classes viewed him as a traitor to their cause.

During 1919–1920 Noske worked energetically with the indefatigable former Prussian War Minister General Walter Reinhardt to rebuild the army. In March 1920, Noske's order to disband the Ehrhardt and Lowenfeld Naval Brigades was rebuffed and led to a bungled comedy, the so-called Kapp Putsch. In the aftermath, Ebert recognized that Noske had "gone native," growing too close to the military, so he forced him from office. Placated with the presidency of the State of Hannover, Noske remained in that post until 1933 and the

Nazi takeover. Jailed in connection with the 1944 attempt on Adolf Hitler's life in 1944, he suffered health problems, culminating in a fatal stroke in Hannover on 30 November 1946. Despite his loyal service to the republic, workers and his own party never forgave him for the excessive violence of the postwar days. Even today the SPD successfully opposes efforts to recognize Noske with a monument.

Michael B. Barrett

See also
Ebert, Friedrich; Germany, Revolution in; Max von Baden, Prince; Scheidemann, Philipp.
References
Bessel, Richard. *Germany after the First World War.* New York: Oxford University Press, 1993.
Gordon, Harold J. *The Reichswehr and the German Republic, 1919–1926.* Princeton, NJ: Princeton University Press, 1957.
Noske, Gustav. *Von Kiel bis Kapp: zur Geschichte der deutschen Revolution.* Berlin: Verlag für Politik und Wirtschaft, 1920.
Wette, Wolfram. *Gustav Noske: Eine politische Biographie.* Düsseldorf: Droste, 1987.

Noyon Offensive (9–15 June 1918)

After launching three massive attacks from March through May 1918, the Germans still had not achieved their objective of a military victory over the British and French before newly arriving U.S. forces could tip the strategic balance irrevocably. By the first week of June, any window of strategic opportunity had closed, and it was too late for the Germans. First Quartermaster General of the German army Erich Ludendorff still refused, however, to yield the initiative by switching to the defensive. He still wanted to launch Operation HAGEN against the British forces in Flanders, even though he had squandered most of his precious reserves trying to exploit the purely tactical gains of the Chemin des Dames attack.

Before the Germans could deal with the British, or even with the still significant French reserve forces north of the Somme River, they had a more immediate tactical problem to address. After Saint-Quentin and Chemin des Dames, the Germans were left holding two huge salients into Allied territory—somewhat in the form of the letter "M." A limited objective attack between Noyon and Montidier, near the two peaks of the "M," would straighten out the inward bulge in the German line, shortening the overall length of that line and freeing up resources for another chance at the HAGEN attack. Another key objective of the German attack was to gain control of a critical rail line that would ease the logistical strain on the huge Chemin des Dames salient.

Operation GNEISENAU, the code name for the offensive, had been planned originally as a supporting attack for the Chemin des Dames offensive. Even before the Chemin des Dames fighting came to an end, the German high command (OHL) issued General Oskar von Hutier's Eighteenth Army a warning order to prepare for an attack on 7 June, to be mounted by his fifteen divisions against the nine divisions of General Georges Humbert's French Third Army.

In sharp contrast to the three previous German offensives, preparations for Operation GNEISENAU were hasty, poorly executed, and difficult to conceal from Allied intelligence. The German activities were so obvious, compared to the first three attacks, that French intelligence first thought it was all part of a crude and rather obvious deception plan. Many of the assets external to the Eighteenth Army, especially the heavy artillery, were still tied up at Chemin des Dames. As a result, the attack had to be delayed forty-eight hours to 9 June so that all the guns could move into position.

The German artillery preparation lasted three and three-quarters hours, with the Eighteenth Army firing a total of 1.4 million rounds that day. The infantry started moving forward at 4:20 A.M. Despite the absence of surprise, initial results were satisfactory. The French apparently had not learned the lessons of Chemin des Dames and still had more than 50 percent of their troops within 2,000 yards of the front line. By the end of the first day the Eighteenth Army had advanced 6 miles, taken 5,000 prisoners, and virtually neutralized three French divisions. But unlike the three previous offensives, the French were not routed; indeed, they fell back in good order.

By the end of 10 June, the Germans pushed across the Matz River in the center of the attack zone, but progress on the flanks was not satisfactory. The following day at 12:30 P.M., French General Charles Mangin launched a five-division counterattack into the German west flank. On 12 June, two corps of the German Seventh Army launched a supporting attack, Operation HAMMERSCHLAG, on the east side of the GNEISENAU attack. HAMMERSCHLAG, however, stalled completely within a matter of hours.

For the next several days the Germans conducted only local attacks, finally terminating GNEISENAU on 15 June. For the first time one of Ludendorff's attacks had failed to produce any worthwhile tactical results. The Germans had failed to reach any of the rail lines they needed to sustain their dangerously extended Chemin des Dames salient. Thus, they still faced the same immediate problems they did when Operation GNEISENAU started. The five days of fighting cost the Germans some 25,000 casualties and the French about 35,000.

David T. Zabecki

See also
Chemin des Dames Offensive; Hutier, Oskar von; Ludendorff, Erich; Ludendorff Offensives; Lys Offensive; Mangin, Charles; Saint-Quentin Offensive.
References
Essame, Hubert. *The Battle for Europe, 1918.* London: Batsford, 1972.
Holmes, Richard. *The Western Front.* New York: TV Books, 2000.

Paschall, Rod. *The Defeat of Imperial Germany, 1917–1918.* Chapel Hill, NC: Algonquin, 1989.

Pitt, Barrie. *1918: The Last Act.* New York: Ballantine, 1963.

Wynne, Graeme. *If Germany Attacks: The Battle in Depth in the West.* London: Faber and Faber, 1940.

Zabecki, David T. *Steel Wind: Colonel Georg Bruchmüller and the Birth of Modern Artillery.* Westport, CT: Praeger, 1994.

Nungesser, Charles (1892–1927)

French fighter pilot and ace. Born on 15 March 1892 in Paris, Charles Nungesser as a young man sought his fortune in South America. He raced cars in Argentina and took his first flight in an airplane. When the First World War began, he joined the 2nd Hussars and earned a commendation during the retreat to the Marne. In January 1915 he began pilot training. He initially joined an observation squadron but continually sought combat.

In November 1915 Nungesser became a fighter pilot with Escadrille N.65. His personal markings were macabre: a skull and crossbones beneath a coffin flanked by candlesticks within a black heart. Nungesser amassed kills and injuries in equal measure. Over his career his injuries included a jaw and both legs broken, a perforated palate, his lip clipped by a bullet, and a dislocated knee. Despite numerous hospital stays, by the time he became an instructor in September 1917, he had thirty aerial victories. In December 1917 Nungesser was injured again, in a car accident. He returned to the front at the end of the month and began competing with René Fonck for highest-scoring French ace. At the end of the war Nungesser had earned fifteen citations and was the third-highest-scoring French ace with forty-five victories.

After the war Nungesser operated a flying school and tried barnstorming in the United States. He entered the race for the first New York–Paris flight, and on 8 May 1927, he and his friend, François Coli, took off from Paris never to be seen again.

Rodney Madison

See also
Aces; Air Warfare, Fighter Tactics; Aircraft, Fighters; Fonck, Paul-René; France, Air Service.

French ace Charles Nungesser shown in 1921. (Library of Congress)

References

Franks, Norman L. R., and Frank W. Bailey. *Over the Front: A Complete Record of the Fighter Aces and Units of the United States and French Air Services, 1914–1918.* London: Grub Street, 1992.

Garreau, Charles. *Nungesser et Coli: Premiers Vainqueurs de l'Atlantique.* Paris: Acropole, 1990.

Robertson, Bruce, ed. *Air Aces of the 1914–1918 War.* Letchworth, Herts, UK: Harleyford, 1964.

O

Oberste Heeresleitung (German Supreme Command)

With the German mobilization, Colonel General Helmuth von Moltke, chief of the peacetime Great General Staff of the Prussian army, became chief of the General Staff of the Field Army (Generalstab des Feldheeres). Although the German emperor was the official commander-in-chief, the actual conduct of operations and strategic planning lay in the hands of Moltke from the very beginning. His staff formed the Oberste Heeresleitung (OHL), the German Supreme Command.

The OHL's Central Section was responsible for the staff's office management and personnel matters. The Operations Section was at the core of the organization. With the industrialization of warfare and the engagement of German forces in the Balkans, Operations was subdivided in 1916 into Operations I (operations), Operations II (heavy artillery, munitions, war economy), and Operations B (operations in the Balkan theater). The Political Section dealt with all questions of military policy, international law, and peace-related questions, as far as the OHL was concerned. On intelligence, the OHL had a peculiar structure: Subsection IIIb (upgraded to full section in 1915) was responsible for secret intelligence gathering, counterintelligence, press censorship, and domestic propaganda, while the analyzing of IIIb's information lay with the Nachrichtenabteilung (Intelligence Section) from 1917, Fremde Heere (Foreign Armies Section). The year 1916 saw the formation of the Militärische Stelle des Auswärtigen Amtes (Military Agency of the Foreign Office), which—despite its name—was not part of the German Foreign Office but rather organized military propaganda in the Allied and neutral countries as a section of the OHL. In prewar years, the position of quartermaster general had been regarded as the chief of staff's prime advisor, but during the war its main task was to relieve the chief of staff from all duties that were not directly operational, such as supply, postal and medical services, and military jurisdiction.

From the beginning of the war to 14 September 1914, the OHL was headed by Helmuth von Moltke, who, after the defeat in the First Battle of the Marne, fell ill and was dismissed. General Erich von Falkenhayn then took over this post, remaining until 29 August 1916. His tenure saw the beginning of the stalemate on two fronts, the general offensive of the Entente in 1916, and the entry of Italy and Romania into the war. Following a series of clashes with Chancellor Theobald von Bethmann Hollweg and the influential commanders in the East, Field Marshal Paul von Hindenburg and General Erich Ludendorff, as well as the German reversal in the Battle of Verdun and Romania's entry into the war, Falkenhayn was dismissed.

Hindenburg succeeded Falkenhayn, and his assistant, Ludendorff, became Erster Generalquartiermeister (first quartermaster general), a cosmetic solution for the fact that Ludendorff had already become the proxy for the officer in the command of the armed forces. At this point, the war had already turned into a total conflict with the OHL taking command of large portions of the German economy and domestic politics. The collapse of Russia in 1917 temporarily eased the difficult strategic situation, but this was soon counterbalanced by entry of the United States into the war (brought about by the decision of Hindenburg and Ludendorff to resume unrestricted submarine warfare) and the failure of the German spring offensive of 1918. On 26 October Ludendorff resigned, and General Wilhelm Groener took his position. Hindenburg's loyalties in this controversy were split between his emperor and Ludendorff, but he decided not to follow his subordinate into resignation, which in turn ended the personal relationship between two men.

The task of the Fourth Supreme Command was unconventional and unpromising. The army had to be returned to Germany and had to be demobilized, two operations that were astonishingly successful given the military and political situation. Simultaneously, the agreement between the OHL and the new republican government demanded the immediate commitment of the army to quell revolutionary unrest within Germany and to defend the Eastern border against Polish, Bolshevik, and local Baltic forces. With the ratification of the Treaty of Versailles, Hindenburg resigned on 3 July 1919, and Groener led the high command until its disbandment on 30 September 1919.

As with most of the General Staffs in the war, the OHL had faced the problem of commanding forces on a scale that had been previously unknown. The failure of the initial German war plan in September 1914 was at least in part due to the temporary loss of operational control. A first organizational response to this dangerous development was the introduction of an Eastern Front command (Oberbefehlshaber Ost, Oberost) in November 1914. But it was not long before the differing strategic preferences of the OHL and Oberost resulted in new problems. The growing and often rather informal influence of young OHL staff officers—the "demigods"—often led to suspicion among the senior commanders. This tension between staff and front deepened with Ludendorff's frequent interference with the commanders' tactical decisions. Considering the dimension of the task and comparing the OHL's performance to the other belligerents' high commands, the German General Staff proved a powerful military institution in the war machine of the empire. Nevertheless, this institution was neither constitutionally authorized nor trained to direct the domestic politics and war economy of Europe's largest industrialized nation-state. When the OHL tried to do so, the consequences were fatal.

Markus Pöhlmann

See also
Bethmann Hollweg, Theobald von; Falkenhayn, Erich von; Groener, Wilhelm; Hindenburg, Paul von; Ludendorff, Erich; Marne, First Battle of the; Moltke, Helmuth von, Count; Third Supreme Command; Verdun, Battle of.

References
Afflerbach, Holger. *Falkenhayn: Politisches Denken und Handeln im Kaiserreich.* Munich: Oldenbourg, 1994.
Asprey, Robert B. *The German High Command at War: Hindenburg and Ludendorff Conduct World War I.* New York: William Morrow, 1991.
Kitchen, Martin. *The Silent Dictatorship: The Politics of the German High Command under Hindenburg and Ludendorff, 1916–1918.* New York: Holmes and Meier, 1976.
Mombauer, Annika. *Helmuth von Moltke and the Origins of the First World War.* Cambridge and New York: Cambridge University Press, 2001.

October Manifesto (16 October 1918)

Royal declaration issued by Habsburg Emperor Karl I. This proclamation of 16 October 1918 was designed to forestall the breakup of the empire. The manifesto was developed by Austrian Prime Minister Baron Max Hussarek von Heinlein, who believed that federal restructuring was the only means whereby the empire might survive. Issued as written by Karl I, it sought to transform the Austrian portion of the Dual Monarchy into a federation of semiautonomous states, each of which would have its own representative parliament. Karl announced, "The reconstruction of the fatherland must be commenced now," and he called for the new state to be reorganized as a "federal country in which each national component in its territory of settlement shall form its own state." This arrangement would include the Austrian lands, Bohemia, and a new autonomous South-Slav state of Croatia, Dalmatia, and Bosnia-Herzegovina. Hussarek hoped that such an arrangement would satisfy the demands of U.S. President Woodrow Wilson's Fourteen Points calling for the "self-determination of peoples."

This proclamation came too late and offered too little. With Austria-Hungary near collapse, South Slav, Polish, and Czech elements were unlikely to accept compromise. Hungarian opposition, in any case, wrecked it. Despite inclusion of a statement that Hungary's status would be left unchanged, Hungarian Prime Minister Sándor Wekerle denounced the document. Even as the empire collapsed, he refused to abandon Hungarian rule over its Romanian, Slovak, Croat, Serbian, and Ruthene minorities.

The rejection of the October Manifesto signaled the effective end of the Austro-Hungarian Empire.

Spencer C. Tucker

See also
Austria-Hungary, Home Front; Czechoslovakia, Role in War and Formation of State; Fourteen Points; Hussarek von Heinlein, Baron Max; Wekerle, Sándor; Wilson, Thomas Woodrow.

References
Brook-Shepherd, Gordon. *The Last Habsburg.* New York: Weybright and Talley, 1968.
Cornwall, Mark, ed. *The Last Years of Austria-Hungary: Essays in Political and Military History, 1908–1918.* Exeter: University of Exeter Press, 2000.
Jászi, Oszkár. *The Dissolution of the Habsburg Monarchy.* Chicago: University of Chicago Press, 1929.
Pick, Robert. *The Last Days of Imperial Vienna.* New York: Dial, 1976.

Ōkuma Shigenobu (1838–1922)

Japanese statesman and prime minister. Born on 11 March 1838 in Saga, Ōkuma Shigenobu was educated in Mito

Japanese Prime Minister Ōkuma Shigenobu, who took Japan into World War I. (Francis J. Reynolds and C. W. Taylor, *Collier's Photographic History of the European War*, P. F. Collier & Son, New York, 1916)

jumped from 95 seats to 150. In April Ōkuma became prime minister.

When World War I began in Europe in 1914, Ōkuma decided to enter the war on the Allied side in order to secure territory in East Asia. Taking advantage of the military situation in Europe, Ōkuma also presented the Twenty-One Demands to China, by which Japan hoped to expand its political and economic influence in that country.

In October 1916 Ōkuma's cabinet resigned en masse because of severe conflicts between him and the elder statesmen or Genro, as well as charges of widespread government corruption. Ōkuma then retired from politics. He died on 10 January 1922 in Tokyo.

Sugita Yoneyuki

See also
China, Role in War; Japan, Home Frot; Katō Takaakira; Twenty-One Demands.
References
Iddittie, Junesay. *The Life of Marquis Shigenobu Ōkuma: A Biographical Study in the Rise of Democratic Japan.* Tokyo: Hokuseido, 1956.
Lebra, Joyce C. *Ōkuma Shigenobu: Statesman of Meiji Japan.* Canberra: Australian National University Press, 1973.
Oka, Yoshitake. *Five Political Leaders of Modern Japan: Itô Hirobumi, Ōkuma Shigenobu, Hara Takashi, Inukai Tsuyoshi, and Saionji Kinmochi.* Trans. Andrew Fraser and Patricia Murray. Tokyo: University of Tokyo Press, 1986.

Domain (now Ibaraki Prefecture) and Nagasaki. He early displayed skills in both finance and diplomacy. Ōkuma served as finance minister from 1873 to 1881, during which time he reorganized the Japanese fiscal system and promoted industrialization. In April 1882 he established the Rikken Kaishinto (Progressive Party); he also founded Waseda University. Ōkuma served twice as foreign minister, during 1888–1889 and 1896–1897.

In March 1896 Ōkuma contributed to the foundation of the Shinpoto (Progressive Party). In June 1898 he and Itagaki Taisuke, who established the Jiyuto (Liberal Party), Japan's first political party, merged their two parties to found the Kenseito (Constitutional Party). Ōkuma served as prime minister from June to November 1898. Winning 260 seats in the general election in August 1898, Kenseito gained an absolute majority in the parliament; however, the cabinet resigned en masse in November 1898, largely because of an internal struggle in Kenseito. Ōkuma left politics in 1907 to became president of Waseda University.

As the movement to establish a constitutional democracy gained ground in the beginning of Taisho era, Ōkuma returned to the political scene. The Rikken Doshikai (Constitutional Comrade Party) headed by Katō Takaakira, advancing Ōkuma as prime minister, won an overwhelming victory in the general election in March 1914. Seiyukai, the former majority party, went from 184 seats to 105, while Rikken Doshikai

Orlando, Vittorio Emanuele (1860–1952)

Italian political leader and premier. Born on 19 May 1860, at Palermo, Sicily, Vittorio Orlando taught law at the University of Palermo and won recognition as an eminent jurist. In 1897 he became a member of the Chamber of Deputies, serving as minister of public instruction from 1903 to 1905 and minister of justice from 1907 to 1909 and again from 1914 to June 1916. In May 1915, a year before Orlando become minister of the interior under Premier Paolo Boselli, Italy joined the Allies in World War I. Domestic antiwar sentiment was increasing, and Orlando, seeking to maintain parliamentary support for the government, initially chose to respond with conciliatory, persuasive tactics rather than repression.

Skilled at maneuvering political shoals, Orlando became premier after Italy's disastrous October 1917 defeat at Caporetto. He successfully organized a patriotic national united front government, the Unione Sacra, dedicated to full-scale domestic mobilization for war. A stirring orator, Orlando revitalized national morale. Antiwar Socialists now encountered domestic repression. Orlando also asked Britain and France for additional forces, reorganized the army, replaced General Luigi Cadorna as chief of staff with the younger General Armando Diaz, and in October 1918 forced the latter to

Italian Premier Vittorio Emanuele Orlando led Italy's delegation to the Paris Peace talks. (S. J. Duncan-Clark and W. R. Plewman, *Pictorial History of the Great War,* with W. S. Wallace, *Canada in the Great War,* 5th ed., John A. Hertel, Toronto, 1919)

launch the successful Vittorio Veneto campaign in which Italy defeated Austria.

At the 1919 Paris Peace Conference, Orlando was one of the Council of Four, the premiers or presidents of the "Big Four" Allied and Associated Powers—the United States, Great Britain, France, and Italy—who effectively decided on the most important issues. The fact that Orlando spoke French but no English handicapped him, especially in his dealings with U.S. President Woodrow Wilson and British Prime Minister David Lloyd George. Moreover, although Orlando genuinely hoped for a lasting peace settlement, the Treaty of London of 1915 promised to Italy the territory of Dalmatia on the Adriatic coast, and this commitment clashed with Wilson's newly expressed ideals of national self-determination. In addition, although this was not covered by the treaty, Orlando coveted the Italian-speaking port of Fiume. Domestic unrest caused by Italy's large war debt and the country's 500,000 casualties made any compromise on these demands extremely problematic.

Orlando hoped to win Fiume in exchange for Italian support for Wilson's greatest objective, the League of Nations, a bargain Wilson refused even though Lloyd George and French Premier Georges Clemenceau initially favored awarding Italy the city. Orlando emotionally demanded both Dalmatia, under the Treaty of London's provisions, and Fiume, as a matter of self-determination, even though it was surrounded by Slavic areas and Yugoslavia therefore also claimed the port. Even Lloyd George and Clemenceau considered Orlando's pleas both inconsistent and unreasonable. Orlando also contended that without Fiume, Italy would experience political upheaval. When Wilson addressed a manifesto directly to the Italian populace, urging them to reject what he considered Orlando's unjust and excessive territorial demands, Orlando left the conference in late April 1919, expecting an apology from Wilson that never came. Orlando only returned in late May, just in time to sign the final treaty.

Overall, the Italian public apparently supported Orlando's position, but this did not affect the conference's settlement on Fiume, which was declared a free port but was annexed by Italian forces in November 1920. Although Italy obtained Trent, Trieste, Istria, and the Brenner, Orlando fell from power in June 1919 under fierce attacks for not securing more for his country.

Orlando initially tacitly endorsed the rise of Benito Mussolini and the Fascist movement, but he left politics in 1925 when the Fascist assassination of the liberal Giacomo Matteotti made it clear that Italian democracy had become a mere facade. After World War II he resumed his political career as president of the postwar constituent assembly. He died in Rome on 1 December 1952.

Priscilla Roberts

See also
Boselli, Paolo; Cadorna, Luigi; Caporetto, Battle of; Clemenceau, Georges; D'Annunzio, Gabriele; Diaz, Armando; Italy, Home Front; League of Nations Covenant; Lloyd George, David; London, Treaty of; Mussolini, Benito; Paris Peace Conference; Versailles, Treaty of; Vittorio Veneto, Battle of; Wilson, Thomas Woodrow.

References
Albrecht-Carré, René. *Italy at the Paris Peace Conference.* Hamden, CT: Archon, 1966.

Burgwyn, H. J. *The Legend of the Mutilated Victory: Italy, the Great War, and the Paris Peace Conference, 1915–1919.* Westport, CT: Greenwood, 1993.

Elcock, Harold. *Portrait of a Decision: The Council of Four and the Treaty of Versailles.* London: Eyre Methuen, 1972.

Lowe, Cedric J., and Frank Marzari. *Italian Foreign Policy, 1870–1940.* London and Boston: Routledge and Kegan Paul, 1975.

MacMillan, Margaret. *Peacemakers: The Paris Conference of 1919 and Its Attempt to End War.* London: Murray, 2001.

Mantoux, Philippe. *The Deliberations of the Council of Four.* 2 vols. Ed. and trans. Arthur S. Link. Princeton, NJ: Princeton University Press, 1992.

Orlando, Vittorio Emanuele. *Memorie (1915–1919).* Milan: Rizzoli, 1960.

Zivojinovic, Dragan R. *America, Italy and the Birth of Yugoslavia, 1917–1919.* Boulder, CO: East European Quarterly, 1972.

Ostend and Zeebrugge Raids (22–23 April 1918)

British navy raid on two Belgian ports in an effort to deny them to German submarines. Ostend and Zeebrugge constituted important connections to the North Sea and the English Channel for the inland German naval base at Bruges. Ostend connected Bruges to the sea in a series of small canals, while a large canal connected Zeebrugge and Bruges. On average two U-boats departed these ports daily, while sixteen German destroyers were based at Bruges. The Germans also based there a number of torpedo craft of their Flanders Flotillas. Ostend and Zeebrugge were only 60 miles from the southern English coast, placing German submarines and torpedo craft in close proximity to British coastal shipping.

Vice-Admiral Roger Keyes had charge of planning and execution of Operation Z.O. Keyes had assumed command of the British navy's Dover Patrol on 1 January 1918. An aggressive, confident commander, he sought to deny the German navy access to Ostend and Zeebrugge by means of block ships, old ships loaded with concrete that would be sunk in the waterways. Keyes's plan received the full support of retiring First Lord Sir John Jellicoe and of the Admiralty in February 1918.

Operation Z.O. called for scuttling two block ships at the entrance to Ostend harbor and three obsolete cruisers at the entrance of the Zeebrugge-Bruges canal channel. The latter operation would be particularly difficult, as the harbor was formed by a lengthy, curved mole (causeway) 1,840 yards long and 80 yards wide with a German battery at the northern end. Keyes planned to neutralize the German defenses by landing the 700-man 4th Battalion of the Royal Marine Infantry and 200 armed sailors to secure the mole before the three cruisers could be moved into place and be scuttled. Another old cruiser, the *Vindictive*, would carry the marines to the mole with the assistance of two Mersey ferries, the *Daffodil* and *Iris III*. All three vessels were modified for the

View of the British cruiser *Vindictive* scuttled at Zeebrugge, May 1918. (National Archives)

operation, with the *Vindictive* receiving ramps that might be lowered onto the mole.

The attack on the mole would be accompanied by an attack on the 300-yard-long viaduct connecting the mole to the coast. The British planned to blow up two decommissioned submarines loaded with explosives under the viaduct connecting the mole to the shore, isolating the German defenders on the mole. British air raids and bombardments by coastal monitors would serve as diversions. Once the marines and sailors had completed the operation, the crews of the block ships would be picked up from their life rafts and boats by British motor launches and torpedo boats. The attackers also planned to rely extensively on smokescreens to conceal their movements.

For two months, British marine and naval personnel trained secretly for the planned assault. Navy leaders saw the operation as an opportunity for the navy to play its part at a time when the British army was locked in desperate combat in France, trying to contain the German Ludendorff offensives.

Conditions of tide and wind were most important to the operation, leading to its postponement four times, once on 11 April when the wind shifted with the attackers only 16 miles from their objectives. The operation was finally carried out on the night of 22–23 April.

The operation involved a total of 116 vessels. They departed England and arrived off Ostend and Zeebrugge during the night of 22–23 April 1918. The assault, begun later that same night, went badly from the first. The wind shifted just before the *Vindictive* reached the mole, and the Germans illuminated the cruiser with starshells and searchlights. Under heavy German fire, the *Vindictive* stopped 340 yards from the intended landing point. Its grapple failed to grip the mole, and its guns could not be brought to bear on the German batteries on the northern end of the mole. The *Daffodil* managed to push the *Vindictive* against the mole, remaining in that position during the entire time the shore party was on the mole. The raiding party was also smaller than planned, as the *Iris* could not anchor alongside the mole and eventually had to move alongside the *Vindictive* and transfer its men that way. With the raiding party unable to reach the German batteries, the *Vindictive*'s commander, Captain Alfred Carpenter, ordered the men recalled after about forty-five minutes.

One of the submarines, *C-3*, did explode and sever the viaduct. The three cruiser block ships, the *Thetis*, *Intrepid*, and *Iphigenia*, initially managed to avoid detection. The *Thetis* grounded and sank before reaching the channel entrance, but under heavy German fire the other two block ships were successfully scuttled by their crews in the Zeebrugge channel.

The simultaneous attack on Ostend, however, failed. The smokescreen shifted there as well, revealing the block ships *Brilliant* and *Sirius* and the calcium light buoys that the British had laid to mark the harbor entrance. The British scuttled both block ships in the wrong place.

The valor of the men taking part in the raid was unquestioned. The British lost a destroyer and two motor launches sunk. Personnel losses amounted to 170 killed, 400 wounded, and 45 missing. Eleven participants were awarded the Victoria Cross.

Keyes tried again on the night of 10–11 May, when the *Vindictive* returned to Zeebrugge and was scuttled there, but in a position that blocked only about a third of the channel. The Admiralty called off another attempt planned for June.

Allied propaganda celebrated the raids as a great victory, with the *Vindictive*'s captain later claiming that the Germans would not be able to use the harbor for six months. Keyes repeated this claim in his postwar memoirs, but the German official history disagreed sharply with this assessment. The Germans soon dredged a new channel at Zeebrugge, and U-boats were able to enter and exit that port within two days of the raids; German destroyers had easy access by mid-May. The raids did, however, give a considerable psychological boost to the British people at a time when it was desperately needed, and Operation z.o. remains one of the most daring episodes in the history of the Royal Navy. The Germans did not abandon Ostend and Zeebrugge until October 1918.

John Thomas McGuire and Spencer C. Tucker

See also

Convoy System; Jellicoe, John Rushworth, 1st Earl; Keyes, Sir Roger; Ludendorff Offensives; Naval Warfare; Submarine Warfare, Central Powers.

References

Cruttwell, C. R. M. F. *A History of the Great War, 1914–1918.* Oxford, UK: Clarendon, 1934.

Gladisch, Walter. *Der Krieg in der Nordsee,* Vol. 7, *Vom Sommer 1917 bis zum Kriegsende 1918.* Frankfurt am Main: Mittler, 1965.

Halpern, Paul G. *A Naval History of World War I.* Annapolis: Naval Institute Press, 1994.

———, ed. *The Keyes Papers: Selections from the Private and Official Correspondence of Admiral of the Fleet Baron Keyes of Zeebrugge.* 3 vols. London: Navy Records Society, 1972–1981.

Keyes, Sir Roger. *The Naval Memoirs of Admiral of the Fleet Sir Roger Keyes.* 2 vols. London: Thornton Butterworth, 1933–1934.

Lake, Deborah. *The Zeebrugge and Ostend Raids.* Barnsley, South Yorkshire, UK: Leo Cooper, 2002.

Lemoine, André H. *Suspense à Zeebrugge, 1918.* Brussels, Belgium: J. M. Collet, 1985.

Newbolt, Henry. *Naval Operations.* Vol. 5. London: Longmans, Green, 1931.

Pitt, Barrie. *Zeebrugge: St. George's Day, 1918.* London: Cassell, 1958.

Stock, James W. *Zeebrugge and Ostend.* New York: Ballantine, 1974.

Otranto Barrage

Generally unsuccessful effort by the Allies to block the passage of German and Austrian submarines through the Strait of Otranto. After the entry of Italy into the war on the side of the

Entente, the Allies sought to take advantage of the relatively narrow entrance (approximately 60 miles wide) to the Adriatic to bar the passage of German and Austrian submarines operating from Pola and Cattaro. The first British drifters arrived in September 1915 and were based in southern Italian ports. The usual tactic was to drag indicator nets and nets with mines attached in an attempt to snag submerged submarines. The drifters were supposed to be supported by Italian and French patrols, preferably destroyers, but the great demand for destroyers meant that few could be spared and thus other less effective craft were often employed. Until mid-1917 protection was often inadequate, especially at night, and the drifters were highly vulnerable. There were at first too few drifters available to cover the entire strait effectively, and their efforts were supplemented by minefields and motor launches near the Italian coast.

In 1917 the French and Italians persuaded the British to implement a scheme for a fixed mine-net barrage. The barrage, however, was porous and failed to stop submarines. It was nonetheless an annoyance, and Austrian fears that it might become more effective resulted in a raid by three Austrian cruisers in the early hours of the morning of 15 May 1917, leading to the Battle of the Otranto Straits, the largest encounter between surface warships in the Adriatic during the war. The Austrians sank fourteen drifters, and the absence of destroyers for proper protection led the British to withdraw the drifters during the hours of darkness.

The curtailment of drifter activity was only temporary, and eventually more destroyers were found and better protection given. It became increasingly difficult for the Austrians to raid the drifter line, and an attempt to use dreadnoughts to support the raiding force was frustrated when the *Szent István* was sunk by an Italian MAS boat on the night of 9–10 June 1918. The same month, the U.S. Navy reinforced the barrage with thirty-six wooden 110-foot "submarine chasers" based in Corfu. These vessels worked in groups of three using hydrophones in an attempt to fix the position of submarines. They never succeeded in sinking one.

The real decision in the antisubmarine war was the result of the success of the convoy system, but the barrage remained a seductive diversion. In early 1918 the British Mediterranean commander-in-chief Admiral Sir Somerset Gough Calthorpe even toyed with the idea of reducing escorts to strengthen the barrage. By the summer of 1918 there were more elaborate schemes, largely pushed by the United States, for more complex barriers and minefields with the objective of forcing a submarine to dive long enough to exhaust its batteries. At the end of the war only two submarines—possibly a third—are known to have been sunk in the barrage. In one of these cases the submarine commander did not realize a known minefield had been extended.

Paul G. Halpern

See also

Adriatic Theater; Antisubmarine Campaign, Allied Powers; Calthorpe, Sir Somerset; Depth Charges; Great Britain, Navy; Horthy de Nagybánya, Miklós; Hydrophones; Indicator Nets; Italy, Navy; MAS Boats; Mediterranean Theater, Naval Operations; Mines, Sea; Otranto Straits, Battle of; Savoia, Luigi Amedeo di, Duke of Abruzzi; Sims, William Sowden; Submarine Warfare, Central Powers; Thaon di Revel, Paolo; United States, Navy.

References

Chatterton, E. Keble. *Seas of Adventures: The Story of the Naval Operations in the Mediterranean, Adriatic and Aegean.* London: Hurst and Blackett, 1936.

Corbett, Julian S., and Henry Newbolt. *Naval Operations: History of the Great War Based on Official Documents.* 5 vols. London: Longman, 1920–1931, 1938, 1940.

Halpern, Paul G. *The Naval War in the Mediterranean, 1914–1918.* London and Annapolis: Allen and Unwin and the Naval Institute Press, 1987.

Wilson, Michael, and Paul Kemp. *Mediterranean Submarines.* Wilmslow, Cheshire: Crécy, 1997.

Otranto Straits, Battle of (15 May 1917)

Largest battle between surface forces in the Adriatic during the war. The action followed a raid by Austrian forces on the British drifters maintaining the barrage in the Strait of Otranto. The raid was led by Captain Miklós Horthy, then in command of the light cruiser *Novara,* together with its sister ships *Helgoland* and *Saida.* Horthy convinced his superiors that a raid was necessary because the Otranto barrage threatened to hamper the operations of German and Austrian submarines operating from Cattaro and Pola. It is not at all certain this was the case, as only two or three submarines were ever lost in the barrage, but Horthy apparently believed the potential threat was real. There was also the morale factor, which created a need to do something, and the three fast cruisers were among the handful of Austrian ships capable of running the risk. Two destroyers, *Csepel* and *Balaton,* were to act as a diversionary force along the Albanian coast. A German submarine, *UC.25,* would take position off Brindisi and lay mines. The operation was not without risk, for the drifter line between Cape Santa Maria di Leuca and Fano Island was south of Brindisi and Valona. The potentially superior Allied forces at Brindisi or in Albanian waters were therefore between the Austrian raiders and their base.

The Austrians sailed the evening of 14 May 1917, the darkened cruisers proceeding to a predetermined point in the southern Adriatic where they separated, each assigned a sector to attack in the straits. *Csepel* and *Balaton* drew first blood, running into an Italian convoy of three ships escorted by the destroyer *Borea* off the coast of Albania. In the sudden encounter and with the advantage of surprise and excellent execution, the Austrians sank *Borea* and one of the merchantmen and left another ablaze. The three cruisers also achieved surprise and did great execution. The wooden drifters were not real warships and were armed, when they were armed at all, with only light guns that were no match for the 10cm guns of the cruisers. The Austrians reportedly displayed a certain amount of chivalry, sounding sirens and giving the crews an opportunity to abandon the drifters before they sank them. A few chose futilely to resist, and one of them, Skipper Joseph Watt of the *Gowan Lea*, survived along with his battered ship to receive the Victoria Cross. The Austrians sank fourteen of the approximately forty-seven drifters on the line that night and damaged another four, three badly. They picked up seventy-two survivors as prisoners.

The Allies had a strong patrol out that night consisting of the flotilla leader *Mirabello* and three French destroyers, but these were well to the north of the drifter line. They were off Durazzo at dawn and were ordered to turn south and intercept. The main Allied forces at Brindisi put to sea as soon as they were ready. The first to sail were the British light cruisers *Bristol* and *Dartmouth*, Italian flotilla leader *Aquila*, and four Italian destroyers. Another Italian scout cruiser plus a flotilla leader and three destroyers were also raising steam to follow. Rear Admiral Alfredo Acton embarked in Dartmouth to take command of the chase.

The Allies were unable to employ their potentially superior forces effectively. Only a portion eventually sailed, and there were also problems with effective signaling between ships of the three different navies. The *Mirabello* group was the first to make contact with the three Austrian cruisers, but the superior guns of the latter kept them at a distance. Furthermore, the three French destroyers could not match *Mirabello*'s speed and gradually fell behind. Acton's force from Brindisi at first encountered the destroyers *Csepel* and *Balaton*, although he did not realize they were destroyers and initially held back his own. When he finally recognized the true situation, there followed a duel at high speed between the light craft until a lucky shot from *Csepel* cut a steam pipe and disabled the boiler of the *Aquila*, the fastest Allied ship. The two Austrian destroyers were able to escape to the shelter of shore batteries at Durazzo. Acton subsequently detached two destroyers to shield Aquila.

The Dartmouth group now spotted the smoke of Horthy's cruisers and turned to engage them. The main action, a running battle at high speed, followed. The Allied superiority rapidly diminished. *Mirabello* dropped out for a time after water contaminated her fuel. Then one of the French destroyers broke down with condenser trouble, and the other two French destroyers remained behind to guard it against submarine attack. The *Bristol*, due for docking, also fell behind, leaving the *Dartmouth* and the two remaining Italian destroyers to bear the brunt of the action. Both sides inflicted damage, but the *Dart-*

mouth's superior 6-inch guns began to tell, and Horthy was wounded, losing consciousness for a brief period. The *Novara* was subsequently disabled and taken in tow by the *Saida* while the *Helgoland* attempted to cover the maneuver. This was a moment of extreme peril for the Austrians, but Acton disengaged when smoke was sighted on the horizon coming from the direction of Cattaro. It was the armored cruiser *Sankt Georg*, accompanied by two destroyers and four torpedo boats. Well astern there were more Austrian ships, the old coast defense battleship *Budapest* and three torpedo boats. The Austrian cruisers were able to escape. Whether or not Acton broke off the action prematurely will always be a subject for dispute.

The Allied warships suffered their worst losses while returning to Brindisi. The *Dartmouth* was torpedoed by the *UC.25*, although eventually salved, and the French destroyer *Boutefeu* exiting from Brindisi hit one of the submarine-laid mines and was sunk. Austrian, French, and Italian aircraft all made attacks on warships, which although annoying were not effective.

The British temporarily withdrew the drifters during the hours of darkness until an adequate destroyer force was available to protect them. The Austrians had been very lucky and had succeeded in achieving to a certain degree their objective. Ironically, the barrage had never been very effective, and the really decisive factor in the submarine war during 1917 would be the extension of the convoy system to the Mediterranean, not the barrage in the Otranto Straits.

Paul G. Halpern

See also

Adriatic Theater; Antisubmarine Campaign, Allied Powers; Austria-Hungary, Navy: France, Navy; Gauchet, Dominique-Marie; Great Britain, Navy; Horthy de Nagybánya, Miklós; Hydrophones; Indicator Nets; Italy, Navy; Mediterranean Theater, Naval Operations; Mines, Sea; Njegovan, Maximilian; Otranto Barrage; Submarine Warfare, Central Powers; Thaon di Revel, Paolo.

References

Halpern, Paul G. *The Battle of the Otranto Straits: Controlling the Gateway to the Adriatic in World War I.* Bloomington: Indiana University Press, 2004.

———. *The Naval War in the Mediterranean, 1914–1918.* London and Annapolis: Allen and Unwin and the Naval Institute Press, 1987.

Newbolt, Henry. *History of the Great War: Naval Operations.* Vol. 4. London: Longmans, Green, 1928.

Sokol, Hans Hugo. *Österreich-Ungarns Seekrieg, 1914–1918.* 2 vols. Vienna: Amalthea Verlag, 1933; reprint, Graz: Akademische Druck-u. Verlagsanstalt, 1967.

Ufficio Storico della Marina Militare. *La Marina italiana nella grande guerra*, Vol. 4, *La guerra al traffico marittimo.* Florence: Vallecchi, 1938.

Ottoman Empire, Army

In terms of troop strength, the Ottoman Empire (Turkey) did not rank among the major belligerents of World War I. It

Turkish cavalry departing Constantinople. (John Clark Ridpath, *Ridpath's History of the World,* Vol. 10, Jones Bros., Cincinnati, 1921)

mobilized about 2.8 million men, even fewer than the United States. In relation to its prewar population of 22 million, however, Turkey raised more men than Russia, and its recruitment ratio of about 13 percent ranked sixth among the major participating nations of the war. The sheer size of the Ottoman Empire, extending as it did from Thrace to the Persian Gulf and from Caucasia to the Suez Canal, ensured it an important role in the war. Turkey fought on five fronts and sent troops to three more to aid its allies.

The Ottoman Empire entered the war with an army that had been badly mauled in the Balkan Wars of 1912–1913. Eight of its thirty-six peacetime divisions were undergoing major reorganization in 1914, and fourteen were being rebuilt from scratch after having been largely destroyed. Moreover, a purge conducted in 1913–1914 rid the army of 1,300 older officers who were considered to be a liability; however, as a result, in 1914 brigadier generals were often found in charge of corps and colonels commanded divisions, a situation that frequently caused problems over the course of the war.

Following decades of German military assistance, Turkey's army in 1914 was closely modeled after that of Germany, with a General Staff as core organization and pool for highly trained general officers. The recruitment system, mobilization procedures, and order of battle also copied the German model. On the other hand, Turkey was largely lacking the material prerequisites for fighting a modern war. As the least industrialized European power, Turkey could not provide its army with modern armaments in sizable quantities and entered the war desperately short of field guns, machine guns, and ammunition. Turkish supply and medical services were woefully inadequate, and motorcars and aircraft were almost completely absent. The Ottoman road and railroad network was pitiful, and moving a division from Thrace to the East could take months.

Considering these shortcomings, the fighting performance of the Turkish soldier was truly astonishing. Poorly clad and ill-fed, Turkish soldiers for the most part endured terrible hardships, marched enormous distances, and fought in the most hostile environments. Turning the Turkish soldier from his defensive positions required massive material and manpower superiority. Significantly, even in defeat the Ottoman army never experienced large-scale mutinies among the rank and file. Desertion, however, became an increasing problem late in the war.

In 1914 Turkey mobilized forty regular army divisions that initially formed thirteen corps, grouped into four field armies. Corps were composed of three infantry divisions, one artillery regiment, and one cavalry regiment; divisions had three infantry regiments and one artillery regiment. In addition, there were regular and irregular cavalry regiments partially formed into (reserve) cavalry divisions. There was also the 40,000-strong Jandarma, a paramilitary police force that formed mobile regiments. Designated for rear-area duties, it occasionally served in the front line.

The authorized Turkish army organization increasingly came apart during the war when new field armies were added, fought-out divisions were replaced, depleted formations were consolidated, and ad hoc detachments were created. In November 1918, eight field armies commanded a force of only twenty-five divisions, almost none of which had been active in 1914.

While the only war plan available in 1914 called for a cordon style defense of the empire and deployed more than half of the army around Constantinople, in fact Turkey began offensive operations almost from the outset. This was in part to fulfill its obligations to its allies and in part to regain territory lost in recent wars. Minister of War Enver Pasha, however, frequently implemented ever more fantastic offensive schemes that were beyond the operational capabilities of the army and necessitated permanent redeployments, which further wore down the troops. In order to underpin Turkey's standing as a major European power, Enver even sent sizable reinforcements to its European allies that fought with distinction in Romania, Galicia, and Macedonia.

While the potentially most dangerous front for Turkey in any war was Thrace, where the frontier was less than 180 miles from the national capital, its major military effort was in Caucasia. Here, the ill-equipped Third Army engaged in a winter offensive in late 1914. After some initial success, it was badly mauled by a Russian counteroffensive. Rebuilt in the spring of 1915, it was almost destroyed in the Russian Erzurum offensive early in 1916. Later in the same year, the Second Army, composed almost entirely of Gallipoli veterans, was nearly destroyed in an offensive farther south in the Caucasus. After that, the war in the East ground to a halt. In 1918, however, after the Russian revolution had resulted in a withdrawal from Caucasia, the Third Army went over to the offensive and penetrated deep into Armenia and Azerbaijan in an effort to incite a "Pan-Turanic" nationalist movement in central Asia.

In European Turkey, the First and Fifth Armies under the able leadership of German General Otto Liman von Sanders turned back the Entente Gallipoli landing with heavy losses in 1915. Thereafter, however, these two veteran armies were abused as a readily available manpower reserve for other fronts. When the Allies broke out from Salonika in 1918, there was nothing left to prevent them from entering Constantinople.

In Palestine, a coup de main aimed at seizing the Suez Canal in 1914 proved abortive. Afterward, the Sinai-Palestinian Front evolved into a state of protracted, indecisive warfare, aggravated by the rising Arab Revolt. During 1916–1917, a British buildup in this theater progressed, and in 1918 the German-Turkish Yıldırım (thunderbolt) army group finally collapsed under repeated attacks, and British forces seized Jerusalem and Damascus.

In Mesopotamia (Iraq), an Anglo-Indian invasion resulted in Turkish triumph in April 1916 when Major–General Charles Townshend surrendered an entire division to the Ottoman Sixth Army at Kut. Thereafter, this theater of war remained more or less quiet until the British renewed their advance in 1918. Several Turkish invasions of Persia secured a temporary foothold in this virtual strategic vacuum but on the whole proved insignificant.

On 30 October 1918 the Ottoman Empire signed an armistice with the Entente on board the British battleship *Agamemnon* off the island of Mudros, ending Turkey's participation in the war. According to recent estimates, Turkey lost 770,000 dead and 760,000 wounded in the war, each an astonishing 27 percent of the mobilized total, and about 145,000 captured.

Dierk Walter

See also

Arab Revolt; Balkan Wars; Black Sea, Naval Operations; Caucasian Front; Dardanelles Campaign; Enver Pasha; Gallipoli Campaign; Kemal, Mustafa; Liman von Sanders, Otto; Mesopotamian Theater; Ottoman Empire, Home Front; Ottoman Empire, Navy; Palestine and Syria, Land Campaign; Persian Front; Sèvres, Treaty of; Sinai Campaign; Suez Canal; Townshend, Sir Charles; Transjordan Campaign.

References

Emin, Ahmed. *Turkey in the World War.* New Haven, CT: Yale University Press, 1930.

Erickson, Edward J. *Ordered to Die: A History of the Ottoman Army in the First World War.* Westport, CT: Greenwood, 2000.

Fewster, Kevin, Hatice Basarin, and Vesihi Basarin. *Gallipoli: The Turkish Story.* London: Allen and Unwin, 2004.

Lewis, Bernard. *The Emergence of Modern Turkey.* 3rd ed. New York: Oxford University Press, 2002.

Shaw, Stanford J., and Ezel Kural Shaw. *History of the Ottoman Empire and Modern Turkey,* Vol. 2, *Reform, Revolution, and Republic: The Rise of Modern Turkey, 1808–1975.* Cambridge: Cambridge University Press, 1977.

Turfan, M. Naim. *The Rise of the Young Turks: Politics, the Military and Ottoman Collapse.* New York: Tauris, 2000.

Ottoman Empire, Entry into the War

In one of the major turning points of the war, in November 1914 the Ottoman Empire entered the war on the German side. When war began in Europe in early August 1914, Turk-

Crowds in Constantinople gather to hear the government declaration of war against the Allies, 1915. (Library of Congress)

ish leaders were torn over the appropriate response for their country: continued neutrality or entering the war on the side of Germany or the Entente. Both the German and British governments had worked hard to win Turkish good will in the years before the war. The British had long sought to uphold Turkey's territorial integrity against Russian encroachments and desire for a Mediterranean port, but efforts by the Turkish government in the years immediately before World War I to secure an alliance with Britain had been rebuffed, largely because London feared alienating its new ally, Russia. The British had, however, sent a naval mission to help train the Turkish navy, and the Turks had ordered warships from Britain. On the other side, Kaiser Wilhelm II had traveled to Turkey and pushed development of a railroad there to exploit Turkish resources (the Berlin-to-Baghdad Railway project). In 1913 Berlin had sent an advisory group under Generalleutnant (major general) Otto Liman von Sanders to Turkey to train its army.

A decision by the British government may have tipped the balance in favor of joining the war on the German side. On the eve of British entry into the war, First Lord of the Admiralty Winston Churchill on 1 August ordered sequestered two powerful battleships being built in British yards that had already been paid for by popular subscription in Turkey. These were the *Sultan Osman I* (renamed *Agincourt*) and the *Reshadieh* (renamed *Erin*). This decision greatly angered public opinion in Turkey against the Entente. The Germans also sought to capitalize on the traditional animosity between Turkey and Russia.

Still, the Turkish leadership was undecided and on 3 August declared its neutrality in the war. While the government in Constantinople vacillated, Vice Admiral Wilhelm Souchon's German Mediterranean Squadron of the battle cruiser *Goeben* (the most formidable warship in the entire Mediterranean) and light cruiser *Breslau* changed the course of the war. Although British and French naval units heavily outnumbered his own squadron, Souchon succeeded in getting them to the Dardanelles and then to Constantinople on 11 August. The presence of these two warships off the Turkish capital was of immense benefit to the pro-German faction. Without Berlin's concurrence, on 16 August Souchon arranged to "sell" both warships to Turkey as replacements for the Turkish dreadnoughts sequestered by Britain. Renamed, the two warships nonetheless retained their German crews, and Souchon became commander of the Turkish navy while retaining his position in the German navy. The Turkish public was elated over the news of the acquisition of the two ships.

With the secret support of Turkish Minister of War Enver Pasha, the leading supporter of the German alliance, Souchon used his warships to provoke war between Russia and Turkey. On 27 October he set sail from Constantinople under the guise of a training exercise in the Black Sea. Early on 29 October he bombarded Russian bases at Odessa and Novorossiysk and laid mines. The Turkish cabinet was not informed in advance, and Souchon falsely reported that the Russians had attacked him first.

On 4 November 1914 Russia formally declared war on Turkey. Despite the resignation of four members of the Turkish cabinet in protest against what Enver and Souchon had engineered, Turkey remained in the war on the side of the Central Powers. This decision resulted in a new theater of war in the Middle East and caused the Western Allies to divert important resources to the Turkish theaters of war, perhaps enabling Germany to prolong the war. Having Turkey as an active military opponent also cut off Russia from easy access to the West and imposed heavy economic burdens on that country, forcing it to divert military resources from the fight against Germany and Austria-Hungary. This added immensely to Russia's internal difficulties, helping to bring about revolutions three years later.

Dino E. Buenviaje and Spencer C. Tucker

See also

Enver Pasha; *Goeben* and *Breslau*, Escape of; Souchon, Wilhelm; Wilhelm II, Kaiser.

References

Hale, William. *Turkish Foreign Policy, 1774–2000*. London: Cass, 2003.

Hamilton, Richard F., and Holger H. Herwig, eds. *The Origins of World War I*. Cambridge and New York: Cambridge University Press, 2003.

Palmer, Alan. *The Decline and Fall of the Ottoman Empire*. London: Murray, 1992.

Van der Vat, Dan. *The Ship That Changed the World: The Escape of the Goeben to the Dardanelles in 1914*. Bethesda, MD: Adler and Adler, 1986.

Weber, Frank G. *Eagles on the Crescent: Germany, Austria, and the Diplomacy of the Turkish Alliance, 1914–1918*. Ithaca, NY: Cornell University Press, 1970.

Ottoman Empire, Home Front

Before the beginning of World War I, Turkish nationalism had increased. In 1909 the Committee of Union and Progress (CUP), part of the Young Turk movement, convinced Sultan Abdul Hamid to restore the parliament. Following an attempted counterrevolution later that year, the CUP deposed the sultan, replacing him with his younger brother, Mehmed V.

Defeats sustained by the Ottoman Empire in the First Balkan War greatly discredited Mehmed V, and in February 1913 the CUP seized power. A triumvirate of leaders dominated: Enver Pasha as minister of war, Talât Pasha as minister of the interior, and Djemal Pasha as minister of marine. Enver Pasha invited Germany to assist in reorganizing the Ottoman army, and a German military mission led by General Otto Liman von Sanders arrived in Istanbul in December 1913. On 2 August Ottoman leaders signed a secret alliance with Germany, promising joint action if Russia intervened militarily in the conflict between Austria-Hungary and Serbia. The next day the Ottoman Empire mobilized its military.

The Entente rejected Enver Pasha's offer of neutrality in return for a large loan and modification of the financial concessions enjoyed by the European powers in the Ottoman Empire. At the same time, London sequestered two Turkish dreadnoughts then under construction in Britain. As these ships had been paid for by Ottoman public subscription, this action turned Turkish public opinion against the Entente. Then, Enver Pasha accepted Germany's offer to give the battle cruiser *Goeben* and light cruiser *Breslau*, which had escaped into the Dardanelles to Turkey.

On 8 September the Ottoman Empire abolished the financial capitulations. On 28 October the *Goeben* and *Breslau* (now renamed the *Sultan Yavuz Selim* and *Midilli*, respectively, but still under German command) attacked Russian ships and ports in the Black Sea. Russia declared war on Turkey on 4 November, followed by Britain and France the next day. On 14 November Mehmed V proclaimed a holy war against the Entente.

The Ottoman Empire's entry into the war had immense consequences. The empire controlled land and sea routes to three continents. The closure of the Dardanelles isolated Russia economically and strategically and severely weakened its ability to wage war. Great Britain was also forced to shift major resources to the protection of the Suez Canal. Soon the Ottoman Empire was fighting in Egypt, Mesopotamia, and Caucasia as well as in Europe at the Dardanelles.

At home under CUP leadership the government instituted many reforms. It reorganized the administration and attempted to introduce the merit system into the state bureaucracy, and it encouraged further reform. It also restructured and updated the taxation system, including introduction of an income tax. The government poured money into infrastructure, improving and expanding transportation and communication systems and laying sewage, electric, and water lines in major urban areas.

The government also challenged the power of the traditionally influential Islamic clerics by placing Islam more under its own control. Prior to the war it subordinated the Islamic courts to its secular system. During the war the government completely secularized the religious courts and schools, and Muslim judges (*kadis*) were appointed and overseen by the secular Ministry of Justice. In 1917 the government took control of family law.

The government also brought about major reforms concerning the emancipation of women, equalizing their legal rights concerning marriage and inheritance. It created opportunities for girls and women in all levels of education, vocational training, and employment. In urban areas, women began to assume greater economic responsibility outside of the home, particularly once mobilization necessitated workforce replacements. More women adopted European-style clothing and discarded the traditional veil. However, complete emancipation did not occur until after the war.

The leaders of the Ottoman Empire believed that the conflict would be over quickly. Consequently, the government did not institute planning to secure sufficient food and civilian supplies for an extended war. By 1915 a grain shortage existed in Constantinople and many other major cities. Famine became widespread because of the lack of agricultural laborers, who had been conscripted into the military; a prolonged drought; and the monopolization of railroads by the military. War refugees fled into major urban areas, bringing instability and a further drain on resources and also spreading typhus. Inflation skyrocketed, perhaps reaching 400 percent in the first year of the war.

The internal stability of the Ottoman Empire was weakened during World War I. Two groups in particular rebelled against rule from Istanbul: the Armenian Christians in eastern Anatolia and the Arabs in the Hejaz. The Armenians, who sought independence, forced the Turks to divert troops there from major campaigns against the British and the Russians. In order to stabilize the situation, the government forcibly relocated the Armenian population to the Syrian desert, an area remote from potential collusion with the Russians. Forced to march through the desert with inadequate water, food, clothing, and medical supplies, as many as 1.2 million Armenians died.

The other major source of revolt was the Arab community of the Hejaz. Its push for independence began in June 1916 under the leadership of Sharif Husayn ibn 'Alī. His third son, Prince Faisal, together with British Colonel T. E. Lawrence, played key roles in supporting a British military campaign in Palestine and Syria in 1917 and 1918. They captured strategic areas, sabotaged Ottoman communication and transportation systems, and forced the Turks to divert troops and attention from the British advances.

Following the armistice signed on 30 October 1918 at Mudros that ended fighting between the empire and the Entente, Allied troops occupied much of the empire. The government at Constantinople disintegrated, and its leaders fled. The Ottoman Empire ended on 15 November when Sultan Mehmed VI, who had succeeded to the throne in October on the death of Mehmed V, established a new government under the control of Greek and British troops. The punitive Allied terms of the Paris Peace Conference, whereby the Allies divided much of the territory of the former Ottoman Empire among themselves, spurred Turkish nationalism and led to a revolution under Mustafa Kemal. Under the terms of the punitive Treaty of Sèvres in 1920, Turkey was largely restricted to Anatolia and its economy was controlled by the Entente powers. After fighting for three years and defeating Greek forces in western Anatolia, the Turks secured new terms under the Treaty of Lausanne in 1923.

Laura J. Hilton and Spencer C. Tucker

See also

Balkan Wars; Djemal Pasha, Ahmed; Enver Pasha; *Goeben* and *Breslau,* Escape of; Husayn ibn 'Alī, King; Kemal, Mustafa; Lausanne, Treaty of; Lawrence, Thomas Edward; Mehmed V, Sultan; Mehmed VI, Sultan; Ottoman Empire, Army; Ottoman Empire, Navy; Ottoman Empire, Postwar Revolution; Sèvres, Treaty of; Talât Pasha, Mehmed.

References

Lewis, Bernard. *The Emergence of Modern Turkey.* 3rd ed. New York: Oxford University Press, 2002.

McCarthy, Justin. *The Ottoman Turks.* London: Longman, 1997.

Palmer, Alan. *The Decline and Fall of the Ottoman Empire.* London: Murray, 1992.

Shaw, Stanford J., and Ezel Kural Shaw. *History of the Ottoman Empire and Modern Turkey,* Vol. 2, *Reform, Revolution, and Republic: The Rise of Modern Turkey, 1808–1975.* Cambridge: Cambridge University Press, 1977.

Turfan, M. Naim. *The Rise of the Young Turks: Politics, the Military and Ottoman Collapse.* New York: Tauris, 2000.

Ottoman Empire, Navy

The once powerful Turkish navy was largely gutted by Sultan Abdul Hamid II (1876–1909). The navy had helped oust his predecessor, and Abdul Hamid II feared that it might be involved in a new revolution. Following the Russo-Turkish War of 1877–1878, he cut naval personnel in half and canceled ironclads on order in Britain and Constantinople. In the late 1880s, two small cruisers and a few torpedo boats and auxiliary vessels were built in Turkish yards, two submarines were acquired from Britain, and some torpedo craft were acquired from Germany. In 1890 a large program was announced, to include rebuilding a number of ships and the acquisition of two new French Hoche-class battleships, as well as cruisers and other ships, but these plans were never realized. About all that was done was to modernize some older ironclads for a coast-defense role and acquire some new gunboats. At the

Turkish torpedo boats. (John Clark Ridpath, *Ridpath's History of the World,* Vol. 10, Jones Bros., Cincinnati, 1921)

beginning of the twentieth century the navy did acquire two new cruisers, some destroyers, and smaller ships.

The 1908 Young Turk Revolution brought about a spirit of reform. That same year the new government announced a program to acquire six battleships, twelve destroyers, twelve torpedo boats, and six submarines as well as a number of smaller craft, but this program was not complete by the time of the Italo-Turkish War of 1911–1912. In the meantime the government secured from Germany two old small battleships and four destroyers. A British naval mission arrived in 1908 to help implement change, but it was not able to accomplish much before the war with Italy, in which the many smaller Turkish navy warships were sunk. Further losses followed at the hands of the Greek navy, the empire's chief naval opponent in the First Balkan War of 1912–1913.

The Ottoman navy had proved utterly incapable of preventing the Italians and Greeks from taking Turkey's Aegean islands, and the Young Turk leaders were determined to build up the empire's naval strength. By 1914 the Turks had two dreadnoughts under construction in British yards and had contracted with the British companies of Armstrong and Vickers to update the government shipyard in Smyrna (Izmir). The seizure in August 1914 by the British government of the dreadnoughts *Reshadieh* (renamed the *Erin*) and the *Sultan Osman I* (renamed the *Agincourt*), both of which

had been paid for by public subscription in Turkey, was a major factor in the Turkish government's decision to enter the war against the Entente.

The Ottoman Empire began the war with a small force indeed. In November 1914 it numbered but two predreadnought battleships, one coastal defense ship, two light cruisers, nine destroyers, three torpedo gunboats, and several torpedo boats, gunboats, and auxiliary vessels. The navy did enjoy a quantum leap in strength on the arrival at Constantinople on 11 August 1914 of the new German battle cruiser *Goeben*. It and its consort, the light cruiser *Breslau*, had escaped British and French ships in the Mediterranean. German Mediterranean Squadron commander Vice Admiral Wilhelm Souchon promptly turned the two ships over to the Turkish navy. The *Goeben* was renamed the *Sultan Yavuz Selim*, and the *Breslau* became the *Midilli*. Both vessels kept their German crews with only a nominal number of Turks added. On 24 September Souchon took command of the entire Ottoman navy. Souchon and Turkish War Minister Enver Pasha conspired to use the two former German ships to shell Russian shore installations in the Black Sea on 29 October and bring Turkey into the war.

The empire lacked submarines, and one French submarine captured in the war did not see active service. Before it entered the war, Turkey requested and received from

Germany a mission headed by Admiral Guido von Usedom of several hundred officers and men who assisted in the maintenance of Turkish warships and improvements to torpedo, mine, and shore batteries at the Dardanelles and Bosporus. During the war the Germans also transferred to the Turks some small warships via Bulgaria.

Souchon ably directed Turkish naval operations during the war, most notably in the Black Sea. On the Dardanelles Front, German-supplied mines, shore batteries, and mobile howitzers, rather than ships, were the key factors in the defeat in early 1915 of a large Allied naval contingent sent to force the straits and steam to Constantinople. With German assistance, the Turks maintained active small flotillas on the Tigris and Euphrates rivers and on Palestinian lakes. During the war the Turks also utilized German submarines to run some supplies, and key personnel to Senussi engaged in fighting Italy in Libya.

The greatest Turkish wartime success came when the minelayer *Nusret* laid mines in the Dardanelles that led to the sinking on 18 March of two Allied battleships and damage to several others, the greatest success of the war by a single Central Powers warship. Not only was this a great tactical success, but it had wide-ranging strategic implications. The Allies now abandoned their effort to force the Dardanelles by naval power alone. Had this gone forward and been successful, it might have driven Turkey from the war and saved imperial Russia from revolution. The other great Turkish naval success was the sinking off the Dardanelles of the British pre-dreadnought *Goliath* on the night of 12–13 May 1915 by the gunboat *Muavenet-i-Millet*, commanded by German Lieutenant Frie.

Most Turkish warships sunk during the war fell to Allied submarines that managed to transit the Dardanelles and enter the Sea of Marmora. During the war the Ottoman navy lost one battleship, one coastal defense ship, one light cruiser, and three destroyers.

Following the 31 October 1918 armistice, on 2 November Souchon handed over control of the *Sultan Yavuz Selim* to a Turkish crew under Admiral Arir Pasha's control. The Turkish navy was then interned in the Gulf of Ismit on the Asiatic shore.

Jack Greene and Spencer C. Tucker

See also
Black Sea, Naval Operations; Dardanelles Campaign; Enver Pasha; *Goeben* and *Breslau*, Escape of; Mediterranean Theater, Naval Operations; Russia, Navy; Souchon, Wilhelm.
References
Gray, Randal, ed. *Conway's All the World's Fighting Ships, 1906–1921.* Annapolis: Naval Institute Press, 1985.
Langensiepen, Bernd, and Ahmet Guleryuz. *The Ottoman Steam Navy, 1828–1923.* Annapolis: Naval Institute Press, 1995.
Miller, Geoffrey. *Straits: British Policy towards the Ottoman Empire and the Origins of the Dardanelles Campaign.* Hull, UK: University of Hull Press, 1997.

Van der Vat, Dan. *The Ship That Changed the World: The Escape of the Goeben to the Dardanelles in 1914.* Bethesda, MD: Adler and Adler, 1986.

Ottoman Empire, Postwar Revolution

In October 1918 the Ottoman Empire lay in ruins. Allied troops controlled the Middle East, much of the Balkans, and even threatened Constantinople itself. Under these pressures, Turkish Sultan Mehmed VI signed an armistice to end the fighting on 31 October 1918. The armistice terms opened the straits, demobilized Turkish armies, and placed all remaining Ottoman territory at the disposal of the Allies.

In the chaos following the armistice, Allied forces moved into Turkish territory on a large scale, beginning with a naval force steaming into Constantinople harbor and British troops pushing into the Caucasus. Over the next six months the British, French, and Italian governments established a three-power administration of Constantinople, garrisoned the Alexandretta-Smyrna-Constantinople railway, and encouraged the creation of independent Georgian and Armenian armies. By the summer of 1919 more troops entered the country, with Italian troops in southwest Anatolia, French troops in the southeast, and a large Greek army at Smyrna.

Turkish nationalist resistance to these maneuvers developed in eastern Anatolia, particularly under General Mustafa Kemal in Samsun and General Kazim Karabekir at Erzurum. In September 1919 the nationalists issued the Declaration of Sivas, affirming the unity of Turkish territory and denying the Allies occupation rights. The nationalists—Karabekir in particular—also turned to the Bolsheviks of Russia for military aid, concluding an agreement the following spring. Contacts with Bolshevik officials served two purposes: they tapped a possible source of funds and provided a bargaining chip to use against the anticommunist British. Over the winter, Turkish nationalist troops skirmished with Allied detachments along the railroad and near Constantinople.

On 16 March 1920, British troops seized government buildings in Constantinople and set up a pro-Allied cabinet, preparatory to forcing the Ottoman government to sign the Treaty of Sèvres. Agreed upon by the British, French, and Italians in April, the treaty made the Kingdom of Hejaz independent, gave Smyrna and many Aegean islands to Greece, ceded the Dodecanese Islands to Italy, internationalized the straits, and made Armenia an independent state. In addition, Syria, Palestine, and Mesopotamia were established as independent states under French and British mandates. The latter two powers also signed the San Remo oil agreement, delimiting their oil interests in Persia, Mesopotamia, and the Caucasus. These demands were presented to the sultan and the pro-Allied cabinet on 10 June. Twelve days later, about 60,000 Greek troops advanced from Smyrna to help enforce these terms. Fighting also began in the Caucasus.

Turkish forces were unprepared for this advance, and Greek military columns soon seized the major cities in western Anatolia and took Adrianople in Thrace. In the East an Armenian attack collapsed near Erzurum, and the Turkish counterattack forced the Armenians to sue for peace. The ensuing peace treaty reduced Armenia to the province of Erivan. On 16 March 1921, Turkish nationalists signed a treaty with Soviet Russia, delimiting the border in the East and securing more military aid.

On 23 March the Greeks opened a new offensive toward Ankara. Although initially stalled, the Greeks regrouped and advanced again in July. The Turks withdrew across the Sakarya River and stood on the defensive. Between 23 August and 16 September, they fought a successful series of meeting engagements over a 120-mile front, known as the Battle of the Sakarya. At this point the French (as with the Italians earlier in the summer) agreed to withdraw from Anatolia in return for economic concessions.

Over the winter the British attempted to negotiate an end to the war through a partial revision of the Treaty of Sèvres. The nationalists in Ankara refused, and the Turks moved over to the offensive on 18 August 1922. In the ensuing war of maneuver, superior Turkish cavalry forced the Greeks back, the retreat then turned into a rout, and the Greeks fled in confusion to the coast.

In response to the Turkish advance toward Constantinople, a British force landed to protect the straits. Armistice negotiations began shortly thereafter. Given Turkish military successes, the opposing sides opened negotiations in November and agreed to the Treaty of Lausanne on 24 July 1923. Although Turkey agreed to relinquish all prewar non-Turkish territory in the Middle East and lost almost all the offshore islands in the Aegean and Mediterranean, the Greeks departed Anatolia, no reparations were paid, and no legal restrictions remained on the Turkish government.

During this same period, the sultanate was abolished. The last British troops evacuated Istanbul on 2 October, and the Turkish Republic was formerly established on 29 October 1923.

Timothy L. Francis

See also

Enver Pasha; Kemal, Mustafa; Lausanne, Treaty of; Mandates; Mehmed VI, Sultan; Sèvres, Treaty of; Tâlat Pasha, Mehmed; Transjordan Campaign; Vardar Offensive.

References

Kent, Marian, ed. *The Great Powers and the End of the Ottoman Empire*. London: Allen and Unwin, 1984.

Kinross, Lord. *Atatürk: Biography of Mustapha Kemal, Father of Modern Turkey*. New York: William Morrow, 1965.

Macfie, A. L. *The End of the Ottoman Empire, 1918–1923*. London: Longman, 1998.

Metz, Helen Chapin. *Turkey: A Country Study*. Washington, DC: Federal Research Division, Library of Congress, U.S. Government Printing Office, 1996.

Palmer, Alan. *The Decline and Fall of the Ottoman Empire*. London: Murray, 1992.

Shaw, Stanford J. and Ezel Kural Shaw. *History of the Ottoman Empire and Modern Turkey*. 2 vols. Cambridge: Cambridge University Press, 1977.

Outbreak of the War (after 28 June 1914)

See Historiography of World War I (back matter)

Owen, Wilfred (1893–1918)

British poet and army officer. Born on 18 March 1893 in Oswestry, England, Wilfred Owen failed to get admitted to a university and decided in 1911 to pursue a career in the Church of England as a lay assistant and pupil to the vicar of Dunsden. After clashing with the vicar, he found part-time employment as a teacher of English in the Berlitz School in Bordeaux, France, in 1913. Owen became a private tutor to a French family in 1914, and in July 1914 he left for Bagnères-de-Bigorre in the Pyrenees to tutor the sons of an English family.

Reluctant to join the war, Owen remained in France until October 1915. He then enlisted in the 28th London Regiment and in June 1916 received a commission as a second lieutenant with the Manchester Regiment. Arriving in France on 1 January 1917, he went as an officer replacement to the front line. His poem "The Sentry" tells of a man he posted on 12 January 1917: "In all my dreams, before my helpless sight, / He plunges at me . . . / Eyeballs, huge-bulged like squids." Owen's poems focus on the waste and horror of war. In "Anthem for Doomed Youth" he asks, "What passing-bell for these who die as cattle?" In "A Terre (Being the Philosophy of Many Soldiers)" he is critical of those who glorify combat: "I have my medals?—Discs to make eyes close. / My glorious ribbons?—Ripped from my own back / In scarlet shreds. (That's for your poetry book.)"

On 2 May 1917, Owen was evacuated to a hospital in Scotland with shell shock. Here he became friendly with the older war poet Siegfried Sassoon, who served as a literary mentor. Declared fit for service in June 1918, Owen won a Military Cross for an October 1918 attack on the Fonsomme Line in which he captured a machine gun and a number of German prisoners. While assisting with construction of a bridge across the Sambre-Oise Canal on 4 November 1918, Owen

British poet Wilfred Owen, shown here with a young boy, possibly his son. Owen was killed in France a week before the end of World War I. (Hulton-Deutsch Collection/Corbis)

was fatally wounded in a fierce fight along the riverbank. On Armistice Day, his parents received notification of his death.

Owen's poems remained largely unpublished until the early 1930s, though Sassoon edited a volume of twenty of them in 1920. Owen's literary reputation gradually appreciated over time, helped by the antiwar mood of the 1960s and the composer Benjamin Britten's musical settings of some of the finer poems in his *War Requiem* (1962). Owen remains one of the most important of British war poets, his popularity attributable both to his condemnation of war and his tragically absurd death.

Caryn E. Neumann

See also
Literature and the War; Sassoon, Siegfried.

References
Hibberd, Dominic. *Owen the Poet*. London: Macmillan, 1986.
———. *Wilfred Owen: A New Biography*. Chicago: Ivan R. Dee, 2003.
Owen, Harold, ed. *Journey from Obscurity: Wilfred Owen, 1898–1918; Memoirs of the Owen Family*. 3 vols. New York: Oxford University Press, 1963–1965.
Owen, Wilfred. *The Complete Poems and Fragments*. Ed. Jon Stallworthy. 2 vols. London: Chatto and Winders, 1983.
———. *Selected Letters*. 2nd ed. Ed. John Bell. New York: Oxford University Press, 1988.
Stallworthy, Jon. *Wilfred Owen*. London: Oxford University Press and Chatto and Windus, 1974.
White, Gertrude M. *Wilfred Owen*. New York: Twayne, 1969.

P

Pacific Islands Campaign

Early campaign undertaken by Allied forces to seize German colonial possessions in Southeast Asia and Oceania. In August 1914 Germany possessed several colonial territories in the South Pacific. Most of these were islands or island chains, too small to support a defensive garrison or modern fortifications. German New Guinea, comprising the northeastern end of the island of New Guinea and several nearby islets, held Germany's largest land force in the theater, with 670 locals led by a few German officers and a small number of German civilians called up as reservists. German Samoa, which included the western Samoan archipelago, had only a police force of 25 locals under German command and a small ceremonial guard. These forces were typically equipped with only rifles and a limited amount of ammunition.

On 6 August 1914 the British government called on the Australian and New Zealand governments to mount a campaign to capture Germany's Pacific possessions, thereby preventing them from supporting operations of the small German East Asia Squadron through resupply and wireless transmissions. Critical to German naval communications in the region were a wireless station on Yap and a similar one on Nauru, located some 2,000 miles apart. A third wireless station was under construction near Rabaul in German New Guinea.

London assigned the takeover of German Samoa to New Zealand, and on 15 August 1914 an expeditionary force of 1,400 men departed by ship for Samoa. It arrived off the Somoan capital of Apia on 30 August. A small party went ashore with a demand for an immediate German surrender and a halt in wireless transmissions. Failing to secure a positive response, the entire Allied force disembarked. Recogniz-

ing the futility of resistance, the German authorities capitulated. Soon most of the New Zealand ships and men were reembarked to participate in other Allied operations. A handful of German prisoners from Samoa were subsequently interned at the British colony of Fiji. Later, the occupiers quelled unrest by Chinese plantation laborers in Samoa by arranging rice shipments from Fiji.

In mid-August 1914 an Australian Naval and Military Expeditionary Force (ANMEF) readied for an attack on German possessions in the Pacific. Enlistment began on 11 August, and following a brief training period an ANMEF force of some 2,000 men sailed for German New Guinea. Its objectives were to seize the wireless station under construction near Rabaul and then seize Rabaul itself, the administrative capital of German Oceania. The ANMEF arrived in Blanche Bay south of Rabaul on 11 September. Two landing parties of 25 men each went ashore, one at the town of Herhertshohe and the other 5 miles south at the Kabakaul village. These groups searched for the station, believed located at the inland village of Bitapaka. The jungle's density impeded progress, and the Kabakaul group encountered makeshift defensive emplacements manned by German reservists and policemen, supplemented by gunmen hidden in treetops, behind foliage, and in hastily dug trenches. Reinforcements supported the Kabakaul party's advance along the roadway approaching Bitapaka, and sentries were posted to maintain security.

One of these sentries, Able Seaman W. G. V. Williams, a 29-year-old employee of the Melbourne City Council, was wounded by fire from the bush and died later aboard the armed merchant cruiser HMAS *Berrima,* the first Australian serviceman killed in the war. Medical Officer Captain Brian

C. A. Pockley was shot by a sniper after he went to Williams's aid. Pockley also died, becoming the first Australian officer killed in the conflict.

Mines and manned trenches blocked the road. Under heavy fire, ANMEF troops attacked the first trench and sent parties into the bush to enfilade the German position. The defenders, recognizing that they were outnumbered, surrendered. A number of the Germans and natives taken prisoner were shot while trying to escape. At the small police barracks near the wireless station, the ANMEF again encountered brief resistance from some thirty Germans, but they too surrendered.

German governor of New Guinea Eduard Haber had withdrawn inland to Toma, some 8 miles inland from Herbertshohe. Too late, he ordered the Bitapaka station relocated to the reserve station at Taulil, just inland from Toma. However, the Germans encountered an advance guard from Herbertshohe, supported by fire from the light cruiser HMAS *Encounter*. After brief negotiations, he surrendered German New Guinea on 17 September 1914. Over the next few months Australian naval and land forces were dispatched to occupy other lightly defended or undefended German possessions, including the Admiralty Islands, the Western Islands, Bougainville, and the German Solomons.

The island of Nauru was administered as a German possession by a private company, the Pacific Phosphates Company. The company was run by German nationals but staffed by British, native, and ethnic Chinese employees. On 4 September the light cruiser HMAS *Melbourne* departed Suva, Fiji, for Nauru to destroy its wireless station. Five days later a landing party of twenty-five Australians landed secretly, captured the Pacific Phosphates Company's German administrator, and accepted his surrender of the island. The wireless station had already been deactivated. To avoid the costs of feeding the company's Chinese laborers who relied upon imported rice, the Allies left the island unoccupied. Pacific Phosphates continued its operations, supplied by ships from neutral governments. In early November, however, Australian forces deported all the Germans on Nauru, and British employees were placed in charge of the company.

In the northern Pacific the chief Allied goal was to destroy the powerful German wireless station on the island of Yap. On 12 August 1914 a landing party from the heavy cruiser HMS *Hampshire* of the British China Squadron easily accomplished the task and soon departed. German engineers rebuilt the station, but on 7 October 1914 Japanese marines landed and again destroyed it. They occupied the island as part of a campaign whereby, in the first ten days of October 1914, Japanese naval forces took over the Mariana, Marshall, and Caroline Islands of Micronesia from Germany, an almost bloodless and largely unpublicized undertaking. Negotiations between Japan and Britain soon produced an agreement that allowed Japan to occupy all German islands north of the equator for the duration of the war, an arrangement that survived into the peace treaties.

Laura M. Calkins

See also
Australia, Army; Australia, Navy; Australia, Role in War; Great Britain, Colonies; Japan, Army; Japan, Home Front; Japan, Navy; New Zealand, Army; New Zealand, Role in War.

References
Hiery, Hermann Joseph. *The Neglected War: The German South Pacific and the Influence of World War I.* Honolulu: University of Hawaii Press, 1995.

Livingston, William S., and Wm. Roger Louis, eds. *Australia, New Zealand, and the Pacific Islands since the First World War.* Austin: University of Texas Press, 1979.

Moses, John A., and Christopher Pugsley, eds. *The German Empire and Britain's Pacific Dominions, 1971–1919: Essays on the Role of Australia and New Zealand in World Politics in the Age of Imperialism.* Claremont, CA: Regina, 2000.

Peattie, Mark R. *Nan'yō: The Rise and Fall of the Japanese in Micronesia, 1885–1945.* Honolulu: University of Hawaii Press, 1988.

Watson, Robert Mackenzie. *History of Samoa.* Wellington, New Zealand: Whitcombe and Tombs, 1918.

Pacifism

Pacifism may be defined as a doctrinaire insistence on peace regardless of the consequences. In the decades before World War I, pacifism was becoming a force in international politics and intellectual thought. Marked by opposition to war, killing, or violence, pacifism means literally "to make peace." Pacifists believed that nations should settle their conflicts by peaceful means, and many pacifists therefore opposed individual or state participation in military activities. Although socialists were represented in the movement, the majority of prewar pacifists were not socialists, and many, indeed, believed that any association with socialism would damage their endeavors. Many were pacifists based on Christian religious convictions. Others were moderates, even conservatives, who nonetheless sought to promote the cause of peace through machinery for international arbitration and disarmament. While all pacifists shared the objectives of peace and justice, the degree of nonviolence they endorsed and the circumstances in which they felt this appropriate varied from individual to individual and group to group, making it quite impossible to characterize pacifism as a single movement.

To facilitate internationalism and encourage steps toward world peace, by the later nineteenth century pacifists had organized. Even before 1870 peace societies existed in Great Britain, the United States, Switzerland, and France. By 1914 there were some 160 such organizations, with many branches and an enormous total membership. One weakness of the peace movement was its failure to fuse the many separate

British conscientious objectors to military service during World War I at the Dyce camp near Aberdeen, Scotland. (Hulton-Deutsch Collection/Corbis)

organizations into one international society with a definite program. By the 1890s, however, peace advocates held yearly international congresses.

Many were drawn into the peace movement not merely by their hatred of war but also for economic reasons. Abolishing war would lift a heavy financial burden from the peoples of the world, freeing up additional funding to promote education and social progress. Ivan Bloch, a Pole, and Norman Angell, an Englishman, both wrote influential books arguing that the great costs of modern warfare would inevitably bring ruin to victor and vanquished alike. Angell's *The Great Illusion,* first published in 1910, became an international bestseller that went through many editions and revisions and helped to win him the 1933 Nobel Peace Prize.

In 1899 a notable advance in the cause of international arbitration occurred when the First Hague Peace Conference resulted in the creation of the Permanent Court of Arbitration, popularly known as the Hague Court because it met at the seat of government of the Netherlands. This court was not a permanent tribunal but rather consisted of a list of 132 distinguished jurists, from among whom disputant states might select arbitrators. The Hague Court had no compulsory jurisdiction and no powers to enforce its decisions; its authority rested solely on the willingness of both parties to a dispute to accept and honor its rulings. The court was eventually housed in a magnificent palace erected at The Hague and funded by Andrew Carnegie, the U.S. steel magnate who devoted his final years to the promotion of peace. By 1914 this tribunal had successfully settled several important international cases. The limitations and imperfections of the system were revealed by its inability on several occasions, including August 1914, to prevent states from resorting to war to resolve disputes.

In much of early-twentieth-century Europe socialist parties enjoyed considerable influence; indeed, on the eve of World War I the Social Democratic Party was the largest single part of the German Reichstag. Socialist leaders such as the Russian Vladimir Ilyich Lenin and the French Jean Jaurès had large followings, and socialists generally opposed colonialism, advocated internationalism, and held that peace could only be achieved at the expense of nationalism and capitalism.

Toward this end, many urged their followers to avoid military service, which was a compulsory obligation in most pre-1914 continental European nations. Others urged the negotiation of arbitration treaties and supported arms reduction proposals. Militant leaders such as the French socialist Gustav Herve advocated industrial sabotage during hostilities so as to impede the war effort. Socialists had organized themselves transnationally in the Second Socialist International, founded in 1889, whose members officially espoused the causes of peace, anti-imperialism, and international brotherhood among the working class as well as supported all efforts to improve the position of labor and the workers. Fears of socialist activities and even of revolution led many European nations to move against socialist organizations once the war began, policies the United States emulated after it finally entered the conflict in spring 1917.

When war came, socialists, the left, labor, and the Second Socialist International split over the war. In each country the majority among them supported their own government, albeit with reservations toward the war that often intensified over time. Some socialists initially tried to prevent the outbreak of war. French Socialist Party leader Jaurès was a staunch opponent of militarism, although since he recognized the need for a national army he therefore acquiesced in his country's military conscription policies. Jaurès favored democratizing the armed forces and converting them into a purely defensive force. As the July Crisis of 1914 intensified, his call for reconciliation rather than war as a means of settling the issues outstanding between France and Germany, and other powers involved, led to his assassination in Paris by a right-wing fanatic at the end of the month.

Once war began, in every European country patriotism trumped class interests, as the great majority of politicians and others rallied around their national governments, while the working class supported the war effort, either as conscripts or as industrial workers. French, British, German, Austrian, and Russian socialists and workers overall had little appetite for opposing their own governments in ways that might give aid and comfort to enemy nations when, for the most part, they shared the general popular dislike of their own country's opponents.

Everywhere, in Britain, France, Russia, Germany, and Austria-Hungary alike, national unity became the watchword. Several antiwar British Liberal politicians resigned from the cabinet of Prime Minister Herbert Asquith over the decision to intervene, but despite his earlier criticism of the Boer War and radical reputation the only potential heavyweight opponent, David Lloyd George, the eloquent, charismatic chancellor of the Exchequer, decided to support the war effort. The majority of Labour Party members decided to do likewise, and for the most part those British politicians who dissented from the war, such as J. Ramsay MacDonald,

who resigned the chairmanship of the Labour Party and gravitated to the more pacifist Independent Labour Party (ILP), simply chose not to accept government office. Although ILP and Liberal Party members who favored peace as soon as possible came together in November 1914 to establish the Union for Democratic Control, favoring open diplomacy, national self-determination, disarmament, and greater parliamentary control of foreign policy, their program implicitly accepted the British commitment to the existing war.

Not all on the left, however, chose to support the war. Russian socialist leader Lenin and the German Rosa Luxemburg, among others, branded the war an imperialist conflict and condemned those who supported it as traitors to socialism who had betrayed the international proletariat. Appalled when at the outbreak of war most socialist leaders supported their national governments, they dedicated their energies to, as Lenin put it, "turning the imperialist war into a civil war." From exile in neutral Switzerland he called on soldiers to turn their rifles on their own officers and inaugurate the world socialist revolution. Lenin became one of the most prominent leaders of the "Zimmerwald Left" transnational grouping of antiwar socialists established in spring 1915. Seeking to turn Lenin's program to its own advantage, in spring 1917 the German government—which, ironically enough, arrested Luxemburg repeatedly for disseminating pacifist propaganda—arranged for his return to Russia, where in November 1917 he and other Bolsheviks seized power and, shortly afterward, fulfilled German hopes by taking Russia out of the war and negotiating peace with the Central Powers.

Throughout the war, pacifism remained relatively strong in the United States and Britain, at least by comparison with the situation in the Central Powers countries, where repression of dissent was particularly pronounced until at least the war's final months. In the United States, the country's neutral status until April 1917 provided particularly fertile soil for peace activities. Secretary of State William Jennings Bryan was an ardent champion of international arbitration treaties as a means of preserving peace, though he resigned in spring 1915 in protest over what he considered the overly harsh line the administration of President Woodrow Wilson adopted toward Germany over the sinking of the passenger liner the *Lusitania* that May. In 1915 Jane Addams, the leading American social reformer and antiwar activist of her time, organized the Women's Peace Party (WPP), whose membership grew to 40,000 by April 1917. In 1915 Addams and others joined with like-minded European women gathered in the International Congress of Women at The Hague to form the Women's International League for Peace and Freedom (WILPF).

Socialist WPP members such as Tracy D. Mygatt and Frances Witherspoon also joined with Jessie Wallace Hughan and John Haynes Holmes in 1915 to organize the Anti-Enlistment League, a body that sought to discourage young

American men from joining the armed forces. In late 1915 the maverick industrialist Henry Ford chartered a passenger liner, the *Oskar II*, to carry a group of American peace activists to Europe to participate in a conference of like-minded European pacifists held at Stockholm in January 1916. Only representatives from the neutral Scandinavian countries joined this gathering, since both the Allied and Central Powers banned participation by their own citizens.

In every belligerent country governments assumed sweeping powers to suppress and punish dissent and could use censorship to silence public opposition to the war. Wartime government repression offered harsh punishment to those who dissented from the war, and censorship soon stilled the voices of conscientious objectors such as the British philosopher Bertrand Russell and such left-wing critics of the war as the Polish-German socialist Rosa Luxemburg. Pervasive waves of intolerant patriotic fervor swept all the belligerents, and only small minorities of radical socialists or labor leaders dared to dissent from the general commitment to war.

In Britain, fears of the introduction of conscription led to the formation in 1914 of the No-Conscription Fellowship. Its numbers swelled substantially when the British government in spring 1916 passed legislation making military enlistments compulsory rather than voluntary. Russell, one of its founders, was imprisoned for urging those of his countrymen who chose to become conscientious objectors to refuse to undertake any work whatsoever related to the war, an option available to those who had strong ethical or religious objections to fighting.

After the United States entered the war in April 1917, the Wilson administration followed suit in repressing dissent. The Sedition Act passed later that spring and its successor, the 1918 Espionage Act, criminalized the making of speeches or publication of materials questioning the validity of the war or encouraging potential enlistees to resist the draft, and newspapers considered insufficiently "patriotic" were closed down. Socialists, radicals, labor activists, and German Americans all became favored targets not just of government repression but also of private vigilante groups, whose actions politicians sanctioned and even encouraged. Conscientious objection was permitted on religious and informally also on ethical grounds, and 25,000 young Americans took advantage of this provision. Five hundred of this number received lengthy prison sentences for refusing to accept any other form of noncombatant service related to the war effort, as did those who refused to register for the draft, such as the young civil rights activist Roger Baldwin, and those who publicly criticized the war, such as the socialist leader Eugene V. Debs.

When pacifistic groups began to raise funds to hire legal counsel for conscientious objectors, many of the organizers were likewise subject to persecution and arrest, while aliens who were for whatever reason considered insufficiently patriotic were liable to deportation. In autumn 1917 the Allied governments also refused passports to labor leaders and leftists from their own countries who wished to attend a conference organized by prominent international socialists in neutral Stockholm, Sweden, its stated purpose to agree on liberal terms for a compromise peace settlement that the governments and, perhaps more important, the peoples of all the belligerent powers would find acceptable.

Although governments sought desperately to maintain enthusiasm for the war and especially the patriotic fervor of those soldiers actually doing the fighting, as the conflict progressed pacifism of a kind made its way into the trenches. Along certain portions of the line, especially the quieter sectors, it was not uncommon for an unstated peace of sorts, or at least the observation of certain understandings as to the timing and nature of aggressive actions, to take hold between the two sides, a situation sometimes known as the "live-and-let-live" system. During the famous 1914 Christmas Truce on the Western Front, soldiers on opposite sides left their trenches to talk and exchange cigarettes and presents with each other, and even, it was alleged, play a soccer game.

After the disastrous Nivelle offensive, in spring 1917 French troops mutinied and refused to go on the attack, disaffection that eventually spread and affected half the entire French army on the Western Front. That same summer complete units of the Russian army also mutinied after the failure of the great Kerensky or second Brusilov offensive, disorders that contributed to the November 1917 Bolshevik Revolution in Russia. It was also in 1917 that the British officer, war hero, and poet Siegfried Sassoon, already a minor celebrity, became disillusioned with his own country's reluctance to contemplate a negotiated peace settlement, publicly stating his belief that soldiers were dying in a conflict that was being continued for no valid objective.

The graphic demonstration of the horrors of modern warfare that World War I provided soon served as an enormous boost to the peace movement. Although or perhaps even because they were often reluctant to break with the prevailing prowar consensus in their own countries, many of those Allied liberals and progressives who supported the war devoted considerable energy to efforts to prevent future conflicts. Within a few months of the outbreak of war, private groups in both Great Britain and the United States, most possessing ties to the prewar international arbitration and peace movement, were organizing in support of the establishment of a postwar international organization that would attempt to prevent future wars. In many though not all cases, members of such groups thought an Allied victory the essential prerequisite of their plans. From late 1914 onward James, Viscount Bryce, Liberal statesman and former ambassador to the United States, took the lead in devising British proposals for a postwar "League of Peace" that would prevent future wars by means of arbitration, backed up, if necessary, by collective economic or military sanctions.

In May 1915 British liberals established a League of Nations Society to promote similar ideas, and for the next two years it carried on quiet propaganda to this effect, gaining a membership of 400 by the end of 1916. The society's supporters were not pacifists, and they carefully avoided criticizing the government's wartime policies or calling for a negotiated peace. Even so, at this time British energies were essentially focused on prosecuting the war effectively rather than on making definite plans for peace.

In the United States, a comparable movement quickly developed. The most prominent group involved was the League to Enforce Peace, established in spring 1915 on the initiative of Hamilton Holt, editor of the *Independent* journal and a leader in the New York Peace Society. Its founding members included several prominent Republicans, including the lawyer ex-President William Howard Taft; Abbott Lawrence Lowell, president of Harvard University; and Theodore Marburg, former U.S. ambassador to Belgium. In June 1915 the newly formed League to Enforce Peace, meeting in Philadelphia, formally adopted a platform calling for U.S. membership in a league of nations with the power to arbitrate international disputes and impose economic and military penalties on countries that went to war and for the promulgation of regular conferences "to formulate and codify rules of international law." Since the United States was still neutral at the time, the organization had greater leeway than its British counterpart to launch a vigorous propaganda campaign throughout the United States, which soon generated considerable public support. Democrats as well as Republicans soon joined the movement, which had the advantage of appealing both to those who supported an Allied victory—and, in many cases, U.S. intervention in the conflict—and those who favored a negotiated peace. In May 1916 U.S. President Woodrow Wilson publicly addressed the first National Congress of the League to Enforce Peace, where he committed the United States in principle to the postwar creation of an international organization to prevent future wars.

British officials had not yet formally endorsed such proposals and would not do so until 1918. In conversations during 1915 and 1916 with Colonel Edward M. House, Wilson's confidential advisor, British Foreign Secretary Sir Edward Grey, probably motivated by a mixture of genuine conviction and a desire to conciliate the U.S. president, expressed broad support for such ideas and his hope that the United States would be a member of any such organization. Grey did, however, stress that he was speaking in a personal rather than official capacity and could not commit his government.

In fall 1916 Lord Robert Cecil, undersecretary of state for foreign affairs, was assigned to draft proposals on behalf of the British government. He produced a memorandum that was circulated around the Foreign Office and the British cabinet, an attempt to imagine how such a body would be organized and would function. Although Cecil's proposals were modified substantially over the next two years, both by himself and by other officials, this marked the beginning of British government efforts to formulate plans for international organization.

After the United States had entered the war, and especially once Woodrow Wilson pressured the Allies to endorse a "new diplomacy," based on "open covenants openly arrived at," nonpunitive peace principles, and the creation of an international association of nations, principles expressed most eloquently in his "Fourteen Points" speech of January 1918, the other Allied governments had greater incentives to make clearer plans for postwar international organization. After close to three years of costly and still inconclusive warfare, they also had to motivate their own populations to continue the fight. From 1917 onward, therefore, British officials allowed nongovernmental organizations to launch much more extensive publicity efforts on behalf of a postwar league of nations, a cause quickly taken up enthusiastically by liberals and the Labour Party. Strong support for a league of nations also developed in France and in neutral states, especially Switzerland, the Netherlands, and the Scandinavian countries, in all of which societies were formed to publicize the need for postwar international organization and develop blueprints.

Although the Paris Peace Conference of 1919 created a League of Nations, the failure of the United States to join that organization, the absence from it of other leading states for much of the subsequent twenty years, the reluctance of several nations to accept its rulings as binding, and the League's lack of any significant coercive mechanisms to enforce its decisions doomed the new body to failure in its efforts to prevent future conflicts. The events of 1914–1918 often left former soldiers and civilians alike permanently scarred, and some—for example, the former British officer Ralph Partridge and the writer and peace activist Vera Brittain—vowed that no matter what the issue supposedly at stake, such violence settled nothing and must never again be repeated. During the 1930s the spread of such sentiments helped to paralyze the Western powers when they sought to confront and check the demands of the fascist or authoritarian regimes of the military in Japan, Adolf Hitler in Germany, and Benito Mussolini in Italy.

T. Jason Soderstrum, Priscilla Roberts, and Spencer C. Tucker

See also
Addams, Jane; Angell (Lane), Sir Ralph Norman; Brittain, Vera Mary; Bryan, William Jennings; Christmas Truce; Conscientious Objectors; Debs, Eugene Victor; Ford, Henry; France, Army Mutinies; Jaurès, Jean; League of Nations Covenant; Lenin, Vladimir Ilyich; Nivelle Offensive; Peace Overtures during the War; Religion and the War; Russell, Bertrand; Sassoon, Siegfried;

Second International; Stockholm Conference; Union of Democratic Control; Women's Peace Party; Zimmerwald Movement.

References

Alonso, Harriet Hyman. *Peace as a Women's Issue: A History of the U.S. Movement for World Peace and Women's Rights.* Syracuse, NY: Syracuse University Press, 1993.

Brock, Peter. *Freedom from War: Nonsectarian Pacifism.* Toronto: University of Toronto Press, 1991.

Brock, Peter, and Nigel Young. *Pacifism in the 20th Century.* Syracuse, NY: Syracuse University Press, 1999.

Ceadel, Martin. *Pacifism in Britain, 1914–1945: The Defining of a Faith.* New York: Oxford University Press, 1980.

———. *Semi-Detached Idealists: The British Peace Movement and International Relations, 1914–1945.* New York: Oxford University Press, 2000.

Chatfield, Charles. *For Peace and Justice: Pacifism in America, 1914–1941.* Boston: Beacon Press, 1973.

Early, Frances H. *A World without War: How U.S. Feminists and Pacifists Resisted World War I.* Syracuse, NY: Syracuse University Press, 1997.

Haupt, Georges. *Socialism and the Great War: The Collapse of the Second International.* Oxford, UK: Clarendon, 1973.

Kennedy, Thomas C. *The Hound of Conscience: A History of the No-Conscription Fellowship, 1914–1919.* Fayetteville: University of Arkansas Press, 1981.

Marchand, C. Roland. *The American Peace Movement and Social Reform, 1898–1918.* Princeton, NJ: Princeton University Press, 1972.

Martin, David A. *Pacifism: An Historical and Sociological Study.* New York: Schocken, 1966.

Millman, Brock. *Managing Domestic Dissent in First World War Britain, 1914–1918.* Portland, OR: Cass, 2000.

Newton, Douglas J. *British Labour, European Socialism, and the Struggle for Peace, 1889–1914.* New York: Oxford University Press, 1985.

Peterson, H. C., and Gilbert C. Fite. *Opponents of War: 1917–1918.* Seattle: University of Washington Press, 1957.

Schorske, Carl E. *German Social Democracy, 1905–1917: The Development of the Great Schism.* Cambridge: Harvard University Press, 1955.

Paderewski, Ignacy Jan (1860–1941)

Polish pianist and politician. Born in the village of Kurilovka on the left bank of the Dnieper (then Russian Poland) on 6 November 1860, Ignacy Paderewski finished his basic musical education at Warsaw Conservatory and studied piano in Berlin and Vienna. His international breakthrough in Paris was followed by several successful tours through the United States and other countries in the 1890s. By the turn of the century, Paderewski was regarded as one of the world's greatest pianists.

Although he settled down near Morges, Switzerland, Paderewski never lost interest in Polish matters. Always a patriot and ready to use his popularity on behalf of his countrymen, he saw a chance for Poland's resurrection in the defeat

Polish concert pianist and politician, Ignace J. Paderewski. (Library of Congress)

of the Central Powers in World War I. His contacts in U.S. government circles and his influence with Polish Americans during the election year of 1916 gave him sufficient leverage to draw President Woodrow Wilson's attention to the Polish question, and the demand for an independent Poland was included in Wilson's Fourteen Points.

In August 1917, Paderewski became the representative of Roman Dmowski's Paris-based Polish National Committee to the United States. The Allies, uncomfortable with both Dmowski and Józef Piłsudski, accepted Paderewski as a figurehead for Poland in 1918. He returned home in triumph and became both prime minister and foreign minister in January 1919. That June Paderewski and Dmowski signed the Versailles Peace Treaty. Criticized for not obtaining the most advantageous conditions for Poland, Paderewski resigned from public office at the end of 1919. Frustrated by his work as a delegate to the League of Nations in 1920–1921, Paderewski returned to the concert stage until the Germans invaded Poland in 1939. He was then chairman of the National Council (the mini parliament) of the Polish government-in-exile in London. The defeat of France in June 1940 led him to return to the United States. Paderewski died in New York City on 29 June 1941.

Pascal Trees

See also
Dmowski, Roman; Fourteen Points; Piłsudski, Józef Klemens; Poland, Role in War; Versailles, Treaty of; Wilson, Thomas Woodrow.

References

Gerson, Louis. *Woodrow Wilson and the Rebirth of Poland, 1914–1920.* New Haven, CT: Yale University Press, 1953.

Hoskins, Janina. *Ignacy Jan Paderewski, 1860–1941.* Washington, DC: Library of Congress, 1984.

MacMillan, Margaret. *Paris, 1919: Six Months That Changed the World.* New York: Random House, 2002.

Wapiński, Roman. *Ignacy Paderewski.* Wrocław: Ossolineum, 1999.

Zamoyski, Adam. *Paderewski.* London: Collins, 1982.

Page, Walter Hines (1855–1918)

American journalist, editor, and publisher; U.S. ambassador to Britain, 1913–1918. Born at Cary, North Carolina, on 15 August 1855, Walter Page graduated from Duke University. His early career was as a journalist. In 1900 he cofounded the publishing house of Doubleday & Page, and he edited the journal *The World's Work* until 1913. In 1911 Page was one of the first to tout Woodrow Wilson for president.

Wilson named Page his ambassador to Britain in March 1913. Close to the social and political leadership in both countries, Page soon came to see the evils of Germany, although he was long unable to persuade Wilson of his views. With the sinking of the liner *Lusitania* (7 May 1915), Page became more outspoken both to Wilson and to Colonel Edward House, arguing that British public opinion was becoming progressively more disgusted and alienated by U.S. reluctance to fight. It is clear from his letters that Page himself believed U.S. entry into the war in 1915 or 1916 could have had a decisive effect.

While President Wilson had long enjoyed his friendship with Page and looked forward to his periodic letters and reports, after the *Lusitania* sinking the two men drifted apart, as Page increasingly identified with the British point of view. While outwardly continuing to reflect official U.S. neutrality, behind the scenes Page argued repeatedly that if the United States hoped to influence the war's outcome at the peace conference, then it must enter the war sooner rather than later. Displeased with this shift in view, Wilson now ignored his letters and arguments. In the summer of 1916 Page returned to Washington for consultations, and many observers (Page included) thought that Wilson would replace him. The two men spent a morning talking over the issues but parted with little accomplished. Somewhat to Page's surprise, he returned to London.

In early 1917, after weeks of effort British code breakers were able to read the Zimmermann Telegram, whereby the German foreign minister sought to persuade Mexico to declare war on the United States by offering German support for Mexican annexation of the U.S. southwest. The British government provided a copy to Page, who forwarded it to Wilson on 24 Feb-ruary. Page and others who handled this incendiary document went to considerable pains to hide the fact that the British had obtained it by breaking German codes rather than utilizing spies or theft. He also feared that Wilson would again procrastinate and delay. Finally published in the United States on 1 March, the telegram became one of the immediate causes of Wilson's decision to seek a declaration of war against Germany.

Page retired because of ill health in August 1917. He died 21 December 1918 at Pinehurst, North Carolina. The British government placed a tablet to his memory in Westminster Abbey, a gesture of gratitude for his pro-British wartime stance.

Christopher H. Sterling

See also

House, Edward Mandell; *Lusitania*, Sinking of; Wilson, Thomas Woodrow; Zimmermann Telegram.

References

Cooper, John Milton, Jr. *Walter Hines Page: The Southerner as American, 1855–1918.* Chapel Hill: University of North Carolina Press, 1977.

Devlin, Patrick. *Too Proud to Fight: Woodrow Wilson's Neutrality.* New York: Oxford University Press, 1975.

Gregory, Ross. *Walter Hines Page: Ambassador to the Court of St. James.* Lexington: University Press of Kentucky, 1970.

Hendrick, Burton J. *The Life and Letters of Walter H. Page.* 3 vols. New York: Doubleday, Page, 1922–1925.

Painlevé, Paul (1863–1933)

French politician and statesman. Born on 5 December 1863 in Paris, Paul Painlevé earned a doctorate in mathematics at age 24. A brilliant mathematician, astronomer, and engineer, his interest in aviation led him to be Wilbur Wright's first European passenger, and the two men set a flight duration record of seventy minutes. Shortly afterward, Painlevé established the first French university course in aeronautical mechanics.

The Dreyfus Affair politicized Painlevé. He joined the Radical Socialists in 1906 and was elected to the French National Assembly in 1910. He then held a variety of cabinet posts from which he closely observed defense matters. Painlevé made a name for himself in 1915 and 1916 as a bitter critic of French army commander General Joseph Joffre and his costly offensives. He was an ardent supporter of fellow Radical Socialist Maurice Sarrail's operations on the Salonika Front.

In March 1917 Painlevé became minister of war in Premier Alexandre Ribot's cabinet. He opposed French army commander General Robert Nivelle's ambitious plan for an offensive in the spring of 1917. When Painlevé confronted Nivelle with his doubts and informed him that key details of the plan were well known in Paris, Nivelle threatened to resign. Painlevé subsequently backed down, but he did secure Nivelle's promise to abandon the offensive if he did not achieve a

French politician and mathematician Paul Painlevé who was briefly premier in 1917. (Hulton-Deutsch Collection/Corbis)

breakthrough in forty-eight hours. After the offensive's spectacular collapse and Nivelle's failure to keep his promise, Painlevé supported Nivelle's removal in favor of General Henri Philippe Pétain. Painlevé deserves some of the credit for restoration of French army morale after the mutinies of 1917.

In September Painlevé replaced Ribot as premier, but he kept the War Ministry portfolio as well. He proved to be a weak premier, lasting just two months. In November Georges Clemenceau assumed the positions of both premier and war minister. Painlevé was again French premier in 1925, minister of war from 1925 to 1929, and minister of aviation twice before his death in Paris on 29 October 1933.

Michael Neiberg

See also
Clemenceau, Georges; France, Army Mutiny; Joffre, Joseph; Nivelle, Robert; Nivelle Offensive; Pétain, Henri Philippe; Ribot, Alexandre; Sarrail, Maurice.

References
Becker, Jean-Jacques. *The Great War and the French People.* Trans. Arnold Pomerans. Providence, RI: Berg, 1985.
Hesse, Germain. *Painlevé: Grand Savant, Grand Citoyen.* Paris: Éditions R.-A. Correa, 1933.
King, Jere Clemens. *Generals and Politicians: Conflict between France's High Command, Parliament, and Government, 1914–1918.* Berkeley: University of California Press, 1951.
Painlevé, Paul. *Paroles et écrits.* Paris: Rieder, 1936.

Paléologue, Georges Maurice (1859–1944)

French diplomat. Born in Paris on 13 January 1859, Maurice Paléologue earned a degree in law and entered the French Foreign Ministry in 1880. The government sent him to Tangiers in 1882, Rome in 1885, and then to China and Korea. Rising through the ranks, Paléologue became ambassador to Bulgaria in 1907. In 1909 he returned to Paris as deputy political director of the Foreign Ministry. In 1911 he became political director. As a result of that appointment, Paléologue was identified as a protégé of French Premier Raymond Poincaré.

In January 1914 Paléologue became ambassador to Russia, a post he held through the first Russian Revolution of 1917. In July 1914 Poincaré, now president, and Premier René Viviani visited St. Petersburg and met with Tsar Nicholas II and Russian officials. The French leaders confirmed and strengthened the French-Russian military alliance, assuring Russia of full support in case of war. Following their departure, Paléologue gave Nicholas even stronger support, claiming that his alleged close ties with Poincaré gave his words even more credence.

When the war began in August, Paléologue urged an immediate Russian offensive in East Prussia to take German pressure off the French, who were facing potential disaster. While the Russians advanced to defeat, their faster than anticipated military offensive caused Chief of the German General Staff General Helmuth von Moltke to divert five divisions from the Western Front, helping the French win the decisive First Battle of the Marne.

Paléologue remained in St. Petersburg after the Russian Revolution of March 1917, but the Bolshevik takeover of November 1918 forced his return to Paris. His subsequent memoir is one of the best eyewitness accounts of the Russian Revolution. Paléologue was then secretary-general of the Foreign Ministry, but he resigned in 1921 to devote his full efforts to writing. Among his works are historical accounts, literary criticisms, his impressions of China and Italy, art books, and several novels. He was elected to the French Academy in 1928. Paléologue died in Paris on 18 November 1944.

Michael Share

See also
Marne, First Battle of the; Moltke, Helmuth von, Count; Nicholas II, Tsar; Origins of World War I; Poincaré, Raymond; Russia, Revolution of March 1917; Russia, Revolution of November 1917; Viviani, René.

References
Jannen, William, Jr. *Lions of July: Prelude to War, 1914.* Novato, CA: Presidio, 1996.
Keiger, John F. V. *France and the Origins of the First World War.* New York: St. Martin's, 1983.
———. *Raymond Poincaré.* Cambridge and New York: Cambridge University Press, 1997.

Paléologue, Georges Maurice. *An Ambassador's Memoirs.* Trans. F. A. Holt. New York: Doran, 1925.

———. *La Russie des Tsars pendant la Grande Guerre.* 2 vols. Paris: Plon-Nourrit, 1921–1922.

Wright, Gordon. *Raymond Poincaré and the French Presidency.* New York: Octagon, 1967; reprint of 1942 ed.

Palestine and Syria, Land Campaign (1914–1918)

British land campaign aimed at liberating Jerusalem and forcing the Ottoman Empire to surrender. The British cabinet discussed an initial plan for the Palestine campaign in January 1915. It proposed an attack on Syria, combined with an advance north from Basra to Baghdad. This plan was shelved, however, in favor of the campaign at Gallipoli.

In February 1915 the Turkish military, urged on by its German ally, attacked the Suez Canal. The British repulsed this effort led by Turkish Minister of Marine General Ahmed Djemal Pasha and assisted by German Chief of Staff Lieutenant General Friedrich Kress von Kressenstein. Because of the great manpower demands of the Western Front, troops in the Egyptian Expeditionary Force (EEF) mostly remained on the defensive until 1917. The Turkish attack of 1915 did, however, force the British to build up fortifications on the eastern side of the Suez Canal. Nuisance raids on the area continued, but the Turks launched no other major offensives there. During 1916 the EEF, led by Lieutenant General Archibald Murray, began construction of a road, a railroad, and a water line across Sinai. Such supply lines and access to water would be crucial in any campaign in Palestine and Syria.

Newly elected British Prime Minister David Lloyd George wanted military victories and believed they could be achieved most easily in the Middle East. He urged Murray to take Gaza and then move up the coast to Jerusalem. The British Palestine offensive began in December 1916 with the capture of El Arish, 25 miles south of the Palestinian border. However, southern Palestine between Gaza and Beersheba was heavily fortified. The Turkish defenders there were led by the German Generals Kress von Kressenstein and Erich von Falkenhayn.

Murray mounted the first attack on Gaza on 26 March 1917. Lieutenant General Sir Charles Dobell led a cavalry attack from the east in combination with an infantry attack from the south. Just as the battle turned to British advantage, Dobell, who was hampered by poor communications, ordered his troops to withdraw. This failure produced more than 3,000 British casualties. A second attempt to take Gaza, beginning on 17 April, also failed, this time with more than 5,000 casualties. In response, Murray was replaced with Major General Sir Edmund Allenby, a cavalryman and veteran of fighting in South Africa and on the Western Front.

Allenby arrived in Egypt at the end of June 1917. After taking stock of the situation, he requested reinforcements and supplies to extend the railroad and water lines. He then reorganized his forces into three corps: XX Corps under Lieutenant General Philip Chetwode, XXI Corps under Lieutenant General Edward S. Bulfin, and the Desert Mounted Corps under Lieutenant General Henry Chauvel. He also moved his headquarters from Cairo to the front. Lloyd George saw to it that the requests were met, and Allenby received two infantry divisions from Europe, one infantry division from Salonika, and artillery and Royal Flying Corps support.

Allenby decided to strike at Beersheba, but with a deception to convince the Turks that he was massing troops to attack at Gaza. For the attack he would have four infantry divisions and three cavalry divisions (80,000 men and 218 guns, supported by 5 tanks). The Turks defended the 30-mile line between Gaza and Beersheba with five infantry divisions and one cavalry division (35,000 men and 200 guns).

Allenby prepared meticulously for the attack. He ordered the construction of new roads, commissioned updated maps, and studied campaigns in the area, including both the Crusades and Napoleon Bonparate's invasion. He also organized 30,000 camels to supply water. Colonel Richard Meinertzhagen, Allenby's chief of intelligence, played an important role. He established a wireless receiving station and used it to intercept Turkish radio transmissions. Meinertzhagen also brought about the death of one of the principal Arab spies by sending him a letter thanking him for service to the British with payment for said services. He then arranged for the letter to be intercepted by the Turks, and the spy was executed. Meinertzhagen also arranged a deception, making it widely known that Allenby would be in Cairo during 29 October–4 November. Lastly, he devised a plan whereby a staff officer would arrange to be pursued by Turkish forces and drop a haversack filled with papers that described an impending attack on Gaza rather than at Beersheba. The first two attempts at the latter failed, until Meinertzhagen took on the task himself and succeeded.

On 31 October the offensive opened with a massive artillery attack against Turkish positions at Gaza, which was well fortified by barbed wire and a formidable trench system. But the artillery attack was a feint. A full-scale attack was then launched against Beersheba. The Desert Mounted Corps (4th Brigade Australian Light Horse) executed a dangerous long ride across the Judean Desert, then charged the Turkish left flank and seized control of the water wells before they could be destroyed.

After the capture of Beersheba, Allenby turned his attention to Gaza, which he secured in four days. XX Corps (10th, 60th and 74th Divisions) steadily pushed back the Turks. Allenby sent XXI Corps up the coast into Palestine, the Turks retreating to the Judean Hills 20 miles south of Jerusalem.

Wounded soldiers being placed on camels for transport to the rear during the Palestine campaign, 1914. (Hulton-Deutsch Collection/Corbis)

Allenby did not want to allow the Turks time to establish a defensive line south of Jerusalem and so refused to let his men and their animals rest. Although his supply and communication lines were stretched, Allenby pushed his forces toward Jerusalem. On 16 November 1917 his forces took Jaffa, on the coast.

Allenby wanted to minimize fighting within the historic city of Jerusalem, and he devised a plan of encirclement. The British brought 18,000 infantry, 8,000 cavalry, and 172 guns to this battle; the Turks had 15,000 infantry, 800 cavalry, and 120 guns. Following fierce fighting on the city's outskirts, on 8 December XXI Corps, supported by artillery fire, broke through from the west. Turkish forces then evacuated Jerusalem, which surrendered on 9 December 1917, ending 401 years of Ottoman control. In anticipation of advancing across the Jordan River, Allenby set a defensive line from the Mediterranean shore east to the Jordan River valley, approximately 10 miles north of Jerusalem.

Allenby wanted to push northward quickly to Damascus, but with the start of the Ludendorff offensive on the Western Front, two of his divisions were recalled and sent there. Allenby then received reinforcements from Mesopotamia. He was also able to take advantage of internal Arab unrest within the Ottoman Empire. The Turks had been weakened by the Arab Revolt led by Husayn ibn ʿAlī, beginning in June 1916. As grand sharif of Mecca, Husayn's family controlled the Hejaz, which contained the holy cities of Mecca and Medina. Husayn's third son, Faisal, became an important Arab military leader and, along with Captain T. E. Lawrence, scored important victories against Turkish forces in 1916 and 1917, including the seizures of Aqaba and Wejh. Allenby integrated Faisal's actions with his own plans and sent the Arabs additional supplies to support their raids on Turkish outposts and railroad lines. Faisal's forces became known as the Arab Army of the North.

On the other side of the battle lines, dramatic changes in personnel occurred. General Otto Liman von Sanders replaced Falkenhayn in March 1918; Liman von Sanders in turn replaced almost all the German staff officers with Turks. Within the Ottoman Empire, the death of Sultan Mehmed V resulted in the ascension of his brother, Mehmed VI, to the throne. Mehmed VI appointed General Mustafa Kemal as commander of the Seventh Army in Syria.

By summer 1918 three Turkish armies were positioned across the Jaffa-Jerusalem line. The Seventh and Eighth

Men of the 3rd Australian Light Horse Regiment firing a machine gun at Khurbetha-ibn-Harith, Palestine. (Australian War Memorial B01697)

Armies were between the coast and the Jordan River; the Third Army lay east of the river. The Turks, however, had been fighting for six months without relief and lacked reserves. Turkish forces consisted of 26,000 infantry, 3,000 cavalry, and 370 guns. An additional 6,000 troops guarded the Hejaz railroad to the east. On this front Allenby enjoyed a two-to-one advantage in manpower as well as a tremendous edge in cavalry and air power. The British had 57,000 infantry, 12,000 cavalry, and 540 guns.

Allenby's goal was to capture Damascus, but first he needed to gain control over the Jordan Plain. After two failed attempts to take Amman, Allenby regrouped and devised a plan to advance northward by which he would outflank Turkish forces to the east while depending on Arab forces to cut the railroad line between Déraa (50 miles south of Damascus) and Haifa.

Early on the morning of 19 September 1918, in the Battle of Megiddo, British forces struck the Turkish right flank. A simultaneous Royal Air Force (RAF) bombing raid on Nazareth destroyed that Turkish communications center, hampering Turkish redeployment. In a few hours the defensive line had been pierced, and soon the 9,000-man 4th Cav-

alry Division advanced 10 miles north and then 30 miles east to Jenin and Megiddo. By nightfall the British had taken 2,500 prisoners and almost captured General Liman von Sanders. Déraa fell on 27 September.

To the north and east the offensive continued. On 23 September the 23rd Cavalry Regiment captured Haifa, Acre, and Es Salt. On 25 September it took Amman, which gave the British control over the Hejaz railroad. On 30 September, British troops entered Damascus with little opposition. On 2 October the city formally surrendered, and 75,000 Turks became prisoners of war. British forces sustained only 5,600 casualties in the capture of Damascus. In the entire campaign, Allenby's forces suffered some 50,000 casualties, the majority of them from disease. The other wing of the British forces took Beirut on 8 October.

In the meantime, Kemal, whose Seventh Army remained intact, was ordered to retreat toward Damascus. When he arrived there in late September, the city was in disarray. Kemal was ordered to hand over his troops to commander of the Fourth Army General Djemal Pasha and proceed to Rayak to gather scattered units. Upon arrival at Rayak, Kemal realized that there were insufficient troops to halt the British offensive. Kemal then took matters into his own hands and ordered all his troops to reassemble north at Aleppo, 200 miles north of Damascus, in the extreme northwest corner of Syria. When the British called on Kemal to surrender and then attacked on 25 October, he withdrew to the northwest outskirts of the city in defense of the southern border of Turkey rather than Aleppo. Kemal's forces attacked repeatedly, forcing the British, outnumbered six to one, to call for reinforcements from Damascus. On 26 October, with reinforcements, the British took Aleppo. The Ottoman Empire surrendered on 30 October 1918, and Liman von Sanders officially handed over his command to Mustafa Kemal.

Laura J. Hilton

See also

Allenby, Sir Edmund, 1st Viscount; Beersheba-Gaza Line, Battles of; Chauvel, Sir Henry George; Damascus, Fall of; Dar'a, Actions around; Djemal Pasha, Ahmed; El Arish, Battle of; Faisal, Prince; Falkenhayn, Erich von; Gallipoli Campaign; Gaza, First Battle of; Gaza, Second Battle of; Husayn ibn 'Alī, King; Jerusalem, Fall of; Kemal, Mustafa; Kress von Kressenstein, Friedrich; Lawrence, Thomas Edward; Liman von Sanders, Otto; Lloyd George, David; Ludendorff Offensives; Megiddo, Battle of; Mehmed V, Sultan; Mehmed VI, Sultan; Murray, Sir Archibald James.

References

Bruce, Anthony P. C. *The Last Crusade: The Palestine Campaign in the First World War.* London: Murray, 2002.

Bullock, David L. *Allenby's War: The Palestinian-Arabian Campaigns, 1916–1918.* London: Blandford, 1988.

Falls, Cyril. *Armageddon, 1918: The Final Palestinian Campaign of World War I.* Philadelphia: University of Pennsylvania Press, 2003.

Gardner, Brian. *Allenby of Arabia: Lawrence's General.* New York: Coward-McCann, 1966.

Hankey, Lord Maurice P. A. *The Supreme Command, 1914–1918.* 2 vols. London: Allen and Unwin, 1961.

Kinross, Lord. *Atatürk: Biography of Mustapha Kemal, Father of Modern Turkey.* New York: William Morrow, 1965.

MacMunn, George, and Cyril Falls. *Official History of the Great War: Military Operations, Egypt and Palestine, from the Outbreak of the War with Germany to June 1917.* London: HMSO, 1928.

Preston, R. M. P. *The Desert Mounted Corps.* Boston: Houghton Mifflin, 1922.

Pallavicini, János Marquis de (1848–1941)

Austro-Hungarian diplomat. Born in Padua on 18 March 1848 into an Italo-Hungarian aristocratic family, János Pallavicini studied law at the University of Vienna. He entered the diplomatic service in 1874 and served in Berlin, Paris, and London. From 1906 to 1918 Pallavicini was ambassador to Constantinople, where he became highly regarded for both his skill and extensive connections.

Pallavicini opposed the 1908 Austro-Hungarian annexation of Bosnia and Herzegovina, which he described as the "cardinal error" of Austro-Hungarian foreign policy. Pallavicini was briefly foreign minister in 1911 during the illness of Aloys Lexa von Aehrenthal, who recommended him as a potential successor, though Count Leopold von Berchtold was instead. Admiral Miklós Horthy de Nagybánya believed that if Pallavicini had been foreign minister in 1914, the crisis that summer would not have ended in war. Pallavicini held that any Austro-Hungarian military intervention in the Balkans would inevitably lead to war with Russia. He urged that the Dual Monarchy renounce all further claims in the Balkans.

Following the assassination of Archduke Franz Ferdinand in Sarajevo in June 1914, Pallavicini took a more belligerent approach, and when war began he concentrated his efforts on bringing Turkey into the war on the side of the Central Powers, although he was entirely pessimistic over the prospects of military victory. In 1916 Pallavicini developed three separate peace proposals, but without effect.

Pallavicini did what he could to halt the massacre of the Armenians. In 1917 new Austro-Hungarian Emperor Karl offered him the post of foreign minister, which he rejected. Pallavicini burned the embassy documents in October 1918 as Allied forces were advancing toward Constantinople. He resigned from the diplomatic service after the war, although from 1927 until his death he was a member of the Upper House of the Hungarian Parliament. Pallavicini died at Pusztaradvány, Hungary, on 4 May 1941.

András Joó

See also

Armenia and the Armenian Massacre; Austria-Hungary, Home Front; Berchtold, Leopold, Count von; Bosnia-Herzegovina, Role in War; Franz Ferdinand, Assassination of; Ottoman Empire, Home Front; Horthy de Nagybánya, Miklós; Karl I, Emperor; Liman von Sanders, Otto; Peace Overtures during the War.

References

Horthy de Nagybánya, Miklós. *Memoirs.* Annotated by Andrew L. Simon. Safety Harbor, FL: Simon Publications, 2000.

Liman von Sanders, Otto. *Five Years in Turkey.* Trans. Carl Reichmann. Annapolis: Naval Institute Press, 1927.

Miller, Geoffrey. *Straits: British Policy towards the Ottoman Empire and the Origins of the Dardanelles Campaign.* Hull, UK: University of Hull Press, 1997.

Palmer, Alexander Mitchell (1872–1936)

American lawyer, legislator, and U.S. attorney general. Born into a Quaker family on 4 May 1872 in Moosehead, Pennsylvania, Alexander Mitchell Palmer graduated from Swarthmore College in 1891. He studied law while working as a stenographer and was admitted to the Pennsylvania State bar in 1893.

U.S. Attorney General Alexander M. Palmer who was at the center of the Red Scare controversy with his use of the Espionage and Sedition Acts. (Library of Congress)

Palmer built up a law practice, became a leader in the state Democratic Party, and served in the U.S. House of Representatives (1909–1915). In 1912, Palmer, who was associated with the progressive wing of the party, helped swing the Democratic Party convention to nominate Woodrow Wilson for president. In 1913 he was appointed judge of the U.S. Court of Claims, and in 1917 President Wilson nominated him for the post of alien property custodian. In this position, Palmer oversaw and confiscated the property of German Americans during World War I.

When Attorney General Thomas Gregory resigned in March 1919, Wilson appointed Palmer to head the Justice Department. He remained in that post until the end of the Wilson administration in 1921. The year 1919 saw a great deal of social conflict: a wave of strikes, the passage of both prohibition and woman suffrage legislation, and the Chicago Race Riots. Worried by the revolution that had taken place in Russia, Palmer became convinced that communist agents were planning to overthrow the U.S. government. His view

was reinforced when a series of bombings occurred in the summer. On 2 June 1919, bombs went off in eight cities including Washington, D.C., where Palmer's residence was partially destroyed.

Palmer recruited John Edgar Hoover as his special assistant, and together they used the Espionage Act (1917) and the Sedition Act (1918) to launch a series of well-publicized raids against radicals and left-wing organizations. On 7 November 1919, the second anniversary of the Russian Revolution, more than 10,000 suspected communists and anarchists were arrested. In January 1920, another 6,000 were arrested and held without trial. These actions took place in several cities and became known as the "Palmer Raids." Palmer and Hoover found no evidence of a proposed revolution, but many of these suspects were held without trial for long periods. The vast majority were eventually released, but 247 were deported to Russia.

When Palmer announced that a communist revolution was likely to take place on 1 May 1920, mass panic took place. In New York, five elected Socialists were expelled from the legislature. When the May revolution failed to materialize, attitudes toward Palmer began to change, and he was criticized for disregarding people's civil liberties. Opposition began to organize. In 1920, the American Civil Liberties Union formed to protest the violation of constitutional rights, such as arrest without warrant, unreasonable search and seizure, the denial of due process, and police brutality. By 1921, the Red Scare was effectively over. Palmer failed to win the nomination as the Democratic presidential candidate in 1920, and the next year he returned to his law practice. Mitchell Palmer died on 11 May 1936 in Washington, D.C.

Katja Wuestenbecker

See also
German Americans and the War; Red Scare; Russia, Revolution of
   November 1917; Wilson, Thomas Woodrow.

References
Coben, Stanley. *A. Mitchell Palmer: Politician.* New York: Columbia
   University Press, 1963; New York: Da Capo, 1972.
Emert, Phyllis Raybin. *Attorneys General: Enforcing the Law.*
   Minneapolis, MN: Oliver Press, 2004.
Feuerlicht, Roberta Strauss. *America's Reign of Terror: World War I,
   the Red Scare, and the Palmer Raids.* New York: Random House,
   1971.
Murray, Robert K. *Red Scare: A Study in National Hysteria,
   1919–1920.* Minneapolis: University of Minnesota Press, 1955;
   Westport, CT: Greenwood, 1980.

Pals Battalions

Great Britain entered World War I as the least prepared of the major powers in 1914 to fight a modern land war. The all-volunteer British army, while a professional force with extensive wartime experience, was minuscule by the standards of the continental armies, which relied on mass conscription. British Secretary of State for War Horatio Lord Kitchener foresaw the need for an army of a million men to fight a war lasting three years. To create this army, the British relied on volunteers.

In order to encourage enlistment for the "Kitchener Army," Major-General Sir Henry Rawlinson advanced the idea that men might be more willing to enlist if they were allowed to serve with men they already knew. British Minister of War Edward George Villiers Stanley, Seventh Earl of Derby, first tested the idea in Liverpool in late August. Within days he had sufficient volunteers to form four battalions. Thus the Pals Battalions were born. Sheffield, Accrington, Leeds, Bradford, and other communities in the industrial midlands and north raised their own battalions. Other battalions were formed on the basis of common professions (the Hull Commercials), employers (the Glasgow Tramways Battalion), or cultural identifications (the Tyneside Irish). Of the 994 battalions raised in Britain between September 1914 and May 1916, 643 were Pals Battalions.

The only large-scale combat test of the Pals Battalions came at the Battle of the Somme (July–November 1916), where more than 57,000 British soldiers fell (19,240 dead) in the initial assault. Although casualties in the Pals Battalions (584 of 720 in the Accrington Pals and 750 of 900 in the Sheffield City Battalion) were proportional to those in other battalions, the long-term effects were more severe. Because the Pals came from limited geographical areas, entire neighborhoods, industries, and even towns had their populations decimated.

Although a few Pals Battalions disbanded in the aftermath of the Somme, the vast majority soldiered on until the British Expedition Force demobilized after the war. When conscription was introduced in Britain in May 1916, replacements diluted the regional character of the surviving Pals Battalions. When Britain again went to war in September 1939, the government immediately introduced conscription, eliminating any need to revive the Pals Battalions concept.

John Lavalle

See also
Great Britain, Army; Kitchener, Horatio Herbert, 1st Earl; Rawlinson, Sir Henry Seymour; Somme Offensive.

References
Middlebrook, Martin. *The First Day on the Somme, 1 July 1916.* New York: Norton, 1972.
Travers, Tim. *The Killing Ground: The British Army, the Western Front, and the Emergence of Modern Warfare, 1900–1918.* Boston: Allen and Unwin, 1987.
Winter, Denis. *Death's Men: Soldiers of the Great War.* New York and London: Penguin, 1978, 1985.

Pankhurst, Emmeline (1858–1928), Christabel (1880–1958), and Sylvia (1882–1960)

British suffragette leaders and political activists. Emmeline Pankhurst was born in Manchester, England, on 4 July 1858. Her father was a successful businessman with radical political beliefs, and her mother was a passionate feminist who began taking her daughter to women's suffrage meetings in the early 1870s. In 1878, Emmeline met the lawyer Richard Pankhurst. A committed socialist, Richard was also a strong advocate of women's suffrage and was chiefly responsible for the drafting of the women's property bill passed by Parliament in 1870.

Emmeline and Richard had four children: Christabel (born on 22 September 1880), Sylvia (born on 5 May 1882), Frank (1884), and Adela (1885). During these years the Pankhursts continued their involvement in the struggle for women's rights, and in 1889 they helped form the pressure group, the Women's Franchise League. Both were active members of the Independent Labour Party. Richard ran unsuccessfully on several occasions for the House of Commons before his death in 1898.

Emmeline continued her involvement in politics, but she grew gradually disillusioned with the existing women's political organizations. In 1901 Christabel met Eva Gore-Booth, who was trying to persuade working-class women in Manchester to join the National Union of Women's Suffrage Societies (NUWSS). Christabel was very impressed with their arguments and decided to join the campaign. Her sister Sylvia and her mother Emmeline also became involved in the suffrage movement at this time. The Pankhursts, however, soon became frustrated by the lack of success of the NUWSS, and in 1903 they formed the Women's Social and Political Union (WSPU). As well as their involvement in the WSPU, Christabel studied law at Owens College, Manchester, and Sylvia won a scholarship to the Royal College of Art in South Kensington.

In 1905 the WSPU decided to use different methods to obtain the publicity they thought would be needed in order to obtain the vote. Christabel and Annie Kenney attempted to disrupt a Liberal Party meeting. In order to gain publicity for their cause, the pair deliberately got themselves arrested and then went to prison rather than pay the fine. The action worked in that the WSPU enjoyed a dramatic increase in its membership.

Christabel obtained her law degree in 1907, but because her gender prevented her from developing that career, she decided to leave Manchester and join the suffragette campaign in London. She disagreed with the way the campaign

British suffragette Emmeline Pankhurst, who was instrumental in securing the vote for women in the early twentieth century. (Library of Congress)

was being run. The initial strategy of the WSPU had been to recruit the support of working-class women. Christabel now advocated a campaign that would appeal to the more prosperous members of society. Whereas her sister Sylvia argued for the vote for all adults, Christabel favored limited suffrage, a system that would only give the vote to women with money and property. She pointed out that the WSPU relied heavily on the money supplied by wealthy women.

Through force of personality and the support of her mother, Christabel gained control of the WSPU in London. Some women left the WSPU in protest; Sylvia, a dedicated socialist like her father, remained out of loyalty to her mother and sister, but she was no longer willing to play a prominent role in the organization. She became very active in the Labour Party and was a close friend of Keir Hardie, leader of that party in the House of Commons.

In 1907, Emmeline moved to London and joined her two daughters in the militant struggle for the vote. Over the next few years all three were imprisoned repeatedly and endured several hunger-strikes. The actions of Emmeline, now in her fifties, inspired many other women to follow her example of committing acts of civil disobedience.

In 1910, Christabel began to support those members of the WSPU who were arguing that the strategy of passive resistance should be replaced by more militant action such as stone-throwing and the destruction of property. When the wholesale smashing of shop windows, vandalizing of art works, and arson attacks took place in 1912, the police began arresting the leaders of the WSPU. Christabel fled to France, where she continued to organize the increasingly militant campaign without fear of imprisonment. Sylvia did not support this policy of violence and concentrated her efforts on helping the Labour Party build up its support in London. This included the production of a weekly paper for working-class women called *The Women's Dreadnought*.

On 4 August 1914, England declared war on Germany, and two days later the WSPU announced that it was suspending all political activity until the war was over. The government then released all suffragettes from prison. In return, the WSPU agreed to end their militant activities and assist the war effort. The war caused further conflict between Sylvia and the WSPU. Sylvia was a pacifist and disagreed with the WSPU's strong support for the conflict. She joined with other women to form the Women's Peace Army, an organization that demanded a negotiated peace. During the war Sylvia worked with Dr. Barbara Tchaykovsky to open four mother-and-baby clinics in London in order to help destitute mothers.

In October 1915, the WSPU changed its newspaper's name from *The Suffragette* to *Britannia*. Emmeline and Christabel's patriotic view of the war was reflected in the paper's new slogan: "For King, For Country, For Freedom." Articles attacked antiwar activists such as Ramsay MacDonald as being "more German than the Germans." The *Britannia* also railed against politicians and military leaders for not doing enough to win the war.

In 1917, the WSPU changed its name to the Women's Party. Christabel and Emmeline had now completely abandoned their earlier socialist beliefs and advocated policies such as the abolition of the trade unions. However, Sylvia's newspaper, *The Women's Dreadnought,* continued to campaign against the war and gave strong support to organizations such as the No-Conscription Fellowship. The newspaper also published Siegfried Sassoon's famous antiwar statement in July 1917. Sylvia Pankhurst supported the Bolshevik Revolution in Russia in November 1917 and visited that country, where she met Vladimir Lenin and ended up arguing with him over censorship. The British government disapproved of Sylvia's pro-Communist articles in her newspaper, and she was imprisoned for five months in 1918 on charges of sedition.

Following passage of the Qualification of Women Act in 1918, which gave the vote to women over age 30, Christabel became one of the seventeen women candidates who stood in the postwar election. She represented the Women's Party in both the 1918 and 1919 elections but was defeated both times. After the war Emmeline and Christabel spent several years on a lecture tour in the United States and Canada. Christabel turned her energies to Christian fundamentalism and carved out a new career as a writer of best-selling evangelical books and as a high-profile speaker on the fundamentalist preaching circuit.

When Emmeline returned to Britain in 1925 she joined the Conservative Party and was adopted as one of its candidates in the East End of London. Sylvia, who still held her strong socialist views, was appalled by this decision. In 1927, Sylvia gave birth to a son, Richard Pankhurst, but upset her mother by refusing to marry the boy's father. Sylvia was totally opposed to signing a marriage contract or taking a man's name.

Emmeline Pankhurst died on 14 June 1928, in London. Christabel returned to Britain in the 1930s. In 1936, she was appointed a dame commander of the British Empire but left for the United States at the start of the Second World War. Christabel Pankhurst died in Los Angeles on 13 February 1958.

Sylvia remained active in politics throughout her life. She was a deeply committed antiracist and antifascist, and in the 1930s she supported the republicans in Spain, helped Jewish refugees from Nazi Germany, and led the campaign against the Italian occupation of Ethiopia. In 1956, she accepted an invitation issued by the Ethiopian government to live there. When she died in Addis Ababa on 27 September 1960, she received a state funeral.

Katja Wuestenbecker

See also

MacDonald, James Ramsay; Pacifism; Sassoon, Siegfried; Women in the War.

References

Bartley, Paula. *Emmeline Pankhurst.* New York: Routledge, 2002.

Bullock, Ian, and Richard Pankhurst, ed. *Sylvia Pankhurst: From Artist to Anti-Fascist.* New York: St. Martin's, 1992.

Castle, Barbara. *Sylvia and Christabel Pankhurst.* New York: Viking Penguin, 1987.

Harrison, Shirley. *Sylvia Pankhurst, A Crusading Life, 1882–1960.* London: Aurum, 2003.

Larsen, Timothy. *Christabel Pankhurst: Fundamentalism and Feminism in Coalition.* Rochester, NY: Boydell, 2002.

Purvis, June. *Emmeline Pankhurst: A Biography.* New York: Routledge, 2002.

Papen, Franz von (1879–1969)

German army officer. Born on 29 October 1879 at Werl, Westphalia, Franz von Papen attended a cadet academy at Bensberg and became a noncommissioned officer at age 15. He transferred to the main corps of the cadet school at Berlin and later entered the Imperial Corps of Pages. Commissioned in the 5th Westphalian Uhlan Regiment at age 19, he became a General Staff officer and received training in intelligence operations. He was promoted to captain in 1913.

Also in 1913, Papen assumed a dual assignment as military attaché in the German Embassy in Washington, D.C., and the German legation in Mexico. After reporting for duty in January 1914 in Washington, Papen traveled in Mexico, which was then in revolutionary turmoil, in search of contracts for German arms makers and in defiance of the U.S. policy of nonrecognition of the regime of General Victoriano Huerta. Papen supervised security measures at the German legation in Mexico City and traveled to Veracruz to observe the U.S. military intervention there.

After the start of World War I in August 1914, Papen returned to Washington and was soon involved in a publicity campaign to influence American public opinion. He also established a network of agents to report on troop movements and the production of war matériel, and he was involved in the forging of U.S. passports to allow German reservists to evade the British blockade and return home. Papen also helped create a dummy corporation to purchase scarce raw materials and thereby hinder production of armaments for the Allies by buying up all available gunpowder and hoarding it. Working with other agents and sympathizers, he also helped finance abortive attempts to blow up the Welland Canal and a key bridge from Canada, foment strikes among German and Irish dockworkers, and sabotage ships loaded with armaments for Great Britain. When the group's plans were discovered, Papen was declared persona non grata by the U.S. government and returned to Germany in December 1915.

Papen then served on the Western Front as a captain in the 4th Guards Infantry Division in 1916 and in Palestine as a major in the German Asia Corps in 1917–1918. After the war he entered politics and was elected to the Prussian Landtag from the Catholic Center Party during 1921–1928 and again during 1930–1932. President Paul von Hindenburg appointed Papen chancellor in May 1932, and he served in that post until December. His decision to end the ban on Nazi armed groups and efforts to convince Hindenburg that he could control Adolf Hitler helped bring the latter to power as chancellor. Papen served as vice chancellor under Hitler during 1933–1934 followed by four years as ambassador to Austria. During World War II he was German ambassador to Turkey. Tried by the International War Crimes Tribunal at Nuremberg, Papen was acquitted. Brought later before a German denazification court,

he was found guilty and sentenced to two years in prison. Papen published his memoirs in 1952 and died in Obersasbach on 2 May 1969.

Gregory Zieren

See also
Intelligence and Counterintelligence; Sabotage.
References
Adams, Henry M., and Robin K. Adams. *Rebel Patriot: A Biography of Franz von Papen.* Santa Barbara, CA: McNally and Loftin, 1987.
Doerries, Reinhard R. "Die Tatigkeit deutscher Agenten in den USA wahrend des Ersten Welkrieges und ihr Einfluss auf die diplomatischen Beziehungen zwischen Washington und Berlin." In *Diplomaten und Agenten: Nachrichtendienste in der Geschichte der deutsch-amerikanischen Beziehungen,* ed. Reinward R. Doekries, 15–52. Heidelberg: Winter Verlag, 2001.
Koeves, Tibor. *Satan in Top Hat: The Biography of Franz von Papen.* New York: Alliance Book Corporation, 1941.
Papen, Franz von. *Memoirs.* Trans. Brian Connell. New York: Dutton, 1953.
Petzold, Joachim. *Franz von Papen: Ein Deutsches Verhängins.* Munich, Germany: Buchverlag Union, 1995.
Rolfs, Richard W. *The Sorcerer's Apprentice: The Life of Franz von Papen.* Lanham, MD: University Press of America, 1996.

German pilot showing the parachute pack attached to his back, along with the rip cord attached to the aircraft, should he fall out unconscious. (National Archives)

Parachutes

Emergency devices allowing aviators to escape from damaged aircraft. Prior to World War I parachutes were largely a curiosity, but the pressures of combat stimulated significant practical development. The crews of observation balloons, motivated by the dangers they faced from attacks on the highly explosive hydrogen-filled gas bags that provided lift, were the first to embrace parachutes. Balloon crewmen wore harnesses that connected to parachutes packed in containers on the outside of the balloon gondolas, and when a crewman jumped overboard his weight pulled the parachute from the container. This technology was also available for airplanes but was not quickly embraced because the early designs were unwieldy and difficult to use.

Both pilots and senior leadership resisted using parachutes on airplanes for a variety of reasons, including the aggressive and macho culture of flying but also because commanders feared that pilots would use this as an excuse not to try to return an airplane to its base. Parachute designs improved late in the war, and their use and acceptance by pilots grew, especially to allow escape from burning airplanes. Parachutes were also used to deliver emergency supplies to ground forces and to insert agents behind enemy lines. U.S. Army Brigadier General Billy Mitchell also suggested that parachutes be used to deliver a large body of troops behind the primary defenses of the enemy as a means to break the stalemate on the Western Front.

Jerome V. Martin

See also
Air Warfare, Fighter Tactics; Lighter-Than-Air Craft; Mitchell, William.
References
Bickers, Richard Townshend. *The First Great Air War.* London: Hodder and Stoughton, 1988.
Kennett, Lee. *The First Air War, 1914–1918.* New York: Free Press, 1991.

Paravanes

Apparatus used by a moving vessel to attack a submerged submarine or, more commonly, to sweep moored mines. A paravane consists essentially of cables attached to a torpedo-shaped float fitted with adjustable fins for setting the depth and direction of its movement. Antisubmarine paravanes were towed astern and equipped with charges set to explode upon contact with a submarine's hull.

Minesweeping paravanes were mounted in pairs, one on either side of a ship's bow with the float set to move at a distance on an angle away from the ship's course, thus maintaining tension on a heavy wire running back to the ship. A submerged mine in the ship's path would be deflected by the bow wave and pushed down the wire to a cable cutter that severed its mooring cable, causing it to rise to the surface for detonation by gunfire.

Related to the floating nets used by commercial fishermen, paravanes were developed by British naval officer Lieutenant Dennistoun Burney who submitted his first proposals in October 1914. Trials began in May 1915, and in August a process of equipping the entire fleet started, at first with capital ships and cruisers, which continued into 1917. Although initially regarded as a nuisance, paravanes soon proved highly effective at low cost, and by the end of the war they had largely negated German use of mines against naval vessels. Some merchant ships also received paravanes, but their crews tended to be wary of them and the results were mixed.

John A. Hutcheson Jr.

See also
Great Britain, Navy; Mine Warfare, Sea; Mines, Sea; Naval Warfare.
References
Marder, Arthur J. *From the Dreadnought to Scapa Flow: The Royal Navy in the Fisher Era, 1904–1919.* 5 vols. London: Oxford University Press, 1961–1970.
Morison, Samuel L. *Guide to Naval Mine Warfare.* Arlington, VA: Pasha Publications, 1995.

Paris Gun

German long-range cannon. The Paris Gun is one of the most remarkable artillery pieces in military history. Its maximum range of 137,800 yards (about 75 miles) by far exceeded any gun ever built to that time. Even to this day, very few conventional artillery pieces actually fired in war have been able to achieve even half that range. Often incorrectly called the Big Bertha, the official name of the Paris Gun was the Wilhelmgeschütz (the Kaiser Wilhelm Gun). It was designed by Krupp's managing director, the brilliant ordnance engineer Professor Fritz Rausenberger, who also designed the Big Bertha.

The Paris Gun was constructed by inserting a 210mm liner tube into a bored-out 380mm naval gun barrel. The liner extended some 39 feet beyond the muzzle of the base barrel. A 19-foot smooth-bore extension was then added to the front of the extended liner, giving the composite barrel a length of 130 feet. The entire assembly required an external truss system mounted on top of the barrel to reduce the droop of the tube. The carriage consisted of a steel box assembly with a pivot in the front and wheels in the rear that ran on a rail track. The gun could only be fired from a prepared concrete firing platform. The barrel alone weighed 200 tons; the carriage weighed 250 tons, and the turntable-type firing platform weighed 300 tons.

Heavy gun supposed to have been the type to shell Paris, a distance of 75 miles. (S. J. Duncan-Clark and W. R. Plewman, *Pictorial History of the Great War*, with W. S. Wallace, *Canada in the Great War*, 5th ed., John A. Hertel, Toronto, 1919)

Despite being a technical marvel, the Paris Gun was a relatively impractical combat weapon. The long and drooping barrel that produced its great range also meant that the fall of shot had a very large circular probable error—which meant wide inaccuracy. The huge and corrosive 400-pound propellant charge caused several centimeters of metal erosion with each shot fired. This meant that the firing chamber volume increased with every round, and each subsequent propellant charge had to be calibrated accordingly. The wear produced by the round as it moved down the tube also caused the bore diameter to grow, meaning that every subsequent round had to be slightly larger than the last. Thus, every barrel and its ammunition had to be supplied as a unit set, with the projectiles and propellant charges precisely numbered. Each barrel was good for a maximum of 60 rounds, after which the barrel had to be replaced. Reportedly, a round loaded out of sequence caused one of the guns to explode on its firing platform.

Virtually all artillery pieces achieve their maximum range when the barrel is elevated to an angle of 45 degrees. Anything over 45 degrees is classified as high-angle fire, and as the elevation increases the range then decreases. The Paris Gun, however, appeared to defy the normal laws of ballistics by achieving its maximum range at an elevation of 50 degrees. The reason is that at 50 degrees elevation the round from the Paris Gun went significantly higher into the stratosphere than at 45 degrees elevation. The reduced air density at the higher altitudes caused far less drag on the body of the projectile, which resulted in the far greater horizontal range.

There were at least three Paris Guns, and there may have been a fourth. The guns were actually manned by naval gunners, with a vice admiral in command of the battery. In early 1918 the Germans had placed three of the guns in the Forest of Crépy, just northwest of Laon. Between March and July the battery fired 303 rounds at Paris. Only 183 of the 265-pound 210mm rounds actually landed in the city, causing 256 deaths and 620 injuries.

The Germans withdrew the guns from action in August 1918 as the Allies were advancing. They were taken back to Germany and presumably destroyed to prevent their capture. The Allied Disarmament Commission was never able to find their remains or determine their exact fate. As with the V-1 and V-2 rockets of World War II, the Paris Gun proved to be little more than a long-range terror weapon that had little influence on the outcome of the war.

David T. Zabecki

See also
Artillery; Big Bertha.

References
Bailey, J. B. A. *Field Artillery and Firepower.* 2nd ed. Annapolis: Naval Institute Press, 2003.
Bull, Gerald V., and C. H. Murphy. *Paris Kanonen—The Paris Guns (Wilhelmgeschütze) and Project HARP.* Herford, Germany: Mittler, 1988.
Hogg, Ian V. *The Guns, 1914–1918.* New York: Ballantine, 1971.
Miller, Henry W. *The Paris Gun.* New York: Jonathan Cape and Harrison Smith, 1930.
Zabecki, David T. *Steel Wind: Colonel Georg Bruchmüller and the Birth of Modern Artillery.* Westport, CT: Praeger, 1994.

Paris Peace Conference (12 January 1919–20 January 1920)

Conference convened by the victorious Allies to decide peace terms with the Central Powers. The main sessions of the Paris Peace Conference debated the terms of peace with Germany

901 Paris Peace Conference

between 19 January and 28 June 1919. The conference climaxed in an elaborate signing ceremony of the Treaty of Versailles on 28 June 1919. Lower-level diplomats continued the conference, leading to subsequent treaties with Austria (Treaty of Saint-Germain-en-Laye, 10 September 1919), Bulgaria (Treaty of Neuilly, 27 November 1919), Hungary (Treaty of Trianon, 4 June 1920), and the Ottoman Empire (Treaty of Sèvres, 10 August 1920). Although the conference opened with much high-minded idealism, it ended with many dashed hopes and great disillusionment. The conference was filled with drama, from the spectacular reception accorded to U.S. President Woodrow Wilson to an attempted assassination of French Premier Georges Clemenceau and the eventual appearance of the German delegation at Versailles.

The conference brought together official and unofficial representatives from around the world. Thirty-two countries were officially represented. Germany and the other defeated Central Powers were not represented. Russia, then in the midst of civil war, was the most notable absentee. Initially the key players were the Big Ten: the chiefs of delegation and the foreign ministers from France, Britain, the United States, Italy, and Japan. The Japanese, however, took little interest in the conference once they had lost their campaign to secure a clause for racial equality and secured both control of the German islands north of the equator and of former German concessions in China (the latter causing a problem with the Chinese delegation). Conference deliberations then were dominated by the Big Eight, which devolved into the delegation heads alone, or the Big Four of French Premier Georges Clemenceau, British Prime Minister David Lloyd George, U.S. President Woodrow Wilson, and Italian Premier Vittorio Orlando. Orlando's position was by far the weakest, and on 24 April he and the Italian delegation left the negotiations after it became obvious that Italy would not receive the city of Fiume. The Big Four thus became the Big Three.

In many ways Wilson was the key figure of the conference. His knowledge of Europe was scant. This was the first time that a sitting U.S. president had journeyed to Europe. As the conference got underway, Wilson had tremendous popular support in Europe, but both Lloyd George and Clemenceau viewed him as meddling, naive, and inexperienced in European affairs. Still, he was crucial to the settlement because of the vital contributions that American men and U.S. finances had made to the Allied victory and because of the leading role that U.S. support would undoubtedly play in the postwar world.

All three of the key leaders largely ignored their own staffs and made most of the critical decisions themselves, turning the deliberations into a clash of personalities and wills. This concentration of decision making also rendered almost impossible the resolution of the immensely complicated conference issues. Complicating matters further, the three leaders mistrusted the advice provided by their military advisors

and kept them as far from the deliberations as possible. The Big Three also believed that in matters of politics soldiers were too politically immature to render sound judgments. "War is too important a business to be left to generals," Clemenceau remarked. He and Marshal Ferdinand Foch, the Big Three's senior military advisor, had a series of vocal public disagreements over the future of the Rhineland. At times Foch's intransigence crossed the line into insubordination, and several politicians believed (incorrectly) that he might be plotting a coup. Even so, the marshal's popularity made it impossible to remove him. Yet, the absence of a military voice at the conference both deprived the politicians of critical advice on security matters and undermined the legitimacy of the process, especially among veterans and conservatives.

Rather than confining themselves to the question of Germany, the conferees attempted to remake the entire global security system. For this task they were immensely unqualified. Lurking in the shadows were many non-German issues, such as the secret French and British accord (the Sykes-Picot Agreement) to divide the former Middle Eastern territories of the Ottoman Empire and the conflict between China and Japan over the latter's claim to the Shandong Peninsula. Issues such as these widened the scope of the conference significantly.

The conferees and their staffs had to resolve more than the dislocations of the war. The issues that had caused the conflict long predated the 1914 assassination of Archduke Franz Ferdinand. The bases for any lasting peace would likewise have to confront three specters of modern European history. The first was unfulfilled nationalism, represented by the Concert of Europe system that had dominated European diplomacy from 1815 to 1870. This haunted Woodrow Wilson most of all. He believed that the Concert system had prevented the peoples of Europe from realizing their nationalist sentiments and had led directly to the outbreak of World War I. He argued that the postwar settlement must therefore address the question of unfulfilled national ambitions. Yet Wilson's goal of national self-determination, even restricted as it was to Europe, faced insurmountable problems. National lines were too blurred to permit the establishment of clear-cut borders. Drawing a tidy border between Russia and the new state of Poland, for example, proved impossible. The settlement was therefore bound to disappoint millions, no matter what the conferees decided.

The second specter, that of the failed revolutions of 1848, haunted all the Big Three, most especially Lloyd George. Made tangible by the triumph of Bolshevism in Russia, political and social unrest threatened the postwar stability and economic growth of the Western powers. The new leaders of Russia preached international revolution, threatening to engulf Europe in war again. Communist rebellions in Germany and Hungary made this all the more terrifying. The disappearance of the Austro-Hungarian Empire and the weakening of Germany left no obvious bulwark against

Bolshevik expansion. The containment of Bolshevism consequently came to occupy a larger role at the conference than had originally been foreseen.

The final specter, unfulfilled Prussian militarism, particularly haunted Clemenceau. He and Foch believed that the war, which for the Germans had come tantalizingly close to victory, had only increased German acquisitiveness and antipathy toward France. Germany and Austria, they argued, might have been defeated, but they still had 75 million inhabitants compared to 45 million in France and Belgium. The war had been largely fought outside German borders, so Germany's industrial infrastructure remained largely intact. Thanks to the Bolshevik Revolution, Russia no longer served France as an eastern ally and counterweight to Germany. Thus French leaders backed a strong Poland. Although Clemenceau and Foch disagreed on how best to contain Germany, both men were intent on using the conference to ensure that Germany could not pose a future threat to France.

The contradictions in the Allied aims created an untenable situation. Every solution posed a new problem: reducing Germany's army would lessen the menace of Prussian militarism but enhance the possibility of a Bolshevik revolution in Germany; separating the Rhineland from Germany would give France and Belgium security but ran the risk of creating an Alsace-Lorraine in reverse; giving Fiume to the Italians would reward them for their wartime sacrifices, but it would also weaken the newly created state of Yugoslavia whose Serbian leadership had also been a member of the alliance; the creation of independent Arab states would fulfill British promises made during the war to Arab leaders but undermine Lloyd George's own desire for a greater British presence in the Middle East and promises made to Zionists in the Balfour Declaration.

Woodrow Wilson's January 1918 pronouncement of the Fourteen Points further complicated matters by creating a pathway to peace that was at once unworkable and immensely popular. Several influential participants (and many Germans) quickly recognized the dilemma that the Fourteen Points created for the conference. If the conferees accepted them as the basis for negotiation, this would heighten the sharp points of disagreement among the victorious powers and enact measures antithetical to the interests of Britain and France. Such a peace would probably be more lenient than most French and British citizens found acceptable. If, on the other hand, the peace conference did not follow the spirit of the Fourteen Points, Germany could claim (as did leaders of the Weimar Republic) that it had been unfairly treated.

Despite their tremendous popular appeal, the Fourteen Points (and Wilsonianism more generally) did not guide the conference as the U.S. president had anticipated. Although the people of Europe may have initially welcomed Wilson and his vision of the postwar world, desires for security soon over-

rode appeals to idealism. The November 1918 British elections, the first in eight years, returned a majority dedicated to a punitive treatment of Germany. In the words of Britain's First Lord of the Admiralty Sir Eric Geddes, Germany should be squeezed like a lemon "until the pips squeak."

A similar situation existed in France, where bitter anger over Germany's invasion, wartime atrocities, and scorched-earth policies prevailed. All French parties, save the Socialists who were divided on the issue, supported either outright annexation of the Rhineland or its separation from Germany. Clemenceau, for his part, had little sympathy for Wilsonian idealism. Upon reading the Fourteen Points he declared, "God Himself only gave us ten [commandments]."

Although many Europeans continued to cling to the idealism that the Fourteen Points represented, resentment toward Germany dominated. Germany's imposition of harsh terms on Russia at Brest Litovsk just two months after the announcement of the Fourteen Points seemed, even to Wilson, to demonstrate that Germany had no right to demand or expect leniency. The scuttling of the German fleet at Scapa Flow highlighted for many the continuing German bad faith.

Unlike their counterparts at the Congress of Vienna a century earlier, the negotiators at Paris were all responsible to electorates. The conferees therefore worked largely behind closed doors but under tremendous scrutiny from the media and their own constituencies. The back-room bargaining that characterized so much of the conference violated Wilson's first point that "diplomacy shall always proceed frankly and in the public view." The Big Three failed to appreciate fully that a people's war could not be followed by a cabinet peace.

Lloyd George and Clemenceau found themselves in the awkward position of speaking favorably about the Fourteen Points in public while undermining many of Wilson's principles behind closed doors. This contradiction helped to discredit the final settlement in the eyes of those European voters who expected a peace based on the Fourteen Points.

Aware that the conference could not please all parties, the conferees agreed on the necessity of implementing Wilson's idea for a League of Nations. Wilson hoped that it would resolve problems emerging from the dissatisfactions, contradictions, and unanticipated problems of any treaty the conference produced. Clemenceau viewed the proposed league as a threat to the security of France, fearing that his people would mistakenly place their confidence in it, rather than in military strength, to contain Germany.

Because of these contradictions, the most important product of the Paris Peace Conference, the Treaty of Versailles with Germany, embodied a series of uncomfortable and untenable compromises that gave all victorious parties only part of what they wanted and so inevitably also left all parties frustrated as well. Worse, it did not significantly diminish German power, permitting a German nationalist resurgence a generation later. The other treaties were also inadequate. The settlements were compromises, their continued survival having been heavily dependent on wise, careful, and far-sighted postwar diplomacy, which was not forthcoming.

All parties were frustrated by the peace conference's many compromises. Foch, who thought the settlement too soft on Germany, and British diplomat Harold Nicolson, who thought it too harsh, both refused to attend the signing. Liberals and the left found the conference's outcome particularly disillusioning, and in their disappointment many turned on Wilson as a failed Messiah. The contradictions and complexities of the Paris peace settlement must be borne in mind when explaining the subsequent Allied failure to enforce many of its provisions.

Michael Neiberg

See also
Atrocities; Balfour Declaration; Brest Litovsk, Treaty of; Bucharest, Treaty of; Clemenceau, Georges; Foch, Ferdinand; Fourteen Points; Franz Ferdinand, Archduke; Germany, Revolution in; League of Nations Covenant; Lloyd George, David; Neuilly, Treaty of; Orlando, Vittorio Emanuele; Reparations; Sykes-Picot Agreement; Saint-Germain, Treaty of; Scapa Flow, Scuttling of German Fleet at; Sèvres, Treaty of; Trianon, Treaty of; Versailles, Treaty of; Wilson, Thomas Woodrow; Zionism.

References
Dallas, Gregor. *1918: War and Peace*. New York: Overlook Press, 2000.

Gmeline, Patrick de. *Versailles: Chronique d'une Fausse Paix*. Paris: Presses de la Cité, 2001.

Henning, Ruth. *Versailles and After*. London: Routledge, 1984.

Howard, Michael. *The Invention of Peace*. New Haven, CT: Yale University Press, 2001.

MacMillan, Margaret. *Paris, 1919: Six Months That Changed the World*. New York: Random House, 2002.

Mayer, Arno. *Politics and Diplomacy of Peacemaking: Containment and Counter-Revolution at Versailles*. New York: Knopf, 1967.

Seaman, L. C. B. *From Vienna to Versailles*. London: Routledge, 1955.

Watt, Richard. *The Kings Depart*. New York: Simon and Schuster, 1968.

Pašić, Nicola (1845–1926)

Serbian politician and statesman. Born at Zajecar, Serbia, on 19 December 1845, Nicola Pašić studied engineering in Belgrade and Zurich. He was elected to the Serbian parliament in 1878, and in 1881 he founded the outspokenly nationalist and anti-Austrian Serbian Radical Party, which he led until his death. Pašić was an active opponent of Serbian Prince Milan Obrenović, and in 1883 Pašić was forced into exile. He returned to Serbia in 1889 and served as prime minister for the first time in 1891–1892. In 1893–1895 he served as minister to Russia. Pašić served again as prime minister during 1904–1905, 1906–1908, and 1909–1911, and he led Serbia through the Balkan Wars of 1912–1913 and World War I, serving as both prime minister and foreign minister from 1912 to 1918.

Prime Minister Nicola Pašić of Serbia, who strengthened ties between Russia and Serbia. (Francis J. Reynolds and C. W. Taylor, *Collier's Photographic History of the European War*, P. F. Collier & Son, New York, 1916)

Pašić apparently had foreknowledge of the involvement of Serbian military and civilian officials in an attempt to assassinate Archduke Franz Ferdinand and ineffectively sought to prevent its implementation. Pašić was largely responsible for drafting the Serbian reply to the Austro-Hungarian ultimatum of July 1914. Following the epic retreat of the Serbian army through Albania in November–December 1915, Pašić set up a Serbian government-in-exile on Corfu.

An ardent advocate of "Greater Serbia" and South Slav unity, Pašić played a major role in the creation of the Kingdom of Serbs, Croats, and Slovenes, which came into being on 1 December 1918. He obtained the agreement of the Croats and Slovenes to the Corfu Pact of 1917 and engineered the deposition of King Nikola I and the annexation of Montenegro by Serbia in December 1918, both of which were major steps toward the creation of a united South Slav kingdom ruled by the Serbian Karageorgević dynasty. Pašić also represented the newly created kingdom at the 1919 Paris Peace Conference and obtained favorable territorial settlements at the expense of the defeated Austria-Hungary and Bulgaria.

Pašić remained a key figure in the kingdom after World War I and served as its prime minister from January 1921 to April 1926. He ensured that the constitution adopted in 1921 provided for strong centralized control of the new kingdom by the Serbs. His pro-Serbian policies aroused the enmity of Montenegrin and Croatian opposition groups and thus contributed to the instability of the new kingdom. Nicola Pašić died at Belgrade on 19 December 1926.

Charles R. Shrader

See also
Balkan Front; Balkan Wars; Corfu Declaration; Franz Ferdinand, Assassination of; Peter I Karageorgević, King; Serbia, Conquest of; Serbia, Role in War; Yugoslavia, Creation of.

References
Cox, John K. *The History of Serbia.* Westport, CT: Greenwood, 2002.
Dragnich, Alex N. *Serbia, Nikola Pašić, and Yugoslavia.* West Orange, NJ: Rutgers University Press, 1974.
Hamilton, Richard F., and Holger H. Herwig, eds. *The Origins of World War I.* Cambridge and New York: Cambridge University Press, 2003.
Pavlowitch, Steven K. *Serbia: The History of an Idea.* New York: New York University Press, 2002.

Passchendaele

See Ypres, Third Battle of

Patton, George Smith (1885–1945)

U.S. Army officer and pioneer of tank warfare. Born on 11 November 1885 in San Gabriel, California, George Patton attended the Virginia Military Institute for a year before graduating from the U.S. Military Academy, West Point, in 1909. Commissioned in the cavalry and an accomplished horseman, Patton represented the United States in the Pentathlon at the 1910 Stockholm Olympics. He served in the Punitive Expedition into Mexico during 1916–1917.

Following U.S. entry into World War I in April 1917, Patton was aide to American Expeditionary Forces (AEF) commander General John Pershing before transferring to the newly formed Tank Corps and organizing the first U.S. tank school at Langres, France. Promoted to temporary lieutenant colonel, he took command of the 304th Tank Brigade and led it in the Saint-Mihiel offensive, where he was wounded. Promoted to colonel, he then participated in the Meuse-Argonne offensive.

U.S. Army Lieutenant Colonel George S. Patton Jr. in front of a Renault FT17 tank in France during World War I. (Corbis)

At the end of the war Patton reverted to his permanent rank of captain and saw the Tank Corps dissolved in 1920. Patton remained a champion of armored warfare. He graduated from the Command and General Staff School (1924) and the Army War College (1932). Returning to armor, he was promoted to temporary brigadier general (1940) and temporary major general (1941), when he assumed command of the 2nd Armored Division. He took command of II Corps in North Africa in March 1943 and the Seventh Army that July. Receiving command of the Third Army (January 1944), he led it across France and into Germany in a brilliant campaign that won him renown as one of the greatest of U.S. generals. Patton died at Heidelberg, Germany, on 21 December 1945 of injuries sustained in an automobile accident.

T. Jason Soderstrum

See also

Meuse-Argonne Offensive; Pershing, John Joseph; Saint-Mihiel Offensive; Tank; Warfare Tanks.

References

Blumenson, Martin. *Patton: The Man behind the Legend, 1885–1945.* New York: William Morrow, 1985.

D'Este, Carlo. *Patton: A Genius for War.* New York: Harper Perennial, 1996.

Farago, Ladislas. *Patton: Ordeal and Triumph.* New York: Ivan Obolensky, 1964.

Hirshson, Stanley P. *General Patton: A Soldier's Life.* New York: HarperCollins, 2002.

Hogg, Ian V. *The Biography of General George S. Patton.* London: Hamlyn, 1982.

French General Paul Pau, brought out of retirement to command the Army of Alsace at the beginning of World War I. (Francis J. Reynolds and C. W. Taylor, *Collier's Photographic History of the European War,* P. F. Collier & Son, New York, 1916)

Pau, Paul (1848–1932)

French army general. Born on 29 November 1848 in Montélimar (Drôme), Paul-Marie-César-Gérald Pau took part in the Franco–German War of 1870–1871, suffering the loss of his lower right arm and hand. Following a variety of assignments, Pau made general in 1903. He retired from the army in 1911 following his failure to obtain the post of chief of the General Staff, which went, instead, to General Joseph Joffre. Pau shared Joffre's views on the doctrine of the offensive, even though Pau differed from Joffre on religious and political matters. Pau was a popular officer and effective administrator, known for his loyalty and his frankness.

Joffre recalled Pau on the outbreak of World War I to take command of the Army of Alsace. Pau led his army in the offensive to recapture Alsace, entering Thann on 14 August 1914 and Mulhouse (Mülhausen) on the 19th, and reaching the outskirts of Colmar on the 21st. Within a few days, German counterattacks retook most of the French gains, but Thann remained in French hands. Following the French army's lack of success in Lorraine, Joffre ordered Pau's divisions westward to join the Sixth Army, and Pau himself went back into retirement. Even though Pau's name was reputed to be the only one known to the French public, Pau did not survive General Joffre's purge of generals after the opening battles of the war.

Although retired from active command, Pau continued to serve. He was a member of the French Supreme War Council (Conseil Supérieur de la Guerre), and he undertook several missions abroad on behalf of the French army. In January 1916 he went to Russia as head of a mission to supervise the delivery of munitions. He visited Australia between September and December 1918 as head of a mission that reported (in 1919) on economic relations between France and Australia. Pau died in Paris on 2 January 1932.

Elizabeth Greenhalgh

See also

Frontiers, Battle of the; Joffre, Joseph; Mulhouse, Battles of.

References

Clayton, Anthony. *Paths of Glory: The French Army, 1914–18.* London: Cassell, 2003.

Porch, Douglas. *The March to the Marne: The French Army, 1871–1914.* Cambridge and New York: Cambridge University Press, 1981.

Spears, Sir Edward. *Liaison, 1914: A Narrative of the Great Retreat.* London: Eyre and Spottiswoode, 1968.

Valluy, J. E. *La Première Guerre Mondiale.* 2 vols. Paris: Larousse, 1968.

Payer, Friedrich von (1847–1931)

German politician. Born on 12 June 1847 at Tübingen, Friedrich von Payer studied law and became a solicitor at Stuttgart in 1871 and a notary in 1899. From 1868 he held several political posts on the local, regional, and national levels in the liberal (South) German People's Party. He was a strong promoter of the fusion of three leftist liberal parties as the Progressive People's Party in 1910 and was elected the chairman of its parliamentary group in 1912.

In August 1914, Payer supported the Reichstag's grant of war credits to the government. During the war, however, he demanded a democratization of the political system and fought to abolish Prussia's three-class franchise. In July 1917 he became chairman of the interparty committee of the Reichstag, a joint group created to facilitate regular consultations among leaders of that body. In this function he was able to mediate between parliament and government. During debate on the Reichstag Peace Resolution that called for peace without annexations, Payer used his influence to have the war declared a defensive struggle.

Payer was appointed vice chancellor under Count Georg von Hertling on 12 November 1917 to replace Karl Helfferich, who had resigned after the dismissal of Chancellor Georg Michaelis. In the spring of 1918, Payer additionally took charge of the new Central Agency for Home Service, a domestic propaganda division. Under the chancellorship of Prince Max von Baden, Payer remained in office and prevented the military leadership from breaking off the already-started armistice negotiations. He was forced to resign on 9 November 1918.

In the German National Assembly (Deutsche Nationalversammlung) of 1919–1920, a forerunner of the Reichstag in the Weimar Republic, Payer was elected chairman of the leftist-liberal German Democratic Party's (DDP) parliamentary group. He voted for the acceptance of the Treaty of Versailles but soon withdrew from politics. Payer died at Stuttgart on 14 July 1931.

Bert Becker

See also

Helfferich, Karl; Hertling, Georg Friedrich von, Count; Max von Baden, Prince; Michaelis, Georg; Reichstag Peace Resolution.

References

Bradler, Günther. "Payer, Friedrich v." *Neue Deutsche Biographie*, Vol. 20. Berlin: Duncker and Humblot, 2001.

Payer, Friedrich von. *Autobiographische Aufzeichnungen und Dokumente*. Ed. Guenther Bradler. Goettingen: A. Kuemmerle, 1974.

———. *Von Bethmann Hollweg bis Ebert: Erinnerungen und Bilder*. Frankfurt am Main: Frankfurter Societaets-Druckerei, 1923.

Sheehan, James J. *German Liberalism in the Nineteenth Century*. Chicago: University of Chicago Press, 1978.

Welch, David. *Germany, Propaganda, and Total War, 1914–1918: The Sins of Omission*. New Brunswick, NJ: Rutgers University Press, 2000.

Peace Overtures during the War

Initiatives aimed at achieving a compromise outcome for World War I reflected the interplay of events on the battlefield, military strategies, diplomacy, and domestic politics in the warring powers. At the beginning of the war, both sides were hopeful of victory, and neither was willing to compromise. Negotiations then became more difficult as the butcher's bill of war mounted. Both sides had invested so much blood and treasure that neither seemed willing to do what was necessary to achieve a lasting peace settlement. When one side in the war seemed in a position of strength and ascendancy militarily, it offered to negotiate, but on its own terms. The strategic stalemate by 1916 on the major fighting fronts and the continually mounting cost of the war, however, intensified attempts by the belligerents, as well as by neutral states, to seek an end to the war through a negotiated settlement.

The neutral United States took a leading role in this process. President Woodrow Wilson feared that if the United States did not bring about a peaceful resolution, his own nation might be drawn into the war. In January 1915 he sent his trusted personal advisor, the pro-Entente Colonel Edward House, to Europe, but House received little positive response from British, French, and German leaders, all of whom seemed to believe that the best way to achieve a meaningful peace was to defeat their enemies.

Early in 1916 House again traveled to Europe on behalf of Wilson. This time he received a favorable reception from British Foreign Secretary Sir Edward Grey. Grey and House agreed that Wilson, on receiving a positive response from France and Britain, would issue a call for a general peace conference. House's conversations with Grey resulted in a memorandum whereby House virtually committed the United States to joining the Allied coalition if Germany rejected a compromise peace.

House clearly exceeded his instructions. Wilson had asked him to propose peace negotiations and to state only that if Germany refused such, the United States would throw its "moral force" against the Central Powers. With Wilson reluctant to give a firm pledge of U.S. participation in the war should Germany reject a comprehensive peace settlement, the plan for a peace conference collapsed. The British government, however, took some comfort from the House-Grey memorandum, which seemed to reveal that the United States morally favored the British cause and thus London believed it did not have to take too seriously U.S. protests against

Drawing showing negotiations between the delegates at the peace conference in Brest Litovsk. The Ukranian delegates plead against Leon Trotsky's centralization policy, 1 February 1918. (Bettmann/Corbis)

British blockade practices. Meanwhile, in November 1916 Wilson won reelection to the presidency. The key issue seems to have been the war. Wilson had campaigned under the slogan "He Kept Us Out of War."

Shortly after his reelection, Wilson prepared another appeal to both sides in the war, drafting a call to both sets of belligerents to present their precise war aims. Before Wilson could issue his appeal, however, Germany itself acted. This move came in the wake of German successes on the Eastern Front, especially victory over Romania, but it also reflected an increasingly desperate German military situation. Austria-Hungary, Germany's chief ally, was reeling; Germany itself had suffered rebuff in the Battle of Verdun; and the winter of 1916–1917 (the "Turnip Winter") was extraordinarily hard on the German population.

Chancellor Theobald von Bethmann Hollweg had rather cynically insisted that Germany undertake peace soundings before it turned to the ultimate solution of trying to win the war through unrestricted submarine warfare. If peace ensued, Germany would not need to resort to unrestricted submarine warfare. If there was no peace conference, then the diplomatic initiative would at least help to justify the resumption of unrestricted submarine warfare. The chancel-

lor also hoped that such an effort would provide a psychological boost for the government at home, convincing many Germans that their leaders were actively seeking a reasonable peace. On 12 December 1916, Bethmann Hollweg proposed peace negotiations between the Central Powers and the Entente. This did not mean that Germany had any intention of yielding its territorial gains to that point, including its occupation of Belgium and northeastern France.

Wilson was now caught in the position of seeming to support the Germans, but he went ahead anyway and on 18 December 1916 issued his own invitation to both sides to formally state their war aims. The Allied leaders were particularly upset over Wilson's apparent effort to force them to reveal the secret arrangements they had made regarding the partition of territories belonging to the Central Powers. On 26 December the German government responded to Wilson, rejecting any role by the U.S. government in peace negotiations and ignoring the central demand in Wilson's proposal, the communication of peace terms. Implicit in this response was the German intention of retaining the bulk of the territory it had conquered by force of arms. The leaders of the Entente, who correctly perceived the German proposal as an attempt to capitalize on military successes, responded on

30 December 1916 by rejecting the German "peace offer" and demanding the withdrawal of German troops from all occupied territories and the liberation of the minorities of Austria-Hungary and the Ottoman Empire.

On 22 January 1917, Wilson expressed his reaction to the Allied response to his appeal in a memorable address to the U.S. Senate. In it Wilson warned the combatants that the only lasting settlement would be "peace without victory." Although the speech did not have its desired effect of bringing the combatants to the peace table, it further established Wilson's position as the world's moral arbiter.

Already, however, German leaders had decided on a desperate gamble. On 31 January Berlin announced to the world that Germany would resume unrestricted submarine warfare the next day. German military leaders imposed their will on policy. They believed that while such an action would undoubtedly bring the United States into the war on the Allied side, within six months a total submarine blockade of the British Isles would force Britain from the war and achieve military victory before U.S. resources could be brought to bear. This German decision not only killed any Wilson peace initiative but soon led to a U.S. declaration of war against Germany on 6 April 1917.

Meanwhile, Austria-Hungary, exhausted by the war, was ready to accept a negotiated settlement. Prodded by Pope Benedict XV and worried by probable U.S. entry into the war, in March 1917 Emperor Karl I summoned his brother-in-law, Prince Sixtus of Bourbon-Parma, and Sixtus's brother Xavier to a secret meeting. The two men were then serving with the Belgian medical services. The meeting resulted in the Sixtus brothers agreeing to act as emissaries for Karl with western European leaders. Karl expressed his desires to see Belgium restored to full sovereignty, Germany evacuate northwestern France, and Alsace-Lorraine returned to France. He was also prepared to make minor territorial concessions to Italy.

The Sixtus mission failed, in part because the Allies were buoyed by U.S. entry into the war and in part because Italian leaders, who hoped to annex significant portions of Austrian territory, strongly denounced the plan as an effort to split the Allied camp. The Serbian government-in-exile also opposed the plan for the same reason. Later, French Premier Georges Clemenceau's publication of the "Sixte Letters" in April 1918 led Kaiser Wilhelm II of Germany to force Karl into signing the Spa Agreements, which definitively subordinated Austro-Hungarian foreign policy to that of Germany.

The German government, believing victory to be within its grasp, did not contemplate any concessions. Indeed, it sought to extend Central Powers influence in Poland, strengthen German domination of the Baltic provinces, and secure Austro-Hungarian hegemony in the Balkans. Moreover, Berlin would make no concessions on Alsace-Lorraine or even Belgium.

Despite intransigence on the part of Germany's leaders, in July 1917 the Reichstag passed a "peace resolution," calling on the government to renounce territorial demands in order to stimulate the search for a solution. The resolution met strong resistance from the kaiser and the German military, but it nevertheless proved that a broad segment of the German public opinion favored a compromise peace.

On 1 August 1917, Pope Benedict XV sent a note to the belligerents proposing a compromise peace without annexations and reparations. The Pope proposed Germany's withdrawal from Belgium and northeastern France; the withdrawal of Allied troops from Germany's colonies; the withdrawal of Germany and other Central Powers forces from Serbia, Montenegro, and Romania; and the creation of an independent Poland. This proposal led to separate bilateral negotiations between the Holy See and both the Entente and the Central Powers.

In these negotiations, the Central Powers, led by Germany, demonstrated their reluctance to withdraw unconditionally from all territories they had occupied, particularly Belgium. The Allies on their part were not prepared to give up their long-term goals, such as regaining Alsace-Lorraine (for France) and securing the ethnic Italian Trentino (for Italy). There were also some German attempts to negotiate with Britain through Spain, but growing disagreements within the German leadership blocked these moves. While the politicians were ready to surrender Belgium and other occupied countries for peace, the German generals, who were actually running Germany, insisted on the retention of some territories for strategic and economic reasons. The generals won. When the German government announced in October 1917 that it would never surrender, all hopes for a negotiated settlement vanished.

The military collapse of Russia in fall 1917 allowed the Central Powers to realize their long-sought goal of fighting on just one major front. Immediately on seizing power in Russia in early November 1917, the Bolsheviks called for a "just" peace without annexations and reparations. They sought peace in order to consolidate their own precarious position in Russia.

The Germans and Russians concluded an armistice and opened peace negotiations at Brest Litovsk. When the Bolshevik leadership learned of the enormity of the German demands, it rejected them and simply announced a policy of "neither war nor peace." The Germans then renewed hostilities. Having destroyed the army in their rise to power, leaving little means of resistance available to them, and with the Germans making great gains, the Russian leadership reluctantly agreed to the German terms. Peace was concluded on the Eastern Front in the punitive Treaty of Brest Litovsk with Russia in March and the Treaty of Bucharest with Romania in May. The severity of the terms of these treaties was unprecedented in modern times. Germany could now shift considerable manpower and other resources to the West and hope to win the war. The Germans came close to success but lacked sufficient manpower to achieve a breakthrough against the western Entente powers, now bolstered by significant numbers of U.S. troops.

The peace overtures of 1916–1918 failed because, from the beginning, all protagonists assumed that the war would end with a military victory, and they were determined to achieve it. There was also a basic asymmetry in the strategic positions of the belligerents. The Central Powers persistently tried at least to preserve the status quo achieved by their armies by 1916, while for the Allies the ideal compromise solution was the restoration of prewar boundaries. This contradiction could be resolved only with a military victory by one side. Neither side was ever ready to negotiate seriously toward a compromise settlement, which in the end would have left both unsatisfied.

Domestic political factors were also important. The dominance of the military over the civilian leadership in Germany by 1916 severely limited Germany's ability to deliver compromise peace proposals. The all-too-obvious weakening position of both Austria-Hungary and Russia in their respective coalitions worked against a peaceful solution, as it enhanced the desire of the leadership of states on the opposite side to press the war forward to a military conclusion. Despite various peace overtures, the war continued until the armistice with Germany on 11 November 1918.

Peter Rainow and Spencer C. Tucker

See also

Benedict XV, Pope; Bethmann Hollweg, Theobald von; Brest Litovsk, Treaty of; Bucharest, Treaty of; Clemenceau, Georges; Grey, Edward, 1st Viscount of Fallodon; House, Edward Mandell; Karl I, Emperor; Mitteleuropa; Reichstag Peace Resolution; Sixtus, Prince of Bourbon-Parma; Sixtus Affair; Submarine Warfare, Central Powers; Sykes-Picot Agreement; Wilson, Thomas Woodrow.

References

Farrar, L. L. *Divide and Conquer: German Efforts to Conclude a Separate Peace, 1914–1918.* New York: Columbia University Press, 1978.

Fischer, Fritz. *Germany's Aims in the First World War.* New York: Norton, 1967.

Rothwell, V. H. *British War Aims and Peace Diplomacy, 1914–1918.* New York: Oxford University Press, 1971.

Stevenson, David. *Cataclysm: The First World War as Political Tragedy.* New York: Basic Books, 2004.

———. *The First World War and International Politics.* Oxford and New York: Oxford University Press, 1988.

———. *French War Aims against Germany, 1914–1919.* Oxford, UK: Clarendon, 1982.

Taylor, Alan J. P. *The Struggle for Mastery in Europe, 1848–1918.* Oxford: Oxford University Press, 1980.

Welch, David. *Germany, Propaganda, and Total War, 1914–1918: The Sins of Omission.* New Brunswick, NJ: Rutgers University Press, 2000.

Pershing, John Joseph (1860–1948)

General of the Armies of the United States and commander of the American Expeditionary Forces (AEF). Born in Laclede, Missouri, on 13 September 1860, John Pershing worked odd jobs and taught school to support his family until receiving an appointment to the U.S. Military Academy in 1882. Commissioned a second lieutenant on graduation in 1886, he joined the 6th Cavalry Regiment in New Mexico, where he saw limited action in the final subjugation of the Apache Indians. In 1891 Pershing participated in the campaign to quiet the Sioux following the tragic confrontation at Wounded Knee.

Later in 1891 Pershing became professor of military science at the University of Nebraska, where he studied law in his off hours. He completed a law degree in 1893 and, frustrated by the lack of military advancement (his promotion to 1st lieutenant did not come until 1892) even considered a legal career. In 1895 he returned to the field with the 10th Cavalry, one of four regiments in the service comprised of African-American soldiers. The following year Pershing joined the

U.S. General John J. "Black Jack" Pershing, who was chasing Pancho Villa in Mexico when World War I began and who commanded the American Expeditionary Forces in France during 1917–1918. (Library of Congress)

HISTORICAL CONTROVERSY
Pershing's Drive on Metz Rejected by Foch, a Wasted Opportunity?

The Saint-Mihiel salient south of Verdun had been in German hands since 1914. Its capture by an independent U.S. army was the dream of American Expeditionary Forces (AEF) commander General John Pershing. His plan to capture the salient that threatened French railway communications was a long time in maturing. Pershing intended to reduce it in an attack from both sides of the salient and then to move eastward into the Woëvre plain, then onward to Metz, an important railway junction in Lorraine, the province that Germany had acquired as a consequence of the Franco-German War of 1870–1871. Thus the U.S. action at Saint-Mihiel—the first as an independent army—had a significance far greater than the small amount of territory gained, important though that was. Success there would prove that the U.S. Army had come of age and that its commanders knew how to plan, prepare, and execute a modern battle.

The operation was to begin in September 1918. However, the stunning Allied successes that started in July on the Marne and continued in August at Amiens revealed that the decisive victorious battle that Allied commander-in-chief Marshal Ferdinand Foch had believed would not come until 1919 might become reality in 1918. Accordingly, Foch changed his plans so as to create a succession of converging blows on the German line, with the British moving from north to south and the French and U.S. forces moving westward. These would force the German army to evacuate the territory it held. To advance toward Metz as Pershing intended would be to undertake a divergent operation. In two angry interviews on 30 August and 2 September 1918, Foch insisted that Pershing reduce the scope of the Saint-Mihiel operation, or give it up altogether if necessary, and transfer his divisions northwestward so as to join in the Meuse-Argonne offensive. The axis of progression would be northwest toward Mézières instead of toward Metz.

Pershing refused to give up his long-planned Saint-Mihiel operation. It began on 12 September, with the U.S. First Army and French divisions easily capturing the salient. The Germans had been caught as they were withdrawing, and their defenses toward Metz were incomplete. The operation ended the next day, and the troops were then transferred to take part in the Meuse-Argonne operation.

The relatively easy capture of the Saint-Mihiel salient led some at the time to complain that Foch had lost a great opportunity to capture a highly important rail hub and strike a huge blow at enemy morale. The corollary was that the enormous casualties suffered by the AEF in the Meuse-Argonne campaign would have been much fewer had they been allowed to continue toward Metz. This is to ignore three important facts. First, the capture of a strongly fortified town in German territory would be a much harder task than taking a small salient that the enemy had already decided to give up. Also, the AEF was totally reliant on the French for both transport capabilities and guns. It lacked the resources to mount an independent campaign toward Metz. Finally, Foch's victorious tactic of successive blows along the whole of the front in a tightening concentric grip on the German front would have been less effective if the U.S. Army had diverged toward Metz.

The controversy is part of the wider struggle between Pershing's obstinate determination to create an autonomous U.S. military force that would win a spectacular battle such as the capture of Metz, thus ensuring his country a more influential place at the peace table, and the Allied need to meet the urgent manpower crisis caused by the German 1918 offensives. The (unjustified) claim that a splendid opportunity was lost when Foch insisted on a change of Pershing's plan for an advance on Metz reflects American disappointment rather than a true appreciation of the merits of the operation.

Elizabeth Greenhalgh

See also
Foch, Ferdinand; Marne, Second Battle of the; Meuse-Argonne Offensive; Pershing, John Joseph; Saint-Mihiel Offensive.

References
Bruce, Robert B. *A Fraternity of Arms: America and France in the Great War.* Lawrence: University Press of Kansas, 2003.

Coffman, Edward M. *The War to End All Wars: The American Military Experience in World War I.* Lexington: University Press of Kentucky, 1998.

Foch, Ferdinand. *The Memoirs of Marshal Foch.* Trans. T. Bentley Mott. New York: Doubleday, Doran, 1931.

Pershing, John J. *My Experiences in the World War.* 2 vols. New York: Frederick A. Stokes, 1931.

Trask, David F. *The AEF and Coalition Warmaking, 1917–1918.* Lawrence: University Press of Kansas, 1993.

staff of commanding General Nelson A. Miles in Washington and in 1897 became an instructor of tactics at West Point. Here, cadets unhappy with his dark demeanor and rigid style labeled him "Black Jack," a derogatory reference to Pershing's 10th Cavalry posting.

In 1898, with war declared on Spain, Pershing rejoined the 10th Cavalry for the Cuba campaign. Although overshadowed by Theodore Roosevelt and his Rough Riders, the African-American soldiers performed admirably during the fight for the San Juan Heights, and Pershing drew praise for his coolness and bravery under fire. Returning to the United States, he entered the Volunteer organization with the rank of major, charged with overseeing the War Department's new Bureau of Insular Affairs. Pershing's diverse experience and legal training prepared him well for the changing role of the U.S. military establishment and the challenges of colonial administration, which he first encountered in 1899 in the Philippines. In 1901, after finally receiving promotion to captain in the Regulars, he campaigned successfully against the Moros, attracting further praise and recognition.

Pershing returned to the United States in 1903 for General Staff service and to attend the Army War College. In 1905, as a military attaché to Japan, he became an official military observer of the Russo-Japanese War. Having won the appreciation of former Secretary of War Elihu Root and President Roosevelt for his handling of Philippine affairs and his reports on the Russo-Japanese War, Pershing in September 1906 experienced a great rarity in U.S. military history when Roosevelt nominated the captain for direct promotion to brigadier general, vaulting him ahead of hundreds of senior officers. Pershing spent most of the next eight years in the Philippines, where he continued to display enlightened leadership. Returning to the United States, he commanded briefly at the Presidio, San Francisco, before moving in 1914 to Fort Bliss near El Paso, Texas, to confront problems associated with the Mexican Revolution. In 1915 his wife Frances Warren and their three daughters, who remained at the Presidio, died in a house fire, but the crisis on the border left Pershing little time to grieve.

In March 1916 Mexican revolutionary leader Francisco "Pancho" Villa led a raid on the small border town of Columbus, New Mexico, that prompted a massive response by the United States. Pershing took charge of a Punitive Expedition into Mexico, with orders to capture or kill Villa and his followers while avoiding conflict with Mexico. The expedition of more than 10,000 men unfolded in a politically charged and naturally hostile environment. It lasted almost a year, cut deep into northern Mexico, and threatened all-out war between the United States and its increasingly unhappy neighbor. Although Villa escaped, Pershing used the expedition to test some of the new technologies of war, including machine guns, aircraft, motorized transport, and radio.

Again Pershing's military skill, administrative ability, and sensitivity to political realities endeared him to his civilian superiors. In May 1917, following the U.S. declaration of war on the Central Powers, President Woodrow Wilson named Pershing, only recently promoted to major general, to command the AEF, which was to fight in Europe as a distinctive U.S. army. Once more Pershing faced an incredibly delicate situation, as he was forced to maintain U.S. military autonomy amid persistent pressure from his European allies for U.S. divisions to fill holes in their deteriorating ranks, a task made even more difficult by the desperate conditions he witnessed upon arriving in France. Pershing, promoted to full general in October 1917, stubbornly refused to have his forces fed piecemeal into the trenches, and he labored to avoid subjecting his men to the failed practices that made this war so horrible. But during the crisis occasioned by Germany's 1918 spring (Ludendorff) offensives, Pershing offered individual U.S. divisions to the Allied command, and the U.S. troops quickly proved their worth in the heavy fighting at Cantigny, Belleau Wood, and Château-Thierry and during the Second Battle of the Marne.

Pershing continued to ready his fighting force—the U.S. First Army—for the long-desired independent action, which Supreme Allied Commander Marshal Ferdinand Foch now reluctantly authorized. In September 1918 the largest U.S. military operation since the Civil War struck and reduced the German-held Saint-Mihiel salient. Pershing hoped to follow up this victory with a drive on Metz and beyond, but Foch refused; Pershing instead redirected U.S. efforts to participate in the massive Meuse-Argonne offensive that began on 26 September and lasted until the armistice in November. Pershing's attention to logistics and his emphasis on maneuver and mobility complemented his soldiers' tenacity in battle and allowed the United States to play the decisive role in the final months of the war. Pershing opposed the armistice, preferring to fight until Germany surrendered, but his views were ignored. After overseeing the demobilization of U.S. forces, in 1919 Pershing returned to the United States a hero.

In September 1919 Congress confirmed Pershing as general of the armies (which did not include a fifth star as would the later general of the army designation of the World War II era). He became army chief of staff in 1921 and entered a busy retirement in 1924. Active in public life, he also excelled as an author, receiving the Pulitzer Prize for his book, *My Experiences in the World War* (1931). Something of a mentor to such future leaders as George Marshall, Dwight D. Eisenhower, and Douglas MacArthur, Pershing, although confined to bed for many of his final years, lived to see the men he influenced triumph in the Second World War. As a soldier, he served in an army that evolved from a frontier constabulary to an international police force and finally to world power, and he played a large role in fostering that evolution. Pershing died at Washington, D.C., on 15 July 1948. He is among the most significant leaders in U.S. military history.

David Coffey

See also

Belleau Wood, Battle of; Cantigny, Battle of; Foch, Ferdinand; Ludendorff Offensives; MacArthur, Douglas; Marne, Second Battle of the; Marshall, George Catlett; Meuse-Argonne Offensive; Roosevelt, Theodore; Saint-Mihiel Offensive; United States, Army; Wilson, Thomas Woodrow.

References

Cooke, James J. *Pershing and His Generals: Command and Staff in the AEF*. Westport, CT: Praeger, 1997.

Smith, Gene. *Until the Last Trumpet Sounds: The Life of General of the Armies John J. Pershing*. New York: Wiley, 1999.

Smythe, Donald. *Guerrilla Warrior: The Early Life of John J. Pershing*. New York: Scribner, 1973.

———. *Pershing: General of the Armies.* Bloomington: Indiana University Press, 1986.

Vandiver, Frank E. *Black Jack: The Life and Times of John J. Pershing.* 2 vols. College Station: Texas A&M University Press, 1977.

Persia

See Iran

Persian Front

A secondary fighting front during World War I but nonetheless one of great strategic importance. A vast empire bordering most of the focal points of Great Power rivalry in Central and South Asia yet stricken with an utterly weak central government and persistent feudal and tribal structures, Persia represented a power vacuum that almost by default became a battleground for the Great Powers in the war. Persia was extremely important to both sides because of its strategic location and because of recently developed British-controlled oil fields. Vulnerable to foreign intervention, Persia was ruled by the weak and vacillating 17-year-old Ahmad Shah. His miniscule military consisted largely of an 8,000-man Cossack Brigade commanded by Russian officers and a Swedish gendarmerie of 7,000 men led by Swedish officers who favored the German side.

Supposedly, foreign troops entered Persia during the war to uphold the shah's authority. In reality, British troops entered south Persia in order to protect the Anglo-Persian oil installations around Abadan and keep open the sea route through the Persian Gulf. Western Persia became a convenient extension of the Anglo-Turkish Front in Mesopotamia and the Russo-Turkish Front in the Caucasus. In central Persia, British, Russian, Ottoman, and German forces and missions battled for dominant influence over what little central power the monarchy possessed, and in eastern Persia, Britain tried to shield its Indian Empire from German, and later Russian, interference. In 1918 northern Persia became the springboard for British intervention in the Russian Civil War.

Turkey was the only power that hoped to take Persian territory. Minister of War Enver Pasha was pursuing his fantastic Pan-Turanic schemes when he ordered the Van Jandarma (paramilitary police) Division into Persia in December 1914, simultaneously with the Caucasian offensive of the Third Army. In spite of some success in bringing local tribes on their side, the Ottoman invaders were unable to secure a permanent foothold in Persia. In the spring of 1915 Russian forces drove them back.

Late in 1915, Russia reinforced its forces, commanded by General Nikolai N. Baratoff. That December they advanced on Hamadan, Tehran, and Qum, driving the Ottomans back farther and bringing most of northwestern Persia under Russian control. See-saw action continued through the winter of 1915–1916 with inconclusive engagements between Turkish, Russian, and Persian tribal forces, but little ground actually changed hands. On 25 February 1916, Baratoff took Kermanshah.

In the spring of 1916, in order to support the Russian defense in the Caucasus, Baratoff received orders to move on Khaniqin. His advance, however, collided with a renewed Turkish effort in Persia. Ali Insan Pasha's Ottoman XIII Corps of three crack infantry divisions totaling 25,000 men hit the scattered Russians and drove them back. On 26 June the Turks were in Karind and on 2 July in Kermanshah. Operating at the extreme end of a fragile supply line through hostile country, Baratoff had no real hope of stopping the Ottoman thrust. The Allies considered a diversionary attack on the Turkish flank by the British Expeditionary Force in Iraq, but this did not materialize. On 9 August Ali Insan took Hamadan. Realizing that he had little chance of permanently holding vast stretches of territory deep in Persia with his small force, he advanced no farther. The Russians remained firmly entrenched on the mountain passes just beyond Hamadan.

A lull occurred in Persia during the winter of 1916–1917. In the spring the Ottoman XIII Corps was withdrawn from Persia in order to help fend off the British advance in Mesopotamia. Baratoff followed, and on 31 March 1917 he retook Qasr-i-Shirin. The Ottoman invasion of Persia was over.

In central and southern Persia, the first two years of the war saw German influence in the ascendant. German diplomatic personnel succeeded in winning over local tribes to oppose the British and Russians, and the Germans even managed to incite revolts in south Persia. The Germans also sent a military mission to Tehran to train Persian troops under German leadership, and German expeditions traversed the country toward Afghanistan, hoping to win Emir Habib Allah of Afghanistan to their side and thus exert pressure on British India. If the British overstated the case in their claim that Persia was virtually a German colony in 1915–1916, it was nevertheless obvious that upholding British influence there would require additional resources.

The British response was multifaceted. Britain asked its Russian allies to bring pressure to bear on the central government by advancing on Tehran. The British also reinforced with units of the Indian army their position in the Persian Gulf and in southern Persia, and in Fars and Kerman the British raised an indigenous force under their control. Known as the South Persian Rifles, the force later expanded to two brigades of more than 6,000 men. Finally, in the vast expanses of eastern Persia, the British established a military cordon to prevent German incursions into Afghanistan. In the southeast, the British maintained throughout the war the so-called Seistan Force, later styled the East Persian Cordon Field Force. It consisted of several Indian squadrons and companies and some 100 indigenous troops. British forces in southern and eastern Persia spent the rest of the war upholding British influence and quelling tribal unrest in continuous small wars.

In the northeast the Russians controlled vast expanses of Persia bordering their central Asian provinces. In 1916 after the Russian advance in northwestern Persia, the Germans found themselves cut off from their lines of communications.

The Russian Revolutions of March and November 1917 dramatically changed the military situation in Persia. Internal unrest sapped Baratoff's force and loosened the Russian hold on northwestern Persia. Simultaneously, the Ottomans again pushed into the Caucasus region with the aim of finally securing a Pan-Turanic empire. Meanwhile, German progress in southern Russia posed a threat not only to the British position in Persia but also to its influence in Afghanistan. To remedy this situation, the British dispatched to northern Persia forces under Major-General L. C. Dunsterville. A confusing strategic situation developed when the Turkish Ninth Army advanced southeast into Persia and took Tabriz, while Dunsterville moved his troops, known as "Dunsterforce," north to secure a road to the vital oil-producing region around Baku. The British forces were finally drawn into the Russian Civil War, at times fighting alongside the counterrevolutionary White forces against the Bolsheviks in northern Persia, Caucasia, and Turkistan.

The Turks, meanwhile, tried to hold on to Azerbaijan even after the Armistice of Mudros (30 October 1918). Only on 7 November 1918 did British forces finally enter Baku. The British intervention in Transcaspia (Turkistan) continued into March 1919, when Russian White forces took over from them.

Dierk Walter

See also

Afghanistan; Azerbaijan; Caucasian Front; Dunsterforce; Enver Pasha; India, Role in War; Iran; Khānaqīn, Battle of; Mesopotamian Theater; Ottoman Empire, Army; Russia, Allied Intervention in; Russia, Civil War.

References

Allen, W. E. D., and Paul Muratoff. *Caucasian Battlefields: A History of the Wars on the Turco-Caucasian Border, 1828–1921.* Cambridge: Cambridge University Press, 1953.

Barker, A. J. *The Bastard War: The Mesopotamian Campaign of 1914–1918.* New York: Dial, 1967.

Ellis, C. H. *The Transcaspian Episode, 1918–1919.* London: Hutchinson, 1963.

Erickson, Edward J. *Ordered to Die: A History of the Ottoman Army in the First World War.* Westport, CT: Greenwood, 2000.

Moberly, Frederick James. *Operations in Persia, 1914–1919.* London: HMSO, 1929.

Pétain, Henri Philippe (1856–1951)

French army marshal. Born at Cauchy-à-la Tour (Pas de Calais) on 24 April 1856, Henri Philippe Pétain graduated from L'École Spéciale Militaire de Saint-Cyr in 1878 and was assigned to the 24th Battalion of Light Infantry. He attended the École Supérieure de la Guerre in 1888–1890. Pétain's early assignments included commander of the marksmanship school at Châlons-sur-Marne and professor of infantry tactics at the École Supérieure de la Guerre, where he took issue with the prevailing cult of the offensive by stressing defensive tactics: *Le feu tue* (Firepower kills). Pétain was only slowly promoted, probably because the French government considered him to be insufficiently republican. In 1911 he finally made colonel and in April 1913 took command of the 4th Infantry Brigade. Undistinguished retirement seemed imminent.

The First World War rescued Colonel Pétain from obscurity. With the excessive casualties of 1914–1915 caused by the offensive doctrine, Pétain's cautious, methodical approach led to rapid promotion. He became a general of brigade in late August 1914 and received command of the 6th Infantry Division in early September. Distinguishing himself in operations in northern France, he received command of the XXXIII Corps in October 1914 and the Second Army in June 1915.

In February 1916 Pétain took charge of the defense of Verdun, where he earned a public reputation for resolution and a private one for pessimism. His policy of rapidly rotating divisions in and out of the battle zone (*roulement*) ensured that French troops were always fresher than the German divisions opposing them. However, it quickly consumed the French army's strategic reserve, reducing from forty to sixteen the number of divisions available for the Somme offensive. As a result, staff officers at French Army Headquarters somewhat unfairly criticized Pétain for having disrupted the strategy of French army commander General Joseph Joffre.

When Premier Aristide Briand replaced Joffre in December 1916, Pétain was bypassed for the more charismatic, offensive-minded General Robert Nivelle, who promised an end to the war in a great offensive. When this spring 1917 offensive ended in disaster, prompting much of the French army to mutiny, in May 1917 Pétain was named commander-in-chief. Working in conjunction with Minister of War Paul Painlevé, he dealt with this crisis through personal visits to the troops, selective punishments, and widespread reforms to improve the lot of the men. Even his detractors admit that Pétain's rehabilitation of the army's morale was a great achievement.

Responding to these new circumstances, Pétain adopted a *stratégie des gages,* or limited war. With the United States having entered the war in April 1917, with Russia having collapsed into a condition of anarchy and revolution, and with

French General Henri Philippe Pétain, who took command of the French Army in 1917. (Library of Congress)

the French army in disarray, Pétain planned to sit on the defensive until more tanks, aircraft, and artillery became available and U.S. troops had arrived in force. In the meantime, he would conduct only limited, carefully prepared offensives designed to restore French prestige and military morale and to capture tactically advantageous ground. Once conditions were ripe, he hoped to seize limited portions of Alsace and Lorraine to increase France's bargaining position in the event of a compromise peace. This strategy, while suited to prevailing political and strategic conditions, earned him the contempt of many offensive-minded officers.

Pétain implemented the first stage of his strategy with very carefully prepared small offensives. French armies won limited tactical victories at Chemin des Dames, Malmaison, and Passchendaele. Yet with revolution in Russia that November, the German victory in the East, the Italian collapse at Caporetto, and the slow arrival of the American Expeditionary Forces (AEF), it became clear that the Allies must prepare for a major German offensive on the Western Front. Tactically, Pétain sought to meet this challenge by imposing defense-in-depth tactics on his senior generals. Strategically, he fought to gain effective control of the Allied reserves on the Western Front. Working in conjunction with his chief of staff General François Anthoine and British Expeditionary Force (BEF) commander Field Marshal Sir Douglas Haig, Pétain

opposed an attempt by General Ferdinand Foch to place Allied reserves under the Supreme War Council. After winning over French Premier Georges Clemenceau, he and Haig defeated Foch on this question at an Allied conference in London in mid-March 1918.

In spite of this political victory, the German offensive on 21 March 1918 caught Pétain and Haig ill-prepared. Taking advantage of superior numbers, a whirlwind barrage, and new storm trooper tactics, the Germans pushed the British Third Army back and overwhelmed the British Fifth Army under General Sir Hubert Gough, threatening to split the British and French armies. Haig had deployed his reserves too far north, and Pétain had deployed his too far south. The two commanders reacted to the crisis at first slowly and then with alarm. Each made provisions for separate retreats and considered the possibility of suing for peace. As a result, they lost the confidence of their governments. After a hurried series of meetings between Clemenceau and British special envoy Lord Alfred Milner at the Doullens conference on 26 March 1918, Foch became coordinator of the Allied armies. After halting the German offensive, in April 1918 Foch became Allied generalissimo.

For some time there was considerable doubt about the extent to which Pétain was Foch's subordinate, but when Pétain complained after the French setback at the Chemin des Dames in May 1918 that Foch had endangered Paris by deploying French reserves too far north in support of the BEF, Clemenceau made it clear that he was to follow Foch's orders. Pétain's prestige was further weakened when Clemenceau removed his chief of staff, Anthoine, an old rival of Foch. Clemenceau then rejected Pétain's offer to step down to command an army corps. For his services as commander-in-chief, Pétain was made a marshal in November 1918. In 1929 he took Foch's place in the Académie Française.

Pétain subsequently played a prominent role in the Third Republic during the interwar period. He sat on the Conseil Supérieur de la Guerre, successfully commanded the French forces in the Rif War, served as minister of war in 1934, and was ambassador to Spain in 1939–1940. As the French army's elder statesman, he played a major role in encouraging the army to adopt a defensive tactical and strategic posture. With the German invasion of France in May 1940, Premier Paul Reynaud recalled Pétain from Spain and brought him into the cabinet as deputy premier to strengthen French resistance against the Germans, but he ended up taking the country in another direction. Following the military defeat, Pétain received full political power. Convinced that the Third Republic had collapsed from internal moral rot, he implemented the controversial Vichy regime, which governed France under collaborationist principles until the liberation in 1944. Pétain's right-wing "national revolution" wished to replace the Republican principles of "Liberty, Equality and

Fraternity" with the conservative values of "Work, Family and Nation."

Pétain was tried for treason after the Second World War. In contrast to his Vichy prime minister, Pierre Laval, who was executed, Pétain was spared the death sentence because of his prestige from the First World War and his extreme age. He died in the prison on the Ile-de-Yeu on 23 June 1953, where he remains buried. Several attempts by right-wingers to remove his remains to rebury them at Verdun have been unsuccessful.

Robert K. Hanks

See also

Anthoine, François Paul; Briand, Aristide; Caporetto, Battle of; Chemin des Dames Offensive; Clemenceau, Georges; Doullens Conference; Foch, Ferdinand; Gough, Sir Hubert de la Poer; Haig, Douglas, 1st Earl; Hindenburg, Paul von; Joffre, Joseph; Ludendorff Offensives; Milner, Alfred, 1st Viscount; Nivelle, Robert; Nivelle Offensive; Painlevé, Paul; Pershing, John Joseph; Supreme War Council; Verdun, Battle of; Voie Sacrée.

References

Ferro, Marc. *Pétain*. Paris: Fayard, 1987.

Griffiths, Richard. *Marshal Pétain*. London: Constable, 1970.

Pedroncini, Guy. *Pétain: Le Soldat et La Gloire*. Paris: Perrin, 1989.

Reynaud, Paul. *In the Thick of the Fight*. New York: Simon and Schuster, 1955.

Ryan, Stephen. *Pétain the Soldier*. New York: A. S. Barnes, 1969.

Serrigny, Bernard. *Trente ans avec Pétain*. Paris: Plon, 1959.

Szaluta, Jacques. "Marshal Pétain and the French Army Mutiny of 1917: A Study in Military Leadership and Political Personality." *Third Republic/Troisième République* (Fall 1979): 181–210.

King Peter I of Serbia, 1914. (Library of Congress)

Peter I Karageorgević, King (1844–1921)

King of Serbia (1903–1918) and subsequently of the Kingdom of Serbs, Croats, and Slovenes (1918–1921). Born at Topcider near Belgrade on 11 July 1844, Peter Karageorgević was the third son of reigning Prince of Serbia Alexander Karageorgević (1842–1858), who was forced to abdicate in 1858. Prince Peter subsequently lived in exile for forty-five years, mostly in France. He graduated from L'École Spéciale Militaire de Saint-Cyr, served gallantly as a sous-lieutenant in the 5th Battalion of the French Foreign Legion in the Franco-Prussian War of 1870–1871, and was decorated with the Cross of the Legion of Honor. In 1875 he organized volunteers to aid the Serbs of Bosnia-Herzegovina in their rebellion against the Turks. In 1883 Peter married Princess Ljubica (Zorka), the eldest daughter of Prince Nikola I of Montenegro, by whom he had three sons: George, Alexander, and Andrei.

Following the assassination of King Alexander Obrenović of Serbia in 1903, Prince Peter was elected king of Serbia by the Serbian National Assembly on 15 June 1903. Having absorbed the principles of liberal democracy during his long stay in France (he translated John Stuart Mills essay "On Liberty" into Serbo-Croatian in 1868), King Peter was a strong advocate of constitutional monarchy. He restored the Serbian Constitution of 1889 and instituted various political, economic, military, educational, and agricultural reforms. His reign ushered in a new era of progress, modernization, and democratization in Serbia.

King Peter I ruled in a time of rising Serbian and South Slav nationalism and struggle against Austro-Hungarian economic and political hegemony. Accordingly, he followed an aggressive, expansionist foreign policy and opposed Habsburg domination, steps that led ultimately to the outbreak of World War I. He cooperated closely with his father-in-law, King Nikola I of Montenegro, and the two monarchs formed a close alliance in the Balkan Wars of 1912–1913 and in World War I. King Peter also favored the idea of a "Greater Serbia" and the union of all the South Slavic peoples under the Karageorgević dynasty. In this he was well-intentioned but prone to manipulation by radical conspirators, such as Colonel Dragutin Dimitrijevic, leader of the notorious Black Hand society, and his own prime minister, Nicola Pašić.

Just before the outbreak of World War I, King Peter, suffering the effects of age and ill-health, named his son, Prince

Alexander, as regent on 24 June 1914. King Peter remained with his people throughout the Serbian army's losing fight against the Central Powers and, borne on a litter, accompanied the army in its epic retreat through the Albanian mountains and then on to Corfu in November–December 1915.

At the end of World War I, King Peter I returned to Belgrade, and on 1 December 1918 he was proclaimed titular king of the newly created South Slav Kingdom of the Serbs, Croats, and Slovenes. King Peter I died at Topcider on 16 August 1921. His son Prince Regent Alexander then assumed the throne as King Alexander II.

Charles R. Shrader

See also
Alexander Karageorgević, Prince; Balkan Front; Balkan Wars; Dimitrijevic, Dragutin; Pašič, Nicola; Serbia, Army; Serbia, Conquest of; Serbia, Role in War.

References
Cox, John K. *The History of Serbia.* Westport, CT: Greenwood, 2002.
Pavlowitch, Stevan K. *Serbia: The History of an Idea.* New York: New York University Press, 2002.

Petragge Raid (22 October 1915)

Russian Baltic Sea amphibious operation, also known as the Demesnes Raid. The little-known Petragge Raid has a significance in inverse proportion to its fame and to what it accomplished. The Petragge Raid is worthy of study because of its innovative tactics and because of the response to the operation.

German army offensives in the Baltic had by mid-1915 forced the Russian army from Poland and were threatening the city of Riga. Both the Russians and the Germans understood the strategic significance of the Kurland Peninsula that formed the western edge of the Bay of Riga. Despite Russian numerical superiority, German forces were driving on Riga by the end of the summer. German naval units had not been able to force their way into the Bay of Riga, and this gave some encouragement to the Russians that they could maintain control there. Hoping to build on its limited success in denying the Germans naval access to the bay and endeavoring to slow the German land advance, the Russian navy conceived an amphibious raid that would come ashore just behind the German front lines.

For the operation the navy committed the predreadnought *Slava,* already a stalwart in operations against the Germans in the Baltic; the seaplane carrier *Orlitsa;* the gunboats *Grozyashchi* and *Khrabryi;* and fifteen destroyers. The goal was to land troops at the coastal town of Demesnes, but the landing actually occurred 7 miles east of the village of Petragge (or Pitragge).

The operation began at 5:50 A.M. on 22 October 1915, with 22 officers and 514 men being put ashore. Caught by surprise,

the Germans had insufficient forces in the area to defeat the attack on the beaches, and such German troops as were on hand immediately fell back. By 1:00 P.M. the raiders had blown several bridges. The Russians had not made allowance for any follow-on operations, and with the Germans regrouping the raiders returned to their ships that same afternoon. The flotilla weighed anchor at 5:50 P.M. and returned to base the next day.

The Petragge Raid was a boldly conceived operation, based on Russian navy control of much of the Baltic and the success of its forces in keeping the German navy from the Bay of Riga, but the failure to provide any supporting forces meant that it could have only limited tactical advantage and no lasting effect. Following the raid, the Germans created a cavalry division for the express purpose of guarding the coast against any repetition. Furthermore, the Petragge Raid awakened the Germans to the feasibility of such ventures, which they later themselves demonstrated so effectively in Operation ALBION.

David A. Smith

See also
ALBION, Operation; Baltic Operations, Land; Baltic Operations, Sea.

References
Mitchell, Donald W. *A History of Russian and Soviet Sea Power.* New York: Macmillan, 1974.
Palovich, Nikolai B., ed. *The Fleet in the First World War.* Vol. 1. *Operations of the Russian Fleet.* Trans. C. M. Rao. Washington, DC: Smithsonian Institution Press, 1979.

Pflanzer-Baltin, Karl von, Baron (1855–1924)

Austro-Hungarian army general. Born on 1 June 1855 at Pecs, Hungary, Karl von Pflanzer-Baltin graduated from the Theresa Military Academy in 1875 and then attended the War Academy during 1879–1880. Prior to the outbreak of World War I, he served on the Austro-Hungarian General Staff, as an instructor at the War Academy, and as chief of staff of XII Corps. In June 1914 Pflanzer-Baltin retired from the army for health reasons.

With the start of World War I Pflanzer-Baltin came out of retirement in October 1914 and was promoted to general of calvary. In late 1914 he received command of the Seventh Army, which was to occupy the southern sector of the Eastern Front. In late 1914 Pflanzer-Baltin commanded the Seventh Army in the Carpathian offensive, a series of battles against Russian forces in early 1915. Between January and mid-April 1915 Austro-Hungarian forces lost over 800,000 men in this campaign, the only success of which occurred in Pflanzer-Baltin's capture of Czernowitz in February 1915.

In late December 1915 Pflanzer-Baltin's Seventh Army, although outnumbered two to one, halted the Russian Bessarabian offensive. Superior numbers of Austro-Hungarian artillery cost Russian forces 50,000 casualties in two weeks. This victory was short-lived, however, as in June 1916 the Seventh Army was destroyed during the Brusilov offensive, the result of Pflanzer-Baltin concentrating too many of his troops in the forward trenches and his being ill at the moment of Russian attack. By mid-June the Seventh Army had sustained more than 100,000 casualties. Following the Brusilov offensive, German troops reinforced the Seventh Army. Pflanzer-Baltin kept nominal command, but in effect his Seventh Army passed under German control, specifically that of the German chief of staff Major General Hans von Seeckt.

In July 1918 Pflanzer-Baltin took command of Austro-Hungarian forces in Albania, where he would lead the last successful offensive of the war by the Central Powers. The news of the armistice was slow to reach him because of the mountainous region, and thus Pflanzer-Baltin did not surrender his forces until 18 November 1918, the last act of the Austro-Hungarian army. Pflanzer-Baltin retired from military service in December 1918, having earned the nickname "Now Here, Now There," for his rapid movement during battle. Pflanzer-Baltin died in Vienna on 8 April 1925.

Jay Morgan

See also
Brusilov Offensive; Carpathian Campaign; Seeckt, Hans von.
References
De Groot, Gerard J. *The First World War.* New York: Palgrave Macmillan, 2001.
Fortescue, Granville. *Russia: The Balkans and the Dardanelles.* London: Melrose, 1915.
Stone, Norman. *The Eastern Front, 1914–1917.* New York: Scribner, 1975.

Philippines

In 1914 the Philippines had been a U.S. possession for more than a decade. The territory officially entered the war with the rest of the United States upon Wilson's declaration of hostilities on 6 April 1917. Immediately thereafter, the U.S. Navy seized twenty-three German merchant ships in Manila harbor; hundreds of German enemy aliens suspected of espionage were subsequently deported to a detention camp in Hot Springs, Arkansas. From a strategic perspective, the Philippines figured almost not at all in the plans of the warring powers except as a source of raw materials; increased demand contributed to rapid economic growth in the islands.

For Filipinos themselves, the war presented an opportunity to demonstrate loyalty to the United States in the hopes of achieving national independence. The administration of President Woodrow Wilson (1913–1921), the first Democrat to govern the Philippines, had initiated a new policy of "Filip-inization," most notably through the implementation in 1916 of the Jones Act, which made a vague promise of independence once Filipinos had established a "stable government." The Jones Act also authorized the formation of a Philippine National Guard under a mixed officer corps of Americans and Filipinos. On 2 June 1917, nationalist leader Manuel Quezon, president of the Philippine Senate, announced that 25,000 men stood ready to join in the U.S. war effort. U.S. policy makers balked at the possibility that Filipinos might give orders to white men, and the Philippine National Guard did not engage in its first public maneuvers until 11 November 1918.

President Wilson's diplomatic rhetoric, which called for national self-determination and the rights of small nations, resonated with nationalist hopes but did not reflect political realities. Filipino nationalists were again sorely disappointed when the question of independence was effectively excluded from discussions at the Paris Peace Conference. The island nation would remain a U.S. colony until 1946.

Christopher Capozzola

See also
Fourteen Points; Pacific Islands Campaign; Paris Peace Conference; Wilson, Thomas Woodrow.
References
Kalaw, Maximo M. *Self-Government in the Philippines.* New York: Century, 1919.
Karnow, Stanley. *In Our Image: America's Empire in the Philippines.* New York: Random House, 1989.

Photo Reconnaissance

Initially, the adaptation of the balloon and airplane to warfare centered on aerial observation. Nearly all of the Great Powers utilized cameras for that task prior to the outbreak of the war. The Germans led in the technical development of aerial photography at the beginning of World War I, with equipment able to take high-quality photos from great altitude. The British lagged most behind with no photographic capability in 1914. Within the British army, observers used their own cameras until 1915; however, during the Battle of the Somme, British aerial observers produced over 19,000 photographs.

Several innovations enhanced the utility of photo reconnaissance, including cameras capable of taking photographs automatically at timed intervals, use of grid maps to aid in interpretation, and stereoscopic photos of great detail. By 1916 photo reconnaissance was the primary means of gathering information on enemy emplacements and movements. By then, ground troops were even receiving photographs of their intended objectives.

Aerial photography was hazardous. The need to fly straight and level for the photographs made such aircraft easy targets. Losses among photo observers remained high throughout

Long-range photographic camera in the gondola of a lighter-than-air craft on the Western Front, June 1917. (National Archives)

This aerial observer is demonstrating the proper use of a respirator, which would be used when the aircraft flew at high altitude. (National Archives)

the war. Though often overlooked, aerial observation in general, and photo reconnaissance in particular, were arguably the most decisive contribution of aviation to the war.

Rodney Madison

See also
Aircraft, Reconnaissance and Auxiliary; Lighter-Than-Air Craft; Somme Offensive.
References
Kennett, Lee. *The First Air War, 1914–1918*. New York: Free Press, 1991.
Mead, Peter. *The Eye in the Air: History of Air Observation and Reconnaissance for the Army, 1785–1945*. London: HMSO, 1983.

Piave River, Battle of the (June 1918)

Austria-Hungary's last major effort on the Italian Front in World War I. At the end of 1917, following the Battle of Caporetto, the front between Austro-Hungarian and Italian forces stabilized along the Piave River and Mount Grappa line.

The German high command considered the Western and Italian Fronts as one, and General Erich Ludendorff,

German army quartermaster general, pressured the Austro-Hungarian high command to launch a major offensive on the Italian Front to tie down Allied troops there while the Germans made a major effort in France in the spring (Ludendorff) offensives to win the war. Vienna resisted at first but, with Austria-Hungary increasingly dependent on Germany for food, reluctantly agreed.

Emperor Karl I visited the German high command at Spa and had to capitulate and accept the offensive, the Germans having made it clear that further supplies of wheat would depend on the offensive being carried out during June. For this reason the Austro-Hungarians dubbed the attack the "Hunger Offensive."

The Austro-Hungarian high command planned two main thrusts. The principal one was to be launched across the Piave River by Field Marshal Svetozar Boroević von Bojna's army group of the Sixth Army and the First Isonzoarmee. The second effort, to be supporting only, would be mounted from the Asiago Plateau and Mount Grappa by Field Marshal Franz Conrad von Hötzendorf's army group of the Tenth and Eleventh Armies. But personal rivalries and the weakness of the new chief of staff, General Artur Arz von Straussenburg, led to modification of the plan and two major efforts, with consequent dispersion of resources.

The Austro-Hungarian forces in the offensive were the most powerful on the Italian Front at the beginning of fighting there, but their effectiveness was decreased by logistical problems (especially food supplies) and by the inability of the country's industry, due in part to transportation difficulties and an undernourished workforce, to supply the large quantities of artillery and ammunition required. Nevertheless, the Dual Monarchy assembled fifty-eight divisions, supported by some 6,833 artillery pieces of all types. Opposing them the Italians had fifty-six divisions, including one Czech, three British, and two French, along with 5,650 guns and 1,570 mortars.

On 13 June the Austro-Hungarians launched a diversionary attack in the mountains at Tonale Pass, but its only effect was to draw off some of the Dual Monarchy's resources from the major efforts. The principal attacks began at 3:00 A.M. on 15 June 1918, on the Asiago front. Thanks to Austro-Hungarian army deserters, the Italians knew the timing of the attack and opened counterbattery fire when the Austro-Hungarian troops were in their assault positions.

Nonetheless, Austro-Hungarian infantry occupied the first line of defenses held by British troops and advanced nearly a mile and a half by noon. Italian artillery fire and counterattacks restored the situation, however. By nightfall it was clear that the offensive had failed and the Eleventh Army was incapable of resuming offensive operations. Better fortune met the Hungarian 27th Division, which broke through four defense lines on Mount Grappa before being halted. On the Piave, attacking Austro-Hungarian troops crossed the river but established few bridgeheads, thanks to strong Italian resistance and artillery fire. Only in the Montello sector to the north and at San Donà del Piave toward the Adriatic did the Austro-Hungarian infantry achieve important advances, penetrating 2 to 3 miles.

All along the front the attackers suffered heavy casualties, especially from highly effective Italian artillery fire. Austro-Hungarian artillery fire was only of marginal value, largely because of a shortage of ammunition. Meanwhile, river flooding and Italian aircraft hindered the daytime supply of the Austro-Hungarian bridgeheads. Although Austro-Hungarian attacks continued over the next days, the advance slowed against stiffening Italian resistance.

On 19 and 20 June Italian army commander General Armando Diaz ordered massive and bloody counterattacks; although these failed to drive the Austrians beyond the Piave, the counterattacks put them under heavy pressure. The Austro-Hungarians were able to improve communications over the river, thanks to the receding river, but Boroević lacked the resources to resume the offensive. On the evening of the 20th, Emperor Karl authorized the withdrawal of Austro-Hungarian forces to the eastern bank of the Piave, an operation accomplished with great tactical skill. The Austro-Hungarian retreat was followed at the end of June and early July by several Italian counterattacks in an effort to regain positions lost during the offensive.

In the Battle of the Piave, the Austro-Hungarians lost 11,643 dead, 80,852 wounded, and 1,072 missing, while 24,475 were taken prisoners; the Italians lost 8,396 men dead, 30,603 wounded, and 48,182 taken prisoner. The offensive had other serious consequences. The Austro-Hungarian army suffered major equipment losses, but far more grievous was the collapse of morale in this last great military offensive of the Dual Monarchy, whose army was once again entrenched along the Piave River but now without hope of victory.

Alessandro Massignani

See also
Arz von Straussenburg, Artur; Boroević von Bojna, Svetozar; Conrad von Hötzendorf, Franz, Count; Diaz, Armando; Karl I, Emperor; Ludendorff, Erich; Ludendorff Offensives.

References
Fiala, Peter. *Die letzte Offensive Altösterreichs.* Boppard am Rhein: Boldt, 1967.
Fucik, Josef. *Piava, 1918.* Prague: Havran, 2001.
Minniti, Fortunato. *Il Piave.* Bologna, Italy: Il Mulino, 2000.
Schindler, John R. *Isonzo: The Forgotten Sacrifice of the Great War.* Westport, CT: Praeger, 2001.
Schubert, Peter. *Piave: Un Anno di Battaglie, 1917–18.* Bassano del Grappa, Italy: Ghedina e Tassotti, 1991.

Piłsudski, Józef Klemens (1867–1935)

Polish military leader, revolutionary, and political leader. Born on 5 December 1867 in Zułów in Wilno Province, Józef Piłsudski was educated at the Russian high school in the Lithuanian capital. At home he grew up with Polish traditions and the belief that armed insurrection alone could free Poland from Russian domination. After an abortive attempt to study medicine in Char'kov, Piłsudski returned to Wilno in 1886. He became involved with the socialist movement, which he believed might help the Polish cause. This earned him a five-year banishment to Siberia.

On his return home in 1892, Piłsudski became a founding member of the Polish Socialist Party (Polska Partia Socjalistyczna [PPS]). Again arrested in 1900 for his activities, he managed to escape to Galicia a year later. From there, Piłsudski exploited Russia's weaknesses at every turn. He tried to talk the Japanese into financing a Polish uprising and considered cooperating with the Russian revolutionary movement in 1905. When the PPS split in 1906, Piłsudski remained at the head of the smaller splinter group, the PPS Revolutionary Faction. When tensions rose between Russia and Austria-Hungary, Piłsudski approached the Austrian military, offering

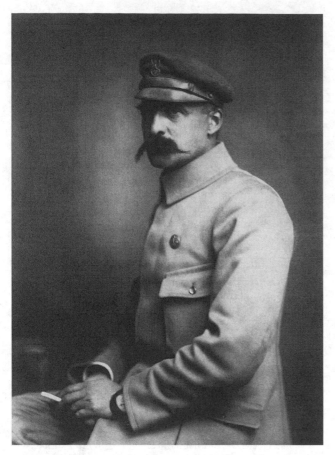

Polish General Józef Klemens Piłsudski. (Hulton-Deutsch Collection/ Corbis)

intelligence services in Russian Poland. This produced no direct results, but the Austrians tolerated the establishment of Polish riflemen's associations in Galicia. These received paramilitary training and became the core of a substantial Polish fighting force in the coming conflict.

When World War I began, Piłsudski obtained Austrian permission to mobilize detachments of riflemen, and a hastily established Polish Commission of Confederated Independence Parties empowered him to take military steps. The numerically unimpressive and ill-equipped riflemen marched on the city of Kielce in Russian Poland on 6 August 1914. They were rebuffed and failed to provoke the national insurrection for which Piłsudski had hoped.

After this, the Austrian Poles formed a surrogate government under the name of Naczelny Komitet Narodowy (Supreme National Committee [NKN]). It absorbed the riflemen into the newly created Polish Legions. Piłsudski accepted temporary subordination to the NKN and was placed in charge of the legions' 1st Brigade. He tried to compensate for this setback by creating the secret Polska Organizacja Wojskowa (Polish Military Organization) for diversionary activities in Russian Poland, thus enlarging his political and military basis.

When the Central Powers occupied Russian Poland in 1915, Piłsudski struggled to demonstrate his independence from them, demanding the formation of a Polish government and the removal of non-Polish officers from the Polish Legions in 1916. When this was refused, he resigned his military position and directed the Polish Military Organization against the Germans.

The situation changed again after the Two Emperors' Proclamation of 5 November 1916. A Provisional Council of State was established, and Piłsudski became the head of its military department. When the Russian Revolution of March 1917 made the Central Powers the bigger obstacle to Polish independence, Piłsudski turned on the latter and the council. The Germans interned him in the fortress of Magdeburg in July 1917 after he had refused to incorporate the Polish Legions into a German-directed Polish army (Polnische Wehrmacht) and to swear an oath of allegiance to Kaiser Wilhelm II.

Piłsudski was released in the midst of the German revolutionary upheaval at the end of the war and arrived in Warsaw as a national hero on 10 November 1918. A day later the Regency Council (which had replaced the Provisional Council of State) transferred military command to Piłsudski and put him at the helm of the Polish state on 14 November. Other political bodies claiming representation of Poland fell in line, accepting the "commander" of the Polish Legions as provisional head of state. The new Polish parliament confirmed Piłsudski in office in February 1919. The next year Piłsudski was appointed the first marshal of Poland and led the Poles to victory against the Russians in 1920.

In the following years, the staunch nationalist Piłsudski became disenchanted with the parliamentary infighting and inattention to national problems that marked Poland's democracy. He staged a coup d'état in May 1926. While democratic institutions continued to operate and criticism of the military regime remained possible, Poland pursued an authoritarian course. Gradually the constitution was recast, placing more authority in Piłsudski's hands. Always dedicated to Poland's regeneration, Piłsudski died at Warsaw on 12 May 1935. He was followed by a succession of largely inept military leaders.

Pascal Trees

See also
Daszyński, Ignacy; Dmowski, Roman; Poland, Role in War; Poland, Two Emperors' Proclamation, Rydz-Śmigły, Edward.

References
Davies, Norman. *Heart of Europe: A Short History of Poland.* Oxford, UK: Clarendon, 1984.

Garlicki, Andrzej. *Józef Piłsudski, 1867–1935.* Ed. and trans. John Coutouvidis. Aldershot, UK: Scolar Press, 1995.

Holzer, Jerzy, and Jan Molenda. *Polska w pierwszej wojnie Światowej* [Poland in the First World War]. 2nd rev. and augmented ed. Warsaw: Wiedza Powszechna, 1967.

Wandycz, Piotr. *The Lands of Partitioned Poland, 1795–1918.* Seattle: University of Washington Press, 1974.

Pistols

During the late nineteenth century revolvers were common. These are weapons in which a number of cartridges (often six) are held in a revolving cylinder that rotates to allow each shot to be fired in sequence. The most famous early revolver was that of Samuel Colt, although earlier designs had been seen. Originally Colt revolvers had to be loaded just like a muzzle-loading musket or rifle, each chamber being slowly and separately loaded, but the advent of the composite cartridge (a complete "round" composed of a cartridge case containing primer and propellant, into which the bullet was fixed) meant that each chamber could be loaded from the rear.

Weapon designers realized that as the cartridge for the pistol was much smaller than that of a rifle, it lent itself to experimentation both in the way cartridges were stored ready for use within the weapon itself and the way in which the weapon worked. The relatively low recoil of the revolver car-tridge meant that the energy on discharge could in itself be used to work the mechanism of a self-loading weapon. Rifles were essentially all manually operated, with few exceptions, but the revolver developed into the semiautomatic pistol in which successive shots were fired simply by pulling the trigger once the first round had been loaded.

Reloading by recoil was achieved by having a heavy breech block closing the breech until most of the gas pressure caused by the cartridge firing was spent, when the inertia of the breech block was overcome and the block was forced back to extract and eject the spent cartfidge. A spring behind the block then forced it forward to reload a fresh cartridge from the magazine.

Some nations used only revolvers as handguns, and the French issued their Modèle d'Ordonnance 1892 8mm revolver throughout the war. Russian officers and others were similarly armed with the 7.62mm Nagant, and this had seven rather than the usual six chambers. The U.S. Army, however, had both revolvers and pistols.

U.S. Army officers inspect the pistols of recruits at a training camp in Indiantown Gap, Pennsylvania during World War I. (Getty Images)

The U.S. revolver was the Smith and Wesson cal .45 M1917, which fired the same ammunition as the automatic. This rimless ammunition was not designed for revolvers, however, and ammunition was issued in clips of three rounds, the clip ensuring that the rounds did not slide forward into the barrel, thus causing stoppages. The most important development in the U.S. arsenal, however, was the M1911A1 automatic pistol cal .45. This solid weapon weighed 39 ounces and fired a cartridge that was a true "man stopper." Although accurate to only 30 or so yards, it was ideal for close-quarter combat.

Such a large caliber was the exception rather than the rule; Germany went with 7.63mm and 9mm. The 7.63mm cartridge was used in the revolutionary, and very effective, Mauser automatic, which had a magazine capacity of ten rounds and could have its accuracy considerably enhanced by the attachment of its wooden carrying case as a stock to make it into a carbine.

The other handgun that Germany issued was perhaps the most famous of all pistols: the Luger Pistole 08. This weapon, with its distinctive toggle cocking action, was used as an officer's pistol originally, but as the war progressed variations appeared. Barrel lengths varied from 4 to 10 inches (the latter in the rare Navy Luger), and special snail magazines were designed to carry thirty-two rounds of 9mm Parabellum ammunition. The 9mm round is still very much in use today, and a number of modern submachine guns (the natural successors of the pistol) use this caliber, although with higher-powered loadings than the original Luger Parabellum cartridge.

The British, as always, tended toward the tried and tested, issuing the Webley .455 Pistol No 1, Mark 1. This was a standard revolver design, using a rimmed .455 cartridge. The British love affair with rimmed cartridges stems from the conception that a rimless cartridge is weaker at the base and therefore more prone to burst. It seems that this has generally not been the case.

One break with tradition for the British came when they issued a semiautomatic revolver, the Webley-Fosbery, in which the chamber was rotated and the action recocked by the recoil of the whole chamber. The other weapon was the Webley .455 automatic, which was a modified M1911 U.S. pistol, designed to use the same cartridge as the British Webley Naval Pistol.

The Austro-Hungarian army used the Steyr 9mm Pistol M12. This shared the same loading system as the Mauser 7.63mm pistol mentioned above, in that the magazine was loaded with a clip and did not detach from the weapon. It also fired a special 9mm cartridge, and unlike other automatic pistols it was a double-action weapon. Although it reloaded automatically, it was cocked and fired by pressing the trigger.

The Japanese employed the Nambu 8mm 1914 Automatic, which was still in use during World War II. It fired an 8mm bottle-necked cartridge similar to the Mauser 7.63 cartridge

in appearance, and the weapon itself bears superficial similarities to the Luger.

The pistol was essentially an officer's weapon, intended to replace the sword in battle, but it became obvious that in close combat such weapons were of great value, especially in the confines of a trench. The pistol reached its design peak in the World War I era and since then has only been modified; there have been no fundamental design changes since that time.

David Westwood

See also
Armaments Production; Assault Weapons; Cavalry; Infantry Tactics; Rifles; Storm Troopers; Trench Warfare.

References
Greener, W. W. *The Gun and Its Development*. Fairfax, VA: Odysseus Press for National Rifle Association, 1995. Reprint of 9th ed. from 1910.
Smith, W. B. B. *Small Arms of the World*. 7th ed. Harrisburg, PA: Stackpole, 1962.
Walter, John. *Allied Small Arms of World War One*. Solihull, West Midlands, UK: Crowood, 2000.

Pleve, Pavel Adamovich (1850–1916)

Russian army general. Born on 11 June 1850 to a Russian noble family of German origin, Pavel Adamovich Pleve (also known as Wenzel von Plehve) graduated from the Nikolaevsky Cavalry School in 1870 and the General Staff Academy in 1877. He first saw action in the 1877–1878 Russo-Turkish War. Pleve remained in the Balkans after the war against Turkey until 1880 as the Bulgarian minister of war.

In 1880 Pleve returned to Russia to follow the customary career pattern of a General Staff officer. He held various command and staff positions, and in 1909 he was appointed commander of forces in the Moscow Military District. Pleve remained in this post until the outbreak of World War I.

Pleve proved to be one of the outstanding senior Russian generals of World War I. At the onset of hostilities, Pleve commanded the Russian Fifth Army in Galicia. With General Aleksei Evert's Fourth Army on its right, the Fifth Army met the initial Austro-Hungarian advance northward from Galicia at the end of August. Pleve's forces sustained 40 percent casualties at Komarów during 26–31 August because of miscalculations by Russian Front commander General Nikolai Ivanov. Pleve was able to avoid encirclement by Austrio-Hungarian forces under General Moritz Auffenberg, skillfully extracting his forces and preventing another Tannenberg.

In November 1914 Pleve marched his forces 70 miles in two and a half days to relieve the Second Army at Łódź. In early 1915 he received command of the newly formed Twelfth Army and received the assignment of attacking East Prussia from the south along with General Barton Rudolf F. Sievers's

Tenth Army. Sievers's army was badly beaten by the Germans and would have totally succumbed had not Pleve mounted an offensive to relieve pressure.

During the summer of 1915 Pleve again commanded the Fifth Army in the northwestern sector of the Eastern Front. That September the Germans mounted an offensive against the Fifth Army in the area from the Gulf of Riga to Kovno. Pleve's forces, the only barrier to a German drive on Petrograd, held their ground, halting the German attack. Pleve, then in poor health, commanded the Northwestern Front from 1915 but left active duty in February 1916 because of health problems. Appointed to the State Council, he died in Moscow on 10 April 1916.

James F. Russell III and Bache M. Whitlock

See also

Auffenberg von Komarów, Moritz, Baron; Evert, Aleksei Ermolaevich; Ivanov, Nikolai Yudovich; Komarów, Battle of; Łódź, Battle of; Russia, Army; Tannenberg, Battle of.

References

Asprey, Robert B. *The German High Command at War: Hindenburg and Ludendorff Conduct World War I.* New York: William Morrow, 1991.

Knox, Sir Alfred. *With the Russian Army, 1914–1917: Being Chiefly Extracts from the Diary of a Military Attaché.* 2 vols. New York: Dutton, 1921.

Rutherford, Ward. *The Russian Army in World War I.* London: Cremonesi, 1975.

Stone, Norman. *The Eastern Front, 1914–1917.* New York: Scribner, 1975.

British Field Marshal Sir Herbert Plumer, 1922. (Library of Congress)

Plumer, Sir Herbert (1857–1932)

British army general. Born on 13 March 1857 at Torquay, England, Herbert Charles Onslow Plumer was educated at Eton. After scoring a high grade on the entrance examination to the Royal Military College, Sandhurst, he was commissioned directly to the 65th Foot in 1876. Plumer served in the 1884 Sudan campaign and the 1896 Matabele campaign. During the 1899–1902 Boer War, he commanded a mounted infantry regiment in the relief of Mafeking and a column during antiguerrilla operations.

Promoted to major-general in 1902, Plumer was appointed quartermaster general to the forces in 1904. In 1906 he received command of the 5th Division in Ireland, and in 1908 he was promoted to lieutenant-general. In 1911 Plumer took over the Northern Command.

In early 1915 Plumer went to France to take command of the newly formed V Corps. He served at Second Ypres and in May 1915 was appointed to command the Second Army in place of General Horace Smith-Dorrien. Plumer was promoted to full general in June 1915. Through 1915 and 1916

Plumer's army held portions of the line but was not involved in the major offensives or battles.

After meticulous preparation, Plumer achieved a limited but complete victory at the Battle of Messines on 7 June 1917. The attack made heavy use of mining, artillery, tanks, and gas to support the attack of nine infantry divisions against Messines Ridge. The objectives of the attack were all achieved by midafternoon with far fewer casualties than had been expected. German counterattacks were easily repulsed, and the British continued their attacks for an additional week, by which time the entire Messines salient had been occupied.

In the Third Battle of Ypres launched on 31 July 1917, Plumer attacked in support of the main British effort carried out by General Sir Hubert Gough's Fifth Army. After Gough suffered heavy casualties and had made only limited progress, British Expeditionary Force commander Field Marshal Sir Douglas Haig shifted the main effort in the offensive to Plumer's Second Army. In September–October 1917, Plumer chose to launch a series of carefully planned small-scale attacks and made gains at the battles of Menin Road, Polygon Wood, and Broodseinde. However, further attacks later in October at Poelcappelle and at Passchendaele (Third Battle of Ypres) were costly failures that did not achieve their objectives.

Shortly before the Passchendaele offensive came to an end in November 1917, Plumer was ordered to Italy to assist Italian forces in restoring the situation following the disastrous Italian defeat at Caporetto. However, the front was stabilized by the Italians at the Piave River before Plumer arrived. On 3 December Plumer's force of six French and five British divisions took over a sector of the Italian Front. While in Italy, Plumer established excellent relations with the Italian generals, working to steady their resolve as they rebuilt the Italian army.

In February 1918 Prime Minister David Lloyd George offered the position of chief of the Imperial General Staff to Plumer in place of General Sir William Robertson, but Plumer declined the offer primarily out of loyalty to Robertson.

Plumer returned to France in March 1918 and resumed command of the Second Army. The brunt of the first of the German spring (Ludendorff) offensives launched that same month fell on the Third and Fifth British Armies. Plumer was called upon to release several divisions to reinforce the embattled portions of the British lines. The second German attack, the Lys offensive launched on 9 April 1918, was directed against the front held by Plumer's forces. Although severely pressed by the Germans, he maintained a steady grip on the situation and only grudgingly gave up ground.

Despite being Haig's most experienced and reliable army commander, Plumer played only a subsidiary role in the Allied offensives of autumn 1918. His army operated outside of British command under the Belgian King Albert's army group. As part of the Allied army group, Plumer served in the Courtrai offensive in October 1918. After the armistice Plumer's army was tasked with crossing the German frontier and establishing the British zone of occupation in Germany.

In 1919 Plumer was promoted to field marshal and appointed governor and commander-in-chief of Malta. In 1925 he was selected as high commissioner for Palestine. Created Baron Plumer of Messines and Bilton in 1919, he was raised to viscount in 1929. Unlike other British generals of the war, Plumer only attempted to achieve what was realistically feasible and never undertook blindly optimistic operations. Plumer died in London on 16 July 1932.

Bradley P. Tolppanen

See also
Albert I, King of Belgium; Caporetto, Battle of; Courtrai Offensive; Gough, Sir Hubert de la Poer; Haig, Douglas, 1st Earl; Italian Front; Lloyd George, David; Ludendorff Offensives; Messines Ridge, Battle of; Robertson, Sir William Robert; Smith-Dorrien, Sir Horace Lockwood; Ypres, Second Battle of; Ypres, Third Battle of.

References
Harington, Charles. *Plumer of Messines.* London: J. Murray, 1935.
Powell, Geoffrey. *Plumer, the Soldier's General: A Biography of Field-Marshal Viscount Plumer of Messines.* London: Leo Cooper, 1990.

Prior, Robin, and Trevor Wilson. *Passchendaele: The Untold Story.* New Haven, CT: Yale University Press, 1996.

Pohl, Hugo von (1855–1916)

German navy admiral. Born in Breslau (Wroclaw) on 25 August 1855, Hugo von Pohl joined the Imperial German Navy as a cadet in April 1872. He became a member of Korvettenkapitaen (commander) Alfred Tirpitz's "Torpedo Gang" in the Torpedo Inspectorate during the 1880s.

During most of the 1890s Pohl was at the Imperial Naval Office, both before and after Tirpitz's appointment as its state secretary in June 1897. Pohl distinguished himself while serving with the international expedition in China in 1900. Pohl was promoted to Kaitaen zur See in May 1900, to Konteradmiral (rear admiral) in July 1906, and to Vizeadmiral (vice admiral) in January 1913. He was ennobled in 1913, and in April 1913 he was appointed head of the Admiralty Staff. He was serving in that position when the war began.

Pohl's strategic thought mirrored that of Kaiser Wilhelm II and Chancellor Theobald von Bethmann Hollweg. Pohl believed that there was no sense in throwing away the High Seas Fleet in a reckless assault against the numerically superior Grand Fleet of the Royal Navy. Instead, Pohl advocated keeping the fleet "in being," as a potential threat to British naval operations and as a bargaining counter during the expected peace negotiations. Consequently, Pohl was critical of those, especially Tirpitz, who called for the fleet to assume offensive operations. This attitude was reflected in the orders issued in August and October 1914 to Admiral Friedrich von Ingenohl, commander-in-chief of the High Seas Fleet, that severely restricted the scope of operations. From the outbreak of war to the end of January 1915, Pohl and Ingenohl met only once to discuss the naval situation. The rest of the time, Pohl was with Kaiser Wilhelm II's retinue in Berlin or the various military headquarters.

After the failure of the Dogger Bank raid on 24 January 1915, Pohl was appointed to replace Ingenohl as the new commander-in-chief of the High Seas Fleet on 2 February. He was not a popular appointment. Under his command the fleet rarely ventured from port, since Pohl had no confidence in his scouting forces.

On 8 January 1916, Pohl became seriously ill and was transferred to a hospital ship, then moved to Berlin for an operation. He was relieved of his command on 23 January. Pohl died of liver cancer in Berlin on 23 February 1916.

David H. Olivier

See also
Dogger Bank, Battle of the; Hipper, Franz von; Ingenohl, Friedrich von; Müller, Georg Alexander von; Scheer, Reinhard; Submarine Warfare, Central Powers; Tirpitz, Alfred von; Wilhelm II, Kaiser.

References

Halpern, Paul G. *A Naval History of World War I.* Annapolis: Naval Institute Press, 1994.

Herwig, Holger H. *"Luxury" Fleet: The Imperial German Navy 1888–1918.* London: Allen and Unwin, 1980.

Pohl, Hugo von. *Aus Aufzeichnungen und Briefen während der Kriegszeit.* Berlin: Siegismund, 1920.

Poincaré, Raymond (1860–1934)

French politician and statesman. Born on 20 August 1860 at Bar-le-Duc in Lorraine, Raymond Poincaré and his family left their home when Lorraine became German territory in 1871. This experience had a profound effect on him. Poincaré committed himself to a political career marked by ardent French nationalism, dedication to French security, and honesty. As a young man he gained prominence as a conservative republican lawyer and essayist before being elected to the National Assembly as a deputy in 1887 and then as a senator in 1903 from the Department of the Meuse. He was elected to the Academie Française in 1909, which began his swift rise to national prominence. He gained a reputation for being able to work across partisan lines, a rare quality during the Third Republic. During his term as premier in 1912–1913 (the first of five such terms) he advocated improved ties with Great Britain and Russia and a stronger French army.

In 1913 Poincaré was elected to a seven-year term as French president. The office had traditionally been ceremonial, but he worked to expand its powers and took advantage of the relative inexperience of premiers such as René Viviani and Gaston Doumergue to increase his own influence.

During the crisis period immediately preceding World War I, Poincaré did all he could to tighten the alliance with Russia and secure British entry on the side of France. During the war he was best known for his vocal support of the Union Sacrée (Sacred Union), and he made an emotional appeal for French unity in August 1914 in the face of a German invasion. This helped silence much of the internecine political battles that had been a hallmark of the Third Republic. As president, Poincaré provided stability as the premiership changed hands seven times during the course of the war; however, he believed that the French people did not fully understand or appreciate his efforts. Although he and Georges Clemenceau were rivals, Poincaré supported Clemenceau for the premiership in the dark days of 1917. Clemenceau then worked to return Poincaré to what he saw as the president's proper place.

Poincaré fought numerous battles with French army Commander Joseph Joffre over the exact lines of demarcation between military and civilian authority. He was instrumental in securing Joffre's retirement at the end of 1916. Poincaré

French president Raymond Poincaré moved to strengthen ties with Russia before World War I. (Library of Congress)

supported Joffre's replacement, General Robert Nivelle, and Nivelle's disastrous offensive in April 1917. His relations with the military improved significantly with the appointment of General Ferdinand Foch as Allied generalissimo. The two men shared Poincaré's political outlook, nationalist spirit, and desire to create a separate Rhenish republic after the war.

Poincaré and Foch worked to counter the authority of Clemenceau, who distrusted both men. Clemenceau successfully kept both Poincaré and Foch from exercising any influential role during the Paris Peace Conference. At one point Poincaré and Foch even considered a joint resignation to dramatize their exclusion from the conference.

After the expiration of his term in 1920, Poincaré broke with tradition by returning to active politics, serving twice as premier (1922–1924 and 1926–1929). When Germany failed to fulfill reparations provisions of the Versailles Treaty, Premier Poincaré authorized the French army occupation of the Ruhr in 1923. He correctly saw that if Germany could break these provisions, it would soon break others of the treaty. He also oversaw the restructuring of French finances that improved the French economy and increased his own popularity. He retired from politics in 1929 and died on 15 October 1934 at Nubécourt (Meuse).

Michael Neiberg

See also

Clemenceau, Georges; Foch, Ferdinand; Joffre, Joseph; Nivelle, Robert; Nivelle Offensive; Paris Peace Conference; Reparations; Versailles, Treaty of; Viviani, René.

References

Keiger, John F. V. *Raymond Poincaré.* Cambridge and New York: Cambridge University Press, 1997.

Miquel, Pierre. *Poincaré.* Paris: Fayard Press, 1984.

Poincaré, Raymond. *Au Service de la France: Neuf années de souvenirs.* 10 vols. Paris: Polon, 1930.

Wright, Gordon. *Raymond Poincaré and the French Presidency.* New York: Octagon, 1967; reprint of 1942 ed.

Poison Gas

See Chemical Weapons

Poland, German Offensive (28 September–16 December 1914)

Poland was a major area of military operations early in the war. Poland had disappeared in the late eighteenth century, absorbed by its neighbors in a series of partitions. Most of Poland was part of Russia, although portions of the former Polish kingdom belonged to Germany (West Prussia, South Prussia, and New East Prussia) and Austria (Galicia). For the most part, Russian Poland was flat and, apart from rivers, without major physical barriers.

World War I had opened in the East with a Russian offensive in East Prussia, which the Germans smashed in the battles at Tannenberg and the Masurian Lakes. At the same time, however, the Russians had met success against the Austro-Hungarians in Galicia, inflicting a near fatal blow there from which the Austro-Hungarian army never really recovered. Austrian morale was at a low point, its armies having been defeated by both the Serbians and Russians. Furthermore, the Russians now held most of Galicia and were poised for further strikes into Silesia and Hungary. Had their pursuit been more determined, they might have secured the crucial passes to the interior of Austria and Hungary. But the Russian army had also suffered heavily.

The Austro-Hungarian defeat in Galicia posed a major problem for the Germans because Silesia, one of Germany's main industrial centers, now was in danger of being outflanked from the south. Russian army commander Grand Duke Nikolai Nikolaevich had also done much to rebuild the Russian army following its defeats at Tannenberg and the Masurian Lakes. German army Chief of Staff General Erich von Falkenhayn ordered his commander in East Prussia, General Paul von Hindenburg, to do something to relieve Russian pressure on Austria-Hungary. On 18 September Generalmajor Erich Ludendorff, Hindenburg's quartermaster general (chief of staff), met with Austro-Hungarian army Chief of Staff General Franz Conrad von Hötzendorf and proposed a flanking attack by German forces in East Prussia should Russian forces move against Kraków (Cracow).

By the end of September both sides were busy preparing new offensives. Hindenburg requested reinforcements from

German troops advancing across the flat country that constituted much of Russian Poland. (Francis J. Reynolds and C. W. Taylor, *Collier's Photographic History of the European War*, P. F. Collier & Son, New York, 1916)

Falkenhayn, but the latter, then mounting his own drive against the Channel ports on the Western Front, had none to spare. Hindenburg then withdrew four of the six German corps in East Prussia along with a cavalry division and formed them into the new Ninth Army under General der Kavallerie August von Mackensen. This left only two German corps to cover East Prussia. Utilizing their superb railroad net, in only eleven days the Germans shifted the Ninth Army's more than 220,000 men, horses, artillery, and equipment some 450 miles south to the vicinity of the Polish city of Częstochowa. Here they linked up with the Austrian First Army in order to protect Silesia. Hindenburg and Ludendorff took direct control of the Ninth Army while also retaining operational control of the Eighth.

The Russian high command (Stavka) had been divided over its next military objective. Grand Duke Nikolai favored another offensive into East Prussia; Commander of the Southwestern Front General Nikolai Yudovich Ivanov and Chief of Staff General Mikhail Alekseyev argued for Silesia, where the possibility existed of forcing Austria from the war. In the end Nikolai compromised by detaching the Russian Ninth Army (under General Platon Alexeevich Lechitski) from the northern force in order to drive on Kraków (Cracow) along with the Fourth Army (under General Aleksei Evert) and the Fifth Army (under General Pavel Pleve). The reforming Second Army (under General Philipp Scheidemann) was to be positioned west of Warsaw, where it could be used to reinforce the offensive. This left only General Rudolf F. Sievers's Tenth Army and General Pavel Rennenkampf's First Army for a northern offensive, but the shortest route to Berlin was in fact through western Poland.

Although in theory the Russians had more available men than the Germans, the invasion was poorly prepared and coordinated, with Ivanov and Northwestern Front commander General Nikolai Ruzsky sharing command. Delays plagued the Russians as elements of the three Russian armies moved into position along a 50-mile front on the east bank of the Vistula River.

On 28 September Mackensen's Ninth Army struck south, opening the German Polish offensive. On 8 October Mackensen received orders to take Warsaw. The Germans reached the Vistula River the next day, but they were slowed because of inferior numbers, supply problems, exhaustion, and unfamiliarity with the terrain. Despite knowledge from a captured Russian order that Stavka was planning to invade Silesia, Hindenburg continued the attack. The Germans got to within a dozen miles of Warsaw before Hindenburg finally ordered a withdrawal on 17 October. By 1 November the Ninth Army was back at its starting point, and Hindenburg was faced with the prospect of an invasion of Silesia by four Russian armies.

Designated commander-in-chief of Central Powers armies on the Eastern Front on 1 November, Hindenburg continued to benefit from intercepts of uncoded Russian radio messages. On 3 November, privy to Russian plans, he made his decision. With a promise by Falkenhayn of twelve new army corps, half of them from the Western Front, Hindenburg sought to replicate Tannenberg. Based on a plan developed by Colonel Max Hoffmann, Hindenburg would strip Silesia and East Prussia of forces in order to hurl all available manpower against the Russian right flank at Łódź and Warsaw in the expectation that they would crush the Russian Second Army and trap remaining Russian forces behind the Vistula River. Between 4 and 10 November, Mackensen's entire Ninth Army was again moved, this time 250 miles north from Częstochowa to Torun at the northern tip of the Polish salient. There it was in position to strike the Russians' right flank as it prepared to invade Silesia. Austro-Hungarian army chief of staff General Franz Conrad von Hötzendorf, acting in concert, moved the Austrian Second Army north from the Carpathians into Mackensen's former positions. The Central Powers thus hoped to trap the Russians in a great pincer movement.

Hindenburg and Ludendorff refused to wait for Falkenhayn's promised reinforcements. Instead, on 11 November Mackensen's Ninth Army attacked up the Vistula into the hinge between the Russian First and Second Armies as the Russians were just completing their dispositions. Mackensen's troops caught Rennenkampf's First Army on its northern flank as it was moving to its staging areas, capturing 12,000 prisoners and fifteen guns in the first two days. This led Stavka to relieve Rennenkampf of his command and replace him with Litvinov. Driving into the wedge between the First and Second Armies, Mackensen then smashed into the flank of Scheidemann's Russian Second Army.

In the ensuing Battles of Łódź and Łowicz (16–25 November), it was again Russian manpower against German firepower as the Russian Second Army sought to extricate itself. On 20 November the Russians repulsed almost all of the German Ninth Army's attacks. The exception was General der Infanterie (lieutenant general) Reinhard Scheffer-Boyadel's force of the XXV Reserve Corps and several attached divisions that penetrated the Russian eastern flank and advanced as far as Rzgow. Russian reinforcements now arrived, and by 22 November they had surrounded the German penetration. XXV Corps managed to fight its way from the trap by reversing direction to the northeast. On 24 November Scheffer won a crucial victory at Brzeziny when his 3rd Guards Division destroyed the Russian 6th Siberian Division and opened a 4-mile-wide escape route to the north. The next day Scheffer's men reached the main German lines. They had suffered 4,500 casualties, including 1,000 killed, but had brought out 2,000 of their own wounded, as well as 16,000 Russian prisoners and sixty-four guns.

Both Russian armies now fell back on their supply center at Łódź. When the pursuing Germans arrived there, they found seven Russian corps on the town's perimeter and were surprised by the Russian Fifth Army's attack. Briefly the Russians were in position to envelop the Germans but were unable to exploit the opportunity.

Fighting continued until early December. On 6 December the Russians evacuated Łódź and by 16 December halted their retreat at the Bzura-Rawka River line some 30 miles southwest of Warsaw. Winter brought an end to the fighting. While the Battle of Łódź could be counted a Russian tactical victory, strategically it went to the Germans because the Russians called off their Silesian offensive, not to be renewed. German losses in the Polish campaign totaled approximately 35,000 men; Russian casualties approached 75 percent of the combined strength of the First and Second Armies, some 95,000 men, including 25,000 POWs and 79 guns. The campaign resulted in a widespread perception that the Russian army was no match for the Germans.

Spencer C. Tucker

See also
Alekseyev, Mikhail Vasilyevich; Below, Otto von; Conrad von Hötzendorf, Franz, Count; Evert, Aleksei Ermolaevich; Hindenburg, Paul von; Hoffmann, Max; Ivanov, Nikolai Yudovich; Łódź, Battle of; Ludendorff, Erich; Mackensen, August von; Nikolai Nikolaevich, Grand Duke; Pleve, Pavel Adamovich; Rennenkampf, Pavel Karlovich; Ruzsky, Nikolai Vladimirovich.

References
Churchill, Winston. *The Unknown War: The Eastern Front, 1914–1917.* New York: Scribner, 1931.
Clark, Alan. *Suicide of the Empires: The Battles on the Eastern Front, 1914–18.* New York: American Heritage Press, 1971.
Herwig, Holger H. *The First World War: Germany and Austria-Hungary, 1914–1918.* New York: St. Martin's, 1997.
Stone, Norman. *The Eastern Front, 1914–1917.* New York: Scribner, 1975.

Poland, Role in War

Poland had a stormy history. Throughout the nineteenth century the Polish lands had been divided among Germany, Russia, and the Habsburg monarchy. Since Napoleon's defeat, tsarist Russia held the so-called Congress Poland, by far the largest part of ethnically Polish territory. Germany had advanced into the Posen area, linking her northern territories with Silesia, while Austria retained control of Galicia with the city of Kraków (Cracow). For a century the central European monarchies systematically crushed all Polish aspirations for independence. Near the end of the nineteenth century, however, a realignment of alliances in Europe pitted Poland's partitioning powers against each other, with Germany and Austria-Hungary on one side and Russia on the other. The Poles themselves attached great expectations to the rising international tensions. Hoping for war, they tried to figure out on which side they could make the greatest gains for the Polish cause.

When World War I began in August 1914, the Russians were amazed to hear the Polish representatives in the Duma declare their loyalty to the tsar, and they answered with a manifesto that promised the Polish people a reunion of their lands under his scepter. Poland would be free in its religion, language, and self-government, although the Russian government did not state publicly that the manifesto would apply only to the Prussian and Austrian parts of Poland.

Whatever projects Russia might have had for Poland, they became irrelevant when the German armies occupied Warsaw in August 1915. The Central Powers created two distinct occupational sectors, with a German governor-general residing in Warsaw and an Austrian one in Lublin. With the exception of the Russian Brusilov offensive in the summer of 1916, the hold of the Central Powers on Polish territory was not seriously challenged until the end of the war.

German plans for the newly occupied territory were hazy. While Kaiser Wilhelm II assured Polish loyalists in Germany that a Polish state would be restored after the war, other German ideas revolved around the Mitteleuropa (Middle Europe) concept and the improvement of Germany's strategic boundaries in the East by the annexation of a border strip carved out of the obsolete Congress Kingdom. Berlin considered the Polish question purely from a military angle and was mainly interested in the Poles as a pawn against Russia. The German government looked with suspicion on ideas voiced by Polish conservatives in Austria. The latter aimed, with the support of Emperor Franz Joseph and his chief ministers, at a Polish state comprising the Congress Kingdom and Galicia and linked with the Habsburg monarchy by ties similar to those between Hungary and Austria.

On the economic level, the Central Powers started immediately on the ruthless requisition of raw materials and the dismantling of industrial establishments. They realized, however, that some support from their Polish subjects was necessary if they wished to tap their potential for military purposes. After some hesitation, the Germans and Austrians tried to make the Poles throw in their lot with the Central Powers. On 5 November 1916, Berlin and Vienna proclaimed an autonomous kingdom of Poland within undefined borders. Germany and Austria wanted to keep complete control of this construct, but this Two Emperors' Proclamation did provide for some basic Polish governmental institutions. For the Poles, this was a step toward independence.

Throughout the war the Poles were far from idle, making various attempts to become more than mere pawns in the hands of the belligerents. Polish leader Roman Dmowski finally realized that Russia could not be relied on to create a postwar order that would be favorable for Poland. Leaving Warsaw in 1915, he went first to Britain and then to Switzer-

Russian troops on patrol in Poland in an armored car. (Francis J. Reynolds and C. W. Taylor, *Collier's Photographic History of the European War*, P. F. Collier & Son, New York, 1916)

land and finally to France, where he established the Polish National Committee in 1917. All of the major Allied Powers recognized the committee. It sent representatives to London, Paris, and Rome and paved the way for establishment of a Polish army in France. The pianist Ignacy Paderewski became its agent in the United States, where there was a very large Polish émigré population, and drew President Woodrow Wilson's attention to the Polish question. Wilson ultimately included the demand for an independent Poland with access to the sea in his Fourteen Points. The Entente governments eventually declared Poland an allied belligerent power in the summer of 1918.

Dmowski's and Paderewski's diplomatic achievements were matched by Józef Piłsudski's activities on eastern Europe's battlefields. Establishing the Polish Legions with Austrian consent in 1914, he tried to incite the populace of the Congress Kingdom to rise against the Russians by marching on Kielce with a small and ill-equipped Polish fighting force. The operation was unsuccessful, but it was useful for propaganda purposes. Piłsudski grew disillusioned with the Central Powers and their policies toward Poland. Interned by the Ger-

mans in July 1917 for refusing an oath of allegiance, Piłsudski was released on the eve of the armistice and entered Warsaw as an uncompromised national hero on 10 November 1918. Taking command of the Polish armed forces, he replaced the Polish Regency Council as head of state and notified the powers that a free Polish state had come into existence.

With Piłsudski's approval, Dmowski and Paderewski represented Poland at the Paris Peace Conference. Poland's frontiers remained a vexing problem and were not settled until 1921 following the end of the 1919–1920 Polish-Soviet War.

While it is obvious that the Central Powers and Russia merely intended to exploit Poland for their respective war efforts in 1914, the development of the conflict forced them to yield gradually to Polish demands. The eventual rebirth of Poland was undoubtedly due primarily to the highly improbable coincidence of the three partitioning powers breaking down simultaneously in defeat and revolution, but it would not be justifiable to ignore or discount the Poles' own resourcefulness in pursuit of their ultimate objective.

Pascal Trees

See also
Brusilov Offensive; Dmowski, Roman; Fourteen Points; Franz
Joseph I, Emperor; Paderewski, Ignacy Jan; Piłsudski, Józef
Klemens; Poland, German Offensive; Poland, Two Emperors'
Proclamation; Wilhelm II, Kaiser; Wilson, Thomas Woodrow.

References
Davies, Norman. *Heart of Europe: A Short History of Poland.* Oxford,
UK: Clarendon, 1984.
Garlicki, Andrzej. *Józef Piłsudski, 1867–1935.* Ed. and trans. John
Coutouvidis. Aldershot, UK: Scolar Press, 1995.
Holzer, Jerzy, and Jan Molenda. *Polska w pierwszej wojnie Światowej*
[Poland in the First World War]. 2nd rev. and augmented ed.
Warsaw: Wiedza Powszechna, 1967.
Komarnicki, Titus. *Rebirth of the Polish Republic.* Melbourne,
Australia: Heinemann, 1957.
Clark, Alan. *Suicide of the Empires: The Battles on the Eastern Front,
1914–18.* New York: American Heritage Press, 1971.
Liulevicius, Vejas Gabriel. *War Land on the Eastern Front: Culture,
National Identity and German Occupation in World War I.*
Cambridge and New York: Cambridge University Press, 2000.
Lukowski, Jerzy, and Hubert Zawadzki. *A Concise History of Poland.*
Cambridge: Cambridge University Press, 2001.
Wandycz, Piotr. *The Lands of Partitioned Poland, 1795–1918.*
Seattle: University of Washington Press, 1974.

Poland, Two Emperors' Proclamation (1916)

Initiative by the Central Powers to create an autonomous Polish state on the occupied territory of Russian Poland. When the prospect of an early decision in the Great War receded, the belligerents began seeking even the most unlikely allies. The three states of Germany, Austria-Hungary, and Russia had partitioned Poland in the late eighteenth century; all now sought to secure and harness the support of their Polish subjects. With the potential of some 1.5 million recruits from Poland, German governor-general in Warsaw Hans von Beseler early in 1916 urged Berlin to establish an autonomous Polish Kingdom.

The Austro-Hungarian government still hoped to realize its concept of an Austro-Polish solution, that is, the de facto inclusion of Poland into the Habsburg monarchy. Vienna accepted the idea of Polish autonomy only grudgingly and under the pressure of the 1916 Brusilov offensive.

On 18 October 1916 leading politicians and representatives of the militaries of Germany and Austria-Hungary met in the Silesian town of Pless (Pszczyna) to discuss Polish matters. As a consequence, on 5 November the German and Austrian general governors in Warsaw and Lublin respectively proclaimed the autonomous Kingdom of Poland in the names of their two emperors.

The new Kingdom of Poland was to be a constitutional hereditary monarchy with its own army, controlled by the Central Powers. Its territory was vaguely confined to the Russian-ruled part of Poland then held by Germany and Austria. Germany was clearly unwilling to relinquish the Posen area, nor did Austria intend to let go of Galicia.

Four days after the ceremonies, the Central Powers issued a call to arms to the yet-to-be established Polish army, thus removing any doubts over the real aims of the proclamation. The number of volunteers was commensurably low. The Poles made it plain that there would be no Polish army without a Polish government.

Given these circumstances and the fact that the Two Emperors' Proclamation made the possibility of a separate peace with Russia unlikely, in early 1917 the Germans accepted the establishment of a Polish Provisional Council of State. This body had only consultative powers, but it gained political weight when Józef Piłsudski agreed to head the kingdom's military department. While these were only embryonic forms of governmental institutions, the act of November 1916 did have the political significance of restoring Poland to the map of Europe and creating an irreversible momentum toward Polish independence.

Pascal Trees

See also
Beseler, Hans Hartwig von; Brusilov Offensive; Eastern Front
Overview; Franz Joseph I, Emperor; Piłsudski, Józef Klemens;
Poland, Role in War; Wilhelm II, Kaiser.

References
Chwalba, Andrzej. *Historia Polski, 1795–1918.* Kraków:
Wydawnictwo Literackie, 2000.
Davies, Norman. *God's Playground: A History of Poland.* 2 vols.
Oxford, UK: Clarendon, 1981.
Holzer, Jerzy, and Jan Molenda. *Polska w pierwszej wojnie Światowej*
[Poland in the First World War]. 2nd rev. and augmented ed.
Warsaw: Wiedza Powszechna, 1967.
Komarnicki, Titus. *Rebirth of the Polish Republic.* Melbourne,
Australia: Heinemann, 1957.
Liulevicius, Vejas Gabriel. *War Land on the Eastern Front: Culture,
National Identity and German Occupation in World War I.*
Cambridge and New York: Cambridge University Press, 2000.
Wandycz, Piotr. *The Lands of Partitioned Poland, 1795–1918.*
Seattle: University of Washington Press, 1974.

Polivanov, Alexei Andreevich (1855–1920)

Russian minister of war. Born in Russia to an influential noble family on 16 March 1855, Alexei Polivanov graduated in 1874 from the Nikolaevsky Engineering School and served in the 1877–1878 Russo-Turkish War. From 1899 to 1904 Polivanov was on the General Staff, becoming chief of the General Staff in 1905.

Minister of War Vladimir Sukhomlinov appointed Polivanov deputy minister of war in 1906. This promotion came as a result of the disappointing and humiliating performance of the Russian army during the 1904–1905 Russo-Japanese War. Polivanov called for far-reaching modernization of the Russian military and the political machine behind it.

In 1912 Polivanov staunchly defended maintaining Russian fortresses as defensive positions despite the sharp disapproval of Sukhomlinov. This and suspicions by the aristocracy concerning his liberal predispositions led to Polivanov's dismissal. Still a prominent political figure, Polivanov served on the State Council from 1912 to 1915. This allowed him the opportunity to plot the dismissal of Sukhomlinov and secure the post of minister of war for himself in June 1915.

Polivanov then set out to reform the Russian military. He implemented a new training regimen and sought to overcome problems of supply and communication. These efforts met only partial success, as was demonstrated by Russia's continuing difficulties in World War I. In September 1915 Tsar Nicholas II decided to take personal command of the army at the front. Polivanov objected to the tsar's interference, incurring the wrath of the Tsarina Alexandra, who then began scheming with Prime Minister Boris Stürmer to bring about Polivanov's termination. Polivanov was dismissed as minister of war in March 1916.

Polivanov's influence during the rest of the war was inconsequential. After the Bolsheviks came to power in November 1917, he offered his services to the Red Army and helped negotiate the 1920 Soviet-Polish peace talks at Riga. While there, he contracted typhus and died on 25 September 1920.

Scott T. Maciejewski

See also

Alexandra Fyodorovna, Tsarina; Nicholas II, Tsar; Nikolai Nikolaevich, Grand Duke; Stürmer, Boris Vladimirovich; Sukhomlinov, Vladimir Aleksandrovich.

References

Golovin, N. N. *The Russian Army in World War I*. Reprint ed. Hamden, CT: Archon, 1969 [1931].

Lincoln, W. Bruce. *Passage through Armageddon: The Russians in War and Revolution, 1914–1918*. New York: Simon and Schuster, 1986.

Rutherford, Ward. *The Russian Army in World War I*. London: Cremonesi, 1975.

Wildman, Allan K. *The End of the Russian Imperial Army*, Vol. 1, *The Old Army and the Soldiers' Revolt (March–April 1917)*. Princeton, NJ: Princeton University Press, 1980.

Portugal

Located on the western portion of the Iberian Peninsula, the state of Portugal in 1914 was poor; socially divided, especially over the church; and ruled by an unstable liberal republican

Portuguese infantrymen in France. (*The Great War in Gravure: The New York Times Portfolio of the War,* The New York Times Co., 1917)

government. Strife, mutinies, and assassinations occurred throughout this period. Although Portugal had been a traditional British ally, on the outbreak of war most Portuguese wished to remain neutral. There was, however, strong national concern over Portugal's African colonies. Portuguese leaders worried that a German military victory in the war would lead to the loss of its African colonies. There were also fears in Portugal that an Allied victory without Portuguese participation on that side might bring the same result. In these circumstances, the republican government acted. On 23 November 1914, the National Assembly voted to declare war against Germany. Any action was delayed, however, by an insurrection of January 1915 led by General Pimenta de Castro, leader of the pro-German faction in the Portuguese army. For the next four months Castro ruled as dictator. In May he was overthrown by a democratic revolt, and Bernardino Machado took power as president.

Beginning on 24 February 1916, Portuguese authorities seized German ships that had sought refuge in Portuguese ports. Germany then declared war on Portugal on 9 March, followed by Austria-Hungary on 15 March.

Portugal rejected an Allied request for labor troops and insisted on sending fighting men. In March 1917 a Portuguese expeditionary force, eventually numbering some 54,000 men, began arriving in Flanders. Commanded by General Gomes de Costa, it first saw action on 17 June. In the April 1918 Battle of Lys during the Ludendorff offensives, the Portuguese 2nd Division suffered heavy losses against the German Sixth Army.

Meanwhile, the political situation in Portugal remained chaotic. On 5 December 1917, General Sidonio Pães carried out another pro-German coup, arresting and deporting the president and declaring himself military dictator. However, Pães was assassinated only nine days later, and the democratic regime was reestablished.

Portugal also sent some 40,000 reinforcements to Angola and Portuguese East Africa (Mozambique), both of which bordered German colonies. On 4 December 1917, German colonial troops under Colonel Paul Emil von Lettow-Vorbeck invaded Portuguese East Africa from neighboring German East Africa. On 8 December the troops captured a Portuguese force at Ngoma (River Rovuma). The Germans fought across Portuguese East Africa for most of 1918.

The war did provide a stimulus to the Portuguese economy with growing orders from the Allied Powers for food, raw materials, and finished goods. The economic effects of this were uneven, however, as wages failed to keep up with inflation. Unrest in Portugal continued after the war, leading in 1928 to the dictatorship of Antonio de Oliveira Salazar.

A. J. L. Waskey and Spencer C. Tucker

See also
Africa, Campaigns in; Lettow-Vorbeck, Paul Emil von; Lys Offensive.

References
Bradford, Sarah. *Portugal*. New York: Walker, 1973.
De Meneses, Filipe Ribeico. *Uniãosagrada e sidonismo: Portugal en guerra (1916–18)*. Lisbon, Portugal: Cosmos Ediçõs, 2000.
Farwell, Byron. *The Great War in Africa, 1914–1918*. New York: Norton, 1986.
Ferrira, José Mederios. *Portugal na Conferência da Paz, Paris, 1919*. Lisbon, Portugal: Quetzal Editores, 1992.
Gallagher, Tom. *Portugal: A Twentieth Century Interpretation*. Manchester, UK: Manchester University Press, 1983.
Teixira, Nuno Severiano. *O poder e a guerera, 1914–1918: Objectivas nacionais e estratégias políticas na entrada de Portugal na Grande Guerra*. Lisbon, Portugal: Editorial Estampa, 1996.

Potiorek, Oskar (1853–1933)

Austro-Hungarian army field marshal. Born in Bleiberg, Carinthia, on 20 November 1853, Oskar Potiorek entered the military school system at the age of 13 and quickly distinguished himself. He rose rapidly through a series of assignments, becoming military-governor of Bosnia-Herzegovina in 1911.

Believing the army better able to run Bosnia-Herzegovina than the joint Ministry of Finance, Potiorek worked to limit

Austro-Hungarian Army Field Marshal Oskar Potiorek was remembered as the man who was unable to protect Archduke Franz Ferdinand from assassination in June 1914. (Corbis)

the authority of the minister's representative and to strengthen ties with local politicians. He argued for a hard line against the Serbian population of Bosnia, playing them off against the other minorities of the territory. Potiorek's policies worked at cross-purposes with the conciliatory line favored by the ministry in Vienna. Simultaneously, Potiorek wooed the Archduke Franz Ferdinand, heir to the Austro-Hungarian thrones, as well as other military leaders, in an attempt to supplant General Franz Conrad von Hötzendorf as the most important military leader of the Dual Monarchy.

The outbreak of the Balkan wars in 1912 undercut Potiorek's plans to stabilize the provinces. Losing faith in internal reforms, he joined Conrad in demanding a forceful resolution of the Serbian menace. If diplomacy could win such a victory, so much the better; barring this, Potiorek favored a preventive war. He believed that delay would adversely affect army morale and leave the Dual Monarchy weakened.

The commander officially responsible for security during Franz Ferdinand's visit to Sarajevo in June 1914, Potiorek escaped responsibility for the lax precautions in place and his failure to heed warnings that tighter security was required. He argued vehemently for war. In August, Potiorek's allies ensured his appointment as commander of the Dual Monarchy's forces in the Balkans, subordinate only to Conrad at Supreme Headquarters. Aware that Conrad had already decided to mobilize the army's resources against Russia, Potiorek nevertheless argued for and received permission to launch an immediate offensive against Serbia.

The Austro-Hungarian invasion of Serbia was soon in reverse, with heavy Habsburg casualties and a Serbian counterinvasion. Nevertheless, Potiorek kept his command and planned a second attack in November that registered significant initial gains. Convinced that the Serbian army was near defeat, Potiorek pushed his forces forward, hoping to defeat Serbia before Christmas. Although his subordinates disliked Potiorek personally (they often received their orders in writing, as Potiorek preferred to isolate himself and make notes for his memoirs), his star had risen so high by the beginning of December that some officers at army headquarters hoped he might replace Conrad as chief of the Imperial General Staff.

Instead, with supply lines overextended and Austro-Hungarian forces exhausted, a Serbian counterattack of 3 December inflicted a crushing defeat on Potiorek's forces, which immediately began a barely controlled retreat. Having kept Conrad and Vienna largely in the dark about events, Potiorek discovered that his support in Vienna quickly evaporated. On 27 December, with the military situation fast deteriorating, Potiorek was replaced as commander by Archduke Eugen. Under pressure, Potiorek immediately submitted his retirement from the army, which became effective on 1 January 1915.

After the war, Potiorek lived quietly in retirement. He died in Klagenfurt, Austria, on 17 December 1933.

Kelly McFall

See also
Balkan Wars; Bosnia-Herzegovina, Role in War; Franz Ferdinand, Archduke; Franz Ferdinand, Assassination of; Kolubara River, Battle of the; Serbia, Conquest of.

References
Dedijer, Vladimir. *The Road to Sarajevo*. New York: Simon and Schuster, 1966.

Jerábek, Rudolf. *Potiorek: General im Schatten von Sarajevo*. Graz: Verlag Styria, 1991.

Rothenberg, Gunther. *The Army of Francis Joseph*. West Lafayette, IN: Purdue University Press, 1976.

———. "The Austro-Hungarian Campaign against Serbia in 1914." *Journal of Military History* 53(2) (April 1989): 127–146.

Pratt, William Veazie (1869–1957)

U.S. Navy admiral. Born in Belfast, Maine, on 28 February 1869, William Pratt graduated from the United States Naval Academy, Annapolis, in 1889. During the Spanish-American War Pratt participated in the blockade of Cuba and helped to suppress the Philippine Insurrection. While an instructor at the Naval War College, Pratt met and became a protégé of the

U.S. Navy Admiral William Veazie Pratt, commander-in-chief of the U.S. Fleet, on board his flagship, the battleship *Texas*. (Corbis)

energetic, innovative, and politically well-connected naval officer William Sims, under whom Pratt served from 1913 to 1915 with the Atlantic Fleet's Torpedo Flotilla, where he became known for his tactical planning and leadership skills.

From 1917 to 1919 Pratt was assistant to Admiral William S. Benson, chief of naval operations, with whom Sims, now commander of U.S. naval forces in Europe, clashed repeatedly over operational matters. Pratt managed to win the respect of both these powerful personalities and remain on good terms with each, probably because he worked intensively and displayed outstanding administrative ability in organizing the naval war effort, personally handling much of the avalanche of paperwork the war generated. Both Sims and Benson urged his promotion to rear admiral, which came in 1921.

After the war Pratt strongly supported naval limitation, on which he became a recognized expert. In the 1920s he served as president of the Naval War College and held several sea assignments, the last as commander-in-chief of the United States Fleet. Promoted to vice admiral in 1927 and admiral in 1928, Pratt served as chief of naval operations from 1930 to 1933, when he retired. He then wrote extensively on naval events and policy. Pratt died in Chelsea, Massachusetts, on 28 February 1957.

Priscilla Roberts

See also
Benson, William Shepherd; Sims, William Sowden; United States, Navy.

References
Symonds, Craig L. "William Veazie Pratt, 17 September 1930–30 June 1933." In *The Chiefs of Naval Operations*, ed. Robert William Love Jr., 69–86. Annapolis: Naval Institute Press, 1980.
Wheeler, Gerald E. *Admiral William Veazie Pratt, U.S. Navy: A Sailor's Life*. Washington, DC: Department of the Navy, Naval History Division, 1974.

Preliminary Bombardment

Artillery fire to disorganize and suppress defending troops prior to an attack. In World War I infantry rarely had sufficient firepower of its own. Support came late in the war from aircraft and tanks, but artillery was essential. Just how much support was required varied with circumstances. Poorly trained or equipped attackers required more help, while weak or demoralized defenders needed less in the way of preliminary bombardments.

Targets changed over time. Early bombardments consisted of general shelling of enemy trenches. By late 1915, with better targeting intelligence, artillery began to focus on enemy headquarters, strong-points, telephone exchanges, and other points critical to the defensive organization. This was especially important given a general shortage of shells. By 1916 production of artillery shells had dramatically increased to the point that quantity of shells fired and duration of the preliminary bombardment were paramount. In 1915 preliminary bombardments lasted a few days (as at Loos and Vimy Ridge), in 1916 about a week (as at Verdun and the Somme), and in 1917 preparations for the Nivelle offensive and Third Ypres took two to three weeks. Late in 1917 and early in 1918 an emphasis on surprise attacks brought the length of the bombardments down to at most a few hours.

Both sides believed that their artillery could smash any given defensive position, and defensive tactics began to emphasize defense in-depth. The defenders spread out, increasing the number of targets the attacker had to hit. This required the attacker to expend more time or employ more artillery, or both. Preliminary bombardments then extended to interdicting enemy reserves from reaching the front (the deep battle) and counterbattery fire against enemy artillery.

Throughout the war a key target for preliminary artillery fire was the defender's wire entanglements. If the wire was intact, then a few defenders could repel overwhelming numbers of attackers. After a few experiences of attacking infantry mowed down by German machine guns, British commanders demanded thorough wire-cutting. In consequence, during the week-long preliminary bombardment (24 June–1 July 1916) in the Battle of the Somme, approximately 30 percent of shells were for wire-cutting. A requirement to demolish wire barriers could dictate the duration of a bombardment.

The Germans developed a different style of preliminary bombardment than the Allies. They generally preferred a short, intense "hurricane" bombardment to the more lengthy and accurate deliberate bombardment. The German goal was to stun and neutralize the defenders. The Germans believed that this was a better combined-arms doctrine than the French philosophy of "artillery conquers, infantry occupies." German artillery doctrine reached its peak under Lieutenant Colonel Georg Bruchmüller, whom many regard as the founder of present-day artillery tactics. When the Allies had sufficient numbers of tanks to destroy the wire in a broad sector, they too experimented with hurricane bombardments. These shorter barrages restored the element of surprise to attacks. Thus the key role of tanks in the war may have been that of restoring operational surprise on the battlefield rather than providing tactical firepower.

Throughout the war both the format and targets of the preliminary bombardment changed dramatically. Armies added many more artillery pieces, especially heavy guns. But until infantry could secure sufficient firepower from other sources, it had to rely on artillery.

Sanders Marble

See also
Artillery; Bruchmüller, Georg; Counterbattery Fire; Creeping Barrage; Nivelle Offensive; Somme Offensive; Uniacke, Sir Herbert; Verdun, Battle of; Vimy Ridge, Battle of; Wire Obstacles.

References

Bailey, J. B. A. *Field Artillery and Firepower*. Oxford, UK: Military Press, 1989.

Farndale, Martin. *History of the Royal Regiment of Artillery: Western Front, 1914–1918*. London: Royal Artillery Institution, 1986.

Zabecki, David T. *Steel Wind: Colonel Georg Bruchmüller and the Birth of Modern Artillery*. Westport, CT: Praeger, 1994.

Prezan, Constantine (1861–1943)

Romanian army general. Born on 27 January 1861 in Romania, Constantine Prezan received his secondary education and early military training in both Bucharest and France. Commissioned in 1880 as a lieutenant, Prezan won promotion to captain in 1887, major in 1892, and lieutenant colonel in 1895. He served on the General Staff and became adjutant to Romanian Tsar Ferdinand. When Romania entered World War I in August 1916, Prezan was a major general commanding the Fourth Army. Crossing the Carpathian Mountains into Hungarian Transylvania, Prezan's army was forced to withdraw in January 1917 under German-led counterat-

Romanian General Constantine Prezan, commander of the Fourth Army when Romania entered the war in 1916. (Corbis)

tacks against armies on Prezan's southern flank. Prezan objected to General Alexandru Averescu's plan that the Romanian army attack Austro-Hungarian forces from the rear. The inadequate Romanian rail system through the Carpathian Mountains made lateral transportation such as this nearly impossible, and as Prezan feared, Averescu's plan failed. In August 1916 Prezan was promoted to lieutenant general and that November was named army chief of staff.

In April 1917 Prezan accompanied Romanian Premier Ionel Brătianu to Petrograd to coordinate Russian support for a summer offensive. The collapse of the Russian army, however, rendered meaningless Romanian military accomplishments at Marasti in July and Marasesti in August. Romania was forced to conclude peace with the Central Powers in the Treaty of Bucharest, under which the Romanian army was demobilized.

When Romania reentered the war in November 1918, Prezan again became army chief of staff. The Romanian military presence in Transylvania and the Banat of Temesvar enhanced Britianu's territorial claims at the Paris Peace Conference. Prezan retired in 1920. He was then promoted to field marshal and asked to form a nonparty government, but that attempt failed. Prezan spent his last years in Italy, returning to Romania only shortly before his death at his Moldavian estate on 27 August 1943.

David R. Loeffler

See also

Averescu, Alexandru; Brătianu, Ionel; Bucharest, Treaty of; Paris Peace Conference; Romania, Army; Romania, Campaign of 1916; Transylvania.

References

Armies of the Balkan States, 1914–1918: The Military Forces of Bulgaria, Greece, Montenegro, Rumania, and Serbia. London: Imperial War Museum, Department of Printed Books in association with Battery Press, 1996.

Preda, Dumitru, and Costica Prodan. *The Romanian Army during the First World War*. Bucharest: Univers Enciclopedic, 1998.

Spector, Sherman David. *Romania at the Paris Peace Conference: A Study of the Diplomacy of Ioan I. C. Bratianu*. Iasi, Romania: Center for Romanian Studies, Romanian Cultural Foundation, 1995.

Torrey, Glenn E. *The Revolutionary Russian Army and Romania, 1917*. Pittsburgh, PA: Center for Russian and East European Studies, University of Pittsburgh, 1995.

———. *Romania and World War I: A Collection of Studies*. Iasi, Romania, and Portland, OR: Center for Romanian Studies, 1998.

Princip, Gavrilo (1894–1918)

Bosnian youth who assassinated Austrian Archduke Franz Ferdinand and his wife Sophie. Princip was born to an Orthodox Serbian peasant family in the Grahovo Valley in Southern Bosnia on 13 July 1894. It was a time of considerable social change. The traditional social institution of the *zadruga*, or

The assassin of Archduke Franz Ferdinand, Gavrilo Princip, is hustled into custody in Sarajevo on 28 June 1914. (The Illustrated London News Picture Library)

extended family, was dissolving, and this disruption affected Princip's family. After four years of primary school, at age 13 Princip left the Grahovo Valley for Sarajevo where his older and economically successful brother intended to enroll him in a Habsburg military school. When he reached Sarajevo, however, his brother had changed his mind (supposedly on the advice of a friend who told him not to make Gavrilo "an executioner of his own people") and enrolled him in the local Merchants' School instead. After three years of study there, Princip transferred to a Gymnasium.

It was in the Gymnasium years that Princip became an ardent Serbian nationalist. In 1911 he joined Young Bosnia, the secret society that hoped to detach Bosnia from Austria and join it a larger Serb state. In 1912 Princip walked as if on pilgrimage from Sarajevo to Belgrade, kneeling down to kiss the soil when he crossed into Serbia.

During the First Balkan War of 1912, Princip and many other members of Young Bosnia sought to join the Serbian army's irregular forces, commanded by Major Vojislav Tankosić, a member of the Central Committee of Unity or Death (popularly known as the Black Hand), the principal conspiratorial organization in Serbia. Turned down in Bel-

grade because of his small stature, Princip finally tracked down Tankosić, who rejected him out of hand with the words, "You are too small and too weak."

The combination of intense Serbian nationalism and rejection for physical weakness are the most common explanations advanced for Princip's determination to commit an act of great consequence on behalf of his people. In fact, during his first interrogation after the assassination of Franz Ferdinand, he told the authorities, "People took me for a weakling . . . which I was not." He and the other conspirators secured their weapons from Tankosić's organization in Serbia, but whether or not they acted on instructions from Tankosić or any other Serbian official is still in question. Princip was one of seven conspirators who plotted to assassinate the archduke during his visit to Sarajevo on 28 June 1914. He was the only one who actually fired a weapon, a pistol with which he mortally wounded both the archduke and his wife (although one other conspirator, Nedjelko Cabrinović, earlier that day did throw a hand grenade, which missed its target).

Princip was arrested immediately after the assassination. Tried at Sarajevo on 28 October, he was convicted but was spared the death penalty because he was a minor. He received a sentence of twenty years in prison, the maximum permissible. Meanwhile, the Austria-Hungarian government held Serbia responsible for the murders of the archduke and his wife and used them as an excuse for a preventive war against Serbia, which led directly to World War I.

Princip lost an arm to tuberculosis while in prison at Theresienstadt, Austria. He died there, probably of this disease, on 28 April 1918.

Karl Roider

See also
Franz Ferdinand, Archduke; Franz Ferdinand, Assassination of.

References
Cassels, Lavender. *The Archduke and the Assassin: Sarajevo, June 28th 1914.* New York: Stein and Day, 1985.

Dedijer, Vladimir. *The Road to Sarajevo.* New York: Simon and Schuster, 1966.

Remak, Joachim. *Sarajevo: The Story of a Political Murder.* New York: Criterion, 1959.

Prisoners of War

At the beginning of the war, all participating governments anticipated a short conflict. In consequence, none of the warring states had given adequate attention to the incarceration of large numbers of prisoners of war (POWs) for a prolonged period of time. The result was considerable chaos and suffering for those taken prisoner early in the war.

Most of the warring powers adhered to the Hague Conventions of 1899 and 1907, which codified humane treatment for POWs and required the capturing state to accord POWs the same conditions as for its own soldiers. The Hague Convention also required governments to compile records on each prisoner and stipulated that prisoners were not to be used for war work, but this regulation was ignored as the need for laborers sharply increased.

Within six months the warring powers had taken almost 1.5 million prisoners. Despite the pressures of total war, most captor states endeavored to treat their prisoners humanely. There were some incidents of mistreatment, but most came from incompetence and lack of foresight rather than intentional cruelty. The original temporary arrangements proved inadequate, and the result was considerable suffering in regard to shelter, food, and clothing. Crowded conditions produced outbreaks of disease. Typhus, typhoid fever, and dysentery were common in the early camps on all sides, especially in the East. Conditions gradually improved as permanent camps were constructed and tents gave way to permanent shelters. The widespread use of POW labor also led to improved conditions for many prisoners, as it gave them access to better food and some income.

The various Red Cross societies began distribution of aid to the POWs from the fall of 1915 onward. The International Committee of the Red Cross compiled information on prisoners and relayed this to family members. It also distributed letters, parcels, and money, and it supervised prison camp conditions on both sides. Red Cross packages included basic foodstuffs as well as luxuries such as tobacco, clothing, chocolate, coffee, and soap. The Red Cross also accounted for those who died in the camps and forwarded their belongings to relatives. The French Bureau de Secours aux Prisonniers de Guerre and the British Prisoners of War Help Committee oversaw volunteer efforts.

Generally speaking, POWs held by the Western Entente powers were the best cared for, while those in the East suffered the most. Living conditions for prisoners in the camps in the East, especially in Russia, were very difficult. Many prisoners held by the Russians were sent to Siberia, where life was especially harsh.

Military enlisted prisoners were required to work. Prisoners worked in quarries, factories, and coal and salt mines. They built roads, cut timber, and worked in agriculture. As demands for labor increased during the war, many prisoners were forced to labor in war-related work. Private employers often hired POW labor, and prisoners often struck up friendships with local civilians who provided them extra food and clothing. While the income was welcome, many prisoners resented the extra work.

Officers were generally accorded better treatment. They had the best quarters, monthly financial allowances, and release from any type of labor. The rampant inflation of the war, however, eroded the purchasing power of their financial stipends.

Infectious diseases were a constant problem. Dysentery, gangrenous wounds, and lice were omnipresent. Nutritional deficiencies caused beriberi and dental problems. Many prisoners suffered from chronic depression, and suicide was not uncommon.

Prisoners could send and receive mail, although their correspondence was censored. To relieve boredom, prisoners organized libraries and formed dramatic groups, orchestras, and choirs. Sports activities proliferated, and the POWs also established school systems with workshops to teach new skills and lectures on such subjects as history and foreign language. Prisoners were also permitted to attend church services.

Many World War I POWs made attempts to escape, which was both far easier and less likely to result in severe punishment than in World War II. Charles de Gaulle, for example, attempted escape a half dozen times, but each time he was foiled, in large part due to his conspicuous height. Prisoners could escape from the poorly guarded camps, from work parties, or from transport trains. Many did so and attempted to reach neutral states such as Switzerland, the Netherlands, and the Scandinavian states. Prisoners escaping in Britain might be able to secure refuge on Dutch ships in British ports.

German prisoners of war in a French prison camp, c. 1917–1919. (National Archives)

Those caught attempting to escape were usually sent to a more secure facility, or they might be placed in solidarity confinement. Prisoners who managed to reach their home countries often provided valuable intelligence information about the enemy.

World War I ushered in a new class of war prisoners: alien civilians. These included students, resident workers, travelers, and merchant seamen. After a brief period in which they could depart, such individuals were often placed in camps but were not required to work. Not until the 1949 Geneva Conventions was there international agreement on the treatment of alien noncombatants.

Western Front

The largest number of prisoners taken by both sides in the war on the Western Front came during the war of maneuver at the beginning of the conflict. Thereafter some prisoners were taken in trench raids, and more fell in general offensives. By early 1915, for example, the Germans held 245,000 French prisoners. The largest number of British prisoners, some 100,000, were taken in the Ludendorff offensives in the spring

of 1918. At the end of the war the Germans held nearly 172,000 British prisoners and another 10,000 from the British Dominions and colonies. The Germans also held 350,000 French and 43,000 U.S. POWs. During the war the British captured about 328,000 Germans, while the French took another 400,000. The French also held a number of Turkish and Bulgarian prisoners, whom they interned on Corsica.

Generally speaking, conditions were best for German prisoners held in camps in Britain and in U.S.-run camps. The British kept some Germans prisoners on prison ships. Conditions there, while cramped, were nonetheless satisfactory. Conditions were slightly worse for Germans in the French-run camps, especially at the beginning of the war when the French were unprepared for the huge influx of German prisoners. Conditions improved rapidly as the French built permanent camps. The French were especially concerned about the German treatment of their many French prisoners, so they were anxious that the German POWs be well cared for under the Hague Convention. They also did not force their POWs to work in war-related industries until they learned that the Germans were doing so. The French did not release their last POWs until 1920, keeping many of them at work repairing war-related damage.

At first U.S. forces transferred Germans they captured to French control, but this practice ended when Americans began to fall into German hands. U.S. authorities decided that they needed to maintain the German prisoners themselves in order to ensure that American POWs held by the Germans were well cared for. Despite considerable time to prepare for this, the United States had given little thought to the care of its POWs, and many were sheltered in tents for some time. The U.S. military also put German POWs to dangerous work, such as disposing of munitions; in one case, twenty-five Germans POWs died in an explosion from such activity, leading to a temporary work stoppage. Later such work for prisoners would be banned by international law.

But the worst conditions for Allied POWs taken on the Western Front were in Germany. Prisoners sent to agricultural areas to do farm work were fortunate in that most could supplement their diets. Many others ended up working in German factories where they were relatively well cared for. POWs sent to work in the lumber industry or coal mines were forced to labor for ten to twelve hours a day in dangerous conditions with poor rations, little pay, and next to no medical treatment in case of injury.

Eastern Front

Both sides took large numbers of prisoners in the more fluid warfare that characterized fighting on the Eastern Front. In the great Battle of Tannenberg at the end of August 1914, the Germans captured more than 90,000 Russian soldiers. At Przemyśl in March 1915 and in the first three days of the Brusilov offensive in June 1916, the Russians took 70,000 Austro-Hungarian soldiers prisoner. During the three and a half years of fighting on the Eastern Front, some 5 million prisoners were taken by both sides. The largest number were Russians: 1.43 million taken by the Germans, and 1.27 million captured by Austro-Hungarian forces. The Russians in turn took 2.11 million Austro-Hungarian soldiers and 167,000 Germans.

Conditions in the camps were at first harsh, especially in Russia, due to lack of foresight and inadequate resources. Disease was rampant in some camps on both sides on the Eastern Front. Perhaps the worst example was in Russia. At the Totskoye POW camp near Samarrah, a typhus epidemic in the winter of 1915–1916 claimed more than 9,000 of 17,000 prisoners housed there. Conditions for prisoners slowly improved with the construction of permanent shelters and the distribution of aid through the Red Cross. The revolutions in Russia in 1917 produced more freedom for the prisoners but also brought chaos, as prisoners were often dependent on local authorities for their support. All three of the major powers fighting on the Eastern Front endeavored to turn POWs to fight against their own state. They segregated prisoners

according to nationality and encouraged them to volunteer for national military formations. Both sides during the war, for example, formed Polish military units and promised that if their side won the war Poland would achieve independence. At the beginning of the war, the Russians formed a brigade of Czechs living in Russia who desired to fight against Austro-Hungary for Czech independence. This brigade swelled into the Czech Legion as the Russians added to it Czechs who had either deserted or been captured from the Austro-Hungarian army. Later the Bolshevik government of Russia had some success in recruiting Hungarian POWs, many of whom were radicalized while incarcerated. The leadership of the short-lived Hungarian Soviet Republic after the war included a number of former Russian POWs, among them Béla Kun.

Unfortunately for the POWs held on the Eastern Front, the end of the war did not bring their speedy repatriation. Revolution, the collapse of public services, and the Russian Civil War all imposed additional problems. Perhaps a half million Central Powers prisoners were trapped in Siberia and Central Asia until the end of the Russian Civil War in 1920. The last POWs were not repatriated until 1922. Norwegian Fridtjof Nansen, appointed by the Council of the League of Nations to coordinate the release of the remaining prisoners, was awarded the Nobel Peace Prize in 1922 for his work in this regard.

Africa

During the initial invasion by South African forces of German South-West Africa (today's Namibia), the Germans took a number of prisoners. Held in camps at Tsumeb and Namutoni in the north of the colony, they were generally treated well. When South African forces finally triumphed in South-West Africa in mid-1915, they reciprocated the favor regarding prisoner treatment. In the prolonged fighting on the other side of the continent in German East Africa, the Germans also took a number of Allied prisoners and held them for much of the war. The principal complaint of Allied soldiers held by the Germans in Africa seems to have been that they were guarded by native African troops.

Middle East

Prisoners held by the Ottoman Empire during the war suffered difficult conditions indeed. The majority of the British prisoners taken by the Turks, most of them in the siege of Kut-al-Amara, suffered terribly despite promises that they would be held under humane conditions. Of more than 8,000 British and Indian troops taken at Kut in April 1916, nearly 5,000 died before the end of the war. In part this was because conditions were so difficult for the Turks themselves. According British prisoners the same standards as Turkish soldiers condemned a large number to death. In all 70 percent of British POWs held in Turkish camps died.

Ottoman prisoners held by the British were significantly better cared for, although there were problems at first, largely due to lack of shelter, and trachoma led to blindness in at least one eye in about 10 percent (15,000) of Turkish prisoners held by the British. Some 18,000 Ottoman prisoners were also held in India and Burma, but little is known about conditions there. The British also extensively recruited Arab prisoners to fight on the side of the Arab Revolt against Turkish rule. As was the case with prisoners from other nations held there, Ottoman prisoners in Russia suffered greatly in the course of the war. Perhaps 25 percent of Ottoman prisoners held in Russia died there during the war.

Far East

During the war the Japanese, Australian, and New Zealand forces captured the German Pacific islands and the German cession at Qingdao (Tsingtao) in China. There was little fighting, save at Qingdao, and the number of prisoners taken was small. There was no general internment of German civilians taken, save on Rabaul where most were soon released. The largest number of prisoners were those taken by the Japanese in the siege of Qingdao. Some 4,600 German POWs were held in twelve (later eight) Japanese camps in Japan, where they were well treated and received assistance from the Japanese YMCA.

Throughout the war, conditions for POWs varied substantially, depending on circumstance. While there were certainly individual acts of violence against prisoners, the Great War also saw an absence of state policies to deny prisoners the rights accorded to them under international law. They were not intentionally starved or worked to death or used in medical experiments, as was the practice of some governments during World War II.

Spencer C. Tucker

See also

Brusilov Offensive; Czech Legion; Hungary, Postwar Revolution; Kun, Béla; Kut, Siege of; Ludendorff Offensives; Max von Baden, Prince; Red Cross; Przemyśl; Qingdao, Siege of; Tannenberg, Battle of.

References

Burdick, Charles, and Ursula Moessner. *The German Prisoners of War in Japan, 1914–1920.* Lanham, MD: University Press of America, 1984.

Dennett, Carl P. *Prisoners of the Great War.* Boston: Houghton Mifflin, 1919.

Farwell, Byron. *The Great War in Africa, 1914–1918.* New York: Norton, 1986.

Fischer, Gerhard. *Enemy Aliens: Internment and the Homefront Experience in Australia, 1914–1920.* St. Lucia: University of Queensland Press, 1989.

Hoffman, Conrad. *In the Prison Camps of Germany: A Narrative of "Y" Service among Prisoners of War.* New York: Association Press, 1920.

Jackson, Robert. *The Prisoners, 1914–18.* London: Routledge, 1989.

Ketchum, J. Davidson. *Ruhleben: A Prison Camp Society.* Toronto: University of Toronto Press, 1965.

Speed, Richard B. *Prisoners, Diplomats, and the Great War: A Study in the Diplomacy of Captivity.* New York: Greenwood, 1990.

Vance, Jonathan F., ed. *Encyclopedia of Prisoners of War and Internment.* Santa Barbara, CA: ABC-CLIO, 2000.

Prittwitz und Gaffron, Maximilian von (1848–1917)

German general. Born on 21 November 1848 in Bernstadt, Silesia, the son of an official from a family with noble antecedents, Maximilian Wilhelm von Prittwitz und Gaffron entered the Prussian army in 1866 as a lieutenant in the 3rd Guards Grenadier Regiment. During 1873–1876 he studied at the Prussian War Academy. Following several promotions, Prittwitz joined the General Staff in 1879 with the rank of captain. He participated in the Franco-Prussian War and won the Iron Cross Second Class. Promoted to lieutenant colonel in 1892, colonel in 1894, and Generalmajor in 1896, he commanded the 20th Infantry Brigade. In 1901 he was promoted to Generalleutnant (major general) and received command of the 8th Division. In 1906 he was advanced to general of infantry and became the commanding general of XVI Army Corps st Metz. In 1913 he was advanced to colonel general and appointed inspector general of the First Army Inspectorate.

With the outbreak of war, Prittwitz assumed command of the Eighth Army, charged with the defense of East Prussia against the Russians while the bulk of the German army was sent west against France. He owed this appointment more to his connections than military ability. Prittwitz's sizable girth earned him the unflattering nickname of "Der Dicke" (Fatty). Although a somewhat indecisive and timid commander, Prittwitz did recognize talent among his staff, especially Lieutenant Colonel Max Hoffmann.

On August 17 General Hermann von François, commanding I Corps, seized the initiative and attacked at Stallupönen units of General Pavel Rennenkampf's advancing First Russian army. This German military success encouraged Prittwitz to launch an attack three days later on the Russians at Gumbinnen. Vastly outnumbered by Rennenkampf's forces, the Germans were repulsed. Prittwitz soon learned that General Aleksandr Samsonov's Russian Second Army had also crossed the southern frontier of East Prussia and would thus be in position to threaten the Eighth Army's rear. Prittwitz now panicked and informed Chief of the German General Staff Helmuth von Moltke at Koblenz that unless reinforcements could be sent at once, he would have to abandon all East Prussia and withdraw behind the Vistula River. Prittwitz did not inform his staff members of his communication to Moltke, and when they objected to the withdrawal, Prittwitz approved their counterproposal of an attack on Samsonov's left flank, for which three divisions were to be switched in haste by rail from the Gumbinnen Front. Hoffmann was the principal architect of this plan, which would culminate in the subsequent Battle of Tannenberg.

Unaware of this change of heart, on 22 August Moltke informed Prittwitz that he was being replaced by General Paul von Hindenburg, with General Erich Ludendorff as Hindenburg's quartermaster general. Prittwitz did not contest the replacement, which marked the effective end of his military career. Meanwhile, Hindenburg and Ludendorff readily confirmed Hoffmann's dispositions, resulting in the German triumph of Tannenberg. Prittwitz died a broken man in Berlin on 29 March 1917.

Peter Overlack and Spencer C. Tucker

See also

François, Hermann von; Gumbinnen, Battle of; Hindenburg, Paul von; Ludendorff, Erich; Moltke, Helmuth von, Count; Rennenkampf, Pavel Karlovich; Samsonov, Aleksandr Vasiliyevich; Stallupönen, Battle of; Tannenberg, Battle of.

References

Clark, Alan. *Suicide of the Empires: The Battles on the Eastern Front, 1914–18.* New York: American Heritage Press, 1971.

Elze, Walter. *Tannenberg: Das deutsche Heer von 1914, seine Grundzüge und deren Auswirkung im Sieg an der Ostfront.* Berlin: F. Hirt, 1928.

Reichsarchiv. *Der Weltkrieg 1914 bis 1918: Militärische Operationen zu Lande.* Vol. 2. Berlin: Mittler, 1925.

Schäfer, Theobald von. *Tannenberg.* Oldenburg and Berlin: Stalling, 1927.

Showalter, Dennis E. *Tannenberg: Clash of Empires.* Hamden, CT: Archon, 1991.

Stone, Norman. *The Eastern Front, 1914–1917.* New York: Scribner, 1975.

A French soldier standing on a battlefield wearing a gas mask around his neck. The phrase "They shall not pass" is written in the clouds of gas behind the soldier. (Library of Congress)

Propaganda

World War I was the first great war in history in which media played an important role. As one German observer put it, propaganda was "more powerful than the navy, more dangerous than the army." Propaganda could be used to arouse hatred of the foe, warn of the consequences of defeat, and idealize one's own war aims in order to mobilize a nation, maintain its morale, and make it fight to the end. It could explain setbacks by blaming scapegoats such as war profiteers, hoarders, defeatists, dissenters, pacifists, left-wing socialists, spies, shirkers, strikers, and sometimes enemy aliens so that the public would not question the war itself or the existing social and political system.

Propaganda could also demoralize the enemy, incite soldiers to desert, and stir up unrest among the enemy state's civilian population. Its favorite targets were dissatisfied elements such as underprivileged classes, revolutionary movements, and national minorities. Propaganda could also win over neutral states by encouraging friendly elements and local warmongers or, at a minimum, keep neutrals out of the war by fostering noninterventionist or pacifist views. Finally, it could help retain allies, break up enemy alliances, and prepare exhausted or dissatisfied nations to defect or make a separate peace.

In each country officials were authorized to suspend press freedom. Governments rapidly established censorship procedures that suppressed news apt to distress their populations, but they hesitated to organize formal propaganda offices. In the first months of World War I such offices hardly seemed necessary, as most people rallied to the defense of their homelands. Internal strife, party fights, and class struggles were voluntarily suspended as citizens closed ranks behind their governments. In Germany this was known as the "Domestic Truce," in France the Union Sacrée, and in Russia the union of tsar and people.

Journalists, writers, artists, and cartoonists all joined in what the writer Thomas Mann called a "spiritual military service." University professors were especially active, glad to assist in organizing the spiritual crusade. They gave lectures to the public and even at the front, in neutral countries, and in occupied territories. They published propaganda brochures and promoted appeals and counterappeals. Numerous private propaganda organizations were founded or reactivated, such as the Committee of the Study and Documentation of the War in France, the League of German Scholars and Artists in Germany, and the Sokolev Committee in Russia.

Schoolteachers and, to a lesser degree, priests, also acted as propaganda agents. Priests supported their nation's cause in their homilies as did teachers in their lessons; both groups also organized patriotic assemblies and campaigns for war bonds.

However, as the number of casualties mounted and war-weariness set in with domestic hardships on the home fronts, dangerous rumors, gossip, and criticism spread, and pacifist and left-wing socialist movements again became active. In order to counter this decline in public morale, and also to boost campaigns in neutral states, each nation involved in the war began the systematic dissemination of propaganda.

British propaganda efforts were initially spread among several agencies. The Parliamentary Recruiting Committee enlisted volunteers for the army and navy; three other offices directed their energies toward neutral countries; and the Foreign Office gave regular press conferences. Even in March 1918, when propaganda was more centralized in the Ministry of Information under Lord Beaverbrook (Max Aitken), there were still competing bureaus, such as the Department of Enemy Propaganda directed by Lord Northcliffe.

In Germany final decisions on censorship and propaganda rested with local military commanders, who assumed the highest executive powers and were, outside Bavaria, responsible solely to the kaiser. Section IIIB of the General Staff, later its War Press Office, coordinated press policy and organized daily press conferences. In October 1914, thirty-six agencies involved in propaganda in neutral countries were centralized in the Foreign Ministry under the Central Office for Foreign Propaganda. All these offices were reorganized several times, and in summer 1917 General der Infanterie Erich Ludendorff, German army first quartermaster general, enlarged the War Press Office into the huge propaganda machine of Patriotic Instruction. It employed hundreds of officers and countless writers, painters, caricaturists, photographers, and technicians. In both Britain and Germany, private agencies and departments of various ministries also continued to present propaganda, and conflicts among them were inevitable.

The French Foreign Ministry established a Press House in December 1915 that was more efficiently reorganized when Georges Clemenceau became premier in 1917. In Russia there was no state propaganda office. The Russian monarchy was afraid to mobilize mass sentiment due to fear that this might turn against the monarchy. In Italy in November 1916 a minister without portfolio was entrusted with supervising propaganda, but he had practically no funds for his operations. Only with the near-catastrophic Italian defeat in the Battle of Caporetto that October was the propaganda office properly financed and real mass propaganda begun. Turkey had a secret Special Organization for propaganda and sabotage abroad. Belgian propaganda was at first directed by several embassies and later centralized in the Belgian Documentary Bureau. On U.S. entry into the war, President Woodrow Wilson appointed journalist George Creel to develop a Committee on Public Information (CPI). Three national movements without a state also had their own propaganda organizations: the Office of Nationalities of Lithuanian politician Juozas Gabrys in Lausanne, Switzerland, and the bureaus of the Czechoslovak National Council and the Polish National Committee in Paris and London.

Propaganda everywhere reflected individual nations' war aims. These objectives were political and economical but were usually camouflaged ideologically in the guise of a clash of civilizations (*Kulturkrieg*). This was most intense between Germany and the Western powers (Kultur versus Civilization). The Entente, later joined by Italians and the United States, denounced the Germans as militarists and barbarians and proclaimed a crusade in the name of freedom and civilization, in order "to make the world safe for democracy." They nonetheless found it embarrassing that until the March 1917 revolution in Russia, they were allied with the most despotic regime in Europe, tsarist Russia.

The Germans denounced Western democracy as a "plutocracy" that was in reality the embodiment of capitalism and materialism and ridiculed its outdated parliamentarianism as failing to represent the genuine will of the people. Helped by the Swede Rudolf Kjellén and the Englishman Houston S. Chamberlain, they proclaimed the "Ideas of 1914." Thus "German freedom" was declared to be "devotion to the community," and other salient values were "order," "performance of duty," and "discipline."

The most important propaganda slogan of the war was certainly the right of peoples to national self-determination. The Central Powers and, rather belatedly, the Allies promised to provide this, but only to oppressed nationalities living under the enemy's yoke. Thus, Germany pledged itself to liberate the subject peoples of tsarist Russia, but when on 5 November 1916 the Kingdom of Poland was proclaimed, it comprised only the former Russian territories; Poles in Poznań and Galicia were to remain under Prussian and Austrian rule. As the war progressed, public opinion in Germany became polarized over war aims. A majority of the people demanded vast annexations, while a minority favored a more flexible solution: the liberated nations in the East would be formally independent but tied to Germany as satellite states in a Mitteleuropa system. Kjellén praised this as "leadership without domination."

In November 1914 Germany's ally Turkey proclaimed jihad (holy war) to liberate all Muslim peoples from the yoke of the Allied Powers. Some success was achieved in North Africa. Turkish propaganda and German gold led to the uprising of the Senussi, which occupied 100,000 Allied soldiers until February 1917. There was also some unrest in Algeria, Morocco, and Persia, but to the great disappointment of the Central Powers, India and Egypt remained quiet.

Topics such as freedom, self-determination, and Kultur might appeal to the cultivated bourgeoisie, but they were ineffective as far as the common people were concerned. For them, simpler and clearer arguments were necessary. The most important of these was vilification of the enemy. Presentations reflected deep-seated national prejudices: the German either in a uniform, with a monocle and spiked helmet, or as a glutton eating sausages and drinking beer; the Frenchman as frivolous and vainglorious; the Englishman greedy and hypocritical; the Italian malicious and treacherous; and the Russian drunken and dirty. Enemy leaders were presented as cruel personalities, wading in blood, allied with death and the devil. Sometimes cultural symbols such as a bloodthirsty Teutonic Valkyrie or a ruthless John Bull were employed. The Germans hated the English for a blockade that was illegal under international law and that starved them and ruined their economy. "God punish England" replaced "Good day" as a greeting in Germany, and the poet Ernst Lissauer wrote his "Hymn of hate" against England.

Atrocity stories were very effective. German soldiers were accused of mutilating children and killing babies, Belgians and French of illegal sniping and gouging out prisoners' eyes, and Russians of cutting off women's breasts and legs. Stories based on unreliable testimony were not only presented in newspapers, brochures, and posters but also in official "whitebooks" and reports by distinguished scholars. The most notable propaganda efforts were the "Bryce-Report" on German atrocities against Belgian civilians and the rumored "Corpse-conversion-factory" where the Germans allegedly used human corpses to make soap.

The Germans were at a disadvantage in this campaign. In their rapid advance into Belgium, northeastern France, and Russia they had indeed proceeded with barbarous cruelty, burning libraries and churches, pillaging houses, raping women, and shooting thousands of innocent civilians before establishing repressive occupation regimes. Allied propaganda was able to exploit the sinking of the liner *Lusitania,* the execution of nurse Edith Cavell, and the Armenian massacres by the Turks. Germany and its allies were forced to use propaganda defensively, denying accusations and justifying their actions. Humorous ridicule of the enemy, especially in cartoons, was also important. Laughter not only alleviated

A U.S. World War I poster emphasizing the imporetance of workers on the home front for the American soldiers in France. (National Archives)

stress and tension, but, as Sigmund Freud explained, "By showing the enemy as small, low, despicable, comic, ridiculous, we give ourselves the enjoyment of a victory."

Specific propaganda was directed toward shoring up the home fronts in such slogans as "The war was imposed by the enemy, we only defend ourselves"; "We must have confidence in our leaders"; "We suffer from the war, but the enemy suffers more"; "To go on strike now helps the enemy"; "We must hold out till victory, otherwise all former sacrifices will be vain"; "Peace at any price will impose disastrous conditions on us, a victorious peace will prevent future aggressions." French writer Henri Barbusse argued in his pseudo-pacifist novel *The Fire* and in subsequent propaganda appeals that the war was terrible but that the French must fight until the end because if German militarism could be crushed, eternal peace would reign.

Arguments inciting soldiers to desert included "You are duped and sacrificed for the interests of your leaders" (Prussian junkers or British plutocrats) and "In our prisoner camps you will be well treated." In 1918 a most convincing argument was presented to the Germans: "2 million Americans are now in France, more than 10 times that number stand ready in America. Your course is hopeless!" In response German propaganda falsified arrival figures and ridiculed the American soldier as incapable of fighting effectively.

In 1914 favorable views of the war penetrated the whole cultural fabric. Plays, operettas, songs, patriotic concerts, "tableaux vivants," conferences, novels, toys, children's books, photos, and cartoons were all related to the war. Newspapers published war poems and even such incredible lies as "80 percent of German shells fail to burst." Millions of patriotic postcards circulated, and ashtrays, plates, match boxes, and tear-off calendars carried propaganda messages. At school traditional instruction was replaced by lessons directly related to the war, such as calculations of enemy losses. There were also discussions of the latest war reports, the singing of patriotic songs, and fund-raising campaigns.

Later in the war, as morale plummeted, governments offered theater troupes, mobile army cinemas (in Germany alone there were some 900 of these), and entertainment groups that toured the front. Military newspapers, which had initially enjoyed a certain amount of freedom, became propaganda organs closely supervised by the high commands. In Britain, which at first avoided conscription, recruiting volunteers was a most urgent task. The poster featuring Horatio Kitchener pointing toward the viewer with the words "Your Country needs YOU!" was perhaps the most famous such image of the war. More successful perhaps were public meetings organized by the Parliamentary Recruiting Committee, where reluctant young men were pushed forward by the enthusiastic crowd and registered on the spot. From the summer of 1917 the German army's Patriotic Instruction employed special propaganda officers who held weekly compulsory courses for soldiers to review materials from the War Press Office. It also recruited priests, professors, teachers, trade union leaders, and reliable soldiers for home front meetings. In the United States official propaganda was organized on a large scale: the CPI published millions of leaflets, booklets, and posters; organized forty-five war conferences; and employed 75,000 speakers, the famous Four-Minute Men, who made some 750,000 speeches.

Film was most important. Newsreels and films depicting military heroism were much in demand. However, as actual filming at the front was not permitted, scenes of battle had to be reenacted, and troops sometimes laughed heartily or reacted angrily when watching such films. From spring 1915, interest in war films decreased. People wanted to forget the war and view traditional light fare. The British were able to recapture the audiences with such documentaries as *The Battle of the Somme* and amusing propaganda films such as *Once a Hun, Always a Hun*. In Germany, despite creation of a Photo and Film Office, feature films were ineffective, and the foundation of the Universum Film Aktingesellschaft (Universum

Film Company [UFA], a new state umbrella organization combining private and government financing to produce propaganda films) by Ludendorff in December 1917, came too late. In Russia, France, and Italy propaganda films were of little importance, but in the United States, thanks to such actors as Charlie Chaplin and Mary Pickford, they played a major role in rallying public opinion and selling war bonds. Films could be shown in the remotest locations, brought there by special trucks that carried the projector and screen.

Some propaganda techniques grew out of specific national traditions. In some Austrian and German cities, enormous wooden emblems and statues of generals were erected into which people would hammer iron or golden nails in exchange for donations of between 1 and 100 marks. In Russia, with its high illiteracy rate, traditional entertainments enjoyed a comeback, at least until 1915. Millions of cheap war "lubki," the Russian version of the popular "broadside," were sold or shown in peep shows. In puppet theaters, Kaiser Wilhelm II was beaten to death by Petruschka, the Russian Punch. In circus pantomimes Wilhelm, Austrian Emperor Franz Joseph, and Ottoman Sultan Mehmed V were brought into the ring in wheel barrows and tormented by devils.

For propaganda in neutral countries a different approach was necessary. Propaganda offices gave interviews to foreign journalists, organized sightseeing tours of the front, translated and analyzed foreign newspapers, sent out speakers and propaganda material, and supported friendly local societies and neutrality committees.

As the British blockaded the North Sea ports and cut the oversea cables, the Germans had to telegraph propaganda by radio (the "1,000 Words Service" of the Transocean Society) and transmit propaganda via neighboring neutral countries, at first through Italy and then by way of Sweden. The material was then distributed by friendly local businessmen, immigrants, and numerous propaganda agents. The German embassy in Bern alone employed 500–600 people and forwarded information to newspapers, libraries, hotels, doctors' waiting rooms, and thousands of private addresses.

Regular bribing of the foreign press and even government purchase of foreign businesses were widespread. On other occasions agents purchased and destroyed the entire circulation of hostile issues, and sometimes distribution firms were bought up in order to assure that only "friendly" papers were sold at newsstands.

Propaganda agencies financed international conferences. The greatest German success was the Third Conference of Nationalities in Lausanne in June 1916, organized by the Lithuanian Juozas Gabrys and presided over by a Belgian, where 400 delegates of various nationalities in Russia, Ireland, and the French and British colonies denounced Allied oppression and the denial of freedom and self-determination. Sometimes propaganda was reinforced by espionage. Czech undercover agents in the German and Austrian embassies in Washington stole compromising photos and sabotage plans that were then widely publicized.

It was more difficult to conduct propaganda in enemy countries because of censorship and controls at the frontiers. Nevertheless, there as well newspapermen were bribed. The Germans bribed the Parisian papers of *Le Journal, La Tranchée républicaine,* and *Le Bonnet rouge,* while the French subsidized the *Kölnische Volkszeitung* in Köln (Cologne). Propaganda could be smuggled across neutral countries such as Switzerland and Holland by placing false titles on newspapers or putting a patriotic newspaper on the top of a bundle; brochures were disguised as philosophical treatises, and leaflets were hidden in chests with a double bottom.

The Germans were especially active in fomenting nationalist or socialist uprisings. By July 1915 they had distributed 5 million marks to support revolutionary propaganda in Russia. In April 1917 they not only transported Lenin from Switzerland to Russia but thereafter provided him with propaganda posters, postcards, brochures, and substantial financial assistance, helping to make the Bolsheviks a mass party and facilitating the Bolshevik Revolution of November 1917. The Germans also supported the Irish uprising of 1916 against British rule, financed socialist and pacifist groups in Italy (200,000 Swiss francs in 1918 alone), and even paid the Sicilian Mafia for assistance. Turkish-German propaganda for the jihad was less successful than were the British in reaching Arab nationalists. British Lieutenant Colonel T. E. Lawrence played an important role in inciting an Arab uprising against the Turks.

There was some propaganda activity directed at prisoners of war, literally a captive audience. The Germans built eighty mosques and employed dozens of mullahs to preach jihad to captured Muslim soldiers from the British, French, and Russian armies. The results were meager compared to the efforts of the Czechoslovak national movement in Russia, where the Czech Legion was recruited from among Czechs living in Russia and also among prisoners and deserters from the Austro-Hungarian army. Propaganda against enemy soldiers was fully developed by 1917–1918. This included leaflets strewn among trenches by "propaganda grenades" fired by mortars or dropped behind the lines by planes and balloons. Loudspeakers also broadcast propaganda across no-man's-land. In appropriate cases, along the Rhine, Isonzo, and Adriatic, propaganda traveled in bottles or buoys.

After the war General Erich Ludendorff blamed Allied propaganda for his defeat, and Adolf Hitler admired the Allied efforts and criticized the German counterpart as weak and inept. Nonetheless, Hitler himself was profoundly influenced by German war propaganda. Later he often repeated one of its major arguments, that Americans lacked moral fiber and fighting ability, a serious mistake in his war calculations during World War II.

No German propaganda could turn the tide against the overwhelming manpower and matériel superiority of the Allies, supported by the United States from the beginning of World War I. It did, however, help persuade the population to hold out, retarding the inevitable downfall of the Central Powers. Propaganda, while not decisive in the war's outcome, was indispensable to all the warring countries. Without effective propaganda, no nation would have endured the terrible casualties and personal privations of four long years of war.

Eberhard Demm and Christopher H. Sterling

See also

Aitken, Sir William Maxwell, Lord Beaverbrook; Atrocities; Caporetto, Battle of; Cavell, Edith Louisa; Censorship; Children and the War; Clemenceau, Georges; Creel, George Edward; Easter Rising; Film and the War; Four-Minute Men; Franz Joseph I, Emperor; Gabrys, Juozas; Harmsworth, Alfred, Viscount Northcliffe; Hindenburg, Paul von; Hitler, Adolf; Kitchener, Horatio Herbert, 1st Earl; Lawrence, Thomas Edward; Lloyd George, David; Ludendorff, Erich; *Lusitania,* Sinking of; Mehmed V, Sultan; Mitteleuropa; Naval Blockade of Germany; Russia, Revolution of November 1917; Senussi and Sultan of Darfur Rebellions; War Aims; Wilhelm II, Kaiser; Wilson, Thomas Woodrow.

References

Buitenhuis, Peter. *The Great War of Words: British, American and Canadian Propaganda and Fiction, 1914–1933.* Vancouver: University of British Columbia Press, 1987.
Demm, Eberhard. *Der Erste Weltkrieg in der Internationalen Karikatur.* Hannover, Germany: Fackelträger-Verlag 1988.
———. *Ostpolitik und Propaganda im Ersten Weltkrieg.* Berne and Frankfurt: Lang, 2002.
Horne, John, and Alan Kramer. *German Atrocities, 1914: A History of Denial.* New Haven, CT: Yale University Press, 2001.
Jann, Hubertus F. *Patriotic Culture in Russia during WWI.* Ithaca, NY: Cornell University Press, 1995.
Lasswell, Harold D. *Propaganda Technique in World War I.* New York: Knopf, 1927; reprint, Cambridge, MA: MIT Press, 1971.
Mock, James R., and Cedric Larson. *Words That Won the War: The Story of the Committee on Public Information, 1917–1919.* Princeton, NJ: Princeton University Press, 1939.
Ostermann, Patrick. *Duell der Diplomaten: Die Propaganda der Mittelmächte und ihrer Gegner in Italien während des Ersten Weltkriegs.* Weimar, Germany: Verlag und Datenbank für Geisteswissenschaften, 2000.
Ross, Stewart Halsey. *Propaganda for War: How the United States Was Conditioned to Fight the Great War of 1914–1918.* Jefferson, NC: McFarland, 1996.
Sanders, Michael, and Philip M. Taylor. *British Propaganda during the First World War, 1914–1918.* London: Macmillan, 1982.
Vaughn, Stephen L. *Holding Fast the Inner Lines: Democracy, Nationalism, and the Committee on Public Information.* Chapel Hill: University of North Carolina Press, 1980.
Welch, David. *Germany, Propaganda, and Total War, 1914–1918: The Sins of Omission.* New Brunswick, NJ: Rutgers University Press, 2000.

Prostitution and Venereal Disease

The spread of syphilis and gonorrhea among troops during the First World War produced heightened worries over the danger that disease posed for soldiers and the general population. It also brought an increase in surveillance of prostitution and women more generally.

Systems of regulated prostitution developed in France and Britain during the nineteenth-century and were designed to ensure the health of prostitutes for customers. Regulation required women working on the streets or in brothels to register with police and receive regular medical exams. Police doctors conducted monthly or bimonthly pelvic and visual examinations on women, looking for chancres or full-body rashes (pox) that indicated infection.

If symptomatic, prostitutes were not certified to receive clients, isolated in the brothels, or sent to a women's prison-hospital (such as the well-known Saint Lazare prison in Paris). Unfortunately, as Dr. Paul Faivre would complain about the French system in 1917, medical exams for prostitutes were often poorly conducted by police doctors who usually used a single speculum, which was not sanitized between exams. Cross-contamination between sick and healthy women during exams was probable, and doctors did not screen male clients. As a result, male clients often spread disease to prostitutes and their families.

By World War I, Germany and France still maintained an active system of medical regulation of prostitution. During the war, concern over the spread of disease on the home front and among troops encouraged military medical services and police to focus almost exclusively on the control and medical regulation of prostitutes. However, the activities of women more generally became linked to worries about prostitution.

After the mobilization of 1914, French and British officials became suspicious of the activities of single working women, those left behind by husbands, or those drawn to attractive young men in uniform (out of a sense of duty, patriotism, or from sheer hero-worship). British officials and social observers understood the sudden increase in unescorted women on the streets as a threat to public morality. Even women working for war charities came under scrutiny. In Britain, organizations such as the National Union for Women Workers, the London Council for the Promotion of Public Morality, and the National Vigilance Association grew concerned that women soliciting funds in the streets for wartime charities placed themselves dangerously close to prostitution and were "a grave menace to morality."

The British government employed a series of measures under the Defence of the Realm Act (DORA) to limit when and where women could appear publicly. During November 1914 British authorities in Cardiff placed women there under curfew from 7:00 P.M. until 8:00 A.M. Breaking the curfew carried serious penalties. Five women arrested during curfew hours were sentenced to detention, but others received fifty-six days of hard labor. Even the National Vigilance Association, though unsympathetic to the idea of a curfew, suggested patrols by groups of women to monitor women's activities and morality in Cardiff and in Bristol.

Concern for morality and ensuring women's "proper" activities would not abate during the war. As the Frenchman Paul Géraldy wrote in his novel, *La guerre, madame* (1916), many soldiers and bystanders were troubled by widows who wore makeup, seemingly oblivious to their period of mourning. Others viewed the thousands of women who worked in war factories, took up jobs traditionally held by men, and made use of their income to buy consumer goods as a sign of a degenerate Europe. Even women of the middle classes, often thought of as morally upstanding and above prostitution, came under suspicion. In March 1916, Dr. E. Gaucher and Dr. Léon Bizard published an article in the *Annales des Maladies Vénériennes* on the number of soldiers who had contracted syphilis. While the article discussed different rates of infection, the doctors speculated on how the spread of disease had changed. They argued that for a variety of reasons (a need for income, sadness, or compassion for soldiers), middle-class women readily entered prostitution and presented a new source of disease and moral degeneration.

While untrue in the vast majority of cases, observers continuously theorized that women on the home front cared increasingly less about the war and their men at war, and more for money, personal comfort, and licentious behavior on the streets. The numbers of single women who worked and newly widowed women as well as fears over the spread of disease combined to create a climate of confusion for police. Prostitutes could no longer be quickly identified as women in the company of men who did not appear to be husbands or fathers.

German police experienced similar difficulties during the war. They kept prostitutes under strict surveillance and required that prostitutes register with police. German authorities identified those women who engaged in sexual activities outside of marriage, even on an irregular basis, as amateur prostitutes, or *Heimliche Prostitutierte*. As elsewhere, police considered most women identified as amateur prostitutes liable to carry disease and to have a high probability of transmitting it to others. To control the spread of disease during the war, German military officials worked to increase police surveillance. They closed bars with hostesses, and military doctors took on the responsibility of conducting prostitutes' medical exams.

Troops themselves did little to aid authorities in controlling disease or ending confusion about identifying "real" prostitutes. In London, soldiers on leave sought out women, not necessarily prostitutes. During a public debate in 1917, Lieutenant General Sir Francis Lloyd, in charge of forces in London, argued that one had to be tolerant of soldiers. "It is difficult when you have been working in dirty wet trenches with bullets flying about . . . to come to London with all its pleasures and temptations, and if you are a virile soldier, not to 'have a go' of some sort." Speaking at the same meeting, Sir Edward Henry noted that parks were often misused through the night, so that "couples may be seen behaving in a most scandalous manner."

In fact, while soldiers were warned about unregistered women, they were also strongly encouraged to treat disease and guard their health. After September 1916, the French Military Health Service required soldiers to attend lectures on venereal disease and distributed leaflets on its dangers and soldiers' duty to the nation to remain healthy. While some officials in the French army suggested that soldiers be regularly inspected for signs of venereal disease, doctors rarely examined soldiers before leave, preferring instead to study new methods of prevention and treatment. The French and the British as well as the American Expeditionary Forces (AEF) all eventually required soldiers to denounce women suspected of passing infection and to utilize chemical cleansing stations after exposure. There, soldiers cleansed themselves and applied calomel, arsenic, or mercury-based ointments to kill any remaining infections. Of course, the disagreeable, invasive nature of the chemical prophylaxis meant that many soldiers avoided the process altogether.

German military doctors also used lectures and tracts to explain the dangers of venereal disease, urging their soldiers to avoid extra or premarital sex for the sake of their honor and duty. One Bavarian army doctor, Georg Reh, told soldiers to avoid contact with French women. He explained that soldiers must be able "to fight and oppress their desires of lust with iron will." But, while appeals to honor and pleas for chastity worked at the front, for men on leave in the rear areas conditions were much like those in England and France: soldiers sought out women. In Brussels, soldiers who arrived at the train station received pamphlets describing the dangers of disease and suggesting the use of prophylactics, but few in any army had access to the latter or used them. Late in the war, the German army placed vending machines in soldiers' barracks. German soldiers who returned from a sexual encounter could purchase a small packet of disinfectant when needed, to be used immediately or carried with them for later use. The anonymity and practicality of this system proved popular with German troops.

Prostitutes did not have to work very hard to convince soldiers to consider their services. Soldiers sought comfort and distraction to erase memories of trench warfare or to ensure they did not die virgins. Prostitution, as sex work, was a booming business during the war. British officer Robert Graves

recorded the interest in brothels in his war memoir, *Goodbye to All That*. Graves was perhaps more fearful of the dangers of venereal disease than most of his colleagues, since many believed "they had a good chance of being killed within a few weeks anyhow." Graves often "excused himself" from visiting brothels with other men, not on moral grounds, he wrote, but "because I didn't want a dose [of venereal disease]."

Getting into a brothel could be difficult. In France, Graves witnessed long lines in front of brothels, up to 150 strong. Complicating matters, visiting a brothel could present more difficulties than simply waiting in line. Some soldiers had trouble finding the money required (about ten francs or eight shillings). Once at the brothel, many soldiers were in for a surprise, as women working as prostitutes quickly learned to exploit young men's eagerness for a sexual encounter so that they could pass rapidly from one client to the next. According to Graves, the demands of the job left the women worn out after three weeks, at which point "she retired on her earnings, pale but proud." (And, in some cases, with a venereal disease that would eventually ruin her health.)

Stories circulated among soldiers and officials that a single prostitute could service a battalion of men a week, or upwards of sixty to eighty men a day, for as long as she was able. According to Robert Graves, three weeks was the maximum a woman could endure. In Paris, French police doctor Léon Bizard reported similar statistics. Near the front especially, women found ample, if disagreeable, work in the sexual economy. "There," Bizard wrote, "it was a pressing crowd, a hard, dangerous and sickening 'business': fifty, sixty, even one hundred men of all colors and races, 'to do' per day," all under the continual threat from aircraft attack and artillery bombardments. The prostitutes who had been on the front lines explained to Bizard that "the profession was so laborious—eighteen hours of 'slaving at it' per day!—that every month, even every 2 weeks, [the women] had to go to Paris to regain their strength." But by that time, Bizard wrote, they had earned nearly a fortune and could begin life anew. "Decidedly," he commented, "the war created some nouveaux riches."

Not all prostitutes left the business quickly or stayed near the front lines to work. Some in Paris made use of the war to turn small brothels into larger businesses, later selling them for a fortune. In one case, Aline Zink, a 25-year-old former *fille soumise* (unregistered prostitute), purchased a small Parisian brothel on the Boulevard la Chapelle for 3,500 francs. Her *maison de rendez-vous* contained a bar area, a salon, and a kitchen on the ground floor. Eight bedrooms existed on the second floor of the house, with many rented out to women who stayed there as *pensionnaires*—those who worked as prostitutes in the rooms, renting the spaces. From eight in the morning until midnight, Zink allowed four women dressed in street clothes to make themselves available to clients with each visit costing a minimum of three francs. Shortly after she opened her brothel, Aline Zink married, and, in typical bourgeois style, lived elsewhere with her husband.

Zink did not allow the women to cause problems and developed a solid working relationship with the police. She made certain that her house had a doctor so that all women received medical exams and documentation to continue working. This provided a trouble-free establishment for the police to monitor. The police closed the Pannier Fleuri only once during the war, for a minor infraction. Zink never tried to avoid interacting with the police or to circumvent regulation. On several occasions Zink assisted the police, offering information they considered useful. Aline Zink and her husband, now a war veteran, later sold the brothel for a tidy profit and began a new life.

Restricting prostitution during the Great War never really slowed the spread of disease. This came only at the end of the war, when soldiers began to return home and resume a more normal life. However, throughout the conflict, each of the warring nations would worry about the role of women and their possible connections to prostitution, the threat of venereal disease, and the importance of ensuring the health of men while simultaneously increasing restrictions on prostitutes.

Michelle K. Rhoades

See also
Defence of the Realm Act; Graves, Robert Ranke; Medicine in the War; Women in the War.

References
Grayzel, Susan. *Women's Identities at War.* Chapel Hill: University of North Carolina Press, 1999.

Rhoades, Michelle K. "'No Safe Women': Prostitution, Masculinity, and Disease in France during the Great War." Unpublished doctoral dissertation, University of Iowa, 2001.

———. "'There Are No Safe Women': Prostitution in France during the Great War." *Proceedings of the Western Society for French History* 27 (2001): 43–50.

Sauertig, Lutz D. H. "Sex, Medicine and Morality during the First World War." In *War, Medicine and Modernity,* ed. Roger Cooter, Mark Harrison, and Steve Sturdy. Phoenix Mill, Stroud, UK: Sutton, 1998.

Protopopov, Aleksandr Dmitriyevich (1866–1918)

Russian politician. Born on 30 December 1866 in Simbirsk Province, Aleksandr Protopopov was of noble descent. After studying law, he returned to his hometown to run his family's textile factory. His work with the local zemstvo (assembly) led eventually to election to the Third and Fourth Dumas as a member of the Octobrist Party. A liberal reputation, gained in part by Protopopov's frequent championing of Jewish rights, led to his selection as a Duma vice-president in 1914.

Russian politician Aleksandr Protopopov was minister of the interior at the time of the 1917 Russian Revolution and was a close friend of Grigory Rasputin. (Corbis)

In 1915 Protopopov was appointed to chair the war industries committee on metals.

In early 1916 Protopopov visited several of the capitals of Russia's allies at the head of a Duma delegation. On his way back to St. Petersburg, he met with a German diplomat in Stockholm who was seeking to extend peace feelers. This encounter, however, led nowhere. Protopopov made a full report on the matter to Tsar Nicholas II and to the Duma, but the incident later gave rise to rumors of treason.

After his return, Protopopov became acquainted with Grigory Rasputin when the holy man was summoned to cure a deteriorating case of late-stage syphilis. Rasputin's influence led Nicholas to appoint Protopopov minister of internal affairs in September 1916. The tsar hoped that Protopopov's political antecedants would help mollify relations with the

Duma, the members of which were increasingly critical of the government. However, the by-now insane Protopopov merely further infuriated his former colleagues by attending Duma sessions wearing a uniform of the hated gendarmerie. His manifest incompetence, increasingly close relationship with Tsarina Alexandra (with whom he conducted seances to contact Rasputin), and rumors of treason inspired repeated calls for his ouster, but Protopopov retained his post until the collapse of the Romanov Dynasty. Arrested after the March 1917 revolution, he was shot by the Bolsheviks on 1 January 1918.

John M. Jennings

See also
Alexandra Fyodorovna, Tsarina; Nicholas II, Tsar; Rasputin, Grigory Yefimovich; Russia, Home Front; Russia, Revolution of March 1917.

References
Hasegawa Tsuyoshi. *The February Revolution: Petrograd, 1917.* Seattle: University of Washington Press, 1981.
Lincoln, W. Bruce. *Passage through Armageddon: The Russians in War and Revolution, 1914–1918.* New York: Simon and Schuster, 1986.

Przemyśl

Austro-Hungarian fortress in Galicia. Controlling the San River and a natural passage through the Carpathian Mountains, Przemyśl had been a fortress town since the eighth century. The Habsburgs converted it to a ring fortress beginning in 1887, and the Archduke Franz Ferdinand was a special patron of Przemyśl. Covering over 9 square miles and comprised of some thirty smaller forts, bastions, and gates, it was the third largest fortification in Europe and, at the beginning of World War I, housed the Austrian Army General Headquarters.

The jewel in the Austro-Hungarian defensive crown, as well as the gateway to Hungary and the key to Galicia, Przemyśl was twice besieged during the conflict of 1914–1918. It held a garrison of 120,000 men and, supposedly, supplies adequate to withstand a three-year siege. The railway line to Budapest was in any case direct, double-tracked and capable of carrying heavy, fast trains that would enable rapid reinforcement. The Austrian commander-in-chief, Field Marshal Franz Conrad von Hötzendorf, placed so much faith in Przemyśl that he slept on a field bed in the Zasani Barracks there during the opening days of the war.

Although the Austrian high command intended Przemyśl to function as a supply depot and rearguard support, the fortress became the launching point for the initial attacks of August 1914. Plagued by uncertainty, the General Staff initially sent several divisions south against Belgrade only to recall them two days later for use in the northward thrust against Russia.

Imperial railroad officials, already overwhelmed by the logistics of mobilization, routed the troop train only to Przemyśl, mistakenly thinking that the track beyond was incapable of bearing the traffic. The Habsburg troops therefore detrained at the fortress and were marching to the planned attack zones nearly 75 miles forward when they encountered the Russians. When Russian forces pushed the Habsburg armies back in mid-September, therefore, the fortress was isolated and then besieged by Russian General Selivanov's Eleventh Army. The Russians, however, could not take Przemyśl.

Reinforced by Germany's newly created Ninth Army, Conrad set out to rescue Przemyśl in early October. The attack caught the Russian troops as they were repositioning, allowing Austro-Hungarian forces to lift the siege of the fortress on 17 October 1914. Success was fleeting, as the numerically superior Russians quickly regrouped and drove Conrad's forces back across the San, with the Eleventh Army once again investing Przemyśl at the end of the month. The multinational garrison now found itself nearly 50 miles behind enemy lines, its stores reduced from having provisioned its would-be rescuers, and winter fast approaching.

Not until January 1915 could Conrad even muster the forces to mount a second relief operation. Employing two and a half German infantry divisions and one of cavalry in combination with an equal Austro-Hungarian force, Conrad struck at the center of the Russian line on 23 January. The attack rolled forward until bad weather struck. The roads, which had briefly thawed, froze again as a cold front swept over the front lines. Entire bivouaced units froze to death while the offensive stalled. Only after a month of fighting did Conrad's troops take the Carpathian passes that had been the first day's objective.

A second offensive launched in mid-February met a similar fate. All told, these two actions cost Conrad 800,000 casualties. Faced with this situation, the defenders of Przemyśl elected to surrender on 22 March 1915, though eyewitnesses reported over a year's worth of supplies remaining. The Russians took 117,000 prisoners. The Austro-Hungarian army forces did explode much of the useful war matériel prior to the surrender, however.

Austro-Hungarian propaganda of the day trumpeted the heroic defense of the bastion. In truth, little fighting took place during the siege. The Russians did not possess sufficient heavy artillery to shell the fortress and could not maneuver what guns they had through the heavy ice and mud. The garrison made only token attempts to break the siege and, according to contemporary reports, appeared indifferent to its capture. Victory at Przemyśl was more a matter of Austrian ineptitude and internecine rivalry among the troops than anything the Russians did. Observers styled the fall of Przemyśl as a "second Metz," noting that the Russians now held a splendid base for an advance into Hungary.

Przemyśl forts after German bombardment. (John Clark Ridpath, *Ridpath's History of the World,* Vol. 10, Jones Bros., Cincinnati, 1921)

On 2 May 1915, however, before the Russians could take advantage of their prize, Conrad launched yet another offensive to retake the fortress. This attack, spearheaded by German troops, carried through to Przemyśl on 4 June. The outnumbered Russians quickly retreated. They had in any case rendered the fortress largely useless by stripping it of most defensive matériel, including entrenching tools and wire. Most of this had been sold to the local populace.

In November 1918, the fortress became a bone of contention between Ukrainian and Polish partisans. Seven days after the Ukrainian coup d'état of 3–4 November, General Władysław Sikorski led the new Polish army to victory at Przemyśl. His campaign ensured that Lvov and Galicia would become part of the new Polish state.

Timothy C. Dowling

See also
Conrad von Hötzendorf, Franz, Count; Franz Ferdinand, Archduke.

References
Herwig, Holger H. *The First World War: Germany and Austria-Hungary, 1914–1918.* New York: St. Martin's, 1997.
Materniak, Ireneusz. *Przemy'sl, 1914–15.* Warsaw: Altair, 1994.
Sondhaus, Lawrence. *Franz Conrad von Hötzendorf: Architect of the Apocalypse.* Boston: Humanities, 2000.
Stone, Norman. *The Eastern Front, 1914–1917.* New York: Scribner, 1975.

Pulkowski, Erich (1877–?)

German army officer. Born into a military family in 1877, Erich Pulkowski joined the German army. While assigned to the Foot Artillery School of Fire in 1917, he developed a system of predicting artillery registration corrections without having to actually fire the guns. This breakthrough greatly increased the element of surprise in the attack, because a battery of guns could then covertly occupy its position on the battlefield and remain silent until the start of the attack. The Pulkowski Method (Pulkowski Verfahren, as it was called in the German army), used correction factors from current weather data combined with previously measured muzzle velocity errors from individual guns to derive the predicted registration corrections. The elements of the calculations were exactly the same as the system still used by all NATO armies at the start of the twenty-first century: wind speed, wind direction, air temperature, air density, rotation of the earth, propellant temperature, and velocity error.

Pulkowski had a hard time convincing the German army to adopt his system. Early in 1918 Colonel Georg Bruchmüller learned about it and realized that it offered a solution to many of the tactical problems he was working to solve. Bruchmüller employed a modified form of the Pulkowski Method during the Eighteenth Army's attack at Saint-Quentin in March 1918. Within a few months the system became standard throughout the German army, with Pulkowski constantly moving up and down the front conducting training classes.

Pulkowski's father was also a Foot Artillery officer, as were two of his brothers. Another brother was a Field Artillery officer. All four Pulkowski brothers served in World War I. Despite his significant technical contribution, Pulkowski was not retained in the postwar Reichwehr. He retired from the German army with the rank of major and took over the management of his family's toy business in Cologne.

David T. Zabecki

See also
Artillery; Bruchmüller, Georg; Infantry Tactics; Ludendorff Offensives; Saint-Quentin Offensive.

References
Paschall, Rod. *The Defeat of Imperial Germany, 1917–1918*. Chapel Hill, NC: Algonquin, 1989.
Zabecki, David T. *Steel Wind: Georg Bruchmüller and the Birth of Modern Artillery*. Westport, CT: Praeger, 1994.

Putnik, Radomir (1847–1917)

Serbian army field marshal. Born on 24 January 1847 at Kragujevac, Serbia, Radomir Putnik was educated at the Serbian Artillery School and commissioned in 1866. He led a brigade in fighting against Turkey in 1876 and in 1877–1878, and he was chief of staff of a division in the war against Bulgaria in 1885. After attending the staff college in 1889, Putnik was appointed deputy army chief of staff and served as an instructor at the military academy. Forced into early retirement in 1895, he was recalled and promoted to general when the Karageorgević dynasty took power in 1903. Putnik then served as army chief of staff from 1903 to 1917, save for three brief periods when he was minister of war (1904–1905, 1906–1908, and 1912). Putnik modernized the Serbian army and led it in the

Serbian Army Field Marshal Radomir Putnik led his army in stunning defeats of Austro-Hungarian invading forces in 1914. (Library of Congress)

Balkan Wars during 1912–1913, defeating the Turks at Kumanovo in October 1912, for which he was promoted to field marshal, and at Monastir in November 1912, and defeating the Bulgarians at Bregalnica during June–July 1913.

In poor health, Putnik was recovering at an Austrian spa when World War I began, but Emperor Franz Joseph ordered his release and return to Serbia. Putnik subsequently led the Serbs to stunning victories over Austro-Hungarian forces at the Battle of the Drina River in August and at the Kolumbara River in December 1914. Overwhelmed by the three-sided attack of the Germans, Austro-Hungarians, and Bulgarians under General August von Mackensen in October–November 1915, Putnik was forced to order a difficult winter retreat through Albania.

Carried over the mountains in a sedan chair by his soldiers, Putnik reached Scutari on 7 December 1915. No longer able to command, Putnik was evacuated to France where he died at Nice on 17 May 1917. Certainly Serbia's greatest soldier of modern times, Field Marshal Radomir Putnik was perhaps the best field commander on either side in the Balkans during World War I. He demonstrated outstanding strategic and tactical competence as well as the ability to inspire his troops and lead them to victory against great odds.

Charles R. Shrader

See also

Alexander Karageorgević, Prince; Balkan Front; Balkan Wars; Drina River, Battle of the; Jadar River, Battle of the; Kolubara River, Battle of the; Mišić, Živojin; Peter I Karageorgević, King; Serbia, Conquest of; Serbia, Role in War.

References

Djordjevic, Dimitrije. "Vojvoda Putnik, the Serbian High Command, and Strategy in 1914." In *East Central European Society in World War I,* ed. Béla K. Király and Nandor F. Dresziger, 569–589. Boulder, CO: Social Science Monographs, 1985.

———. "Vojvoda Radomir Putnik." In *East European War Leaders: Civilian and Military,* ed. Béla K. Király and Albert A. Nofi, 223–248. Boulder, CO: Social Science Monographs, 1988.

Skoko, Savo. *Vojvoda Radomir Putnik.* 2 vols. Belgrade: Beogradski izdavaichko-graiichki zavod, 1984.

Q

Qingdao, Siege of
(23 August–7 November 1914)

Only major World War I land battle in east Asia. The siege of Qingdao (Tsingtao) pitted Japan and Germany against one another. It also marked the first time that a unit of the British army fought under non-European command.

Between 1897 and 1913 Germans built from scratch a European-style fortress city on the tip of China's Shandong (Shantung) Peninsula. Located halfway between Tianjin (Tientsin) in Hobei (Hopeh) province and Shanghai in Jiangsu (Kiangsu) province, Qingdao commanded the entrance to Kaiochow Bay, the principal German navy base in the Pacific.

Qingdao contained extensive port facilities, including one of the largest dry docks in the world. The city was defended by a ring of small sea forts around the lower end of the peninsula, anchored by a major fort on the bay side and another on the Yellow Sea side. The main forts mounted 210mm and 240mm guns in revolving turrets.

Remembering all too well the Russian experience at Port Arthur (called by the Chinese Lushang) during the 1904–1905 Russo-Japanese War, the Germans also constructed land defenses to thwart any ground attack from China. Qingdao's main defenses were set into two ranges of low hills that spanned the peninsula above the city. Four miles from the city, the inner defensive line was based on powerful Fort Bismarck in the center, supported by a fort at either end of the line. Fort Bismarck was armed with 280mm howitzers and 210mm guns in reinforced concrete casemates, while the two flank forts had 105mm and 120mm guns in open batteries. Interspersed between the forts the Germans placed some 90 guns, ranging in size from 37mm to 90mm.

The far weaker outer line was 8 miles above the city, where the peninsula was 12 miles wide. Unfortunately for the Germans, the Qingdao garrison was never large enough for them to man both defensive lines adequately. The key terrain on the outer line, 1,200-foot-high Prinz Heinrich Hill on the southern flank, was never sufficiently fortified. Between the two lines of forts, the German intermediate defensive zone in the flat, marshy Haipo (Hai P'o) River valley contained five reinforced concrete redoubts, each with a garrison of about 200 troops.

Japan had signed an alliance with Great Britain in 1902, and the leaders in Tokyo saw in World War I an opportunity to eject Germany from east Asia. On 15 August 1914, using the justification of the Japanese-British alliance, Japan issued an ultimatum to the Germans in Qingdao. They had until 23 August to evacuate and abandon the colony without compensation. The German governor, navy Captain Alfred Meyer-Waldeck, rejected the ultimatum and prepared for a siege as the Germans began to evacuate nonessential civilians. Even before the Japanese ultimatum, on 4 August the German cruiser squadron under the command of Vice Admiral Maximilian von Spee departed Qingdao for the safety of open waters, not wishing to repeat the mistake the Russians had made ten years earlier in allowing their ships to be bottled up at Port Arthur.

Even after calling in German reservists from all over Asia, Meyer-Waldeck still had only about 4,600 troops. His sole remaining naval units were the obsolete Austrian cruiser *Kaiserin Elizabeth*, the torpedo boat *S-90*, and five small gunboats. His air force consisted of one observation balloon and one Rumpler Taube monoplane, piloted by navy Lieutenant Günther Plueschow.

Japanese sailors coming ashore near Qingdao (Tsingtao), 1914. (Library of Congress)

Believing themselves obligated to support the Japanese operation, the British sent the old predreadnought *Triumph* and a token land force consisting of the 2nd Battalion, South Wales Borders from Tianjin, and a half battalion of the 36th Sikhs. British ground troops were under the command of Brigadier-General Nathaniel Barnardiston, who was outraged at being the first British commander to serve in the field under a non-European superior commander.

On 2 September the Japanese ground force, commanded by Lieutenant General Kamio Mitsuom, began coming ashore at Longkou (Lungkow) Bay some 100 miles north of Qingdao. By the time the Japanese were ready to mount their main attack, they had more than 50,000 troops ashore, with another 10,000 still in reserve offshore. The 24th Heavy Artillery Brigade alone had in excess of 100 guns and howitzers larger than 120mm. The German defenders were outnumbered at least thirteen to one.

On 28 September the Japanese attacked and captured Prinz Heinrich Hill, and the rest of the outer defensive line fell within hours. Continuing the fight from the intermediate defensive zone, the German artillery put up a stiff and effective resistance. But on 7 October, the sole German observa-

tion balloon broke loose of its mooring and drifted to sea. From that point on the German artillery was firing blind.

It took the Japanese most of October to move their heavy artillery forward for the attack on the intermediate defensive zone. In the meantime, most of the fighting took place at sea, with the German coastal batteries exchanging fire with the Japanese fleet, and the small handful of German fighting ships carrying out hit-and-run raids. On 17 October the torpedo boat *S-90* managed to sink the minelayer *Takashio,* with the loss of 250 Japanese sailors.

On 31 October the Japanese heavy artillery began firing on Qingdao itself. Their ground forces simultaneously began attacking the intermediate defensive zone using classic siege techniques. By 1 November Meyer-Waldeck knew that the end was near, and he ordered the start of the systematic destruction of anything in Qingdao that might be useful to the Japanese. By 5 November Japanese artillery fire had neutralized almost all the German minefields and wire entanglements, and the German artillery was almost out of ammunition. Early on 6 November, under orders from Meyer-Waldeck, Lieutenant Gunther Plüschow loaded Qingdao's war diaries and other secret papers into his monoplane and headed for neutral Chinese territory. Plüschow eventually made it back to Germany.

The last German position surrendered at 9:30 A.M. on 7 November. The operation had cost the Japanese 1,445 killed and 4,200 wounded. The British lost 14 killed and 61 wounded. Despite the massive pounding they had taken from both sea- and land-based heavy artillery, the Germans suffered only 200 killed and 500 wounded. Qingdao is significant as one of history's last large-scale actions involving coastal artillery. It also was one of the first major battles in which air, land, and sea power all combined to play key and mutually supporting roles. Despite their relatively high casualty rate, the Japanese military demonstrated a mastery of joint operations far beyond the capability of most armies of 1914.

David T. Zabecki

See also

Amphibious Warfare; Japan, Army; Japan, Home Front; Kamio Mitsuomi; Spee, Maximilian von, Count.

References

Burdick, Charles B. *The Japanese Siege of Tsingtao*. Hamden, CT: Archon, 1976.

Edgerton, Robert B. *Warriors of the Rusing Sun: A History of the Japanese Military*. New York: Norton, 1997.

Hoyt, Edwin P. *The Fall of Tsingtao*. London: A. Barker, 1975.

Jones, Jefferson. *The Fall of Tsingtau: With a Study of Japan's Ambitions in China*. Boston: Houghton Mifflin, 1915.

Q-Ships

During World War I the term "Q-ship" or "Mystery Ship" referred to a disguised British submarine hunter. Also known as "Decoy Vessels" or "Towed Service Ships," they were usually former merchant, cargo, supply, or collier ships. Some were even ex-fishing vessels or Flower-class sailing ships. Most British Q-ships were relatively small and apparently poorly maintained, in order to lull German submarine captains into a false sense of security. Most flew the flags of a variety of neutral nations and posed as ships on peaceful commercial missions. Under international maritime law of the day, such deception was legal as long as the British naval ensign was displayed just prior to an engagement.

The British Admiralty adopted the Q-ships because of the heavy loss of merchant shipping to German U-boats, especially during the first year of World War I. Standard tactics

British Navy Q-ship *Suffolk Coast*, was used as a decoy to capture or destroy submarines. Here is a view of the dummy deckhouse, showing the gun that was concealed until the doors fell at a signal from the bridge. (S. J. Duncan Clark and W. R. Plewman, *Pictorial History of the Great War*, with W. S. Wallace, *Canada in the Great War*, 5th ed., John A. Hertel, Toronto, 1919)

involved the Q-ship attempting to decoy a German submarine to the surface, often by coming to a complete stop, lowering its colors, and launching lifeboats, generally a sure sign of surrender. If the submarine surfaced and came within range, the real crew, hidden during the initial contact, would rush to their guns to fire on the U-boat and attempt to sink it.

Q-ships were usually armed with one 4-inch and two 12-pounder guns. These were hidden behind hinged bulwarks, inside false superstructures and false deck cargoes, or under dummy lifeboats. Out of necessity Q-ships frequently changed their names and disguises. Q-ships were often equipped with a bladder or other device to increase their buoyancy sufficient to survive one or two torpedo hits to the hull. Some Q-ships towed older submarines just below the surface. When contacted by the enemy U-boat, the trawler crew kept the attention of the U-boat while they released their own submarine to attack the enemy sub and attempt to torpedo it. Such tactics had some success early in the war when German submarines, often on unescorted patrols, preferred to attack smaller unarmed ships by firing from their deck guns rather than using torpedoes, a tactic that allowed the U-boat to remain longer at sea.

Numbers vary widely, depending on the source, but the Royal Navy deployed between 200 and 300 Q-ships and lost between 38 and 61 of them. One official source states that 30 percent of all U-boats destroyed by surface ships in the war were the victims of Q-ships.

Predictably, the greatest successes of Q-ships came early. As the war progressed, only the ablest and craftiest captains still sank U-boats. Indeed, many Q-ships were lost. After the war most surviving Q-ships were returned to commercial service. In 1939, with the advent of World War II, the Royal Navy resurrected the Q-ships. Beginning in 1942, the U.S. Navy also deployed Q-ships in the Pacific theater.

William Head

See also
Antisubmarine Campaign, Allied Powers.
References
Bridgland, Tony. *Sea Killers in Disguise: The Story of the Q-Ships and Decoy Ships in the First World War.* Annapolis: Naval Institute Press, 1999.
Chatterton, E. Keble. *Q-Ships and Their Story.* Annapolis: Naval Institute Press, 1972.
Dower, John W. *War without Mercy.* New York: Pantheon, 1986.

Queen Elizabeth-Class Battleships

A class of five British superdreadnoughts completed in 1915 and 1916 that served extensively in both world wars. Besides the *Queen Elizabeth,* the class included the *Warspite, Valiant, Barham,* and *Malaya.* Their design was developed from that of the Iron Duke-class that immediately preceded them but enlarged and modified to carry a principal armament of 15-inch guns, a new standard. The Queen Elizabeth-class ships were also the first capital ships designed for oil-fired boilers. Displacing 27,500 tons, they were 646 feet long and 90.5 feet wide, armed with 8 × 15-inch guns in four superimposed midline turrets and 16 × 6-inch guns, protected by armor with a 13-inch maximum on the main belt and turrets. Their rated speed was 23 knots, and they carried a crew of 925 men.

Originally planned as a four-ship squadron, the class received a fifth unit, the *Malaya,* financed by a gift from the Federated Malay States. Except for the *Queen Elizabeth,* refitting after service at the Dardanelles in 1915, all fought as the 5th Battle Squadron at Jutland on 31 May–1 June 1916, where *Warspite* was heavily damaged. In 1917–1918 the *Queen Elizabeth* served as flagship of the Grand Fleet, receiving the surrender of the German High Seas Fleet on 17 November 1918.

In the later 1920s all the Queen Elizabeth-class ships were fitted with trunked funnels, antitorpedo bulges, and antiaircraft guns. The *Queen Elizabeth, Warspite,* and *Valiant* received more extensive rebuilds after 1934, including new engines, aircraft facilities, and modernized superstructures.

In World War II the *Barham* was lost in the Mediterranean on 25 November 1941 to three torpedoes from the German submarine *U-331.* The other units of the class survived the war. The *Warspite* was sold for scrap in 1946; the *Malaya, Valiant,* and *Queen Elizabeth* followed in 1948.

John A. Hutcheson Jr.

See also
Battleships; Great Britain, Navy; Naval Balance; Naval Warfare.
References
Gibbons, Tony. *The Complete Encyclopedia of Battleships.* New York: Crescent, 1983.
Moore, John. *Jane's Fighting Ships of World War I.* London: Random House, 1990.

Qurna, Battle of (4–9 December 1915)

British amphibious operation against the Turks in Mesopotamia. Qurna is located at the junction of the "Old" Euphrates River with the Tigris River, 40 miles north of Basra. For half of the year the Euphrates flooded its shallow bed, turning the surrounding desert into an immense lake.

Following their defeat at Basra in November 1914, Colonel Subhi Bey's Turkish forces fell back on Qurna to resupply and reinforce. British area commander Lieutenant General Sir Arthur Barrett's orders called for him to secure Basra but also allowed him to move up the river as far as he believed necessary to protect that port.

On 3 December Barrett dispatched upriver in steamers a combined force of two Indian battalions and a double company from the Royal Norfolk Regiment, along with some sappers and several field guns. The next morning the assault force went ashore, covered by naval gunfire from accompanying British gunboats.

Concealed Turkish guns in Muzereh Village opened heavy fire on the British vessels. The guns were difficult to locate from the river, and the ships took a number of hits. Hit at the waterline, the *Miner* was forced to withdraw. Despite taking damage, the British ships lent effective gunnery support to the troops ashore. Shells from the *Espiègle* set Muzereh on fire and forced the Turks from their concealed positions in date palm groves.

Because Turkish defensive positions were only partially completed, British and Indian land forces were able to control the riverbank opposite Qurna. Heavy Turkish gunfire, however, forced the British to retire for the night and await reinforcements.

At dawn on 6 December Major General C. I. Fry arrived with the remaining Norfolks, two additional Indian army battalions, and a mountain battery. Subhi Bey's troops, meanwhile, had reoccupied their old positions and both sides were forced to re-engage once again along the same lines. British land forces made steady progress, and the Turks were eventually forced to retreat again across the Tigris to Qurna.

On the morning of 8 December, British ships moved past the river junction, enabling them to fire into the town. Two Indian battalions and some sappers, supported by mountain guns, marched up the left bank well away from the river, then turned toward it. Soon the British were ferrying troops a mile and a half north of Qurna. Turkish communications were now cut and the escape route closed.

British vessels continued shelling Qurna until the next day, 9 December, when Fry demanded and received Subhi Bey's unconditional surrender. In the battle the British land force sustained 27 dead and 292 wounded; 2 sailors were also killed and 2 wounded. Some 1,000 Turks (including 42 officers) surrendered. The capture of Qurna solidified the British hold on Basra.

Christopher J. Richman

See also
Mesopotamian Theater.

References

Barker, A. J. *The Bastard War: The Mesopotamian Campaign of 1914–1918.* New York: Dial, 1967.

McEntee, Girard Lindsley. *Military History of the World War.* New York: Scribner, 1943.

Moberly, F. J. *The Campaign in Mesopotamia, 1914–1918.* 3 vols. Nashville, TN: Battery Press, 1997–1998.

R

Race to the Sea (September–November 1914)

Series of battles in northern France and Belgium in the autumn of 1914. Following the Anglo-French counteroffensive at the Marne, stalemate emerged along the Aisne River valley in mid-September. Consequently, in the area from the Aisne north to the English Channel, both Allied and German forces initiated a series of attempts to outflank the other.

This process, the so-called Race to the Sea, was in fact a race to find an open flank on which to resume mobile operations with the intent of bringing the war to decisive conclusion. From late September until mid-November, however, neither side was able to reach open territory in advance of the other. The result was a series of violent collisions that ended with Belgian, French, and British forces facing their German adversaries in static positions extending from the English Channel to the Swiss border.

On 14 September, following the German defeat in the First Battle of the Marne, General Erich van Falkenhayn replaced General Helmuth von Moltke as chief of the German General Staff. Falkenhayn decided to revive the failed Schlieffen Plan by sending German forces around the French left flank on the Aisne. Simultaneously French army commander General Joseph Joffre resolved to outflank the German right at Noyon. Consequently, in the second half of September, units of General Noël de Castelnau's French Second Army collided with those of Crown Prince Rupprecht's German Sixth Army as both formations stretched to the northwest in an effort to find open territory.

Fighting intensified in early October as the two forces clashed around Arras, an important transportation hub in northern France. On 1 October two French infantry corps and one cavalry corps under General Louis Ernest de Maud'huy began pushing toward Arras from the west. At the same time, units of the German Sixth Army were approaching the city from the east. Crown Prince Rupprecht intended to hold the French at Arras while wheeling forces to the north of the city, thereby outflanking the French wing. By the evening of 4 October, Maud'huy's force was in danger of being encircled. German units had occupied the city of Lens to the north, while French Territorial units south of Arras were giving way under heavy German pressure.

Both Castelnau and Maud'huy suggested retreat. Unwilling to concede Arras, Joffre quickly reorganized the French forces in the vicinity. Detaching Maud'huy's force from the Second Army, he designated it the Tenth Army and placed both formations under General Ferdinand Foch. From 5 October Foch forbade retirement from Arras. Despite heavy losses, French forces held their positions. By the evening of the 6th, German pressure had diminished, as Falkenhayn decided to cease attacks in the vicinity. Both he and Joffre subsequently turned their attention northward.

While Rupprecht's German Sixth Army attempted to turn the Allied flank in northern France in late September, Falkenhayn had directed III Reserve Corps, commanded by General Hans von Beseler, to besiege the fortified Belgian port city of Antwerp. The capture of Antwerp and destruction of the Belgian army, which was using the city as a base, would ensure the safety of German lines of communication west. It would also remove any impetus for the dispatch of British forces to Belgium. This, combined with the operations of the Sixth Army to the south, would leave the Germans in control of

German General Erich von Falkenhayn, who became Chief of the German General Staff in mid-September 1914, following the dismissal of General Helmuth von Moltke. (Library of Congress)

French and Belgian territory from the Somme River north to the English Channel, enabling their forces to outflank the Anglo-French armies and march on Paris.

With this intent, Beseler's forces opened the siege of Antwerp on 28 September. After subjecting the city to an intense artillery bombardment, on 1 October Beseler initiated infantry attacks. With only limited French and British assistance forthcoming, Antwerp capitulated on the 10th. The Belgian army, however, escaped and retired behind the River Yser. This development presented a problem for Falkenhayn. In early October he had assembled in Belgium the Fourth Army under Albrecht, Duke of Württemberg. Falkenhayn intended to send the Fourth Army southward into France in an attempt to outflank the Allied left wing, but the presence of 53,000 Belgian troops at the Yser inhibited Württemberg's freedom of movement.

Consequently, on 18 October the German Fourth Army attacked Belgian positions along the Yser. Although they were supported by French forces and British naval guns in the English Channel, the Belgians were slowly forced to give

ground. In desperation, on the 27th King Albert I ordered the locks at Nieuport opened, inundating the countryside. By 31 October the rising water level had created an impassable barrier for the Germans, thereby securing the Allied left flank.

By this point German and Allied efforts were concentrated around the Belgian town of Ypres. In early October the British Expeditionary Force (BEF) had begun transferring from positions on the Aisne to northern France and Flanders. As elements of the BEF arrived in the area between La Bassee and Ypres, British commander Sir John French directed them to advance. By mid-October, however, they faced increasing resistance from German cavalry, which preceded the arrival of more substantial forces. By 19 October elements of Württemberg's Fourth Army and Rupprecht's Sixth Army had assembled and began advancing westward, north and south of Ypres, respectively. The BEF was forced onto the defensive, but the timely arrival of French and Indian reinforcements prevented a German breakthrough.

By late October, Falkenhayn's search for open ground was becoming increasingly desperate. In an effort to resume mobile operations before the arrival of additional Allied troops, he quickly assembled a new force between the Fourth and Sixth Armies. It consisted of six divisions and more than 250 heavy guns formed into Army Group Fabeck. Falkenhayn now directed these forces to punch through the fragile British line south of Ypres.

British units at Ypres weathered fierce German attacks during 29–31 October. On the afternoon of the 31st, elements of Army Group Fabeck nearly broke through at Gheluvelt. In early November, however, pressure on the BEF subsided, as French reinforcements launched counterattacks around Ypres and mounting losses diminished the intensity of the German offensive. Falkenhayn made a final effort on 10–11 November. On the 11th the Prussian Guards managed to crack the British line south of Ypres, but the British again recovered. By 13 November the fighting around Ypres had largely subsided, and the Race to the Sea was over.

The Race to the Sea left both German and Allied forces exhausted. For the balance of 1914, both sides could do little more than replenish their losses and fortify the continuous lines that now covered the Western Front from the Swiss border to the English Channel. The elaborate trench systems that developed would not be breached until 1918.

Nikolas Gardner

See also

Aisne, First Battle of the; Albert, First Battle of; Albrecht, Duke of Württemberg; Antwerp, Siege of; Arras, First Battle of; Castelnau, Noël de; Falkenhayn, Erich von; Foch, Ferdinand; French, John, 1st Earl of Ypres; Joffre, Joseph; Marne, First Battle of the; Maud'huy, Louis Ernest de; Rupprecht, Crown Prince; Schlieffen Plan; Ypres, First Battle of; Yser, Battle of.

References

Farrar-Hockley, Anthony. *Death of an Army*. New York: Morrow, 1968.

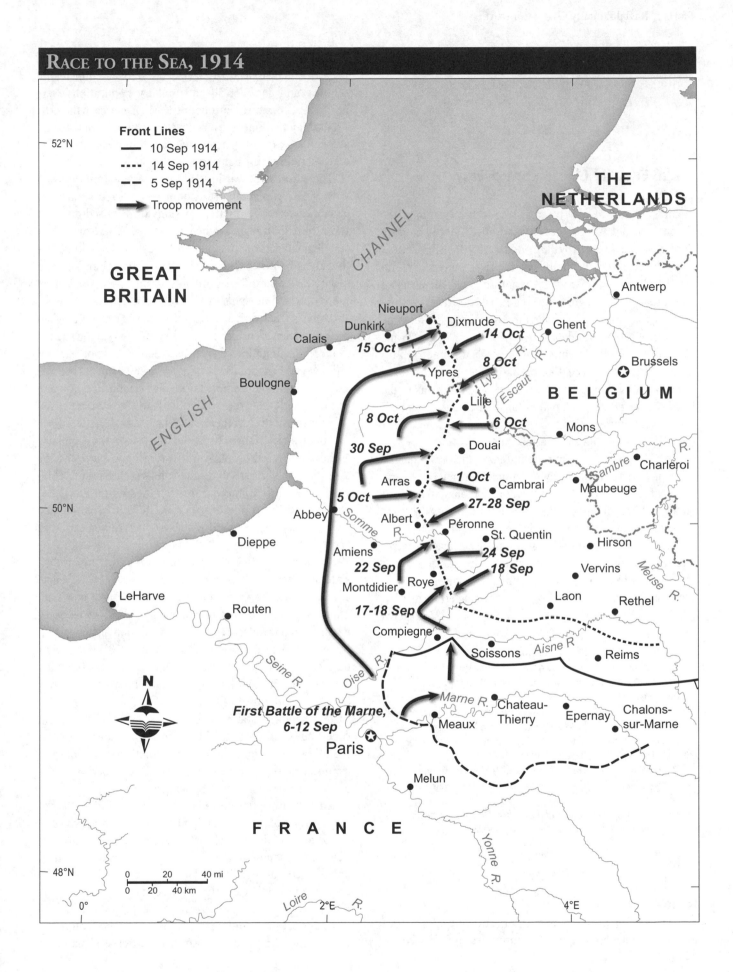

RACE TO THE SEA, 1914

Front Lines
— 10 Sep 1914
···· 14 Sep 1914
– – 5 Sep 1914
→ Troop movement

52°N

GREAT BRITAIN

THE NETHERLANDS

ENGLISH CHANNEL

Antwerp

Calais
Dunkirk
Nieuport
Dixmude **14 Oct**
15 Oct
Ghent
Brussels
Boulogne
Ypres **8 Oct**
Lys R.
Escaut R.
BELGIUM
8 Oct
Lille
6 Oct
Mons
Douai
30 Sep
Sambre R.
Charleroi
Arras **1 Oct**
Cambrai
Maubeuge
5 Oct
50°N
Abbey
Somme R.
Albert
27-28 Sep
Péronne
St. Quentin
Hirson
Dieppe
Amiens
22 Sep
Roye **24 Sep**
18 Sep
Vervins
Meuse R.
LeHarve
Montdidier
17-18 Sep
Laon
Rethel
Routen
Compiegne
Soissons
Aisne R.
Reims
Seine R.
Oise R.
First Battle of the Marne, 6-12 Sep
Marne R.
Chateau-Thierry
Epernay
Chalons-sur-Marne
N
Paris
Meaux
Melun

FRANCE

Yonne R.

48°N

0   20   40 mi
0   20   40 km

0°
Loire R.
2°E
4°E

Herwig, Holger H. *The First World War: Germany and Austria-Hungary, 1914–1918*. New York: Arnold, 1997.

Strachan, Hew. *The First World War*, Vol. 1, *To Arms*. Oxford: Oxford University Press, 2001.

Racial Equality Clause Controversy (1919)

Japan's attempt to insert a racial equality clause into the Covenant of the League of the Nations drafted by the Paris Peace Conference was checked by the United States, Great Britain, and Australia. As one of the five major victorious powers of World War I and as the only "colored" nation among them, Japan on 13 February 1919 sought to insert a racial equality clause into the League's covenant. However, three prominent figures at the conference—U.S. President Woodrow Wilson, British Prime Minister David Lloyd George, and Australian Prime Minister William Hughes—rejected incorporating the principle of racial equality into the covenant. Anti-Japanese movements in the United States, British colonial expansionists, and Australia's exclusionary immigration policy combined to militate against those nations' acceptance of racial equality.

On 11 April Japan again sought to have the racial equality clause inserted into the covenant. In spite of a majority vote by eleven of eighteen members in favor of the request, the United States and Britain blocked the vote on the grounds that such important issues as racial equality required a unanimous as opposed to majority vote. The racial equality clause was therefore rejected. Japan's failure to secure such a clause aroused considerable resentment in Japan, but also among many "colored" nations that faced issues of racial self-determination.

Majima Ayu

See also

Fourteen Points; Hughes, William Morris; League of Nations Covenant; Lloyd George, David; March First Movement, Korea; Paris Peace Conference; Wilson, Thomas Woodrow.

References

Dickinson, Frederick R. *War and National Reinvention: Japan in the Great War, 1914–1919*. Cambridge: Harvard University Press, 1999.

MacMillan, Margaret. *Paris, 1919: Six Months That Changed the World*. New York: Random House, 2002.

Mayer, Arno J. *Politics and Diplomacy of Peacemaking: Containment and Counter-Revolution at Versailles, 1918–1919*. New York: Knopf, 1967.

Naoko Shimazu. *Japan, Race and Equality: The Racial Equality Proposal of 1919*. New York: Routledge, 1998.

Radio

Wireless (as the British termed it) or radio telegraph (code) and radio telephone (voice) communications played an expanding part in fighting, diplomacy, and propaganda. Experimental wireless had developed in the late nineteenth century, and commercial and military applications were becoming common in Europe and North America in the early 1900s. Major military powers developed significant land and sea wireless capability before the war, though its use in aircraft was still experimental.

The outbreak of war in 1914 led to severe limitations on any private use of radio in the countries involved, as virtually all commercial and amateur stations were closed down or taken over by the governments involved. The Royal Navy supplemented its own facilities in August 1914 by taking over the extensive Marconi-developed "All-Red" or Empire chain of wireless stations. These provided useful links, especially in the Southern Hemisphere where little else existed. Likewise, Washington took over all foreign-owned radio facilities when the United States entered the war in 1917. Those who tried to evade these limitations were prosecuted because of fear that radio would be employed by enemy agents. During the war extensive training programs were also established in many countries to develop the thousands of radio operators needed to supplement the few then available.

Enemy radio transmitters were often targets for military strikes, an indication of their growing importance. At the same time, the British cut German undersea telegraph cables in the early days of the war, forcing the Central Powers to employ radio transmissions, on which the British could tune and eventually understand as their code-breaking expertise expanded.

Army radio in 1914 was crude on both sides of the conflict. Antennas were obvious targets, and equipment was fragile, cumbersome, and vulnerable to weather or enemy action. There were few trained operators, and there were never enough radios available (a U.S. Army division of 20,000 men rarely had more than six radios even in 1918). But radio's biggest drawback was the lack of senior commanders willing to use or trust it in battlefield conditions. Poorly organized at first, army radio users also suffered from security breaches such as sending vital messages in the clear rather than in code. Radio was most useful away from the Western Front (in the Middle East, for example) where alternative modes of communication were rare, as was the likelihood of signal interference or enemy code breaking.

An early exception to radio's limitations was the use of radios in aircraft for artillery spotting. Demand for such service led to rapid development of lighter equipment with sufficient transmission range and various means of avoiding interference. Voice (radio telephony) communication from aircraft became possible by 1917. By the end of the war some 600 British fighter and bomber aircraft were equipped with radios.

Radio direction-finding techniques, developed before but vastly improved during the war, made wireless signaling at

German radio station on the Eastern Front, August 1917. (National Archives)

sea dangerous because triangulation could readily locate a ship's transmitter, thus placing the vessel at risk from submarine attack. Knowing this danger, Allied convoys of merchantmen usually maintained radio silence (relying on visual signals), as did most military vessels while on patrol. The German light cruiser *Emden,* for example, was successful as a commerce raider for a long period largely by keeping wireless silence. Electronic jamming of enemy radio signals was often attempted, usually with little effect.

On the other hand, radio was generally effective in both the British and German fleets and became an essential element in such large naval battles as Jutland (31 May–1 June 1916). Distance, darkness, or smoke would have made visual signals impossible. As spark-gap equipment was replaced (1916–1917) by better arc and then (1918) vacuum tube-powered equipment, naval radio's value improved further.

Wartime needs and growing equipment procurement greatly increased the pace of radio's technical development. Tube-based equipment, rare in 1914 (when obsolete spark-gap wireless telegraphy was still widespread), was becoming standard by 1918, vastly increasing radio's capabilities by adding voice to code communication. The U.S. Navy supervised a mandatory pooling of private patents "for the duration" to encourage manufacture of the best possible equipment. The U.S. Army established a large Signal Corps research center that became Fort Monmouth, New Jersey, which developed improved transmitters for use on land and in the air. Working in Paris, Signal Corps officer Major E. H. Armstrong perfected his superheterodyne receiver in 1918, an example of equipment growing from wartime needs but developed too late to be applied during hostilities.

Radio was not used for direct propaganda, as broadcasting had not yet developed. But large government stations (such as Nauen outside of Berlin and the U.S. Navy's NAL outside of Washington) were often used to transmit news reports (for use by newspapers), to stay in touch with distant bases or colonies, or to communicate important diplomatic messages such as President Woodrow Wilson's Fourteen Points in 1918.

Christopher H. Sterling

See also

Codes and Code Breaking; *Emden,* SMS; Fourteen Points; Jutland, Battle of; Propaganda; Room 40; Wilson, Thomas Woodrow; Zimmermann Telegram.

References

Hezlet, Vice Admiral Sir Arthur. *Electronics and Sea Power*. New York: Stein and Day, 1975.

Howeth, L. S. "The Golden Age." In *History of Communications: Electronics in the United States Navy*, 207–296. Washington: Government Printing Office, 1963.

Nalder, R. F. H. *The Royal Corps of Signals: A History of Its Antecedents and Development*. London: Royal Signals Institution, 1958.

Report of the Chief Signal Officer to the Secretary of War, 1919. Washington: Government Printing Office, 1919 (reprinted by Arno Press, 1974).

Schubert, Paul. "Era of Military Use." In *The Electric Word: The Rise of Radio*, 85–187. New York: Macmillan, 1928.

Thompson, George Raynor. "Radio Comes of Age in World War I." In *The Story of the U.S. Army Signal Corps*, ed. Max L. Marshall, 157–167. New York: Watts, 1965.

Wedlake, G. E. C. *SOS: The Story of Radio Communication*. North Pomfret, VT: David and Charles, 1973.

Bulgarian Premier and Minister of Foreign Affairs Vasil Hristov Radoslavov. (Francis J. Reynolds and C. W. Taylor, *Collier's Photographic History of the European War*, P. F. Collier & Son, New York, 1916)

Radoslavov, Vasil Hristov (1854–1929)

Bulgarian prime minister during 1913–1918. Born on 15 July 1854 in Lovech in what is now central Bulgaria, Vasil Radoslavov studied in Germany and received a doctorate of law from the University of Heidelberg. Upon his return to Bulgaria he joined the generally russophobic Liberal Party and served as Bulgarian minister of justice from 1884 to 1886. From 1886 to 1887 he was prime minister of Bulgaria. After this he joined the cabinet of Prime Minister Stefan Stambulov. After Stambulov's assassination in 1895, Radoslavov formed his own Liberal Party. He again served as prime minister from 1901 to 1903.

In foreign policy Radoslavov was strongly russophobic. When Russia failed to intervene to spare Bulgaria the catastrophic defeats of the Second Balkan War in 1913, Radoslavov once again assumed the office of prime minister on 4 July 1913, at the head of an anti-Russian and pro–Austro-Hungarian coalition government. The supercilious Tsar Ferdinand regarded Radoslavov as a coarse but effective advocate of his own desires in foreign policy. With the approval of Tsar Ferdinand, Radoslavov pursued a strategy that favored the Triple Alliance. Nevertheless, despite Austro-Hungarian and German entreaties, he kept Bulgaria out of the First World War in 1914.

Radoslavov then negotiated with both sides in an effort to secure territories in Macedonia and Thrace in return for Bulgarian military intervention. The Central Powers were able to make the best offer, and on 16 September Radoslavov signed agreements committing Bulgaria to that alliance. On 14 October 1915 Bulgaria joined Austria-Hungary and Germany in an attack on Serbia. The next year Bulgaria joined its allies in attacking Romania.

A strong advocate of Bulgaria's territorial claims, Radoslavov resigned on 21 June 1918 because of the growing dispute between Bulgaria and Germany over the disposition of northern Dobrudzha, which the Central Powers forces had seized from Romania in 1916. As a result of the Bulgarian collapse in September 1918, Radoslavov fled to Germany. He died in Berlin on 31 October 1929. Radoslavov was an ambitious and tenacious advocate of Bulgarian nationalism and the most important russophobic politician in Bulgaria from the turn of the century until the end of the First World War.

Richard C. Hall

See also
Bulgaria, Role in War; Ferdinand I, Tsar of Bulgaria.

References

Radoslavov, Vasil. *Dnevni belezhki, 1914–1916*. Ed. by Ivan Ilchev. Sofia, Bulgaria: Kliment Ohridski, 1993.

Radoslawoff [Radoslavov], Vasil. *Bulgarien und die Weltkrise*, Berlin: Ullstein, 1923.

Silberstein, Gerard. *The Troubled Alliance: German-Austrian Relations, 1914–1917*. Lexington: University of Kentucky Press, 1970.

Railway Artillery

Any piece of artillery mounted on a rail carriage designed to run on conventional rail lines. Railway artillery first appeared during the American Civil War, when Union forces during the

German long-range railway gun. (National Archives)

Richmond campaign mounted a 13-inch mortar on a flatcar. Both the Confederate and Union Armies subsequently made extensive use of all variations of rail-mounted guns. Most armies lost interest in the concept following the Civil War, but after the Franco-Prussian War of 1870–1871 the French army started experimenting with railway artillery. By the end of World War I, both the Allies and the Germans had advanced systems of railway guns, which saw extensive service in the static environment of trench warfare on the Western Front.

Rail-mounted guns used primarily for offensive purposes were large-caliber weapons on special mountings that could be moved rapidly from position to position, either on existing or specially laid tracks. Before they could be fired, however, these guns normally required special preparations to the track or to the railcar and platform. Rail-mounted guns used for defensive purposes were generally smaller in caliber and mounted as integral components of an armored train. During the Russian civil war immediately following World War I, the Red Army made extensive use of such trains to move troops and to conduct patrols in force.

The type of mount that a particular railway gun had was a function of the weapon's size. A pivot mount affixed directly to the rail car allowed the gun to traverse and fire in any direction relative to the line of the track. A larger-caliber gun using a pivot mount required outriggers or other stabilizing systems to prevent the recoil from tipping the whole thing over when firing perpendicular to the track. Almost all guns larger than 200mm had mountings that aligned the gun semirigidly to the rail car, allowing for only a very slight movement a few degrees in either direction. These guns were aimed for firing either by rotating the entire car on a track turntable or by pushing or pulling the car along a specially laid length of curved track, known as an épée. Once the gun was within a degree or two of the required azimuth, the onboard traverse made the final adjustments.

Although the Schneider Company of France had been experimenting with railway artillery prior to World War I, the French army never officially adopted any such guns before 1914. As soon as the war started and the French recognized the mistake they had made in arming their army almost exclusively with the light 75mm field gun, they immediately initiated a crash program to convert naval and fortress heavy guns for field use. The key technical problem was that the French had no suitable field carriages on which to mount the heavier guns. As a wartime expedient, the heavy naval guns were mounted on rail carriages—with no form of recoil control at all. It was a messy solution, but it did work to get heavier guns up behind the French front lines rapidly. Purpose-built railway guns soon followed, and by the end of the war France had some nineteen different models in service, ranging from 240mm to the huge Obusier de 520, which threw a 520mm, 3,640-pound shell only 15,970 yards.

Despite having the best-developed rail infrastructure in Europe, Germany too was slow to recognize the potential of railway guns. Among the earliest of the German railway guns was the 17cm K (E) Samuel. Introduced in 1916, it was little more than a standard 170mm heavy field gun bolted down into the bed of a flatcar. The most numerous of the purpose-built German rail guns was the 21cm SKL/40 (E) Peter Adelbert, which fired a 210mm, 253-pound shell out to a maximum range of 28,000 yards. The largest German railway gun of World War I was the 38cm SKL/45 (E) Max. The gun's rail carriage had four bogies of five pairs of wheels each. The gun and its carriage had a combined weight of 297 tons. It fired a 380mm, 1,652-pound projectile to a maximum range of 26,250 yards. Both the Peter Adelbert and the Max were based on existing naval guns. The "(E)" in a German artillery nomenclature stood for Eisenbahnartillerie (Railway Artillery).

As with the French, the initial British railway guns of World War I were retrofitted naval and coastal guns. The first British railway gun was the 9.2-inch Gun Mk–3, introduced in 1915. It fired a 380-pound projectile to a maximum range of 12,900 yards. The largest British railway gun of the war was the 14-inch Gun Mk–3, introduced in 1916. Weighing 277 tons in action, it fired a 1,582-pound shell to a maximum range of 34,800 yards. During the latter part of the war, the British started designing the even larger 18-inch Howitzer Mk-1, but that system only entered service after the war ended.

After pioneering railway artillery during the Civil War, the U.S. Army promptly forgot about it, only to rediscover it in 1917. Since it seemed most unlikely that the German High Seas Fleet would be appearing off the east coast any time during the war, the United States followed the European lead of converting coastal guns into railway guns. Some fifty 8-inch coastal guns and twice as many 12-inch coastal howitzers were converted to railway guns, but none of the 12-inchers and only three of the 8-inchers actually reached France before the war ended. The U.S. Navy, meanwhile, pursued its own program to retrofit its M-1909 14-inch battleship gun to a railway carriage. The navy actually got five of them built, shipped to France, and into action with their own crews by October 1918, where they supported the operations of the U.S. First and Second Armies.

David T. Zabecki

See also
Artillery; Big Bertha; French 75 Gun; Paris Gun.

References
Bailey, J. B. A. *Field Artillery and Firepower.* 2nd ed. Annapolis: Naval Institute Press, 2003.
Hogg, Ian V. *The Guns, 1914–1918.* New York: Ballantine, 1971.
Hogg, Ian, and John Batchelor. *Rail Gun.* Poole, Dorset, UK: John Batchelor, 1973.

Ramadi, Battles of (8–14 July and 22–29 September 1917)

Mesopotamian Front battles. Ramadi lies on the Tigris River 25 miles upstream from Falluja and provides easy access to the Euphrates districts. Its strategic importance caused Ramadi to be the scene of several important World War I battles. British area commander General Sir Stanley Maude decided to attack Ramadi and sent British forces against it twice in 1917, during 8–14 July and 22–29 September.

Following the loss of Falluja in March 1917, Turkish forces retreated up the Tigris to Ramadi and set up positions there to cover the Madhij Defile from different positions. The Turks had about 1,000 men and six guns. Maude launched the attacks primarily because work on the Sakhlawiya Dam was a prerequisite to a flood protection scheme, and safeguarding the workers on this project meant occupying Dhibban, 20 miles south of Ramadi, and removing Turkish forces from the area.

The July British assault was the only military operation during the hot weather in 1917 when marching and fighting were both necessary. In consequence it saw the first serious attempt to employ motorized infantry in the Mesopotamian theater.

The main problem for the British was in massing troops for the attack. Maude assembled a force at Dhibban, but it faced a 20-mile march. The intense July heat both day and night prompted the British to employ trucks. A strike force of some 600 men departed Dhibban for Ramadi on the night of 7 July in 127 Ford vans and trucks. Three airplanes provided reconnaissance.

By the night of the 8th the British had occupied the Madhij Defile without incident. Cavalry reached Ramadi by sunrise on the 9th. The first Turkish resistance came from along the Euphrates River, where artillery fire and their own disorganization caused the British to halt. Reinforcements were halted by a sand storm that also interrupted communications and prevented British gunners from locating their targets. The British took heavy casualties in the battle and from the intense heat, forcing them to call off the attack. Of 566 British casualties, 321 were from the heat.

The British mounted a second assault on 22 September when Major General H. T. Brookings and the 12th and 42nd Infantry Brigades moved from Madhij to take Muskaid Ridge to the west of Ramadi with little resistance. Instead of trying to move along the riverbank as the Turks expected, Brookings's men then moved to the left and by midafternoon reached the Euphrates Valley Canal. At the same time the 14th Hussars, operating independently of the infantry, swung south of Muskaid Ridge and gained the Aleppo road. There they dismounted and entrenched. Meanwhile, the 42nd Brigade captured Ramadi Ridge and the 12th took Aziziyeh Ridge under Turkish shelling and machine-gun fire. The Turks found their withdrawal blocked by the 14th Hussars and were cut down by their machine-gun fire. The remaining Turks were rounded up the next day by British cavalry and armored cars.

Christopher J. Richman

See also
Maude, Sir Frederick Stanley; Mesopotamian Theater.

References
Barker, A. J. *The Bastard War: The Mesopotamian Campaign of 1914–1918.* New York: Dial, 1967.
Moberly, F. J. *The Campaign in Mesopotamia, 1914–1918.* 3 vols. Nashville, TN: Battery Press, 1997–1998.

Rapallo Conference (16 April 1922)

Clandestine meeting between German and Russian Foreign Ministers Walther Rathenau and Georgi V. Chicherin. The conference occurred at Rapallo, Italy, on Easter Sunday, 16 April 1922. The ministers of these two states had been attending the European Economic Conference at Genoa and repaired to nearby Rapallo to sign a far-reaching agreement under which Germany extended de jure recognition to the Soviet government, the first of that government by a major power. Both states also renounced all war claims and prewar indebtedness against the other.

Military cooperation between Germany and Russia was not specified in the Rapallo agreement but flowed from it. The two states exchanged officers for training, and Germany established three secret training areas in Russia for tanks, aviation, and chemical warfare. The Germans experimented with advanced war techniques forbidden by the Versailles Treaty and trained their military personnel on Soviet territory, while the Soviets received the help of German experts to build up Russia's military and industrial strength. The Russians also benefited from military information, loans, and the construction of modern tank and airplane factories on Soviet soil by the Germans. On a broader scale, Rapallo was the first significant diplomatic victory for the new Bolshevik government of Russia.

Arthur T. Frame and Spencer C. Tucker

See also
Rathenau, Walther; Reparations; Versailles, Treaty of; War Debts.

References
Carr, Edward H. *German-Soviet Relations between the Two World Wars, 1919–1939.* Baltimore: Johns Hopkins University Press, 1951.
Dziewanowski, M. K. *A History of Soviet Russia.* Englewood Cliffs, NJ: Prentice-Hall, 1979.
Eyck, Erich. *A History of the Weimar Republic,* Vol. 1, *From the Collapse of the Empire to Hindenburg's Election.* Trans. Harlan P. Hanson and Robert G. L. Waite. Cambridge: Harvard University Press, 1967.
Felix, David. *Walter Rathenau and the Weimar Republic: The Politics of Reparations.* Baltimore: Johns Hopkins University Press, 1971.
Jacobson, Jon. *When the Soviet Union Entered World Politics.* Berkeley: University of California Press, 1994.
Kochan, Lionel. *Russia and the Weimar Republic.* Westport, CT: Greenwood, 1978.
Rubinstein, Alvin Z. *The Foreign Policy of the Soviet Union.* New York: Random House, 1968.

Rasputin, Grigory Yefimovich (1864–1916)

Siberian peasant and wandering mystic who became an advisor and confidant to the Russian imperial family. Born near the Ural Mountains in the western Siberian village of Pokrovskoe sometime between 1864 and 1872, Grigory Yefimovich Rasputin was a precocious child who learned to read the Bible at an early age. As a young man he ran afoul of the law for petty thievery and dalliances with young girls. Rasputin came under the influence of a religious sect known as the Khlysty (Flagellants) and became a self-declared holy man who claimed healing powers.

Rasputin was a wandering "holy man," a *Strannik* (pilgrim) in search of God in the tradition of many Orthodox Russians. He was known alternately as a *Starets* (unofficial spiritual guide) and a *Yurodiviy* (holy fool). Though he was careful not to wander too far from Orthodoxy, many of his practices were akin to those of the quasi-Christian sects, which fit his personal licentiousness.

Rasputin arrived in the capital of St. Petersburg in the first years of the new century, and in October 1905 his contacts within the religious hierarchy and among the nobility secured him access to the imperial family. The politics and ideologies of the era created a growing crisis of faith for Orthodoxy that emphasized saints, holy men, and miracle workers. This trend opened the way for Rasputin's rise to prominence. Rasputin was said to possess two miraculous powers: healing and precognition. He seemed able to "read" a person's character and quickly assess his or her strengths and weaknesses. His greatest ability, however, was to calm people in distress, which drew him to the attention of the imperial couple.

Grigory Rasputin, Russian mystic and religious advisor to Tsarina Alexandra. (The Illustrated London News Picture Library)

Nicholas II and Alexandra were extremely devout members of the Russian Orthodox Church, but they also believed in miracles and faith healing. Young Tsarevich Aleksey Nikolaevich, heir to the throne, suffered from hemophilia. Called to the boy's bedside on occasions of distress, Rasputin seemed able to stop the tsarevich's hemorrhaging. Explanation of Rasputin's success in controlling the bleeding, either through hypnosis or positive thinking, is elusive, but certainly his perceived success endeared him to the tsarina especially and gave him an intimacy with the royal family enjoyed by few. Soon his unfettered advice extended to state business, as he attempted to influence the tsar's decisions in ministerial and policy matters. From 1910 he is believed to have exercised considerable political power.

Rasputin's frequent affairs with women and his drunkenness are well documented. He opposed Russia's involvement in World War I, reportedly telling the tsar that if Russia went to war it "would drown in its own blood." When Tsar Nicholas II took personal command of the war effort in the fall of 1915, the tsarina came to exercise political power in his absence. Rasputin held considerable influence over her and the selection of cabinet ministers. Rumors spread that the tsarina was Rasputin's lover. Convinced that Rasputin now threatened the very survival of the Romanov dynasty, members of the nobility and right-wing supporters of autocracy plotted his assassination. After a half dozen unsuccessful attempts, in the early morning hours of 17 December 1916 Prince Feliks Iusupov, son-in-law of the tsar's sister, supported by others in the imperial family and government, poisoned, shot, and finally drowned Rasputin. Upon learning of Rasputin's death from drowning, the tsar abandoned his command of the army, leaving no one in authority, and replaced every able minister of his government. Even members of the imperial family who asked for leniency for the assassins were exiled from the capital. With the breakdown of capable governance and command of the war effort, as well as the widening chasm between the monarchy and the people, Russia stood on the brink of revolution. Although Rasputin did not materially affect the coming of the revolution that would sweep away the tsarist regime, he did perhaps hasten it.

Arthur T. Frame

See also
Alexandra Fyodorovna, Tsarina; Nicholas II, Tsar; Nikolai
    Nikolaevich, Grand Duke; Russia, Revolution of March 1917.
References
De Jonge, Alex. *The Life and Times of Grigorii Rasputin.* New York:
    Coward, McCann and Geoghegan, 1982.
Florinsky, Michael T. *The End of the Russian Empire.* New York:
    Collier, 1931.
Fuhrmann, Joseph J. *Rasputin: A Life.* New York: Praeger, 1990.
Lincoln, W. Bruce. *Passage through Armageddon: The Russians in
    War and Revolution, 1914–1918.* New York: Simon and Schuster,
    1986.
———. *The Romanovs: Autocrats of All the Russias.* Garden City,
    NY: Doubleday, 1981.
Minney, R. J. *Rasputin.* New York: McKay, 1973.
Moynahan, Brian. *Rasputin: The Saint Who Sinned.* New York:
    Random House, 1997.
Radzinsky, Edvard. *The Rasputin File.* Trans. Judson Rosengrant.
    New York: Nan A. Talese, 2000.
Shukman, Harold. *Rasputin.* Stroud, UK: Sutton, 1997.

Rathenau, Walther (1867–1922)

German industrialist and statesman. Born on 29 September 1867 at Berlin, Walther Rathenau came from an important Jewish family. He was the son of Emil Rathenau, founder of the German public utilities company Allgemeine Elektrizitätsgesellschaft (AEG), which had acquired Thomas Edison's European patent rights. Young Rathenau studied physics, chemistry, engineering, and philosophy at the universities of Berlin and Strasbourg. Having finished his doctorate, Rathenau had difficulty finding a position at AEG that

German politician Walter Rathenau, head of the Economic War Management Department. (Library of Congress)

suited his intellectual ambitions. However, articles he contributed to the influential periodical *Die Zukunft* (The Future) attracted some recognition.

Rathenau established himself as an influential businessman and political advisor to the entourage of Kaiser Wilhelm II, also becoming the friend of leading intellectuals such as Gerhard Hauptmann, Hugo von Hofmannsthal, Rainer Maria Rilke, Frank Wedekind, and Stefan Zweig. At the outbreak of war in 1914, Rathenau assumed direction of the Economic War Management Department (Kriegs-Rohstoff Abteilung) and contributed to the formulation of war aims with several memoranda for Chancellor Theobald von Bethmann Hollweg.

In August 1914 Germany had reserves of gunpowder for only four months, but before this deadline arrived the chemical industry was already producing a wide range of synthetics. Rathenau arranged for Germany's supply of vital raw materials to be allocated according to priority and industrial production to be focused on war essentials such as ammunition and army supplies. Research facilities were commissioned to find replacements for vital imports such as rubber, saltpeter, and natural fertilizer, all of which now were subject to British blockade. As such Rathenau played a key role in the German war effort.

After the war, Rathenau became one of the few positive symbols of the Weimar Republic. Renowned as an excellent negotiator and an internationalist, he was chosen by Chancellor Karl Wirth in May 1921 as minister of reconstruction and then in January 1922 as foreign minister. Rathenau represented Germany at the Cannes and Genoa reparations conferences. He upset right-wing nationalists by arguing that Germany should fulfill its obligations under the Treaty of Versailles. However, he simultaneously worked with Minister of Finance Matthias Erzberger to try to convince the Allies that the treaty terms were too harsh. In October 1921 with the fall of Wirth, Rathenau left government officially but continued to be entrusted with important foreign negotiations. He signed the Treaty of Rapallo with the Soviet Union on 16 April 1922. Although a fervent nationalist, Rathenau was also a key proponent of international cooperation, and his initiatives played an important part in breaking Germany's postwar diplomatic isolation.

In his academic writings, Rathenau contended that the days of unfettered capitalism were over and argued that technological change and industrialization were pushing civilization toward a stage of extreme mechanization in which the human soul would be lost. In an attempt to find an alternative to laissez faire capitalism that did not involve state socialism and Marxism, Rathenau proposed a decentralized, democratic social order in which the workers would have more control over production and the state would exert more control over the economy. His translated works include *In Days to Come* (1921) and *The New Society* (1921).

As a Jew, Rathenau was depicted as part of the supposed anti-German conspiracy, the existence of which was postulated by right-wing elements who opposed his attempts to fulfill reparations obligations. On 24 June 1922 two right-wing army officers assassinated Rathenau on his way to the Foreign Office in Berlin.

Peter Overlack

See also
Bethmann Hollweg, Theobald von; Erzberger, Matthias; Max von Baden, Prince; Paris Peace Conference; Rapallo Conference; Versailles, Treaty of; Wilhelm II, Kaiser.

References
Buddensieg, Tilmann, Thomas P. Hughes, and Jürgen Kocka, eds. *Ein Mann vieler Eigenschaften: Walther Rathenau und die Kultur der Moderne.* Berlin: Wagenbach, 1990.
Felix, David. *Walter Rathenau and the Weimar Republic: The Politics of Reparations.* Baltimore: Johns Hopkins University Press, 1971.
Strandmann, H. Pogge von, ed. *Walther Rathenau: Industrialist, Banker, Intellectual, and Politician: Notes and Diaries, 1907–1922.* Oxford and New York: Clarendon, 1985.
Wilderotter, H., ed. *Die Extreme berühren sich: Walther Rathenau, 1867–1922.* Berlin: Argon-Verlag, 1993.

Rawlinson, Sir Henry Seymour (1864–1925)

British army general. Born 20 February 1864 at Trent Manor, Dorset, Henry Rawlinson was educated at Eton and the Royal Military College, Sandhurst. He joined the King's Royal Rifle Corps in 1884 and served in the 1886–1887 Burma campaign, the 1898 reconquest of the Sudan, and the 1899–1902 Boer War. In 1903 he was appointed commandant of the Staff College, Camberley, as a brigadier-general. Promoted to major-general in 1909, Rawlinson received command of the 3rd Division in 1910.

After the outbreak of the First World War, Rawlinson briefly served at the War Office before being appointed to command the 4th Division in France. In October 1914 he was sent to Antwerp to command IV Corps with the task of holding the city. However, Antwerp fell before he arrived, and he was then ordered to cover the flank of the Belgian army as it retreated southwest.

As a corps commander in France in 1915, Rawlinson served at Neuve-Chapelle, Festubert, and the Third Battle of Artois. In early 1916 Rawlinson was promoted to lieutenant-general and appointed to command the newly formed Fourth Army. British Expeditionary Force commander General Sir Douglas Haig assigned Rawlinson's army the leading role in the Somme offensive of 1916. Rawlinson envisioned a limited attack but was overruled by Haig, who hoped for a break-through and complete victory. On 1 July 1916, the opening day of the Battle of the Somme, Rawlinson's men absorbed 57,470 casualties in what was the bloodiest single day in British military history. Haig continued the offensive with enormous cost of life until November 1916.

Despite being promoted to full general in January 1917, Rawlinson was relegated to a secondary role for that year. While Generals Sir Hubert Gough and Sir Herbert Plumer directed the Passchendaele offensive (Third Battle of Ypres), Rawlinson was tasked with planning a combined naval-army landing on the Belgian coast that was never executed. When Plumer departed for Italy in November 1917, Rawlinson replaced him at the Second Army. In February 1918 the

British General Sir Henry Rawlinson who commanded the Fourth Army at the end of the war. (National Archives)

British command structure was reorganized, and Rawlinson was appointed British military representative to the Supreme War Council at Versailles. In March 1918 Rawlinson was recalled to army command, taking over the remnants of the Fifth Army, later renamed the Fourth Army.

On 4 July 1918, Rawlinson carried out a successful limited attack at Le Hamel. A month later, on 8 August 1918, he launched a much larger attack at Amiens. This latter attack was a complete victory and was described by General Erich Ludendorff as "the black day of the German Army in the history of this war."

Rawlinson's army, which had a strength of 24 Allied divisions and 450 tanks, spearheaded the British offensives of autumn 1918. His army defeated the Germans at the Second Battle of Albert, captured Peronne on 31 August, stormed the Saint-Quentin Canal and drove the Germans from the Hindenburg Line, and participated in the Selle and Sambre offensives. Between 8 August and 11 November, Rawlinson's army advanced 60 miles, capturing 80,000 German prisoners and taking 1,100 artillery pieces.

In 1919 Rawlinson directed the evacuation of the Allied forces from Murmansk and Arkhangelsk (Archangel) in North Russia. After briefly commanding Aldershot, Home Forces, in 1919–1920, Rawlinson was appointed commander-in-chief of India in 1920. Created a baron in 1919, Rawlinson died in Delhi on 28 March 1925.

Bradley P. Tolppanen

See also

Albert, Second Battle of; Amiens Offensive; Antwerp, Siege of; Artois, Third Battle of; Gough, Sir Hubert de la Poer; Haig, Douglas, 1st Earl; Le Hamel, Battle of; Ludendorff, Erich; Neuve-Chapelle, Battle of; Plumer, Sir Herbert; Russia, Allied Intervention in; Saint-Quentin Offensive; Sambre Offensive; Somme Offensive; Supreme War Council.

References

Blaxland, Gergory. *Amiens: 1918*. London: Frederick Muller, 1968.

Maurice, Sir Frederick. *Soldier, Artist, Sportsman: The Life of General Lord Rawlinson of Trent, GCB, GCVO, GCSI, KMG*. New York: Houghton Mifflin, 1928.

Prior, Robin, and Trevor Wilson. *Command on the Western Front: The Military Career of Sir Henry Rawlinson, 1914–1918*. Oxford, UK: Blackwell, 1992.

Red Baron

See Richthofen, Manfred von, Baron

Red Cross

International medical aid society. The Red Cross, and its Muslim counterpart the Red Crescent, offered humanitarian

Italian children waiting for supplies from the American Red Cross, c. 1917–1918. (Library of Congress)

relief during the war. The organization was founded in 1863 by Jean Henri Dunant, a Swiss citizen who was deeply affected by the suffering of soldiers in the 1859 Battle of Solferino during Austria's war with France and the Kingdom of Sardinia. Dunant organized a field ambulance corps to assist the wounded after the battle. A book he wrote drew the attention of the Public Welfare Society in Geneva, which formed the International Committee of the Red Cross (ICRC) in 1863. In 1864 a number of nations sent delegates to a conference in Geneva, and on 22 August 1864 eleven nations signed the Geneva Convention for the Amelioration of the Condition of the Wounded in Armies in the Field. The convention agreed that its symbol would be a red cross on a white field.

In 1867 the First International Conference of the Red Cross occurred, with representatives of nine governments and sixteen national committees in attendance. In 1876 the organization took the name of the International Committee of the Red Cross. That same year the Ottoman Empire formed a similar organization. Understandably reluctant to embrace the Christian cross, it adopted the crescent as its symbol. During the Franco-Prussian War of 1870–1871, the ICRC took on the additional task of assisting prisoners of war, which was formally added to its mandate in an ICRC conference in Washington, D.C.

The ICRC grew into an organization with chapters in many countries. It became the primary agency for providing sanitary services for armies in the field in order to alleviate suffering as well as the chief body for ameliorating conditions of captivity for prisoners of war (POWs). The ICRC's ambitious goal of working for the abolition of war was rendered impossible by the lack of support from the national branches, which backed the goals of their own governments.

The Red Cross actively sought to reduce the suffering of war by improving the wholly inadequate medical service typically provided to soldiers in the field. As far as its medical services were concerned, Red Cross organizations typically supplied nurses, medical equipment, medical supplies, ambulances, and field hospitals. Assisting the Red Cross became a means by which those who were ineligible for military service could support their nation's troops in the field.

Opposition to the idea of a civilian-run auxiliary to the military and naval authorities made the establishment of a British Red Cross particularly difficult. Military leaders feared a loss of control, while famed British nurse Florence Nightingale feared that such an organization would make war easier to conduct and therefore more readily waged. While France, Germany, and Japan all had enthusiastic and large national chapters, Britain and the United States were slower to develop them. The British Red Cross Society (BRCS) was formed in 1905 from several different organizations. The British army already had a well-developed medical corps and was reluctant to depend on the BRCS. During World War I the army came to use not only the BRCS but the rival Order of St. John Ambulance Brigade. These two organizations contributed more than 2,000 voluntary aid detachments (VADs) to assist in providing medical services and other duties. In 1915 the BRCS organized ambulance convoys, which moved millions of patients in France. During the war 7,800 men and women, both paid and volunteer, served overseas.

The United States entered the war in better shape but with a much more heavily militarized Red Cross. A War Department circular in 1912 had granted the Red Cross monopoly status as the only volunteer society authorized by the government to render aid to U.S. armed forces in time of war. In 1916, the army named surgeon Colonel J. R. Kean to organize Red Cross field and hospital columns as part of President Woodrow Wilson's preparedness campaign. Former U.S. President William Howard Taft chaired the Central Committee of the American Red Cross (ARC). ARC obligations, as specified by the army, included the raising of private funds to purchase a hospital ship, three railway surgical operating cars, and the material for field hospitals, as well as supplying the personnel to staff the medical centers. Mirroring contemporary American society, the Red Cross established separate facilities for white and black wounded. By the end of the war, the ARC had abandoned the practice of confining its work solely to the sick and wounded, instead functioning as a service organization for all combatants.

Joining and contributing to the Red Cross became a patriotic duty of every loyal citizen, regardless of age or gender. Red Cross societies relied on the public for donations to support their work with the appeals for funds often implying that a soldier's fate could be determined by a civilian's generosity. A popular U.S. poster showed a Red Cross nurse aiding a fallen soldier with the caption "If You Fail, He Dies." Another U.S. poster, "The Greatest Mother in the World," showed a giant nurse cradling an infantilized wounded man like a baby, suggesting that parents need not fear for the well-being of their soldier sons if the Red Cross had sufficient money to do its job.

Working for one's national Red Cross society became an outlet for patriotism and also a measure of a citizen's loyalty. The need for Red Cross nurses afforded women opportunities for national service. French Red Cross officials emphasized that a woman could pay her debt to her homeland by serving as a nurse for wounded men who had already paid their debt by serving in the armed forces. French conservatives also took the opportunity presented by the war to advance the Red Cross as an instrument for ridding the nation of undesirable influences such as feminism and pacifism. Red Cross nurses, passively obedient to medical and military authority, would serve as a militia to restore the values of an earlier France.

Indifference to the Red Cross was viewed by many as disloyalty to the nation. One U.S. poster showed the American and Red Cross flags side by side, with the caption "Loyalty to One Means Loyalty to Both." Patriots turned fundraisers into attacks on those citizens who questioned the value of the war or national leadership. One Wisconsin man who criticized the Red Cross in the belief that it was just another charitable organization was convicted under the Espionage Act for hindering the U.S. government in its prosecution of the war.

The ICRC, headquartered in Geneva, found itself lost in the nationalistic fervor that marked the war. Members of the Allied Red Cross branches, especially that of the United States, did not want to work with enemy Red Cross members, even to promote peaceful activities. With international dialogue often impossible, the ICRC was severely restricted in its activities. Its wartime role was chiefly that of a clearinghouse for gifts and correspondence to soldiers as well as a source of information about POWs, not yet regulated under the Geneva Convention. On 21 August 1914 the ICRC formed the International Prisoner of War Agency (IPOWA). It established a Tracing Service that kept a great card index of millions of captives on both sides, POWs as well as civilian internees. ICRC representatives visited hundreds of POW camps on both sides and reported on conditions. The ICRC also sought to force both sides to conform to international law. In 1917 the ICRC condemned the Germans for torpedoing appropriately marked hospital ships, and in 1918 it condemned chemical warfare as a "barbarous innovation." At the end of the war, the ICRC assisted in the repatriation of POWs.

By war's end, members of the ICRC had already begun formulating an agenda for the postwar organization, including international agreement regarding the treatment of civilians and POWs. The ICRC strongly supported the League of Nations, while the national branches found a peacetime role providing assistance for victims of natural disasters and diseases.

Caryn E. Neumann

See also
League of Nations Covenant; Prisoners of War; Wilson, Thomas Woodrow.

References
Boissier, Pierre. *From Solferino to Tsushima: History of the International Committee of the Red Cross.* Geneva: Henry Dunant Institute, 1985.
Davison, Henry P. *The American Red Cross in the Great War.* New York: Macmillan, 1919.
Durand, André. *From Sarajevo to Hiroshima: History of the International Committee of the Red Cross.* Geneva: Henry Dunant Institute, 1984.
Forsyth, David. *Humanitarian Politics: The International Committee of the Red Cross.* Baltimore: Johns Hopkins University Press, 1977.
Gilbo, Patrick F. *The American Red Cross: The First Century.* New York: Harper and Row, 1981.
Hutchinson, John F. *Champions of Charity: War and the Rise of the Red Cross.* Boulder, CO: Westview, 1996.
Moorehead, Caroline. *Dunant's Dream: War, Switzerland and the History of the Red Cross.* New York: HarperCollins, 1998.
Morrah, Dermot. *The British Red Cross.* London: Collins, 1944.

Red Scare

Term applied to two distinct periods of intense anticommunism in U.S. history: in 1919–1920 and in the early 1950s. Both periods were characterized by widespread fears of communist influence on American society and communist infiltration of the U.S. government. These fears spurred aggressive investigation and jailing of persons associated with communist and socialist ideology or political movements.

Directly following World War I, much of the nation was still in a frenzy of patriotic and anti-German sentiment. Hatred of the "Huns" was quickly replaced by a fear of anarchists, communists, and immigrants. In 1901 an anarchist had shot and killed President William McKinley, and in November 1917 the Bolsheviks had seized power in Russia and the next year murdered the royal family. Fears of a communist plan to overthrow the government of the United States, far-fetched as this seems in retrospect, created paranoia in some government officials. This concern merged with the long-standing worry of many Americans over the large eastern European immigrant population in the United States. To many, the communities forming in the big cities were associated with atheism, anarchism, and communism, values seen as antithetical to those of the United States.

To many Americans, 1919 was a time of uncertainty and social conflict, with a wave of strikes, the passage of both prohibition and woman suffrage, and the Chicago race riot. One of the first major strikes after the war occurred when 60,000 shipyard workers in the Seattle area walked off the job on 6 February. Despite the absence of any violence or arrests, management claimed that the strikers were "Reds" and charged that they were trying to incite revolution. On 1 May rallies were held throughout the country, and riots ensued in several cities including Boston, New York, and Cleveland. On 9 September the Boston police went on strike. Two weeks later, a nationwide steel strike occurred when 365,000 workers walked off their jobs. In Gary, Indiana, unrest was so prevalent that officials declared martial law there on 5 October.

Fear of strikes leading to a Communist revolution spread throughout the country, and hysteria took hold. "Red hunting" became the national obsession. Many held colleges to be hotbeds of Bolshevism, and several professors were labeled as radicals. A number of schoolteachers were fired for current or prior membership in leftist organizations.

A series of bombings by suspected anarchists began that summer. Between April and June 1919, forty-three bombs sent to leading politicians and businessmen in eight cities were either discovered in the mail or exploded killing two people and destroying property in eight cities. In Washington, D.C., an Italian anarchist blew himself up outside Attorney General Mitchell Palmer's home, which was partially destroyed. On 16 September 1920 a bomb exploded in Wall Street, near the leading banking firm of J. P. Morgan and Company. The blast killed thirty people by the next day, and nine others died from it over the following month. Several hundred others were injured in this worst domestic terrorist episode in the United States to that time. In response to the bombings, a surge of public patriotism swept the country, often involving violent denunciations of communists, radicals, and foreigners, and resulting in several lynchings of suspected anarchists.

Palmer recruited John Edgar Hoover as his special assistant, and together they used the Espionage Act (1917) and the Sedition Act (1918) to launch a campaign against radicals and left-wing organizations. Encouraged by Congress, which had refused to seat duly elected socialist Victor Berger from Wisconsin, Palmer began a series of well-publicized raids against union offices and the headquarters of communist and socialist organizations. The first in a series of so-called Palmer Raids occurred on 7 November 1919, the second anniversary of the Bolshevik seizure of power in Russia. More than 10,000 suspected anarchists and communists were rounded up, many of whom were detained for long periods without being formally charged. In December, in a highly publicized move, more than 200 alien detainees were deported to Russia, among them the prominent radical Emma Goldman. Despite no credible evidence that a communist plot was underway, Palmer staged more raids in January 1920. Assisted by local law enforcement, officials throughout the country arrested and detained as many as 6,000 suspects.

Another incident that fueled the fear of anarchism was the trial of Nicola Sacco and Bartolomeo Vanzetti. The two had been arrested in May 1920 and charged with a robbery in which two guards were killed. Both men were Italian immigrants and known anarchists. Despite weak evidence, they were convicted of murder and sentenced to death. In 1927, following many public protests and petitions, both men were executed.

When Attorney General Palmer announced that a communist revolution was likely to take place on 1 May 1920, there was something akin to panic. In New York, five elected Socialists were expelled from the legislature. When the May revolution failed to materialize, however, attitudes began to change and Palmer came under criticism from a number of prominent lawyers for his disregard of basic civil liberties. Most damning were charges that Palmer had manufactured the crisis as a means to gain the Democratic presidential nomination in 1920. The national mood began to return to normal, and by the summer of 1920 the Red Scare was largely over. Many historians, however, believe that the Red Scare presaged the antiradicalism and McCarthyism that became highly influential in the United States during the late 1930s and 1950s.

Katja Wuestenbecker

See also
German Americans and the War; Goldman, Emma; Palmer, Alexander Mitchell; Russia, Revolution of November 1917; United States, Home Front.
References
Lindop, Edmund. *America in the 1920s.* Brookfield, CT: Twenty-First Century Books, 2004.
Murray, Robert K. *Red Scare: A Study in National Hysteria, 1919–1920.* Minneapolis: University of Minnesota Press, 1955; Westport, CT: Greenwood, 1980.
Nielsen, Kim E. *Un-American Womanhood: Antiradicalism, Antifeminism, and the First Red Scare.* Columbus: Ohio State University Press, 2001.
Schmidt, Regin. *Red Scare: FBI and the Origins of Anticommunism in the United States, 1919–1943.* Copenhagen, Denmark: Museum Tusculanum Press, University of Copenhagen, 2000.

Reichstag Peace Resolution (19 July 1917)

Important German peace initiative. When Germany's policy of unrestricted submarine warfare failed to bring Britain to its knees in six months as the German navy leadership had

promised, Matthias Erzberger, leader of the Catholic Center Party, unexpectedly exposed the navy's miscalculations during a speech to the Reichstag's Budget Committee on 6 July 1917. Convinced that a German victory was no longer possible, Erzberger demanded that the Reichstag go on record as favoring "a peace of understanding" without territorial annexations. Such a resolution, he believed, would find widespread support abroad.

Erzberger's proposal, which caused a panic among Reichstag deputies, was enhanced by the presumption that Erzberger was acting for Chancellor Theobald von Bethmann Hollweg, which was not the case. In this situation, the Center Party agreed to form an informal coalition with the leftist Progressive Party and the Majority Social Democratic Party. Leaders of all three parties joined with the right-of-center National Liberals in establishing a joint committee (Interfraktioneller Ausschuss) to facilitate regular discussions. These parties dominated the Reichstag, and their coalition suggested the emergence of a common front for domestic political reform.

Following hectic debate about the contents of the resolution, on 12 July 1917 the Socialists, the Progressives, and the Center Party agreed on a text that called for a "peace of understanding."

Both the chancellor and the army high command (OHL) immediately opposed the resolution. Bethmann Hollweg, however, earned the enmity of both sides. The generals accused him of letting the domestic situation get out of hand, and the Reichstag parties that had previously supported him now expressed their lack of confidence in him or remained indifferent. OHL pressure forced Kaiser Wilhelm II to dismiss the chancellor on 13 July. Having triumphed over Bethmann Hollweg, the OHL gave up its opposition to the resolution, which the Reichstag passed overwhelmingly on 19 July 1917 by a vote of 212 to 126 (17 abstentions). The Reichstag called for "a peace of understanding" with no "forced territorial acquisitions" and no economic penalties. It also called for freedom of the seas and the rule of international law.

The wording of the resolution was vague, and new Chancellor Georg Michaelis, who took office on 14 July, accepted it only with the qualification of "as I understand it." Michaelis's chief objection was not the statement eschewing territorial acquisitions but rather what he perceived as the belief of deputies that they had a say in foreign policy.

Rejecting territorial annexations or economic exactions still made it possible to come to "agreements." Thus the same Reichstag overwhelmingly approved the annexationist Treaty of Brest Litovsk with Russia the next March.

The resolution had little effect abroad but was immensely important within Germany. Only seven weeks later, rightists formed the Fatherland Party, an obvious attempt by annexationist leaders to counter the resolution. In spite of criticism leveled against it, the Reichstag Peace Resolution of 1917 was a spectacular act of defiance by the Reichstag and signaled a major rift in the domestic consensus in Germany behind the war.

Bert Becker

See also

Bethmann Hollweg, Theobald von; Brest Litovsk, Treaty of; Erzberger, Matthias; Fatherland Party; Germany, Home Front; Michaelis, Georg; Peace Overtures during the War; Submarine Warfare, Central Powers; War Aims.

References

Chickering, Roger. *Imperial Germany and the Great War, 1914–1918.* Cambridge: Cambridge University Press, 1998.

Epstein, Klaus. *Matthias Erzberger and the Dilemma of German Democracy.* Princeton, NJ: Princeton University Press, 1959.

Farrar, L. L. *Divide and Conquer: German Efforts to Conclude a Separate Peace, 1914–1918.* New York: Columbia University Press, 1978.

Feldman, Gerald D. *German Imperialism, 1914–1918: The Development of a Historical Debate.* New York: Wiley, 1972.

Religion and the War

Both Allied and Central Powers states employed religion to rally support for the war; religion also played a significant role in soldiers' wartime experiences. When the Great Powers of Europe became embroiled in war in 1914, both Protestant and Catholic clergy all over Europe enlisted in the nationalist causes of their respective nations, urging congregations and parishioners to support the war as a Christian endeavor. Both sides believed that the war would prove to be a major turning point for Europe.

At the beginning of the conflict, British Christians placed the Great War in the tradition of the Just War, a Christian standard for conflict dating back to St. Augustine in the fourth century. The principles of a just war do not legitimize war in itself. They suggest that one should only participate in a war if it is declared by the state, if its purpose is to protect one's homeland or redress a wrong, and if the declaration of war derives from pure motives. Many Englishmen admired German arts and the military and saw England mirrored in Germany, sharing common linguistic and cultural roots. Anglican clergy reminded their congregations that Germany was a respectable nation that had temporarily gone astray.

As it became clear, however, that the soldiers would not be home by Christmas and that this was a total war, Anglican clergy began to change their perception of the war. The concept of a just war could not explain a war so violent, protracted, and destructive. They began to see the conflict as a holy war, using the evocative language of the crusades to suggest that this was a war against an enemy that Britain had to vanquish completely in the name of righteousness. Despite their earlier acknowledgment of Germany's contributions to Western civilization, Anglican clergy now began to emphasize German exceptionalism in Western society. Germany, the clergy charged, had begun to decline when intellectuals began to question the legitimacy of the Bible. In addition, Germans did not have recourse to a strong church: Germany's Lutheran Church was a state church, subordinate to the dictates of the government. Perhaps most worrisome of all, many clergy argued, was its governmental structure. Germans had a penchant for militarism, or Prussianism, that emphasized the importance of the military in elevating the nation's prestige in the world. As Germany came to be depicted as the equivalent of the Antichrist in rousing, patriotic sermons, so were its actions presented as increasingly heinous and wicked. The clergy repeated tales of German atrocities against Belgium and French citizens. Biblical analogies magnified the charges against Germany; thus, sermons connected Germany's moral decline to that of Babylon.

German clergy were no less dedicated to their own country's cause in the war. Recent scholarship suggests that some leaders in Germany (and elsewhere) saw the war as a means to unite their peoples behind the government in a holy crusade. One minister described the unity of Germans in language reminiscent of the Biblical account of the first Pentecost, the occasion when the Holy Spirit descended upon the disciples following the crucifixion of Christ. Germany was seen as surrounded by enemies, but ministers urged that it could remain strong by eschewing the materialism of other western nations and returning to the essential values of the German Volk: resolve, courage, and spiritual devotion. Clergy cast Germany in the role of David, who as a result of his purity and faith defeated Goliath; Germany's primary enemy, Britain, played the role of Goliath.

Germans laid much of the blame for Britain's descent into depravity on its imperialistic ambitions, which had created an empire that subjected a long list of the world's peoples to British rule. Great Britain, German ministers charged from the pulpit, believed itself to represent an ideal that other nations should follow. Germans saw this arrogance as leading Britons to believe they could conquer any weaker peoples. British leaders were viewed as hypocritical, since in advertising German atrocities in Belgium and casting itself as the savior of that small country, Great Britain was ignoring its own history of crushing small nations. Given this history of world dominance, Britain was actually performing the part of Cain, who slew his brother Abel out of jealousy.

While Germany's and England's churches were culling biblical metaphors and casting the war in clear Manichean terms, France's Catholics also saw the war through the lens of their faith. With a historic animosity toward Germany, from the beginning of the war French priests easily cast the enemy as the devil incarnate. French Catholics also viewed

British Army chaplain saying a prayer after the Battle of Cambrai over the bodies of two British soldiers killed in a frontline trench. (National Archives)

this war as a crusade and its casualties as martyrs imitating Christ. Indeed, priests and chaplains could see the war as a Good Friday writ large, with French Christians willingly sacrificing their lives as Christ did to prevent evil from triumphing. The war brought a great religious revival in France, on which U.S. soldiers commented when they arrived in the country in 1917. Rather than casting France as the epitome of purity, French Catholics perceived the war as a rejuvenating experience for their country.

France, however, differed from both England and Germany in its emphasis upon ecumenicism. French Catholic, Protestant, and Jewish religious personnel found surprising sympathy for and bonds to one another, particularly in the trenches. Parallel to the French government's effort to forge a united national front to win the war, France's religious groups found powerful national connections as spiritual brothers.

In Russia, where the Orthodox Church and state had a close relationship, the clergy similarly supported the war. The Synod sent a patriotic message to the churches and also requested that the Imperial Manifesto justifying the war be read to churchgoers. The Synod urged priests to say special prayers for soldiers and the tsar and to instruct their parishioners to support the war and bear any sacrifices necessary. Newspapers reported wartime miracles suggesting that God was on Russia's side, such as bullets hitting crosses worn around men's necks instead of flesh and visions of the Virgin.

By 1915, however, church activity in support of the war declined, and tensions surfaced between liberal and conservative factions within the clergy. Already weakened in the eyes of the Russian people because of its attachment to the increasingly unpopular state, Orthodox Church influence waned among the soldiers. Although the church continued to play a prominent role in official patriotic events, its decreased authority became evident in the *lubki* (broadsides) that were printed and distributed throughout the countryside. To inspire patriotism, the *lubki* increasingly relied on traditional folklore and historical and legendary heroes. The war focused attention on patriotism and national identity, but it also spurred discussion of political issues. Mounting casualties, territorial losses, and starvation in the big cities brought on revolution and direct attacks on the Russian Orthodox Church.

When Protestants in the United States contemplated the war from a distance, they largely did so in the spirit of Progressivism that had overtaken the country since Theodore Roosevelt's presidency. This movement had won the support of both major political parties in the nation; in response to industrialization, urbanization, and immigration, Progressive reformers strove to root out corruption in government, restrain big business, and apply scientific methods of management to public institutions. Liberal Protestants, sympathetic to the Progressive cause, created a complementary theology: the social gospel. Progressive-minded clergy believed that they were living at the dawn of a new age, a period that would be marked by the growth of Christianity and world moral health. These Progressive Christians did not see the world heading toward a preordained demise as outlined in the Biblical book of Revelation but rather had a boundless optimism that they could create God's kingdom on earth through the reform of social institutions. Also known as "applied Christianity," social gospel devotees stressed collective efforts toward improvement in society over individual conversion.

When World War I began, Progressive clergymen saw it as an opportunity to establish a world order, based not on competition and trade but on democracy and world peace. They were not pacifists, however. Engaging in war to eventually realize these goals was a worthy, if not morally obligatory, cause. American clergy viewed the war as a revitalizing force that could spread the Progressive ideals of international peace and establish the millennium on earth. Progressive clergy tended to be pro-Allied from the onset, seeing the conflict as the chance to usurp monarchy and end ongoing international rivalries. They rightly saw President Woodrow Wilson as an ally in establishing a Christian brotherhood; as a Progressive, Wilson shared the optimistic vision of a future international peace brokered by Americans. His Fourteen Points resonated with the millennialist goals of the social gospelers, as Wilson emphasized that morality must underpin international relations and imagined a world that could be peacefully managed through a League of Nations. When the United States did go to war, it posited itself as a messianic nation destined to lead the way toward righteousness with God's blessing while painting Germany as a satanic nation that could only destroy God's plan for the world.

In the trenches, troops on both sides accepted their clergy's interpretations of the war but also engaged in more intimate rituals and symbolic acts to cope with the total war that they were obliged to fight. Not only Catholics but also Protestant troops collected religious medals and rosaries. Soldiers in letters and in writings after the war recounted occasions when hymn singing alleviated tense situations. Protestants in particular placed importance on reading the Bible; some soldiers kept it close to their hearts in battle in the faith that it would help save their lives—indeed, on occasions a well-placed Bible did stop a bullet from penetrating flesh. While Protestants on the home front tended to read the Old Testament for a vision of an angry God that they could reconcile with the war's brutality, soldiers in the trenches tended to read the New Testament, seeking resonance with Christ's sacrifice on the cross.

Not all Christians living in the combatant nations supported the war or accepted the clergy's analysis of the conflict. Conscientious objectors such as Mennonites in the United States embraced pacifism as the only position consistent with Christianity. With a muscular, aggressive Christianity buttressing the war, pacifists often found themselves in difficult positions. Objectors found themselves unsupported by the U.S. government and often accused of insincerity or cowardice. When the Selective Service Act went into effect in 1917, local draft boards could assign conscientious objectors to noncombatant positions, but many Mennonites could not even accept a noncombatant role that would indirectly support the war. Other Mennonites accepted service in agriculture or in the Red Cross. Often conscientious objectors ended up in detention camps while officials debated their status; these camps often became the site for humiliating insults and abuses in retaliation for the refusal of such groups to fight.

Protestants, from both the Allied and Central Powers alike, tended to use the same imagery but reverse the roles. Although they shared many of the same beliefs, Protestants could easily see in one denomination or another characteristics of the Antichrist. Roman Catholics, however, found themselves divided in ways foreign to the splintered Protestants around the world. Pope Benedict XV steadfastly opposed the war and several times attempted to end it through negotiations; his stance provoked constant tensions with the Italian government, which had joined the Allied side in 1915. Just as Italy found itself separated from the Vatican, U.S. Catholics viewed the war as an opportunity to Americanize the church. Catholics, who wanted to rid the church of its foreign and ambiguously loyal image in Protestant eyes, endorsed Protestant explanations of the war. In the United States as in France, ecumenicism pervaded as Americans attempted to mobilize all of society. Although after the war the sense of ecumenicism dissipated, the experience led Roman Catholics in the United States to create a national body, the National Catholic Welfare Council, to agitate on its behalf and gain acceptance as a vital moral U.S. institution. The war may have done much to increase the acceptance of Catholics in American society; in 1928, Al Smith became the first Catholic to run for president on the ticket of a major political party.

While the war revealed religious problems and tensions in the major European powers, it also prompted religious upheaval in the Middle East. Just as certain Protestants viewed the war as an opportunity to advance their cause, in Constantinople Ottoman Sultan-Caliph Mehmed V issued a call to jihad (holy war) against the Allied Powers in order to rally his Arab subjects behind the decision to side with the Central Powers but also to gain support among Arabs living under British and French control. The Ottoman Arab subjects remained loyal for the most part, but the proclamation failed to generate significant response in the Arab regions under the control of the Entente powers. Ultimately the British were successful in supporting an Arab Revolt against Ottoman rule. Western intrusion into Arab affairs eventually led to the disastrous religious conflict over Palestine between the Jews and Arabs after World War II.

When the war finally ended in 1918 with Europe devastated and fragmented, Christians on both sides had to reevaluate their concepts of the war. German Christians, having insisted that God would not fail to support their country, were unable therefore to see the war as a failure on God's part. Rather, many chose to attribute the defeat to the failure of the Volk to remain steadfast in their faith and principles; God used defeat as purification. People in the Allied countries tended to envisage their military victory as a moral one and the new League of Nations as the extension of Christian ethics into world history. Wilson and Progressive Christians in the United States agreed, but the president's refusal to compromise with the Republican leadership on the League of Nations led the U.S. Congress to reject the treaty, lengthening the odds against the League's survival. While the Progressive vision in the United States was not abandoned immediately, it had been dealt a sharp blow. By the time of the Great Depression, liberal theologians began contemplating the limits of humanity's moral efforts.

While World War I should not be viewed as exceptional in its use of religion—the clergy have often insinuated themselves into national politics and foreign affairs—religion in this war did contribute to the concept of total war, making the use of more effective weaponry and attacks against civilians morally acceptable. The war also spelled the end of boundless optimism so evident in the prewar years among many Christians. American theologians would come to reject the utopian vision of the Progressives, while many German Protestants would grant Adolf Hitler and the Nazis their blessing in their attempt to establish a new order.

Lisa Roy Vox

See also

Arab Revolt; Atrocities; Benedict XV, Pope; Conscientious Objectors; Fourteen Points; Hitler, Adolf; League of Nations Covenant; Mehmed V, Sultan; Pacifism; Peace Overtures during the War; Red Cross; Roosevelt, Theodore; Salvation Army; Selective Service Act; Wilson, Thomas Woodrow.

References

Becker, Annette. *War and Faith: The Religious Imagination in France, 1914–1930.* New York: Oxford University Press, 1998.

Gamble, Richard. *The War for Righteousness: Progressive Christianity, the Great War and the Rise of the Messianic Nation.* Wilmington, DE: ISI Books, 2003.

Hoover, A. J. *God, Germany, and Britain in the Great War: A Study in Clerical Nationalism.* New York: Praeger, 1989.

Marrin, Albert. *The Last Crusade: The Church of England in the First World War.* Durham, NC: Duke University Press, 1974.

McKeown, Elizabeth. *War and Welfare: American Catholics and World War I.* New York: Garland, 1988.

Mock, Melanie Springer. *Writing Peace: The Unheard Voices of Great War Mennonite Objectors.* Telford, PA: Pandora, 2003.

Piper, John F., Jr. *The American Churches in World War I.* Athens: University of Ohio Press, 1985.

Schweitzer, Richard. *The Cross and the Trenches: Religious Faith and Doubt among British and American Great War Soldiers.* Westport, CT: Praeger, 2003.

Williams, John. *The Other Battleground: The Home Fronts; Britain, France and Germany, 1914–1918.* Chicago: Regnery, 1972.

Remarque, Erich Maria (1898–1970)

German soldier and novelist. Born on 22 June 1898 in Osnabruck, Erich Remarque was attending teacher's college in the fall of 1916 when he was drafted into the German army. He served as an infantryman on the Western Front and was known as being cool-headed and brave in combat; twice he rescued wounded comrades under fire. He was wounded several times, the last time severely, and he spent the last months of the war convalescing in a hospital in Duisburg, Germany.

Remarque made several unsuccessful forays into writing in the 1920s. He finally wrote *All Quiet on the Western Front* as a personal attempt to come to terms with the bleakness and difficulty adjusting to normal life that he and so many veterans had experienced after the war. Published in Germany in 1929, *All Quiet on the Western Front* remains today one of the most widely read and influential works of literature by a combat veteran. The novel depicts the experiences of a common infantryman in the trenches on the Western Front with all its horrors and hardships. Quickly hailed as a masterpiece, the novel's straightforward style and frank portrayal of the war's impersonal destruction immediately struck a chord with veterans and the public at large. Translated into other languages, the book sold 3.5 million copies in a year and a half. It was also made into a very successful and critically acclaimed U.S. film in 1930.

Remarque followed with another novel, *The Road Back*, in 1931. It detailed the difficulties veterans experienced in adjusting to civilian life after the Great War. Remarque also attracted the ire of the National Socialists, who forced him from Germany when they took power. They accused Remarque of being a leftist and a Jew, neither of which was true. In 1933 they banned his novels as unpatriotic and pacifistic. Remarque lived in Switzerland until he immigrated to the

United States in 1939. He continued writing and became a U.S. citizen in 1947. Among his later works were two dealing with the German experience under Nazi rule: *Arch of Triumph* (1946) and *Spark of Life* (1952). Remarque died in Locarno, Switzerland, on 25 September 1970.

Thomas J. Stuhlreyer

See also
Jünger, Ernst; Literature and the War.
References
Eksteins, Modris. *Rites of Spring: The Great War and the Birth of the Modern Age.* Boston: Houghton Mifflin, 1989.
Fussell, Paul. *The Great War and Modern Memory.* New York: Oxford University Press, 1975.
Linder, Ann P. *Princes of the Trenches: Narrating the German Experience of World War I.* Columbia, SC: Camden House, 1996.
Owen, C. R. *Erich Maria Remarque: A Critical Bio-Bibliography.* Amsterdam Rodopi Bv Editions, 1984.
Remarque, Erich Maria. *All Quiet on the Western Front.* New York: Little, Brown, 1930.
Wagner, Hans. *Understanding Erich Maria Remarque.* Columbia: University of South Carolina Press, 1991.

Russian General Pavel Karlovich Rennenkampf, commander of the First Army that invaded East Prussia in August 1914. (Francis J. Reynolds and C. W. Taylor, *Collier's Photographic History of the European War,* P. F. Collier & Son, New York, 1916)

Rennenkampf, Pavel Karlovich (1854–1918)

Russian general who played a major role in battles in East Prussia early in the war. Born on 29 April 1854 to a family of Baltic German (and possibly Austrian) nobility, Pavel Rennenkampf graduated from the Helsingfors Cadet School in 1873. After several field assignments as a cavalry officer, he graduated from the General Staff Academy in 1882. He received command of a cavalry regiment in the Kiev Military District in 1895. By 1900 Rennenkampf had been transferred to Siberia, where his service with the Transbaikal Cossacks earned him a reputation for courage.

At the outbreak of the 1904–1905 Russo-Japanese War, Rennenkampf commanded the Transbaikal Cossack Division, and by the time of the Battle of Mukden he had received temporary command of the bulk of the Russian cavalry. His courage enhanced his reputation in the army, however, he was ineffective in handling large units and displayed an ignorance of cavalry's shortcomings on the modern battlefield. In 1905 he received command of a punitive expedition to put down revolutionary activities near Chita. His firm, legalistic actions earned him a reputation for harshness that was probably undeserved, but they endeared him to political conservatives. In 1907 Rennenkampf took command of III Corps, and then in 1913 he received command of the Vilna Military District.

Rennenkampf commanded the Russian First Army at the start of World War I. In accordance with the Russian war plan, his mission was to invade East Prussia along with General Aleksandr Samsonov's Second Army and trap the Ger-

man forces between the two Russian pincers. Rennenkampf engaged the Germans at Stallupönen (17 August 1914) and Gumbinnen (20 August 1914). After Gumbinnen, a tactical Russian victory, the First Army's advance slowed to a crawl. Both Rennenkampf and his front (Army Group) commander, General Yakov Zhilinski, mistakenly believed that the Germans were routed and hoped that Samsonov's Second Army would complete the victory. Partly due to Rennenkampf's sluggish movements, the Germans annihilated Samsonov's force in the Battle of Tannenberg.

The Germans quickly turned their attention to Rennenkampf's First Army and on 7 September launched an offensive near the Masurian Lakes. Rennenkampf had spread his forces along the front without retaining adequate reserves, and the Germans achieved a breakthrough. The Russians were forced to retreat. Some scholars claim that Rennenkampf kept his forces from destruction during the withdrawal, while others accuse the First Army commander of incompetence. In any event, the Russians suffered heavy casualties before reestablishing a new defensive line near the East Prussian border.

In November 1914, Rennenkampf again proved slow to advance his army during the conflicts at Thorn and Łódź. These latest failures, coupled with the mistakes at Tannenberg and the Masurian Lakes, led to his relief from command at the end of the month.

After his dismissal, a court inquiry scrutinized Rennenkampf's actions. He was officially exonerated of gross malfeasance, but he was still held responsible for his army's failure to support Samsonov at Tannenberg. Rennenkampf retired from active service and remained in Saint Petersburg until late 1917. He then moved toward south Russia, where he was captured and executed by the Bolsheviks in late March 1918.

Curtis S. King

See also

Gumbinnen, Battle of; Łódź, Battle of; Masurian Lakes, First Battle of the; Russia, War Plan; Samsonov, Aleksandr Vasiliyevich; Stallupönen, Battle of; Tannenberg, Battle of; Zhilinski, Yakov Grigorevich.

References

Clark, Alan. *Suicide of the Empires: The Battles on the Eastern Front, 1914–18.* New York: American Heritage Press, 1971.

Lincoln, W. Bruce. *Passage through Armageddon: The Russians in War and Revolution, 1914–1918.* New York: Simon and Schuster, 1986.

Showalter, Dennis E. *Tannenberg: Clash of Empires.* Hamden, CT: Archon, 1991.

Stone, Norman. *The Eastern Front, 1914–1917.* New York: Scribner, 1975.

Reparations

Indemnity payments imposed upon defeated Germany, Austria, and Hungary in compensation for the damage the war had inflicted on the Allied Powers. At the Paris Peace Conference of 1919, the victorious Allied leaders agreed that the Central Powers, especially Germany, were guilty of starting World War I and therefore should be liable for the financial burden of the devastation other European powers had suffered. Precedence for this existed, as Germany had imposed heavy indemnities on France in the Treaty of Frankfurt of May 1871 and on Russia in the Treaty of Brest Litovsk of March 1918. The United States acquiesced in this principle at Paris but demanded no reparations for itself. U.S., British, and French leaders found it impossible to reach a mutually acceptable figure at the conference, while German officials protested that their devastated country lacked the resources to pay even 60 billion gold marks over several decades, the smallest of the figures Allied economic experts at Paris envisaged.

To resolve the deadlock the Allies created a Reparation Commission mandated to determine the total liabilities of Germany and its allies no later than May 1921. After the U.S. Senate repeatedly refused to ratify the Treaty of Versailles, the U.S. government formally withdrew from this body; however, it still kept unofficial but influential "observers" in place. In May 1921 the commission set a total German liability of 132 billion gold marks—50 billion to be funded over thirty-seven years, the remainder at some unspecified future date if and when the commission should decide that Germany could afford to pay.

An unexpressed but widely acknowledged hope was that the U.S. government would cancel a substantial portion of the approximately $12 billion in war debts that the former Allied governments had incurred to purchase war supplies from U.S. sources, thereby enabling the Allies to be equally lenient toward Germany's obligations. U.S. officials rejected all attempts to link war debt payments to reparations and strongly resented the 1922 British Balfour Note. The note stated that Britain would seek no more in reparations from its enemies and debt repayments from its allies than it required to repay its own obligations to the United States. Austria and Hungary encountered more modest reparation bills, and having accepted these in principle they were able to raise international loans through the League of Nations for postwar reconstruction, whereupon the Allied governments suspended their reparation payments for twenty years.

The new republican government of Germany, a far wealthier state, initially acquiesced in reparations arrangements, but leading Ruhr industrialists were determined to resist such transfers of funds to the Allies. An exchange crisis quickly resulted, followed by hyperinflation as Germany printed money to meet its internal budget deficit. In early 1922 the German government defaulted on scheduled reparation payments. After lengthy but fruitless negotiations, in January 1923 French Premier Raymond Poincaré sent French troops into Germany's wealthy Ruhr district with the stated intention of extracting payment in kind and forcing Germany to live up to its treaty obligations. Poincaré feared that if Germany could break its obligations in this area, it would do so with the remainder of the treaty as well. The German government now encouraged a program of "passive resistance" from workers in the Ruhr, promising to pay for their patriotic idleness while it appealed to Britain and the United States to press France to withdraw its troops. This pressure was forthcoming, but Poincaré refused to budge; the result was catastrophic, with ruinous inflation in Germany that pauperized the middle class and had much to do with the coming to power of Adolf Hitler a decade later. The occupation also proved costly to France financially, and in the national elections of 1924, the left came to power in that country.

The impasse was broken in 1924 when an international committee of government officials and financiers, headed by the American banker Charles G. Dawes, convened at Paris to reassess Germany's reparations burden. Under the so-called Dawes Plan, German payments were substantially reduced, and both Germany and France obtained large international loans on the European and U.S. financial markets. Although the U.S. government supposedly remained aloof from the Dawes Plan, U.S. officials followed its evolution closely. Dawes and Owen D. Young, another prominent American businessman, took the lead in the committee's deliberations, working closely with the top New York investment bank, J. P.

Morgan and Company, the partners of which negotiated the loans underpinning the Dawes Plan. In practice, reparations were paid not from German production but from the proceeds of massive private loans on behalf of assorted German enterprises issued in the U.S. market during the later 1920s.

Even in 1924 many of those involved thought Germany's payments still impracticably high, and in 1929 another committee, headed by Young, reduced the annuities by an additional 20 percent. As the Great Depression gradually intensified after 1929, U.S. loans to Germany dried up, leading Germany to threaten to default on its reparation payments. In 1931 President Herbert Hoover negotiated a one-year moratorium for intergovernmental payments on both reparations and war debts. At the 1932 Lausanne Conference, the former Allies effectively canceled the remaining reparations burden, demanding only a final token payment, and even this Germany ultimately failed to pay.

Then and later critics such as the highly influential economist John Maynard Keynes attacked the reparations settlement as unworkable economically and part of a broader vengeful attempt to wreak retribution upon Germany and keep that country weak, which was likely to breed future German resentment and precipitate forcible efforts to reverse it. More recently, historians have suggested that economically it would have been quite feasible for Germany to pay those sums fixed by the various reparations settlements, but that whatever their political outlook German leaders would nonetheless have found it politically impossible to continue such protracted payments over the lengthy timespans envisaged.

Priscilla Roberts

See also
Brest Litovsk, Treaty of; Hoover, Herbert Clark; J. P. Morgan and Company; Keynes, John Maynard; Paris Peace Conference; Poincaré, Raymond; Rathenau, Walther; Stresemann, Gustav; Versailles, Treaty of; War Debts.

References
Costigliola, Frank. *Awkward Dominion: American Political, Economic, and Cultural Relations with Europe, 1919–1933.* Ithaca, NY: Cornell University Press, 1984.
Ferguson, Niall. *The Pity of War: Explaining World War I.* New York: Basic Books, 1999.
Hogan, Michael J. *Informal Entente: The Private Structure of Cooperation in Anglo-American Economic Diplomacy, 1918–1928.* Columbia: University of Missouri Press, 1977.
Kent, Bruce. *The Spoils of War: The Politics, Economics, and Diplomacy of Reparations, 1918–1932.* Oxford, UK: Clarendon, 1989.
McNeil, William C. *American Money and the Weimar Republic: Economics and Politics on the Eve of the Great Depression.* New York: Columbia University Press, 1986.
Schuker, Stephen A. *The End of French Predominance in Europe: The Financial Crisis of 1924 and the Adoption of the Dawes Plan.* Chapel Hill: University of North Carolina Press, 1976.
Silverman, Daniel P. *Reconstructing Europe after the Great War.* Cambridge: Harvard University Press, 1982.
Trachtenberg, Marc. *Reparation in World Politics: France and European Economic Diplomacy, 1916–1923.* New York: Columbia University Press, 1980.
Wheeler-Bennett, John W. *The Wreck of Reparations: Being the Political Background of the Lausanne Agreement, 1932.* London: Allen and Unwin, 1932.
Wilson, Joan Hoff. *American Business and Foreign Policy, 1920–1922.* Lexington: University Press of Kentucky, 1971.

Reuter, Ludwig von (1869–1943)

German navy admiral. Born on 9 February 1869 in Guben, Germany, Ludwig von Reuter participated in the 3 November 1914 raid on Scarborough, Scotland, as commander of the battle cruiser *Derflinger.* In January 1915 he took part in the Battle of the Dogger Bank, where the *Derflinger* provided effective gunnery support. Reuter also participated in the 1916 Battle of Jutland where he commanded the 4th Scouting Group of five light cruisers with his flag in the *Stettin.* After this battle Reuter was transferred to the Baltic, where he took part in Operation ALBION against Russian-held islands. He returned to the North Sea in November 1917 and participated in the second Helgoland Bight skirmishes. Following this action he was promoted to rear admiral and took command of the Scouting Forces of the High Seas Fleet.

At the end of the war Reuter was placed in charge of the ships surrendered to the British and held at Scapa Flow in the Orkney Islands. On 21 June 1919, acting on secret orders from Berlin, Reuter ordered the vessels of the High Seas Fleet scuttled. A total of fifty-three major German warships went down, including ten battleships, five battle cruisers, five light cruisers, and thirty-three destroyers. The British managed to save a battleship, three light cruisers, and eighteen destroyers.

As the scuttling of the fleet was a direct violation of the terms of the armistice, Reuter and his men were held as prisoners of war. Reuter returned to Germany in February 1920, where he was regarded as a national hero for safeguarding the honor of the German navy. Reuter died in Potsdam on 18 December 1943.

Alex Correll

See also
ALBION, Operation; Dogger Bank, Battle of the; Jutland, Battle of; Scapa Flow, Scuttling of German Fleet at; Scarborough Raid.

References
Herwig, Holger H. *"Luxury" Fleet: The Imperial German Navy, 1888–1918.* London: Allen and Unwin, 1980.
Reuter, Ludwig von. *Scapa Flow: The Account of the Greatest Scuttling of all Time.* London: Hurst and Blackett, 1940.
Ruge, Friedrich. *Scapa Flow 1919: The End of the German Fleet.* London: Ian Allan, 1973.
Van der Vat, Dan. *The Grand Scuttle: The Sinking of the German Fleet at Scapa Flow in 1919.* Annapolis: Naval Institute Press, 1986.

Revel, Paolo Thaon di
See Thaon di Revel, Paolo.

Ribot, Alexandre (1842–1923)

French political leader and premier. Born at St. Omer, France, on 6 February 1842, Alexandre Ribot was a brilliant student who earned a law degree in 1863 and became a judge. Ribot was elected to the National Assembly in 1878, initiating a parliamentary career of forty-five years. An Anglophile and moderate republican, Ribot focused on the areas of government finance and foreign affairs. He was premier during 1892–1893 and again in 1905, but he made his most important contribution to France in this period as foreign minister during 1890–1893, when he was responsible for negotiating the 1892 Franco-Russian Military Convention against Germany.

The Dreyfus Affair nearly ended Ribot's political career, his centrist position alienating both sides. He moved to the Senate in 1909 and failed in a bid for the presidency of France in 1912. He supported the three-year military service law of 1913 and the direct income tax of 1914.

In August 1914 Ribot took the portfolio of minister of finance in the Union Sacrée government, with the heavy responsibility of directing France's finances during the war. A fiscal conservative, Ribot was forced to change his views thanks to the mounting government expenditures for the war. He helped meet these by negotiating loans from Great Britain and from private U.S. bankers, notably the firm of J. P. Morgan and Company. Despite the presence of associated Morgan banking houses in both Paris and London, France found its relationship with the predominantly Anglophile Morgan firm far more difficult than did its British ally and tended to contemplate turning to other sources of U.S. finance, tactics that generated yet further tensions with the somewhat arrogant Morgan partners.

On 20 March 1917, Ribot succeeded Aristide Briand to become the third French premier of the war. Once premier,

French Prime Minister and Premier Alexandre Ribot named Henri Philippe Pétain as French commander-in-chief. (National Archives)

Ribot initially opposed but eventually capitulated to the demands of French army commander General Robert Nivelle for an offensive against Germany in the Champagne area. The disastrous April 1917 Nivelle offensive caused heavy casualties and extensive mutinies by French troops. Ribot faced attacks from the French left when he rejected overtures for a separate peace with Germany, on the grounds that he would not embark on any negotiations unless these were predicated on the return of Alsace-Lorraine to France. Radicals also resented Ribot's refusal of passports to French Socialists who sought to attend an international socialist peace conference in Stockholm. The right, meanwhile, assailed him as a defeatist whose handling of internal security matters was inadequate. Ribot resigned as premier on 7 September 1917, although he remained as foreign minister for an additional month.

Ribot spent the remainder of the war in the Senate. Appalled by the heavy damage to his home district of France, he became a strong advocate of hefty reparations against Germany, but he also opposed territorial acquisitions for France that might lead to a new war. Ribot died in Paris on 13 January 1923.

Priscilla Roberts and Spencer C. Tucker

See also
Briand, Aristide; J. P. Morgan and Company; Nivelle, Robert; Nivelle Offensive; Reparations; Stockholm Conference; War Aims.
References
Horn, Martin. *Britain, France, and the Financing of the First World War.* Montreal: McGill-Queen's University Press, 2002.
King, Jere Clemens. *Generals and Politicians: Conflict between France's High Command, Parliament, and Government, 1914–1918.* Berkeley: University of California Press, 1951.
Ribot, Alexandre. *Journal d'Alexandre Ribot et Correspondances Inédites, 1914–1922.* Paris: Librairie Plon, 1936.
Schmidt, Martin E. *Alexandre Ribot: Odyssey of a Liberal in the Third Republic.* The Hague: Martinus Nyhoff, 1974.
Stevenson, David. *French War Aims against Germany, 1914–1919.* Oxford, UK: Clarendon, 1982.

Rice Riots (July–September 1918)

Largest and last popular movement in Japan that took place without any leadership or solid organization. The Rice Riots occurred from July to September 1918 and were a protest against economic hard times during World War I caused by inflation, especially the sharp rise of rice prices. Other factors contributing to the riot were the development of Taisho democracy, the influx of a large number of workers into urban areas that raised the level of rice consumption, the stagnation of rice production, and private hoarding of rice for profit during the Japanese intervention in Siberia.

In July 1918 a group of wives of fishermen in Toyama devised a plan to halt rice shipments, a protest that quickly spread to other parts of Japan. Approximately 700,000 people—not only farmers and fishermen but also day laborers, cartmen, roustabouts, factory workers, and the middle class—joined the movement. Since the police could not control the situation, the army dispatched more than 100,000 men to suppress riots in over 100 locations, and 25,000 people were taken into custody.

The widespread rioting led to the resignation of Prime Minister Masataki Terauchi and his cabinet. Takashi Hara then became prime minister. His was the first cabinet based on a leading political party, the Seiyukai. The Rice Riots spawned a number of specific protest movements that advocated labor and political reforms, including universal suffrage.

Sugita Yoneyuki

See also
Hara Takashi; Siberian Intervention, Japan; Terauchi, Masatake.
References
Dickinson, Frederick R. *War and National Reinvention: Japan in the Great War, 1914–1919.* Cambridge: Harvard University Press, 1999.
Duus, Peter, ed. *The Cambridge History of Japan,* Vol. 6, *The Twentieth Century.* New York: Cambridge University Press, 1988.
Silberman, Bernard S., and H. D. Harootunian, eds. *Japan in Crisis: Essays on Taisho Democracy.* Ann Arbor, MI: Center for Japanese Studies, University of Michigan, 1999.
Young, Arthur Morgan. *Japan in Recent Times, 1912–1926.* Westport, CT: Greenwood, 1973.

Richthofen, Manfred von, Baron (1892–1918)

German air service officer and leading ace of the war. Born in Breslau, Germany (today Wroclaw, Poland) on 2 May 1892 to a wealthy titled family, Manfred Albrecht von Richthofen graduated from Prussian cadet school in 1912 and joined a cavalry regiment. At the outbreak of World War I, he was a cavalry lieutenant in the 1st Uhlans on the Russian Front. In January 1915 he transferred to the air service as an observer. A chance meeting with ace Oswald Boelcke convinced him to become a pilot. Richthofen received his pilot's badge on Christmas Day 1915 and joined a squadron on the Russian Front. Boelcke then induced him to join his Jagdstaffel (fighter squadron) 2.

Richthofen scored his first victory on 17 September 1916 over Cambrai, France. By January 1917, his victory total had reached sixteen and he commanded his own squadron, Jagdstaffel 11. Two days later he received the Pour le Mérite, or "Blue Max." Richthofen's squadron became a scourge over the Western Front. Each aircraft had its tail painted red with distinct individual markings. Richthofen's plane was entirely red. The unit became known as the "Flying Circus" and Richthofen "The Red Baron."

The infamous "Red Baron," Manfred von Richthofen, commander of the Flying Circus and with eighty kills, the leading ace of the war. (Library of Congress)

On 1 July 1917, Richthofen took command of Jagdgeschwader (Fighter Wing) 1, comprising four squadrons with forty-eight aircraft. Instead of regularly scheduled patrols, his fighters scrambled only when enemy aircraft were spotted. On 6 July Richthofen received a severe head wound in combat and spent more than a month on leave. During this time the government used him for propaganda duties, and he wrote his memoirs. He also pressed army leaders and aircraft manufacturers to produce better fighters. The result appeared in late 1917 in the form of Anthony Fokker's DR1 Dreidecker (tri-wing). Not satisfied, Fokker in January 1918 produced the exquisite D-VII. Armed with these superior weapons, Richthofen's pilots wreaked havoc throughout the spring of 1918. Ultimately the Red Baron had eighty aerial victories.

On 21 April while patrolling near British lines in the area of Vaux-sur-Somme, Richthofen pursued an opposing aircraft. As they dived near an Australian machine-gun antiaircraft battery, Richthofen's aircraft was attacked by Canadian pilot Roy Brown. Brown and the Australians on the ground both fired at Richthofen, who then crash-landed near a group of ground troops, who also fired at him. When the British forces reached Richthofen, he was dead, killed by a single shot through the heart.

Brown received credit for the kill, but recent studies by experts have suggested that the Australians brought down the Red Baron. In any case, the British Royal Flying Corps buried him in France with full military honors. Later, his body was returned to Wiesbaden. Although he was best known for his eighty victories, Richthofen's efforts to secure better fighters and his development of large-formation fighter tactics were of great importance.

William Head

See also
Air Warfare, Fighter Tactics; Aircraft, Fighters; Boelcke, Oswald; Fokker, Anthony Herman Gerard.
References
Kilduff, Peter. *The Red Baron*. New York: Doubleday, 1969.
Morrow, John H., Jr. *German Air Power in World War I*. Lincoln: University of Nebraska Press, 1982.
Nowarra, Heinz J., and Kimbrough S. Brown. *Von Richthofen and the Flying Circus*. 3rd ed. Letchworth, UK: Harleyford, 1964.
Richthofen, Manfred Albrecht von. *The Red Baron*. Trans. Peter Kilduff. Garden City, NY: Doubleday, 1969.

Rickenbacker, Edward Vernon (1890–1973)

U.S. aviation pioneer. Born on 8 October 1890 in Columbus, Ohio, Edward Rickenbacker had little formal schooling. After a succession of jobs, he became a race car driver and at one point held the land speed record of 134 miles per hour.

On U.S. entry into World War I, Rickenbacker joined the army and went to France in the American Expeditionary Forces (AEF). Originally a chauffeur for General John Pershing's staff, he secured the assistance of Colonel William Mitchell to transfer to the air service in August 1917. After training at Issoudun, France, Captain Rickenbacker was assigned to the 94th Aero Pursuit "Hat in the Ring" Squadron, the first U.S. squadron to see action. In May 1918 he became commander of the 94th and was promoted to temporary major. Rickenbacker flew his first combat mission on 14 April and shot down his first plane two weeks later. By May he had shot down six planes. He was later awarded the Medal of Honor for his actions on 25 September 1918, when he attacked seven German planes and shot down two of them. By the end of the war, he had shot down twenty-two airplanes and four observation balloons in less than seven months, making him the leading American ace of the war. His 94th Squadron was credited with shooting down sixty-nine German aircraft.

Returning to the United States in 1919, Rickenbacker started Rickenbacker Motor Company, which failed in 1926. He went on to buy a controlling interest in the Indianapolis

American ace Major Eddie Rickenbacker of the 94th Aero Squadron, standing up in his Spad plane, at an airfield near Rembercourt, France, 18 October 1918. (National Archives)

Motor Speedway, worked for the Cadillac Division of the General Motors Corporation, and become president and director of Eastern Airlines. During World War II Rickenbacker carried out two special assignments, one to the Soviet Union and the other to inspect air bases in the Pacific. In October 1942 his B-17 crashed 600 miles north of Samoa, and he spent twenty-two days in a life raft before rescue. After the war Rickenbacker continued to direct Eastern Airlines. He retired in 1954 and died on 23 July 1973 in Zurich, Switzerland.

T. Jason Soderstrum

See also
Air Warfare, Fighter Tactics; Mitchell, William; Pershing, John
   Joseph; United States, Army Air Service.
References
Farr, Finis. *Rickenbacker's Luck: An American Life.* Boston:
   Houghton Mifflin, 1979.
Garlin, Sender. *The Real Rickenbacker.* New York: Workers Library,
   1943.
Jeffers, H. Paul. *Ace of Aces: The Life of Capt. Eddie Rickenbacker.*
   New York: Presidio/Ballantine, 2003.
Rickenbacker, Eddie. *Rickenbacker.* Englewood Cliffs, NJ: Prentice-
   Hall, 1968.

Riezler, Kurt (1882–1955)

German government official and scholar. Born on 11 February 1882 at Munich, Kurt Riezler studied classical philology, history, and economic history at Munich University during 1901–1906. Extensive European travel stimulated his interest in political journalism. In 1906 Riezler entered the press office of the German Foreign Office and was made legation councilor in 1910.

When Theobald von Bethmann Hollweg became imperial chancellor in 1909, Riezler soon became one of his closest confidants. He developed the concept of "calculated risk," which influenced the politics of the chancellor in the July Crisis of 1914. Riezler also developed the 1914 September Memorandum, listing German war aims. He hoped for a Central Europe (Mitteleuropa) led by Germany but without major annexations of territory. In contrast to army leaders and many German nationalists, Riezler suggested imperialism based not on coercion but on persuasion and demonstrated

German cultural superiority. His war diaries, published by Karl-Dietrich Erdmann in 1972, renewed discussion among historians concerning German war guilt.

After Bethmann Hollweg's departure from office on 13 July 1917, Riezler became section head for Russian affairs in the German legation at Stockholm that November. Following the Treaty of Brest Litovsk with Russia in March 1918, Riezler was promoted to councillor at the German Embassy in Moscow that April and undertook development of plans whereby Germany might assist a counterrevolution to overthrow the Bolsheviks. Under Chancellor Max von Baden, Riezler became cabinet chief to Minister of Foreign Affairs Wilhelm Solf in October 1918. During the German Revolution of November 1918–January 1919, he served as a permanent representative of the German government to the Bavarian state government in Bamberg and strongly supported military actions undertaken to recapture Munich. He was head of the secretariat of first president of the German Republic Friedrich Ebert during 1919–1920.

During the Weimar Republic, Riezler became an honorary professor at the University of Frankfurt am Main in 1928. He immigrated to the United States in 1938 and became a professor at the New School for Social Research in New York and also a guest professor at the University of Chicago. He returned to Europe in 1954 and died in Munich, Germany, on 5 September 1955.

Bert Becker

See also
Bethmann Hollweg, Theobald von; Ebert, Friedrich; Germany, Revolution in; Max von Baden, Prince; Mitteleuropa; Solf, Wilhelm Heinrich; War Aims.

References
Becker, Bert. "Riezler, Kurt." In *Neue Deutsche Biographie*, Vol. 21, 618–619. Berlin: Duncker and Humblot, 2003.
Erdmann, Karl-Dietrich, ed. *Kurt Riezler: Tagebücher, Aufsätze, Dokumente.* Goettingen: Vandenhoeck and Ruprecht, 1972.
Fischer, Fritz. *Germany's Aims in the First World War.* New York: Norton, 1967.
Moses, John A. *The Politics of Illusion: The Fisher Controversy in German Historiography.* London: Prior, 1975.

Rifles

Rifle manufacture came of age in the nineteenth century when the bolt action was perfected, allowing the rifleman to reload by mechanical means. The principal significance of this was that riflemen could now reload from a prone position, a significant tactical advance. The rifle fired a composite cartridge, with bullet, propellant, and primer contained in one factory-made load; sights were developed that enabled accurate fire to 800 yards and volley fire up to around 2,000 yards. Further rifles were now of smaller calibers (between 0.25-inch and 0.3-inch bore), and they were lighter and easier to carry over long distances.

All World War I armies were armed with bolt-action magazine rifles that fired a composite cartridge. The operation of the rifles was relatively simple. A clip (charger in the British army) containing between three and five cartridges was used to load the magazine. The bolt action was used to open the breech on a rearward movement, and the subsequent forward movement chambered a cartridge from the magazine. Once fired, the manual retraction of the bolt extracted the empty case from the chamber, and the ejector threw the spent case away from the rifle. Rates of fire of up to fifteen aimed rounds per minute were possible.

The rifle was cocked (the firing pin being held back mechanically, with a spring to force it forward when fired) either on the rearward or the forward movement of the bolt. Perhaps the smoothest action from the rifleman's point of view was the Short Magazine Lee Enfield series, which saw service right through World War I as well as, with some modification, World War II.

The Germans were issued the Mauser Gewehr G98 in 7.92mm caliber. Mauser was a famous name in the firearms world, and rifles were made for a number of other countries by the company or under license in the country concerned. The G98 appeared in 1898 and was a design that achieved fame both in its original form and in World War II in its shortened form as the Karabine K98, the standard rifle for the German army throughout war.

The rifle fired a 7.92 × 57mm cartridge (the second figure denotes the overall length of the cartridge) with a muzzle velocity of 2,854 feet per second (fps) to a sighted range of 2,000 yards. Total weight of the rifle was just 9 pounds, and the overall length was 49.25 inches. It was loaded from a five-round integral box magazine. The rifle had one slight drawback in that the bolt action was none too smooth, but it was nevertheless an excellent weapon.

The new British rifles had been designed at the turn of the century. Weapons designers needed to increase the depth of rifling when cordite was introduced as a propellant, as the older Lee-Metford system of rifling was easily damaged by this hotter new powder. The result was the Lee-Enfield rifling system. Added to this was the need for the British army to have one rifle for all troops rather than rifles and carbines, all themselves adapted variously for use by cavalry, engineers, and infantry.

The short-magazine Lee-Enfield Mark III rifle (SMLE) was the 1902 version. It had a Lee bolt action. James P. Lee had a long history of successful firearms design to his credit. The turning-bolt was adopted by the British, improved, and used to form this famous action, renowned for its smoothness of operation. The S.M.L.E. had a ten-round magazine, was 44.50 inches in length, weighed 8.66 pounds, and had a muzzle velocity of 2,060 fps.

U.S. troops being instructed in the proper care and maintenance of their rifles, near Moulle, France, 22 May 1918. (National Archives)

In 1914 the French army was equipped with the rather ancient Lebel 8mm Modèle 86. The first small bore military rifle to be adopted by any nation, it featured a tube magazine under the barrel. The design, similar to early Winchester repeating rifles, had one significant drawback. Pointed-nosed bullets could not be used because the point of one bullet came into contact with the primer of the bullet in front of it, making an explosion in the magazine highly likely. This meant that the French army used rounded-nosed bullets, which were ballistically inferior. Rounds also had to be loaded individually, which gave the Lebel an inferior rate of fire. The rifle itself was a workmanlike design, and many were used by snipers and for grenade launching, something for which the French Berthier rifle was not suitable. The Lebel had an eight-round magazine, was 51.1 inches in overall length, weighed 9.22 pounds, and had a muzzle velocity of 2,380 fps.

In 1916 the French army adopted the Mannlicher-Berthier rifle, also of 8mm caliber. It had a five-round magazine and an overall length of 51.3 inches, weighed 9.34 pounds, and fired its bullets at 2,380 fps.

The Russian army was equipped with the Moisin-Nagant rifle in 7.62mm (0.3-inch) caliber. It was a bolt-operated rifle designed by Colonel Sergei I. Mosin of the Russian army and first appeared in 1891. The five-round magazine design was by a Belgian company, Émile and Léon Nagant in Liège. The weapon was not well designed, having only moderate accuracy with the 7.62mm bullet. The cartridge, like the British 0.303-inch, was rimmed. The Moison-Nagant was 48.5 inches in length and weighed nearly 9 pounds. It fired its rounds at 1,985 fps.

Rimmed cartridges were common to Russia and Britain in the war, but all other main protagonists had adopted the rimless cartridge. Rimless cartridges are easier to load and handle, despite the British criticism that they were weaker at the base than the rimmed cartridge. U.S. weapons, however, were designed around the .30-06 cartridge, a rimless cartridge that served U.S. troops well until the late 1950s.

The rifle the American Expeditionary Forces (AEF) infantry brought with them to France in 1917 was the Springfield .30-06 M-1903. This rifle had a Mauser-type bolt action and was superbly accurate. Even today the .30–06 Springfield will be found both on the target range and in the sporting field. Although its action is slower than the Lee-Enfield system, the rifle served well and was regarded highly by all troops who used it. The Springfield had a five-round magazine, weighed 8.5 pounds, was 43.25 inches in length, and fired its M2 ammunition at 2,800 fps. U.S. troops also used the British M1917 Lee-Enfield.

The U.S. troops brought another rifle with them, if "rifle" is a true description; in European parlance it was a light machine gun. This was the Browning Automatic Rifle (BAR), caliber .30, Model 1918. The need for local fire support on the battlefield had become common knowledge, and the BAR was a superb design for the time and far lighter than its British counterpart, the Lewis Gun, or the German Maxim MG 08/15, and was much more reliable than the French Chauchat.

True automatic rifles had, however, existed from early in the twentieth century. The French Saint-Étienne or M1917 and M1918 rifles were true semiautomatic weapons, the first such rifles to be on limited general issue to troops. They fired an 8mm round, one shot per trigger pull, from a five-round magazine. Interestingly, the Russians also had a semiautomatic rifle, the 6.5mm caliber Federov Model 1916 3 Avtomat2. This began as a design for the standard Russian 7.62mm × 54R (round point) cartridge, but that proved too powerful and the Japanese 6.5mm × 50 semirimmed round was chosen instead. The October Revolution in 1917 brought work to an end.

The majority of rifles were, however, the bolt-operated magazine rifles mentioned above, although many smaller nations had their own designs in the field. The rifles were used by line infantry as well as rear-area troops, but they also had specialist uses. Many were developed into sniper rifles with the adoption of telescopic sights. These sights gave a much better resolution, enabling snipers to engage individual, small targets at much greater ranges than the ordinary infantry, whose sighting was by means of the iron sights issued with their rifles. Snipers could shoot at ranges of up to 800 yards.

Rifles were also employed to launch grenades. The British, for example, designed a tube to fit on the muzzle of the Lee-Enfield that was secured by the bayonet lug. This tube had a hole at its base corresponding to the rifle muzzle. Into the tube was placed a Mills hand grenade, which fitted snugly but not tightly. A special round with no bullet was then fired in the rifle, which projected the grenade beyond the ordinary throwing range that a man could manage. This cup discharger is still seen on many museum weapons.

The World War I rifle was sufficiently accurate to engage targets at 800 yards and was durable in the mud, ice, and dust of all fronts during the conflict.

David Westwood

See also
Armaments Production; Assault Weapons; Bayonets; Grenades, Hand; Infantry Tactics; Machine Guns; Pistols; Snipers; Storm Troopers; Trench Warfare.
References
Allen, W. G. B. *Pistols, Rifles and Machine Guns.* London: EUP, 1953.
Huon, Jean. *Military Rifle and Machine Gun Cartridges.* Alexandria, VA: Ironside International, 1988.
Lugs, Jaroslav. *Firearms Past and Present.* London: Greenville, 1973.
Smith, W. B. B. *Small Arms of the World.* 7th ed. Harrisburg, PA: Stackpole, 1962.
Walter, John. *Dictionary of Guns and Gunmakers,* London and Philadelphia: Greenhill and Stackpole, 2001.

Riga, Battle of (1–3 September 1917)

Key battle of the war. On the strategic level, the battle for the Baltic coastal city of Riga effectively eliminated Russia from the war and allowed Germany to focus the majority of its military resources against the Allies in the West in 1918. On the operational level, it was the war's first successful large-scale penetration and breakthrough. On the tactical level, the Germans for the first time applied on a large scale many of the war-fighting innovations they had developed between 1914 and 1918, foreshadowing the end of the battlefield stagnation that characterized ground combat in World War I.

Riga was the extreme right anchor of the Russian line, which ran roughly east and west along the Dvina River and was held by the 10.5 divisions of the Russian Twelfth Army under General Vladislav N. Klembovski. North of the river the Russian defenses consisted of two parallel positions. The forward position began on the dunes along the riverbank and had three and in some places four lines of trenches. The rearward position began 2 miles back from the river and had two sets of trench lines. The Russians also heavily fortified several of the islands in the river.

Along the south bank of the river, General Oskar von Hutier's Eighth Army had 7.5 divisions deployed along the 80-mile sector from the coast to Jacobstadt. The Russian defenses were oriented to directly repel a German attack against Riga. Hutier, however, planned an attack across the Dvina near Uxkull, about 20 miles east of Riga. Once they were across the river, Hutier planned that his forces would then maneuver behind Riga and cut off the Russian garrison. Hutier believed that 10 divisions would be necessary for the river crossing, and the German high command accordingly reinforced Eighth Army with 8 more infantry and 2 cavalry divisions for the operation.

At 9:10 A.M. on 1 September 1917, the German LI Corps launched the assault across the 200-yard-wide Dvina on a 6-mile front. The 19th Reserve Division on the right and the 2nd Guards Infantry Division on the left crossed in assault boats.

Weapons captured by the Germans from the Russians in the 1918 Battle of Riga. (Hulton-Deutsch Collection/Corbis)

In the center, the 14th Bavarian Infantry Division captured and neutralized heavily fortified Borkum Island before continuing on to the north bank.

Once the three first echelon divisions consolidated on the far bank, they quickly overran the forward Russian defensive position. As the lead divisions moved against the rear defensive position, German pioneers finished building pontoon bridges across the Dvina in each of the three divisional attack sectors. Three second-echelon divisions then crossed the river on the bridges and closed up rapidly behind the lead divisions, ready to exploit the breakout from the second defensive positions.

The Russian Twelfth Army began to crumble only three hours into the attack. By the end of the first day, the Germans had six divisions on the far bank in an 8-mile-wide bridgehead. Riga fell late on the afternoon of 3 September. The Russians suffered more than 25,000 casualties in the battle, while the Germans sustained only 4,200 casualties. On 21–22 September the German army again attacked across the Dvina, this time at Jackobstadt on the other end of the Russian line. The two German victories in rapid succession effectively eliminated any Russian military threat to the Baltic sector.

Although Riga initially was regarded as one of the great feats of arms of World War I, some historians in recent years have argued that Riga was not so much captured by the Germans using new tactics as it was given up by a dispirited and broken Russian army. There is probably a certain level of validity to this hypothesis, yet the Riga battle retains its significance as a test bed for the tactics that the Germans would use with such devastating effectiveness at Caporetto two months later, and then on an even larger scale during the Ludendorff offensives on the Western Front in 1918.

Riga was the first large-scale application of the infantry infiltration tactics that had been developed by the Germans in lower-level counterattacks on the Western Front. Popularly known as Storm Troop Tactics, they were also incorrectly called Hutier Tactics by the surprised Allies. Hutier had almost nothing to do with their development. He was simply the first commander to use them in a multicorps operation. More significantly, Riga was the first time that the new infantry tactics were combined with the new artillery fire support tactics that had been developed primarily under the direction of Colonel Georg Bruchmüller on the Eastern Front. Bruchmüller was seconded to the Eighth Army as Hutier's artillery commander for the Riga operation. In early 1918, when Hutier moved to the Western Front to assume command of the newly organized Eighteenth Army, Bruchmüller went with him.

David T. Zabecki

See also

Artillery; Bruchmüller, Georg; Caporetto, Battle of; Hutier, Oskar von; Ludendorff Offensives; Storm Troopers.

References

Fuller, J. F. C. *The Conduct of War: 1789–1961.* Rutgers, NJ: Rutgers University Press, 1961.

Hoffmann, Max. *Der Krieg der Versäumten Gelegenheiten.* Berlin: Verlag für Kulturpolitik, 1929.

Pitt, Barrie. *1918: The Last Act.* New York: Ballantine, 1963.

Zabecki, David T. *Steel Wind: Colonel Georg Bruchmüller and the Birth of Modern Artillery.* Westport, CT: Praeger, 1994.

References

Halpern, Paul G. *A Naval History of World War I.* Annapolis: Naval Institute Press, 1994.

Nekrasov, George. *North of Gallipoli: The Black Sea Fleet at War, 1914–1917.* Boulder, CO: East European Monographs, 1992.

Stone, Norman. *The Eastern Front, 1914–1917.* New York: Scribner, 1975.

Rize Landing (7 April 1916)

Russian navy's amphibious landing on the Turkish coast during the Black Sea and Caucasus campaigns. Conducted on 7 April 1916, it was part of a series of Russian amphibious landings that spring. Rize was a larger version of landings made at Erzurum in February and Atina in March. Commanded by Admiral Nikolay Yudenich, the Rize landing was in support of operations by the Russian army, which was moving through the Turkish coastal areas toward the Black Sea port of Trabzon. Russian capture of this port would mean completion of the second stage of the Russian campaign on the Caucasian Front and would cement Russian control of the Caspian Sea.

Cognizant of the failure at Gallipoli the previous year, Russian naval planners made certain that the landing at Rize had sufficient naval support. They also selected Rize because its geography and lack of defenses favored a successful operation. Yudenich committed to the operation a force consisting of the dreadnought *Imperatritsa Maria,* three cruisers, and three improvised seaplane carriers as well as minesweepers and smaller craft. They had also developed special flat-bottomed landing craft to take the troops ashore. The Russians tested their landing procedures in an early March landing of 2,100 troops at Atina and west of Riza.

Indicator nets protected the bay at Rize from submarines. Although the major Russian warships left the area on sighting a submarine, the landing on 7 April was successful. The navy had all 16,000 troops ashore within a nine-hour span. Within twenty-four hours half of the Russian forces were engaged with Turkish forces. Trabzon fell on 19 April. The landing further consolidated the gains Russia had made in March, solidified its hold on the Black Sea, and led to an expansion of the navy's coastal support role. Geopolitically, the landing affirmed Britain's decision in March to let Russia extend its influence into Persia (Iran).

Chris Tudda

See also

Amphibious Warfare; Black Sea, Naval Operations; Caucasian Front; Mine Warfare, Sea; War Aims; Yudenich, Nikolay.

Rizzo, Luigi (1887–1951)

Italian navy officer and successful exponent of MAS (motor torpedo boat) small attack craft. Born on 8 October 1887 in the Sicilian town of Milazzo, Luigi Rizzo followed the maritime tradition of his family and ancestors, graduating from the Istituto Nautico of Messina in 1905 and serving in the merchant marine until appointed Danube navigation inspector in 1912 at the Romanian Black Sea port of Sulina. Anticipating war, Rizzo returned to Italy in the summer of 1914 and that August was called to active naval service as a sublieutenant, training in torpedo applications and mine warfare.

From May 1916 Rizzo commanded a MAS squadron on the island of Grado. Benefiting from frequent reconnaissance in the upper Adriatic, Rizzo led the *MAS 9* and *MAS 13,* driven only by auxiliary electric motors, into the harbor of Trieste on the night of 9–10 December 1917. The two torpedoes launched from Rizzo's *MAS 9* struck and sank the Austro-Hungarian battleship *Wien.* Promoted to lieutenant commander amid much public acclaim, Rizzo found new admirers such as Admiral Paolo Thaon di Revel, the activist writer Gabriele D'Annunzio, and King Victor Emmanuel III, who presented him with the gold medal for valor.

In February 1918 the Italian navy's MAS inspector, Captain Costanzo Ciano, joined Rizzo and "volunteer seaman" D'Annunzio for a daring night incursion soon known as the "Beffa di Buccari" (Bakar Jest), in which three of the fastest new MAS boats streaked undetected into that enemy harbor near Fiume (Rijeka) and "launched" three bottles festooned with Italian tricolor ribbons containing satirical messages penned by D'Annunzio expressly for the surprised Austrian defenders.

Rizzo's crowning achievement came during an early morning patrol near Zara (Zadar) 10 June 1918, when he weaved his *MAS 15* through an Austro-Hungarian destroyer screen off the island of Premuda and torpedoed the dreadnought *Szent Istvan,* which capsized and sank. This high seas attack created a sensation, establishing Rizzo's reputation as a brilliant tactical artist, heroically nicknamed "L'Affondatore" (The Sinker).

In 1919 Rizzo was elected the parliamentary delegate from Fiume, and he also began a long career in shipping and shipyards. In 1932 Rizzo was promoted to rear admiral (naval reserve) and proclaimed Count of Grado; his resistance activities against Nazi authority in Trieste after the 1943 armistice resulted in his 1945 imprisonment in Germany. Rizzo died in Rome on 27 June 1951.

Gordon E. Hogg

See also
Adriatic Theater; Austria-Hungary, Navy; D'Annunzio, Gabriele; Italy, Navy; MAS Boats; Thaon di Revel, Paolo; Torpedo Boats; Victor Emmanuel III, King.
References
Andriola, Fabio. *Luigi Rizzo*. Roma: Ufficio Storico della Marina Militare, 2000.
Bagnasco, Erminio, and Achille Rastelli. *Navi e Marinai Italiani nella Grande Guerra*. Parma: Albertelli, 1997.
Halpern, Paul G. *The Naval War in the Mediterranean, 1914–1918*. Annapolis: Naval Institute Press, 1987.

British Admiral Sir John De Robeck, commander of the Allied fleet in the Dardanelles. (Francis J. Reynolds and C. W. Taylor, *Collier's Photographic History of the European War*, P. F. Collier & Son, New York, 1916)

Robeck, Sir John de (1862–1928)

British admiral. Born at Gowran Grange, Naas, County Kildare, Ireland, on 10 June 1862, John de Robeck entered the Royal Navy in 1875 and attained the rank of rear-admiral in 1911. Recalled from half pay at the beginning of World War I, Robeck was assigned to command the 9th Cruiser Squadron. At the beginning of 1915 he was second-in-command of Vice-Admiral Sackville Carden's Eastern Mediterranean Squadron. Carden was then preparing to lead a naval assault to force the Dardanelles and steam to Constantinople, in hopes of driving the Ottoman Empire from the war.

The plan, drawn up by Carden, called for a deliberate reduction of Turkish defenses at the entrance to the straits, minefield sweeps, and the advances of the battleships to Constantinople. First Lord of the Admiralty Winston Churchill, the driving force behind the operation, believed that if the British ships could steam to Constantinople and bring the Turkish capital under threat of naval bombardment, then Turkey would withdraw from the war.

The assault, which began with a bombardment of the outer Turkish forts on 19 February 1915, went poorly from the start. The British were able to silence the outer forts but could not destroy the mobile Turkish howitzers, which made it impossible for British minesweepers to clear the channel. On 16 March 1915, only two days before the attempt to force the narrows with the big ships was to be made, Carden suffered a nervous collapse. Robeck then assumed command and planned to press forward.

On 18 March, Robeck launched the attack. Eighteen allied battleships exchanged fire with the Turkish shore batteries with some success, but as the big ships made their way through the channel they ran into an unexpected minefield. One French and two British battleships were sunk, and other major war-ships sustained damage. Robeck at first was prepared to renew the attack but, following a weather delay, on 22 March changed his mind and recommended waiting until troops could be landed to secure the commanding heights on the Gallipoli Peninsula. Churchill and Robeck's chief of staff, Captain Roger Keyes, urged him to proceed, but the War Council upheld the right of the commander on the spot to make the decision. Robeck held firm. He did not realize that the Turks were low on both ammunition and mines, and had he pressed the attack it would have had a good chance of success. Although Robeck allowed Keyes to return to London to urge a renewed naval assault, his own statements to London also undercut this. Robeck worried not so much about breaking through the Dardanelles and reaching Constantinople with his ships as about what he would do if the Turks then refused to surrender.

During 1916–1918 Robeck commanded the 3rd Battle Squadron in the Grand Fleet. He was then high commissioner at Constantinople from 1919 to 1920 and commander-in-chief of the Atlantic Fleet in 1922–1924. Robeck died in London on 30 January 1928.

Harold Wise and Spencer C. Tucker

See also
Carden, Sir Sackville Hamilton; Churchill, Sir Winston; Dardanelles Campaign; Gallipoli Campaign; *Goeben* and *Breslau*, Escape of; Hamilton, Sir Ian; Mine Warfare, Sea.
References
Halpern, Paul G. "De Robeck and the Dardanelles Campaign." In *The Naval Miscellany*, Vol. 5, ed. N. A. M. Rodger. London: Allen and Unwin, 1984.

Keyes, Sir Roger. *The Naval Memoirs of Admiral of the Fleet Sir Roger Keyes*, Vol. 1, *The Narrow Seas to the Dardanelles, 1910–1915.* London: Thornton Butterworth, 1934.

Marder, Arthur J. "The Dardanelles Revisited: Further Thoughts on the Naval Prelude." In *From the Dardanelles to Oran: Studies of the Royal Navy in War and Peace, 1915–1940*, 1–32. London: Oxford University Press, 1974.

Penn, Geoffrey. *Fisher, Churchill and the Dardanelles.* Barnsley, South Yorkshire, UK: Pen and Sword, 1999.

Wallin, Jeffery D. *By Ships Alone: Churchill and the Dardanelles.* Durham, NC: Carolina Academic Press, 1981.

British Chief of the Imperial General Staff General Sir William Robertson. (Francis J. Reynolds and C. W. Taylor, *Collier's Photographic History of the European War*, P. F. Collier & Son, New York, 1916)

Robertson, Sir William Robert (1860–1933)

British army general and chief of the Imperial General Staff. Born in Welbourn, Lincolnshire, on 29 January 1860, the son of a village tailor, William "Wully" Robertson entered domestic service at age 13 and later enlisted underage and against his parents' wishes in the 16th Lancers in 1877. From this humble beginning he began an unprecedented rise from private to field marshal. Commissioned a lieutenant in 1888, Robertson came to know the army inside out, serving in India and South Africa as well as commandant of the Staff College as a major-general in 1910.

At the outset of World War I Robertson became quartermaster general of the British Expeditionary Force (BEF) in France, successfully keeping it supplied during its retreat under heavy German assault. Coolness under pressure earned him an appointment in January 1915 as chief of staff to BEF commander Field Marshal Sir John French. A stalwart "Westerner," Robertson opposed diversions of effort to ancillary theaters, arguing that the war would be won or lost in France and Belgium.

Robertson became chief of the Imperial General Staff in December 1915. He worked effectively with Field Marshal Lord Kitchener, secretary of state for war, and was promoted to general in June 1916. Kitchener's death the same month led David Lloyd George to take the secretaryship; six months later Lloyd George was prime minister. Gruff and with a no-nonsense approach, Robertson often silenced debate with a terse "I've 'eard different." Lloyd George was an uncommonly gifted orator given to strategic flights of fancy, and the two men clashed repeatedly.

As the war cabinet's principal advisor on military strategy yet also the point man for Field Marshal Douglas Haig and the BEF, Robertson was in a nearly impossible situation. Appalled by casualties at the Somme in 1916, the new prime minister initially proposed that Britain aid Italy with attacks on Austria or else devote more resources to the Middle East or the Balkans. These proposals struck Robertson as dangerous diversions of effort. Lloyd George eventually agreed to a major offensive on the Western Front in 1917 while placing the BEF directly under French General Robert Nivelle's command. Robertson never forgave him for this affront to the honor and autonomy of the BEF; meanwhile, Nivelle's offensive proved disastrous.

Few options remained to the BEF after Nivelle's failure and French army mutinies. Robertson favored an attrition strategy, relying on massive artillery barrages and measured infantry attacks to "bite and hold" territory. Lloyd George, however, continued to float ideas for Eastern sideshows that looked feasible on paper, yet for Robertson these posed insuperable difficulties, especially in logistics. Ultimately, both men fell prey to Haig's grandiose offensive scheme in Flanders that led to catastrophe in the Third Battle of Ypres (Passchendaele).

Unable to fire Haig, Lloyd George vented his frustration and anger by sacking Robertson instead, replacing him with General Sir Henry Wilson in February 1918. Robertson's service as chief of the Imperial General Staff testified to his integrity, energy, and resolution. While an ally of Haig, he was no man's lapdog. After serving as commander-in-chief of Home Forces in 1918 and of Britain's Rhine occupation army in 1919, Robertson made field marshal in March 1920, retiring the next year. He died in London on 12 February 1933.

William J. Astore

See also

Great Britain, Army; Haig, Douglas, 1st Earl; Kitchener, Horatio Herbert, 1st Earl; Lloyd George, David; Nivelle Offensive; Somme Offensive; Wilson, Sir Henry Hughes; Ypres, Third Battle of.

References

Bonham-Carter, Victor. *The Strategy of Victory, 1914–1918: The Life and Times of the Master Strategist of World War I: Field-Marshal Sir William Robertson.* New York: Holt, Rinehart and Winston, 1963.

Robertson, William R. *From Private to Field Marshal.* London: Constable, 1921.

———. *Soldiers and Statesmen, 1914–1918.* 2 vols. London: Cassell, 1926.

Woodward, David R. *Field Marshal Sir William Robertson: Chief of the Imperial General Staff in the Great War.* London: Praeger, 1998.

Rodman, Hugh (1859–1940)

U.S. Navy admiral. Born on 6 January 1859 at Frankfort, Kentucky, Hugh Rodman graduated from Annapolis with the class of 1880. As a junior officer he had a succession of sea assignments, including service on the screw steamer *Essex* during an extended Pacific cruise (1886–1889). He also had billets ashore, including the Bureau of Navigation, Hydrographic Office, and Naval Observatory. With the U.S. Coast and Geodetic Survey during 1891–1895, he helped map the Alaskan and Canadian coasts and later served conspicuously as a gunnery officer on the cruiser *Raleigh* during the Battle of Manila Bay in the Spanish-American War.

By the time of his promotion to captain in 1911, Rodman had served extensively in the Pacific, the Far East, and on both U.S. coasts. During 1912 and 1913 he commanded the battleships *Connecticut* and *Delaware* with the Atlantic Fleet, touring European waters. In 1917 Rodman was promoted to rear admiral and took command of Battleship Squadron 1. Assuming command of Division 9 that November, he raised his flag in the battleship *New York.*

The United States entered World War I in April 1917. After prolonged deliberations over the nature of U.S. naval assistance to its allies, in November 1917 Secretary of the Navy Josephus Daniels directed that Rodman lead his battleships across the Atlantic to join forces with the Royal Navy. Upon arrival at Scapa Flow in the Orkney Islands, Division 9 became the 6th Battle Squadron of the British Grand Fleet.

Rodman recognized that the U.S. Navy contingent had much to learn from the battle-tested Royal Navy, and he set about integrating the U.S. activities and protocols with those of the British as they undertook joint maneuvers. The U.S. squadron was soon distinguished by its alarmingly poor gunnery marks under wartime conditions. By late 1918 the U.S. squadron had markedly improved its abilities and had earned British respect, undertaking antisubmarine patrols, nearly intercepting the German High Seas Fleet during its last sortie on 24–25 April 1918, and on 20 November 1918 witnessing the surrender of the High Seas Fleet at Scapa Flow.

U.S. Navy Admiral Hugh Rodman. (John Clark Ridpath, *Ridpath's History of the World,* Vol. 10, Jones Bros., Cincinnati, 1921)

After the war Rodman served as commander of the Pacific Fleet during 1919–1921. He retired from the navy in January 1923. In 1937 he and the battleship *New York* represented the U.S. Navy at King George VI's coronation naval review. Rodman died in Washington, D.C., on 7 June 1940.

Gordon E. Hogg

See also

Antisubmarine Campaign, Allied Powers; Grand Fleet; Great Britain, Navy; High Seas Fleet; United States, Navy.

References

Jones, Jerry W. *U.S. Battleship Operations in World War I.* Annapolis: Naval Institute Press, 1998.

Reynolds, Clark G. *Famous American Admirals.* Annapolis: Naval Institute Press, 2002.

Rodman, Hugh. *Yarns of a Kentucky Admiral.* Indianapolis, IN: Bobbs-Merrill, 1928.

Rodzianko, Mikhail Vladimirovich (1859–1924)

Russian politician. Born on 12 April 1859 to a family of wealthy landowners in Ekaterinoslav Province, Mikhail Rodzianko received his early education in the elite Corps of Pages and served in the Imperial Guards cavalry. After returning home to manage his family's property, he served in the local zemstvo (assembly), which led to his election to the Duma in 1907. A member of the Octobrist Party, Rodzianko was elected president of the Third Duma in 1911 and was reelected president of the Fourth Duma.

As the wartime Duma president, Rodzianko, at heart a constitutional monarchist, grew increasingly pessimistic about the monarchy's prospects for surviving the war. He repeatedly urged the replacement of incompetent and corrupt ministers such as Ivan Goremykin and Boris Stürmer, only to be ignored by Tsar Nicholas II, who disliked and distrusted Rodzianko. Nor could Rodzianko persuade Nicholas to prevent Tsarina Alexandra and her advisor Grigory Rasputin from meddling in political decisions. Appalled by the tsar's decision to take personal command of the army in 1915, Rodzianko came to believe that the Duma should play a greater political role, but the tsar and his ministers rebuffed his efforts.

The outbreak of the March 1917 revolution placed Rodzianko in a difficult position. On the one hand, he realized that the tsar's government was hopelessly incapable of carrying on the war effort. On the other, he was essentially conservative and loyal to the institution of the monarchy. Caught between the revolutionaries and the tsar, Rodzianko urged Nicholas to abdicate in favor of his son Alexis and appoint his younger brother Mikhail regent. By that time, however, the monarchy was already irretrievably lost.

After the revolution, Rodzianko was not invited to join the provisional government. He eventually went into exile in Yugoslavia, where he died in poverty on 19 January 1924.

John M. Jennings

See also

Alexandra Fyodorovna, Tsarina; Nicholas II, Tsar; Rasputin, Grigory Yefimovich; Russia, Home Front; Russia, Revolution of March 1917.

References

Hasegawa Tsuyoshi. *The February Revolution: Petrograd, 1917.* Seattle: University of Washington Press, 1981.

Lincoln, W. Bruce. *Passage through Armageddon: The Russians in War and Revolution, 1914–1918.* New York: Simon and Schuster, 1986.

Romani, Battle of (4–9 August 1916)

Battle during the Sinai campaign. Bir er Romani lay 22 miles to the east of the Suez Canal and 3 miles south of the Mediterranean coast. By late May 1916 the British had established a railhead at Romani as the first step in their planned advance across the Sinai Peninsula. However, local Ottoman forces, reinforced with troops fresh from the Ottoman victory at Gallipoli, were determined to disrupt these plans and launch another attack against the Suez Canal.

To this end an 18,000-strong Ottoman expedition (with the veteran 3rd Infantry Division at its core) set out for Romani in July under the command of Colonel Friedrich Kress von Kressenstein. Progress was slow because of the presence of two Austrian heavy artillery batteries and the difficulties encountered trying to transport them across the sandy terrain. Kressenstein planned to trap and destroy the British garrison at Romani by outflanking it. The heavy guns and a single infantry regiment were to pin down the British defenders while the bulk of his force attempted to encircle the position by attacking the British right flank.

British commander Lieutenant General Sir Archibald Murray anticipated Kressenstein's line of attack and had deployed his forces accordingly. An infantry force of 11,000 men built around the 52nd (Lowland) Division manned the Romani defenses while approximately 3,000 horses and men of Major General "Harry" Chauvel's Australian and New Zealand Mounted Division screened the desert expanses to the south of the railhead.

With his mounted troops in the path of the main Ottoman attack, Murray intended to use two brigades to fight a delaying action until it was clear that the Ottoman force was fully engaged in battle. Thereupon the remaining two brigades of the Australian and New Zealand Mounted Division were to counterattack and take the Ottomans in the flank. As the Ottoman expedition approached the outskirts of Romani, Murray reinforced the position and added the British 5th Mounted Brigade to his Dominion mounted force.

At 2:00 A.M. on the morning of 4 August, Kressenstein launched his main assault. Ottoman infantry and Australian light horsemen shot and bayoneted each other in the darkness as the Ottomans strove to break through to the rear of Romani. The Ottoman attack was pressed home with fierce determination, and it drove the Australians back farther than Murray had planned. Nonetheless, by midmorning the Australian line was still intact, and the momentum of the Ottoman advance had been halted. At that point, Chauvel ordered the rest of his division and the 5th Mounted Brigade to attack the now exposed Ottoman left flank. Fighting continued throughout the day, but by nightfall the Ottoman troops were forced to withdraw. Meanwhile, at Romani itself the garrison had come under sustained bombardment, but the Ottoman diversionary attack had been easily contained.

The following day the British began their pursuit of the retreating Ottoman troops. To Murray's disappointment, this was not as effective as he had hoped. The British infantry were unable to meet the required pace under the harsh Egyptian sun, and the task was left to the five mounted brigades, which had already borne the brunt of the battle. For the next five days, and under increasingly unfavorable and trying conditions, the Australian, New Zealand, and British horsemen harried the Ottoman force as it fell back to prepared positions at Bir el Abd, but they could not destroy it.

Despite this, Romani was still a significant British victory, and the Ottoman army would never again threaten the Suez Canal. Total Ottoman casualties were approximately 6,000 men, of which more than 4,000 were taken prisoner. British forces sustained 1,130 casualties, the bulk of which were suffered by the Australians.

Damien Fenton

See also
Chauvel, Sir Henry George; Egypt; Kress von Kressenstein, Friedrich; Murray, Sir Archibald James; Sinai Campaign.

References
Erickson, Edward J. *Ordered to Die: A History of the Ottoman Army in the First World War.* Westport, CT: Greenwood, 2000.

Gullet, Henry S. *Official History of Australia in the War of 1914–18,* Vol. 7, *The Australian Imperial Force in Sinai and Palestine.* Melbourne, Australia: Government Printer, 1923.

MacMunn, George, and Cyril Falls. *Official History of the Great War: Military Operations, Egypt and Palestine, from the Outbreak of the War with Germany to June 1917.* London: HMSO, 1928.

Powles, Charles G. *Official History of New Zealand's Effort in the Great War,* Vol. 3, *The New Zealanders in Sinai and Palestine.* Wellington, New Zealand: Whitcombe and Tombs, 1922.

Romania, Army

When Romania entered World War I on 17 August 1916, the country faced a potential two-front war: Bulgaria to the south

Troops of the Romanian Army pass in review. (S. J. Duncan Clark and W. R. Plewman, *Pictorial History of the Great War,* with W. S. Wallace, *Canada in the Great War,* 5th ed., John A. Hertel, Toronto, 1919)

and Austria-Hungary to the west and north. Although Romanian military leaders were optimistic about the potential outcome, their nation's military lacked the leadership, training, equipment, and resources necessary to achieve victory.

Romania had a compulsory military service law. Conscripts who were selected by ballot at age 21 served seven years. They then passed into the reserve for twelve additional years before spending a further six years in the militia. The army consisted of the regular army, its reserve, a territorial militia, and the Gloata or home militia of all citizens ages 36–46 to be mobilized for local defense only.

In 1913 the regular standing army numbered about 92,000 men organized into four corps, an independent cavalry brigade, and an independent brigade in the Dobrudja. When the army was mobilized the next year, it numbered some 382,000 men. When Romania declared war in 1916, some 750,000 men were called to the colors and formed into twenty-three infantry and two cavalry divisions. The First Army, commanded by General Ioan Culcer, consisted of three infantry divisions with three other infantry divisions held in reserve. General Alexandru Averescu commanded the Second Army of four infantry divisions, one cavalry division, and two infantry divisions held in reserve (approximately 126,000 men). The Third Army, under the command of General Mihail Aslan, consisted of six infantry divisions (some 142,000 men). General Constantine Prezan commanded the Fourth Army of 107,000 men organized in three infantry divisions, one cavalry division, and one infantry division held in reserve.

Unfortunately for Romania this mobilization for war fatally weakened the army. With some notable exceptions, such as General Alexandru Averescu, its leadership was inept and many of the officers were poorly trained. The army also lacked equipment of all kinds. In 1916 it had only 440,000 rifles, 110,000 of which were outdated; 1,300 artillery pieces, of which only half were modern; and only about 900 machine guns. Ammunition and transport were both in short supply. The government was well aware of these shortcomings, but it counted on Russian assistance, faulty Austro-Hungarian troop strength along the Romanian border, and a quick and victorious campaign. Much effective work was done toward military reorganization by a French military mission beginning in September 1916 and headed by General Henri M. Berthelot.

From the Allied standpoint, the performance of the Romanian army in the war was a great disappointment, especially to the Russians. Many Romanian units fought effectively, and about half of the army survived the defeat at the hands of the Central Powers to rejoin the war at its end. Several reequipped and retrained Romanian divisions gave good account of themselves in subsequent fighting. Romania also paid a high price for its involvement in the war. Of 750,000 men mobilized, 335,706 died, 120,000 were wounded, and 80,000 were taken prisoner or missing in action. Casualties

thus totaled 71 percent of those mobilized, one of the highest rates for any nation in the war.

Laura J. Hilton and Spencer C. Tucker

See also
Averescu, Alexandru; Berthelot, Henri Mathias; Romania, Campaign of 1916; Romania, Role in War.

References
Alexandrescu, Vasile. *Romania in World War I: A Synopsis of Military History*. Bucharest: Military Publishing House, 1985.

Petrescu-Comnene, Nicolae. *The Great War and the Romanians: Notes and Documents on World War I*. Iasi: Center for Romanian Studies, 2000.

Torrey, Glenn E. *Henri Mathias Berthelot: Soldier of France, Defender of Romania*. Portland, OR: Center for Romanian Studies, 2001.

———. *Romania and World War I: A Collection of Studies*. Iasi, Romania, and Portland, OR: Center for Romanian Studies, 1998.

Romania, Campaign of 1916

Before World War I, King Carol I of Romania cultivated ties with imperial Germany in order to balance French efforts to gain influence there. The sympathies of most Romanians, however, lay with France, and popular feeling over the alleged mistreatment of ethnic Romanians in Transylvania (Ardeal) was a constant source of friction with Austria-Hungary. As public sentiment favored the Entente side, Romania adopted a policy of armed neutrality at the outbreak of the Great War in August 1914.

As the monarchy's influence in Romania shrank (Carol died in October 1914 and was succeeded by King Ferdinand), Prime Minister Ionel Brătianu increased his influence. Primarily concerned with domestic politics, Brătianu opened negotiations with both sides in an attempt to gain lands inhabited by ethnic Romanians. Although courted by both the Entente side, which promised to deliver Transylvania, and the Central Powers, which promised Bukovina and Bessarabia, the Romanian government decided to remain neutral until the opportune moment. Tacit approval for this course of action was received when Britain advanced Romania a £5 million loan in January 1915. Nor was Brătianu averse to profiting financially from Vienna and Berlin, as he encouraged Romanian firms to sell petroleum to the Central Powers. This amounted to about 400,000 tons in 1915 alone, a valuable contribution to those powers' war-making ability.

Russian success in the summer of 1916 provided the key to unlock Romanian policy. The Russian Brusilov offensive, launched on 4 June and targeted against weakened Austro-Hungarian forces, produced widespread and impressive Russian gains. Although they suffered heavy losses (about 1.4 million men), the Russians moved the entire Southern Front forward an average of 30 miles, driving the Austro-Hungarians back in confusion. In the Bukovina region in

Romanian troops, parading through the streets of Bucharest. (Bettmann/Corbis)

particular the Austrians suffered devastating losses, and the Russians marched into the Carpathians on the Transylvanian border. Although the front stabilized following the arrival of German reinforcements, the Austro-Hungarians lost up to 750,000 men (including 380,000 taken prisoner) and the empire teetered on the edge of collapse.

At this point Brătianu obtained another offer from the Entente, including promises of troops and military aid from Russia, help from the expeditionary force at Salonika, and the gain of Transylvania upon the defeat of the Central Powers. The Entente, eyeing the shaky Austro-Hungarians, hoped to break Vienna's resistance, as a major defeat in Transylvania might knock them from the war, allowing Entente armies to isolate Bulgaria and the Turks and thus end the fighting in the entire region. The Romanians were especially optimistic about the plan since they had broken the Austrian diplomatic code and knew that the ambassador from Vienna suspected nothing.

The Romanians mobilized four large armies of perhaps 440,000 men and declared war on 27 August 1916. Three of the armies were positioned on the Transylvanian frontier—two in Wallachia and one farther north in Moldavia—while a reserve army guarded the Danube and the Dobrudja salient on the Black Sea facing Bulgaria. About 350,000 Romanian troops, although poorly trained and inexperienced, marched into eastern Transylvania with little difficulty.

Russian troops pushed from the Kirilibaba Pass in Galicia in early September and made contact with the Romanian right on 11 September. The combination of early snow in the Carpathians and the diversion of troops north to battles around Halicz, however, stalled the offensive a few days later, crippling any further movement into northern Transylvania.

Austro-Hungarian forces, comprising roughly 30,000 reservists, militia, and local police, meanwhile fell back in the face of these attacks, losing control of the frontier railway and the important city of Kronstadt. At the same time, however, the excellent Austrian radio intercept service began decrypting Romanian message traffic, made verbose by the lack of telephone lines and carelessness by Romanian code clerks and telegraphers. This intelligence allowed the Central Powers to discern plans for future Romanian movements and position blocking forces.

In the south, meanwhile, the Entente forces in Greece tried without success to pin down the Bulgarian army. Faced with strong Bulgarian forces in the east, a combined Serbian and French attack advanced up the Tcherna Valley in early September. Supported by diversionary British attacks on the Struma River, these forces ground their way north, eventually liberating Monastir in November. While ultimately successful, this slow, set-piece offensive failed to divert Bulgarian troops south or prevent Central Powers operations on the Danube.

Indeed, the first countermove against Romania came on 1 September, a mere four days after the declaration of war, when Field Marshal August von Mackensen led a ten-division force of Bulgarians, Austro-Hungarians, Turks, and Germans across the Bulgarian frontier into the Dobrudja. Supported by efficient air reconnaissance units as well as an Austrian radio intercept section in Sofia, the attackers destroyed two Romanian divisions and drove the rest back to the Tchernavoda-Constanza rail line. Three Russian divisions under Andrei Zaionchkovsky, supported by three Romanian divisions from Transylvania, stabilized this defensive line by the end of September. This maneuver protected the important port of Constanza, although the Russians, appalled by the incompetence of their Romanian allies, worried about the future.

Meanwhile to the northwest, former chief of staff of the German army General Erich von Falkenhayn arrived in Transylvania in early September and took command of the new Ninth Army, formed from troops shipped east in more than 1,500 trains from France. As these divisions were positioned, the Austrians continued to withdraw into the interior of Transylvania, drawing the Romanians farther into the mountains. Falkenhayn's headquarters kept track of the Romanian advance through situation reports, provided every three hours by the Austrian intercept service, and prepared a counterattack later called the "judgment of God."

Falkenhayn's first move occurred in mid-September with an attack against the Romanian First Army near the Danube, pushing the invaders from the city of Hartzeg. Although the Romanians clung to the Vulkan Pass, the advance cleared the flank for the main counterattack on 22 September. Bavarian Jaegers outflanked their opponents near Hermannstadt on the 26th, took the Rother Tharm pass, and forced the Romanians to retreat in some disorder. Falkenhayn then turned east again and on 4 October hit the flank of the Romanian Second Army, which was then busy pushing toward Schassburg to the north. With their supply lines in danger, the Romanians fell back toward Moldavia, abandoning the vital rail crossroads at Kronstadt on 9 October.

The initial blows against Romanian troops revealed several advantages possessed by the Central Powers. In addition to much better operational intelligence, Falkenhayn's troops possessed superior artillery and greater freedom of movement. Indeed, the Romanians were now pinned in a deep crescent position in an attempt to hold the Carpathian passes. The Austrian intercept service also knew that the Reserve Romanian troops were deployed covering the railroad passes before Ploeshti in the center of the line, so Falkenhayn quickly planned another outflanking offensive.

Reinforced with heavy artillery, the Ninth Army's right wing pushed through the Vulkan Pass in mid-October. Although stopped by tenacious resistance in the Jiu Valley, Falkenhayn regrouped and launched a five-division attack on 10 November. Within a week, superior numbers and guns crushed the Romanian defense, and German cavalry advanced into the Danube plain on a wide front. Two days later Mackensen, supported by a flotilla of monitors and gunboats, began crossing the Danube in force at Sistovo and Belene; this was completed by 25 November. Bulgarian cavalry detachments soon roamed the countryside, sacking towns and creating havoc in southern Wallachia.

With the Romanian left flank crumbling, the strong forces guarding the central frontier passes fell back to avoid encirclement. Many disintegrated as the Romanian peasant conscripts deserted and went home. The remnants of two armies, supported by a single Russian division railed south in support, tried to defend Bucharest but were broken on the Argesh River in early December. Mackensen's force entered the capital of Bucharest on 6 December.

Meanwhile, Falkenhyan's main force pushed through the central passes and advanced on Ploesti, the center of the Romanian oil region. In response, Colonel John Norton-Griffiths, a member of the British Parliament connected with British intelligence, and the many American engineers employed in the oil fields, set about destroying the wells, refineries, stores, and fuel tanks.

Covered by forlorn rearguard actions, the broken remnants of the Romanian army retired behind the Sereth River in Moldavia. The Central Powers continued their advance, sweeping through eastern Wallachia in late December. Although the important railhead at Focsani was taken in January 1917, winter stalled any future operations on the Sereth or in the Moldavian passes.

The campaign had been a disaster for Romania, with 160,000 men killed, wounded, or missing and another 150,000 taken prisoner. Romania had also lost the Dobrudja and Wallachia. Penned up in Moldavia and abandoned by Russia when that nation collapsed into revolution in 1917, the army did well to maintain its position in the field until the conclusion of the Treaty of Bucharest in May 1918, by which Romania left the war. Although the Central Powers were forced to extend their Eastern Front to the Black Sea (adding 250 miles to the line), the successful campaign helped protect Bulgaria, removed a major threat to the Austro-Hungarian flank, and opened an improved communications line to the Ottoman Empire.

Timothy L. Francis

See also
Balkan Front; Brătianu, Ionel; Brusilov Offensive; Carol I, King of Romania; Falkenhayn, Erich von; Ferdinand I, King of Romania; Galicia Campaigns; Mackensen, August von; Monastir Offensive; Salonika Campaign; Zaionchkovsky, Andrei Medarovich.

References
Bujac, Jean. *Campagnes de l'Armée Roumaine, 1916–19.* Paris: Charles-Lavauzelle, 1933.
Herwig, Holger H. *The First World War: Germany and Austria-Hungary, 1914–1918.* New York: St. Martin's, 1997.
Jukes, Geoffrey. *Carpathian Disaster: Death of an Army.* New York: Ballantine, 1971.
Torrey, Glenn E. "Indifference and Mistrust: Russian-Romanian Collaboration in the Campaign of 1916." *Journal of Military History* 57 (April 1993): 279–300.
———. "The Redemption of an Army: The Romanian Campaign of 1917." *War & Society* 12 (October 1994): 22–42.

Romania, Navy

Romania's decision to enter World War I on the side of the Entente spelled disaster for Romania. Its army suffered heavy losses and watched helplessly as the Germans pushed into Bucharest in December 1916. The small Romanian navy, while it performed rather more effectively than the army, was likewise unable to influence events.

Of the navy's two major components, the Maritime Division was chronically underequipped, while the Danube Division, in relative terms, flourished. The Maritime Division made do with several auxiliary cruisers and guardships, one being the retired and disarmed cruiser *Elisabeta*. Its four new destroyers, ordered in 1913 from yards in Italy, had been requisitioned by the Italian navy in 1915; two were finally handed over to Romania in 1920. The Danube Division received rather more attention and was well-equipped with monitors, gunboats, and patrol craft, and it deployed in coordinated operations with the Romanian army that prevented the Central Powers advance to the Danube delta.

While in action against Bulgarian positions at Turtucaia and Silistra in August 1916, the Romanian 2nd Monitor Division (*Bratianu, Kogalniceanu,* and *Catargiu*), effected the safe evacuation of the Romanian army's 9th Infantry Division. The 4.7-inch gun emplacements removed from the old cruiser *Elisabeta* were mounted ashore and used to good effect alongside the monitors' batteries. Teaming up with army artillery components during the summer and fall of 1917, the monitor division formed the River and Delta Forces Command, which held the line against the Germans in Moldavia, and by early 1918 both the Danube Division and the Maritime Division were primarily occupied with sweeping enemy mines from seaports, shipping channels, and rivers.

With the capitulation of the Central Powers in November 1918, Romania found its coastline doubled with ceded territory. This prompted a modest expansion in its navy through Austro-Hungarian reparations and, later, orders from Italy and France.

Gordon E. Hogg

See also
Balkan Front; Bulgaria, Role in War; Romania, Army; Romania, Campaign of 1916; Romania, Role in War.

References
Alexandrescu, Vasile, "Kampfe der Rumanischen Kriegsmarine im Ersten Weltkrieg." *Marine-Rundschau* 77(7) (1980): 394–399.
Bardeanu, Nicolae. *Contribuții la Istoria Marinei Romane.* Vol. 1. Bucuresti, Romania: Editura Științifica și Enciclopedica, 1979.
Gray, Randal, ed. *Conway's All the World's Fighting Ships, 1906–1921.* Annapolis: Naval Institute Press, 1985.

Romania, Role in War

Romania occupied an important position in the northeastern Balkan region. It extended over 46,000 square miles and had a population of some 9 million people. Romania consisted of three major areas: Wallachia, Moldavia, and the Dobrudja. While the inhabitants of Wallachia and Moldavia were predominantly ethnic Romanians and practiced Eastern Orthodox Christianity, the Dobrudja contained a much more diverse population, including many Muslims. Indeed, in this area Romanians were in the minority. Romania was rich in grains with abundant arable land, and its oil fields at Ploesti were the largest in Europe.

On 27 August 1916, Romania declared war on the Central Powers. This came as something of a surprise, as Romania had signed a defensive military alliance with Germany in 1883 that had been renewed by Romanian King Carol I in 1913. Carol was also of the Hohenzollern-Sigmaringen line and related to German Kaiser Wilhelm II.

At the beginning of World War I, the Romanian government declared its neutrality. The vast majority of King Carol's cabinet favored such a course, and Premier Ionel Brătianu justified it on the basis that Romania was bound to support Germany and Austria-Hungary only in the event of a defensive war. More importantly, Romania coveted Transylvania, then part of Hungary and home to 3 million ethnic Romanians.

The sole rail line connecting Germany and the Ottoman Empire ran through Romania, and Russia pressured Romania to block this route that allowed transit of goods from Germany to the Turks. Romania bowed to this demand. It also moved closer to the Entente when in December 1914 it accepted a loan from Britain to strengthen its military.

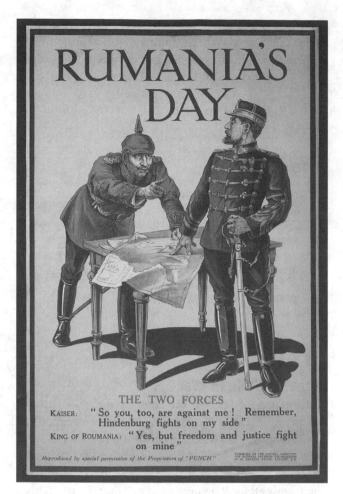

British poster. In the caption, German Kaiser Wilhelm II says, "So, you, too are against me! Remember, Hindenburg fights on my side." King Ferdinand I of Romania replies, "Yes, but freedom and justice fight on mine." (Library of Congress)

Romanian foreign policy clearly favored the Entente. In October 1914 Carol I died. He was succeeded by his nephew, Ferdinand I, who allowed Brătianu to control foreign policy. Throughout 1915 the Romanian premier bargained with the Entente. He demanded simultaneous Allied offensives on the Eastern and Western Fronts to exert maximum pressure on the Central Powers, which came in 1916 with the Somme and the Brusilov offensives. He also asked for, and obtained, stocks of war matériel from the Allies. Most importantly, he secured promises of Romanian territorial aggrandizement, including Transylvania but also the Banat of Temesvar, a rich agricultural region; Bukovina; and southern Galicia. Russia also agreed that if Romania entered the war, it would provide 200,000 troops to protect that country from a potential Bulgarian attack from the south. The Western Allies also assured Brătianu of assistance from a half million Allied troops at Salonika and an expanded effort against Bulgaria.

On 17 August 1916, Romania officially signed the Treaty of Bucharest with the Triple Entente. Ten days later the Romanian government declared war on the Central Powers and sent 80 percent of its army in an invasion of Austria-Hungary to secure Transylvania. The Allies were caught off guard by the Romanian attempt to take Transylvania, as they had anticipated that Romania would concentrate its military efforts against Bulgaria.

Bulgarian forces, taking advantage of the weakened Romanian troop deployment along the Danube, then attacked north. Romania soon found itself fighting on two fronts: combined German and Austro-Hungarian forces to the west and north, and the Bulgarian army to the south. In addition, promised Russian assistance did not materialize, and the French commander of Allied forces at Salonika, General Maurice Sarrail, failed to support the Romanians by promptly attacking the Bulgarians.

Fighting on two fronts and lacking adequate supplies and reinforcements, the poorly trained and equipped Romanian forces were on the defensive from September to December 1916. British forces, fearing the imminent fall of Romania, sabotaged the Ploesti oil fields on 5 December and set fire to more than 800,000 tons of oil. The Central Powers occupied the capital of Bucharest on 6 December 1916, and the Romanian army was forced into the northeast corner of the country, across the Serit River, in Moldavia to regroup.

Combined Romanian and Russian forces launched an attack across the Serit in July 1917, and in the battles of Marasti, Marasesti, and Oituz they defeated the Central Powers forces, although with high casualty rates. The collapse of the Russian military and the second Russian revolution in November 1917 ended this effort. In December 1917 almost all Russian troops were withdrawn by the provisional Russian government, forcing Romania to sign an armistice with Germany on 9 December, known as the Truce of Foscani.

Romania had no choice but to accept the preliminary surrender terms of 5 March 1918, which ceded the Dobrudja to Bulgaria and brought the demobilization of its armed forces. The Treaty of Bucharest signed on 7 May 1918 formally ended Romanian hostilities between Romania and the Central Powers. It provided for the demobilization of five of fifteen Romanian army divisions and placed manpower restrictions on the remaining ten. It also set limits of the munitions Romania could retain. In addition, Romania was forced to cede the Dobrudja to Bulgaria, border regions to Austria-Hungary, and control over the Danube to the Central Powers (including the right to station warships on the river). This treaty and Romania's catastrophic personnel losses—535,706 in all, 71.4 percent of all Romanians who took up arms, of whom approximately 200,000 were wounded or prisoners and 335,706, 44 percent of the total, were dead—were devastating to the country. The treaty also gave Germany a ninety-year lease on the Ploesti oil fields and access to its grain production.

Romania was saved by the ultimate Allied victory in the war. In September 1918 Bulgaria was forced to sue for peace. Taking heart from this development and the collapse of the Austro-Hungarian war effort, on 12 October Romania reconstituted its government with the formation of a national council. On 10 November 1918, one day before the Allied armistice with Germany took effect, Romania abrogated the Treaty of Bucharest and reentered the war on the Allied side.

In summer 1919 Romanian forces advanced into Hungary to assist with the overthrow of the Communist government of Béla Kun that had seized power in Budapest the previous March. Romanian forces remained in place as occupiers for several months, extracting heavy reparations (or looting) and seeking an advantageous military and territorial position prior to Hungary's eventual conclusion of the Treaty of Trianon with the Allies in June 1920.

Although Allied pressure forced Romania to withdraw its forces from Hungary in late 1919, in practice Romania benefited greatly from the Allied victory. In an effort to strengthen that country against a resurgence of Austria and Hungary and also to bar Communist Russia from expansion in a southwesterly direction, the conferees at the Paris Peace Conference granted Romania important territorial gains that it had not won on the battlefield. These included Transylvania; the eastern Banat, including Temesvar (the remainder was awarded to Yugoslavia); and the Dobrudja. Much to the surprise of Romanian leaders, the country also received Bessarabia and Bukovina, which contained many Romanians and Ukrainians. These two regions, through their governments, had declared a desire to be part of Romania. The acquisition of this territory doubled the size of Romania, but it brought complex minority problems that served to weaken the country in the decades that followed.

Laura J. Hilton

See also
Brătianu, Ionel; Brusilov Offensive; Bucharest, Treaty of; Bulgaria, Role in War; Carol I, King of Romania; Ferdinand I, King of Romania; Hungary, Postwar Revolution; Kun, Béla; Marghiloman, Alexandru; Paris Peace Conference; Romania, Army; Romania, Campaign of 1916; Romania, Navy; Salonika Campaign; Sarrail, Maurice; Somme Offensive; Wilhelm II, Kaiser.

References
Alexandrescu, Vasile. *Romania in World War I: A Synopsis of Military History.* Bucharest: Military Publishing House, 1985.
MacMillan, Margaret. *Paris, 1919: Six Months That Changed the World.* New York: Random House, 2002.
Petrescu-Comnene, Nicolae. *The Great War and the Rumanians: Notes and Documents on World War I.* Iasi: Center for Romanian Studies, 2000.
Torrey, Glenn E. *Romania and World War I: A Collection of Studies.* Iasi, Romania, and Portland, OR: Center for Romanian Studies, 1998.

Rome Congress of Oppressed Nationalities (April 1918)

In the wake of the military disaster at Caporetto in late 1917, the Italian government allowed a Congress of Oppressed Nationalities to meet in Rome in April 1918. It included Transylvanian, Polish, and Czechoslovak representatives as well as Italian politicians and members of the Yugoslav Committee, previously disdained by the Italians for their lack of an independent military force. The congress appealed to the Allies to make the principle of national self-determination applicable to the Austro-Hungarian Empire.

Earlier, the Habsburg Empire had been offered a separate peace with its territory relatively intact, but the Austrians had sealed their fate by signing the Treaties of Brest Litovsk and Bucharest. In addition, for the first time Vienna sent troops to the Western Front. Failing to detach Austria-Hungary from the Central Powers, the Allies instead decided to encourage the oppressed nationalities and did so formally on 3 June 1918, with U.S. approval, in the Versailles Declaration issued by the Supreme War Council.

Errol M. Clauss

See also
Austria-Hungary, Home Front; Beneš, Edvard; Czechoslovakia, Role in War and Formation of State; Dmowski, Roman; Fourteen Points; Masaryk, Tomáš Garrigue; Paderewski, Ignace Jan; Poland, Role in War; Supreme War Council; Yugoslavia, Creation of.

References
Lederer, Ivo. *Yugoslavia and the Paris Peace Settlement: Yugoslav-Italian Relations and the Territorial Settlement, 1918–1920.* Princeton, NJ: Princeton University Press, 1957.
Stevenson, David. *The First World War and International Politics.* Oxford and New York: Oxford University Press, 1988.

Rommel, Erwin (1891–1944)

German infantry officer. Born at Heidenheim near Ulm on 15 November 1891, Erwin Rommel was solidly bourgeois and saw the army as a chance for advancement. He joined the Württemberg 124th Infantry Regiment in July 1910 as an officer-cadet, gaining his commission in January 1912.

Attached to the 19th Field Artillery Regiment when World War I began, Rommel rejoined the 124th Infantry Regiment and served with distinction on the Western Front in Belgium and France. He won the Iron Cross Second Class in September 1914 for aggressively attacking three French soldiers despite being wounded himself and the Iron Cross First Class at the Argonne in January 1915 for his role in leading his platoon through 100 yards of barbed wire to assault a French position. In September 1915 he was promoted to first lieutenant and named commander of the 2nd Company in the elite Württemberg Mountain Battalion, then forming. He led this unit in both Romania and Italy.

Rommel made his reputation in the Battle of Caporetto in October–November 1917. Leading his company of 100 infantrymen with six machine guns, he succeeded in capturing 150 Italian officers, 9,000 men, and eighty-one guns for the loss of 6 German dead and 30 wounded. In just over two days he advanced 12 miles and climbed more than 7,000 feet. For this feat Rommel won Germany's highest decoration, the Pour le Mérite (Blue Max). Promoted to captain, Rommel finished the war in a staff position.

Rommel captured the essence of German infiltration tactics in his book *Infanterie Greift An* (Infantry Attacks). Published in 1937, the text served as an unofficial "how-to" manual for the German infantry, whom Rommel praised for their "tremendous combat power." He claimed that his book showed "the superiority of the junior German commander to his enemy counterpart." Rommel's emphasis on surprise, flank attack, infiltration, and aggressive pursuit caught the eye of Adolf Hitler, who rewarded him with the command of his bodyguard detachment and later the 7th Panzer Division in the campaign against France in 1940. Rommel became one of Hitler's favorites, winning command of Afrika Korps (January 1941) and a field marshal's baton (June 1942), but he grew increasingly critical of Hitler as the war turned against Germany. Implicated for having foreknowledge of the failed plot to assassinate Hitler, Rommel was allowed to commit suicide by poison on 14 October 1944. He was buried with considerable pomp in a state funeral.

William J. Astore

See also
Alpine Warfare; Caporetto, Battle of; Germany, Army; Hitler, Adolf; Infantry Tactics; Isonzo, Battles of the; Storm Troopers.

References
Fraser, David. *Knight's Cross: A Life of Field Marshal Erwin Rommel.* London: HarperCollins, 1993.
Lewin, Ronald. *Rommel as Military Commander.* London: Batsford, 1968.
Rommel, Erwin. *Infantry Attacks.* Mechanicsburg, PA: Stackpole, 1994.
———. *The Rommel Papers.* Ed. B. H. Liddell Hart. New York: Da Capo, 1953, 1982.

Ronarc'h, Pierre (1865–1940)

French navy admiral. Born at Quimper (Finistère) on 22 February 1865, Pierre-Alexis-Marie-Antoine Ronarc'h entered the École Navale in 1880. He held ship assignments in both the Indian Ocean and the South Atlantic. In 1898 he studied at the École des Hautes Études de la Marine. He then served in the Far East as aide-de-camp to the commander of the French Squadron there. He next participated in fighting against China and in the Boxer Uprising. Promoted to commander in 1902, he was stationed at Rochefort. In 1906 he commanded a destroyer in the Mediterranean. Promoted to captain in 1910, he commanded torpedo boats and submarines at Brest. In 1912 he took command of marines in the Mediterranean.

Promoted to rear admiral in June 1914, Ronarc'h rose to national prominence during World War I in the October–November 1914 Flanders campaign, when he led a brigade of marines to support the Belgian army under King Albert I along the Yser River. Advancing between Dixmude and Nieuport, Ronarc'h and his men demonstrated great determination and even attempted limited attacks. But the Germans, who greatly outnumbered the marines, turned Ronarc'h's flanks.

French General Ferdinand Foch, in overall command of Allied forces in Flanders, nevertheless envisioned that Ronarc'h's men would advance while elements of the French 42nd Infantry Division secured their northern flank. German strength made such an advance impossible, but Ronarc'h held his ground against long odds, allowing the Belgians to reposition.

The Allies held on the Yser and in the Ypres salient despite furious German attacks. Ronarc'h thus played a prominent role in helping to save both the Belgian army and the Channel ports. His efforts also had ramifications away from Ypres. The actions near Dixmude proved to be an important event for Brittany, a region whose language and culture had always been more Celtic than Gallic. Almost all men in Ronarc'h's brigade were Bretons, and Ronarc'h became Brittany's first hero of the war.

Promoted to vice admiral in November 1915, Ronarc'h in March 1916 became commander of French naval forces in the English Channel, his principal mission being cooperation with the Royal Navy to ensure the uninterrupted flow of men and supplies from Britain to the continent. Named in April 1919 as head of the naval General Staff, Ronarc'h retired from the navy in February 1920. He died in Paris on 1 April 1940.

Michael Neiberg

See also
Albert I, King of Belgium; Flanders Campaign; Foch, Ferdinand.

References
Halpern, Paul G. *A Naval History of World War I.* Annapolis: Naval Institute Press, 1994.
Mabire, Jean. *La Bataille de l'Yser: Les Fusiliers Marins à Dixmude.* Paris: Fayard, 1979.

Room 40

Cryptographic office of the British Naval Intelligence Division (NID). Primarily a code-breaking operation, Room 40 obtained its name from its location in the old Admiralty building. All powers involved in World War I recognized the need to intercept and analyze enemy communications, and in August 1914 Sir Alfred Ewing, director of naval education, was appointed to head a new cryptological office for the Royal Navy, which in November was transferred to Room 40. Its work was closely identified with Rear-Admiral Reginald "Blinker" Hall, head of the NID. The seizure of German naval code books in the first few months of the war, most notably from the German cruiser *Magdeburg*, greatly facilitated Room 40's work.

Among its successes, Room 40 provided to the Royal Navy information on the cruise of the German battle cruiser *Goeben* and light cruiser *Breslau* in the Mediterranean at the beginning of the war, the German naval raid on Scarborough in December 1914, the movement of Admiral Maximilian von Spee's squadron to the Falkland Islands, German naval dispositions that led to the Battle of the Dogger Bank of January 1915, and several zeppelin raids on Britain. Room 40 accurately warned the Admiralty of German High Seas Fleet preparations to put to sea at the end of May 1916, but the Admiralty failed to act effectively on this invaluable intelligence. Many of its code-breakers had been civilians before the war and were thus suspect to many staff officers. Indeed, a problem never completely solved during the war was the ineffective utilization and coordination of intelligence information produced by Room 40.

On 15 August 1916, Room 40 became aware of German intentions to sortie with a large force, but decisions on both sides prevented a decisive engagement. Room 40's work proved invaluable in the convoy system instituted in 1917, enabling the Royal Navy to reroute convoys away from known U-boat positions. In 1917 Room 40 intercepted the Zimmermann Telegram, the publication of which helped bring the United States into the war. Following World War I, in 1919 the remnants of Room 40 were combined with MI-8 into the Government Code and Cypher School, located at Bletchley Park.

Mark D. Mills

See also

Dogger Bank, Battle of the; Hall, Sir William Reginald; Jutland, Battle of; *Magdeburg*, SMS; Scarborough Raid; Spee, Maximilian von, Count; Zimmermann Telegram.

References

Beesly, Patrick. *Room 40: British Naval Intelligence, 1914–1918*. New York: Harcourt Brace Jovanovich, 1982.

Deacon, Richard. *A History of British Secret Service*. London: Panther Granada, 1984.

Halpern, Paul G. *A Naval History of World War I*. Annapolis: Naval Institute Press, 1994.

Santoni, Alberto. *Il primo Ultra Secret: l'influenza delle decrittazioni britanniche sulle operazioni navali della guerra, 1914–1918*. Milan: Mursia, 1985.

Roosevelt, Franklin Delano (1882–1945)

Assistant secretary of the navy, later president of the United States. Born on 30 January 1882 in Hyde Park, New York, Franklin Roosevelt graduated from Harvard University in 1904. After attending Columbia Law School, he rose quickly in New York politics. Woodrow Wilson rewarded Roosevelt for his support in the 1912 presidential race with the position of assistant secretary of the navy under Josephus Daniels in 1913, a position that Roosevelt held until 1920.

Roosevelt aggressively promoted the navy and helped ready it for World War I. He was a vocal advocate of expansion and contingency planning, and his aggressive policies often put him at odds with Wilson, Daniels, and a majority of the cabinet. An internationalist in foreign policy, Roosevelt was an early advocate of war against Germany. He also supported U.S. intervention in Haiti.

Roosevelt demonstrated remarkable administrative skills and worked well with unions, department employees, and

Assistant Secretary of the Navy Franklin Delano Roosevelt. (Library of Congress)

naval leaders. He helped reorganize the administrative system of the navy and oversaw the introduction of new management techniques in the naval yards. He investigated collusion and price-fixing by defense contractors.

When the United States entered the war in April 1917, Roosevelt oversaw a significant naval construction program. He also pushed the mining of the North Sea between Scotland and Norway, and he made two inspection tours of navy bases in the European war zone. At the end of the war Roosevelt was a firm supporter of a league of nations.

Roosevelt resigned his naval post in 1920 to become the vice-presidential candidate on the Democratic ticket headed by James M. Cox. This bid for national office was not successful. Elected president of the United States as a Democrat in 1932, Roosevelt led the nation during the Great Depression and World War II. The only U.S. president ever elected to four terms, he died in office at Warm Springs, Georgia, on 12 April 1945.

T. Jason Soderstrum

See also
Daniels, Josephus; United States, Navy; Wilson, Thomas Woodrow.
References
Davis, Kenneth S. *FDR: The Beckoning of Destiny, 1882–1928*. New York: Putnam, 1972.
Freidel, Frank. *Franklin D. Roosevelt*. 4 vols. Boston: Little, Brown, 1952–1973.
Marolda, Edward J., ed. *FDR and the U.S. Navy*. New York: St. Martin's, 1998.
Ward, Geoffrey C. *Before the Trumpet: Young Franklin Roosevelt*. New York: Harper and Row, 1985.
———. *A First-Class Temperament: The Emergence of Franklin Roosevelt*. New York: Harper and Row, 1989.

Former President of the United States Theodore Roosevelt. He offered to raise and command a division of men in 1917, but President Woodrow Wilson refused. (Library of Congress)

Roosevelt, Theodore (1858–1919)

U.S. politician and president of the United States during 1901–1909. Born on 27 October 1858 in New York City, Theodore Roosevelt graduated from Harvard University in 1880 and briefly attended Columbia Law School before entering politics. Appointed assistant secretary of the navy under President William McKinley in 1897, he resigned the next year during the Spanish-American War to organize, along with Leonard Wood, the 1st U.S. Volunteer Cavalry Regiment (the "Rough Riders"). He fought with that unit in Cuba as a lieutenant colonel and then colonel. Returning home a hero, he was elected governor of New York in 1899. He became vice-president of the United States in 1901 and assumed the presidency upon William McKinley's assassination on 14 September 1901. Roosevelt was elected president in his own right in 1904.

During his presidency Roosevelt sought to advance U.S. interests abroad. He secured the independence of Panama from Colombia and began construction of the Panama Canal; he brought the warring parties together to end the Russo-Japanese War, which won him the Nobel Prize for Peace (1906). He also expanded the navy and sent the Great White Fleet around the world. Domestically he attacked the great business trusts and promoted conservation of natural resources.

Retiring to private life in 1909, Roosevelt remained active in politics and public life. Upon the outbreak of World War I, Roosevelt's sympathies were immediately strongly pro-Allied. Roosevelt hoped his county would follow policies that would lead to war with Germany, a preference he deliberately muted in his public statements on the conflict. By 1916 he actively sought to promote military preparedness, convinced that the United States would soon go to war. He also expressed alarm over pacifist sentiment in the nation.

Roosevelt strongly attacked the policies of President Woodrow Wilson for doing too little to protect U.S. rights against Germany, criticisms he expressed particularly strongly during the 1916 presidential campaign. When the United States entered the war in April 1917, Colonel Roosevelt, as he now styled himself, volunteered to raise a division of "horse riflemen" to fight in France after only six weeks' training. Premier Georges Clemenceau of France supported this as a boost to morale, but President Woodrow Wilson rejected the request. Roosevelt then sought to mobilize the United States behind the war effort. Crisscrossing the nation on speaking tours, he not only helped unite the country behind the war but also was an active recruiter in Liberty Loan drives. He supported both governmental and private efforts to suppress antiwar dissent, force all Americans to demonstrate patriotic enthusiasm for the war, and abjure radical political principles.

While Roosevelt himself was unable to serve in the military, all five of his children from his second marriage aided the U.S. cause in Europe. Daughter Ethel served as a nurse in the American Ambulance Hospital in Paris where her husband was a doctor. Son Kermit was a captain in the British army in the Middle East, and when the United States entered the war he became a major in a U.S. artillery unit. Archibald, a captain in the army, was severely wounded in France. Awarded the Croix de Guerre, he was invalided from the service. Theodore Jr., a U.S. Army lieutenant colonel, was also wounded and won the Distinguished Service Cross for his actions in the battles at Soissons and at the Argonne. Roosevelt's youngest son, Quentin, a pilot in the Army Air Corps, was shot down and killed over France in 1918, a great blow to his father.

Shortly after the war ended, Roosevelt publicly stated his opposition to the establishment of a postwar league of nations as envisaged by Wilson, though he apparently supported a continuation of the U.S. wartime alliance with Britain and France. Roosevelt died on 6 January 1919 at his Sagamore Hill estate at Oyster Bay, New York.

T. Jason Soderstrum and Priscilla Roberts

See also
Clemenceau, Georges; United States, Home Front; Wilson, Thomas Woodrow; Wood, Leonard.

References
Brands, H. W. *T. R.: The Last Romantic*. New York: Basic Books, 1997.

Chessman, G. Wallace. *Theodore Roosevelt and the Politics of Power*. Boston: Little, Brown, 1969.

Dalton, Kathleen. *Theodore Roosevelt: A Strenuous Life*. New York: Knopf, 2002.

Gardner, Joseph L. *Departing Glory: Theodore Roosevelt as Ex-President*. New York: Scribner, 1973.

Hagedorn, Hermann. *The Bugle That Woke America: The Saga of Theodore Roosevelt's Last Battle for His Country*. New York: The John Day Company, 1940.

Morris, Edmund. *Theodore Rex*. New York: Random House, 2001.

Pringle, Henry F. *Theodore Roosevelt: A Biography*. New York: Harcourt, Brace Jovanich, 1956.

Roques, Pierre Auguste (1856–1920)

French army general. Born on 28 December 1856 in Marseilles, Pierre Roques attended the École Polytechnique. Roques joined the army and won rapid promotion. He held a number of colonial assignments, beginning with service in Algeria. As a colonel he had charge of railroad construction in Madagascar during 1897–1905 and won promotion to general of brigade in 1906. As inspector of military aviation during 1910–1912, he helped promote French air power.

Roques's record as a combat commander in World War I was undistinguished. At the beginning of the war he commanded XII Corps in the Fourth Army. This army had been designated to carry out the major offensive action against Germany in the event of war, and on 22 August 1914 it attacked in the Ardennes with the goal of securing Neufchâteau. XII Corps was to support the main effort, mounted by the Colonial Corps, but the latter was surrounded by German forces and defeated at Rossignol. Roques then halted his own advance, which left XII Corps on the left exposed to a German counterattack, leading to heavy French casualties. The Fourth Army withdrew from the Ardennes on 24 August. Roques took command of the First Army in January 1915.

Appointed minister of war in March 1916, Roques—who had been a classmate of Joseph Joffre, served with him, and was a close friend—soon became embroiled in a personal conflict between Joffre and General Maurice Sarrail, who commanded the Allied Balkan Eastern Force at Salonika. In October 1916 Joffre sent Roques on an inspection trip to evaluate Sarrail's force. Sarrail had been largely ineffective, and Allied leaders wanted him removed from command; however, contrary to what Joffre had expected, Roques produced a favorable report, allowing leftists in the Chamber who supported Sarrail to attack Joffre, whom they accused of withholding troops and reinforcements from a leftist general. This and the poor performance of French and Allied forces at Verdun, on the Somme, and in Romania led French Premier Aristide Briand to remove Joffre as commander-in-chief. Briand was furious at Roques and removed him from his post as minister of war that December.

Roques then returned to the field briefly to command the Fourth Army before serving in technical posts from July 1917 to February 1919. Retired from the military in March 1919, Roques died at St. Cloud on 26 February 1920.

Joshua J. Robinson

See also
Briand, Aristide; Joffre, Joseph; Sarrail, Maurice.

References
Horne, Alistair. *The French Army and Politics, 1870–1970*. New York: Harper and Row, 1964.

Joffre, Joseph J. C. *The Personal Memoirs of Joffre: Field Marshal of the French Army*. 2 vols. Trans. T. Bentley Mott. New York: Harper, 1932.

King, Jere Clemens. *Generals and Politicians: Conflict between France's High Command, Parliament, and Government, 1914–1918*. Berkeley: University of California Press, 1951.

Musgrave, George Clarke. *Under Four Flags for France*. New York: Appleton, 1918.

Rothmaler, Karl Wilhelm von

See Einem, Karl Wilhelm von

Rufiji Delta Campaign (September 1914–July 1915)

Extended Allied naval campaign to destroy a German warship menacing Indian Ocean shipping. The German light cruiser *Königsberg* entered service in 1907. She was 376'8" long, displaced about 3,814 tons, had a maximum speed of 23 knots, and was armed with 10 × 4.1-inch guns, 8 × 2-inch guns, and 2 × 17.7-inch torpedo tubes. She had a crew of 322 men.

The *Königsberg* was patrolling in eastern African waters when the war began. A Royal Navy attack on Dar-es-Salaam in German East Africa on 8 August 1914 resulted in loss of the *Königsberg*'s port facilities. Meanwhile, on 6 August the *Königsberg*, commanded by Captain A. D. Looff, captured and sank the merchant ship *City of Winchester*. She then rendezvoused with the collier *Somalia* on the 21st before retiring to the Rufiji River delta.

Following a radio intercept on 19 September, the *Königsberg* emerged to sink the British cruiser *Pegasus* at Zanzibar the following day, subsequently retiring to the Rufiji Delta for extensive overhaul. Three British light cruisers arrived on 30 September to bottle up the *Königsberg*. Fortunately for the Germans, it proved easy to conceal the vessel in the Rufiji's maze of mangrove-lined channels. Defense was enhanced by sandbars, a minefield, and the *Königsberg*'s secondary armament, removed and emplaced ashore.

On 10 November the British sank the collier *Newbridge* in a channel of the Rufiji in an attempt to trap the *Königsberg* permanently. In reality, this would have merely forced the German cruiser to use another channel if Looff had been foolish enough to challenge the superior British forces. Looff, however, realized that by merely preserving his ship, he would force the Royal Navy to deploy significant forces. During November and December the British attempted with limited success to use spotter aircraft to target the German warship.

In February the German collier *Rubens,* sent from Germany to refuel the cruiser for an escape attempt to Germany, was intercepted by the British and sunk. Recognizing the inevitable, Oberstleutnant (Lieutenant Colonel) Paul von Lettow-Vorbeck, German commander in German East Africa, ordered many of *Königsberg*'s crew ashore to help defend the German colony. British aircraft finally spotted the trapped German warship in April. On 5 July, the newly arrived Royal Navy monitors *Mersey* and *Severn,* armed with 6-inch guns, entered the delta in the face of heavy German shore fire.

Despite the aid of spotter aircraft, the *Mersey* was damaged by shells from the *Königsberg* and forced to retire, followed by the *Severn*. On 11 July the monitors resumed their attack and, firing with devastating effect, forced the crew of the *Königsberg* to abandon their now wrecked ship. German forces subsequently salvaged everything useful on the ship. Taken ashore, the ship's powerful guns provided artillery support to the Germans as they continued their struggle in East Africa until war's end.

Glenn E. Helm

See also
Africa, Campaigns in; Battle Cruisers; Battleships; *Königsberg,* SMS; Lettow-Vorbeck, Paul Emil von; Monitors.

References
Corbett, Julian S., and Henry Newbolt. *Naval Operations: History of the Great War Based on Official Documents.* 5 vols. London: Longman, 1920–1931, 1938, 1940.

Farwell, Byron. *The Great War in Africa, 1914–1918.* New York: Norton, 1986.

Hoyt, Edwin P., Jr. *The Germans Who Never Lost: The Story of the Königsberg.* New York: Funk and Wagnalls, 1968.

Miller, Charles. *Battle for the Bundu: The First World War in East Africa.* New York: Macmillan, 1974.

Rupprecht, Crown Prince (1869–1955)

Bavarian crown prince and commander of Bavarian army forces in World War I. Born in Munich on 18 May 1869, Rupprecht Maria Luitpold Ferdinand von Wittelsbach (usually known as Rupprecht von Bayern) joined the army in 1886 and rose through the ranks. Service included the usual command and staff positions in the infantry and cavalry, which included attending the Bavarian Kriegsakademie (War Academy) and qualifying for the General Staff corps. He also studied at the universities of Munich and Berlin during 1889–1891.

A skillful and much-admired leader in the field, Rupprecht and Prussian Crown Prince Wilhelm were earmarked for major field commands before the war, but both were assigned to armies intended to serve as the anvil of the German offensive plan. Disliking such a secondary role, both placed political pressure on Chief of the German General Staff General Helmuth von Moltke and his operations director, Lieutenant Colonel Erich Ludendorff, for a greater role. The result was that their Fifth and Sixth Armies were strengthened and allowed to make a spoiling attack in Lorraine at the expense of the strength and power of the attacking northern wing, composed of the First through Fourth Armies.

At the beginning of the war, Rupprecht took command of the Bavarian army's three active and one reserve corps along with the Prussian XXI Corps as the newly constituted German Sixth Army. His subsequent aggressive attack in Lorraine brought the French offensive there to a bloody halt on the fron-

Crown Prince Rupprecht of Bavaria inspects Saxon storm troops at Cambrai. (National Archives)

tier. This action, however, had unintended consequences in that it enabled French army commander General Joseph Joffre to more easily extract French forces in Lorraine to meet the major German threat from the north through Belgium in the form of the First through Fourth Armies. The relocated French forces helped turn the tide in the First Battle of the Marne. Following the German failure on the Marne, Rupprecht's Sixth Army shifted to northwestern France and Flanders during the so-called Race to the Sea. It remained in that area for the duration of the war and there engaged in some of the conflict's hardest fighting with the British Expeditionary Force (BEF).

In 1915, Lieutenant General Hermann von Kuhl became Rupprecht's chief of staff, a relationship that lasted throughout the war. Rupprecht gained a reputation as a first-class defensive fighter, and in July 1916 he was promoted to field marshal in both the Bavarian and Prussian armies, taking command a month later of the newly constituted Army Group Crown Prince Rupprecht in Flanders. His was one of the three major army groups on the Western Front, the other two being that of German Crown Prince Wilhelm and Duke Albrecht of Saxony.

Rupprecht directed the German defensive campaigns on the Somme in 1916 and in Flanders in northwestern France in 1917. He then led two of the five great German (Ludendorff) offensives in the spring of 1918, despite misgivings he expressed to Ludendorff over German strategy. When Rupprecht questioned the operational objective, Ludendorff shouted, "I cannot abide the word operations. We'll blow a hole in the middle and the rest will follow of its own accord. That is what we did in Russia." Rupprecht's Second Army under Lieutenant General Georg von der Marwitz and his Seventeenth Army under Lieutenant General Otto von Below, along with Crown Prince Wilhelm's Eighteenth Army under Lieutenant General Oskar von Hutier, indeed "blew a hole" some 50 miles wide, but faulty operational design, exhaustion, lack of manpower, and stiffening Allied resistance combined to halt the Germans.

Rupprecht handled with skill the long, painful German retreat that began in August, but German losses were so great the Allies could not be denied. Following the armistice, Rupprecht retired from the army and abdicated his claim to the Bavarian throne. He returned to live in Bavaria, eschewing efforts to restore the monarchy and a political role. An opponent of the Nazis, he moved to Italy in 1939 and remained there until war's end. He escaped Gestapo arrest in the sweep after 20 July 1944 by hiding; his wife and children were interned by the Nazis. Rupprecht returned to Bavaria after the war and died at his palace near Starnberg on 2 August 1955.

Michael B. Barrett

See also

Albrecht, Duke of Württemberg; Below, Otto von; Frontiers, Battle of the; Hutier, Oskar von; Joffre, Joseph; Kuhl, Hermann von; Lorraine, Invasion of; Ludendorff, Erich; Ludendorff Offensives; Marne, First Battle of the; Marwitz, Georg von der; Messines Ridge, Battle of; Moltke, Helmuth von, Count; Schlieffen Plan; Somme Offensive; Tannenberg, Battle of; Vimy Ridge, Battle of; Wilhelm, Crown Prince.

References

Asprey, Robert B. *The German High Command at War: Hindenburg and Ludendorff and the First World War.* New York: Morrow, 1991.

Gray, Randal. *Kaiserschlacht, 1918: The Final German Offensive of World War One.* Westport, CT: Praeger, 2004.

Middlebrook, Martin. *The Kaiser's Battle, 21 March 1918: The First Day of the German Spring Offensive.* London: Penguin, 1978.

Rupprecht von Bayern. *Mein Kriegstagebuch.* 3 vols. Munich: Deutscher National Verlag, 1929.

Sendtner, Kurt. *Rupprecht von Wittelsbach.* Munich: R. Pflaum, 1954.

British philosopher and noted pacifist Bertrand Russell. (Library of Congress)

Russell, Bertrand (1872–1970)

British mathematician, philosopher, and peace activist. Born on 18 May 1872 in Trelleck, Monmouthshire, Bertrand Arthur William Russell was the grandson of Lord John Russell, who served twice as prime minister under Queen Victoria. Following the death of his mother (1874) and of his father (1876), Russell and his older brother lived with their grandparents. Educated at first privately and later at Trinity College, Cambridge, Russell obtained first-class honors degrees in both mathematics and philosophy. In addition, he studied and lectured on economics and political science. In 1910, he was appointed lecturer at Trinity College.

In 1907, several supporters of voting rights for women formed the Men's League for Women's Suffrage, which Russell joined. He also became a member of the Fabian Society, where he met the pacifist Clifford Allen. In July 1914, Russell collected signatures from fellow professors for a statement urging England to remain neutral in the imminent European war. Soon after the outbreak of that war, Russell, Allen, and Fenner Brockway formed the No-Conscription Fellowship (NCF), an organization to campaign against the introduction of conscription. Russell was also a founding member of the Union of Democratic Control (UDC), the most important of the British antiwar organizations during the war. Other members of the organization included Joseph Rowntree, Ramsay MacDonald, Edmund Dene Morel, Charles Trevelyan, and Norman Angell. The UDC argued for a foreign policy that was under parliamentary control and called for immediate peace negotiations.

With the passing of the Military Service Act in January 1916, the NCF concentrated its efforts on persuading men to refuse call-up into the armed services. Although he was elected to the Royal Society in 1908, Russell's career at Trinity came to an end in 1916 when he was convicted and fined for his antiwar activities. After U.S. President Woodrow Wilson's reelection in 1916, Russell wrote an open letter to the president in which he appealed to the U.S. government to make peace between the European governments.

In July 1917, Russell helped the war poet and serving army officer Siegfried Sassoon draft a statement of protest against "this evil and unjust war." During the war Russell published several books on politics, war, and peace. He strongly advocated the need for an international government to secure peace in the world by means of effective international law. In 1918, Russell was convicted a second time for his antiwar efforts and spent six months in prison. Russell originally welcomed the Russian Revolution. After the war, he paid a short visit to Russia and China and, after meeting Vladimir Lenin and Leon Trotsky, wrote a book that was sharply critical of communism.

In 1931 Bertrand succeeded his elder brother as 3rd Earl Russell. He used the forum of the House of Lords to promote his views on pacifism. He also generated controversy when he wrote against Victorian notions of morality and sexuality. In 1938, Russell went to the United States and during the next years taught at many of the country's leading universities. In 1940, he was involved in legal proceedings when his right to teach philosophy at the College of the City of New York was questioned because of his views on religion and morality.

In the years leading to World War II, Russell supported the policy of appeasement, but in the late 1930s he ceased to be a pacifist with the rise of Adolf Hitler in Germany. Russell argued that although war was always a great evil, in some particularly extreme circumstances it might be a lesser of multiple evils.

For his scientific works, Russell was awarded the Sylvester medal of the Royal Society and the de Morgan medal of the London Mathematical Society in 1934; he was reelected a fellow of Trinity College in 1944 and received the Nobel Prize for Literature in 1950. The last twenty years of Russell's life were devoted primarily to warnings about the nuclear danger, advocacy of world government, and the active work of peacemaking. Together with Albert Einstein, he released the Russell-Einstein Manifesto in 1955, which was also signed by a Communist scientist and several Nobel Prize-winners, calling for the curtailment of nuclear weapons. In 1957, he was a prime organizer of the first Pugwash Conference on Science and World Affairs, which brought together scientists concerned about the proliferation of nuclear weapons. Russell became the founding president of the Campaign for Nuclear Disarmament in 1958. Three years later at the age of 88 he was once again briefly imprisoned, this time in connection with antinuclear protests. In 1962, Russell acted as a mediator in two serious international crises (Cuba and the border dispute between China and India).

The Bertrand Russell Peace Foundation was formed in 1963 and worked to free political prisoners in more than forty countries. Russell began publishing articles criticizing the Vietnam War, and along with Jean-Paul Sartre he organized a tribunal intended to expose alleged U.S. war crimes; this came to be known as the Russell Tribunal. Russell died at his home in Penrhyndeudraeth in North Wales on 2 February 1970.

Katja Wuestenbecker

See also

Angell (Lane), Sir Ralph Norman; Hitler, Adolf; Lenin, Vladimir Ilyich; MacDonald, James Ramsay; Morel, Edmund Dene; No-Conscription Fellowship; Russia, Revolution of March 1917; Russia, Revolution of November 1917; Sassoon, Siegfried; Trotsky, Leon; Union of Democratic Control; Wilson, Thomas Woodrow.

References

Irvine, Andrew, ed. *Bertrand Russell: Critical Assessments.* London: Routledge, 1998.

Moorehead, Caroline. *Bertrand Russell: A Life.* London: Sinclair-Stevenson, 1992.

Russell, Bertrand. *The Autobiography of Bertrand Russell.* 3 vols. London: Allen and Unwin, 1967–1969.

Ryan, Alan. *Bertrand Russell: A Political Life.* London: Allen Lane, 1988; London: Penguin, 1990.

Vellacott, Jo. *Bertrand Russell and the Pacifists in the First World War.* Brighton, UK: Harvester, 1980.

Russia, Air Service

The Russian army entered the air age when two officers flew a balloon from St. Petersburg to Novgorod in 1885. The Russians employed balloons for observation and reconnaissance during the Russo-Japanese War of 1904–1905 but did not make effective use of them. However, as lighter-than-air ships gained acceptance, heavier-than-air craft drew interest. In 1910 the War Ministry established an aviation branch of the St. Petersburg Aeronautics School at Gatchina and authorized the purchase of aircraft abroad. A second school was established at Sevastopol shortly thereafter.

Russian heavy bomber Sikorsky Ilya Muronetz. (Art-Tech)

Aircraft participated in Russian army maneuvers in 1911, and in 1912 a special aviation section established by the Main Directorate of the General Staff took control of military aviation. In 1913 the Russians employed chiefly French aircraft, most of them assembled in Russian factories. While the Russian aircraft industry struggled, talented native engineers such as Igor Sikorsky came on the scene.

At the outbreak of World War I, the Russian army had 244 airplanes in its inventory; however, shortages of spare parts kept most grounded. After only one month of fighting, by the beginning of September only 145 frontline aircraft remained in service. Often Siberian peasant-infantrymen, believing that only Germans were cunning enough to develop aircraft, shot down the Russian reconnaissance planes returning from enemy lines.

Early in the war France provided nearly 50 aircraft to Russia, but most were obsolete. Despite efforts by the Allies and domestic industry to increase the numbers of aircraft supporting the Russian army, Russian aircraft production was less than a third that of Germany. Another problem was the shortage of trained air crews. Between 1910 and 1914, the two pilot training schools produced only some 300 pilots. After the start of the war, Russia opened new schools in Odessa and Moscow and expanded the facilities at Gatchina and Sevastopol. Nonetheless, Russia lagged in the production both of aircraft and pilots. By 1917 Russia still had only about 500 trained pilots and fewer than that number of aircraft at the front.

There were limited successes, however. Sikorsky four-engine bombers penetrated up to 150 miles into the enemy's rear areas in 442 long-range bombing raids between 1915 and 1917. In the same period, Russian reconnaissance aircraft took more than 7,000 photographs, and despite the concentration of aviation assets in support of ground formations, the Russians organized a fighter branch in 1916 to counter German attacks on their reconnaissance aircraft.

Despite some successes, the Russian air arm proved inadequate in the war. In air power, as in other areas, the backwardness of Russian industry and dependence on foreign imports were telling. The Russians were never able to free themselves of foreign engine designs, nor could they produce sufficient wireless sets or synchronized machine guns to support their needs. With the Bolshevik seizure of power in 1917, the air service disintegrated, along with the rest of the Russian military establishment.

Arthur T. Frame

See also

Air Warfare, Fighter Tactics; Air Warfare, Strategic Bombing; Aircraft, Bombers; Aircraft, Fighters; Aircraft, Production; Aircraft, Reconnaissance and Auxiliary; Antiaircraft Weapons; Photo Reconnaissance.

References

Jones, David R. "The Beginnings of Russian Air Power, 1907–1922." In *Soviet Aviation and Air Power: A Historical View,* ed. Robin Higham and Jacob Kipp. Boulder, CO: Westview, 1977.

Kennett, Lee. *The First Air War, 1914–1918.* New York: Free Press, 1991.

Kilmarx, Robert A. *A History of Soviet Airpower.* New York: Praeger, 1962.

Lincoln, W. Bruce. *Passage through Armageddon: The Russians in War and Revolution, 1914–1918.* New York: Simon and Schuster, 1986.

Menning, Bruce W. *Bayonets Before Bullets: The Imperial Russian Army, 1861–1914.* Bloomington: Indiana University Press, 1992.

Stroud, John. *The Red Air Force.* London: The Pilot Press, 1943.

Russia, Allied Intervention in (1918–1922)

Immediately upon seizing power in Petrograd in November 1917, the Bolsheviks announced that Russia was withdrawing from World War I. Russia's former allies of Britain, France, and the United States wanted to keep that country in the struggle against the Central Powers and prevent stocks of weapons from falling into the hands of the Central Powers by reversing the political situation in Russia, but they had no coordinated plans to accomplish this end. Even after the Allied Supreme War Council decided to intervene on the side of the White (anti-Bolshevik) forces in Russia, the action was haphazard and ineffective. In part this was because the Allied governments provided only military assistance and not the economic support indispensable to victory. Throughout, the Western powers pursued short-range military goals, but they never seriously discussed the political future of a non-Bolshevik Russia.

During a conference of Allied leaders at Rapallo in November 1917 concerning military cooperation, the British and French representatives were unsuccessful in securing agreement on a common policy toward Russia. Then on 23 December 1917, London and Paris signed a convention agreeing to enter the Russian Civil War in support of the White forces against the Reds (Bolsheviks). This gave rise to the Bolshevik charge that the Western Allies had agreed to a program to dismember Russia.

German occupation of the strategically and economically important Ukraine triggered the Allied intervention. Also, negotiations at Brest Litovsk between the Bolshevik government and the Germans led to concern in the Allied capitals that the Baltic states, eastern Poland, Ukraine, and part of the Caucasus would come under either German or Turkish control.

The French took the lead in the Allied intervention. French General Ferdinand Foch, later supreme Allied military commander, strongly favored intervention in Russia to keep that state in the war against Germany. His plan envisaged a multinational military force under his own command. On 24 December 1917, the Allied Supreme War Council proclaimed

Machine-gun company of the U.S. 31st Infantry in Vladivostok, Siberia, following World War I. (Bettmann/Corbis)

that the Allied Powers would provide military assistance to any political faction in Russia supporting their country's participation in the war against Germany. The French government strongly supported the Czech Legion in Russia, and between March and May 1918, during the Ludendorff offensive on the Western Front, that government made every effort to reopen the Eastern Front and encouraged Japan to take part.

The Allied intervention in Russia began with the landing of British troops at Murmansk on 9 March 1918, although London was less concerned than Paris about a Bolshevik Russia and feared a Japanese thrust into the Russian Far East. The British government was also far more pragmatic in its Russian policy in that it was willing to support any Russian government, including the Bolsheviks, that would guarantee British economic interests in the Russian market. In Ukraine, British economic interests met French competition; White leaders were able to use this rivalry to play the Allies off against each other.

In early 1919 during the Paris Peace Conference, British Prime Minister David Lloyd George and U.S. President Woodrow Wilson encouraged negotiations with the Bolsheviks. Wilson suggested a conference of all factions in the Russian Civil War to begin on 15 February 1919, on Prinkipo Island in the Sea of Marmara. This effort came to nought

because leading White Generals Aleksandr Kolchak and Anton Denikin, as well as the Bolshevik leaders, sought to continue their military offensives. The Bolsheviks also feared that a peace conference under Allied auspices would necessarily favor the Whites, as they were the clients of the Western powers. But Lloyd George and Wilson believed that the Whites only deserved to win if they could gain the support of the Russian population. Moreover, there was no agreement between the Allies and the White leaders concerning Russia's political future after an end to the Bolshevik regime. The political values of the Western democracies and the authoritarian White generals were so different that the Allies could not be certain that a White regime in Russia would be an improvement on the Bolsheviks.

Meanwhile, the civil war continued. Although the Allies provided military equipment and advisors, they made no effort to force political change that would bring about an efficient political system on territory occupied by the Whites. Moreover, French-British and U.S.-Japanese rivalries prevented unified action in the Russian Civil War.

Following the death of Admiral Kolchak in February 1920, the Western Allies did seek a modus vivendi with the Bolshevik regime. As a first step toward that end, in January 1920 they lifted the economic blockade of Bolshevik Russia. At the

Soldiers and sailors from many countries parading in front of the Allied Headquarters Building, Vladivostok, Russia, September 1918. (National Archives)

same time, the Allied Powers began their withdrawal from Russian territory. According to an official French government report of October 1919, France alone had spent more than 7 billion francs in its Russian intervention, with nothing to show for the outlay. There was also some sentiment among Western politicians to cultivate Bolshevik Russia as an ally against a resurgent Germany.

Japan's approach was quite different. Even before Japan's gains of the 1904–1905 Russo-Japanese War, that nation's leaders had sought to expand Japanese influence on the Asian mainland in Korea and Manchuria. Japanese expansionists perceived in the Russian Civil War a splendid opportunity to enhance their holdings in Russia's eastern territories. Japanese General Tanaka Giichi in Manchuria proposed the creation of an independent non-Communist Siberian state, allied with, and presumably dominated by, Japan. Whereas the United States sent to Siberia 9,000 soldiers, Great Britain 7,000, China 2,000, Italy 1,400, and France 1,200, Japan dispatched some 73,000 troops to eastern Siberia and the Russ-

ian Far East. In addition, Japan had 60,000 soldiers deployed in neighboring Manchuria.

Some Japanese leaders predicted that Siberia would be the site of an eventual clash between the civilizations of the "Yellow" and "White" races in the Far East. Thus the Japanese intervention into Siberia was directed not only against Russia but also to forestall U.S. engagement in the region. Most White leaders, however, harbored strong patriotic, and often racist, suspicions of the Japanese, seeing in them only a temporarily useful force in the struggle against Bolshevism. They saw no long-term advantage in an alliance with Japan. This was one reason for the Japanese failure in Siberia. Finally, in large part due to the financial strain of the enterprise, the Japanese withdrew from Siberian territory. Japan's departure was completed by the end of October 1922.

Eva-Maria Stolberg

See also

Brest Litovsk, Treaty of; Czech Legion; Denikin, Anton; Kolchak, Aleksandr Vasiliyevich; Lloyd George, David; Ludendorff

ALLIED INTERVENTIONS IN WESTERN RUSSIA, 1918 – 1922

Canadians
Americans

British
French
Canadians
Italians
Serbs

Finns

Finns

British

Latts

Latts

Baltic
Germans

Poles

Romanians

French

British

British

Legend:
- - - Boundary of Russian Empire, 1914
••• Eastern Front, Autumn 1918
—— Area of Soviet Territory, Mar 1921
• Main locations of Bolshevik Uprisings
← Attacks by Allied Powers

NORWAY

SWEDEN

FINLAND

Helsinki

ESTONIA

Baltic
Sea

LATVIA

Riga

LITHUANIA

GERMANY

Warsaw

POLAND

CZECHOSLOVAKIA

HUNGARY

YUGOSLAVIA

GREECE

Constantinople

ROMANIA

Bucharest

BULGARIA

Murmansk

Archangel

Shelkursk

Petrograd

Pskov

Minsk

Kaluga

Smolensk

Moscow

RUSSIA

Perm

Kazan

Nizhni
Novgorod

Samara

Orenburg

Penza

Tambov

Saratov

Kiev

Zhitomir

Kharkov

Poltava

Don R.

Ural R.

Dniester R.

Dnieper R.

Yekaterinoslav

Odessa

Rostov

Astrakhan

Volga R.

Sea
of Azov

Sevastopol

Novorossiysk

Maikop

Caspian
Sea

Black   Sea

Batumi

Baku

OTTOMAN EMPIRE

Tehran

PERSIA

Mediterranean
Sea

Trans-Siberian Railway

60°N

50°N

40°N

10°E   0°   10°W   20°W   30°W   40°W   50°W

0   100   200 mi
0   100   200 km

N

Offensives; Paris Peace Conference; Russia, Civil War; Siberian Intervention, Japan; Supreme War Council; Tanaka Giichi; Wilson, Thomas Woodrow.

References

Bradley, John. *Allied Intervention in Russia, 1917–1920.* New York: Basic Books, 1968.

Foglesong, David S. *America's Secret War against Bolshevism: U.S. Intervention in the Russian Civil War, 1917–1920.* Chapel Hill: University of North Carolina Press, 1995.

Kennan, George F. *Soviet-American Relations, 1917–1920,* Vol. 2, *The Decision to Intervene.* Princeton, NJ: Princeton University Press, 1958.

Kettle, Michael. *Churchill and the Archangel Fiasco, November 1918–July 1919 (Russia and the Allies, 1917–1920).* 3 vols. London: Routledge, 1981–1992.

Melton, Carol Willcox. *Between War and Peace: Woodrow Wilson and the American Expeditionary Force to Siberia, 1918–1921.* Macon, GA: Mercer University Press, 2001.

Silverlight, John. *The Victors' Dilemma: Allied Intervention in the Russian Civil War.* New York: Weybright, 1970.

Stolberg, Eva-Maria. "Japan's Strategic and Political Involvement in Siberia and the Russian Far East, 1917–1922." In *Japan's National Identity and Its Asian Neighbours in Imperial Era,* ed. Robert Cribb and Li Narangoa. im Druck: Curzon Press.

Ullman, Richard H. *Anglo-Soviet Relations, 1917–1921.* 3 vols. Princeton, NJ: Princeton University Press, 1961–1972.

Wandycz, Piotr S. *France and Her Eastern Allies, 1919–1925.* Minneapolis: University of Minnesota Press, 1962.

Willett, Robert L. *Russian Sideshow: America's Undeclared War, 1918–1920.* London: Brassey's, 2003.

Russia, Army

The Imperial Russian Army symbolized the institution of the empire and support for the emperor more than any other element of Russian society. It was the embodiment of strength against outside threats and the bulwark of internal order. The army was inextricably bound to the autocracy and the monarchy to the army; this had been the case for centuries. Even the outward emblem of status and prestige in Russian society was the table of ranks, an imitation of army ranks. Those who served the state received these marks of distinction, with the uniform and its decorations as the badge of loyalty and status for both the military and civilian bureaucracy. The army was also an engine for upward social mobility, at least after a series of reforms that began in the 1870s.

Through the 1850s, army recruits came exclusively from the peasantry. Conscription was mourned like a death sentence by those involved because the twenty-five-year term of service separated the soldier permanently from his family and village. The military constituted a separate caste, in practice considered lower than bonded serfs. Soldiers suffered from severe discipline, inhuman punishments, and indifference to basic human needs. Reforms in the 1860s and 1870s intro-duced universal military obligation for all males regardless of class and a reduction in terms of service to six years active and nine years reserve. In 1888 active service was reduced to four years, and reserve time was increased to eighteen. After the Russo-Japanese War of 1904–1905, the term of active service shrank to three years and the reserve service was reduced to fifteen. The empire's leaders hoped to maintain an active peacetime force of 800,000 men with a trained reserve force of 550,000. Justifications advanced for this large standing force and length of service were Russia's vast physical size and poor railroad system that impeded speedy reserve mobilization. Illiterate peasants also took longer to train.

There were numerous severe inequities in the conscription mechanism. Young, healthy bachelors were sometimes exempted while older sole breadwinners were called to the colors, leaving their families destitute. No matter how heavy a man's family responsibilities had become, at the outbreak of war every trained male up to 39 years of age would immediately be mobilized. While the Russo-Japanese War revealed many inequities and exposed the dissatisfaction within the force and potential for revolutionary reaction, the same system was still employed with only minor changes in 1914.

Upon conscription, the Russian recruit was issued three uniforms, unfinished boot leather, a greatcoat, knapsack, and a rifle. In cantonment he slept on a straw mattress on a wooden bunk, with only his greatcoat as cover. In the field his greatcoat was his bedroll. His unchanging daily fare was bread for breakfast, cabbage soup with meat for lunch, and a porridge of cereal grain for supper, but most soldiers actually ate better in the army than in their villages.

Corporal punishment could still be administered but only by court-martial, not on the authority of a single officer. This latter provision was abolished during the Russo-Japanese War but was unwisely reintroduced just before World War I and could be inflicted without court-martial proceedings at the discretion of the commanding officer. For minor infractions, typical punishments included terms in the guardhouse on bread and water or periods of standing at attention for long hours with rifle in hand and a pack full of rocks or dirt on the offender's back. The most common forms of discipline, however, were blows to the face of the miscreant by his sergeant, accompanied by derogatory epithets.

Russian peasant-soldiers generally did not identify with the abstractions of the nation, the state, or most especially the empire. These attitudes were normally inculcated through socialization and education, which were not for the most part available to Russian peasants. While tremendous numbers of Russians were killed or became life-long cripples for "tsar and fatherland" over the generations, they accepted this because of a fatalistic belief that once conscripted it was their lot in life and could not be avoided except through divine intervention. Even the mystical attitude of Russian peasants

Regiments of Russian soldiers are greeted by lines of French cavalry, while people throng the roadsides to see the troops pass. (Francis J. Reynolds and C. W. Taylor, *Collier's Photographic History of the European War*, P. F. Collier & Son, New York, 1916)

that the tsar would be some type of father-protector, if only their plight were not hidden from him, was not carried over to military authority. Events of the Russo-Japanese War and the subsequent 1905 revolution disrupted this mystical relationship and began the process of dissolution of the soldiers' fatalistic acceptance of their military lot.

Officer service in the Russian army was linked to a bond of service to the person of the tsar. Every tsar and member of the imperial family, male and female, held honorary commissions in one or more of the guards units and wore its uniform on ceremonial occasions. It was expected that young grand dukes would choose a regiment and serve as an ordinary officer in it. For centuries the officer corps was the domain of the landholding Russian nobility; however, the mid-nineteenth-century process of reform began to alter that bias, and by 1895 only 73 percent of the officer corps came from the nobility. On the eve of World War I, nobles constituted only 51 percent of the officer corps. The remainder were professionally motivated middle- and lower-class men who had come to service through a system of military schools developed for that purpose.

The remote relationship between officers and soldiers of the Imperial Russian Army was not due to officers' participation in physical punishment or abuse, both of which were offi-

cially discouraged, but rather the distance imposed by society and military regulation. Officers were considered noblemen in uniform, no matter what their class background. And despite reforms, fear and distrust of the nobility was ingrained in peasant-soldiers. Officers generally maintained an attitude of aloofness and separation from their men.

The Russo-Japanese War of 1904–1905 and the revolution of 1905 shook the foundations of the Imperial Russian Army and led to some reverses in reform. For two years after the war, the army was preoccupied with restoring domestic peace and eliminating revolutionary elements from its ranks. Between 1909 and 1914 the army made great strides toward reform and recovery, but it was still a peasant army, weak in leadership and supported by a barely adequate economy. The beginning of 1914 saw the introduction of a program of increased expenditures intended to modernize the force over the next three years. This "Great Program" would have increased annual recruitment and firepower by 20 percent and added heavy artillery for the first time. As early as 1901, France offered aid in building strategically located railroads to speed the Russian mobilization and perhaps nullify the German offensive plan. Their construction was a factor prompting German army leaders to believe that the longer a general European war was delayed, the less chance Germany would have of winning it.

The Great War intervened, however, before much had been accomplished.

In August 1914 the army numbered some 5.25 million men. The bulk of the army was on two fronts. The Northwestern Front facing Germany consisted of one army group of two armies: the First Army of four corps on the north and the Second Army of five corps south of the East Prussian salient. North from the Baltic to the Northwestern Front, the Sixth Army provided security. The Ninth Army was formed just before the war began. Its assignment was to thrust from Warsaw north toward Berlin. On the Southwestern Front facing Austria-Hungary, two army groups of two armies each prepared to thrust into Galicia. One army group consisted of the Fourth and Fifth Armies, with seven corps between them. The second army group consisted of the Third and Eighth Armies, dividing nine corps between them. The Russian Seventh Army provided security and covering operations between the Southwestern Front and the Black Sea coast. Later the Tenth Army was created and entered the line in the Northwestern Front to deal with German advances there.

Under the Fundamental Laws of the Russian Empire, the tsar was the supreme commander-in-chief of Russian armed forces. Believing, however, that possible setbacks would expose him to personal criticism, the tsar's ministers urged him to appoint someone else. Despite Nicholas II's belief that kingship included armed forces command in national emergency, he reluctantly appointed his uncle, Grand Duke Nikolai Nikolaevich, to supreme command. By August 1915 the Russian war effort was near collapse, and Tsar Nicholas II, against the advice of his cabinet, decided to take supreme command himself. His decision to place himself at Stavka, the Russian high command, isolated him from governmental decision making and had little impact on military matters.

Despite the massive size of the Russian army, its greatest shortcoming on the battlefield was in military hardware. Russian artillery relied almost exclusively on a rapid-fire 3-inch gun organized into six batteries per infantry division, with each corps adding another two batteries of 4.8-inch light howitzers. The army had only 164 guns of 6-inch bore, organized into two separate formations, a total less than half the number fielded by their opponents. The situation for machine guns was even worse, and in 1914 the Russian army had only about 4,000.

Drawing on the Russo-Japanese War, the Russian General Staff calculated usage rates for artillery and stockpiled 1,000 shells per gun but made no plans for increasing production in wartime. The first weeks of fighting revealed those stockpiles to be inadequate, because the rapid-fire 3-inch guns expended enormous quantities of shells. Believing that commanders at various levels were simply hoarding stocks, the Artillery Administration maintained that its production of 300,000 shells a month was sufficient, despite pleas from front commanders. Although over 6.5 million rounds were stockpiled at the front by the end of November 1914, there had been no effort to increase production. Not knowing the tremendous effort involved in moving this stockpile of shells, commanders saw no reason to economize and fired off the whole amount by the end of 1914. The Russian army was short of shells for most of 1915.

As the shell shortages began to bite, small-arms and ammunition shortages also became evident. The General Staff had planned for sufficient rifles for mobilization; in fact, so many were manufactured that production was slowed in favor of machine guns. Tremendous manpower losses in the early fighting also meant loss of soldiers' individual weapons. Shortfalls were met by taking rifles from noncombatants, but by early 1915 recruits were being trained and sent forward as replacements without weapons. Commanders were instructed to equip them with rifles recovered from the battlefield.

During the war the Russian army sustained unprecedented casualty rates. Some estimates for losses by the end of 1914 are as high as 1.8 million men, 396,000 of them dead. Nearly half of the prewar trained manpower had been effectively lost by the end of 1914. These casualties were replaced by raw, barely trained recruits. By the end of 1916, 14.6 million men had been conscripted for the army. Of these, 6.9 million were in the field army and another 2 million were in rear garrisons. This left more than 5.5 million accounted for in casualties. The Germans listed 2.1 million taken prisoner. By the fall of 1917 the total recruitment figure reached 15.3 million in uniform with just over 3.6 million killed and wounded.

Perhaps surprisingly, by 1916 and 1917 shortages of munitions, weapons, and supplies no longer constituted major shortcomings. Domestic increases in production and increased support from allies had taken care of the shortfall. But the previous shortages had taken their toll on the front-line troops, who had been forced to absorb mounting casualties. Even successful offensives, such as the Brusilov offensive of 1916, cost massive bloodshed. In late 1916 Russian soldiers despaired of the slaughter ever stopping. Replacements were badly trained peasant youths and older family men who resented being torn from their families and villages. Many replacement officers were recruited from among previously deferred students and workers who had been infected with revolutionary ideas and did not support the tsarist government. The replacements infected veteran troops with their worries over domestic and civilian concerns, while the veterans told the recruits of the traumas they had endured and still faced. This combination undermined the fighting will of the army and led to a series of mutinies in the fall of 1916, sometimes involving entire regiments.

To soldier dissatisfaction were added food shortages caused by disruptions in distribution. These struck the army in December 1916 and January 1917, just as they did the civilian populace. By February 1917 soldiers feared starvation, often going several days without rations. News from home told soldiers that conditions there were no better. Letters complained of long lines, shortages, and skyrocketing prices, which added to the men's feelings of helplessness. After the March 1917 revolution brought the fall of the autocracy, soldiers began to vote for peace by fleeing their units.

Order Number One, pushed through the Petrograd Soviet Executive Committee in February 1918 by soldiers' deputies and issued by the Soviet despite its lack of governmental authority, abolished the death penalty in the army, directed the establishment of political commissars at every military level, and established command by committee where privates' votes equaled those of officers, effectively removing army control from the latter. By mid-April Russia's frontline soldiers were fraternizing with their enemies. All attempts to enforce discipline met with hostility from the troops. Meanwhile, Bolshevik Party agitators, bent on ending Russia's participation in the war, worked among the troops.

In March 1917, the provisional government had named General Lavr Kornilov commander of the Petrograd garrison. Frustrated in efforts to restore order and discipline in the capital garrison, Kornilov was allowed to return to the front lines to command the Eighth Army. Early successes in the so-called Kerensky offensive of July 1917 were reversed when the German counteroffensive drove the Russians back in disarray. Kornilov's attempts to restore order and discipline failed, and Russian soldiers deserted. From the Baltic to Romania, the Russian army simply collapsed.

In August 1917, Prime Minister Aleksandr Kerensky appointed Kornilov supreme commander of the army. When the Germans took Riga shortly after, causing panic in Petrograd, Kerensky ordered Kornilov to come and restore order. When Kornilov called upon the government to resign and hand over control to him, Kerensky dismissed Kornilov and ordered his arrest. In defiance of Kerensky's orders, Kornilov ordered his forces to march on Petrograd. Kerensky then called on the Bolsheviks for assistance. The Bolsheviks organized massed railroad workers and some soldiers and sailors to block Kornilov's path, convincing his forces to disperse.

With the aid of radicalized army units in the capital, the Bolsheviks seized power from the provisional government beginning on the night of 6–7 November 1917. The new Bolshevik government immediately faced a dilemma. It had gained soldier support with the motto "Peace, Land and Bread," and it now ordered an end to Russian participation in the war. When negotiations broke down over Germany's punitive peace terms, the Bolsheviks attempted to follow a strategy of "no peace, no war." There followed a major German army offensive that the collapsed Russian army could not withstand, forcing the Bolsheviks to conclude the Treaty of Brest Litovsk on German terms in March 1918. Over the

next three years, the rise of the counterrevolutionary White armies and the challenge of intervention from former allies caused the new Soviet government to establish the Red Army from the ashes of the Imperial Russian Army.

Arthur T. Frame

See also

Brusilov Offensive; Carpathian Campaign; Caucasian Front; East Prussia, Campaigns in; Eastern Front Overview; Galicia Campaigns; Gumbinnen, Battle of; Kerensky Offensive; Kornilov, Lavr Georgyevich; Masurian Lakes, First Battle of the; Masurian Lakes, Second Battle of the; Nicholas II, Tsar; Nikolai Nikolaevich, Grand Duke; Russia, Home Front; Russia, Revolution of 1905; Russia, Revolution of March 1917; Russia, Revolution of November 1917; Russia, War Plan; Tannenberg, Battle of.

References

Kagan, Frederick W., and Robin Higham, eds. *The Military History of Tsarist Russia*. New York: Palgrave, 2002.

Knox, Sir Alfred. *With the Russian Army, 1914–1917: Being Chiefly Extracts from the Diary of a Military Attaché.* 2 vols. New York: Dutton, 1921.

Lincoln, W. Bruce. *Passage through Armageddon: The Russians in War and Revolution, 1914–1918.* New York: Simon and Schuster, 1986.

Menning, Bruce W. *Bayonets Before Bullets: The Imperial Russian Army, 1861–1914.* Bloomington: Indiana University Press, 1992.

Sanborn, Joshua. *Drafting the Russian Nation: Military Conscription, Total War, and Mass Politics, 1905–1925.* DeKalb: Northern Illinois University Press, 2003.

Schimmelpenninck van der Oye, David, and Bruce W. Menning, eds. *Reforming the Tsar's Army: Military Innovation in Imperial Russia from Peter the Great to the Revolution.* New York: Cambridge University Press, 2004.

Solzhenitsyn, Aleksandr. *August 1914.* New York: Farrar, Straus, 1971.

Taylor, Brian D. *Politics and the Russian Army: Civil-Military Relations, 1689–2000.* New York: Cambridge University Press, 2003.

Wildman, Allan K. *The End of the Russian Imperial Army*, Vol. 1, *The Old Army and the Soldier's Revolt (March–April 1917)*. Princeton, NJ: Princeton University Press, 1980.

Russia, Civil War (1918–1920)

Not even the Treaty of Brest Litovsk with Germany that ended Russia's participation in the First World War brought peace to Russia. On 9 March 1918 the new Bolshevik government moved the capital from Petrograd to Moscow. This was partly because of the exposed position of Petrograd in relation to the Germans and their satellite states, and partly due to threats from counterrevolutionary forces now gathering in the border areas. Monarchists, members of the propertied classes, liberals, moderate socialists, and Russian nationalists of all political persuasions were more or less united in their refusal to accept the disastrous Treaty of Brest Litovsk. Many of

Bolsheviks on the streets during the November 1917 Revolution in Russia. (Library of Congress)

them now sought to use armed force to overthrow the Bolsheviks, whose policies they bitterly opposed. Collectively, those against the Bolsheviks came to be known as the Whites; the Bolsheviks and their supporters were the Reds.

The Civil War began in February 1918 in a revolt of the Don Cossacks under Ataman Dutov. The Don Cossacks had previously enjoyed special privileges under the tsars. But in faraway provinces such as in Siberia and Central Asia, where the Bolsheviks were poorly organized, local authorities held on to power. The situation in the Don region became uncertain when the Don Cossacks there under Ataman Krasnov opened negotiations with the Germans; the anti-Bolshevik movement in the Don region ultimately split into pro-German and pro-Allied factions. Meanwhile, the Germans installed a satellite regime in Ukraine under hetman Pavlo Skoropadsky but supported him only halfheartedly, not helping him create an Ukrainian army.

The situation in the Far East was confused with the establishment there of independent Siberian governments. In November 1918 Admiral Aleksandr Kolchak seized power in Omsk and tried to unify the White forces in Siberia. In Siberia the Whites gained the support of the Czechoslovak Legion, 45,000 Czechs who had fought in World War I for Russia against Austria-Hungary to secure independence for their

homeland and now wished to continue that fight. They literally fought their way across Russia on the Trans-Siberian Railroad to Vladivostok, which they reached in May 1918. In July 1918 a joint U.S. and Japanese force landed at Vladivostok in support of the Czechs, who held much of Siberia for Kolchak. However, Kolchak was not an effective military commander. Indeed, the Bolshevik or Red forces seem to have gotten the best commanders, most of them junior officers hastily promoted on the basis of ability.

The British and French encouraged and supported those opposed to Bolshevik rule. The major Allied governments, including the United States, sent supplies, money, and troops to help White forces, although there was no coordination to this effort. The Allied governments hoped initially that if the Bolsheviks were overthrown, then Russia would reenter the war against Germany. Also, the Allies wanted to keep war supplies given the Russians from falling into the hands of the Germans, and they sought to topple Communism.

The Bolshevik government faced war with nothing resembling a trained force, especially as the Bolsheviks had set out to destroy the army in the process of seizing power. During the first period of the Civil War, the central government suffered one reverse after another, but gradually a new Red Army was organized. Under the leadership of Commissar for War Leon Trotsky, it developed into a regular army based on conscription and subject to strict discipline.

The Bolsheviks had the advantage of fighting on interior lines. The White forces were widely scattered on the periphery, in the northwest (Baltic provinces), in the south (Ukraine, Caucasus), and in the east (Siberia). The Reds also had the vast stocks of arms and munitions that had been produced by 1917 under the tsarist war effort. The White forces secured much of their arms and munitions from the Allies, chiefly Britain and France.

The Reds also derived a certain measure of support from the fact that they were defending Russian territory. Lack of cohesion among the counterrevolutionary movements and the fitful attitude of the Allied governments constantly hampered the operations of the Whites.

Leading commander of the counterrevolutionary White forces General Lavrenti Kornilov was killed in battle in April. General Anton Denikin took over command in the South, where he carried the brunt of the fighting. The last commander in the south was General Baron P. N. Wrangel.

Key factors in the Red victory included the hard-core of dedicated, disciplined Bolsheviks who provided the leadership of the Red Army, above all Leon Trotsky. A dedicated, ruthless, and supremely confident commander, the tireless Trotsky proved to be a revolutionary general of high caliber. Geography also benefited the Reds. Initially the territory firmly in their control coincided approximately with that of medieval Muscovy around the city of Moscow. Here they

Russian troops marching through the streets of Petrograd after returning from the war. (Edgar Allen Forbes, ed., *Leslie's Photographic Review of the Great War,* Leslie-Judge Co., New York, 1919)

enjoyed the advantage of interior lines, with short supply lines radiating out around Moscow that enabled the rapid movement of men and supplies. Also, the White forces were bitterly divided and could never coordinate their efforts or their ideology. Neither did they win the support of the Don, Kuban, and Siberian cossacks and numerous nationalities of the empire because, as centralists, they persistently rejected the idea of autonomy. By contrast, the Bolsheviks had troops drawn from the various nationalities, and they also trained native communist cadres.

In September 1918 the various White factions met in conference in Ufa in the Urals, but the effort to unify their many factions failed on the issue of autonomy for the Cossacks and national minorities. The Whites simply put off spelling out a detailed program for fear it would antagonize one or more groups of supporters.

The peasants were probably the key factor in the outcome. The vast majority probably believed that if the Whites triumphed they would lose the land they had gained from the revolution. Another factor was certainly the Polish attitude. The Poles might have cooperated with the White forces, but they preferred instead to see the conflict continued as long as possible so they could push their own frontier to the east in the process. Many Russians, moreover, considered the Whites as mere tools for the Allies, and this worked against them.

The Russian Civil War was a fight to the death by hungry and ragged soldiers with neither side asking nor giving quarter and both committing horrible brutalities and atrocities. Hundreds of thousands of Russians died. Before the end of 1920, all the White armies had been pushed back and forced to evacuate Russian soil.

Eva-Maria Stolberg and Spencer C. Tucker

See also

Brest Litovsk, Treaty of; Czech Legion; Denikin, Anton; Kerensky, Aleksandr Fyodorovich; Kolchak, Aleksandr Vasiliyevich; Kornilov, Lavr Georgyevich; Lenin, Vladimir Ilyich; Russia, Allied Intervention in; Skoropadsky, Pavlo Petrovich; Trotsky, Leon; Ukraine, Role in War and Revolution in.

References

Bradley, John F. N. *Civil War in Russia, 1917–1920*. London: Batsford, 1975.

Brovkin, Vladimir N. *Behind the Front Lines of the Civil War: Political Parties and Social Movements in Russia, 1918–1922*. Princeton, NJ: Princeton University Press, 1994.

Lehovich, Dimitry V. *White against Red: The Life of General Anton Denikin*. New York: Norton, 1974.

Lincoln, W. Bruce. *Red Victory: A History of the Russian Civil War, 1918–1921*. Simon and Schuster, 1989.

Luckett, Richard. *The White Generals: An Account of the White Movement and the Russian Civil War*. New York: Viking, 1971.

Strod, Ivan I. *Civil War in the Taiga: A Story of Guerilla Warfare in the Forests of Siberia*. Moscow: Progress, 1933.

Swain, Geoffrey. *The Origins of the Russian Civil War*. London: Longman, 1996.

Russia, Home Front

A discussion of Russia's home front during World War I must begin with the revolution of 1905 and the manifesto of October 1905 that ended the rebellion. That manifesto introduced to Russia a quasi-parliament, the State Duma, and upper house, the State Council. It promised a parliamentary regime with limited freedoms of press, speech, and association. But autocracy, represented by police, prisons, and censorship of speech, though not the press, continued in force. Despite his promises, the tsar dissolved the Duma and gradually narrowed the franchise until its composition suited his desire.

The first two Dumas were short-lived and had no control of finances or the military. Legislative power still rested primarily with the tsar. The tsar used the Fundamental Laws to alter the franchise, and the Third Duma, elected in 1907, was unrepresentative of the masses and composed primarily of conservatives and moderates from the nobility and wealthy propertied classes. This Duma did, however, introduce some semblance of representative government and influenced internal and external trade relations. The Third Duma survived its full five years to 1912, and the Fourth Duma followed suit.

Tsar Nicholas II had only limited exposure to Russian political affairs and social conditions before ascending the throne in 1894. Both he and Tsarina Alexandra resolutely believed in the traditional concepts of autocracy, orthodoxy, and Russian nationality and his right to rule. They also believed in the mystical union of the tsar and the people, with peasants looking to the tsar as father-protector.

The imperial couple were devout, believing in miracles and faith healing. The heir to the throne, Aleksey Nikolaevich, was a hemophiliac. Because reputed faith healer Grigory Rasputin was believed to have stopped the tsarevich's hemorrhaging, he gained great influence with the royal couple. During World War I Rasputin's advice, through the tsarina, influenced decisions relating to ministerial and military matters.

Government ministers were appointed by the tsar, who also appointed half the membership of the State Council annually. The other half was elected by regional legislative bodies, known as zemstvos; the Orthodox Church; and other conservative organizations. The system ensured that the tsar's legislative decisions would not be blocked from becoming law.

In 1914 the population of the Russian Empire was about 180 million people. Peasants constituted approximately 80 percent of that number and were the mainstay of the empire. They provided its food, the manpower for its armed forces, and most of its taxes. Although Russia was industrializing and losing its feudal character, factory workers constituted only a small minority of the population. Before the war, Russian industry grew rapidly, fueled by increases in internal and external trade, while foreign markets and investments were readily available to Russian enterprises. Unfortunately, almost one-third of all Russian foreign trade was with Germany.

Because of the demands of industry and some overcrowding on the land, many peasants joined the growing pool of industrial workers. The class of independent peasant landowners was also steadily though slowly rising, and agricultural productivity increased so that Russia became a net grain exporter prior to World War I. During the twelve-year-long experiment with so-called parliamentary government, however, the masses grew more and more alienated from their tsar and government and more influenced by radical intellectuals.

Freedom of the press had burgeoned apace. Between 1905 and 1914 weekly periodicals grew threefold and daily newspapers increased tenfold. This phenomenon resulted from the government's abandonment of press censorship in 1905. With this growth came a surge in literacy among the peasantry to about one-quarter by 1914, with two-thirds of army recruits being literate. These factors worked to increase the portion of the population considered the obshchestvenost (informed public).

Russian workers were prohibited from forming guilds, unions, and associations. This denied them access to culture and society and excluded them from the political process. Workers were thus attracted to study groups and libraries established by radical intellectuals. Those set up by Marxists were especially popular, but populist groups also attracted many. In the course of studying social sciences and European socialism, peasant-workers often abandoned the vestiges of faith in Orthodoxy and the tsar that they had brought with

Refugees of the civil war, mostly women and children, at a Russian railroad station awaiting a train. (Edgar Allen Forbes, ed., *Leslie's Photographic Review of the Great War,* Leslie-Judge Co., New York, 1919)

them from their villages. The tsar, however, attributed this alienation to the establishment of the Duma and the Council of Ministers, considering them layers of unresponsive and self-seeking bureaucrats separating him and his subjects.

These weaknesses in the social structure, the failure to move toward progressive government, and the pressure of radical ideas accompanied Russia into World War I. Initially, patriotic euphoria brought cooperation. The Duma voluntarily adjourned so that its members could contribute directly to the war effort instead of making speeches, even if these supported the government. Even the name of the capital was changed from St. Petersburg to Petrograd, because the former sounded too German.

By the spring of 1915 cooperation between society and the government had soured. Early wartime successes in East Prussia were reversed within days due to senior military commanders' ineptitude in the field. Initial gains in Galicia lasted somewhat longer because they were won from an equally unprepared foe, Austria-Hungary, but by April 1915 shortages of arms and ammunition reversed those, too. Bureaucratic inefficiency and waste were overwhelming. The military was left short of arms and ammunition, while projected army reforms had not been implemented. Industries could not secure essential materials formerly obtained from German suppliers, and there were shortages of skilled labor.

Russia's relative geographical isolation limited the ability of its western Allies to assist.

By mid-1915 the Russian war effort was near collapse. That summer Russian businessmen, liberals, and would-be reformers in the Duma seized on the munitions difficulties to establish a War Industries Committee that included representatives from the Duma and private business as well as the various government ministries; they hoped the War Industries Committee would prove the spearhead for further erosion of the tsarist regime's powers. To add to the bureaucratic confusion, several other public-private supplementary organizations to improve the administration of the war effort were established. Some historians suggest that especially given the existing disadvantages, including the enlistment of many skilled workers and decreases in per capita output of essential raw materials, the expansion of Russian munitions production during the war was remarkably impressive, with dramatic fifteenfold growth in shell production and tenfold increases in the output of guns in the period from August 1914 to December 1916.

Prompted by his concept of kingly duty and the military reverses suffered in 1915, in September that year Tsar Nicholas II assumed personal command of the armies. His lack of military experience made him unequal to the task, and he succeeded only in isolating himself at army headquarters away from contact with his ministers and government.

Empire affairs drifted, and Nicholas came increasingly under the influence of his wife and Rasputin. The tsar frequently changed the make-up of his Council of Ministers based on the half-literate Rasputin's advice through the tsarina, further disrupting government functioning. Rumors spread that the tsarina was Rasputin's lover and, because of her German heritage, that she was leading a plot to conclude a treacherous peace with Germany. Even supporters of the tsar began to consider the possibility of forcing him to abdicate, questioning whether the regime's shortcomings were due to incompetence or treason.

By 1916 patriotic enthusiasm had subsided. Some 15 million men had been mobilized for the military, but the economy had been grievously disrupted, and success in the field was lacking. In spring 1916 the Allies called for a Russian offensive to relieve pressure in France, and the leadership obliged. The cost of the resulting Brusilov offensive in men and matériel was high, however, undermining army morale. Neither peasant soldiers nor the masses understood the causes or objectives of the war, and the frightful losses and poor conditions incited mass desertions. Confidence in the military and government leadership failed, and war-weariness infected the Russian people.

By the end of 1916 the situation inside Russia was unstable, and the question was not *if* revolution would come but *when*. In the Duma in November 1916, Pavel Milyukov, leader of the moderate Kadet Party, made a speech denouncing government inefficiency, and Socialist Revolutionary Party deputy Aleksandr Kerensky called for the tsar's abdication. In December, Rasputin's assassination by a well-connected aristocrat and a conservative Duma leader temporarily reduced tension, but raging inflation reinvigorated it. Coal prices had quadrupled in Petrograd, and prices of other commodities had increased even more. At the beginning of 1917, food prices soared catastrophically. Bread prices rose 2 percent a week, vegetables 3 percent, meat 7 percent, and sugar 10 percent. Firewood in Petrograd grew so expensive that workers had to choose between starving or freezing. In February food riots broke out in Petrograd followed by strikes that daily increased in intensity.

The president of the Duma and others pleaded with the tsar to appoint a government that would regain the people's confidence, but he refused. Clashes between strikers and police continued, culminating on 12 March when military units sent to reinforce police refused to fire on strikers, turned on their officers, and joined the strikers. The tsar, rushing back from army headquarters to Petrograd, was stopped in Pskov and persuaded to abdicate on 14 March 1917.

On that day a Duma committee met to establish a governing body to rule provisionally until a permanent government could be chosen by the Constituent Assembly. On 15 March both the Provisional Committee of the Duma and the Executive Committee of the Petrograd Soviet (a shadow government organized in the capital and based on the soviets or councils of the 1905 revolution) agreed on a provisional government, its members drawn primarily from the Duma and volunteer organizations. From the beginning, the provisional government was weakened because authority from the Duma meant nothing to workers and peasants who owed no allegiance to it, and it shared power with the Petrograd Soviet, which had already won their loyalties. The new government also announced freedoms unprecedented for Russia, which contributed to increasing chaos both in Russian society and in the army, where discipline broke down.

The war became the crucial issue. The government made the fateful decision to continue the war, both to justify the costs already incurred and to realize Russia's historic ambitions. When the provisional government initiated an offensive in the summer of 1917, the compromise with the Petrograd Soviet collapsed. The desires of the people and the continuation of any war were incompatible, and, directed through the Soviets and encouraged by the Bolsheviks, soldiers and workers toppled the provisional government. Promising peace, land, and bread, the Bolsheviks carried out a coup d'état in early November 1917.

Having helped to destroy the army in his rise to power, the first action of Bolshevik leader Vladimir Lenin was to declare an armistice with the Germans. The Bolsheviks first attempted to negotiate an end to the war, but the Germans demanded too much. The government then embarked on a program of "no peace, no war," whereupon the Germans renewed hostilities. The virtually unchecked German advance forced the Bolsheviks to conclude the Treaty of Brest Litovsk in March 1918. Russia did not regain all the territory it lost in this treaty until after the Second World War.

Russia then dissolved into civil war as counterrevolutionaries, supported by the Allied governments, sought to topple the Bolsheviks. The Russian Civil War lasted through 1920. From June 1918 to March 1921, in response to the crisis of the Civil War, the Bolsheviks adopted a policy of War Socialism. This attempted to prevent a total collapse of the economy and mobilize national resources for the struggle as well as reshape the socioeconomic structure of the country into a centrally planned and state-controlled economy. Unfortunately for the long-suffering Russian people, the Bolsheviks failed to deliver on their promises, and the outcome was a regime far more repressive than its predecessor.

Arthur T. Frame

See also

1905; Russia, Revolution of March 1917; Russia, Revolution of November 1917; War Socialism.

References

Ferguson, Niall. *The Pity of War: Explaining World War I*. New York: Basic Books, 1999.

Hardach, Gerd. *The First World War, 1914–1918*. Trans. Peter and Betty Ross. London: Allen Lane, 1977.

Hosking, Geoffrey. *Russia, People and Empire*. Cambridge: Harvard University Press, 1997.

Jahn, Hubertus F. *Patriotic Culture in Russia during World War I*. Ithaca, NY: Cornell University Press, 1995.

Lincoln, W. Bruce. *Passage through Armageddon: The Russians in War and Revolution, 1914–1918*. New York: Simon and Schuster, 1986.

Lynch, Michael. *Reaction and Revolutions: Russia, 1881–1924*. 2nd ed. New York: Hodder and Stoughton, 2000.

Marwick, Arthur. *War and Social Change in the Twentieth Century: A Comparative Study of Britain, France, Germany, Russia, and the United States*. London: Macmillan, 1974.

Neilson, Keith. *Strategy and Supply: The Anglo-Russian Alliance, 1914–1917*. Boston: Allen and Unwin, 1984.

Pearson, Raymond. *The Russian Moderates and the Crisis of Tsarism, 1914–1917*. New York: Barnes and Noble Books, 1977.

Sanborn, Joshua A. *Drafting the Russian Nation: Military Conscription, Total War, and Mass Politics, 1905–1925*. DeKalb: Northern Illinois University Press, 2003.

Shapiro, Leonard. *The Russian Revolutions of 1917: The Origins of Modern Communism*. New York: Basic Books, 1984.

Siegelbaum, Lewis H. *The Politics of Industrial Mobilization in Russia, 1914–17: A Study of the War-Industries Committees*. New York: St. Martin's, 1983.

Russia, Navy

Any discussion of the Russian navy of World War I must begin with the Russo-Japanese War of 1904–1905. The near destruction of the navy during that war, especially the traumatic loss of the Baltic fleet in the Battle of Tsushima Straits in May 1905, was catastrophic to the navy and the nation.

In 1907 the Naval General Staff proposed a massive rebuilding program, but the army and State Defense Council, presided over by Grand Duke Nikolai Nikolaevich, opposed it as going beyond the defensive role envisioned for the navy. A less ambitious construction plan, known as the "Small Program" and proposed in April 1907, still met opposition from the State Defense Council, based on its proposed expanded fleet mission to "act as a free naval force for supporting the interests of the empire in foreign waters." Nonetheless, Tsar Nicholas II approved the Small Program, which could have made the Baltic fleet competitive with or superior to the German fleet normally in that sea. However, while the Duma had little authority to approve budgets or raise taxes, it could debate the issues, and the government desired Duma support. The controlling conservative parties supported strengthening military forces in general but insisted on giving the army pri-

ority, and the Duma therefore refused to support the Small Program. Hence, little naval rebuilding occurred before 1913.

Eventually in 1912, the Duma voted to approve a long-term building program to begin in 1913, with most new construction to be stationed in the Baltic. Construction suffered from delays and cost overruns, caused by shortages of skilled labor and the general inefficiency of Russian industry as well as by corruption and political and labor unrest. In any case, even in ideal circumstances capital ships took years to construct, with the result that the program's vessels were not ready by August 1914.

Russia had seven dreadnought battleships under construction at the beginning of the war, and all were completed during the war. Four Gangut-class dreadnoughts (12×12-inch guns) were completed by the end of 1914, while the remaining three Imperatritsa Maria-class (12×12-inch and 20×5.1-inch guns) were completed later during the war. Under the Small Program, four battle cruisers, eight light cruisers, thirty-six destroyers, and eighteen submarines were also under construction; however, the battle cruisers were not completed during the war, and the light cruisers never reached completion. Many of the destroyers were ready by 1915–1916, but the submarines were not delivered until just prior to the 1917 revolution.

In August 1914 the Russian navy consisted of 8 predreadnought battleships, 14 cruisers, 105 destroyers, 25 torpedo boats, and 25 submarines. The majority of these ships were concentrated in the Baltic and Black Seas. The Russian Black Sea Fleet consisted of 5 battleships, 2 cruisers, 9 new destroyers, 17 torpedo boats, and 6 submarines, together with miscellaneous gunboats, minelayers, and smaller craft.

In the Black Sea, Turkey was the principal potential opponent, and its navy was even more obsolete than the Russian. In the Pacific, the Russians had only two cruisers and some obsolete destroyers, plus a few submarines and torpedo boats. The White Sea station was covered primarily by torpedo boats.

Perhaps 80 percent of the Russian fleet was obsolete in August 1914. Russia was also obtaining less for its money than its competitors. Even though it cost 40 percent more to build ships in Russian yards than in Britain, the Duma had stipulated that the ships of the Small Program be built in Russia. Moreover, the myriad classes and designs within the fleet required the maintenance of extensive stockpiles of ordnance and supplies of spare parts. Nonetheless, the Naval Ministry and General Staff were fairly efficient in supplying the naval depots, in sharp contrast with the situation in the army.

The prewar manpower strength of the navy was some 56,000 men, including officers. This grew during the war to a peak strength of some 90,000 men. Most of the manpower for the army was recruited from the peasantry, whereas sailors came primarily from the urban working classes. About 60 percent were recruited from port and industrial cities. Senior officers came from the nobility, while middle- and lower-grade officers were drawn from the rising middle classes, because modern vessels required technically qualified personnel. Many Russian naval officers came from non-Russian backgrounds and were Baltic-Germans, Finns, and Swedes.

Although previously administratively and financially independent of the army, at the beginning of the war the navy was subordinated to the land forces. The navy's mission was to protect the Northern Front's right flank and then sweep German ships from the Baltic when the army attained offensive superiority. The chain of command ran from the Russian high command (Stavka) to the commander of the Northern Front, then to the commander of the Sixth Army and finally to the commander of the Baltic Fleet.

Since the Northern Front never succeeded in mounting a sustained offensive, the Baltic Fleet remained in defensive reserve throughout the war with the exception of an early mine-laying campaign. Baltic Fleet commander Vice Admiral Nikolai von Essen, on his own initiative, began a mine-laying campaign on 31 July 1914, two days before the outbreak of war. In three days four Russian minelayers laid 2,124 mines in the Gulf of Finland and across both entrances to the Gulf of Riga.

The Black Sea Fleet remained bottled up throughout the war once Turkey joined the Central Powers in October 1914. There the primary threat came from the powerful German battle cruiser *Goeben*. However, for most of the war the Black Sea Fleet controlled that body of water and was able to support army operations. Of the two Russian cruisers in the Pacific at the start of the war, one was sunk early by a German raider disguised as a British cruiser, and the other was transferred to the Mediterranean during the Dardanelles campaign and then to the North Sea to support Allied supplies shipments to Russia.

By 1917 Russian sailors, particularly in the Baltic where spare time abounded, had become heavily influenced by revolutionary intellectuals. In November 1917 men from the Kronstadt naval base near Petrograd played a significant role in the Bolshevik seizure of power. Sailors of the cruiser *Aurora* fired a blank shot to signal the start of the uprising. With the Bolshevik takeover, on 2 January 1918 the Imperial Russian Navy ceased to exist and the Red Fleet officially came into being.

Arthur T. Frame

See also
Baltic Operations, Sea; Black Sea, Naval Operations; Dardanelles Campaign; East Prussia, Campaigns in; Eastern Front Overview; Essen, Nikolai Ottovich von; Kolchak, Aleksandr Vasiliyevich; Galicia Campaigns; Nicholas II, Tsar; Nikolai Nikolaevich, Grand Duke; Russia, Army; Russia, Home Front; Russia, Revolution of 1905; Russia, Revolution of March 1917; Russia, Revolution of November 1917.

References
Mawdsley, Evan. *The Russian Revolution and the Baltic Fleet: War and Politics, February 1917–April 1918*. New York: Macmillan, 1978.
Mitchell, Donald W. *A History of Russian and Soviet Sea Power*. New York: Macmillan, 1974.
Nekrasov, George M. *Expendable Glory: A Russian Battleship in the Baltic, 1915–1917*. Boulder, CO: East European Monographs, 2004.
Saul, Norman E. *Sailors in Revolt: The Russian Baltic Fleet in 1917*. Lawrence: Regents Press of Kansas, 1978.
Westwood, J. N. *Russian Naval Construction, 1905–45*. Basingstoke, UK: Macmillan, 1994.
Woodward, David. *The Russians at Sea: A History of the Russian Navy*. New York: Praeger, 1965.

Russia, Revolution of 1905

The Russian Revolution of 1905 was a series of disturbances and uprisings that spanned the period of 1905–1907 and proved to be both a rehearsal and a harbinger for events in 1917. Russia's defeat in the Russo-Japanese War of 1904–1905 brought a loss of national pride and sparked societal and military disaffection. Although the army allowed the tsarist government to weather the storm, disaffection and revolutionary ideas influenced events in 1917.

Trouble began with mobilization for the war. Changes in recruiting procedures and terms of service had brought inequities in conscription. Educational deferments and exemptions were granted, but only for sons and sole breadwinners. Those eligible for army service were drafted by lot. Individuals not drafted were liable to be called up as replacements in national emergencies following mobilization of regular and reserve forces. In wartime every trained male from ages 21 to 39 was liable for military service despite family situation, a procedure that sometimes left young bachelors untouched.

The Russian government in St. Petersburg was hopelessly removed from the people, and most Russians did not understand the necessity of a war against Japan to decide control of Manchuria. The mobilization of 1904 summoned to the army a wide variety of disaffected individuals, including officers infected by revolutionary ideas circulating in the universities. Indiscriminate mobilization patterns, accompanied by a five-week train trip across Siberia, exposed the disgruntled reservists to revolutionary propaganda and led to previously unheard of numbers of desertions and disorders. At the same time, 1904 saw a series of political assassinations of tsarist officials, events that were greeted largely by indifference from most of the population. Loss of respect for legal authority, rampant corruption at every level, and the central government's refusal to grant basic rights all fueled revolutionary agitation.

The revolutionary spark came on 22 January 1905, when tsarist troops in St. Petersburg fired on peaceful worker-demonstrators attempting to petition the tsar for economic and civil rights. This day, known as Bloody Sunday, saw more than 100 civilians killed and another 300 wounded. News of the bloodshed touched off strikes in virtually every Russian industrial center. During the next month more strikes occurred than in the previous decade. In June, a mutiny aboard the warship *Potemkin* in the Black Sea triggered several similar military upheavals. Throughout the summer, strikes spread from industry to railway shops, effectively shutting down rail transportation. Peasant disturbances also occurred.

In addition, Russia lost the war with Japan in large part due to poor leadership and inadequate equipment. Once the war was over, millions of soldiers waited at railroad sidings to ship home and be demobilized. Some, still bearing arms and nursing grievances against the regime, joined in the growing disturbances.

In early October 1905, the strikes lost momentum and conditions calmed deceptively, surprising radical agitators. Then, during 7–17 October, the empire spontaneously erupted in a massive general strike. Without incitement from agitators, workers in the factory, transportation, and service industries left their shops and peasants left their fields in order to take up arms and carry banners demanding civil rights.

The tsar's advisors were indecisive, and fearing the overthrow of the government, Nicholas II gave the St. Petersburg police chief full authority to deal ruthlessly with disorder. Ominous quiet overtook the capital. The tsar's first minister, Sergei Witte, saw two ways to address the problem: crush the rebellion with still-loyal portions of the army led by a military dictator or grant a constitution allowing some civil rights and establishing a State Duma or parliament. Nicholas preferred the former and offered the military dictatorship to his uncle, Grand Duke Nikolai Nikolaevich, who refused and urged the tsar to grant a constitution.

Bowing to the inevitable, the tsar gave way. On 17 October 1905, Witte published the Manifesto on the Improvement of Order in the State. Known as the October Manifesto, this was supposedly a comprehensive guarantee of civil rights and called for the establishment of a broadly elected legislative assembly, the State Duma. The October Manifesto effectively ended the 1905 revolution. However, the revolution did not run its full course until 1907.

With the restoration of order, Nicholas II and his government chipped away at the reforms and freedoms. The tsar dissolved a succession of elected Dumas, restricted the powers of this elected body, and sharply reduced the franchise. Gradually the clock was turned back. The experience of 1905–1907, however, was not lost on the people and would be evoked in 1917, especially in the establishment of representative councils, known as soviets, which had been the hallmark of the Revolution of 1905.

Arthur T. Frame

See also

Lenin, Vladimir Ilyich; Milyukov, Pavel Nikolayevich; Nicholas II, Tsar; Nikolai Nikolaevich, Grand Duke; Russia, Army; Russia, Home Front; Russia, Revolution of March 1917; Russia, Revolution of November 1917.

References

Ascher, Abraham. *The Revolution of 1905.* 2 vols. Stanford: Stanford University Press, 1988–1992.

Ferro, Marc. *Nicholas II: Last of the Tsars.* Trans. Brian Pearce. New York: Oxford University Press, 1993.

Lincoln, W. Bruce. *In War's Dark Shadow: The Russians before the Great War.* New York: Dial, 1983.

Lynch, Michael. *Reaction and Revolution: Russia, 1881–1924.* 2nd ed. New York: Hodder and Stoughton, 2000.

Pipes, Richard. *The Russian Revolution.* New York: Knopf, 1990.

Rogger, Hans. *Russia in the Age of Modernisation and Revolution, 1881–1917.* New York: Longman, 1983.

Shanin, Teodor. *Russia, 1905–07: Revolution as a Moment of Truth.* New Haven, CT: Yale University Press, 1986.

Shukman, Harold. *Lenin and the Russian Revolution.* New York: Capricorn, 1966.

Surh, Gerald D. *1905 in St. Petersburg: Labor, Society, and Revolution.* Stanford, CA: Stanford University Press, 1989.

Verner, Andrew M. *The Crisis of the Russian Autocracy: Nicholas II and the 1905 Revolution.* Princeton, NJ: Princeton University Press, 1990.

Wolfe, Bertram D. *Three Who Made a Revolution: A Biographical History.* 2 vols. New York: Dial, 1948, 1964.

Russia, Revolution of March 1917

The first of two internal Russian uprisings in 1917 resulting in the transformation of Russian government and society and the country's eventual withdrawal from World War I. It is often referred to as the February Revolution, because when it occurred Russia followed the Julian calendar, which was thirteen days behind the Gregorian calendar used in the West.

After twelve years of experimenting with so-called representative government, the Russian people believed that little had changed, and they came more under the influence of radical intellectuals. Adding to their burden was the enormous cost of two and a half years of war, replete with military disasters, incompetent leadership, inefficient bureaucracy, arms and ammunition shortages, rampant inflation, and tremendous sacrifices in casualties. By 1917 the Russian masses had suffered enough.

Tsar Nicholas II, out of touch with his people and government and strongly influenced by his wife Alexandra, focused more on preserving the autocracy than on saving Russia. Attempts to pressure him to do otherwise only stiffened his stubborn resolve. In December 1916, conservative members

National burial of the victims of the March 1917 Revolution, 23 March 1917, in the national capital of Petrograd, Russia. (Library of Congress)

of the nobility and Duma assassinated Grigory Rasputin, who held considerable influence over the royal couple. The tsar, who had been nominally commanding the army at the front, secluded himself with his family at Tsarkoe Selo, 15 miles from Petrograd, isolating himself from people and events and leaving no one at army headquarters with authority to act. Nicholas did not return to army headquarters in Mogilev until 5 March 1917.

Throughout January and February, conditions deteriorated everywhere but were the worst in Petrograd. Worker dissatisfaction led to periodic strikes in war industries. Inflation and food shortages due to mismanagement and an inadequate transportation net brought food riots. On 22 January 1917, 150,000 workers in Petrograd took to the streets to commemorate the twelfth anniversary of Bloody Sunday in 1905. Across Russia other workers did likewise. This marked only the beginning of the wave of strikes across Russia in the following weeks. Every day the masses, especially in the capital, became more embittered.

On 5 March, workers—primarily women frustrated by long hours and inadequate wages that bought little food for their families while their husbands were at the front—poured into the streets of Petrograd demanding "Bread!" As more workers joined the strikers, soon totaling 90,000, those cries were joined with shouts of "Down with the war!" and then

"Down with the Tsar!" By nightfall the police had restored apparent calm, but strike fever simmered through the night in the workers' quarters. The next morning, 40,000 people filled the streets. They were met initially by 500 mounted Cossacks ordered to restore calm. Facing demonstrators led by women, the Cossacks hesitated and then gave way as the strikers marched to the city center. Others joined in until by nightfall a reputed 160,000 workers had gathered in the city's center. Not since the 1905 revolution had so many strikers converged in central Petrograd.

The police were unable to control the situation, and after three days the government ordered in regular army units to augment them. By 10 March the city had become an armed camp, and periodic gunfire erupted as police and strikers clashed. On the evening of 11 March, upon returning to their barracks, soldiers of a Guards regiment mutinied and vowed not to fire on crowds again. The next morning they refused to obey their officers' orders and joined the demonstrators in the street. Soon the entire Petrograd garrison joined the revolution.

On the afternoon of 12 March, members of the Duma, which the tsar had that day ordered dissolved, elected a Temporary Committee to restore public order. The same day in the same building, the Petrograd Soviet, comprised of delegates from factories, workshops, rebelling military units, and representatives from socialist parties, established itself to take hold of the revolution and restore order. Technically neither body possessed governmental authority, although the central administration had ceased to function since the tsar was back at army headquarters where he still controlled most of the army.

Removed from the scene, the tsar and his advisors misunderstood the situation in the capital and underestimated its seriousness. Nicholas II first ignored pleas from his advisors to appoint a government the people could trust and instead directed military commanders to suppress the rebellion. That task force simply melted away when the soldiers came in contact with revolutionaries. On 13 March the tsar left Mogilev by train for Petrograd to take personal control, but his train was diverted to Pskov where the army leadership, including his uncle Grand Duke Nikolai Nikolaevich, convinced him that his only option was abdication.

On 15 March the Duma Temporary Committee dissolved itself and established the provisional government under Prince Georgy Lvov, a nonparty-affiliated liberal, as prime minister. Pavel Milyukov, a Duma deputy and leader of the Kadet Party, became foreign minister, and Aleksandr Guchkov, a Kadet and Octobrist Party leader, was made minister of war. Aleksandr Kerensky, a Socialist Revolutionary member of the Duma, became minister of justice. Kerensky was simultaneously vice-chairman of the Petrograd Soviet and, given his role in both, acted as liaison between the two.

The provisional government's position was weakened from the start because it inherited all of the problems of its predecessor, while its authority came from the Duma from which Russian workers and peasants had been disenfranchised. It was weakened further by sharing power with the Petrograd Soviet, which had the support of the vast majority of the capital's populace and persistently second-guessed and undercut the provisional government's decisions.

Ominously, the leaders of the provisional government, responding to Allied pressure in the form of loans, decided to continue Russia's involvement in the war, a course taken despite war-weariness and the disintegration of discipline in the army. The latter was intensified by Order Number One, issued by the Petrograd Soviet, a decree that destroyed the authority of military officers over their troops. Kerensky's dream of a great successful military offensive that would win the people's support for the government ended in military defeat and the army's collapse. The provisional government's authority declined steadily. In July 1917 the Bolsheviks mounted an unsuccessful coup in Petrograd (as St. Petersburg was called). Shortly afterward the new military commander-in-chief, General Lavr Kornilov, demanded that Kerensky restore the powers of officers over their men and reinstate the death penalty. When Kerensky refused, Kornilov tried in early September to stage a military takeover of the government, an effort Kerensky repelled with the help of swiftly rearmed

workers and Bolsheviks. Many of those who assisted Kerensky at this time soon afterward helped to launch a second revolution, in reality a coup d'état, carried out in November (October by the Russian calendar) by the antiwar Bolsheviks.

Arthur T. Frame

See also

East Prussia, Campaigns in; Eastern Front Overview; Galicia Campaigns; Kerensky, Aleksandr Fyodorovich; Kerensky Offensive; Kornilov, Lavr Georgyevich; Lenin, Vladimir Ilyich; Nicholas II, Tsar; Rasputin, Grigory Yefimovich; Russia, Home Front; Russia, Revolution of 1905; Russia, Revolution of November 1917.

References

Figes, Orlando. *A People's Tragedy: The Russian Revolution, 1891–1924.* New York: Viking Adult, 1997.

Hasegawa Tsuyoshi. *The February Revolution: Petrograd, 1917.* Seattle: University of Washington Press, 1981.

Hosking, Geoffrey. *Russia, People and Empire.* Cambridge: Harvard University Press, 1997.

Keep, John L. H. *The Russian Revolution: A Study in Mass Mobilization.* New York: Norton, 1976.

Lincoln, W. Bruce. *Passage through Armageddon: The Russians in War and Revolution, 1914–1918.* New York: Simon and Schuster, 1986.

Pipes, Richard. *The Russian Revolution.* New York: Knopf, 1990.

Shapiro, Leonard. *The Russian Revolutions of 1917: The Origins of Modern Communism.* New York: Basic Books, 1984.

Wildman, Allan K. *The End of the Russian Imperial Army,* Vol. 1, *The Old Army and Soldier's Revolt (March–April 1917).* Princeton, NJ: Princeton University Press, 1980.

Russia, Revolution of November 1917

The second of two internal uprisings in 1917 Russia. Led by the Bolshevik Party, this revolution (really a coup d'état) resulted in the transformation of the Russian government and society and the country's withdrawal from World War I. It is often referred to as the October Revolution because at the time Russia followed the Julian calendar, thirteen days behind the western Gregorian calendar.

Spontaneous uprisings of March 1917 led to the collapse of the imperial government and the abdication of Tsar Nicholas II. Two self-appointed governing bodies—the provisional government and the Petrograd Soviet—sought to fill the vacuum. The provisional government lacked the allegiance of the masses of the people, especially in the capital, because its authority derived from the Duma. On the other hand, the Soviet had limited popular support, since it was elected by workers and soldiers in the capital only. It hesitated to lead, fearful of being tainted by the "bourgeois" nature of the revolution. Instead, its leaders second-guessed and undercut provisional government decisions. Thus from March to November, Russia had two governing bodies, one having formal authority without power, and the other with power but no authority.

An example of the cross purposes at which the two worked was the Soviet's Order Number One. It removed control and discipline in the armed forces by abolishing the death penalty, establishing political commissars at every level and directing command by committee where privates and officers had equal votes. Spurred on by the antiwar Bolshevik Party, Russia's frontline soldiers began to fraternize with the enemy, and officer attempts to enforce discipline encountered hostile resistance.

The revolution early that year in March allowed thousands of veteran revolutionaries to return from internal and external exile. From Switzerland via Germany and Sweden came thirty-eight exiles, including Vladimir Lenin, leader of the Bolsheviks. Lenin arrived in Petrograd on 16 April and presented speeches over the next two days that were later printed as the April Theses. Lenin claimed that the revolution marked the beginning of the international revolution of the proletariat, rejected cooperation with the provisional government, and called for all power to the soviets (the councils that had sprung up across Russia mirroring those of the revolution of 1905). Lenin also demanded an end to what he called the "predatory" war.

One compromise between the provisional government and the soviet was continuation of the war. The Western Allied governments insisted on this as a condition of financial loans. When the provisional government proclaimed support for Russia's original war aims and initiated an offensive supporting the Allies, the compromise fell apart. This mid-July Kerensky offensive, named for Minister of War Aleksandr Kerensky, collapsed in part due to war-weariness and the indiscipline prompted by Order Number One. Some units of the Petrograd garrison, fearing they would be sent to the front, revolted and were joined by idle workers and radical sailors from the nearby Kronstadt naval base. Eventually the uprising was quelled, though with some loss of life. Since Bolsheviks had joined the uprising, believing they would be blamed for it in any case, the provisional government ordered Bolshevik leaders arrested, but Lenin escaped into hiding in Finland.

On 7 August, a prolonged government crisis developed following the resignation of Prince Georgy Lvov over anticipated labor and agrarian policies. Kerensky then succeeded him as prime minister. His cabinet was moderately left-oriented with twelve of the sixteen ministers divided between Socialist Revolutionaries (the largest political party in Russia, representing the peasants) and the Mensheviks (an evolutionary socialist party). Kerensky tried to placate both the left and the right, but fearing the Bolsheviks, he ordered recently appointed commander of the armed forces General Lavr Kornilov to prepare to march on Petrograd if the Bolsheviks stirred insurrection.

In early September, when the German army occupied Riga and the road to Petrograd lay open, Kornilov sent a cavalry corps toward the capital, ostensibly to protect it. His action was seen as a right-wing attempt to reverse the revolution, however. Sensing the approaching danger, the soviet organized to protect the revolution. The Petrograd garrison and Kronstadt sailors, joined by idle workers, all strongly influenced by Bolshevik calls for peace, land, and bread, were mobilized to barricade and protect the capital. In desperation, Kerensky appealed to the Bolsheviks to assist in defending against counterrevolution, released imprisoned leaders such as Leon Trotsky, and armed the Bolshevik's Red Guard. Meanwhile, Bolshevik-influenced railroad workers stopped Kornilov's troops short of the capital, convincing even the most trusting soldiers that they were helping to restore the hated monarchy.

The Bolsheviks, able to claim that they had saved the revolution, now gained 50 percent of the seats in the Petrograd Soviet. In October, backed by leftist socialist revolutionaries, Trotsky was elected chairman of the Petrograd Soviet. He immediately withdrew that body's support from the provisional government. When in October the rumor circulated that the government might move the capital to Moscow to protect it from the German army, the soviet claimed full control of troop deployments in and around Petrograd. On 26 October the soviet appointed a Military Revolutionary Committee, outwardly to defend the capital; however, its members became the General Staff of the Bolshevik Revolution.

Although many leading Bolsheviks balked at Lenin's suggestion that the time was ripe for an armed uprising, on 29 October in a secret meeting the Central Committee of the party voted narrowly in favor of seizing power. The provisional government remained passive, although it was vaguely aware of Bolshevik preparations. The non-Bolshevik Executive Committee of the All-Russian Congress of Soviets postponed its meeting until 7 November and ordered a halt to all demonstrations and issuing of arms without the committee's approval.

On 5 November, the Bolsheviks sent regiments under their control to occupy strategic sites around the capital. On the evening of 6 November, the provisional government announced a state of emergency and declared the Soviet's Military Revolutionary Committee, controlled by Trotsky, to be illegal and ordered his arrest along with other Bolshevik leaders, including Lenin who had slipped back into Petrograd in October. The provisional government, barricaded in the Winter Palace, called too late for loyal troops to deal with the Bolsheviks. On the morning of 7 November, sailors on the cruiser *Aurora,* anchored in the Neva River, fired blank rounds from its guns, the signal for the uprising to begin. Bolshevik forces seized, almost without bloodshed, key buildings and facilities in the capital and on 8 November stormed the Winter Palace, arresting thirteen members of the provisional government. Kerensky managed to escape and fled into exile.

Lenin declared the victory and announced the formation of the Soviet of People's Commissars with himself as chairman. The new Soviet government immediately ordered an end to Russian participation in the war. When the Germans insisted on punitive peace terms, the government balked and attempted to follow a strategy of "neither war or peace." This proved impossible when the German army initiated a major offensive, forcing the Bolsheviks to conclude the Treaty of Brest Litovsk on German terms in March 1918. Lenin concluded that even yielding vast amounts of territory was preferable to renewal of the war and the possibility of the Bolsheviks in turn being driven from power. The new leadership also set aside the results of national elections, planned before their seizure of power, that had gone strongly against them. Meanwhile, civil war had erupted between the Bolsheviks and their supporters (the Reds) and conservative counterrevolutionary forces (the Whites). This ended with the Reds victorious in 1920. The Bolsheviks gradually—at great cost to the Russian people—reshaped the socioeconomic structure of the country.

Arthur T. Frame

See also

Brest Litovsk, Treaty of; Eastern Front Overview; Galicia Campaigns; Kerensky, Aleksandr Fyodorovich; Kerensky Offensive; Kornilov, Lavr Georgyevich; Lenin, Vladimir Ilyich; Nicholas II, Tsar; Russia, Allied Intervention in; Russia, Army; Russia, Civil War; Russia, Home Front; Russia, Navy; Russia, Revolution of March 1917; Trotsky, Leon.

References

Carr, E. H. *The Bolshevik Revolution, 1917–1923*. 3 vols. London: Macmillan, 1950.

Figes, Orlando. *A People's Tragedy: The Russian Revolution, 1891–1924*. New York: Viking Adult, 1997.

Keep, John L. H. *The Russian Revolution: A Study in Mass Mobilization*. New York: Norton, 1976.

Lincoln, W. Bruce. *Passage through Armageddon: The Russians in War and Revolution, 1914–1918*. New York: Simon and Schuster, 1986.

Pipes, Richard. *The Russian Revolution*. New York: Knopf, 1990.

Rabinowitch, Alexander. *The Bolsheviks Come to Power: The Revolution of 1917 in Petrograd*. New York: Norton, 1976.

Service, Robert. *The Russian Revolution, 1900–1927*. 3rd ed. New York: St. Martin's, 1999.

Shapiro, Leonard. *The Russian Revolutions of 1917: The Origins of Modern Communism*. New York: Basic Books, 1984.

Trotsky, Leon. *The History of the Russian Revolution*. Trans. Max Eastman. 3 vols. New York: Simon and Schuster, 1932.

Russia, War Plan (1914)

Also known as Plan "A," the basic operational plan developed by the Russians on the eve of World War I envisioned that if Germany threw its main attack against France, Russia would launch its main effort against Austria-Hungary in Galicia with a strong secondary attack into East Prussia against the Germans. A variant, Plan "G," provided for the unlikely contingency of Germany first moving east. Russian preparation concentrated on "A."

The concept for Plan "A" originated with the 1879 Dual Alliance between Germany and Austria-Hungary. When in 1890 Kaiser Wilhelm II refused to renew Otto von Bismarck's Reinsurance Treaty of 1887 between Russia and Germany, Russia was cast adrift. Russia needed money for its industrialization, and France needed an ally. The two countries, assumed by the kaiser to be ideologically incompatible, then moved together and became allies, concluding a military convention in 1894. This obliged Russia to respond to an attack on France by Germany, or Italy supported by Germany, by attacking Germany with all forces at its disposal. France would reciprocate with an attack on Germany if Germany, or Austria-Hungary supported by Germany, attacked Russia.

In the ensuing years, France continued to focus on Germany as the primary threat, while the Russians saw the Habsburgs as their main military adversary, chiefly because it was at the expense of the Dual Monarchy that Russia hoped to realize its long-cherished hopes of securing hegemony over the Balkans and an outlet on the Mediterranean. By 1900 the French had convinced the Russians to divide their land forces into two fronts or army groups, the Northern Front against Germany and the Southwestern Front against the Dual Monarchy. The French, who correctly worried about German plans to concentrate first against them while a slow-moving Russia mobilized, secured Russian agreement to conduct an invasion of East Prussia by the fifteenth day of the start of a Russian mobilization. Russia argued that its slower mobilization would provide only a portion of its force by day fifteen, but in the ensuing years France pressed its demands and even offered technical and financial aid to build strategically located railroads to speed the Russian mobilization. These, however, were incomplete by the start of war, but their construction was one factor prompting German army leaders to believe that the longer a general European war was delayed, the less chance Germany would have of winning it.

Despite the setbacks of the Russo-Japanese War of 1904–1905 and the revolution of 1905, by 1910 Russian leaders had agreed to the basics of French desires. In 1911 they promised France to send 800,000 troops against Germany by the fifteenth day of mobilization. In 1912 the Russians approved a convention, Plan 19. First developed by Quartermaster General Yuri Danilov, it contained variants of Plans "A" and "G" and called for two simultaneous offensives, the main one against Austria-Hungary but with a second, strong thrust into East Prussia, with forces to be more or less in place by the fifteenth day of mobilization.

By early 1914, Plan "A" directed that 33 percent of Russia's forces would be allocated to prepare for a drive on Berlin by first occupying East Prussia with a coordinated drive around the Masurian Lakes. Fifty-two percent of the army would concentrate on Galicia to defeat the Austro-Hungarians, while the remaining 15 percent would be divided between protection of the Baltic and Black Sea coasts. While the Russians expected to execute Plan "A," the supreme commander-in-chief of Russian land forces had until day nine of mobilization to decide between it and variant "G." According to their mobilization timetable, however, only one-third of Russia's army would be available for deployment on day fifteen of the mobilization.

Mobilization for war began on 31 July 1914, and two days later Grand Duke Nikolai Nikolaevich, the tsar's uncle, was appointed supreme commander of the army. On 6 August he chose Plan "A." On 9 August, responding to desperate pleas from the French government, the grand duke ordered a final alteration of the planned concentrations in order to strengthen the drive into East Prussia and threaten Berlin. On 14 August operations in East Prussia were ordered to begin, fifteen days into the Russian mobilization. The other Russian armies received orders to begin their offensives on 18–19 August.

Most historians charge that the effort to assist France by embarking on a premature offensive in East Prussia led to the early Russian disasters on that front. However, these defeats stemmed as much from poor leadership and faulty coordination between the two armies at the front than from any defective prewar planning.

Arthur T. Frame

See also
Danilov, Yuri Nikiforovich; East Prussia, Campaigns in; Galicia Campaigns; Masurian Lakes, First Battle of the; Nikolai Nikolaevich, Grand Duke; Rennenkampf, Pavel Karlovich; Samsonov, Aleksandr Vasiliyevich; Sazonov, Sergey Dmitriyevich; Sukhomlinov, Vladimir Aleksandrovich; Tannenberg, Battle of; Wilhelm II, Kaiser.

References
Kennon, George F. *The Fateful Alliance: France, Russia and the Coming of the First World War.* New York: Pantheon, 1984.
Lincoln, W. Bruce. *Passage through Armageddon: The Russians in War and Revolution, 1914–1918.* New York: Simon and Schuster, 1986.
———. *In War's Dark Shadow: The Russians before the Great War.* New York: Dial, 1983.
Turner, L. C. F. "The Russian Mobilization in 1914." In *War Plans of the Great Powers, 1880–1914,* ed. Paul M. Kennedy. London: Allen and Unwin, 1979.

Ruzsky, Nikolai Vladimirovich (1854–1918)

Russian army general. Born into a Russian noble family on 18 March 1854, Nikolai Ruzsky graduated from Konstantinovsky Military College in 1872 and was commissioned an infantry officer. He served in the Russo-Turkish War of 1877–1878. He was deputy chief of staff of the Kiev Military District during 1896–1902 and chief of staff of the Second Manchurian Army in the Russo-Japanese War of 1904–1905.

In mid-September 1914 Ruzsky took command of the Northwestern Front. Idolized by his staff and known as a clear thinker with a rapid grasp of problems, he also suffered from poor health. That November Ruzsky participated in the defense of Łódź, in which he demonstrated both caution and indecisiveness.

In March 1915 Ruzsky took command of the Sixth Army, and that August he assumed command of the new Northwestern Front of three armies to defend approaches to Riga and Dvinsk. In March 1916 Ruzsky left this command because of illness. He returned to service that November in command of the Northern Front from the Gulf of Riga to Lake Narocz. During the March 1917 revolution, Tsar Nicholas II found himself stranded at Ruzsky's Pskov headquarters, where Ruzsky played a key role in persuading him to abdicate.

Following the March Revolution, Ruzsky was dismissed from his command, possibly for cooperating with revolutionary innovations of elected army committees and political commissars. He then traveled south to the Caucasus, where he joined other tsarist generals. Taken prisoner by the Bolsheviks, he was executed at Piatogorsk on 19 October 1918.

Michael G. Uranko Jr.

See also
Nicholas II, Tsar; Russia, Army; Russia, Revolution of March 1917; Russia, Revolution of November 1917.

References
Knox, Sir Alfred. *With the Russian Army, 1914–1917: Being Chiefly Extracts from the Diary of a Military Attaché.* 2 vols. New York: Dutton, 1921.
Menning, Bruce W. *Bayonets Before Bullets: The Imperial Russian Army, 1861–1914.* Bloomington: Indiana University Press, 1992.
Pipes, Richard. *The Russian Revolution.* New York: Knopf, 1990.
Stone, Norman. *The Eastern Front, 1914–1917.* New York: Scribner, 1975.
Wandycz, Piotr. *The Lands of Partitioned Poland, 1795–1918.* Seattle: University of Washington Press, 1974.

Rydz-Śmigły, Edward (1886–1941)

Polish army marshal and leader of Poland. Born on 11 March 1886 in Brzeżany near Tarnopol (then Austrian Poland), Edward Rydz studied fine arts in Cracow, where he made the acquaintance of Józef Piłsudski. From 1908 he worked in various Polish patriotic groups, both legal and underground. Rydz continued those activities after completing his compulsory service in the Austro-Hungarian army in 1911 and soon occupied leading positions. He took the pseudonym Śmigły, which he later added to his original name.

In August 1914, the Austrians allowed Rydz-Śmigły to join the Polish force that formed the 1st Brigade of Piłsudski's "Polish Legions," formally part of the Austro-Hungarian army. As a consequence of Rydz-Śmigły's distinguished service in fighting against Russia, Piłsudski promoted him to colonel in 1916. When the Germans interned Piłsudski in 1917, he entrusted Rydz-Śmigły with command of the underground Polska Organizacja Wojskowa (Polish Military Organization), which he had designed for diversionary and intelligence operations.

Left to his own devices in dealing with rivalries between the different Polish factions, Rydz-Śmigły mobilized the Polish Military Organization as soon as the Habsburg monarchy showed signs of dissolution in Galicia, on 1 November 1918, and took over control there from the Austrians. Invited to join Ignacy Daszyński's Lublin-based provisional government, Rydz-Śmigły became minister of war and commander-in-chief of the army until the return of Piłsudski from internment in November 1918.

During the 1919–1920 Polish-Soviet War, Rydz-Śmigły served as a general under Piłsudski's command. He became an army inspector in 1921, rising in 1935 to the post of general inspector of the armed forces. In 1936, on Piłsudski's death, Rydz-Śmigły succeeded him as marshal of Poland. The German invasion of Poland in September 1939 found Poland with its military modernization program incomplete, and Rydzy-Śmigły's centralized system of command worked to the disadvantage of the Polish armed forces. With the Polish military defeat, Rydz-Śmigły crossed into Romania with the remainder of the government and was interned. In 1940 he escaped to Hungary and then returned to Poland. He died in German-occupied Warsaw under an assumed name on 2 December 1941.

Pascal Trees

See also

Daszyński, Ignacy; Piłsudski, Józef Klemens; Poland, Role in War.

References

Jabłonowski, Marek, and Piotr Stawecki. *Następca komendanta: Edward Śmigły-Rydz, Materiały do biografii.* Pułtusk: Wyższa Szkoła Humanistyczna, 1998.

Komarnicki, Titus. *Rebirth of the Polish Republic.* Melbourne, Australia: Heinemann, 1957.

Mirowicz, Ryszard. *Edward Rydz-Śmigły: Działalność wojskowa i polityczna.* Warsaw: Instytut Wydawniczy Związków Zawodowych, 1988.

Watt, Richard M. *Bitter Glory: Poland and Its Fate, 1918–1939.* New York: Simon and Schuster, 1979.